The Nebraska hardcover edition includes:

The Journals of the Lewis and Clark Expedition, Volume 1
Atlas of the Lewis and Clark Expedition

The Journals of the Lewis and Clark Expedition, Volume 2
August 30, 1803–August 24, 1804

The Journals of the Lewis and Clark Expedition, Volume 3
August 25, 1804–April 6, 1805

The Journals of the Lewis and Clark Expedition, Volume 4
April 7–July 27, 1805

The Journals of the Lewis and Clark Expedition, Volume 5
July 28–November 1, 1805

**The Journals of the Lewis and Clark Expedition, Volume 6
November 2, 1805–March 22, 1806**

The Journals of the Lewis and Clark Expedition, Volume 7
March 23–June 9, 1806

The Journals of the Lewis and Clark Expedition, Volume 8
June 10–September 26, 1806

The Journals of the Lewis and Clark Expedition, Volume 9
The Journals of John Ordway, May 14, 1804–September 23, 1806,
and Charles Floyd, May 14–August 18, 1804

The Journals of the Lewis and Clark Expedition, Volume 10
The Journal of Patrick Gass, May 14, 1804–September 23, 1806

The Journals of the Lewis and Clark Expedition, Volume 11
The Journals of Joseph Whitehouse, May 14, 1804–April 2, 1806

The Journals of the Lewis and Clark Expedition, Volume 12
Herbarium of the Lewis and Clark Expedition

The Journals of the Lewis and Clark Expedition, Volume 13
Comprehensive Index

Sponsored by the Center for
Great Plains Studies,
University of Nebraska-Lincoln
and the American
Philosophical Society, Philadelphia

A Project of the Center for Great Plains Studies, University of Nebraska–Lincoln
GARY E. MOULTON, EDITOR   Thomas W. Dunlay, Assistant Editor

The Definitive Journals of
Lewis & Clark

*Down the Columbia
to Fort Clatsop*

VOLUME 6 of the Nebraska Edition

University of Nebraska Press
Lincoln and London

©1990 by the University of Nebraska Press. All rights reserved.
Manufactured in the United States of America. First paperback
printing: 2002

◎

LIBRARY OF CONGRESS CATALOGING-IN-PUBLICATION DATA
Journals of the Lewis and Clark Expedition. Volume 2–8
The definitive journals of Lewis and Clark / Gary E. Moulton,
editor ; Thomas W. Dunlay, assistant editor.
p. cm.
Vols. 7–8: Gary E. Moulton, editor.
"A project of the Center for Great Plains Studies, University of
Nebraska–Lincoln."
Paperback edition of v. 2–8 of the Journals of the Lewis and
Clark Expedition, originally published in 13 v. by the University
of Nebraska Press, c1983–2001.
Includes bibliographical references and index.
Contents – v.2. From the Ohio to the Vermillion – v.3. Up the
Missouri to Fort Mandan – v.4. From Fort Mandan to Three
Forks – v.5. Through the Rockies to the Cascades – v.6. Down
the Columbia to Fort Clatsop – v.7. From the Pacific to the
Rockies – v.8. Over the Rockies to St. Louis.
ISBN 0-8032-8009-2 (v.2: alk. paper)– ISBN 0-8032-8010-6 (v.3:
alk. paper)– ISBN 0-8032-8011-4 (v.4: alk. paper)– ISBN 0-8032-
8012-2 (v.5: alk. paper) – ISBN 0-8032-8013-0 (v.6: alk. paper) –
ISBN 0-8032-8014-9 (v.7: alk. paper)– ISBN 0-8032-8015-7 (v.8:
alk. paper).
1. Lewis and Clark Expedition (1804–1806). 2. West (U.S.) –
Description and travel. 3. Lewis, Meriwether, 1774–1809 – Diaries. 4. Clark, William, 1770–1838 – Diaries. 5. Explorers –
West (U.S.)–Diaries I. Lewis, Meriwether, 1774–1809. II. Clark,
William, 1770–1838. III. Moulton, Gary E. IV. Dunlay, Thomas
W., 1944– . V. University of Nebraska–Lincoln. Center for Great
Plains Studies. VI. Title.
F 592.4 2002 917.804'2–dc21   2002018113

Contents

List of Figures, vi

Preface, ix

Editorial Symbols and Abbreviations, xi

Special Symbols of Lewis and Clark, xi

Common Abbreviations of Lewis and Clark, xii

Introduction to Volume 6, 1

Chapter 25
From the Cascades of the Columbia to the Sea,
November 2–21, 1805, 7

Chapter 26
At Fort Clatsop, November 22, 1805–
January 6, 1806, 79

Chapter 27
At Fort Clatsop, January 7–20, 1806, 174

Chapter 28
At Fort Clatsop,
January 21–March 17, 1806, 226

Chapter 29
The Start for Home,
March 18–22, 1806, 429

Chapter 30
Fort Clatsop Miscellany, 445

Sources Cited, 497

Index, 509

FIGURES

Map of Expedition's Route, November 2, 1805–March 22, 1806, 6

1. Mouth of the Columbia River, Washington and Oregon, ca. November 16–25, 1805, 52
2. Flounder (starry flounder, *Platichthys stellatus*), November 18, 1805, 63
3. Area about Cape Disappointment, ca. November 18, 1805, 64
4. Fort Clatsop Environs, December 7, 1805–March 23, 1806, 80
5. Point Adams, Oregon, ca. December 1, 1805, 102
6. Plan of Fort Clatsop Drawn over Area of Youngs Bay, ca. December 7, 1805, 110
7. Plan of Fort Clatsop, ca. December 7, 1805, 111
8. Location of Fort Clatsop, ca. December 17, 1805, 128
9. Necanicum River, Oregon, ca. December 17, 1805, 129
10. Conic Hat, December 29, 1805, 141
11. Conic Hat, December 29, 1805, 143
12. Two Swords, a Bludgeon, and a Paddle, January 1, 1806, 152
13. Route to the Whale Site, ca. January 6–10, 1806, 170
14. Skate (big skate, *Raja binoculata*), January 7, 1806, 176
15. Arrow, January 15, 1806, 207
16. Arrow, January 15, 1806, 209
17. Bone Fishhook and Line, January 16, 1806, 212
18. Bone Fishhook and Line, January 16, 1806, 213
19. Digging Instrument, January 23, 1806, 232
20. Digging Instrument, January 24, 1806, 234
21. Conic Hat and Double-edged Knife, January 29, 1806, 247
22. Conic Hat and Double-edged Knife, January 30, 1806, 250
23. Method of Head-flattening and Adults with Skull Deformation, ca. January 30, 1806, 252
24. Paddle, Small Canoe, Canoe with High Bow, and Most Common Canoe, February 1, 1806, 264
25. Canoe with Carved Images, February 1, 1806, 266
26. Paddle, Small Canoe, and Sharp-pointed Paddle, February 1, 1806, 268
27. Another Small Canoe, Canoe with High Bow, and Most Common Canoe, February 1, 1806, 269
28. Canoe with Carved Images, February 1, 1806, 271
29. Stalk and Leaves of the Shallon (salal, *Gaultheria shallon*), February 8, 1806, 289
30. Fir Leaf (Douglas fir, *Pseudotsuga taxifolia*), February 9, 1806, 291
31. Fir Cone (Sitka spruce, *Picea sitchensis*), February 9, 1806, 292
32. Maple Leaf (vine maple, *Acer circinatum*), February 10, 1806, 294
33. Maple Leaf (vine maple, *Acer circinatum*), February 10, 1806, 296
34. Evergreen Shrub Leaf (Oregon grape, *Berberis aquifolium*), February 12, 1806, 300
35. Evergreen Shrub Leaf (dull Oregon grape, *Berberis nervosa*), February 12, 1806, 301
36. Fern Leaf (Christmas fern, *Polystichum munitum*), February 13, 1806, 304
37. Fern Leaf (Christmas fern, *Polystichum munitum*), February 13, 1806, 306
38. Head of a Vulture (California condor, *Gymnogyps californianus*), February 16, 1806, 320

39. Head of a Vulture (California condor, *Gymnogyps californianus*), February 17, 1806, 323

40. Pine Cone (Sitka spruce, *Picea sitchensis*), February 18, 1806, 326

41. Eulachon (*Thaleichthys pacificus*), February 24, 1806, 343

42. Eulachon (*Thaleichthys pacificus*), February 25, 1806, 350

43. Head of Cock of the Plains (sage grouse, *Centrocercus urophasianus*), March 2, 1806, 369

44. Cock of the Plains (sage grouse, *Centrocercus urophasianus*), March 2, 1806, 372

45. Head of a White Gull (northern fulmar, *Fulmarus glacialis*), March 6, 1806, 386

46. Head of a White Gull (northern fulmar, *Fulmarus glacialis*), March 7, 1806, 389

47. Head of a Brant (greater white-fronted goose, *Anser albifrons*), March 15, 1806, 417

48. Head of a Brant (greater white-fronted goose, *Anser albifrons*), March 15, 1806, 419

49. White Salmon Trout (coho salmon, *Oncorhynchus kisutch*), March 16, 1806, 422

50. White Salmon Trout (coho salmon, *Oncorhynchus kisutch*), March 16, 1806, 424

51. Tongue Point, Oregon, Winter 1805–6, 460

Preface

Numerous persons have helped us in bringing this volume to completion. Their subject knowledge or love of the Lewis and Clark expedition and their selfless sharing of time and talents have increased the worth of the annotations to the text tremendously. The great captains and their party may have been able to accomplish their explorations without the help of native guides, but the going would have been far more difficult, time consuming, and hazardous. We too, may have completed our work without the assistance of specialists and dedicated laypersons, but the quality of the work would have suffered and our journeys into unknown areas would have been more burdensome without them. Our guides were friendly, wise, and generous.

Three special friends of this project have died since the publication of the last volume: Donald Jackson, Paul Russell Cutright, and Robert B. Betts. These men aided this endeavor with their writings, their advice, and their good will; they will be sorely missed. Their good names and good works will live on.

A number of people have continued helping the project. Robert E. Lange of Portland, Oregon, assisted in tracking down Columbia River nomenclature and provided numerous other services. James P. Ronda and W. Raymond Wood were always at hand with comments, encouragement, and friendly advice. Robert B. Betts (New York City), Gladys Watkins Allen (Alton, Illinois), William P. Sherman (Portland, Oregon), and Lyle S. Woodcock (St. Louis, Missouri) contributed financially to the project. Likewise, the Lewis and Clark Trail Heritage Foundation provided financial aid, and its many members have been steadfast friends and supporters.

At the principal repositories of Lewis and Clark materials we again had the professional and capable assistance of Beth Carroll-Horrocks, Martin L. Levitt, Roy E. Goodman, Edward C. Carter II, and Randolph S. Klein, all of the American Philosophical Society, Philadelphia, and Duane R. Sneddeker and Bryan Stephen Thomas of the Missouri Historical Society, St. Louis. Staff, office, and administrative help came from the Center for Great Plains Studies and the project itself at the University of Nebraska-Lincoln. We can thank Frederick C.

Luebke, Rosalind K. Carr, and Lori L. Gourama of the Center, and Cindy L. Donnelly of the project for their important work.

We again turned to scholars in areas where we had little experience. As usual, we found these persons to be knowledgeable, patient, and generous.

ARCHAEOLOGY: Rick Minor, Heritage Research Associates, Eugene, Oregon; Kenneth M. Ames, Portland State University. BOTANY: A. T. Harrison, Westminster College, Salt Lake City; Margaret R. Bolick, University of Nebraska-Lincoln. GEOLOGY: Robert N. Bergantino, Montana Bureau of Mines and Geology, Butte; John Eliot Allen, Portland State University (emeritus). LINGUISTICS: American Indian linguistic data in the notes were collected by Raymond J. DeMallie, Indiana University, and were provided by the following individuals: *Algonquian.* Ives Goddard, Smithsonian Institution. *Chinookan.* Michael Silverstein and Robert E. Moore, both of the University of Chicago. *Makah.* Ann M. Bates, Indiana University. *Salishan and Alsea.* M. Dale Kinkade, University of British Columbia. *Latin.* John D. Turner, University of Nebraska-Lincoln. ZOOLOGY: Patricia Freeman, University of Nebraska-Lincoln (mammals, taxonomy); Gary L. Hergenrader, University of Nebraska-Lincoln (fish); Thomas O. Holtzer, University of Nebraska-Lincoln (insects); John Janovy, University of Nebraska-Lincoln (coastal marine life); John D. Lynch, University of Nebraska-Lincoln (fish); Jim R. Rosowski, University of Nebraska-Lincoln (coastal marine life); Thomas B. Thorson, University of Nebraska-Lincoln (emeritus) (coastal marine life).

It is not expected that these persons' generosity extends to accepting blame for errors that may appear herein; we reserve that right.

EDITORIAL SYMBOLS AND ABBREVIATIONS

[roman]	Word or phrase supplied or corrected.
[roman?]	Conjectural reading of the original.
[*italics*]	Editor's remarks within a document.
[*Ed:italics*]	Editor's remarks that might be confused with EC, ML, NB, WC, or X.
[*EC:italics*]	Elliott Coues's emendations or interlineations.
[*ML:italics*]	Meriwether Lewis's emendations or interlineations.
[*NB:italics*]	Nicholas Biddle's emendations or interlineations.
[*WC:italics*]	William Clark's emendations or interlineations.
[*X:italics*]	Emendations or interlineations of the unknown or an unidentified person.
⟨roman⟩	Word or phrase deleted by the writer and restored by the editor.

SPECIAL SYMBOLS OF LEWIS AND CLARK

α	Alpha
∠	Angle
☽	Moon symbol
☞	Pointing hand
★	Star
☉	Sun symbol
♍	Virgo

COMMON ABBREVIATIONS OF LEWIS AND CLARK

Altd., alds.	altitude, altitudes
Apt. T.	apparent time
d.	degree
do.	ditto
h.	hour
id., isd.	island
L. L.	lower limb
L., Larb., Lard., Lbd., or Ld. S.	larboard (or left) side
Lad., Latd.	latitude
Longtd.	longitude
m., mts.	minute, minutes
M. T.	mean time
mes., mls., ms.	miles
obstn.	observation
opsd.	opposite
pd., psd.	passed
pt.	point
qde., quadt., qudt.	quadrant
qtr., qutr.	quarter
s.	second
S., St., Star., Starbd., Stb., or Stbd. S.	starboard (or right) side
sext., sextn., sextt.	sextant
U. L.	upper limb

Note: abbreviations in weather entries are explained at the presentation of the first weather data, following the entry of January 31, 1804.

Introduction to Volume 6

Cascades of Columbia River, Washington-Oregon, through Winter at Fort Clatsop, Oregon

November 2, 1805 – March 22, 1806

Below the Cascades of the Columbia River the Corps of Discovery passed into yet another natural region, the thick rain forest of the Northwest Coast. Many Indian villages dotted the banks of the Columbia, some of them inhabited by people frightened by the coming of strangers. Fortunately the sight of Sacagawea and her baby convinced them that the newcomers were not a war party. Near the mouth of the Willamette River they reentered the world of previously known geography, for boats of George Vancouver's British expedition had penetrated this far up the Columbia in 1792.

For November 7, 1805, Clark was able to note "Ocian in view! O! the joy." In fact, he was premature, for what they were seeing was only the wide estuary of the Columbia. Within a few days, however, Lewis and a few men pushing ahead did reach the coast. Their satisfaction at attaining their long-sought goal was considerably dampened by the weather, the characteristic rain and storms of the Northwest Coast winter. The party was trapped for days on the northern shore of the estuary, unable to move because of high winds and gigantic waves. "All wet and disagreeable" is an expression occurring frequently in Clark's journals, and on November 22, still immobilized, he burst out, "O! how horriable is the day." Their discomfort was not altered by seeing the Chinook Indians paddle their canoes across rough waters the explorers did not dare attempt.

They had arrived where they had longed to be, and they knew that the mountain winter would make the return east impossible for some months. Their immediate problem was to find a place near the coast to wait out the winter. There seemed to be no really suitable spot on the north side of the Columbia. Considering whether to winter on the coast, intolerably wet but offering the possibility of contact with a ship, or to seek some drier inland spot up the Columbia, the captains took the step, rare in the annals of exploration, of taking a vote of the party. Even York, the slave, and Sacagawea, the Indian woman, had their opinions recorded. The final decision was to cross to the south side of the Columbia to seek a location with adequate game and proper timber to build a stockade. After a few days of searching, on December 7 they picked a site on the banks of what is now called Lewis and Clark River some miles from the coast. While Clark set out on the next day for the coast to find a site for a saltmaking camp, Lewis and the men began felling trees for what they would call Fort Clatsop after the local Indian tribe. Here would be their home for the next three and one half months, until March 23, 1806.

It was a sojourn marked not by the fierce cold and snow of the previous winter at Fort Mandan but by rain, storms, and gray skies. They did not starve, but food was neither plentiful nor good. The inability to preserve meat in the damp climate meant that they lived much of the time on spoiled elk, fish, and roots. Relations with the local Indians were not as satisfactory as they had been at Fort Mandan. The captains found many of the natives' customs and attitudes repugnant and thought they demanded too high a price for the food and other goods they furnished. Although the Indians never manifested real hostility, the commanders took strict security measures to insure the safety of the party.

The quest for food kept hunting parties out constantly, elk being the chief game animal. Reports of a whale stranded some distance down the coast led Clark to set out on January 6 to seek this possible source of meat, with a party of eleven men. Sacagawea insisted on going to see the ocean and the big fish, taking her baby and her husband with her. Clark found that the Tillamook Indians had already stripped the whale, but he was able to purchase a few hundred pounds of meat and a few gallons of oil and returned to the fort on January 10.

The captains had had hopes of meeting American or British seagoing traders, from whom they might obtain supplies and send dispatches home, but none were in the area during the winter although there was abundant evidence of their contact with the local people. A Russian ship seeking a location for a new settlement arrived off the mouth of the Columbia just before the Americans left, but they were unable to enter the river and the two parties never met.

The captains did not lack occupation. Lewis resumed his journal-keeping on the first day of 1806, after a lapse of over three months. For the remainder of his stay at Fort Clatsop he devoted himself to making a detailed record of the natural history and human culture of the coast and the region west of the Rockies. Clark has occasionally received credit for the first descriptions of many new species, but it now appears that he simply borrowed material originally written by Lewis, while copying Lewis's journals. At no other time did they devote so much space to the description of plants and animals and the life and material culture of the native peoples, the record of a land little known to the outside world. Included with these descriptions were an unprecedented number of sketches, in the journals themselves, of plants, animals, and artifacts. The number of drawings other than maps in these Fort Clatsop journals far surpasses those found in the rest of the captains' writings, the product of enforced leisure in a strange, new environment. Besides the many plant and animal species pictured, there was a record of the great variety of canoe types, of native clothing, implements and weapons, and diagrams of the local methods of deforming the heads of infants, with the results.

The captains first noted the transition in the Columbia gorge from the dry ponderosa pine–white oak forest on the east to the moist Douglas fir–western hemlock–Sitka spruce forests on the west. Among plant species first described by Lewis are the Oregon crabapple, Oregon grape, dull Oregon grape, and salal (all sketched in the journals and appearing in this volume), along with trees like Sitka spruce, grand fir, and western white pine. Among new animal discoveries were the greater white-fronted goose, the northern fulmar, the eulachon, and the sage grouse (all pictured herein), and also the Columbian black-tailed deer, the steelhead trout, the mountain beaver (which is not a beaver), and the Oregon bobcat. While Lewis wrote, Clark worked on his maps of the first transcontinental journey by Anglo-Americans.

We know much less about the enlisted men, except that they were kept busy hunting and making moccasins for the return trip, and that the captains were sufficiently concerned about venereal disease that they finally asked for a pledge that none of the party would have anything more to do with the native women. Minor illnesses flourished because of the dampness and cold.

Boredom, sickness, a monotonous diet, and the dreary weather all enhanced their impatience to start on the trip for home as soon as they reasoned that the melting snows of the Rockies would allow their passage. The captains knew that the Nez Perces, with whom they had left their horses on the trip west, would head east of the Rockies to hunt buffalo as soon as the snow in the higher mountains receded. They were anxious to secure their horses, cross the mountains, and explore new trails the Shoshones had told them about—a more direct route from the eastern end of the Indian road across the mountains to the Great Falls of the Missouri and also to carry out a separate exploration of the Yellowstone River.

They had planned to leave on April 1, after preparing what food and clothing they could obtain and leaving messages in the fort and with the Indians for any sea traders who arrived after their departure. If any disaster overwhelmed the Corps on the journey home, some record of their achievement might thus still reach the United States. Eagerness to be on the move prompted them to move up the date to March 20, then bad weather and the need to secure additional canoes held them another two days. Lewis and Clark feared that the price the Indians wanted for another canoe would so badly deplete their small stock of trade goods as to cripple their ability to obtain needed supplies on the way home. The captains succumbed to temptation and violated their longstanding and consistently observed rule against stealing Indian property and sent out a party to take an unattended canoe nearby, rationalizing that the Clatsops had taken elk that the expedition hunters had shot and left.

On March 22, Lewis wrote, "we determined to set out tomorrow at all events."

The Journals of the Lewis and Clark Expedition, Volume 6

November 2, 1805 – March 22, 1806

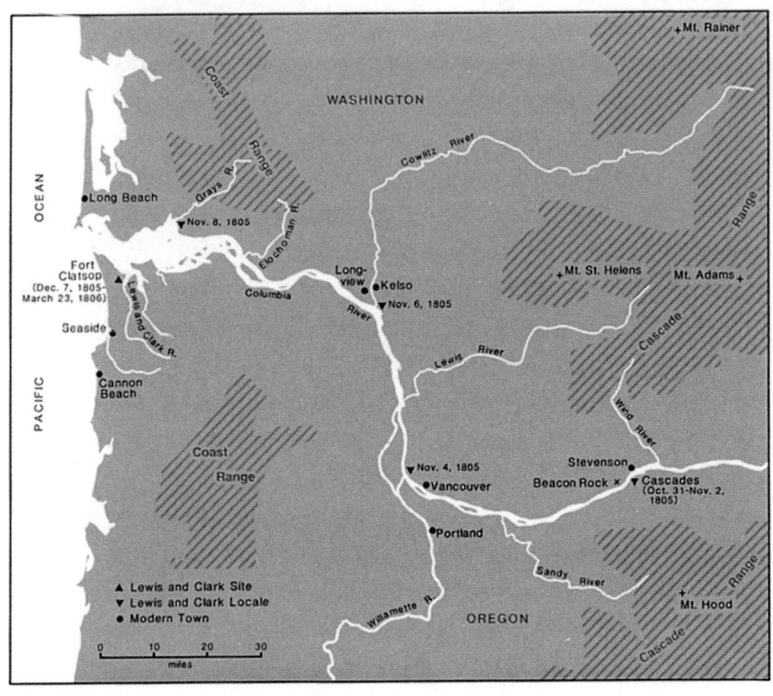

The Expedition's Route, November 2,
1805–March 22, 1806

Chapter Twenty-Five

From the Cascades of the Columbia to the Sea

November 2–21, 1805

[Clark] *Novr. 2d Saturday 1805*[1]

Meridian altitude 59° 45′ 45″ made a portage of about 1½ miles with half of the Baggage, and run the rapid with the Canoes without much damage,[2] one Struck a rock & Split a little, and 3 others took in Some water   7 Squars Came over the portage loaded with Dried fish & *Beargrass*,[3] Soon after 4 men Came down in a Canoe   after takeing brackfast, & after taking a meridian altitude we Set out   Passed 2 bad rapids one at 2 & the other at 4 mile below the Isd on Lard. and upper end of Strawberry Island[4] on the Stard. Side from the Creek end of last Course

> S. 50° W.   5   miles to a timbered bottom on the Lard. Side, passed the Lowr. point of Strawbery Isd. at 3 miles, a Isd Covd with wood below on Stard. Side a remarkable high rock on Stard. Side about 800 feet high & 400 yds round, the *Beaten* Rock.[5] The mountains and bottoms thickly timbered with Pine Spruce Cotton and a kind of maple   Passed 2 Small wooded Islands on Std. Side, ⟨opsd⟩ below the lower Island on the Stard. Side   at 4 miles an Indian village of 9 Houses, The river wider and bottoms more extencive.

From the Cascades of the Columbia to the Sea

S. 47° W.   12   miles to a ⟨Lard.⟩ Stard. point of rocks of a high clift of black rocks.⁶ passed a Stard. Point at 4 miles. here the mountains are low on each Side & thickly timbered with pine. river about 2 miles wide, passed a rock at 10 miles in the middle of the river this rock is 100 feet high & 80 feet Diameter, a deep bend to th Stard. Side,

We Labiech killed 14 Geese & a Brant, Collins one Jos. Fields & R 3 those gees are much Smaller than Common, and have white under their rumps & ⟨abov⟩ around the tale,⁷ The tide rises here a fiew 9 Inches, I cannot assertain the prosise hite it rises at the last rapid or at this place—of Camp.⁸

The Indians we left at the portage passed us this evening one other Canoe Come up

S. 58° W.   4   miles ⟨to a⟩ Stard. point of a large bottom. Encamped on the
            21   21 Lard Side river about 2 miles wid Country thickly timbered we Encamped behind a large rock in the Lard. Bend, a Canoe with 7 Inds. came down & Encamped with us

[Clark]   *November 2nd Saturday 1805* ⁹

Examined the rapid below us more pertcelarly the danger appearing too great to Hazzard our Canoes loaded, dispatched all the men who could not Swim with loads to the end of the portage below, I also walked to the end of the portage with the carriers where I delayed untill everry articles was brought over and canoes arrived Safe. here we brackfast and took a Meridn. altitude *59° 45′ 45″* about the time we were Setting out 7 Squars came over loaded with Dried fish, and bear grass neetly bundled up, Soon after 4 Indian men came down over the rapid in a large canoe. passed a rapid at 2 miles & 1 at 4 miles opposit the lower point of a high Island on the Lard Side, and a little below 4 Houses on the Stard. Bank,¹⁰ a Small Creek on the Lard Side opposit Straw berry Island, which heads below the last rapid, opposit the lower point of this Island passed three Islands covered with tall timber opposit the Beatin rock Those Islands are nearest the Starboard Side, imediately below on the Stard. Side passed a village of *nine* houses,¹¹ which is Situated between 2 Small Creeks, and are of the Same construction of those above; here the river widens to near a mile, and the bottoms are more extensive and thickly timbered, as also the high mountains on each Side, with Pine, Spruce pine, Cotton wood, a Species of ash, and alder. at 17 miles passed a rock near the middle of the river, about 100 feet high and 80 feet Diamuter,[12] proceed on down a Smoth gentle Stream of about 2 miles wide, in which the tide has its effect as high as the Beaten rock or the Last rapids at Strawberry Island,— Saw great numbers of waterfowl of Different kinds, Such as Swan, Geese, white & grey brants,[13] ducks of various kinds, Guls, & Pleaver. Labeach killed 14 brant Joseph Fields 3 & Collins one. we encamped under a high projecting rock on the Lard. Side,[14] here the mountains leave the river on each Side, which from the great Shute to this place is high and rugid; thickly Covered with timber principalley of the Pine Species. The bottoms below appear extensive and thickly Covered with wood. river here about 2½ miles wide. Seven Indians in a Canoe on their way down to trade with the nativs below, encamp with us, those we left at the portage passed us this evening and proceeded on down The ebb tide rose here about 9 Inches, the flood tide must rise here much higher— we made 29 miles to day from the Great Shute—

1. Here continues Clark's first draft found in the Elkskin-bound Journal, beginning at September 11, 1805, and running to December 31, 1805. The second entry is from Codex H, covering the period October 11–November 19, 1805. See Appendix C, vol. 2.

2. This is the area of today's Cascades of the Columbia River, Skamania County, Washington, and Hood River County, Oregon. The rapids are now inundated by Bonneville Dam. The area is discussed in notes for October 30 and 31, 1805. *Atlas* map 79.

3. Beargrass, *Xerophyllum tenax* (Pursh) Nutt. Hitchcock et al., 1:812; Gunther (EWW), 23.

4. Hamilton Island, Skamania County. The larboard island is Bradford Island, in Hood River County, crossed by Bonneville Dam. The creek mentioned next is probably Hamilton Creek, unnamed on *Atlas* map 79; it is "dry run" on *Atlas* map 88, and "Broad run" or "Broad Brook" on figs. 28 and 29 in volume 5 of this edition. Strawberry is woodland strawberry, *Fragaria vesca* L. var. *crinita* (Rydb.) C. L. Hitchc.

5. At the top of this page in the Elkskin-bound Journal, Clark has "S 58 W." Perhaps this is a reminder for which course he is writing up, but it is different than the one given at the start and in the codex journal. "Beaten Rock" is Beacon rock, in Beacon Rock State Park, Skamania County. Clark's size estimate is remarkably close, its height is generally given as 840 feet above the river. See note at October 31, 1805. *Atlas* map 79.

6. The black rocks are basalts of the Miocene-age Columbia River Basalt Group; the point is today's Cape Horn, Skamania County.

7. The brant is *Branta bernicla* [AOU, 173], while the common goose is the Canada

From the Cascades of the Columbia to the Sea

goose, *B. canadensis* [AOU, 172]. The smaller goose is evidently one of the subspecies of the Canada goose, perhaps the lesser Canada goose, *B. canadensis leucopareia* [AOU, 172.1], but other subspecies are possible. See above, May 5, 1805; below, March 8, 1806. Burroughs, 192–96.

8. In Multnomah County, Oregon, in the vicinity of present Latourell, within Rooster Rock State Park. *Atlas* maps 79, 88. At the top of the next page after this entry Clark has written "17," a subtotal of the day's mileage.

9. The courses for this entry to November 16 are grouped with the codex entry of November 16, as Clark had them.

10. This sentence has a vertical line drawn through it.

11. Identified on *Atlas* map 79 as the "Wah-clallah Tribe of Shahala Nation," probably the same people also referred to as the Watlalas, an Upper Chinookan-language people. The term Shahala is from Chinookan *šáxl(a)*, "upriver, above," and *šáxlatkš*, "those upriver." These people, who resided along the "Cascades of the Columbia," are often labeled under the general name of Cascades Indians. Like many Chinookan-speaking peoples, this group was greatly reduced by disease later in the nineteenth century, with most of the survivors eventually joining the Wascoes on the Warm Springs Reservation or the Wishrams on the Yakima Reservation. Hodge 2:922; Spier, 21, 24; Berreman, 18–19; Hajda, 67, 119–20. The village of nine houses was in Skamania County, in the vicinity of present Skamania. Spier & Sapir, 167–68, vaguely place several villages of the Cascades Indians in this area. The village observed by Lewis and Clark may correspond with a known archaeological site, where test excavations encountered evidence of late prehistoric occupation. Warren (RSWA), 10–11. Prehistoric occupation in the Cascades area has a limited time depth, as all sites investigated to date are situated on landforms created as a result of the Bonneville landslide around 800 years ago. Minor, Toepel, & Beckham; Minor (PH).

12. "Phoca" or "Seal rock" on *Atlas* map 79. "Phoca" is Greek for "seal." Lewis and Clark's name has been restored to this formation, rising about thirty feet in the Columbia River. The name is for the harbor seal, *Phoca vitulina richardii*. See October 23, 1805. The rocks in this area are basalts of the middle Miocene Yakima Basalt Subgroup of the Columbia River Basalt Group.

13. The white and blue color phases of the snow goose, *Chen caerulescens* [AOU, 169], described on March 8, 1806.

14. Probably Crown Point, Multnomah County, with its scenic vantage of the Columbia gorge, and today's Vista House atop.

[Clark] *November 3rd Sunday 1805*

The fog So thick this morning we did not think it prudent to Set out untill ⟨it Cleared away at⟩ 10 oClock we Set out and proceeded on verry well,[1] accompanied by our Indian friends— This morning *Labich* killed 3 Geese flying Collins killed a Duck— The water rose ⟨2⟩ Inches last night the effects of *tide*. The Countrey has a handsom appearance in ad-

Chapter Twenty-Five

From the Cascades of the Columbia to the Sea

November 2–21, 1805

[Clark] *Novr. 2d Saturday 1805*[1]

Meridian altitude 59° 45′ 45″ made a portage of about 1 ½ miles with half of the Baggage, and run the rapid with the Canoes without much damage,[2] one Struck a rock & Split a little, and 3 others took in Some water 7 Squars Came over the portage loaded with Dried fish & *Beargrass*,[3] Soon after 4 men Came down in a Canoe after takeing brackfast, & after taking a meridian altitude we Set out Passed 2 bad rapids one at 2 & the other at 4 mile below the Isd on Lard. and upper end of Strawberry Island[4] on the Stard. Side from the Creek end of last Course

S. 50° W.   5   miles to a timbered bottom on the Lard. Side, passed the Lowr. point of Strawbery Isd. at 3 miles, a Isd Covd with wood below on Stard. Side a remarkable high rock on Stard. Side about 800 feet high & 400 yds round, the *Beaten* Rock.[5] The mountains and bottoms thickly timbered with Pine Spruce Cotton and a kind of maple Passed 2 Small wooded Islands on Std. Side, ⟨opsd⟩ below the lower Island on the Stard. Side at 4 miles an Indian village of 9 Houses, The river wider and bottoms more extencive.

S. 47° W.   12   miles to a ⟨Lard.⟩ Stard. point of rocks of a high clift of black rocks.⁶ passed a Stard. Point at 4 miles. here the mountains are low on each Side & thickly timbered with pine. river about 2 miles wide, passed a rock at 10 miles in the middle of the river this rock is 100 feet high & 80 feet Diameter, a deep bend to th Stard. Side,

We Labiech killed 14 Geese & a Brant, Collins one Jos. Fields & R 3 those gees are much Smaller than Common, and have white under their rumps & ⟨abov⟩ around the tale,⁷ The tide rises here a fiew 9 Inches, I cannot assertain the prosise hite it rises at the last rapid or at this place— of Camp.⁸

The Indians we left at the portage passed us this evening   one other Canoe Come up

S. 58° W.   4   miles ⟨to a⟩ Stard. point of a large bottom. Encamped on the
             21   21 Lard Side   river about 2 miles wid   Country thickly timbered   we Encamped behind a large rock in the Lard. Bend, a Canoe with 7 Inds. came down & Encamped with us

[Clark]   *November 2nd Saturday 1805* ⁹

Examined the rapid below us more pertcelarly   the danger appearing too great to Hazzard our Canoes loaded, dispatched all the men who could not Swim with loads to the end of the portage below, I also walked to the end of the portage with the carriers where I delayed untill everry articles was brought over and canoes arrived Safe.   here we brackfast and took a Meridn.   altitude *59° 45′ 45″*   about the time we were Setting out 7 Squars came over loaded with Dried fish, and bear grass neetly bundled up, Soon after 4 Indian men came down over the rapid in a large canoe.   passed a rapid at 2 miles & 1 at 4 miles opposit the lower point of a high Island on the Lard Side, and a little below 4 Houses on the Stard. Bank,¹⁰ a Small Creek on the Lard Side opposit Straw berry Island, which heads below the last rapid, opposit the lower point of this Island passed three Islands covered with tall timber opposit the Beatin rock Those Islands are nearest the Starboard Side, imediately below on the Stard. Side passed a village of *nine* houses,¹¹ which is Situated between 2 Small Creeks, and are of the Same construction of those above; here the river widens to near a mile, and the bottoms are more extensive and

November 2–21, 1805

vance no mountains extensive bottoms— the water Shallow for a great distance from Shore—. The fog continued thick untill 12 oClock, we Coasted, and halted at the mouth of a large river on the Lard Side,[2] This river throws out emence quanty of ⟨quick⟩ Sand and is verry Shallow, th narrowest part 200 yards wide bold Current, much resembling the river Plat, Several Islands about 1 mile up and has a Sand bar of 3 miles in extent imedeately in its mouth, discharging it waters by 2 mouths, and Crowding its Corse Sands So as to throw the Columbian waters on its Nothern banks,[3] & confdg it to ½ ms. in width Passed a Small Prarie on the Stard. Side above, a large Creek[4] opposit *qk Sand* River on the Stard. Side, extensive bottoms and low hilley Countrey on each Side (*good wintering Place*) a high peaked mountain Suppose to be Mt. Hood is on the Lard Side S. 85° E. 40 miles distant from the mouth of quick Sand river.—

Course Nov. 3d

West	3	miles to the upper mouth of quick Sand ⟨mountain⟩ river, Country low on each Side rising to a hilley Countrey passed a large Creek opposit Std. Side & 2 Sand bars
S. 70° W.	7	miles to the upper point of a large Island Covered with [*blank*] passed the Lower mouth of Sandy river at 3 miles opposit the head of a large Island Std. Side faced with rocks and the ⟨edge⟩ Side is pine & Cotton a large Creek falls in oppost to the head of this Island Isld of Fowls[5] as I Saw Som 1000 pass over to the head of this Island on the Stard Sd. passed Some ruged rocks in the middle of the river opposit the Island— river wide The Countrey below quick Sand river on the Lard Side is low Piney Countrey. Passed the lower point of the Island at 3½ miles long & 1½ wide— emence quantity of Geese, Brants, Ducks & Sea otter, Some of the large & Small kind of Swan, & Sand hill Cranes—also luns & White gulls
S. 87° W.	3 13	miles on the North Side of the Island and Encamped we met 2 Canoes, of Indians 15 in number who informed us they had Seen 3 Vestles 2 days below us, we Camped on the Island, and Sent out hunters on it and Capt. Lewis walked out, after Dark Capt. Lewis with 3 men went into a large Pond on this Island & killed a Swan & Several ducks. ⟨we⟩ The Party killed this

From the Cascades of the Columbia to the Sea

day 3 Swan 8 Brant, & 5. The Canoe was borrowed of the Inds. here & taken over by 4 men into the pond. I gave the Indians a Brant to eate.

[Clark] *November 3rd Sunday 1805*

The Fog So thick this morning that we could not See a man 50 Steps off, this fog detained us untill 10 oClock at which time we Set out, accompanied by our Indian friends who are from a village near the great falls, previous to our Setting out Collins killed a large Buck, and Labiech killed 3 Geese flying. I walked on the Sand beech Lard. Side, opposit the canoes as they passed allong. The under groth rushes, vines &c. in the bottoms too thick to pass through, at 3 miles I arrived at the enterance of a river which appeared to Scatter over a Sand bar, the bottom of which I could See quite across and did not appear to be 4 Inches deep in any part; I attempted to wade this Stream and to my astonishment found the bottom a quick Sand, and impassable— I called to the Canoes to put to Shore, I got into the Canoe and landed below the mouth, & Capt Lewis and my Self walked up this river about 1½ miles to examine this river which we found to be a verry Considerable Stream Dischargeing its waters through 2 Chanels which forms an Island of about 3 miles in length on the river and 1½ miles wide, composed of Corse Sand which is thrown out of this quick Sand river Compressing the waters of the Columbia and throwing the whole Current of its waters against its Northern banks, within a Chanel of ½ a mile wide, Several Small Islands 1 mile up this river, This Stream has much the appearance of the *River Platt*: roleing its quick Sands into the bottoms with great velocity after which it is divided into 2 Chanels by a large Sand bar before mentioned, the narrowest part of this River is 120 yards—on the Opposit Side of the Columbia a ⟨large Creek⟩ [*NB: Small river called Seal river*] falls in above this Creek on the Same Side is a Small prarie. extensive low country on each Side thickly timbered.

The Quick Sand river appears to pass through the low countrey at the foot of those high range of mountains in a Southerly direction,— The large Creeks which fall into the Columbia on the Stard. Side rise in the Same range of mountains to the N. N. E. and pass through Some ridgey land— A Mountain which we Suppose to be Mt. Hood is S. 85° E about

47 miles distant from the mouth of quick sand river This mtn. is Covered with Snow and in the range of mountains which we have passed through and is of a Conical form but rugid— after takeing dinner at the mouth of this river we proceeded on passed the head of a Island near the lard Side back of which on the Same Side and near the head a large Creek falls in, and nearly opposit & 3 miles below the upper mouth of quick Sand river is the lower mouth, [for?] This Island is 3½ miles long, has rocks at the upper point, Some timber on the borders of this Island in the middle open and ponney [NB: pondy]. Some rugid rocks in the middle of the Stream opposit this Island. ⟨proceeded in⟩ [NB: proceeded on] to Center of a large Island in the middle of the river which we call Dimond Isld. from its appearance, here we met 15 Indn men in 2 canoes from below, they informed us they Saw 3 vestles below &c. &c. we landed on the North Side of this Dimond Island and Encamped,[6] Capt. L walked out with his gun on the Island, Sent out hunters & fowlers— below quick Sand River the Countrey is low rich and thickly timbered on each Side of the river, the Islands open & Some ponds river wide and emence numbers of fowls flying in every direction Such as Swan, geese, Brants, Cranes, Stalks [NB: Storks], white guls, comerants & plevers &c.[7] also great numbers of Sea Otter in the river—[8] a Canoe arrived from the village below the last rapid with a man his wife and 3 children, and a woman whome had been taken prisoner from the Snake Inds. [NB: on a river from the South which we found to be Mulknoma] on Clarks River[9] I Sent the Interpreters wife who is a *So So ne* or Snake Indian of the Missouri, to Speake to this Squar, they Could not understand each other Sufficiently to Converse. This familey and the Inds. we met from below continued with us Capt Lewis borrowed a Small Canoe of those Indians & 4 men took her across to a Small lake in the Isld. Cap L. and 3 men Set out after night in this Canoe in Serch of the Swans, Brants Ducks &c. &c. which appeared in great numbers in the Lake, he Killed a Swan and Several Ducks which made our number of fowls this evening 3 Swan, 8 brant and 5 Ducks, on which we made a Sumptious Supper. We gave the Indian—who lent the Canoe a brant, and Some meat to the others. one of those Indians, the man from the village near the lower Rapids has a gun with a brass barrel & Cock of which he prises highly— note the mountain we Saw from near the forks proves to be Mount *Hood*

1. Between the camp of November 2 and the mouth of Sandy (Quicksand) River they passed the highest point on the Columbia reached by Lieutenant William Broughton of George Vancouver's expedition in 1792. This was on a large sand island, today's Reed Island, much of which had disappeared by 1805. Thus they returned, for the first time since April 1805, to country previously explored by whites. They also passed the point Broughton named Point Vancouver, having sighted it from the island; the point is about four miles east of Washougal, Clark County, Washington, and across the river from Oregon's Rooster Rock State Park. Barry (BOC); Anderson (SSGV), 116–117; Meany, 264–65; *Atlas* maps 79, 88.

2. Sandy River, "Quick Sand River" on *Atlas* map 79, in Multnomah County, Oregon.

3. The sand deposited by Sandy River is derived by erosion of mudflows from Mt. Hood containing abundant volcanic ash and volcaniclastic fragments. The mudflow is the last of many and may have occurred less than two hundred years ago—probably just a few years before Lewis and Clark passed through here. Clark was correct about the impact of the Sandy on the Columbia, as its delta has diverted the main stream's channel two miles to the north. Allen (MG), 82.

4. Washougal River, meeting the Columbia near present Washougal; "Seal R" on *Atlas* map 79.

5. "White Brant Isld" on *Atlas* map 79, and "Fowl I" on *Atlas* map 88; apparently later Lady Island. Archaeological work here, although largely unpublished, is noteworthy for the discovery of prehistoric ceramic artifacts associated with occupation of a site on the island approximately 2,000–2,500 years ago. Woodward (ECT).

6. Diamond Island is later Government and McGuire islands, opposite Portland, Multnomah County. The camp was on the island, about three miles west of present Camas, Clark County, Washington. *Atlas* map 79.

7. Some of these birds may be identified as the sandhill crane, *Grus canadensis* [AOU, 206], the wood stork, *Mycteria americana* [AOU, 188], and the double-crested cormorant, *Phalacrocorax auritus* [AOU, 120]. The swans (noted as the "large & Small kind" in the first entry) would be the trumpeter swan, *Cygnus buccinator* [AOU, 181], and the tundra, or whistling, swan, *C. columbianus* [AOU, 180]. See below, March 9, 1806. The other references are too obscure for precise identification. Holmgren, 33; Burroughs, 199–200.

8. The harbor seal.

9. The "Snake" woman was probably a Paiute, but perhaps a Shoshonean whose language was unfamiliar to Sacagawea. Biddle added the red-inked note about the "Mulknoma" knowing the party's discovery of this river on their return journey in April 1806; it is the present Willamette River, meeting the Columbia at Portland. Actually their original supposition that these Indians were living on the "Clark's" River (present Deschutes) was probably correct. Ray & Lurie, 365; *Atlas* maps 77, 79.

[Clark] *Novr. 4th Monday 1805*

A Cloudy Cool morning, wind West, we Set out at ½ past 8 oClock having dispatched 4 men in the Small canoe to hunt

November 2–21, 1805

Course

West	6	miles to the North Side & Lower point of a large Island, passed the lower point of dimon Island at 3 miles, a little below the head of a large Island on the Lard Side. (river wide and Countrey low on both Sides & thickly covered with pine)—. this Island is Seperated from one on its Lard. by a narrow Chanl. in which there is only water in high tide— which rises here ab. 18 Inches. high tide at 6 oClock P m ⟨passed the Lower point the Isld. at 1 mile lower, a large Indian⟩

⟨Those people men & women ⟨flatten the⟩ heads ⟨village⟩ are flat⟩

We landed at a village 200 men of Flatheads of 25 houses 50 canoes built of Straw, we were treated verry kindly by them, they gave us round root near the Size of a hens egg roasted which they call *Wap-to* to eate [1]

N. 88° W.	6	miles to Point on the Stard Side passed a village 25 Houses on the Lard. main Shore, those houses are differently built from those above all except one verry large house covered with bark & Thached with Straw. verry worm
N. 80° W.	3	miles on the Stard. Side, a Pon and a Small plain on Std. Side passed the head of an Island at 1 miles near the middle of the river to a 2d Island opsd. the end of this Course
N. 76° W.	4	miles on the Stard. Side passed a Island near the large Island Lbd. a range of high hills on the Lard. Side running S E & N W. leaving a large bottom on the river.

I walked out on the Stard. Side found the country fine, an open Prarie for 1 mile back of which the wood land comence riseing back, the timber on the edge of the Prarie is white oke, back is Spruce pine [2] & other Species of Pine mixed Some under groth of a wild crab [3] & a Specis of wood I'm not acquainted, a Specis of maple & Cotton wood grow near this river,[4] Some low bushes [5]

Indians continue to be with us, Several Canoes Continue with us, The Indians at the last village have more Cloth and uriopian trinkets than above I Saw Some Guns, a Sword, maney Powder flasks, Salers Jackets, overalls,[6] hats & Shirts, Copper and Brass trinkets with few Beeds only. dureing the time I was at Dinner the Indians Stold my tomahawk which I made use of to Smoke I Serched but Could not find it, a Pond on the Stard Side, off from the river. Raspberries[7] and [blank] are also in the bottoms— met a large and Small canoe with 12 men from below the men were dressed with a variety of articles of European manufactory the large Canoe had emeges on the bow & Stern handsomly Carved in wood & painted with the figur of a Bear in front & man in a Stern. Saw white geese with black wings—[8] Saw a Small Crab-apple with all the taste & flavor of the Common— Those Indians were all armed with Pistols or bows and arrows ready Sprung war axes &c.[9]

N W.	3	miles on the Stard. Side passed the Lower point of Immage canoe Island and 4 Small Islands at its lower point all on the Lard Side—
N. 35° W.	1	mile on the Stard Side, bottoms low and extensive, not Subject to over flow, river about 1½ miles wide
North	3	miles to a white tree on the Stard. Side. high tide here at 5 oClock P M.

⟨Encamped on the Lard. Side.[10] Mt. Ranier⟩ Mount Hellen[11] bears N. 25° E about 80 miles, this is the mountain we Saw near the foks of this river. it is emensely high and covered with Snow, riseing in a kind of Cone perhaps the highest pinecal from the common leavel in america passed a village of 4 hs. on the Stard Side at 2 mils, one at 3 mls.

One deer 2 Ducks & Brant killed

N. 28° W.	3 29	miles to a Stard bend & campd. near a village on the Std. Side passed one on each Side, proceded on untill after dark to get Clere of Indians we Could not 2 Canoes pursued us and 2 others Came to us, and were about us all night we bought a fiew roots &c.

[Clark] *November 4th Monday 1805*

A cloudy cool morning wind from the West we Set out at ½ past 8 oClock, one man Shannon Set out early to walk on the Island to kill Something, he joined us at the lower point with a Buck. This Island is 6 miles long and near 3 miles wide thinly timbered[12] (Tide rose last night 18 inches perpndicular at Camp) near the lower point of this dimond Island is The head of a large Island Seperated from a Small one by a narrow chanel,[13] and both Situated nearest the Lard Side, those Islands as also the bottoms are thickly Covered with Pine &c. river wide, Country low on both Sides; on the Main Lard Shore a Short distance below the last Island we landed at a village of 25 *Houses:*[14] 24 of those houses we[re] thached with Straw, and covered with bark, the other House is built of boards in the form of those above, except that it is above ground and about 50 feet in length and covered with broad Split boards This village contains about 200 men of the *Skil-loot* nation I counted 52 canoes on the bank in front of this village maney of them verry large and raised in bow. we recognised the man who over took us last night, [*NB: our pilot who came in his canoe*] he invited us to a lodge in which he had Some part and gave us a roundish roots about the Size of a Small Irish potato which they roasted in the embers until they became Soft, This root they call *Wap-pa-to* which the *Bulb* of the *Chinese* cultivate in great quantities called the *Sa-git ti folia* [*NB: we believe it to be the Same*] or common arrow head—.[15] it has an agreeable taste and answers verry well in place of bread. we purchased about 4 bushels of this root and divided it to our party,

at 7 miles below this village passed the upper point of a large Island[16] nearest the Lard Side, a Small Prarie in which there is a pond opposit on the Stard. here I landed and walked on Shore, about 3 miles a fine open Prarie for about 1 mile, back of which the countrey rises gradually and wood land comencies Such as white oake, pine of different kinds, wild crabs with the taste and flavour of the common crab and Several Species of undergroth of which I am not acquainted, a few Cottonwood trees & the Ash[17] of this countrey grow Scattered on the river bank, Saw Some Elk[18] and Deer Sign and joined Capt. Lewis at a place he had landed with the party for Diner. Soon after Several Canoes of Indians from the village above came down dressed for the purpose as I Supposed of Paying us a friendly visit, they had Scarlet & blue blankets Salors jackets, overalls, Shirts and Hats independant of their Usial dress; the most of them had either war axes Spears or Bows Sprung with quivers of arrows, Muskets or pistols, and tin flasks to hold their powder; Those fellows we found assumeing and disagreeable, however we Smoked with them and treated them with every attention & friendship.

dureing the time we were at dinner those fellows Stold my pipe Tomahawk which They were Smoking with, I imediately Serched every man and the canoes, but Could find nothing of my Tomahawk, while Serching for the Tomahawk one of those Scoundals Stole a Cappoe [*NB: Capotte (gr: coat)*]¹⁹ of one of our interpreters, which was found Stufed under the root of a treer, near the place they Sat, we became much displeased with those fellows, which they discovered and moved off on their return home to their village, except 2 canoes which had passed on down— we proceeded on met a large & a Small Canoe from below, with 12 men the large Canoe was ornimented with *Images* carved in wood the figures of ⟨man &⟩ a Bear in front & a man in Stern, Painted & fixed verry netely on the ⟨bow & Stern⟩ of the Canoe, rising to near the hight of a man two Indians verry finely Dressed & with hats on was in this canoe passed the lower point of the Island which is *nine* miles in length haveing passed 2 Islands on the Stard Side of this large Island, three Small Islands at its lower point. the Indians make Signs that a village²⁰ is Situated back of those Islands on the Lard. Side and I believe that a Chanel is Still on the Lrd. Side as a Canoe passed in between the Small Islands, and made Signs that way, probably to traffick with Some of the nativs liveing on another Chanel, at 3 miles lower, and 12 Leagues below quick Sand river passed a village of four large houses [*NB: Mulknomaws*]²¹ on The Lard. Side, near which we had a full view of *Mt. Helien* which is perhaps the highest pinical in America from their base it bears N. 25° E about 90 miles— This is the mountain I Saw from the Muscle Shell rapid on the 19th of October last Covered with Snow, it rises Something in the form of a Sugar lofe—²² about a mile lower passed a Single house on the Lard. Side, and one on the Stard. Side, passed a village on each Side and Camped near a house on the Stard. Side²³ we proceeded on untill one hour after dark with a view to get clear of the nativs who was constantly about us, and troublesom, finding that we could not get Shut of those people for one night, we landed and Encamped on the Stard. Side Soon after 2 canoes Came to us loaded with Indians, we purchased a fiew roots of them.

This evening we Saw vines much resembling the raspberry which is verry thick in the bottoms. A range of high hills at about 5 miles on the Lard Side which runs S. E. & N W. Covered with tall timber the bottoms below in this range of hills and the river is rich and leavel, Saw White geese with a part of their wings black. The river here is 1½ miles wide, and current jentle. opposit to our camp on a Small Sandy Island the brant & geese make Such a noise that it will be impossible for me to Sleap. we *made 29 miles* to day

Killed a Deer and Several brant and ducks. I Saw a Brarow[24] tamed at the 1st village to day The Indians which we have passd to day [*NB: in their boats were of*] of the *Scil-loot* nation [*NB: going up to the falls.* differ a little] in their language from those near & about the long narrows of the *Che-luc-it-te-quar* or *E-chee-lute*, their dress differ but little, except they have more of the articles precured from the white traders, they all have flatened heads both men and women, live principally on fish and *Wap pa toe* roots, they also kill Some fiew Elk and Deer, dureing the Short time I remained in their village they brought in three Deer which they had killed with their Bow & arrows. They are thievishly inclined as we have experienced.[25]

1. Wapato, *Sagittaria latifolia* Willd. Lewis and Clark describe the importance and ethnobotanical use of the wapato in entries for March 29, 1806. Biddle describes the gathering process under April 4, 1806. Hitchcock et al., 1:147; Coues (HLC), 3:929. See also October 22, 1805.

2. "White oke" is Oregon white, or Garry, oak, *Quercus garryana* Dougl. ex Hook. Hitchcock et al., 2:85; Little (CIH), 166-W. "Spruce pine" is probably not the same tree as noted on September 9, 1805, near Missoula, Montana, where it was identified as Engelmann spruce, *Picea engelmannii* Parry. Pine is clearly being used in a general sense, as it is today, to refer to any evergreen coniferous species. Spruce refers to species with sharply pointed, square needles, not in bundles. The spruce pine of this day at this low elevation is probably Sitka spruce, *P. sitchensis* (Bong.) Carr., which reaches its easternmost distributional limit in this region of the Columbia gorge in southwestern Skamania County, Washington, and northern Hood River County, Oregon. Little (CIH), 42-W. Lewis describes the tree more fully on February 4, 1806, where he calls it a species of fir. An important and interesting ecological feature of the Columbia gorge here is the transition from dry ponderosa pine-white oak forest on the east to the moist Douglas fir-western hemlock forests (with Sitka spruce) on the west, and the complex interdigitation of vegetation zones at this low elevation. Franklin & Dyrness, 310–11. There remains a possibility that the spruce pine could be Douglas fir, *Pseudotsuga menziesii* (Mirb.) Franco. Little (CIH), 80-W.

3. The wild crab, then new to science, is Oregon crabapple, *Malus diversifolia* (Bong.) Roem., given by Hitchcock et al. as western crabapple, *Pyrus fusca* Raf. Little (MWH), 100-W; Hitchcock et al., 3:164; Cutright (LCPN), 268, 274, 416. See Lewis's detailed description at January 28, 1806.

4. The maple is probably bigleaf maple, *Acer macrophyllum* Pursh (new to science), and

the final tree is black cottonwood, *Populus trichocarpa* T. & G. Little (CIH), 95-W, 153-W; Franklin & Dyrness, 72; Cutright (LCPN), 288–89, 401.

5. A subtotal of "19" appears at the top of the next page following these words.

6. Not the bib overalls of later usage, but trousers of strong material worn over regular clothes for their protection. Criswell, 60.

7. The raspberry of the floodplain ("bottoms") is the Pacific blackberry, *Rubus ursinus* Cham. & Schlecht., a common, low-elevation blackberry that is ethnobotanically important in the area. The captains usually call it the green brier because it retains its green leaves late in the fall. Hitchcock et al., 3:182–83; Gunther (EWW), 35–36; Franklin & Dyrness, 74.

8. Snow goose.

9. Again the number "19" at the top of the next page.

10. An error; elsewhere in both entries Clark indicates a camp on the starboard side, which may account for striking the passage.

11. Mt. St. Helens in Skamania County, Washington, still an active volcano although it did not erupt during Lewis and Clark's stay on the Pacific Coast. Vancouver named it in 1792 after the island of St. Helena in the South Atlantic.

12. There is a blank space equivalent to several lines after this sentence.

13. This island ("White Goose Isd." of *Atlas* map 79) may be Government and McGuire islands and adjoining islands and sandbars; it is "Twin Islds." of *Atlas* map 88. See also Diamond Island of entry of November 3.

14. Designated "Sha-hala N." on *Atlas* map 79, evidently a part of the Upper Chinookan-language Watlalas. Hodge, 2:519; Berreman, 16, 18–19; Swanton, 476; Hajda, 67. The village was within present Portland, Multnomah County, Oregon, and was probably destroyed by the construction of the city's airport. "Skil-loot" ("Skil-lute" on *Atlas* map 79) is probably the Chinookan imperative form *s(i)ḱlútk*, "look (at him)!" which Silverstein suggests Clark misconstrued as an ethnonym. Cf. Hodge, 2:519; Hajda, 65–66, 108–9.

15. The Chinese species is *Sagittaria sagittifolia* L., old-world arrowhead, and is not the same species as the North American arrowhead, more commonly called wapato. Bailey, 130. Here Clark may have been borrowing from Lewis's knowledge of the Linnaean Latin nomenclature.

16. "Image Canoe Island" on *Atlas* map 79, evidently later Hayden and Tomahawk islands. An adjacent island is named "Tomahawk" on *Atlas* map 88, in reference to the item's loss. Archaeological work here has failed to locate any prehistoric materials. The pond on the adjacent north shore is present Vancouver Lake, Clark County.

17. Probably bigleaf maple of the first entry, rather than ash. There is some confusion between the two species, as discussed at February 10, 1806. However, the Oregon ash, *Fraxinus latifolia* Benth., is commonly found along watercourses with the black cottonwood and bigleaf maple. Franklin & Dyrness, 72.

18. Elk (or more properly, wapiti), *Cervus elaphus*.

19. The capote, or blanket coat, a long, hooded coat of heavy blanket material, was popular in the Canadian fur trade of the period. Criswell, 21.

20. The village may be one of several shown on *Atlas* map 80 on the Oregon shore behind Sauvie ("Wappâto") Island. In this vicinity on the island is the so-called Sunken

Village, a deeply stratified, partially submerged archaeological site. Many perishable artifacts have been found in the water-logged deposits; radiocarbon dates indicate submergence of this site within the last 500 years. Warren (RSWA), 19; Butler (PLCV), 7, 10.

21. An Upper Chinookan-language group living on Sauvie Island ("Multnomahs" on "Wappâto Island" on *Atlas* map 80), Multnomah County. The term is Chinookan *mátnuma(x)*, "(those) at/toward the body of water." They are identified by tribe on *Atlas* maps 80, 88, and in the Estimate of Western Indians (see Chapter 30). Berreman, 16–17; Hajda, 66, 109–15. Both Sauvie Island and the Vancouver Lake area on the Washington side are very rich and important archaeologically, but neither has been intensively studied. The bulk of the archaeological record pertains only to the last 3,000 years of prehistory. Pettigrew. At the time of historic contact, this area had one of the densest Indian populations in western North America. Hajda, 67–75; Boyd & Hajda, 309–26. Indian settlements in the Lower Columbia Valley referred to in historic accounts are listed by Hajda and by Saleeby & Pettigrew.

22. The mountain seen on October 19 was Mt. Adams, but Clark is now seeing Mt. St. Helens. Allen (PG), 312 n. 15.

23. The camp was probably near the entrance of present Salmon Creek in Clark County, Washington. The creek is not shown on *Atlas* maps 79, 80, while the lake shown near the camp may be one of the lakes north of present Vancouver Lake (probably the "Pond" on *Atlas* map 79), perhaps Post Office Lake or Green Lake.

24. A badger, *Taxidea taxus*; see above, July 30, 1804; below, February 26, 1806.

25. The remaining one-quarter of p. 107 here in Codex H is blank.

[Clark]   *Novr. 5th Tuesday 1805*

a Cloudy morning Som rain the after part of last night & this morning. I could not Sleep for the noise kept by the Swans, Geese, white & black brant, Ducks &c. on a opposit base, & Sand hill Crane, they were emensely numerous and their noise horrid. We Set out at Sun rise &

                              Courses

N. 35° W.	3	miles to a Stard. point river about ¾ of a mile wide a Small prarie on the Std.
N. 30° W.	3	miles to the South West Side of an Island ⟨near⟩ Seperated from the Stard. Side by a narrow channel river widens to about 1½ miles *Green bryor Isd.*
N. 12° W.	3	miles to a Lard. point of 2 rocks ⟨psd. Ind.⟩ opposit the upper pt. of an Isd. on Std. Side psd. 2 house on the Lard. Sid, passed the lower pt. of the Island Std. at 2 miles. behind this Island a little above the lower point on the Std. side is a large village of ¼ of a mile in extent. I counted 14 large houses in

		front next the slew 7 canoes loaded with Indians Came up to See us. low rock
N. 22° W.	6	miles to a Stard point passed a large Slew ¼ of a mile wide or at a ½ of a mile on th Lard. Side Some low rockey clifts below. The language of those people have a great Similarity to those above. met 3 canoes of Indians
N. 30° W.[1]	5	miles to a point of woodland Stard. Side. a range of high hills here forms the Stard. bank of the river, the Shore bold and rocky covered with a thick growth of pine timber an extensive low ⟨bottom⟩ Island & bottoms on the Lard. side passed 2 Islands on Std. & the Lard. pt. on 3d
N. 40° W.	7	m. to a point of woodland Std. passed the Lower point of the Island Close under the Lard Side at 5 miles a Small Island in the middle of the river. passed an old village on the Island at 3 miles, The high hills leave the river on the Stard. at 3 miles, a high bottom below met 4 canoes of Indians one of those canoes had emigies bow & Stern & 26 Indians in them all[2]
N. 40° W.	5 ― 32	miles to a point of high piney land on the Lard Side the Stard. Shore bold and rockey passed a Creek at 2 miles on the Stard Side, below which is an old village. rained all the evening and Some fine rain at intervals all day river wide & Deep

our hunters killed 10 Brant 4 of which were white with black wings 2 Ducks, and a Swan which were divided, we Came too and Encamped on the Lard. Side under a high ridgey land,[3] the high land come to the river on each Side. the river about 1½ mile wide. those high lands rise gradually from the river & bottoms— we are all wet Cold and disagreeable, rain Continues & encreases. I killed a Pheasent which is very fat—[4]   my feet and legs cold. I saw 17 Snakes to day on a Island, but little appearance of Frost at [tear] this place.

[Clark] November 5th Tuesday 1805

Rained all the after part of last night, rain continues this morning, I [s]lept but verry little last night for the noise Kept dureing the whole of the night by the Swans, Geese, white & Grey Brant Ducks &c. on a Small Sand Island close under the Lard. Side; they were emensely noumerous, and their noise horid— we Set out ⟨at about Sun rise⟩ early here the river is not more than ¾ of a mile in width, passed a Small Prarie on the Stard. Side passed 2 houses about ½ a mile from each other on the Lard. Side a Canoe came from the upper house, with 3 men in it mearly to view us, passed an Isld. Covered with tall trees & green briers Seperated from the Stard. Shore by a narrow Chanel⁵ at 9 [8?] miles I observed on the Chanel which passes on the Stard Side of this Island a Short distance above its lower point is Situated a large village, the front of which occupies nearly ¼ of a mile fronting the Chanel, and closely Connected, I counted 14 houses [*NB: Quathlapotle nation*]⁶ in front here the river widens to about 1½ miles. Seven canoes of Indians came out from this large village to view and trade with us, they appeared orderly and well disposed, they accompanied us a fiew miles and returned back. about 1½ miles below this village on the Lard Side behind a rockey Sharp point, we passed a Chanel ¼ of a mile wide,⁷ which I take to be the one the Indian Canoe entered yesterday from the lower point of *Immage Canoe Island* [X: *So named*] a Some low clifts of rocks below this Chanel, a large Island Close under the Stard Side opposit,⁸ and 2 Small Islands, below, here we met 2 canoes from below,— below those Islands a range of high hills form the Stard. Bank of the river, the Shore bold and rockey, Covered with a thick groth of Pine an extensive low Island,⁹ Seperated from the Lard side by a narrow Chanel, on this Island we Stoped to Dine I walked out found it open & covered with ⟨Small⟩ grass interspersed with Small ponds, in which was great numbr. of foul, the remains of an old village on the lower part of this Island, I saw Several deer our hunters killed on this Island a Swan, 4 white 6 Grey brant & 2 Ducks all of them were divided, below the lower point of this Island a range of high hills¹⁰ which runs S. E. forms the Lard. bank of the river the Shores bold and rockey & hills Covered with pine, The high hills leave the river on the Stard. Side a high bottom between the hill & river. We met 4 Canoes of Indians from below, in which there is 26 Indians, one of those Canoes is large, and ornimented with *Images* on the bow & Stern. That in the Bow the likeness of a Bear, and in Stern the picture of a man— we landed on the Lard. Side & camped a little below the mouth of a creek¹¹ on the Stard. Side a little below the mouth of which is an Old Village which is now abandaned—;¹² here the river is about one and a half miles wide, and deep, The high Hills which run in a N W. & S E. derection form both banks of the river the Shore boald and rockey, the hills rise gradually & are Covered with a thick groth of pine &c. The valley which is from above the mouth of Quick Sand River to this place may be computed at 60 miles wide on a Derect line, & extends a great Distanc to the right & left rich thickly Covered with tall timber, with a fiew Small Praries bordering on the river and on the Islands; Some fiew Standing Ponds & Several Small Streams of running water on either Side of the river; This is certainly a fertill and a handsom valley, at this time Crouded with Indians. The day proved Cloudy with rain the greater part of it, we are all wet cold and disagreeable— I Saw but little appearance of frost in this valley which we call ⟨*Wap-pa-too* Columbia⟩ [*NB: Columbian Valley*][13] from that root or plants growing Spontaniously in this valley only In my walk of to Day I saw 17 Striped Snakes I killed a grouse which was verry fat, and larger than Common. This is the first night which we have been entirely clear of Indians Since our arrival on the waters of the Columbia River. We made 32 miles to day by estimation—

1. This course and remarks and part of the next appear to be in Lewis's handwriting.

2. A subtotal of "27" appears on the top of the next page after this course.

3. In Columbia County, Oregon, southeast of present Rainier, perhaps near Prescott. *Atlas* map 80.

4. Perhaps the Oregon ruffed grouse (called a grouse in Clark's second entry), *Bonasa umbellus sabini,* now combined with *B. umbellus* [AOU, 300], and new to science. See descriptions below, February 5 and March 3, 1806. Burroughs, 218–19; Cutright (LCPN), 430; Holmgren, 32.

5. Apparently the outlet of Lewis River, now the boundary between Clark and Cowlitz counties, Washington. The island may be Bachelor Island ("green bryor Isd" on *Atlas* map 89). Lewis River is "Chah wah na hi ook" on *Atlas* maps 79, 80.

6. The Cathlapotles were an Upper Chinookan-language group living on the Columbia and lower Lewis rivers in Clark County. Hodge, 1:217; Spier, 21; Swanton, 414–15; *Atlas* maps 80, 89. The name is Chinookan *gaɫápuλx*, "(those of) Lewis River," from *nápuλx,* "Lewis River." Silverstein. The Cathlapotle village at the mouth of Lewis River was called Nahpooitle (Hodge 2:217); it is shown on *Atlas* map 80 on the Washington shore across from the lower of end of Sauvie ("Wappâto") Island. There are two archaeological sites in this vicinity. The principal Cathlapotle village has not been formally excavated, but a large artifact collection from this area has been described. Minor (CAC). The other site, consisting of a series of seasonal camps located along Lake River upstream from the village, has been extensively tested. The occupation of these camps spans the last 2,000 years. Abramowitz; Minor & Toepel. Biddle wrote the interlineation in red ink.

7. The channel behind Sauvie ("Wappâto") Island, in Washington and Columbia counties, Oregon. *Atlas* map 80.

8. The supposed island was apparently crossed out on *Atlas* maps 80, 88, but the two small islands were retained, perhaps today's Burke and Martin islands.

9. "E-lal-lar or Deer Isd." on *Atlas* map 80; still Deer Island, in Columbia County. The term is Upper Chinookan *iláłx̣*, "deer." Gibbs (AVC), 11.

10. Part of the Coast Ranges.

11. The Kalama River, nameless but labeled "20 yds." on *Atlas* map 80, in Cowlitz County.

12. This may be the village of the Lakjalamas (or Klakalama or Thlakalama), an Upper Chinookan-language group residing at the mouth of the Kalama River, Cowlitz County. Hodge, 2:743; Spier, 23, Hajda, 111–12. The place is named "Cath-la-haw's Village" on *Atlas* map 80, which is from Chinookan *gałáx̣awš*, "the ones who have cous roots," and the people are called "Cal-la-maks" in the Estimate of Western Indians (see Chapter 30).

13. It appears that Clark had substituted "Columbia" for "Wap-pa-too," then Biddle crossed both out in red and placed his interlineation.

[Clark]   November 6th Wednesday

a cold wet morning. rain Contd. untill [*blank*] oClock we Set out early & proceeded on the Corse of last night &c.

N. 50° W.	1	mile on the Lard. Side under Some high land. bold rockey Shore
N. 60° W.	1	mile under a bold rockey Shore on the Lard Side, opsd. the upper point of a Island close under the Stard Side the high lands closeing the river on that Side above river wide
N. 75° W.	12	miles to a point of high land on the Lard Side, passed *two* Lodges on the Lard Side at 2 miles in a bottom, The high land leave The river on the Stard. Side. passd. a remarkable [described?] Knob of high land on the Stard. Side at 3 miles Close on the Waters edge—[1] we purchased of the Indians who cam in their Canoes to us with Salmon—trout—and *Wap-to* roots. Some of their Salmon [t]rout roots & 2 Dressed Beaver Skins for which I gave 5 Small fishing hooks. passed a Island nearest the Lard. Side at 10 mile the head of a Isd. on Std. opposit High Cliffs, with Several Speces of Pine Cedars &c. arber vita & different Species of under groth.
N. 80° W.	2	miles under a high clift on the Lard Side the lower point of the Island on Stard. opposit those hills are Covered thickly

N. 88° W.	5	miles to a high Clift a little below an old village in the Stard. bend and opposit an old village on a Lard. point of a handsom & extensive bottom. passed a Island in the middle of the river 3 miles long and one wide, passed a Small Island Close on the Stard Side & a lower point of a former Isld. below which the lands high & with Clifts to the river Stard. Side
S. 45° W.	5	miles under a Clift of verry high land on the Stard. side wind high a head. We over took 2 Indian Canoes going down to trade
S. 50° W.	1	mile under a high rockey Hill of pine. The Indians leave us, Steep assent, Som Clifts³
S. 75° W.	1	mile under a high hill with a bold rocky Shore, high [X: Steep] assent river about 1 mile wide
West	1	mile under a high Steep hill bold rockey Shore, Encampd under the hill on Stones Scercely land Sufficent between the hills and river Clear of the tide for us to lie. Cloudy & rain all wet and disagreeable. this evening made large fires on the Stones and dried our bedding. The flees are verry troublesom which collects in our blankets, at every old village we encamp at— we killed nothing to day, we halted to dine and the bushes So thick that our hunters Could not get through, red wood, green bryors, a kind of Burch, alder, red holley⁴ a kind of maple &c. &c. The Species of Pine is Spruce Pine fir⁵ arber vitia &c. red Loril, the bottoms have rushes grass & nettles, the Slashes long grass bulrushes flags &c. Som willow on the waters edge
	29	

with Spruce pine *arbor vita* Hackmatack² as called a kind of alder red wood &c. &c. rain Continu

[Clark]   *November 6th Wednesday 1805*

A cool wet raney morning we Set out early at 4 miles pass 2 Lodges of Indians in a Small bottom on the Lard Side I believe those Indians to be travelers. opposit is ⟨the head of a long narrow Island close under the Starboard Side, back of this Island two Creeks fall in about 6 miles apart,⟩ [*NB: an* ⟨*this*⟩ *Island in the mouth of the large river Cow e lis kee*⁶ *150 yds wide— 9 miles lower a large creek Same Side*] and appear to head in the high hilley countrey to the N. E. opposit ⟨this long Island is 2 others one Small and about the middle of the river⟩ [*NB: between the mouths of these* *rivers are 3 Small islands*[7]   *one on the Ld. Shore one near the middle*] the other larger and nearly opposit its lower point, and opposit a high clift of Black rocks[8] on the Lard. Side at 14 miles [*NB: from our camp*]:   here the Indians of the 2 Lodges we passed to day came in their canoes with Sundery articles to Sell, we purchased of them *Wap-pa-too* roots, *Salmon trout*, and I purchased 2 beaver Skins for which I gave 5 Small fish hooks. here the hills leave the river on the Lard. Side, a butifull open and extensive bottom in which there is an old Village, one also on the Stard. Side a little above both of which are abandened by all their inhabitents except Two Small dogs nearly Starved, and an unreasonable portion of flees—   The Hills and mountains are covered with Sever kinds of Pine—*Arber Vitea* or white Cedar, *red Loril*,[9] alder[10] and Several Species of under groth, the bottoms have common rushes, ⟨bull rushes,⟩ nettles, & grass   the Slashey parts have Bull rushes & flags—[11]   Some willow on the waters edge,[12] passed an Island [*NB: near Ld Shore*] 3 miles long and one mile wide,[13] [*NB: & two Sm: isl.*[14] *both*] ⟨one⟩ close under the Stard. Side below the ⟨long narrow Island⟩ [*NB: large creek*] below which the Stard Hills are verry from the river bank and Continues high and rugid on that Side all day, [*NB: called Fanny's Island the large one.*]   we over took two Canoes of Indians going down to trade one of the Indians Spoke a fiew words of english and Said that the principal man who traded with them was Mr. Haley,[15] and that he had a woman in his Canoe who Mr. Haley was fond of &c.   he Showed us a Bow of Iron and Several other things which he Said Mr. Haley gave him.   we came too to Dine on the long narrow Island   found the woods So thick with under groth that the hunters could not get any distance into the Isld.   the red wood, and Green bryors interwoven, and mixed with pine, alder, a Specis of Beech [Berch?], ash &c.[16] we killed nothing to day   The Indians leave us in the evening, river about one mile wide hills high and Steep on the Std.   no place for Several Miles suffcently large and leavil for our camp   we at length Landed at a place which by moveing the Stones we made a place Sufficently large for the party to lie leavil on the Smaller Stones Clear of the Tide[17] Cloudy with rain all day we are all wet and disagreeable, had large fires made on the Stone and dried our bedding and Kill the flees,[18] which collected in our blankets at every old village we encamped near   I had like to have forgotten a verry remarkable Knob[19] riseing from the edge of the water to about 80 feet high, and about 200 paces around at its Base and Situated ⟨on the long narrow Island⟩ [*NB: below the mouth of Cow e liske riv.*][20] above and nearly opposit to the 2 Lodges we passed to day, it is Some distance from the high land & in a low part of the Island

[*NB: Camped ⟨nearly⟩ opposite to the upper point of an Isl. aftds called Sturgeon Island*][21]

1. An asterisk to the side of this entry may have some reference to the knob. A "Knob" is shown on *Atlas* map 80 (see note below). Also a subtotal of "14" is at the bottom of this page and at the top of the next.

2. Arborvitae is western redcedar, *Thuja plicata* Donn. Hitchcock et al., 1:111. Apparently Clark is saying that it is also called hackmatack, although that term was previously used for western, Montana, or mountain larch, also called tamarack and hackmatack, *Larix occidentalis* Nutt. (see September 14, 1805), but it is found only at higher elevations. In the second entry of this day he uses the term "white cedar" for the western redcedar.

3. A subtotal of "27" appears at the top of the next page after this course.

4. Possibly either dull Oregon grape, *Berberis nervosa* Pursh, or Oregon grape, *B. aquifolium* Pursh. The term red could be describing the reddish-purple color of the plants' leaves in winter. See the detailed description of February 12, 1806.

5. Probably grand fir, *Abies grandis* (Dougl.) Lindl., described by Lewis on February 6, 1806. Little (CIH), 6-W.

6. The Cowlitz River, meeting the Columbia at present Longview and Kelso, Cowlitz County, Washington. *Atlas* maps 80, 81, 89. The name is from káwliƚs, in the Cowlitz and Lower Chehalis languages. The island is apparently not shown on the maps but may be present Cottonwood Island.

7. The possibilities for the islands include Dibblee (formerly Lord), Walker, and Fisher islands. The creek is presumably Coal Creek (labeled "not known" on *Atlas* map 81) in Cowlitz County. The island marked with the camp of March 26, 1806 on *Atlas* map 81 is probably either Dibblee Island or Walker Island or a former combination of the two. Two islands are shown on *Atlas* map 89, with the camp of March 26 apparently on Walker Island. The island on the north shore at the entrance of Coal Creek is probably Fisher Island. Cf. Coues (HLC), 2:699 n. 16, 3:909 n. 11.

8. The rocks in this area are composed of basalt of the Columbia River Basalt Group of middle Miocene age and of the Goble Volcanics of Eocene-Oligocene age.

9. Lewis's laurel is probably the California rhododendron, *Rhododendron macrophyllum* G. Don, a large-leaved evergreen understory shrub of the old-growth forest west of the Cascade Range. References to laurel by the captains indicate the extent of the western hemlock vegetation zone. The men were probably familiar with the Eastern species mountain laurel, *Kalmia latifolia* L., which is similar to the rhododendron in appearance, hence the use of the term laurel. The flowers of the rhododendron vary from pink to deep rose-purple and appear in late spring or early summer but are gone by the time Lewis made his observation. His use of the term "red" is thus unclear; he may have been

informed of its flower color by natives or some red coloring may be apparent in winter. Hitchcock et al., 4:27; Franklin & Dyrness, 45, 74, 77; Bailey, 764; Cutright (LCPN), 417.

10. The alder is red, or Oregon, alder, *Alnus rubra* Bong., and new to science. Little (CIH), 104-W; Cutright (LCPN), 274, 401.

11. Rushes and bulrushes are *Scirpus* sp.; nettles are stinging nettle, *Urtica dioica* L.; "Slashey," in Virginia and Kentucky, are wet or swampy places overgrown with bushes, while here it would be flooded marshes, oxbows, or sloughs of the river; "flags" are common cat-tail, *Typha latifolia* L. Hitchcock et al., 2:91, 1:731; Criswell, 79.

12. The willow would be one or more of the following, low-elevation species: Pacific willow, *Salix lasiandra* Benth.; Scouler willow, *S. scouleriana* Barratt; Sitka willow, *S. sitchensis* Sanson. Little (MWH), 173-W, 179-W, 182-W.

13. Probably present Crims (sometimes given as Grim's) Island, Columbia County. "Fanny's Isd." on *Atlas* map 81 and later in the text, perhaps named on the return in March 1806. It is unnamed on *Atlas* map 89. Coues considers Clark to have given the name in honor of his sister Frances. Coues (HLC), 3:909 n. 11.

14. Only one island is shown on *Atlas* map 81. It was apparently Biddle who crossed out "one" in this entry, in his red ink. In the first entry Clark calls the second one "a former Isld."

15. "Haley" may have been Captain Samuel Hill of Boston, skipper of the brig *Lydia*, who traded with the Lower Columbia Indians in April 1805, reportedly going upriver in a boat as far as the "Great Rapids" (Cascades). He would return in April or July 1806, after the expedition had left. See notes for November 24, 1805. It is also possible that Haley was Captain William Shaler of the brig *Lelia Bird*, who visited the Columbia in May 1804, but the facts learned from the Indians fit Hill better. Ruby & Brown (CITC), 88–90, 110–11; Howay (1931), 143, 146, 149.

16. "Red Wood" is possibly red osier dogwood, *Cornus sericea* L. (or *C. stolonifera* Michx.). If the word is birch, it is water, or river, birch, *Betula occidentalis* Hook., which is mainly east of the Cascade Range with only a small population in the gorge. From this entry, however, the word appears to be beech. If so, it could be the red alder again, confused for a beech. See a similar discrepancy at November 30, 1805. Hitchcock et al., 3:588–90, 2:77–81; Little (MWH), 22-NW.

17. In southwestern Wahkiakum County, Washington, on the point later called Cape Horn and opposite "Sturgeon Isd.," perhaps today's Wallace Island, Columbia County, Oregon. *Atlas* map 81. However, on *Atlas* map 89, Sturgeon Island relates better to the position of modern Puget Island. There may have been an error in transferring information between maps and texts. *Atlas* map 81 appears more reliable. See the next entry and cf. Thwaites (LC), 3:206.

18. Fleas are of the family Pulicidae.

19. Mt. Coffin, which was given that name by Broughton of Vancouver's expedition in 1792 because of several Indians being buried in canoes in the vicinity. Franchère (JV), 78, 78 n. 6. Clark's wording gives the impression it was on an island, but its historic location is on the mainland in the area of Longview, just downstream from the mouth of the Cowlitz River. Clark's estimate of 80 feet is considerably short of its 225 (or 240) feet height when

it existed. Beginning early in this century it was extensively quarried and leveled. It was composed of the volcanic unit of the Eocene-age Cowlitz Formation.

20. Biddle struck out the passage when he substituted his own, all in red ink.

21. Perhaps Wallace Island, but see n. 17 above. *Atlas* map 81. Nearly one-quarter of the remaining p. 113 of Codex H is blank.

[Clark] *November 7th Thursday 1805*[1]

a Cloudy fogey morning, a little rain. Set out at 8 oClock proceeded on

N. 82° W.	2½	miles on the Std Side under a high hill Steep assent
N. 45° W.	1½	miles and the high Land on the Std. Side Steep assent
N. 60° W.	1	mile on the Std. Sid high hill a thick fog. Can't See across the Riv opposit the lower pt. of an Isd.[2]
West	2	miles on the Stard Side under a hill high and rockey
N W.	1	mile to the head of an Island Close under the Stard Side, Sept. by a narrow Chanel. 2 Canoes of Indians met us, and returnd. with us, a Island in the middle of the river, we followed those Inds. on the North Side of the Island thro a narrow Chanel to their village on the Stard. Side of 4 houses, they gave fish to eate, and Sold us fish Salmon trout, some *Wapto* roots and 3 Dogs, the language of those peopl have a Similarity with those above. The women ware a kind of Srand made of the fur cedar bark but Soft in place of a tite pice of leather as worn by the women above. the men have nothing except a robe about them, they are badly made and use but fiew ornements

The womens peticoat is about 15 Inches long made of *arber vita* or the white Cedar bark wove to a String and hanging down in tossles and [t]ied So as to cover from their hips as low as the peticoat will reach and only Covers them when Standing, as in any other position the Tosels Seperate. Those people Sold us otter Skins for fish hooks of which they wer fond

We delayed 1½ hour & Set out the tide being up in & the river So Cut with Islands we got an Indian to pilot us into the main chanel one of our Canoes Seperated from us this morning in the fog— great numbers of water fowls of every descriptn. common to this river

N. 10° W.	15	miles to a white tree in a Stard. bend under a high hill passed Several marshey Isld. on the Stard. Side opposit to which &

on the Stard. Side is a village of 4 houses   passed Several marshey Islands on the Lard sd. an Indian village on one of those Islands. they came and traded 2 beaver skins for fishing hooks and a fiew *Wapto* roots. The rivr. verry wide. The beaver Skins I wish for to make a robe as the one I have is worn out. to an old village of 7 houses under the hill Stard. Side. Several Slashey Isld. on Stard Side, we called and bought a Dog & Some fish.

SW.	3	miles to a point of high land on the Stard. Side passed a Small Island on Stard. Side the head of a large low marshy Island on the middle river about from 5 to 7 miles wide
S. 62° W	5	miles ⟨lard side⟩ to a point Stard. Side a Deep bend to the Stard Side under a high mountain. pine
S. 70° W	3 34	miles to a point on the Stard Side high mountains Some high mountains on the Lard Side off the river— we encamped on the Stard Side under a high hill Steep and mountanious we with dificulty found leavel rocks Sufficent to lie on, Three Indians followed us they Could Speake a little English, they were detected in Stealing a knife & returned late to their village. The rain Continued untill 9 oClock moderately. we are in view of the opening of the Ocian, which Creates great joy. a remarkable rock of about 50 feet high and about 20 feet Diameter is situated opposit our Camp about ½ a mile from Shore Several marshey Islands towards the Lard Side the Shape of them I can't See as the river is wide and day foggey

[Clark]   *November 7th Thursday 1805*

A cloudy foggey morning Some rain. we Set out early   proceeded under the Stard Shore under a high rugid hills with Steep assent the Shore boalt and rockey, the fog So thick we could not See across the river, two Canos of Indians met and returned with us to their village which is Situated on the Stard Side behind a cluster of Marshey Islands, on a narrow chanl. of the river through which we passed to the *Village* of 4 Houses,[3] they gave us to eate Some fish, and Sold us, fish, *Wap pa to* roots three *dogs* and 2 otter Skins for which we gave fish hooks principally of which they were verry fond.

Those people call themselves *War-ci-â-cum*[4] and Speake a language dif-

From the Cascades of the Columbia to the Sea

ferent from the nativs above with whome they trade for the *Wapato* roots of which they make great use of as food. their houses differently built, raised entirely above ground eaves about 5 feet from the ground Supported and covered in the same way of those above, dores about the Same size but in the Side of the house in one Corner, one fire place and that near the opposit end; around which they have their beads raised about 4 feet from the flore which is of earth, under their beads they Store away baskets of dried fish Berries & *wappato,* over the fire they hang the flesh as they take them and which they do not make immediate use. Their Canoes are of the Same form of those above. The Dress of the men differ verry little from those above, The womin altogether different, their robes are Smaller only Covering their Sholders & falling down to near the hip— and Sometimes when it is Cold a piec of fur curiously plated and connected So as to meet around the body from the arms to the hips— ⟨Their peticoats are of the bark of the white Cedar⟩[5] "The garment which occupies the waist and thence as low as the knee before and mid leg behind, cannot properly be called a petticoat, in the common acception of the word; it is a *Tissue* formed of white Cedar bark bruised or broken into Small Strans, which are interwoven in their center by means of Several cords of the Same materials which Serves as well for a girdle as to hold in place the Strans of bark which forms the tissue, and which Strans, Confined in the middle, hang with their ends pendulous from the waiste, the whole being of Suffcent thickness when the female Stands erect to conceal those parts useally covered from familiar view, but when she stoops or places herself in any other attitudes this battery of Venus is not altogether impervious to the penetrating eye of the amorite. This tissue is Sometimes formed of little Strings of the Silk grass twisted and knoted at their ends"[6] &c. Those Indians are low and ill Shaped all flat heads

after delaying at this village one hour and a half we Set out piloted by an Indian dressed in a Salors dress, to the main Chanel of the river, the tide being in we Should have found much dificuelty in passing into the main Chanel from behind those islands, ⟨if⟩ without a pilot, a large marshey Island[7] near the middle of the river near which Several Canoes Came allong Side with Skins, roots fish &c. to Sell, and had a temporey residence on this Island, here we See great numbers of water fowls about those marshey Islands; here the high mountanious Countery approaches the river on the Lard Side, a high mountn. to the S W. about 20 miles, the high mountains. Countrey Continue on the Stard Side, about 14 miles below the last village and 18 miles of this day we landed at a village of the Same nation.[8] This village is at the foot of the high hills on the Stard Side back of 2 Small Islands it contains 7 indifferent houses built in the Same form of those above, here we purchased a Dog Some fish, *wappato* roots and I purchased 2 beaver Skins for the purpose of making me a *roab*, as the robe I have is rotten and good for nothing. opposit to this Village the high mountaneous Countrey leave the river on the Lard Side below which the river widens into a kind of Bay & is Crouded with low Islands Subject to be Covered by the tides— we proceeded on about 12 miles below the Village under a high mountaneous Countrey on the Stard. Side. Shore boald and rockey and Encamped under a high hill on the Stard. Side opposit to a rock Situated half a mile from the Shore, about 50 feet high and 20 feet Diamieter,[9] we with dificuelty found a place Clear of the tide and Sufficiently large to lie on and the only place we could get was on round Stones on which we lay our mats rain Continud. moderately all day & Two Indians accompanied us from the last village, they we detected in Stealing a knife and returned, our Small Canoe which got Seperated in the fog this morning joined us this evening from a large Island Situated nearest the Lard Side below the high hills on that Side, the river being too wide to See either the form Shape or Size of the Islands on the Lard Side.

Great joy in camp we are in *View* of the *Ocian*,[10] [*NB: in the morning when fog cleared off just below last village just on leaving the village of Warkiacum*], this great Pacific Octean which we been So long anxious to See. and the roreing or noise made by the waves brakeing on the rockey Shores (as I Suppose) may be heard distictly[11]

we made 34 miles to day as Computed

1. It is not clear why an asterisk follows this line. It may be related to one below after the words "but fiew ornements" or at "great numbers," but in what way is unknown.

2. Perhaps Puget Island, Wahkiakum County, Washington, and labeled "[Sea] otter Isd." on *Atlas* map 81, apparently "Sturgeon Isd." on *Atlas* map 89.

3. The village of "4 Large Houses" shown on *Atlas* map 81 may correspond to the Wahkiakum settlement of *wáqaiqam*, from which the name of these people was derived, or to the nearby village of *ıloˊxumın* or *Loˊxumin*. Ray (LCEN), 38; Sw n, 414; Martin, 44.

4. These people were the Wahkiakums, a Chinookan group who lived along the Columbia River in Wahkiakum County, from Grays Bay upstream to the vicinity of Oak Point. Hodge, 2:890; Ray (CI), 127–28; Ruby & Brown (CITC), 5–6; Martin, 40–52; Hajda, 105–6; Ronda (LCAI), 184–86. Their name comes from Chinookan *wáqaiqam* or *qáiqamix*, "region downriver." Silverstein. Clark observed that the language of the Wahkiakums was different from that of the Chinookan peoples upriver. The Wahkiakums, and the neighboring Cathlamets across the river, spoke a dialect known as Kathlamet. Kathlamet is similar to the dialects spoken by other Chinookan peoples farther upriver, and all of these dialects are commonly grouped together as the Upper Chinook language. Clark's observation, however, is in accord with the recently proposed idea that Kathlamet had sufficiently different pronunciation, grammar, and lexical items for it to be considered a third language, standing between Lower and Upper Chinook, for which the name Middle Chinook has been suggested. Hymes, 16. It was apparently Biddle who substituted in his red ink "ki" for "ci" in the tribal name.

5. In addition to the language difference, the Wahkiakums and neighboring Cathlamets differed from Chinookan peoples upstream in constructing their houses entirely above ground, in women's dress, and in their greater use of the smallest of the canoe types among the marshy islands in their territory (see entry for February 1, 1806). At this point, the party approached the upper estuary of the Columbia River. The archaeology of this area is known almost entirely from the work of Minor (ASCR).

6. The passage in quotation marks was copied from Lewis's Codex J entry for March 19, 1806. See the Introduction, vol. 2; Dunlay. The line following appears to have been added later.

7. Thwaites (LC), 3:209 n. 1, considers this present Tenasillahe Island. That island may have been formed out of the "Mashey Islands" shown on *Atlas* map 82. Clark's curve of the river at this point is exaggerated. It is shown more properly on *Atlas* map 89.

8. A Wahkiakum village near present Skamokawa, Wahkiakum County. This is the village of "7 Houses" on *Atlas* map 81, which may correspond to the Wahkiakum villages of *Chahulklilhum* or *Tlashgenemaki*. Curtis, 8:182; Boas (KT), 6; cf. Spier, 22. Archaeological work has been reported at two Wahkiakum settlements in this area. The Skamokawa site was occupied as early as 2,300 years ago but was apparently abandoned some time before historic contact. Minor (SS); Minor (FSS). The inhabitants may have relocated slightly downstream to the Bay View site which appears to have been occupied in the early historic period. Gehr. In addition to their villages along the north shore of the Columbia River, the Wahkiakums also occupied seasonal camps on islands in the river. One of these was on Tenasillahe Island and was famous as a fishing site. Ray (LCEN), 39.

9. They were opposite Pillar Rock, between Brookfield and Dahlia and west of Jim Crow Point in Wahkiakum County. Its height varies with the tide but may have risen seventy to one hundred feet above the water before the top was removed in later years for the installation of light and navigational aids. The rock is composed of a resistant block of basalt of the middle Miocene Pomona Basalt flow. It is shown as "rock" on *Atlas* maps 82, 89, opposite the camp of this day. The landmark figures prominently in the only surviving Wahkiakum myth, which exists in three versions. Martin, 43.

10. They were actually looking at the Columbia estuary, not the ocean.
11. A space of two blank lines occurs before the final sentence.

[Clark] Novr. 8th Friday 1805

a cloudy morning Some rain and wind we Changed our Clothes and Set out at 9 oClock proceeded on Close under the Stard. Side

S. 63° W.	2	miles to a point on the Stard. Side passing under high Mountainious Country Som low Islands opposit at about 3 miles 3 Inds. in a Canoe over took us
S. 60° W.	6 $\underline{8}$	miles to Cape ⟨disappointment⟩¹ Swells on the Stard Side, a Deep bend to the Stard Side high country on both Sides, passed an old village 2 Hs. at 1 ⟨¼⟩ mile on an ⟨Std.⟩ 4 houses at 3 miles and halted to dine at an old village of Several in a deep bay on the Stard. Side of 5 miles Deep Several arms still further into the land Saw great [numbers] of Swan Geese and Ducks in this Shallow bay, Cloudy and disagreeable all the Day. Great maney flees at this old village,

R. Fields Killed a goose & 2 Canvis back Ducks² in this bay after Dinner we took the advantage of the returning tide & proceeded on to the 2d point,³ at which place we found the Swells too high to proceed we landed and drew our canoes up So as to let the tide leave them. The three Indians after Selling us 4 fish for which we gave Seven Small fishing hooks, and a piece of red Cloth. Some fine rain at intervales all this day. the Swells Continued high all the evening & we are Compelled to form an Encampment on a Point Scercely room Sufficent for us all to lie Clear of the tide water. hills high & with a Steep assent, river wide & at this place too Salt to be used for Drink. we are all wet and disagreeable, as we have been Continually for Severl. days past, we are at a loss ⟨to⟩ & cannot find out if any Settlement is near the mouth of this river.

The Swells were So high and the Canoes roled in Such a manner as to cause Several to be verry Sick. Reuben fields, Wiser McNeal & the Squar wer of the number

[Clark] November 8th Friday 1805

A Cloudy morning Some rain, we did not Set out untill 9 oClock, haveing Changed our Clothing— proceeded on Close under the Stard. Side, the hills high with Steep assent, Shore boald and rockey Several low Islands in a Deep bend or Bay to the Lard Side,[1] river about 5 or 7 miles wide.   three Indians in a Canoe overtook us, with Salmon to Sell, passed 2 old villages on the Stard. Side and at 3 miles entered a nitch of about 6 miles wide and 5 miles deep with Several Creeks makeing into the Stard Hills, this nitch we found verry Shallow water and Call it the Shallow ⟨nitch⟩ [*NB: Bay*][5]   we came too at the remains of an old village at the bottom of this nitch and dined, here we Saw great numbers of fowl, Sent out 2 men and they killed a Goose and two *Canves back* Ducks   here we found great numbers of flees which we treated with the greatest caution and distance; after Diner the Indians left us and we took the advantage of a returning tide and proceeded on to the Second point on the Std.   here we found the Swells or waves So high that we thought it imprudent to proceed; we landed unloaded and drew up our Canoes. Some rain all day at intervales; we are all wet and disagreeable, as we have been for Several days past, and our present Situation a verry disagreeable one in as much; as we have not leavel land Sufficient for an encampment and for our baggage to lie Cleare of the tide, the High hills jutting in So Close and Steep that we cannot retreat back, and the water of the river too Salt to be used, added to this the waves are increasing to Such a hight that we cannot move from this place, in this Situation we are compelled to form our Camp between the hite of the Ebb and flood tides, and rase our baggage on logs—   We are not certain as yet if the whites people who trade with those people or from whome they precure ther goods are Stationary at the mouth, or visit this quarter at Stated times for the purpose of trafick &c.[6]   I believe the latter to be the most probable conjucture—   The Seas roled and tossed the Canoes in Such a manner this evening that Several of our party were Sea Sick.

    1. In 1775 Captain Bruno de Heceta, a Spanish explorer, sighted the Columbia estuary; although he did not enter it he correctly concluded that he had found the mouth of a great river, which he called the San Roque. Captain James Cook in 1778 and La Pérouse in 1785 (see below, November 15, 1805) missed the river. In 1788 Captain John Meares, a British sea captain and fur trader, found the location but concluded that the river did not exist; he therefore called the northern headland "Cape Disappointment." Not until May 19, 1792, did Captain Robert Gray, in the American trading ship *Columbia Rediviva*, enter the estuary and confirm the existence of the river, which he named for his ship. Cape Disappointment he renamed Cape Hancock, but Meares's name has persisted. As indi-

cated by the crossing out of the name, Lewis and Clark had not actually reached Cape Disappointment, but were near Grays Point, which they called "Cape Swells."

2. The canvasback, *Aythya valisineria* [AOU, 147], was already known to hunters in the East but was not recognized as a species until described by Alexander Wilson in 1814. See Lewis's description below, March 9, 1806. Burroughs, 188.

3. They camped here this day and the next, on the west side of Grays Bay ("Shallow Bay" on *Atlas* maps 82, 89) probably near the Wahkiakum-Pacific county line, Washington, or farther west near Frankfort, Pacific County, and Grays Point.

4. Cathlamet Bay, in Clatsop County, Oregon, east of Tongue Point ("Point William" on *Atlas* map 82).

5. Grays Bay, in Pacific and Wahkiakum counties; shown as "Shallow Bay" on *Atlas* map 82. Named after Robert Gray, first known Euro-American to enter the Columbia estuary in 1792 (see n. 1, above). A concentration of Wahkiakum villages occurred along the shores of Grays Bay, with other settlements extending up Grays River and Deep River into the interior. Work at an archaeological site on Grays River recovered evidence of occupation dated between 2,000 and 2,700 year ago. Minor (ASCR). It was apparently Biddle who crossed out "nitch" and replaced it with his own word, all in red ink.

6. Trading vessels visited the area fairly often after Gray's entry in 1792, but no permanent trading station seems to have been established until the Astorians arrived in 1811. Irving (Astor).

[Clark] Novr. 9th Saturday 1805

The tide of last night obliged us to unload all the Canoes one of which Sunk before She was unloaded by the high waves or Swells which accompanied the returning tide, The others we unloaded, and 3 others was filled with water Soon after by the Swells or high Sees which broke against the Shore imediately where we lay, rained hard all the fore part of the day, the [tide] which rose untill 2 oClock P M to day brought with it Such emence Swells or waves, added to a hard wind from the ⟨S W⟩ South which Loosened the Drift trees which is verry thick on the Shores, and tossed them about in Such a manner, as to endanger our Canoes very much, with every exertion and the Strictest attention by the party was Scercely Suffient to defend our Canoes from being Crushed to pieces between those emensely large trees maney of them 200 feet long and 4 feet through. The tide of this day rose about [*blank*] feet & 15 Inches higher than yesterday this is owing to the wind which Sets in from the ocian, we are Compelled to move our Camp from the water, as also the loading every man as wet all the last night and this day as the rain Could make them which Contind. all day. at 4 oClock the wind Shifted about to the S. W imediately from the ocian and blew a Storm for about 2 hours, raised the tide verry high all wet & cold   Labiech killed 4 Ducks very fat & R. Fields Saw Elk Sign.

not withstanding the disagreeable time of the party for Several days past they are all Chearfull and full of anxiety to See further into the ocian. the water is too Salt to Drink, we use rain water. The Salt water has acted on some of the party already as a Pergitive.   rain continus.

[Clark] *November 9th Saturday 1805*

The tide of last night did not rise Sufficintly high to come into our camp, but the Canoes which was exposed to the mercy of the waves &c. which accompanied the returning tide, they all filled, and with great attention we Saved them untill the tide left them dry—   wind Hard from the South and rained hard all the fore part of the day, at 2 oClock P M the flood tide came in accompanied with emence waves and heavy winds, floated the trees and Drift which was on the point on which we Camped and tosed them about in Such a manner as to endanger the Canoes verry much, with every exertion and the Strictest attention by every individual of the party was Scercely Sufficient to Save our Canoes from being crushed by those monsterous trees maney of them nearly 200 feet long and from 4 to 7 feet through.   our camp entirely under water dureing the hight of the *tide*, every man as wet as water could make them all the last night and to day all day as the rain Continued all day, at 4 oClock P M the wind Shifted about to the S. W. and blew with great violence imediately from the Ocian for about two hours, notwithstanding the disagreeable Situation of our party all wet and Cold (and one which they have experienced for Several days past) they are chearfull and anxious to See further into the Ocian, The water of the river being too Salt to use we are obliged to make use of rain water—   Some of the party not accustomed to Salt water has made too free a use of it on them it acts as a pergitive.

at this dismal point we must Spend another night as the wind & waves are too high to proceed.

[Clark] *November 10th Sunday 1805*

rained verry hard the greater part of the last night & Continus this morning, the wind has layed and the Swells are fallen.   we loaded our

Canoes and proceeded on, passed a Deep Bay on the Stard. Side I Call [*blank*]

S. W.	8	miles to point on the Stard. Side passed a deep Bay and
	10	6 points on the Stard. Side rained hard Saw enoumurable quantites of Sea guls and Ducks

The wind rose from the N W. and the Swells became So high, we were Compelled to return about 2 miles to a place where we Could unld. our Canoes, which was in a Small Bay on Driftwood, on which we had also to make our fires to dry our Selves as well as we could the Shore being either a Clift of Purpendicular rocks or Steep assents to the hight of 4 or 500 feet, we continued on this drift wood untill about 3 oClock when the evening appearing favourable we loaded & Set out in hopes to turn the Point below and get into a better harber, but finding the *waves* & *Swells* continue to rage with great fury below, we got a Safe place for our Stores & a much beter one for the Canoes to lie and formed a Campment[1] on Drift logs in the Same little Bay under a high hill at the enterence of a Small drean which we found verry convt. on account of its water, as that of the river is Brackish— The logs on which we lie is all on flote every high tide— The rain Continud all day— we are all wet, also our beding and many other articles.   we are all employed untill late drying our bedding.   nothing to eate but Pounded fish

[Clark] November *1oth Sunday 1805*

Rained verry hard the greater part of last night and continues this morning.   the wind has luled and the waves are not high; we loaded our canoes and proceeded on   passed Several Small and deep nitch on the Stard. Side, we proceeded on about 10 miles   Saw great numbers of Sea Guls, the wind rose from the N. W. and the waves became So high that we were compelled to return about 2 miles to a place we Could unload our Canoes, which we did in a Small nitch at the mouth of a Small run on a pile of drift logs where we Continued untill low water, when the river appeared calm we loaded and Set out; but was obliged to return finding the waves too high for our Canoes to ride, we again unloaded the Canoes, and Stoed the loading on a rock above the tide water, and formed a camp on the Drift Logs which appeared to be the only Situation we could find to lie, the hills being either a perpendicular Clift, or Steep assent, riseing to about 500 feet— our Canoes we Secured as well as we could— we are all wet the rain haveing continued all day, our beding and maney other articles, employ our Selves drying our blankets— nothing to eate but dried fish pounded which we brought from the falls. we made 10 miles today—

1. They remained at this campsite until November 15; it was on the eastern side of Point Ellice, Pacific County, Washington, east of the Astoria Bridge and near the town of Meglar. Appleman (LC), 360: *Atlas* maps 82, 89.

[Clark] *November 11th Monday 1805*

a hard rain all the last night we again get wet the rain continue at intervals all day. Wind verry high from S W and blew a Storm all day Sent out Jo. Fields & Collins to hunt. at 12 oClock at a time the wind was verry high and waves tremendeous five Indians Came down in a Canoe loaded with fish of Salmon Spes. Called *Red Charr*,[1] we purchased of those Indians 13 of these fish, for which we gave, fishing hooks & some trifling things, we had Seen those Indians at a village behind Some marshey Islands a few days ago. they are on their way to trade those fish with white people which they make Signs live below round a point, those people are badly Clad, one is dressd. in an old Salors Jacket & Trouses, the others Elk Skin robes. we are truly unfortunate to be Compelled to lie 4 days nearly in the Same place at a time that our day are precious to us, The Wind Shifted to [blank] the Indians left us and Crossed the river which is about 5 miles wide through the highest Sees I ever Saw a Small vestle ride, their Canoe is Small, maney times they were out of Sight before the were 2 miles off Certain it is they are the best canoe navigators I ever Saw[2] The tide was 3 hours later to day than yesterday and rose much higher, the trees we camped on was all on flote for about 2 hours from 3 untill 5 oClock P M, the great quantities of rain which has fallen losenes the Stones on the Side of the hill & the Small ones fall on us, our Situation is truly a disagreeable one our Canoes in one place at the mercy of the waves our baggage in another and our Selves & party Scattered on drift trees of emense Sizes, & are on what dry land they can find in the Crevices of the rocks & hill Sides

[Clark]   *November 11th Monday 1805*

A hard rain all the last night, dureing the last tide the logs on which we lay was all on float   Sent out Jo Fields to hunt, he Soon returned and informed us that the hills was So high & Steep, & thick with undergroth and fallen Timber that he could not get out any distance; about 12 oClock 5 Indians came down in a canoe, the wind verry high from the S. W. with most tremendious waves brakeing with great violence against the Shores, rain falling in torrents, we are all wet as usial and our Situation is truly a disagreeable one; the great quantites of rain which has loosened the Stones on the hill Sides, and the Small Stones fall down upon us, our canoes at one place at the mercy of the waves, our baggage in another and our Selves and party Scattered on floating logs and Such dry Spots as can be found on the hill Sides, and Crivices of the rocks.   we purchased of the Indians 13 red charr which we found to be an excellent fish   we have Seen those Indians above and are of a nation who reside above and on the opposit Side who call themselves ⟨Calt-har-ma⟩ [NB: Cath lah ma][3] they are badly clad & illy made, Small and Speak a language much resembling the last nation, one of those men had on a Salors Jacket and Pantiloons and made Signs that he got those Clothes from the white people who lived below the point &c.   those people left us and Crossed the river (which is about 5 miles wide at this place) through the highest waves I ever Saw a Small vestles ride. Those Indians are Certainly the best Canoe navigaters I ever Saw.   rained all day

 1. The sockeye (or blue-backed) salmon, *Oncorhynchus nerka*, already known to science. See Lewis's description below, March 13, 1806. Burroughs, 262–63; Cutright (LCPN), 270.
 2. Biddle gathered additional information from Clark in 1810 about native seamanship. Biddle Notes [ca. April 1810], Jackson (LLC), 2:540.
 3. The Cathlamets, or Kathlamets, lived across the Columbia River from the Wahkiakums and both peoples spoke the Kathlamet language. The Cathlamets occupied settlements along the south shore of the Columbia River from the vicinity of Tongue Point upstream to the neighborhood of Puget Island in Clatsop County, Oregon. Hodge, 1:216; Berreman, 15; Hajda, 104–5. Some investigators extend Cathlamet territory farther upstream to Oak Point and beyond, but it is unclear if these writers are referring to the local group named the Cathlamets or to the distribution of the Kathlamet linguistic dialect. Boas (KT), 6; Curtis, 8:181–82; Ray (LCEN), 38. The village for which these people were named, *gaɬámat* in the Upper Chinook language, was located on Aldrich Point

From the Cascades of the Columbia to the Sea

(formerly called Cathlamet Head). About 1810 the Cathlamets moved across the Columbia and joined the Wahkiakums in a village at the present site of Cathlamet. Silverstein; Strong (CC), 60–61; Ray (LCEN), 39. See also November 26, 1805. Biddle's insertion is not in his usual red ink.

[Clark]   November 12th Tuesday 1805

a tremendious thunder Storm abt. 3 oClock this morning accompanied by wind from the S W. and Hail, this Storm of hard Clap's thunder Lighting and hail untill about 6 oClock at intervals   it then became light for a Short time when the heavens became darkined by a black Cloud from the S, W, & a hard rain Suckceeded which lasted untill 12 oClock with a hard wind which raised the Seas tremendiously high braking with great force and fury against the rocks & trees on which we lie, as our Situation became Seriously dangerous, we took the advantage of a low tide & moved our Camp around a point a Short distance to a Small wet bottom at the mouth of a Small Creek, which we had not observed when we first Came to this Cove, from its being very thick and obscured by drift trees & thick bushes, Send out men to hunt   they found the woods So thick with Pine & [decay?] timber and under groth that they could not get through, Saw Some Elk tracks, I walked up this creek & killed 2 Salmon trout, the men killd. 13 of the Salmon Species, The Pine of fur Specs, or Spruc Pine grow here to an emense Size & hight maney of them 7 & 8 feet through and upwards of 200 feet high. It would be distressing to a feeling person to See our Situation at this time all wet and cold with our bedding &c. also wet, in a Cove Scercely large nough to Contain us, our Baggage in a Small holler about ½ a mile from us, and Canoes at the mercy of the waves & drift wood, we have Scured them as well as it is possible by Sinking and wateing them down with Stones to prevent the emence [waves] dashing them to pices against the rocks—   one got loose last night & was left on a rock by the tide Some distance below without recving much damage. fortunately for us our Men are helthy. It was clear at 12 for a Short time. I observed the Mountains on the opposit Side was covered with Snow— our party has been wet for ⟨Seven Six⟩ 8 days and is truly disagreeable, their robes & leather Clothes are rotten from being Continually wet, and they are not in a Situation to get others, and we are not in a Situation to restore them—   I observe great numbers of Sea guls, flying in every derection—   Three men Gibson Bratten & Willard attempted to decend in a Canoe built in the Indian fashion and abt. the Size of the one the Indians visited us in yesterday, they Could not proceed, as the waves tossed them about at will, they returned after proceeding about 1 mile— we got our Selves tolerable Comfortable by drying our Selves & bedding Cought 3 salmon this evining in a Small branch above about 1 mile

[Clark]   *November 12th Tuesday 1805*

A Tremendious wind from the S. W. about 3 oClock this morning with Lightineng and hard claps of Thunder, and Hail which Continued untill 6 oClock a. m. when it became light for a Short time, then the heavens became Sudenly darkened by a black Cloud from the S. W. and rained with great violence untill 12 oClock, the waves tremendious brakeing with great fury against the rocks and trees on which we were encamped. our Situation is dangerous. we took the advantage of a low *tide* and moved our camp around a point to a Small wet bottom at the mouth of a Brook, which we had not observed when we Came to this cove; from it being verry thick and obscured by drift trees and thick bushes It would be distressing to See our Situation, all wet and Colde our bedding also wet, (and the robes of the party which Compose half the bedding is rotten and we are not in a Situation ⟨not⟩ to supply their places) in a wet bottom Scercely large enough to contain us, ⟨with⟩ our baggage half a mile from us and Canoes at the mercy of the waves, altho Secured as well as possible, Sunk with emence parcels of Stone to wate them down to prevent their dashing to pieces against the rocks; one got loose last night and was left on a rock a Short distance below, without rciving more dammage than a Split in her bottom— Fortunately for us our men are healthy. 3 men Gibson Bratten & Willard attempted to go aroud the point below in our Indian Canoe, much Such a canoe as the Indians visited us in yesterday, they proceeded to the point from which they were oblige to return, the waves tossing them about at will I walked up the branch and giged 3 Salmon trout. the party killed 13 Salmon to day in a branch about 2 miles above. rain Continued

[Clark]   *November 13th Wednesday 1805*

Some intervales of fair weather last night, rain and wind Continue this morning, as we are in a Cove & the Mountains verry high & Pine Spruce[1]

verry high & thick Cannot deturmine the procise course of the winds. I walked to the top of the first part of the mountain with much fatigue as the distance was about 3 miles thro' intolerable thickets of Small Pine, arrow wood a groth much resembling arrow wood with briers,[2] growing to 10 & 15 feet high interlocking with each other & Furn, aded to this difficulty the hill was So Steep that I was obliged to drawing my Self up in many places by the bowers, the Countrey Continues thick and hilley as far back a I could See. Some Elk Sign, rained all day moderately. I am wet &c. &c. The Hail which fell 2 night past is yet to be Seen on the mountain on which I was to day. I Saw a Small red Berry which grows on a Stem of about 6 or 8 Inches from the Ground, in bunches and in great quantity on the Mountains, the taste insiped.[3] I saw a number of verry large Spruce Pine one of which I measured 14 feet around and verry tall. My principal objects in assdg. this mountain was ⟨not⟩ to view the river below, the weather being So Cloudey & thick that I could not See any distance down, discovered the wind high from the N. W. and waves high at a Short distance below our Encampment, (Squar displeased with me for not [Sin?] &c &) *Wap-to* a excellent root which is rosted and tastes like a potato[4] I Cut my hand   despatched 3 men in a Indian canoe (which is calculated to ride high Swells) down to examine if they can find the Bay at the mouth & good harbers below for us to proceed in Safty. The Tides at every flud come in with great Swells & Breake against the rocks & Drift trees with great fury—   the rain Continue all the evening   nothing to eate but Pounded fish which we have as a reserve See Store, and what Pore fish we can kill up the branch on which we are encamped   our canoe and the three men did not return this evening—   if we were to have cold weather to accompany the rain which we have had for this 6 or 8 days passed we must eneviatilbly Suffer verry much as Clothes are Scerce with us.

[Clark]   *November 13th Wednesday 1805*

Some intervales of fair weather last night, rain continue this morning. I walked up the Brook & assended the first Spur of the mountain with much fatigue, the distance about 3 miles, through an intolerable thickets of Small pine, a groth much resembling arrow wood on the Stem of which there is thorns; this groth about 12 or 15 feet high inter lockd into each other and Scattered over the high fern & fallen timber, added to this the hills were So Steep that I was compelled to draw my Self up by the assistance of those bushes— The Timber on those hills are of the pine Species large and tall maney of them more than 200 feet high & from 8 to 10 feet through at the Stump those hills & as far back as I could See, I Saw Some *Elk* Sign, on the Spur of the mountain tho' not fresh. I killed a Salmon trout on my return. The Hail which fell 2 nights past is yet to be Seen on the mountains; I Saw in my ramble to day a red berry resembling Solomons Seal berry which the nativs call *Sol-me* and use it to eate. my principal object in assending this mountain was to view the countrey below, the rain continuing and weather proved So Cloudy that I could not See any distance on my return we dispatched 3 men Colter, Willard and Shannon in the Indian canoe to get around the point if possible and examine the river, and the Bay below for a god harber for our Canoes to lie in Safty &c. The tide at every floot tide Came ⟨in⟩ with great swells brakeing against the rocks & Drift trees with great fury The rain Continue all day. nothing to eate but pounded fish which we Keep as a reserve and use in Situations of this kind.

1. Sitka spruce, as noted on November 4; it is the dominant species of this region. The Sitka spruce vegetation zone is a narrow coastal temperate rain forest, generally only a few miles in width except where it extends up river valleys. It has a uniform wet and mild climate with rich soils. The forests are dense, tall, and among the most productive in the world. The three most common trees are Sitka spruce, western hemlock, *Tsuga heterophylla* (Raf.) Sarg., and western redcedar. Douglas fir and grand fir are also important. The mature forests have lush understories with dense growth of shrubs, herbs, ferns, and mosses. Hitchcock et al., 1:132–33; Franklin & Dyrness, 58–59; Cutright (LCPN), 239.

2. The small pine are possibly shore pine, *Pinus contorta* Dougl. var. *contorta*, unless Clark is using "pine" in a general sense. Little (CIH), 50-W; Franklin & Dyrness, 59. Clark's growth resembling arrowwood is the first description of devil's club, *Oplopanax horridum* (J. E. Smith) Miq. The irregularly toothed leaves indeed resemble the arrowwood or American cranberrybush, *Viburnum trilobum* Marsh., both have similar red fruits, and the height is correct. Devil's club is a characteristic and important understory species in this vegetation zone. Hitchcock et al., 3:506; Franklin & Dyrness, 61.

3. This is clearly bunchberry, dwarf cornel, puddingberry, *Cornus canadensis* L. Hitchcock et al., 3:588; Gunther (EWW), 43. It is "*Sol-me*" in the day's second entry. Confusion has occurred in identifying this plant because of the use of the native term here, since Lewis also uses the word solme to identify another species on January 27, 1806. The men are apparently applying the Chinookan word *šul(a)mix* to two entirely different plants. The problem is compounded by the fact that solme apparently refers to the wild cran-

berry or serviceberry, which is not the plant noted here or on January 27. Language difficulties may be the cause of these problems. Thwaites (LC), 3:221 n. 1; Cutright (LCPN), 266; Gibbs (AVC), 11; Ray (LCEN), 122.

4. This sentence is inserted upside down to the rest of the page in the Elkskin-bound Journal. Some slight rearranging of the text was necessary for clarity.

[Clark]   Novr. 14th Thursday 1805[1]

Rained last night without intermission and this morning the wind blew hard from the [blank] We Could not move, one Canoe was broken last night against the rocks, by the waves dashing her against them in high *tide* about 10 oClock 5 Indians Come up in a Canoe thro emence waves & Swells, they landed and informed us they Saw the 3 men we Sent down yesterday, at Some distance below   Soon after those people Came Colter one of the 3 men returned and informed us that he had proceeded with his Canoe as far as they Could, for the waves and Could find no white people, or Bay, he Saw a good Canoe harber & 2 Camps of Indians at no great distance below and that those with us had taken his gig & knife &c. which he forcably took from them & they left us, after our treating them well.   The rain Continue all day   all wet as usial, killed only 2 fish to day for the whole Party, at 3 oClock Capt. Lewis Drewyer Jo. & R. Fields & Frasure Set out down on the Shore to examine if any white men were below within our reach,[2] they took a empty Canoe & 5 men to Set them around the Point on a Gravelley Beech which Colter informed was at no great distance below. The Canoe returned at dusk half full of water, from the waves which dashed over in passing the point Capt Lewis is object is also to find a Small Bay as laid down by Vancouver just out of the mouth of the Columbia River.[3]   rained as usial ⟨untill⟩ all the evening, all wet and disagreeable Situated

[Clark]   November 14th Thursday 1805

rained all the last night without intermition, and this morning.   wind blows verry hard but our Situation is Such that we Cannot tell from what point it comes—   one of our Canoes is much broken by the waves dashing it against the rocks—   5 Indians Came up in a Canoe, thro' the waves, which is verry high and role with great fury—   They made Signs to us that they Saw the 3 men we Sent down yesterday.   only 3 of those

Indians landed, the other 2 which was women played off in the waves, which induced me to Suspect that they had taken Something from our men below, at this time one of the men Colter returnd by land and informed us that those Indians had taken his Gigg & basket, I called to the Squars to land and give back the gigg, which they would not doe untill a man run with a gun, as if he intended to Shute them when they landed, and Colter got his gig & basket   I then ordered those fellows off, and they verry readily Cleared out   they are of the *War-ci-a-cum* N. Colter informed us that "it was but a Short distance from where we lay around the point to a butifull Sand beech, which continud for a long ways, that he had found a good harber in the mouth of a creek near 2 Indian Lodges— that he had proceeded in the Canoe as far as he could for the waves, the other two men Willard & Shannon had proceeded on down["]

Capt Lewis concluded to proceed on by land & find if possible the white people the Indians Say is below and examine if a Bay is Situated near the mouth of this river as laid down by Vancouver in which we expect, if there is white traders to find them &c.   at 3 oClock he Set out with 4 men Drewyer Jos. & Reu. Fields & R. Frasure, in one of our large canoes and 5 men to Set them around the point on the Sand beech.   this canoe returned nearly filled with water at Dark which it receved by the waves dashing into it on its return, haveing landed Capt. Lewis & his party Safe on the Sand beech. The rain Continues all day all wet. The rain &c. which has continued without a longer intermition than 2 hours at a time for ten days past has distroyd. the robes and rotted ⟨a great maney⟩ nearly one half of the fiew Clothes the party has, perticularley the leather Clothes,—   fortunately for us we have no very Cold weather as yet and if we have Cold weather before we Can kill & Dress Skins for Clothing ⟨we⟩ the bulk of the party will Suffer verry much.

1. Two asterisks precede the dateline, but their purpose is unknown.
2. Apparently it is Lewis's route that is shown as a dotted line on *Atlas* map 89, ending at Cape Disappointment at the words, "Capt Lewis left the Sea Coast here." Lewis moved inland for his return somewhere south of Seaview, Pacific County, Washington, and arrived at the main party on November 17.
3. Baker (Haleys) Bay, just east of Cape Disappointment in Pacific County. *Atlas* maps 82, 89. Lewis had with him on the expedition copies of Vancouver's maps. *Atlas*, 16 n. 21. Broughton of the Vancouver party named the bay after Captain James Baker who had a

ship anchored in the bay when Broughton arrived in 1792. Barry (BOC), 398. Clark gave it as Haleys after the locals' favorite trader. See Clark's second entry of November 15, 1805; for Haley, see note at November 6, 1805.

[Clark] *November 15th Friday 1805*

Rained all the last night at intervales of Sometimes of 2 hours, This morning it became Calm & fair, I prepared to Set out at which time the wind sprung up from the S. E. and blew down the River & in a fiew minits raised Such Swells and waves brakeing on the Rocks at the point as to render it unsafe to proceed. I went to the point in an empty canoe and found it would be dangerous to proceed even in an empty *Canoe* The Sun Shown untill 1 oClock p. m. which gave an oppertunity for us to dry Some of our bedding, & examine our baggage, the greater Part of which I found wet Some of our Pounded fish Spoiled I had all the arms put in order & amunition examined.

The rainey weather Continued without a longer intermition than 2 hours at a time from the 5th in the morng. untill the 16th is *eleven* days rain, and the most disagreeable time I have experienced Confined on a tempiest Coast wet, where I can neither get out to hunt, return to a better Situation, or proceed on: in this Situation have we been for Six days past.— fortunately the wind lay about 3 oClock we loaded I in great haste and Set out passed the blustering Point[1] below which is a Sand beech, with a Small marshey bottom for 3 miles on the Stard. Side, on which is a large village of 36 houses deserted by the Inds. & in full possession of the flees, a Small Creek fall in at this village, which waters the Country for a few miles back; Shannon & 5 Indians met me here, Shannon informed me he met Capt. Lewis Some distance below & he took willard with him & Sent him to meet me, the Inds with him wer rogues, they had the night before Stold both his and Willards guns from under their heads, Capt. Lewis & party arrived at the Camp of those Indians at So Timely a period that the Inds. were allarmed & delivered up the guns &c. The tide meeting of me and the emence Swells from the main Ocean (imedeately in front of us) raised to Such a hite that I concluded to form a Camp on the highest Spot I could find in the marshey bottom,[2] and proceed no further by water as the Coaste becomes verry [dangerous] for Crafts of the Size of our Canoes—and as the Ocian is imedeately in front and gives us an extensive view of it from Cape disapointment to Point addams,[3] ⟨except 3 small Islands off the mouth and West of us.⟩ my Situation is in the upper part of Haley Bay S. 86° W. [blank] miles Course five ⟨from⟩ to Cape Disapt. and S. 35° W. Course [blank] miles from point Addams

The River here at its mouth from Point addams to the enterance of Haley Bay above is [blank] Miles or thereabouts, a large Isd. the lower point of which is immediately in the mouth above[4]

4 Indians in a Canoe Came down with *papto* roots to Sell, for which they asked, blankets or robes, both of which we could not Spare I informed those Indians all of which understood Some English that if they Stole our guns &c the men would Certainly Shute them, I treated them with great distance, & the Sentinal which was over our Baggage allarmed them verry much, they all Promised not to take any thing, and if any thing was taken by the Squars & bad boys to return them &c. the waves became very high Evening fare & pleasent, our men all Comfortable in the ⟨Huts⟩ Camps they have made of the boards they found at the Town above

[Clark] November 15th Friday 1805

Rained all the last night, this morning it became Calm and fair, I preposed Setting out, and ordered the Canoes Repared and loaded; before we could load our canoes the wind Sudenly Sprung up from the S. E and blew with Such violence, that we could not proceed in Safty with the loading. I proceeded to the point in an empty Canoe, and found that the waves dashed against the rocks with Such violence that I thought it unsave to Set out with the loaded Canoes— The Sun Shown untill 1 oClock P M which afford us time to Dry our bedding and examine the baggage which I found nearly all wet, Some of our pounded fish Spoiled in the wet; I examined the amunition and Caused all the arms to be put in order.

About 3 oClock the wind luled, and the river became calm, ⟨we⟩ I had the canoes loaded in great haste and Set Out, from this dismal nitich where we have been confined for 6 days passed, without the possibility of proceeding on, returning to a better Situation, or get out to hunt, Scerce of Provisions, and torents of rain poreing on us all the time— proceeded on passed the blustering point below which I found a butifull Sand beech thro which runs a Small [*NB?: river from the hills*]   below the mouth of this Stream is a *village* of 36 houses uninhabited by anything except flees, here I met G. Shannon and 5 Indians. Shannon informed me that he met Capn. Lewis at an Indian Hut about 10 miles below who had Sent him back to meet me, he also told me the Indians were thievish, as the night before they had Stolen both his and Willards rifles from under their heads, [*NB: they threatened them with a large party from above which Cap. Lewis's arrival confirmed*] that they Set out on their return and had not proceeded far up the beech before they met Capt Lewis, whose arival was at a timely moment and alarmed the Indians So that they instantly produced the Guns— I told those Indians who accompanied Shannon that they Should not Come near us, and if any one of their nation Stold anything from us, I would have him Shot, which they understoot verry well. as the tide was Comeing in and the Seas became verry high imediately from the *Ocian* (imediately faceing us) I landed and formed a camp on the highest Spot I could find between the hight of the tides, and the Slashers in a Small bottom   this I could plainly See would be the extent of our journey by water, as the waves were too high at any Stage for our Canoes to proceed any further down.   in full view of the *Ocian* from *Point Adams* [*NB: or Rond /see La Payrouse*][5] to Cape Disapointment, I could not See any Island in the mouth of this river as laid down by Vancouver.[6] The Bay which he laies down in the mouth is imediately below me. This Bay we call Haleys bay from a favourate Trader with the Indians which they Say comes into this Bay and trades with them   Course to Point adams is S. 35° W. about 8 miles   To Cape Disapointment is S. 86° W. about 14 miles   4 Indians of the *War-ki a cum* nation Came down with ⟨pap-pa-too⟩ [*NB: Wappatoo*] to Sell &c. The Indians who accompanied Shannon from the village below Speake a Different language from those above, and reside to the north of this place The Call themselves *Chin nooks*,[7] I told those people that they had attempted to Steal 2 guns &c. that if any one of their nation stole any thing that the Sentinl. whome they Saw near our baggage with his gun would most certainly Shute them, they all promised not to tuch a thing, and if any of their womin or bad boys took any thing to return it imediately and Chastise them for it. I treated those people with great distance.   our men all Comfortable in their Camps which they have made of boards from the old Village above.   we made 3 miles to day.

1. Point Ellice, Pacific County, Washington. *Atlas* map 82. "Point Distress" on the map in Codex I, p. 152 (fig. 1).

2. Southeast of Chinook Point, on the east side of Baker Bay (Lewis and Clark's "Haley's Bay"), in Pacific County, and west of present McGowan; the site is in a small state roadside park adjacent to Fort Columbia State Park. From here Clark and the main body of the party got their first actual sight of the Pacific. Appleman (LC), 357–59; *Atlas* maps 82, 89, 90, 91.

3. The southern headland at the mouth of the Columbia retains the name given it by Robert Gray in 1792, in Clatsop County, Oregon. *Atlas* map 82.

4. Present Sand Island, Pacific County, which does not appear on *Atlas* maps 82, 91, or fig. 1. Lines have been drawn vertically through this paragraph.

5. Jean-François de Galaup, Comte de La Pérouse, a French naval officer, sailed from France in 1785 with two ships for the Pacific. He explored the west coast of North America from southern Alaska to Monterey, California, besides visiting the east coast of Asia and many Pacific islands. After his departure from Botany Bay, Australia, in March 1788, nothing more was heard from him; forty years later the wreckage of his ships was found in the Santa Cruz Islands. La Pérouse had sent home his expedition journal and maps by way of Siberia and these were published in 1797. Biddle's interlineation presumably refers to the 1798 English edition, *The Voyage of La Perouse Round the World*, for the names the Frenchman gave coastal features. Gassner; Coues (HLC), 2: 713–14 nn. 32–33. It was apparently Biddle who underscored the phrase beginning "I could not" to "mouth of" in red ink. That and the next several lines have a vertical line through them, but not in red.

6. Biddle provides additional comments on Vancouver, perhaps from Clark in their 1810 conversations. Biddle Notes [ca. April 1810], Jackson (LLC), 2: 540–41.

7. The Chinooks, or Chinooks proper, occupied the north bank of the Columbia River from Cape Disappointment at the mouth and upstream at least as far as Megler and probably as far upstream as the vicinity of Grays Bay in Pacific County. Their territory extended north along the Washington coast to Willapa (formerly Shoalwater) Bay. Curtis, 8:182; Hodge, 1:272–73; Spier, 31; Taylor (CkI); Hajda, 100–102. The Chinooks proper practiced a biseasonal settlement pattern, occupying villages along the Columbia River during the summer fishing season, moving to villages on Willapa Bay for the winter. This accounts for Lewis and Clark having seen very few Indians along the river in November. One of their principal settlements was the summer village of činúk (a Salish Chehalis term) on Baker Bay, from which both the name of this group and the name of the linguistically related peoples upstream along the Columbia River was derived. Boas (Ch), 563.

[Clark] *November 16th Satturday 1805*[1]

a fine morning cool the latter part of the night, I had all our articles of every discription examined, and found much wet, had all put out & dried, The 5 Indians Theves left me. I took a meridean altd. with Sextt. $50° 36'$

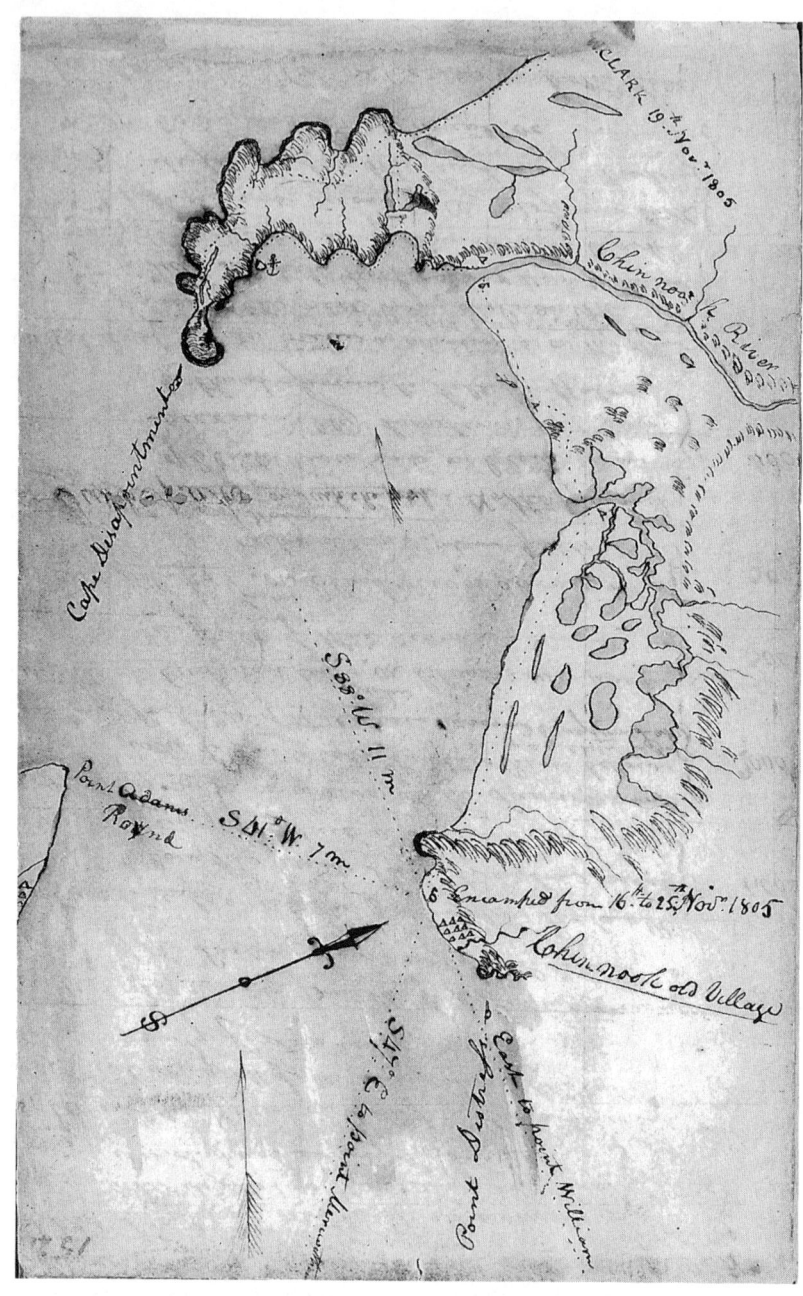

1. Mouth of the Columbia River, Washington and Oregon,
ca. November 16–25, 1805, Codex I, p. 152

15 the Shakeing emige below— I Sent out Several hunters Some to kill fowl others to hunt deer or Elk. The Sea is fomeing and looks truly dismal to day, from the wind which blew to day from the S. W. an Indian Canoe passed down to day, loaded with roots &c. three Indians Came up from below I gave them Smoke but allowed them no kind of Privelages what ever, they camped with the 4 which Came down yesterday, near us, The evening provd. Cloudy & I could make no lunar observations. one man Sick with a violent Cold, Caught by lying in his wet Clothes, Several nights   Course from Stormey point to Cape Disapointment is ⟨West⟩ [blank] Miles, passd a Small Creek and an old village at 2 miles on the Stard Side   a Small Creek at 1 mile   we Encamped just above a Point in a Deep bay to the Stard. Side into which falls 2 Small rivers Std.[2] Grat many Indians liveing on the Bay & those two rivers, the ⟨lower End of a large Island in the Mouth of the Columbia opsd. to us, we See Islands at Some distance from Land S. W.⟩ the Countrey on the Stard. Side high broken & thickly timbered, that on the Lard. at Some distance from Point Adms high and mountains on a Pinecal of a which is Snow at this time—   near the Point is Low bottom land—

our hunters and fowlers killd 2 Deer 1 Crane & 2 ducks, my Servt. York killed 2 Geese & 8 white, black and Speckle Brants,[3] The White Brant, with part of their wings black is much the largest, the black brant is verry Small, a little larger than a large Duck—   the deer pore but large

[Clark]   November 16th Saturday 1805

Cool the latter part of the last night this morning Clear and butifull; I had all our articles of every discription examined and put out to Dry. The 5 *Chin nooks* left us   I took a meridenal altitude with the Sextn. 50° 36' 15 which gave for Lattitude *46° 19' 11 1/10''* North. I Sent out Several hunters and fowlers in pursute Elk, Deer, or fowls of any kind. wind hard from the S W   The Waves high & look dismal indeed breaking with great fury on our beech   an Indian canoe pass down to day loaded with *Wap-pa-toe* roots; Several Indians came up to day from below, I gave them Smoke but allowed them no kind of privilage whatever in the camp, they with the 4 which came down yesterday encamped a Short distance from us. The evening proved Cloudy and I could not take any Luner observations— One man Sick with a violent cold, Caught by laying in his wet leather Clothes for maney nights past.

The Countrey on the Stard Side above Haley Bay is high broken and thickley timbered on the Lard Side from Point Adams the Contrey appears low for 15 or 20 miles back to the mountains, a pinical of which ⟨is⟩ now is ⟨either⟩ Covered with Snow or hail, as the opposit is too far distant to be distinguished well, I Shall not attempt to describe any thing on that Side at present.[4] our hunters and fowlers killed 2 Deer 1 Crain & 2 Ducks, and my man York killed 2 geese and 8 Brant, 3 of them white with a part of their wings black and much larger than the Grey brant which is a Sise larger than a Duck.

2nd November 1805[5]

South	1	Mile to the enterence of a Creek under a bluff on the Lard Side, passed the upper point of large Island Seperated from the Stard Shore by a narrow Chanel at this time without any running water. a Creek falls into this Chanl. from the mountains on the Stard Side, which is also without water at this time. This Island is high rich and open, covered with Strawberry vines and grass narrow open bottom on the Lard Side.
S. 50° W.	5	Miles to a timbered bottom on the Lard Side passed the lower point of Straw berry Island at 3 miles opposit an Island covered with wood, 2 other Islands a little below Covered with wood also, all Small. opposit on the Stard. Side is a rock Situated in a bottom at Some distance from the hills about 800 feet high and about 400 yards arround which we Call the *Beaten* rock, both bottoms and mountains thickly timbered passed a village of houses at 4 miles on the Stard. Side
S. 74° W.	12	Miles to a Stard. point of rocks on Stard. Side a high clift of black rocks. A Stard point at 4 miles. here the mountains are become lower on each side and thickly timbered, the river about 2 miles wide. passed a rock in the middle of the river at 10 miles of 100 feet high and 80 feet diamiuter deep bend to Stard.
S 58° W.	4	Miles to the a point of a large bottom on the Stad Side encamped on the Sard. Side the mountains leave the river on both Sides

3rd November 1805

West	3	Miles to the upper mouth of a river on the Lard Side 120 yards wide the bottom is a quick Sand we Call this *Quick Sand river* a large Creek opposit below a Small prarie. passed Several Sand bars in the river. Country low
Q. Sand R.	25	Miles to the Lower rapid & above tide water.[6]
S 70° W.	7	Miles to the upper point of a large Island resembling a dimond passed the lower mouth of quicksand river at 3 miles opposite to a Creek on the Stard. Side and head of a large Island near the Stard. Side faced with rock passed the lower point of Said Island at 6½ miles 1½ mile wide. Great numbers of fowl flying and Sea Otter in the river.
S 87° W.	3	Miles on the North Side of the Island and Encamped. met 2 Canous &c. &c.

4th November 1805

West	6	Miles to the North Side and lower point of a large Island passing the lower point of dimont Island at 3 miles a little below the head of the large Island near the Lard. Side. river wide and Countrey low on both Sides below quick Sand river and Covered with pine generally. this Island is only Seperated from one imediately below it on the Lard by a narrow Chanel in which there is only water at high tide.
N. 88° W.	6	Miles to a point on the Stard. Side. passed a village of 25 *houses* on the Lard. Side a little below the Islands, built of Straw & bark 50 Canoes and about 200 men *Ske luters* N.
N. 80° W	3	Miles on the Stard Side a pon & Small prarie on the Stard. passed the head of a Verry large Island near the middle of the river at 1 mile, and 2d Island opsd. the end of this Course Situated on the N. Side of the large Island.
N. 76° W.	4	Miles on the Stard. Side passed an island near the large Island on its North Side (I walked) on Std. open bottoms and Some ponds Small
N. 45° W.	3	Miles on the Stard. Side passed the lower point of the large Island which I call *image Canoe* Island from 2 Canoes which we met at this island with tall images on them. 4 Small Islands at its lower point all nearest the Lard Side.

From the Cascades of the Columbia to the Sea

N. 35° W.	1	Mile on the Stard. Side bottoms low & extencive not subject to overflow. river 1 ½ ms. wide
North	3	Miles to a white tree on the Stard. Side. *Mt. St Helian bears N 25° E. about 80 miles* high and Covered with Snow passed a village of 4 houses on the Stard. Side at 2 miles. one house at 3 miles
N. 28° W.	3	Miles to a Stard. Bend and Encamped near a house on the Stard. Side, haveing passed a village on each Side which I could not See distinctly at it was dusk.

5th November 1805

N. 35° W.	3	Miles to a Stard. point a Small prarie on the Stard. Side river at this place ¾ of a mile.
N. 30° W.	3 / 45	Miles to the S W. Side of an Island Sepperated from the Stard Side by a narrow Chanel this Island Covered with green bryors &c the river here widenes to 1 ½ miles passed 2 huts of Indians on the Lard Side.
N. 12° W.	3	Miles to a Lard point of Rocks opposit the upper point of an island on the Stard. Side passed the lower point of Green bryor Island at 2 miles. behind this island a little above the lower point on the Stard. is a large village of *Skil-lutes Nation* nearly ¼ of a mile in length I counted 14 large houses in front next to the Chanel
N. 22° W.	6	Miles to a Stard. point passing a Stream or Chanel behind an island at ½ a mile nearly ¼ of a mile wide on the Lard Side. a point of rocks, above, and Some low Clifts below.
N. 30° W.	5	Miles to a point of wood land on the Stard. Side of the river, the Shore boald & rockey covered with a thick groth of pine timber as above. an extincive low isld. and bottom on the lard Side. passed 2 Islands on the Stard. and the lower point of a third island.
N. 40° W. *E-cal-lar* Isd.	7	Miles to a point of wood land Stard. passed the lower point of the large island Close under the Lard. Side at 5 miles. a Small island in the middle of the river. psd. an old Village on the island at 3 miles The high hills leave the river on the ⟨Stard.⟩ Ld. at 3 miles leaveing a high bottom on that Side for 6 miles. whin the hills close on each Side

November 2–21, 1805

N. 40° W.	5	Miles to a point of high piney land on the Lard Side the Stard Side high bold and rockey here the rainge of low mountains which run S. E & N W. Cross the Columbia leaveing a Valliee of 74 miles on the river passed a creek at 2 miles on the Stard. Side about 20 yards wide. [*EC: Kalama R.*] an old village a little below. river wide and Deep.
mountains ☞		

6th November 1805

N. 50° W.	1	Mile on the Lard Side, under Som high land boald rockey Shore
N. 60° W.	1	Mile under a boald rockey Shore on the Lard. Side opposit to the upper point of an island Close under the Stard. Side the high lands bordering the opposit Side. river wide.
N 75° W.	12	Miles to a point of high land on the Lard. Side. passed 2 ⟨Houses⟩ Lodges in a Small bottom on the Lard. at 2 miles in a bottom. the high land leave the river on the Stard. Side for a feiw miles back, and a long narrow Island is Situated Close under the Stard. Shore behind which 2 Creeks falls in. on this Island near it upper point a verry remarkable Knob of high land which we passed at 3 miles Passed an Island near the Lard Side at 10 miles both of those islands thickly timbered.
N 80° W	2	Miles under a high Clift on the Lard. Side the lower point on the long Island on Stard. as also one Smaller is opposit mountains high and rugid thickly Covered with pine &c.
N. 88° W.	5 92	Miles to a high Clift a little below an old village on the Stard. Side and opposit to a old Village on the Lard. point of a handsom open extincive bottom. passed an Island in the middle of the river 3 miles long and one wide. a Small Island Close under the Stard. Side below which the mountains border the Std. bank with rugid Clifts.
S. 45° W.	5	Miles under a clift of verry high land on the Stard. Side. wind high a hed.
S. 50° W.	1	Mile under a high hill Shore bold and rockey clifts of rocks &c.
S. 75° W.	1	Mile under a high hill with a bold rockey Shore with a Steep assent river 1 m
West	1	Mile under a high hill Steep assent Encamped on the Stones under the Stard. mountain rained &c.

57

7th November 1805

N. 82° W.	2½	Miles ⟨on⟩ along the Stard Side under the high hills. Steep assent. thick fog:
N. 45° W.	1½	Miles along the Stard. Side under the high hills very Steep assent &c.
N. 60° W.	1	Mile along the Stard. Side under high hills opposit the lower point of a Island
West	2	Miles along the Stard. Shore under a high rockey hill. [*EC: Cathlamet (town) here*]
N. 45° W.	1	Mile to the head of an Island close under the Stard. Side Seperated from the Stard Shore by a narrow Chanel which we decended piloted by Indians &c.
N. 10° W.	15	Miles to a high Clift of rocks in a bend to the Stard. Side passed a Village of *War-ci-a-cum* Nation 4 houses behind Several marshey Islands, which is Scattered on the Stard. Side behind which 2 Small Creeks falls in, I believe them to be Small a large marshey Island [*EC: Tenasillihee Island*] in the middle of the river on which Some indians are camped river wide passed an old village of 7 houses behind 2 Small Marshey Islands under the high hills on the Stard Side at 12 miles of the Same Nation of those above.
S. 45° W.	3	Miles to a point of high land on the Std. Side passing under high hills. The river appears to widen into a kind of bay on the Lard Side and crouded with Small islands. the mountains leaveing the river opsd. the last village. behind those Islands a nation of *Calt har-mar* reside
S. 62° W.	5	Miles to a point on the Stard Side thro a Deep bend on the Std. under a high mtn.
S. 70° W.	3	Miles to a point on the Stard Side passg. under a high mountanious Countrey and Encamped on the rocks Stard. Side. opposit a rock Situated ½ a mile in the river 50 feet high & 20 Diamuter Some high mountains to the S W. on the top of one is Snow. *Ocian in view*! O! the joy.

8th November 1805

S. 63° W	2	Miles to a point on the Stard. Side a high mountanious Countrey Std. Several low islands in the Bay or deep bend opposit towards the Lard Shore.

November 2–21, 1805

S. 60° W.	6	Miles to a point on the Stard Side passed old vilgs. at 1 and 3
	142	miles entered a Deep bay or *nitch* about 5 miles deep coasted around it Severl. Creeks or inlets makeing into the land Std. a old village in this nitch which we Call Shallow nitch and land Encamp at the Point.

10th November 1805

S. 45° W.	10	Miles to a Point Distress[7] on the Std. side passed a Deep nitch and Six iner points on the Stard Side. the Shore bold and rockey. mountains high on the Stard and thickly Covered with timber principally of the pine kind. wind rose Swills high we encamped at 9 miles in a Small nitch 6 days. rained &c. a deep bay on the Lard Sid opposit. The Countrey high to the river above the bay on the opposit Side.

16th November 1805

S 80° W.	2	Miles to a point of a low bottom on the Stard. Side (where we Encamped 10 days in a narrow bottom Slashey in full view of the Ocian) passed a Small Creek at 1 mile an old *Chin nook* Village of 36 houses at 1½ miles a butifull Sand beech and narrow bottom below the Creek on Stard.
S. 86° W.	11	Miles Computed to Cape Disapointment the enterance of this great river into the great Pacific Ocian a large Sand bar off Point Adams. a Deep bay to the Stard. with 2 Creeks falling into it and the Coast for a fiew Leagues to the N W Shall be discribed here after.

Ocian 165 Miles from *Quick Sand river*.
Ocian 190 Miles from the first rapid.
Ocian 4142 Miles from the Mouth of *Missouri* R.

1. Again asterisks precede the dateline for unknown reason.

2. Both this entry and the Codex H courses and distances indicate a movement of two miles west on this day. However, *Atlas* map 82 and fig. 1 show the campsite of November 15 as being the one at which the main party remained until November 25, and Biddle's entry for the day also indicates no movement. An "X" next to the usual camp symbol on that map may indicate a move. On *Atlas* map 89 the November 15 camp is labeled "Encamped the 15 16 17." See also *Atlas* map 90. Gass, Ordway, and Whitehouse do not refer to any movement on November 16. Coues (HLC), 2:709–10.

3. The black brant is the western race of the brant; the speckled brant may be the east-

ern race, lighter than the western race and less common on the Pacific Coast. The white brant is the snow goose. Burroughs, 192–93; Holmgren, 28.

4. A vertical line is drawn through this paragraph to here.

5. Clark's course and distance table is from Codex H, pp. 132–48, and is split across two volumes. The material covering October 18–November 1, 1805, is found after the codex entry of the latter date; the remainder is placed here at the concluding date where it is found in the notebook. See also the note at October 18, 1805.

6. This is a subtotal at the bottom of p. 141 of Codex H. Other subtotals appear throughout the table.

7. The word "Distress" appears to have been added to a blank space.

[Clark] *November 17th Sunday 1805*

a fair cool windey morning wind from the *East*. every tide which rises 8 feet 6 Inches at this place, ⟨is acomp⟩ comes in with high Swells which brake on the Sand Shore with great fury.

I Sent out 6 men to kill deer & fowls this morning—

Took Equal altitude with Sextt.

	h	m	s		h	m	s
A. M.	8	47	7	P. M.	2	34	49
"	8	50	29	"	2	37	10
"	8	53	56	"	2	39	35

Altitude produced 27° 58′ 00

at half past 1 oClock Capt. Lewis and his Party returned haveing around passd. Point Disapointment and Some distance on the main Ocian to the N W. Several Indians followed him & Soon after a canoe with *wapto* roots, & ⟨Lickorish⟩ [*ML: Liquorice*][1] boiled, which they gave as presents, in return for which we gave more than the worth to Satisfy them a bad practice to receive a present of Indians, as they are never Satisfied in return. our hunters killed 3 Deer & th fowler 2 Ducks & 4 brant I Surveyed a little on the corse & made Some observns. The Chief of the nation below us Came up to See us[2] the name of the nation is ⟨Chin-noo⟩ *Chin-nook* and is noumerous live principally on fish roots a fiew Elk and fowls. they are well armed with good Fusees. I directed all the men who wished to See more of the Ocean to Get ready to Set out with me on tomorrow day light. the following men expressed a wish to accompany me i'e' Serj. Nat Pryor Serjt. J. Ordway, Jo: Fields R. Fields, Jo. Shannon, Jo Colter, William Bratten, Peter *Wiser*, Shabono & my Servant York. all others being well Contented with what part of the Ocean & its curiosities which Could be Seen from the vicinity of our Camp.

[Clark] November 17th Sunday 1805

A fair cool morning wind from the East. The tide rises at this place 8 feet 6 inches and comes in with great waves brakeing on the Sand beech on which we lay with great fury Six hunters out this morning in serch of Deer & fowl.[3]

At half past 1 oClock Capt Lewis returned haveing travesed Haleys Bay to Cape Disapointment and the *Sea* Coast to the North for Some distance. Several *Chinnook* Indians followed Capt L— and a Canoe came up with roots mats &c. to Sell. those Chinnooks made us a present of a rute boiled much resembling the common liquorice in taste and Size: [ML?: *thy call cul-wha-mo*] in return for this root we gave more than double the value to Satisfy their craveing dispostn. It is a bad practice to receive a present from those Indians as they are never Satisfied for what they reive in return if ten time the value of the articles they gave. This *Chin nook* Nation is about 400 Souls inhabid the Countrey on the Small rivrs which run into the bay below us and on the Ponds to the N W of us, live principally on fish and roots, they are well armed with fusees and Sometimes kill Elk Deer and fowl. our hunters killed to day 3 Deer, 4 brant and 2 Ducks, and inform me they Saw Some Elk Sign. I directed all the men who wished to See more of the main *Ocian*[4] to prepare themselves to Set out with me early on tomorrow morning. The principal Chief of the Chinnooks & his familey came up to See us this evening—

1. Seashore lupine, *Lupinus littoralis* Dougl., whose underground rhizome was prepared for eating by Chinook Indians after roasting and pounding it. The common liquorice used for comparison is the cultivated *Glycyrrhiza glabra* L. Hitchcock et al., 3 : 319; Gunther (EWW), 38; Ray (LCEN), 119; Bailey, 561. It is the "cul-wha-mo" of the day's second entry, from Chinookan *qałxwima* for the lupine. Gibbs (AVC), 14. See Clark's entry of January 22, 1806 (apparently copied from Lewis's entry of January 24), for an extended discussion of the plant.

2. Evidently Comcomly (*Qanqmli*), a one-eyed chief of whom there is written mention from 1795. He was an important figure on the lower Columbia, a shrewd businessman and diplomat who eventually came to dominate the Chinooks. He was generally friendly with the whites, which enhanced his business and political interests. He was on good terms with the Astorians when they established their post in the area in 1811, and at first urged

them to resist the British takeover in 1812, offering the assistance of his warriors. When the British seized the fort, however, he adroitly became their friend and ally. He remained the dominant figure of the Columbia mouth until his death in about 1829 or 1830, of a disease imported by the whites. Ruby & Brown (CITC); Ross; Franchère (AA), 45, 58, 80, 121; Franchère (JV), 76–77, 90–91, 122–23, 193; Cox, 49, 147, 157; Irving (Astor); Coues (NLEH), 2:750; Silverstein.

3. The astronomical observation given at this point is the same as that in the Elkskin-bound Journal.

4. A vertical line runs from "The *Chinnook* Nation" to about this point.

[Clark]   Novr. 18th Monday 1805

a little Cloudy this morning   I set out at day light with 10 men & my Sevent, Shabono, Sergt. Pryer odderway Jos. & R. Fields Shannon Colter, wiser, Lebiech & york   proceeded on Down the Shore from the 1st point[1]

N. W	6	miles to a lodge at the enterance of a river[2] on the Std. in the middle of a boggey Bay
S. 79° W.	7	miles to the mouth of a River old Cabins open bogs above for 2 ms. back we Call after the nation *Chin-nook* River[3] from this river to Camp Point is
S. 64° E		to Bluff Point (a small Island in a nitch of the Bay in the Same Course) is
S. 20° W.	1½	miles psd. a to *Cape Disapt.* is South— To point *adams* is S. 22° E—About 25 miles— passed a part of a fish about 1 mile above I supposed to be a Grampass—[4] The men killed 4 brants & ⟨we⟩ Lab. Killed 48 pliver of 2 different kinds yellow & black legs— I had them picked cooked and we Dined on them.
S. 80° W.	1	mile to the bottom of a nitch at a branch from a pond
South 8° W.		to an Isd. in the 2d nitch from this passed 2 points in the Course To the center of the 1s Nitch a run is 1 mile To the do. of th 2 do is 1 mile

At a run & Island near the Shore here the Traders ancher & trade.[5]   we passed at each point a Soft Clifts of yellow, brown & dark Soft Stones[6] here Capt Lewis myself & Severl. of the men marked our names day of the month & by Land &c. &c.   from this S. W. 3 miles to the Iner pt. of Cape Disapointmt passed a point & 2 Small nitches   (Reuben Fields

2. Flounder (starry flounder, *Platichthys stellatus*),
November 18, 1805, Elkskin-bound Journal

killed a Vulter)[7] we found a Curious flat fish Shaped like a turtle, with fins on each side, and a tale notched like a fish, the Internals on one Sid and tale & fins flat wise   This fish Flownder[8] has a white ⟨belly⟩ on one Side & lies flat to the Ground—   passed from last nitch across to the ocean ½ a mile low land   the Cape is a high Partly bald hill, founded on rock, I assended a high Seperate bald hill[9] Covered with long corse grass & Seperated from the hight of Country by a Slashey bottom 2 miles S. 60 W of the Cape—   thence to a 2d Grassey pt is N. 50° W. 2 miles, Those

3. Area about Cape Disappointment,
ca. November 18, 1805, Elkskin-bound Journal

hills are founded on rocks & the waves brake with great fury against them, the Coast is Sholey for Several miles of this Cape & for Some distance off to the N W a Sand bar in the mouth. Sholey Some distance out from the mouth   The Coast from the Cape N W is open for a Short distance back then it becomes thick piney Countrey intersperced with ponds

Point addams is ⟨S. W⟩ S 20° W about 20 miles the Course on that Side bears S 45 W. I cannot assertain the prosise Course of the Deep water in the mouth of the river, the Channel is but narrow. I proceeded on up above the 2d point and Encamped on the Shore above the high tide,[10] evening Clear, for a Short time. Supd. on Brant and pounded fish men all Chearfull, express a Desire to winter near the falls this winter.—

[Clark] *November 18th Monday 1805*[11]

A little cloudy this morning I Set out with 10 men and my man York to the Ocian by land. i. e. Serjt. Ordway & Pryor, Jos. & Ru. Fields, Go. Shannon, W. Brattin, J. Colter, P. Wiser, W. Labieche & P. Shabono one of our interpreters & York. I Set out at Day light and proceeded on a Sandy beech

N. 80° W.	1	Mile to a point of rocks about 40 feet high, from the top of which the hill Side is open and assend with a Steep assent to the tops of the Mountains, a Deep nitch and two Small Streams above this point, then my course was
N. W.	7	Mile to the enterance of a creek at a lodge or cabin of Chinnooks passing on a wide Sand bar the bay to my left and Several Small ponds Containing great numbers of water fowls to my right; with a narrow bottom of alder & Small balsam between the Ponds and the Mountn. at the Cabin I saw 4 womin and Some Children one of the women in a desperate Situation, covered with Sores Scabs & ulsers no doubt the effects of venereal disorder which Several of this nation which I have Seen appears to have. This Creek appears to be nothing more than the conveyance of Several Small dreans from the high hills and the ponds on each Side near its mouth. here we were Set across all in one Canoe by 2 Squars to each I gav a Small hook

From the Cascades of the Columbia to the Sea

S. 79° W.	5	Miles to the mouth of *Chin nook* river, passed a low bluff of a small hite at 2 miles below which is the remains of huts near which place is also the remains of a whale on the Sand,[12] the countrey low open and Slashey, with elivated lands interspersed covered with [NB?: Some] pine & thick under groth This river is 40 yards wide at low tide— here we made a fire and dined on 4 brant and 48 Pliver which was killed by Labiech on the coast as we came on. Rubin Fields Killed a Buzzard [NB?: Vulture] of the large Kind near the meat of the whale we Saw: W. 25 lb. measured from the tips of the wings across 9½ feet, from the point of the Bill to the end of the tail 3 feet 10¼ inches, middle toe 5½ inches, toe nale 1 inch & 3½ lines, wing feather 2½ feet long & 1 inch 5 lines diamiter tale feathers 14½ inches, and the *head* is 6½ inches including the beak. [NB: head in Peale's Mus.][13] after dineing we crossed the river in an old canoe which I found on the Sand near Som old houses & proceeded on—
S. 20° W.	4	Miles to a Small rock island in a deep nitch passed a nitch at 2 miles in which there is a dreen from Some ponds back, the land low opposite this nitch a bluff of yellow Clay and Soft Stone from the river to the Comencement of this nitch below the Country rises to high hills of about 80 or 90 feet above the water— at 3 miles passed a nitch— this rock Island is Small and at the South of a deep bend in which the nativs inform us the Ships anchor, and from whence they receive their goods in return for their peltries and Elk Skins &c. this appears to be a very good harber for large Ships. here I found Capt Lewis name on a tree. I also engraved my name & by land the day of the month and year, as also Several of the men.
S. 46° E.	2	Miles to the iner extremity of *Cape Disapointment* passing a nitch in which there is a Small rock island, a Small Stream falls into this nitch from a pond which is imediately on the Sea Coast passing through a low isthmus. this Cape is an ellivated ⟨Situat⟩ Circlier point Covered with thick timber on the iner Side and open grassey exposur next to the Sea and rises with a Steep assent to the hight of about 150 or 160 feet above the leavel of the water ⟨from the last mentioned nitch—⟩ this cape as also the Shore both on the Bay & Sea coast is a dark brown rock. I crossed the neck of Land low and ½ of a mile wide to the main Ocian, at the foot of a high open hill project-
Miles ☞	19	

ing into the ocian, and about one mile in Sicumfrance. I assended this hill which is covered with high corse grass. decended to the N. of it and camped. I picked up a flounder on the beech this evening.—

from Cape Disapointment to a high point of a Mountn. which we shall call [*NB: Clarke's Point of View*]¹⁴ beares S. 20° W. about ⟨40⟩ [*WC?:* 25] miles, point adams is verry low and is Situated within the direction between those two high points of land, the water appears verry Shole from off the mouth of the river for a great distance, and I cannot assertain the direction of the deepest Chanel, the Indians point nearest the opposit Side. the waves appear to brake with tremendious force in every direction quite across   a large Sand bar lies within the mouth nearest to point Adams which is nearly covered at high tide. I suped on brant this evening with a little pounded fish. Some rain in the after part of the night.   men appear much Satisfied with their trip beholding with estonishment the high waves dashing against the rocks & this emence ocian

1. Clark's route is shown as a dotted line on *Atlas* map 91 and on fig. 1.

2. Chinook River, in Pacific County, Washington, and given as such on *Atlas* map 89, but in opposition to what Clark apparently applied that name on *Atlas* maps 82, 83. It is unnamed on *Atlas* map 91; fig. 1.

3. Now Wallacut River, flowing into Baker Bay in Pacific County. *Atlas* maps 82 and 83 note it as "Chin-nook Nation," while *Atlas* map 89 gives it as "White brant creek," probably incorrectly.

4. Perhaps *Grampus griseus*, grampus or Risso's dolphin, a cetacean rather than a fish. Hall, 2:892.

5. On *Atlas* maps 89 and 91 a boat is shown at the anchoring spot, while fig. 1 has an anchor drawn at the spot. *Atlas* map 90 has the word "ankerage." It is on the east side of Cape Disappointment between Ilwaco and Fort Canby State Park, Pacific County.

6. The cliffs are composed of siltstone and coarse-grained sandstone of the Miocene-age Astoria Formation. There is also a Quaternary-age landslide near this point containing rubble derived from the Astoria Formation.

7. Their first actual specimen of the California condor, *Gymnogyps californianus* [AOU, 324], now nearly extinct. See above, October 30, 1805; below, February 16, 1806. Burroughs, 201–3.

8. Here in the Elkskin-bound Journal Clark has inserted a sketch of the fish (see fig. 2); it is probably a starry flounder, *Platichthys stellatus*. See below, March 13, 1806. Burroughs, 266; Lee et al., 830.

9. Probably McKenzie Head in Fort Canby State Park.

10. Clark's camp is shown on *Atlas* map 91, near McKenzie Head in Fort Canby State

Park. A map, perhaps of the area, is overwritten by text on this page of the Elkskin-bound Journal (see fig. 3). Included with the map are the words, "Shoals & Swells," in Clark's hand. The camp was in the vicinity of the Fishing Rocks archaeological site. Archaeological work at this shell midden encountered evidence that Chinook Indians used the site as a hunting and fishing camp beginning around 1,000 years ago and continuing into early historic times. Minor (ASCR).

11. There is a great deal of variation between the two entries for the courses of Clark's route.

12. The whale is pictured on *Atlas* map 91.

13. Biddle's interlineation was obviously added much later, probably in 1810, but not in his usual red ink. For Charles Willson Peale see above, September 10, 1803.

14. Tillamook Head, in Clatsop County, Oregon. See *Atlas* map 90. The correction in distance may have resulted from Clark's visit to the area in January. *Atlas* map 84.

[Clark] November 19th Tuesday 1805

began to rain a little before day and Continued raining untill 11 oClock I proceeded on thro emencely bad thickets & hills crossing 2 points to a 3rd on which we built a fire and Cooked a Deer which Jos. Field Killd. from this point I can See into a Deep bend in the coast to the N. E. ⟨N 40° E⟩ for 10 miles. after Brackfast I proceeded on N. 20 E. 5 miles to Comcement a large Sand bar at a low part ponds a little off from the Coast here the high rockey hills end and a low marshey Countrey Suckceed. I proceeded up the Course N. 10° W. 4 miles & marked my name & the Day of the Month on a pine tree,[1] the waters which Wash this Sand beach is tinged with a deep brown Colour for Some distance out. The Course Contd. is N. 20° W. low Coast and Sand beech, Saw a Dead Sturgen[2] 10 feet long on the Sand, & the back bone of a Whale, as I conceived raind I then returned to the Cape & dined, Some curious Deer[3] on this Course darker large boded Shorte legs Pronged horns & the top of the tale black under part white as usial passed a nitch in the rocks below into which falls a Stream, after Dinner I Set out on my return S. E. passed over a low ridge & thro a piney countrey 2½ miles to the Bay, thence up the Bay to the mouth of the *Chen-nook* River Crossed in the Canoe we had left there & Encamped on the upper Side[4] The Hills in the point of this bay are not high, & imedeately below this River the present yellow Bluffs—[5]

above the River and up for about 2 miles the land is low Slashey and Contains much drift wood, the Countrey up this Creek is low with ⟨places or) Copse of high land or as I may Say elevated. The Buzzard which Ruben Fields killed diameter of one feather is—1¼ & 1 Line from the tip of one to the tip of the other wing is 9 feet 0 Inches, from the point of the Bill to the tale is 3 feet 10¼ Ins.   middle Toe 5½ Inches, Toe nale 1 Inches [3½? *and one mark illegible*]   wing feather 2 feet ½ In. Tale feathers 14¼ In.   Head is 6¼ Inch long including the [beek?]

[Clark] November 19th Tuesday 1805[6]

a Cloudy rainey day   proceeded up the Coast which runs from my camp 1¼ miles west of the iner extry of the Cape N. 20° W. 5 miles through a rugged hilley countrey thickly [*NB?: timbered*] off the Sea coast to the Comencment of an extencive Sand beech which runs N. 10° W. to point Lewis about 20 miles distance. I proceeded up this coast 4 miles and marked my name on a low pine.   and returned 3 miles back (The Countrey opsd. this Sand Coast is low and Slashey,[)] Crossed the point 2 miles to the bay and encamped on Chinnook river—   See another book for perticulars   [*EC: see Codex I.*]

[Clark] Tuesday November the 19th 1805[7]

I arose early this morning from under a wet blanket caused by a Shower of rain which fell in the latter part of the last night and Sent two men on a head with directions to proceed on near the Sea Coast and Kill Something for brackfast and that I Should follow my Self in about half an hour.   after drying our blankets a little I Set out with a view to proceed near the Coast the direction of which induced me to conclude that at the distance of 8 or 10 miles, the Bay was at no great distance across. I overtook the hunters at about 3 miles, they had killed a Small Deer on which we brackfast   it comened raining and Continud moderately untill 11 oClock A M.

after takeing a Sumptious brackfast of venison which was rosted on Stiks exposed to the fire, I proceeded on through ruged Country of high hills and Steep hollers on a course from the Cape N 20° W. 5 miles on a Direct line to the Commencement of a Sandy Coast which extended N. 10° W. from the top of the hill above the Sand Shore to a Point of high land distant near 20 miles.   this point I have taken the Liberty of Calling after my particular friend Lewis— at the commencement of this Sand beech the high lands leave the Sea coast in a Direction to Chinnook river, and does not touch the Sea Coast again ⟨untill⟩ below point Lewis leaveing a low pondey countrey, maney places open with small ponds in which there is great numbr. of fowl I am informed that the *Chinnoo*k Nation inhabit this low countrey and live in large wood houses on a river which passes through this bottom Parrilal to the Sea coast and falls into the Bay

I proceeded on the Sandy Coast 4 miles, and marked my name on a Small pine, the Day of the month & year, &c. and returned to the foot of the hill, from which place I intended to Strike across to The Bay, I saw a Sturgeon which had been thrown on Shore and left by the tide 10 feet in length, and Several joints of the back bone of a whale which must have foundered on this part of the Coast. after Dineing on the remains of our Small Deer I proceeded through over a land S E with Some Ponds to the bay distance about 2 miles, thence up to the mouth of Chinnook river 2 miles, crossed this little river in the Canoe we left at its mouth and Encamped on the upper Side in an open Sandy bottom— The hills next to the bay Cape disapointment to a Short distance up the Chinnook river is not verry high thickly Coverd. with different Species of pine &c. maney of which are large, I observed in maney places pine of 3 or 4 feet through growing on the bodies of large trees which had fallen down, and covered with moss and yet part Sound. The Deer of this Coast differ materially from our Common deer in a much as they are much darker deeper bodied Shorter ledged horns equally branched from the beem the top of the tail black from the rute to the end Eyes larger and do not lope but jump—.[8]

    1. Clark advanced about nine miles up the coast from his camp, the extent of which is marked as "W. Clark 19th Novr. 1805" on fig. 1. This may indicate also the marking Clark placed on the tree. On *Atlas* map 91 that point may be the spot marked "Turned back." He was in the area of present Long Beach, Pacific County, Washington. Willapa Bay is a short distance inland, but it does not appear that he saw it. Archaeological work in this area has been confined almost entirely to excavations at the Martin site, a shell midden near Nahcotta, Pacific County, occupied between approximately 1,900 and 500 years ago. Kidd; Shaw.

    2. Given the size (somewhat exaggerated here) it is probably the green sturgeon, *Acipenser medirostris*. Lee et al., 40.

    3. The Columbian black-tailed deer, *Odocoileus hemionus columbiana*, previously un-

known to science. See Lewis's description below, February 19, 1806. Burroughs, 127–28; Cutright (LCPN), 242, 244, 441; Hall, 2:1088–89.

4. On the east side of Wallacut River, a mile or more northeast of present Ilwaco, Pacific County. The spot is clearly indicated on *Atlas* map 91.

5. The hills in this area are composed of Oligocene and Miocene sedimentary rocks, some of which are not especially indurated.

6. This is the last entry in Codex H. A longer entry for the day follows in Codex I.

7. This begins the first daily entry in Codex I, which continues to January 29, 1806. Preceding this entry on the front flyleaf are the following words, in pencil and apparently in Clark's hand: "Gentlemen To meet the approbation of my Country." At the bottom of the page and upside down are some random arithmetic figures, probably relating to astronomical calculations. They read as follow, although the placement of the numbers may not be exact:

$$
\begin{array}{c}
7 \\
34.57
\end{array}
\qquad
\begin{array}{c}
70 \\
\underline{7} \\
44\overline{)490} \quad 11 \\
\underline{44} \\
40
\end{array}
$$

$$
[H?] \qquad 1 \quad 44\text{—}7 \qquad 7
$$

$$
\begin{array}{l}
\text{Lat. } 39°\ \ 46.{}^{6}\!/_{10} \\
\phantom{\text{Lat. }}46\ \ \underline{41\ {}^{6}\!/_{10}} \\
\phantom{\text{Lat. }}2\overline{|88\ {}^{2}\!/_{10}} \\
\phantom{\text{Lat. }}44
\end{array}
\Bigg\} 4
\qquad
\begin{array}{r}
46.6 \\
\underline{34\ 6} \\
279\ 6 \\
1864 \\
\underline{1398} \\
1612\ 36
\end{array}
$$

This entry is also preceded by thirty-three pages of statistical and meteorological material. First comes a table of distances from Fort Mandan to the Pacific Coast (pp. 2–12); it is found in Chapter 30 of this volume. The weather data (pp. 13–33) are placed monthly by chronology. In this journal the weather tables are for the months of April 1805 through January 1806. See Appendix C, vol. 2. Clark also defines his weather table abbreviations on p. 13. This is a copy (with some changes in dates and places) of the explanatory notes found in the Weather Diary which are placed with the January 1804 weather table. Here Clark gives the position of Fort Mandan as 47° 12' 47" north latitude and 99° 24' 45 $^{1}\!/_{10}$" west longitude, somewhat different than earlier calculations. Finally, the date for the entry is immediately preceded by a heading: "Cape Disappointment at the Enterance of Columbia River into the Great *South Sea* or *Pacific Ocean*. (See Journal N 6)." "Journal N 6" is Clark's designation for Codex H.

8. This material about the deer has a red vertical line through it, perhaps done by Biddle.

[Clark]   *Novr. 20 Wednesday 1805*

Some rain last night   despatchd. 3 men to hunt   Jo. Fields & Colter to hunt Elk & Labich to kill some Brant for our brackfast   The Morning

Cleared up fare and we proceeded on by the Same rout we went out, at the River we found no Indians. made a raft & Ruben Fields Crossed and took over a Small Canoe which lay at the Indian Cabin— This Creek is at this time of high tide 300 yards wide & the marshes for Some distance up the Creek Covered with water. not an Indian to be Seen near the Creek. I proceeded on to Camp & on my way was over taken by 3 Indians one gave ⟨me⟩ us Sturgeon & *Wapto* roots to eate I met Several parties on way all of them appeared to know me & was distant, found all well at Camp,[1] maney Indians about one of which had on a robe made of 2 Sea Orter Skins. Capt Lewis offered him many things for his Skins with others a blanket, a coat all of which he refused we at length purchased it for a belt of Blue Beeds which the Squar had— The tide being out we walked home on the beech—

[Clark]   *Wednesday November the 20th 1805*

Some rain last night dispatched Labiech to kill Some fowl for our brackfast he returned in about 2 hours with 8 large Ducks on which we brackfast I proceeded on to the enterance of a Creek near a Cabin no person being at this cabin and 2 Canoes laying on the opposit Shore from us, I deturmined to have a raft made and Send a man over for a canoe, a Small raft was Soon made, and Reuben Fields Crossed and brought over a Canoe— This Creek which is the outlet of a number of ponds, is at this time (high tide) 300 yds wide— I proceeded on up the Beech and was overtaken by three Indians one of them gave me Some dried Sturgeon and a fiew *wappato* roots, I employd Those Indians to take up one of our Canoes which had been left by the first party that Came down, for which Service I gave them each a fishing hook of a large Size— on my way up I met Several parties of Chinnooks which I had not before Seen they were on their return from our Camp. all those people appeard to know my deturmonation of keeping every individual of their nation at a proper distance, as they were guarded and resurved in my presence &c. found maney of the *Chin nooks* with Capt. Lewis of whome there was 2 Cheifs *Com com mo ly* & *Chil-lar-la-wil*[2] to whome we gave Medals and to one a flag. one of the Indians had on a roab made of 2 Sea Otter Skins the fur of them were more butifull than any fur I had ever Seen both Capt. Lewis & my Self endeavored to purchase the *roab* with differant articles   at length we precured it for a belt of blue beeds which the Squar—wife of our interpreter Shabono wore around her waste. in my absence the hunters had killed Several Deer and fowl of different kinds—

   1. Clark had returned to the Chinook Point campsite. See above, November 15, 1805.
   2. Very likely the same as Shelathwell, prominent among the Chinooks in the 1790s, when he was reported by traders; he was often in company with Comcomly. In another place his name is given as "Shil-lar-la-wit." See note at an undated entry at January 1, 1806. Ruby & Brown (CITC), 64, 69–73, 106.

[Clark]   *November 21st Thursday 1805*

   a Cloudy morning   most of the Indians left us, The nation on the opposit Side is Small & Called *Clap-sott*,[1] Their great chief name *Stil-la-sha*— The nation liveing to the North is Called *Chieltz*.[2] The chief is name *Ma-laugh*   not large nation and wore ⟨their⟩ his beards as informed by the Inds. In my absence the hunters Kild. 7 Deer, 4 brants & a Crane.

   Great numbers of the dark brant passing Southerley, the white yet Stationary, no gees & Swan to be Seen. The wind blew hard from the S. E. which with the addition of the flood tide raised emence Swells & waves which almost entered our Encampment   morng. dark & Disagreeable, a Supriseing Climent. We have not had One cold day Since we passed below the last falls or great Shute & Some time before   the Climent is temperate, and the only change we have experienced is from fair weather to rainey windey weather—   I made a chief & gave a medel   this man is name *Tow-wâll* and appears to have Some influence with the nation and tells me he lives at the great Shute—[3]   we gave the Squar a Coate of Blue Cloth for the belt of Blue Beeds we gave for the Sea otter Skins purchased of an Indian.   at 12 oClock it began to rain, and continued moderately all day, Some wind from the S. E., waves too high for us to proceed on our homeward bound journey. Lattitude of this place is $46° 19'$ $11^{1}/_{10}''$ North   Several Indians and Squars came this evening I beleave for the purpose of gratifying the passions of our men, Those people appear to View ⟨horedom⟩ Sensuality as a necessary evile, and do not appear to abhore this as Crime in the unmarried females. The young women Sport openly with our men, and appear to receive the approbation of their friends & relations for So doing   maney of the women are handsom.

They are all low both men and women, I saw the name of J. Bowmon marked or picked on a young Squars left arm. The women of this nation Pick their legs in different figures as an orniment. the[y] were their hair loose, Some trinkets in their ears, none in the nose as those above, their Dress is as follows, i,e the men, were a roabe of either the skins of [*blank*] a Small fured animal, & which is most common, or the Skins of the Sea orter, Loon, Swan, Beaver,[4] Deer, Elk, or blankets either red, blu, or white, which roabes cover the sholders arms & body, all other parts are nakd.

The women were a Short peticoat of the iner bark of the white Ceder or *Arber Vita,* which hang down loose in Strings nearly as low as the knee, with a Short Robe which fall half way down the Thigh. no other part is Covered. The orniments are beeds, Blue principally, large Brass wire around their rists Som rings, and maney men have Salors Clothes, many have good fusees & Ball & Powder— The women ware a String of Something curious tied tight above the anckle, all have large Swelled legs & thighs The men Small legs & thighs and Generally badly made—[5] They live on Elk Deer fowls, but principally fish and roots of 3 Kinds, Lickorish, *Wapto* &c. The women have more privalages than is Common amongst Indians— Pocks & Venerial [X: *venereous*] is Common amongst them[6] I Saw one man & one woman who appeared to be all in Scabs, & Several men with the venereal, their other Disorders and the remides for them I could not lern we divided Some ribin between the men of our party to bestow on their favourite Lasses, this plan to Save the knives & more valueable articles.

Those people gave me Sturgion Salmon & wapto roots, & we bought roots, ⟨high bush Cranberies,⟩ Some mats &c. &c. for which we were obliged to give emence prices— we also purchased a kind of Cranberry[7] which the Indians Say the geather in the low lands, off of Small either vines or bushes just abov the ground— we also purchased hats made of Grass &c.[8] of those Indians, Some very handsom mats made of flags—[9] Some fiew curious baskets made of a Strong weed & willow or [*blank*] Splits—[10], also a Sweet Soft black root,[11] about th Sise & Shape of a Carrot, this root they Value verry highly— The *Wapto* root is Scerce, and highly valued by those people, this root they roste in hot ashes like a potato and the outer Skin peals off, tho this is a trouble they Seldom perform.

[Clark] *Thursday November 21st 1805*

a cloudy morning most of the Chinnooks leave our Camp and return home, great numbers of the dark brant passing to the South, the white Brant have not yet commenced their flight. The wind blew hard from the S. E. which with the addition of the flood tide raised verry high waves which broke with great violence against the Shore throwing water into our Camp— the fore part of this day Cloudy at 12 oClock it began to rain and Continud all day moderately, Several Indians Visit us to day of differant nations or Bands Some of the *Chiltz* Nation who reside on the Sea Coast near Point Lewis, Several of the *Clotsops* who reside on the opposit Side of the Columbia imediately opposit to us, and a Chief from the Grand rapid to whome we gave a Medal.

An old woman & wife to a Cheif of the *Chinnooks*[12] came and made a Camp near ours She brought with her 6 young Squars [*NB: her daughters & nieces*] I believe for the purpose of gratifying the passions of the men of our party and receving for those indulgiences Such Small as She (the old woman) thought proper to accept of, Those people appear to view Sensuality as a Necessary evel, and do not appear to abhor it as a Crime in the unmarried State— The young females are fond of the attention of our men and appear to meet the sincere approbation of their friends and connections, for thus obtaining their favours; the womin of the Chinnook Nation have handsom faces low and badly made with large legs & thighs which are generally Swelled from a Stopage of the circulation in the feet (which are Small) by maney Strands of Beeds or curious Strings which are drawn tight around the leg above the anckle, their legs are also picked with different figures, I Saw on the left arm of a Squar the following letters *J. Bowmon*, all those are Considered by the natives of this quarter as handsom deckerations, and a woman without those deckorations is Considered as among the lower Class they ware their hair lose hanging over their back and Sholders maney have blue beeds ⟨in⟩ threaded & hung from different parts of their *ears* and about ther neck and around their wrists, their dress other wise is prosisely like that of the Nation of *Wa ci a cum* as already discribed. a Short roab, and *tissue* or kind of peticoat of the bark of Cedar which fall down in Strings as low as the knee behind and not So low before maney of the men have blankets of red blue or Spotted Cloth or the common three & 2½ point blankets,[13] and

Salors old Clothes which they appear to prise highly, they also have robes of *Sea Otter*, Beaver, Elk, Deer, fox and Cat[14] common to this countrey, which I have never Seen in the U States. They also precure a roabe from the nativs above, which is made of the Skins of a Small animal[15] about the Size of a Cat, which is light and dureable and highly prized by those people— the greater numbers of the men of the Chinnooks have Guns and powder and Ball— The Men are low homely and badly made, Small Crooked legs ⟨and Small thighs⟩ large feet, and all of both Sects have flattened heads— The food of this nation is principally fish & roots the fish they precure from the river by the means of nets and gigs, and the Salmon which run up the Small branches together with what they collect drifted up on the Shores of the Sea coast near to where they live—

The roots which they use are Several different kinds, the *Wappato* which they precure from the nativs above, a black root which they call *Shaw-na tâh que*[16] & the wild licquorish is the most Common, they also kill a fiew Elk Deer & fowl— maney of the Chinnooks appear to have venerious and pustelus disorders. one woman whome I saw at the beech appeared all over in Scabs and ulsers &c.

we gave to the men each a pece of ribin We purchased Cramberies Mats verry netely made of flags and rushes, Some roots, Salmon and I purchased a hat made of Splits & Strong grass, which is made in the fashion which was common in the U States two years ago also Small baskets to hold Water made of Split and Straw, for those articles we gave high prices—.[17]

1. The Clatsops, for whom the party's winter quarters on the coast were named, occupied the south bank of the Columbia River from Point Adams at the river's mouth and upstream as far as Tongue Point, and south along the Oregon coast to Tillamook Head, all in Clatsop County, Oregon. *Atlas* map 82; Hodge, 1 : 305; Berreman, 15; Taylor (CkI); Hajda, 102–4. Their name derives from Chinookan *ɬaċǝp* or *ɬakílak* (two dialectical variants), "those who have pounded salmon," while one of their main villages on Point Adams was called *ɬakílaki(x)*, "where there is pounded salmon." Silverstein. The Clatsops and the Chinooks across the river spoke dialects which were practically identical and which together comprise the Lower Chinook language. These languages were distinct from the related but mutually unintelligible Upper Chinook language spoken by Chinookan peoples upriver. Although they possessed many skills which the newcomers admired, many aspects of their culture aroused negative reactions in Anglo-Americans and British. The ambivalence of the captains was far from unique. The chief's name as given here

does not appear again. The name is not recorded on the undated list placed with entries of January 1, 1806. Perhaps it was an error in communication.

2. The Chehalis, or more precisely the Lower Chehalis, were a Salish-speaking people living in Grays Harbor and Pacific counties on the southern Washington coast. Their term is apparently čxi'ls, from Chinookan giłáčxi'ls, "Lower Chehalis Salish people." Their Salish name is ƛ'əxil'əs, "sand," for a large and important village at Westport on Grays Harbor. Lower Chehalis territory centered around Grays Harbor and extended southward to Willapa Bay, where the north shore was claimed by both the Lower Chehalis and the Chinooks proper. Hodge, 1 : 241; Spier, 29–31; Ray (LCEN), 36; Swanton, 415–16; Taylor (CsI); Hajda, 96; Silverstein. "Ma-laugh" may be the same as "Mar-lock-ke" in an undated entry at January 1, 1806. His name is not identifiable linguistically.

3. A vertical line runs through these words in the Elkskin-bound Journal, beginning with "I made a chief." Also in a passage below, from "otter skins" to "homeward bound journey." Tow-wâll (*Túwal*) is unknown.

4. American beaver, *Castor canadensis*.

5. One word is added interlinearly near here in the Elkskin-bound Journal but is difficult to read. It appears in the same hand and ink as "venereous" below and may be "Perstetus" for "prostitutes."

6. The pox, or syphilis, and venereal disease.

7. Wild cranberry, *Vaccinium oxycoccos* L., much used by the natives of the lower Columbia. The cranberry was plentiful in the Lower Chinook territory and was an item of trade. Hitchcock et al., 4 : 34–35; Gunther (EWW), 45; Ray (LCEN), 122; Swan (NC), 89.

8. These hats were made of cedar bark and beargrass; see illustrations of the conical style in figs. 10, 11, 21, 22. Clark's brief notes here about the ethnobotany of the Lower Chinooks are treated more expansively by Lewis during the winter at Fort Clatsop. Cutright (LCPN), 264–69.

9. Flags are again the common cat-tail, and woven mats of the plant were widely used by coastal Indians. Gunther (EWW), 21.

10. Here Clark does not clearly distinguish between baskets for cooking, woven watertight of cedar bark and beargrass, and other baskets, less closely woven of the same materials or of rushes, grasses, and sedges. Split willow stems or willow bark, as well as split spruce roots, were often used with rushes for making baskets. Gunther (EWW), 17, 26–27; Ruby & Brown (CITC), 15; Cutright (LCPN), 267–68. See also Swan (ICF), as a source for the material culture of Northwest Coast Indians.

11. Edible thistle, *Cirsium edule* Nutt., a species new to science. See below, January 21, 1806, for Lewis's description. Hitchcock et al., 5 : 137–38; Ray (LCEN), 120; Cutright (LCPN), 264, 274, 406.

12. Evidently the wife of Delashelwilt. See below, March 15, 1806. Ruby & Brown (CITC), 106.

13. A 2½ point blanket would be 5 feet 4 inches by 4 feet 3 inches; see August 20, 1805.

14. Probably the Oregon bobcat, *Lynx rufus fasciatus*, a subspecies then unknown to

science. See below, February 18 and 21, 1806. Burroughs, 92–93; Cutright (LCPN), 273, 387, 442; Hall, 2:1053.

15. The mountain beaver, *Aplodontia rufa*, Lewis and Clark's "sewelel." A rodent, not a beaver, it was then unknown to science. See below, February 26, 1806. Cutright (LCPN), 263, 271, 387, 439; Hall, 1:334–36.

16. The term may be Lower Chinookan *[i/a]šanáta(n)qi*, "thistle" for the edible thistle above. Gibbs (AVC), 19.

17. It is apparent that strong weed (of first entry), strong grass, and straw all refer to beargrass which was used to weave both watertight hats as well as baskets. Swan (NC), 162–63; Gunther (EWW), 23. There is a vertical line through the botany passage, perhaps done by Biddle but not in his red ink. The hat mentioned here is not the typical, conical style of hat worn by the natives (see below, December 29, 1805, and January 29, 30, 1806). It is probably one like that pictured in Gunther (ILNC), 185. The popular hat of the United States was similar to a top hat, but with a lower crown and a wider brim. See Lewis's entry, January 19, 1806.

Chapter Twenty-Six

At Fort Clatsop

November 22, 1805–January 6, 1806

[Clark] *Novr. 22nd Friday 1805*

Some little rain all the last night with wind, before day the wind increased to a Storm from the S. S. E. and blew with violence throwing the water of the river with emence waves out of its banks almost over whelming us in water, O! how horriable is the day— This Storm Continued all day with equal violence accompanied with rain, Several Indians about us, nothing killed the waves & brakers flew over our Camp, one Canoe Split by the Tossing of those waves— we are all Confined to our Camp and wet. purchased some *Wapto* roots for which was given, brass armbans & rings of which the Squars were fond. we find the Indians easy ruled and kept in order by a Stricter indifference towards them

[Clark] *Friday November 22nd 1805*

a moderate rain all the last night with wind, a little before Day light the wind which was from the S S. E. blew with Such violence that we wer almost overwhelmned with water blown from the river, this Storm did not Sease at day but blew with nearly equal violence throughout the whole day accompaned with rain. O! how horriable is the day waves brakeing with great violence against the Shore throwing the Water into our Camp &c. all wet and Confind to our Shelters, Several Indian men and women Crouding about the mens Shelters to day, we purchased a fiew wappato roots for which we gave armbans, & rings to the old Squar, those roots are equal to the Irish potato, and is a tolerable Substitute for bread

The threat which I made to the men of this nation whome I first Saw,

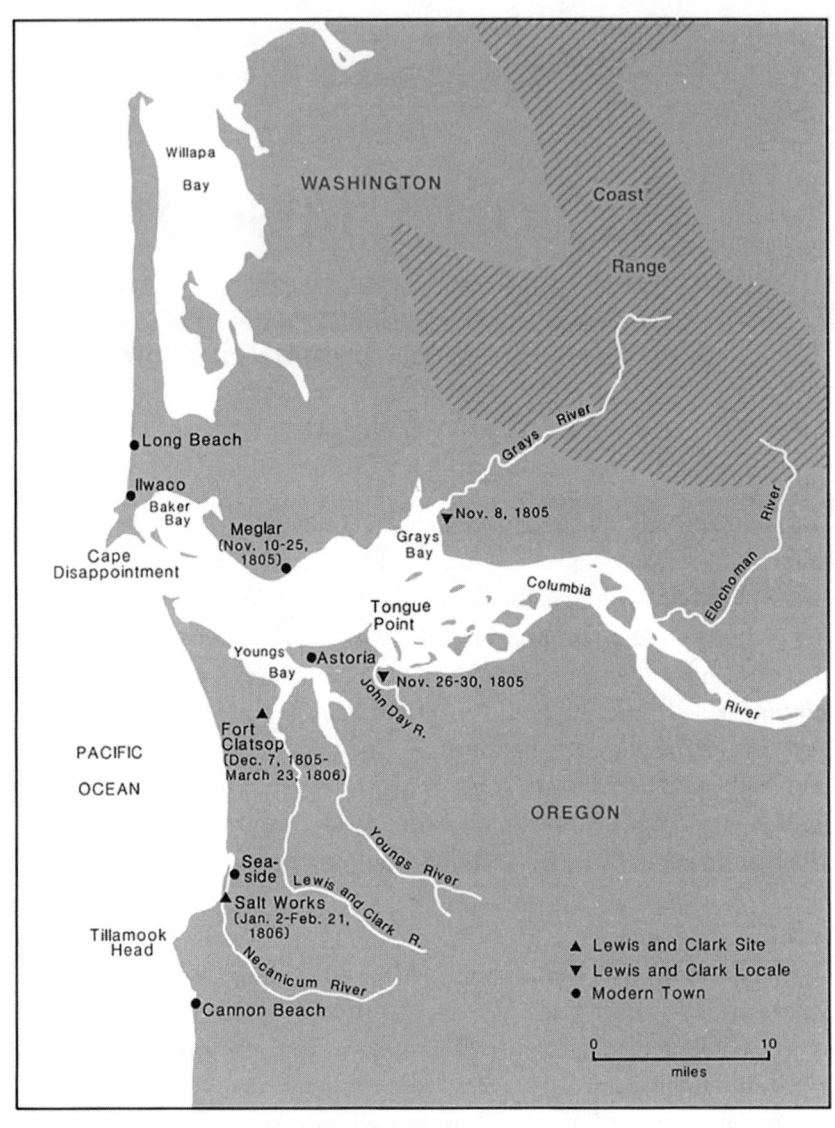

4. Fort Clatsop Environs,
December 7, 1805–March 23, 1806

and an indifference towards them, is: I am fulley Convinced the Cause of their Conducting themselves with great propriety towards ourselves & Party.

[Clark] November 23rd Saturday 1805[1]

The Cloudy and Calm, a moderate rain the greater part of the last night, Sent out men to hunt this morning and they Killed 3 Bucks, rained at intervals all day. I marked my name the Day of the month & year on a [2?] Beech trees & (By Land) Capt Lewis Branded his and the men all marked their nams on trees about the Camp.[2] one Indian Came up from their village on some lakes near Haleys bay. In the Evening 7 Indians of the *Clatt Sopp* nation,[3] opposit Came over, they brought with them 2 Sea orter Skins, for which the asked Such high prices we were uneabled to purchase, with[out] reduceing our Small Stock of merchindize on which we have to depend in part for a Subsistance on our return home, Kiled 4 brant & 3 Ducks to day

[Clark] Saturday November 22rd 1805.[4]

A calm Cloudy morning, a moderate rain the greater part of the last night, Capt Lewis Branded a tree with his name Date &c. I marked my name the Day & year on a Alder tree, the party all Cut the first letters of their names on different trees in the bottom. our hunters killed 3 Bucks, 4 Brant & 3 Ducks to day.

in the evening Seven indians of the *Clot Sop* Nation Came over in a Canoe, they brought with them 2 Sea otter Skins for which they asked blue beads &c. and Such high pricies that we were unable to purchase them without reducing our Small Stock of merchendize, on which we depended for Subcistance on our return up this river— mearly to try the Indian who had one of those Skins, I offered him my Watch, handkerchief a bunch of red beads and a dollar of the American Coin, all of which he refused and demanded "*ti-â, co-mo-shack*[*"*][5] which is *Chief beads* and the most common blue beads, but fiew of which we ⟨happen to⟩ have at this time

This nation is the remains of a large nation destroyed by the Small pox or Some other which those people were not acquainted with, they Speak the Same language of the Chinnooks and resemble them in every respect except that of Stealing, which we have not Cought them at as yet.

    1. The purpose of an asterisk above the dateline in the Elkskin-bound Journal is unknown.
    2. Lewis is using his branding iron again. See above, October 5, 1805, and accompanying note.
    3. The word "Clatt Sopp" appears to have been added later to a blank space.
    4. A mistake on the date which was not carried forward.
    5. The word is Chinookan *tiaqmušakš*, "chief beads."

[Clark]   *November 24th Sunday 1805*

   a fare morning. Sent out 6 hunters and Detained to make the following observations i, e,

Took time dis. & azomith of the Sun A M.

Time			*Dists.*			*azmth.*
h.	m.	s.				
8	33	20	22°	16'	30"	S 64° E.
8	37	48	23	19	45	S 63° E
8	41	35	24	13	0	S 62° E

Equal altitudes with Sextant

	H.	m	s		h	m	s
A. M.	8	53	5.5	P. M			
	"	55	33			(lost)	
	"	58	3				

Altitude produced [*blank*]

observed Time & Distance of Sun & Moons nearest Limbs Sun West   P M

Time			*distance*		
h.	m.	S.			
2	42	11	40°	32'	45"
"	43	38	40	33	15
"	44	53	"	33	30
"	46	9	"	34	15
"	47	29	"	34	30[1]
"	48	53	"	34	45
"	51	29	"	35	15
"	52	50	"	35	30

"	54	00	"	36	00
2	55	38	40	36	15

Several of the *Chenn nook* N. Came, one of them brought an Sea orter Skin[2] for which we gave Some blue Beeds— This day proved to be fair and we dried our wet articles bedding &c. The hunters killed only 1 brant no Deer or any thing else

Observed time and Distance of Moons [*blank*] Limb an *a´ pegasi* Star East P. M.

Time			distance		
h	m	s			
6	16	46	67°	56'	30"
"	19	29	"	54	15
"	25	39	"	50	45
"	28	20	"	50	15
"	31	53	"	48	30
⟨"	37	51⟩	⟨blocked⟩		

The old chief of Chinn-nook nation and Several men & women Came to our camp this evening & Smoked the pipe

Sergt J. Ordway	Cross & examine	S[3]
Serjt. N. Pryor	do do	S
Sgt. P. Gass	do do	S
Jo. Shields	proceed to Sandy R	
Go. Shannon	Examn. Cross	falls
T. P. Howard	do do	falls
P. Wiser	do do	S. R
J. Collins	do do	S. R
Jo Fields	do do	up
Al. Willard	do do	up
R Willard[4]	do do	up
J. Potts	do do	falls
R. Frasure	do do	up
Wm. Bratten	do do	up
R. Fields	do do	falls
J: B: Thompson	do do	up
J. Colter	do do	up
H. Hall	do do	S. R.
Labeech	do do	S R

Peter Crusatte	do do	S R
J. B. Depage	do do	up
Shabono	— —	—
S. Guterich	do do	falls
W. Werner	do do	up
Go: Gibson	do do	up
Jos. Whitehouse	do do	up
Geo Drewyer	Examn other side	falls
McNeal	do do	up
York	" "	lookout

falls	Sandy River	lookout up
6	10	12

Janey[5] in favour of a place where there is plenty of Potas.

Cp L [& F?] Proceed on to morrow & examine The other side if good hunting to winter there, as Salt is an objt. if not to proceed on to Sandy it is probable that a vestle will come in this winter,[6] & that by proceeding on at any distance would not inhance our journey in passing the Rockey mountains, &c.

W C. In favour of proceding on without delay to the opposit Shore & there examine, and find out both the disposition of the Indians, & probibilaty of precureing Subsistance, and also enquire if the Tradeing vestles will arrive before the time we Should depart in the Spring, and if the Traders, Comonly arive in a Seasonable time, and we Can Subsist without a depends. on our Stores of goods, to Continue as the Climent would be more favourable on the Sea Coast for our naked men than higher up the Countrey where the Climate must be more Severe— The advantage of the arival of a vestle from whome we Can precure goods will be more than an over ballance, for the bad liveing we Shall have in liveing on Pore deer & Elk we may get in this neighbourhood. If we Cannot subsist on the above terms to proceed on, and make Station Camps, to neighbourhood of the Frendly village near the long narrows & delay untill we Can proceed up the river. Salt water I view as an evil in as much as it is not helthy— I am also of opinion that one two or three weeks Exemination on the opposide if the propects are any wise favourable, would not be too long

Variation of the Compass is 16° East

[Clark]   *Sunday November 24th 1805.*

A fair morning Sent out 6 hunters, and we proceeded to make the following observations[7] a Chief and Several men of the *Chin nook* nation Came to Smoke with us this evening one of the men brought a Small Sea otter Skin for which we gave Some blue beads— this day proved fair which gave us an oppertunity of drying our wet articles, bedding &c. &c. nothing killed to day except one Brant. the variation of the Compass is 16° East.

being now determined to go into Winter quarters as Soon as possible, as a convenient Situation to precure the Wild animals of the forest which must be our dependance for Subsisting this Winter, we have every reason to believe that the nativs have not provisions Suffient for our Consumption, and if they had, their price's are So high that it would take ten times as much to purchase their *roots & Dried fish* as we have in our possesion, encluding our Small remains of merchindz and Clothes &c. This Certinly enduces every individual of the party to make diligient enquiries of the nativs the part of the Countrey in which the wild Animals are most plenty. They generaly agree that the most *Elk* is on the opposit Shore, and that the greatest numbers of *Deer* is up the river at Some distance above—

The Elk being an animal much larger than Deer, easier to kiled better meat (in the winter when pore) and Skins better for the Clothes of our party: added to—, a convenient Situation to the Sea coast where we Could make Salt, and a probibility of vessels Comeing into the mouth of Columbia ("which the Indians inform us would return to trade with them in 3 months["]) from whome we might precure a fresh Supply of Indian trinkets to purchase provisions on our return home: together with the Solicitations of every individual, except one of our party induced us Conclude to Cross the river and examine the opposit Side, and if a Suffcent quantity of Elk could probebly be precured to fix on a Situation as convenient to the Elk & Sea Coast as we Could find— added to the above advantagies in being near the Sea Coast one most Strikeing one occurs to me i' e, the Climate which must be from every appearance ⟨must be⟩ much milder than that above the 1st range of Mountains, The Indians are Slightly Clothed and give an account of but little Snow, and the weather which we have experiened Since we arrived in the neighbourhood of the

Sea Coast has been verry warm, and maney of the fiew days past disagreeably So. if this Should be the Case it will most Certainly be the best Situation of our naked party dressed as they are altogether in leather.

1. It is given as "3" in Codex I, p. 42.
2. For the sea otter, *Enhydra lutris*, see Lewis's description below, February 23, 1806.
3. Gass says that the captains consulted the men on where to spend the winter; this table evidently represents the vote taken. "Cross and examine S" could mean to cross the Columbia and explore the south side of the estuary for a campsite; however, "S" might stand for "Sandy River" (see below). "Falls" must stand for the Great Falls of the Columbia, at The Dalles, Wasco County, Oregon (*Atlas* maps 77, 78). "S. R." must stand for "Sandy River," the Quicksand River of *Atlas* map 79, present Sandy River in Multnomah County, Oregon. "Lookout" and "up" must mean exploring up the Columbia for a site. "Falls" adds up to 6. "S," "S. R.," and "Sandy R" together make 9. "Lookout" and "up" make 14. It is worth noting that York and Sacagawea voted.
4. A mistake for Richard Windsor.
5. A nickname for Sacagawea.
6. In his 1803 instructions to Lewis, Jefferson had suggested that the captains might wish to send some members of the party back with a copy of their journals, and that the whole party might return by sea if the route by land seemed too dangerous. At the time of leaving Fort Mandan Lewis wrote to the president that they would probably return by way of the Yellowstone. The possibility of sending duplicate journals by sea and obtaining supplies of food and trade goods would still have been attractive, but they met no trading vessels on the Pacific Coast. Although Jefferson informed various sea captains sailing for the Northwest of the possible presence of the Corps of Discovery in the region, there is no evidence that he ever planned to send a vessel for that purpose, or that he led Lewis and Clark to expect one. Possible diplomatic problems with Spain, the difficulty of obtaining money from Congress, and the inherent problem of a rendezvous with a group whose schedule was so uncertain, all stood in the way of such a project. Some writers have stated that Captain Samuel Hill's *Lydia* was present off the mouth of the Columbia in November and December 1805, and that the Indians failed to inform Lewis and Clark of the fact. It would appear, however, that Hill's visits to the Columbia occurred in April-May 1805 and in April or July 1806. Jefferson's Instructions to Lewis, June 20, 1803, Jackson (LLC), 1:61–66; Lewis to Jefferson, April 7, 1805, Jackson (LLC), 1:234; Chuinard (TJCD); Ruby & Brown (CITC), 88–90, 107n, 110; Large (EA); Lavender, 397–400.
7. These observations are the same as those in the Elkskin-bound Journal, except as noted, and are not repeated here.

[Clark] November 25th Munday 1805

a fine day Several Indians Come up from below, we loaded and Set out up the river, and proceeded on to the Shallow Bay,[1] landed to dine, The Swells too high to cross the river, agreeabley to our wish which is to examine if game Can be precured Sufficent for us to winter on that Side, after dinner which was on Drid pounded fish we proceeded on up on the North Side to near the place of our Encampment of the 7th Instant and encamped after night[2] The evening cloudy wind of to day Generally from the E S. E, Saw from near of last Campment Mount Ranier bearing[3] [blank]

[Clark]   Monday 25th November 1805

The Wind being high rendered it impossible for us to Cross the river from our Camp, we deturmind to proceed on up where it was narrow, we Set out early accompanied by 7 *Clât Sops* for a fiew miles, they left us and Crossed the river through emence high waves; we Dined in the Shallow Bay on Dried pounded fish, after which we proceeded on near the North Side of the Columbia, and encamp a little after night near our Encampment of the 7th instant near a rock at Some distance in the river. evening Cloudy the Winds of to day is generally E. S. E which was a verry favourable point for us as the highlands kept it from us Mt. St. Hilians Can be Seen from the mouth of this river.

    1. Grays Bay, in Wahkiakum County, Washington, as before.
    2. Near present Pillar Rock, in Wahkiakum County. The campsite is not marked on *Atlas* maps 82, 89, but the camp of November 7 is noted on both maps.
    3. Mt. Rainier, now in Mt. Rainier National Park in Pierce County, Washington, is the highest point in Washington. It was named for Admiral Peter Rainier of the British Navy by Vancouver in 1792. Anderson (SSGV), 85.

[Clark]   November 26th Tuesday 1805

Cloudy and Some rain this morning at daylight wind blew from the E N. E, we Set out and proceeded on up on the North Side of this great river to a rock in the river from thence we Crossed to the lower point of an [blank] Island passed between 2 Islands to the main Shore, and proceeded down the South Side,[1] passed 2 Inlets & halted below the 2d at a Indian village of 9 large houses— those Indians live on an emenence behind a Island or a Channel of the river not more than 300 yds wide, they live on fish & Elk and Wapto roots, of which we bought a few at a high price they Call them Selves *Cat-tar-bets*[2] description

We proceeded on about 8 miles and Encamped in a deep bend to the South,³ we had not been Encamped long ere 3 Indians Came in a Canoe to trade the⁴ Wapto roots— we had rain all the day all wet and disagreeable a bad place to Camp all around this great bend is high land thickly timbered brushey & almost impossible to penetrate we Saw on an Island below the village a place of deposit for the dead in Canoes—

Great numbers of Swan Geese Brant Ducks & Gulls in this great bend which is Crouded with low Islands covered with weeds grass &c. and overflowed every flood tide The people of the last village is—[*blank*]

they ask emence prices for what they have to Sel Blue Beeds is their great trade they are fond of Clothes or blankits of Blue red or brown

We are now decending to see if a favourable place should offer on the So Side to winter &c.

from a high Point opsd. a high Isd down the South Side is S. 30° W 6 mls to a point of low land opsd. upr. pt of Isd. passed lowr. pt. 1st Isd. marshey. at the upr. pt. of 2 low Isd. opsd. each other at 4 miles

S. 12° E	2	miles to an Indn. *Cat-tar-bet* vilg of 9 houses passed an inlet 300 yds wide on Std at ½ a mile
S. 60° W	1	mile to high land on the South
S. 70° W	1	do. to a South point Low land a low Isd. opsd. pass the former
S. 50° W	6	miles to a high point S.
South	2	miles to a bend Camped
N. 70° W.	6	miles to a point No. 1 a deep bend to the left
S. 50° W	8	miles to Point No. 2 passing a deep bend to the South⁵
S. 50° W	1½	miles
S. 40 W	1½	miles to Pt in Bay

From the *Peninsolu* to the upper point is	N. 65° E—
To Point [*blank*] miles across the river is	N. 25° W 4 miles—
from Pt. No. 2 to Cape Disapointmt	N. 70° W
To point Adams is	west
To 1st Creek Small above Adams	S. 60 W.
To 2nd Creek do do	S. 40 W
to 3d do do do	S. 20 W.

November 22, 1805 – January 6, 1806

To Fort River⁶ is imedeately cross	S 10° E
To the opening of the mouth of River	S. 50 E

The bay turns to the N of East & recves 2 other small Brooks

[Clark] *Tuesday 26th November 1805*

Cloudy and Some rain this morning from 6 oClock. wind from the E. N. E, we Set out out early and crossed a Short distance above the rock out in the river, & between Some low marshey Islands to the South Side of the Columbia at a low bottom about 3 miles below Point *Samuel*⁷ and proceeded near the South Side leaveing the Seal Islands to our right and a marshey bottom to the left 5 Miles to the *Calt-har-ma*r [*NB: Cathlahma*] Village of 9 large wood houses on a handsom elivated Situation near the foot of a Spur of the high land behind a large low Island Seperated from the Southerly Shore by a Chanel of about 200 yards Wide, This nation appear to differ verry little either in language, Customs dress or appearance from the *Chin nooks* & *War-ci â cum* live principally on fish and *pappato*   they have also other roots, and Some Elk meat.

We purchased Some green fish, & *wap pa to* for which we gave Imoderate pricie's.   after dining on the fresh fish which we purchased, we proceeded on through a Deep bend to the South and encamped under a high hill, where we found much difficuelty in precureing wood to burn, as it was raining hard, as it had been the greater part of the day.   Soon after we encamped 3 Indians of the last town Came in a Canoe with *wappato* roots to Sell to us   Some of which we purchased with fish hooks—from the Village quite around this bend to the West the land is high and thickly timbered with pine balsom &c.   a Short distance below the *Calt har mer* Village on the Island which is Opposit I observed Several Canoes Scaffold in which Contained their dead, as I did not examine this mode of deposing the dead, must refer it to a discription hereafter.

1. These islands (called "Seal Islands" in second entry and on *Atlas* map 82) in Clatsop County, Oregon, are now within the Lewis and Clark National Wildlife Refuge. *Atlas* maps 82, 89.

2. For the Cathlamets see above, November 11, 1805. The village of "9 large houses" is shown on *Atlas* maps 82, 92; it was named *Hlilusqahih* and was located at the present town of Knappa, Clatsop County. Archaeological excavations at this site uncovered house re-

mains and artifacts relating to the Cathlamet occupation in the early historic period. Curtis, 8:182; Minor (ASCR).

3. In Clatsop County, near present Svenson. *Atlas* maps 82, 92.

4. A page of bearings and distances interrupts the narrative here in the Elkskin-bound Journal; it may have been written first and the day's narrative written around it later. It has now been placed at the end of the text.

5. Apparently the asterisk at the end of this line refers to two courses in the left margin, at right angles to the rest of page. They have been placed after this course.

6. Probably the river on which they built Fort Clatsop, "Netul River" in later entries, today's Lewis and Clark River, Clatsop County. *Atlas* map 84.

7. Present Cathlamet Point, Clatsop County. Coues (HLC), 2:721 n. 3, suggests that the captains may have named it for Samuel Lewis, the copyist of Clark's 1814 map, *Atlas* map 126, who he conjectures might have been a relative of Meriwether Lewis. In Clark's Estimated Distances (Chapter 30) it seems to be "Point Samuel g—." *Atlas* maps 81, 82, 92. The word here appears as if it could have been added to a blank space.

[Clark] November 27th Wednesday 1805

Some rain all the last night & this morning   at day light 3 Canoes and 11 men Came down with roots meat, Skins &c. to Sill, they asked Such high prices we were unable to purchase any thing, and as we were about Setting out, discovered that one of those Indians had Stole an ax, we Serched and found it under the roabe of one man whome we Shamed verry much

we proceeded on, around Point William[1]   th Swells became high and rained so hard we Concluded to halt and dry our Selves,[2] Soon after our landing the wind rose from the East and blew hard accompanied with rain, this rain obliged us to unload & draw up our Canoes, one of which was Split to feet before we got her out of the river, this place the Peninsoley is about 50 yards and 3 miles around this point of Land.   water Salt below not Salt above.

[Clark] Wednesday 27th November 1805

Rained all the last night and this morning it Continues moderately— at day light 3 Canoes and 11 Indians Came from the Village with roots mats, Skins &c. to Sell, they asked Such high prices that we were unable to purchase any thing of them, as we were about to Set out missed one of our axes which was found under an Indians roab   I smamed [*NB: Shamed*] this fellow verry much and told them they should not proceed

November 22, 1805–January 6, 1806

with us— we proceded on between maney Small Islands passing a Small river[3] of [blank] yds wide which the Indians Call—[NB: Kekemar⟨qu⟩ke] and around a verry remarkable point which projects about 1½ Miles directly towards the Shallow bay the isthmus which joins it to the main land is not exceding 50 yards and about 4 Miles around. we call this Point William

below this point the waves became So high we were Compelled to land unload and traw up the Canoes, here we formed a Camp on the neck of Land which joins Point William to the main at an old indian hut. The rain Continued hard all day we are all Wet and disagreeable. one Canoe Split before we Got her out of the Water 2 feet— The water at our Camp Salt that above the isthmus fresh and fine—

1. Presumably after William Clark; present Tongue Point, Clatsop County, Oregon. *Atlas* maps 82, 92.

2. On the west side of the neck of Tongue Point, in Clatsop County, just east of present Astoria. The majority of the party under Clark remained here until December 7, while Lewis and five men scouted for a suitable wintering camp. *Atlas* maps 82, 92.

3. Present John Day River, in Clatsop County; "Ke ke mar que Creek" on *Atlas* maps 81, 82. The term is from the Chinook language; its phonetic form is uncertain but may be *kigimaxix*. The river should not be confused with the larger John Day River (Lewis and Clark's River La Page; see above, October 21, 1805), reaching the Columbia between Sherman and Gilliam counties, Oregon. Both were named for an Astorian who went insane during the overland journey of 1811–12. Coues (HLC), 2:655 n. 2.

[Clark] *November 28th Thursday 1805*

Wind Shifted about to the S. W. and blew hard accompanied with hard rain all last night, we are all wet bedding and Stores, haveing nothing to keep our Selves or Stores dry, our Lodge nearly worn out, and the pieces of Sales & tents So full of holes & rotten that they will not keep any thing dry, we Sent out the most of the men to drive the point for deer, they Scattered through the point; Some Stood on the *pensolu*, we Could find no deer, Several hunters attempted to penetrate the thick woods to the main South Side without Suckcess, the Swan & gees wild and Cannot be approached, and wind to high to go either back or forward, and we have nothing to eate but a little Pounded fish which we purchasd. at the Great falls, This is our present Situation,! truly disagreeable. aded to this the robes of our Selves and men are all rotten from being Continually wet, and we Cannot precure others, or blankets in their places. about 12 oClock the wind Shifted about to the N. W and blew with great violence for the remainder of the day   at maney times it blew for 15 or 20 minits with Such violence that I expected every moment to See trees taken up by the roots, Some were blown down. Those Squals were Suckceeded by rain,   ! O how Tremendious is the day. This dredfull wind and rain Continued with intervales of fair weather, the greater part of the evening and night.

[Clark]   *Thursday 28th November 1805*

Wind Shifted about to the S. W. and blew hard accompanied with hard rain.   rained all the last night   we are all wet our bedding and Stores are also wet, we haveing nothing which is Sufficient to keep ourselves bedding or Stores dry   Several men in the point hunting deer without Suckcess, the Swan and brant which are abundant Cannot be approached Sufficently near to be killed, and the wind and waves too high to proceed on to the place we expect to find Elk, & we have nothing to eate except pounded fish which we brought from the Great falls, this is our present Situation; truly disagreeable.   about 12 oClock the wind Shifted around to the N W. and blew with Such violence that I expected every moment to See trees taken up by the roots, maney were blown down. This wind and rain Continued with Short intervales all the latter part of the night. O! how disagreeable is our Situation dureing this dreadfull weather.

[Lewis]   *November 29th 1805.*[1]

the wind being so high the party were unable to proceed with the perogues.   I determined therefore to proceed down the river on it's E.[2] side in surch of an eligible place for our winters residence and accordingly set out early this morning in the small canoe accompanyed by 5 men.   drewyer R. Fields, Shannon, Colter & labiesh.   proceeded along the coast.

S. 40 W.	5	m. to a point of land passing twow points one at 3 m. bearing S 10 W. and the 2ed at 1 ½ further a little retreating from the 1st land high and woods thick.
S. 35 W.	2	ml. along the point, land still high and thickly timbered here a deep bay commences runing[3]

S. 40 E.   2   m. along the bay.   the land more open, pass a small prarie at
                1 M.

send out the hunters they killed 4 deer 2 brant a goos and seven ducks, it rained upon us by showers all day. left three of these deer and took with us one   encamped[4] at an old Indian hunting lodge which afforded us a tolerable shelter from the rain, which continued by intervales throughout the night.—

[Clark]   *November 29th Friday 1805*

Blew hard and rained the greater part of the last night and this morning, Capt Lewis and 5 men Set out in our Small Indian canoe (which is made in the Indian fashion Calculated ride the waves) down the South Side of the river to the place the Indians informed us by Signs that numbers of Elk were to be found near the river—   The Swells and waves being too high for us to proceed down in our large Canoes, in Safty—

I Sent out two hunters to hunt deer, & one to hunt fowl, all the others employed in drying their leather and prepareing it for use, as but fiew of them have many other Clothes to boste of at this time, we are Smoked verry much in this Camp   The Shore on the Side next the Sea is Covered with butifull pebble of various Colours—[5]   our diat at this time and for Severall days past is the dried pounded fish we purchased at the falls boiled in a little Salt water—.

[Clark]   *Friday 29th of November 1805*

The wind and rain Continued all the last night, this morning much more moderate.   the waves Still high and rain Continues. Capt Lewis and 5 hunters Set out in our Indian Canoe (which is Calculated to ride wave) dow to the place we expected to find Elk from the Inds. information, the[y] pointed to a Small Bay which is yet below us—   I Sent out 2 men to hunt Deer which I expected might be on the open hill Sides below, another to hunt fowl in the deep bend above the point, all the others engaged drying their leather before the fire, and prepareing it for use— they haveing but fiew other Species of Clothing to ware at this time

The winds are from Such points that we cannot form our Camp So as to provent the Smoke which is emencely disagreeable, and painfull to the eyes— The Shore below the point at our Camp is formed of butifull pebble of various colours. I observe but fiew birds of the Small kind, great numbers of wild fowls of Various kinds, the large Buzzard with white wings, grey and bald eagle's,[6] large red tailed Hawks,[7] ravens & Crows in abundance,[8] the blue Magpie,[9] a Small brown bird[10] which frequents logs & about the roots of trees— Snakes, Lizards, Small bugs, worms, Spiders, flyes & insects of different kinds are to be ⟨found⟩ Seen in abundance at this time.[11]

  1. Here begins Lewis's fragmentary Codex Ia, running through December 1, 1805. It consists of five loose sheets, perhaps drawn from one of the marbled-covered notebooks. See Introduction and Appendix C, vol. 2.

  2. Probably meaning "L." for larboard, the southern bank of the Columbia facing downstream.

  3. On this point, in Clatsop County, Oregon, members of John Jacob Astor's Pacific Fur Company founded the trading post of Astoria in 1811, having arrived by sea in the ship *Tonquin*. They sold the post to the British in 1812, and it became the North West Company post of Fort George. The present city on the point is named Astoria. The bay is Youngs Bay, unnamed on *Atlas* map 82, but called Meriwether's Bay by the party (see entry of December 7, 1805). Irving (Astor); Ross; Cox; Franchère (JV); Franchère (AA).

  4. Not marked on *Atlas* maps 82 or 92 (nor are Lewis's route or other camps on this journey), but on the shores of Youngs Bay, in Clatsop County, probably within the present bounds of Astoria.

  5. The colored pebbles were probably derived from the Pliocene-age Troutdale Formation which contains rounded quartz and chert gravels derived from sources upstream in the Columbia Plateaus and deposited in this area by the Columbia River.

  6. The "grey and bald eagle's" are, respectively, golden eagle, *Aquila chrysaetos* [AOU, 349], and bald eagle, *Haliaeetus leucocephalus* [AOU, 352]. Burroughs, 204–8. See a discussion of the gray eagle at July 11, 1805.

  7. Red-tailed hawk, *Buteo jamaicensis* [AOU, 337], a widespread species already known to science. Ibid., 208; Coues (HLC), 2:724.

  8. Probably the common raven, *Corvus corax* [AOU, 486], and the American crow, *C. brachyrhynchos* [AOU, 488]. See also September 22, 1805. Burroughs, 248; Cutright (LCPN), 432.

  9. Steller's jay, *Cyanocitta stelleri* [AOU, 478], first noted by Lewis on September 20, 1805. The captain gives a full description in an undated entry, ca. December 18, 1805. Burroughs, 248–49.

  10. Perhaps the winter wren, *Troglodytes troglodytes* [AOU, 722], and if so, then new to science; see below, March 4, 1806. Burroughs, 252; Cutright (LCPN), 274, 438.

  11. These zoological observations have a red vertical line running through, drawn perhaps by Biddle.

[Lewis] November 30th 1805.

cloudy morning   set out before sun rise and continued our rout up the bey—

S. 60 E.	1½	to a point. land not very high and open woods a little back from the bay
S. 80 E.	3	m. to the center of a bend passing a point at 1 m. land the ⟨same as in last course⟩ from the commenct. of this course
S. 35 W.	2½	m across the bay to a point of marshey ground which for three miles in width borders this coast—
S. 60 W	2	m. to a point of marshey ground—
S. 50 W	¾	m. to a marshey point at arm of the bay. from this point a point of highland bore S. 25 E. 3 miles distant—
N. 80 W.	2½	to a marshey point passing the arm of the bey ¼ of a mile wide—[1] the country to the S. E. appears to be low for a great distance and is marshey and untimbered for three miles back, from this point, the eastern point or commencement of the bay bore N. 15 E. 3 miles.—
N. 60 W.	3[2]	miles passing an inlet[3] of 100 yds. wide at 4 m. to a point of marshey ground, here an inlet[4] of from 40 to 60 yds. in width comes in just opposite to the upper point of a shore which we have heretofore thought and island but which I am now convinced is the main land. we asscended this stream about 2 m. it's course being S. 15 E. we halted near a small cops of timbered land to which we walked and dined ⟨after which⟩

Sent out three men to examin the country to the S. & W.   they returned after about 2 hours and informed me that the wood was so thick and obstructed by marrasses & lakes that they were unable to proceed to the ocean which could not be at any considerable distance fom the apparent sound of the waves breaking on the Coast.   we now returned and asscended the inlet which we had last passd[5]   no fresh appearance of Elk or deer in our rout so far.   asscend the inlet as we intended about 1 m. found it became much smaller and that it did not keep it's direction to the high land which boar S. 10 W. but inclined West.   therefore returned to the large arm of the bay which we passed this morning.[6]   here we expect to meet with the Clât-sop Indians, who have tantilized us with there being much game in their neighbourhood. this information in fact was the cause of my present resurch, for where there is most game is for us the most eliguble winter station.— continued our rout up the large arm of the bay about 6 miles and encamped on the Stard. side on the highland. the water was quite sweet. therefore concluded that it must be supplyed from a large crick. at our camp it is 120 yds. wide, tho' it gets narrower above. ⟨about 2 miles⟩ it rained but little on us today tho' it was cloudy generally.— Wind from N. E.— saw a great abundance of fowls, brant, large geese, white brant sandhill Cranes, common blue crains,[7] cormarants, haulks, ravens, crows, gulls and a great variety of ducks, the canvas back, duckinmallard,[8] black and white diver,[9] brown duck— &c &c—

[Clark] *November 30th Saturday 1805*[10]

Some rain and hail with intervales of fair weather for 1 and 2 hours dureing the night and untill 9 oClock this morning at which time it Cleared up fair and the Sun Shown, I Send 5 men in a Canoe in the Deep bend above the Peninsulear to hunt fowles, & 2 men in the thick woods to hunt Elk   had all our wet articles dried & the men all employed dressing their Skins, I observe but few birds in this Countrey of the Small kinds— great numbers of wild fowl, The large Buzzard with white under their wings Grey & Bald eagle large red tailed hawk, ravins, Crows, & a small brown bird which is found about logs &c.   but fiew small hawks or other smaller birds to be seen at this time   Snakes, Lizzards, Snales bugs worms Spiders, flies & insects of different kinds are to be Seen in plenty at this time.   The Squar, gave me a piece of Bread to day made of Some flower She had Cearfully kept for her child, and had unfortunately got wet— The hunters killed only 3 hawks, saw 3 Elk but Could not git a Shot at them, The fowlers, killed 3 black ducks,[11] with white Sharp bills, a brown Spot in their foward, Some white under the tail, which Short, and a fiew of the tips of the wing feathers white, Their toes are long Seperated and flaped, no Craw, keep in emence large flocks in the Shallow waters & feed on Grass &c.—   Several men Complaining of being unwell to day—   a Broock comes in to the bend above the 1st point above, and a river falls in the next nitch above this river is Small,—   I observe rose bushes Pine, a kind of ash[12] a Species of Beech[13] and a Species of Maple, in addition to the pine Lorrel[14] and under groth Common to the woods in this Lower Countrey   the hills are not high & Slope to the river

[Clark] *Saturday 30th of November 1805*

Some rain and hail with intervales of fair weather for the Space of one or two hours at a time dureing the night untill 9 oClock this morning, at which time it Cleared away and the Sun Shewn for [*blank*] hours, Several men out hunting   I Send 5 men in the bend above to hunt fowl &c. in a Canoe, employ all the others in drying our wet articles by the fire— Several men Complain of a looseness and gripeing[15] which I contribute to the diet, pounded fish mixed with Salt water, I derect that in future that the party mix the pounded fish with fresh water—   The Squar gave me a piece of bread made of flour which She had reserved for her child and carefully Kept untill this time, which has unfortunately got wet, and a little Sour—   this bread I eate with great Satisfaction, it being the only mouthfull I had tasted for Several months past.   my hunters killed *three* Hawks, which we found fat and delicious, they Saw 3 Elk but Could not get a Shot at them. The fowlers killed 3 black Ducks with Sharp White beeks keep in large flocks & feed on Grass, they have no Craw and their ⟨feet⟩ toes are Seperate, Common in the U. States

The Chinnooks *Cath lâh mâh* & others in this neighbourhood bury their dead in their Canoes.[16]   for this purpose 4 pieces of Split timber are Set erect on end, and sunk a fiew feet in the ground, each brace having their flat Sides opposit to each other and Sufficiently far assunder to admit the width of the Canoe in which the dead are to be deposited; through each of those perpindicular posts, at the hight of 6 feet a mortice is Cut, through which two bars of wood are incerted; on those Cross bars a Small Canoe is placed, in which the body is laid after beaing Carefully roled in a robe of Some dressed Skins; a paddle is also deposited with them; a larger Canoe is now reversed, overlaying and imbracing the Small one, and resting with its gunnals on the Cross bars; one or more large mats of flags or rushes are then rold. around the Canoe and the whole Securely lashed with a long Cord usially made of the bark of the arbar vita or white Cedar.   on the Cross bars which Support the Canoes is frequently hung or laid various articles of Clothing Culinary utensils &c.   we cannot understand them Sufficiently to make any enquiries relitive to their religious opinions, from their depositing Various articles with their dead, beleve in a State of future ixistance.

I walked on the point and observed rose bushes different Species of pine, [*NB: Copy for Dr Barton*]¹⁷ a Spcies of ash, alder, a Species of wild Crab Loral and Several Species of under groth Common to this lower part of the Columbia river— The hills on this Coast rise high and are thickly covered with lofty pine maney of which are 10 & 12 feet through and more than 200 feet high. hills have a Steep assent.

1. Present Youngs River, Clatsop County, Oregon, nameless on *Atlas* maps 82, 92; Lewis and Clark's "Kilhowanahkle." The term is Chinookan *giɬawanaxt*.

2. Lewis has crossed out the following at this point: "5 me to a marshey point at 1½ m."

3. Lewis and Clark River, the captains' "Netul," in Clatsop County, nameless on *Atlas* maps 82, 92. It is Chinookan *níɬul*.

4. Evidently the present Skipanon River, Clatsop County; "Skip â nor win C" on *Atlas* maps 82, 84. The name is again Chinookan *sqipanawnx*. The point mistaken as an island is Point Adams.

5. Apparently Lewis and Clark River.

6. Youngs River.

7. Probably the great blue heron, *Ardea herodias* [AOU, 194], also called a blue crane in weather remarks for February 13, 1804. See also March 6, 1806. Burroughs, 183–84.

8. Mallard, *Anas platyrhynchos* [AOU, 132].

9. Perhaps the bufflehead, *Bucephala albeola* [AOU, 153], already known to science. See below, March 9, 1806. Ibid., 187–88. Holmgren considers it the western grebe, *Aechmophorus occidentalis* [AOU, 1], on the basis of the word "diver" being an old term for loons and grebes. Personal communication. See mention of other divers on March 10, 1806.

10. The purpose of the asterisk at the end of this line is not known.

11. The American coot, *Fulica americana* [AOU, 221], and a known species; it is not a duck. See below, March 10, 1805. Burroughs, 224–25.

12. Possibly Oregon ash, then unknown to science. But see February 10, 1806, about the confusion of ash and maple when seeing these deciduous trees without leaves. Little (CIH), 127–W; Cutright (LCPN), 409.

13. Clark is again confusing the eastern beech with the red alder; he calls it alder in the second entry.

14. Again perhaps the California rhododendron, as on November 6, 1805.

15. Here indicating a pinching and spasmodic pain in the bowels, along with the "looseness" of diarrhea.

16. In addition to the more common use of burial canoes as described here by Clark, the Chinookan peoples around the mouth of the Columbia River also sometimes placed

the dead in boxes. A combination of these methods was employed by the Tillamook Indians of the northern Oregon coast (see Clark's entry for January 8, 1806). The use of burial canoes was a common mortuary practice among native peoples of the Northwest Coast. Ray (LCEN), 74–77; Hajda, 139.

17. The red vertical line drawn through this paragraph may be Biddle's further reminder not to use this passage in his *History*.

[Lewis and Clark] [*Weather, November 1805*][1]

Day of the Month	Wind	State of the Weather
1st	N. E	f.
2nd	S W.	f.
3rd	N. E.	f a fog
4th	W.	c. a. r
5th	S W.	r. c. r
6th	S W.	r. a. r
7th	S W.	r. a. fog[2]
8th	S W.	f. a. r.
9th	S	r
10th	N W.	r. a. r
11th	S W.	r
12th	S. W.	h. r. T & L.
13th	S W.	r
14th		r
15th	S E	f. a. r
16th	W. S. W.	f
17th	E	c. a. f
18th	S. E	f. a. c
19th	S E	c. a. r
20th	S E	f. a. r.
21st	S E	c. a. r
22nd	S S E	r
23rd	S W.	c. a. r.
24th	W	f a r
25th	E S E	C a r
26th	E N E	r
27th	S W	r
28th	S W. & N W.	r
29th	S W.	r
30th	S W.	f a r. & H

[*Remarks*]³

3rd   a thick fog which continud untill meridian   cleared off and was fair the remainder of the day.⁴

5th   Commenced raining at 2 P. M. and continued to rain with intervales throughout the day.   Saw 14 Garter Snakes⁵

6th   rained the greater part of the day moderately.

7th   Thick fog this morning which Continued untill 11 A. M. Cleared off and was fair until meridian,⁶   Several havy Showers dureing the evening

8th   rained moderately

9th   rained all day with wind

10th   do   do

11th   do   do

12th   violent wind from the S W. acompanied with Hail thunder and Lightning, the Claps of Thunder excessively loud and Continued from 3 to 6 A. M. Cleared off a Short time & raind untill 12 oClock   Cleared off an hour and rained again.⁷

14th   a blustering rainey day

15th   The after part of this day is fair and calm for the first time since the 5th instant.⁸

18th   Cloudy   Reubin Field Killed a Vulture⁹

20th   rained moderately from 6 A. M.¹⁰

21st   rained all last night untill 1 P. M and Cleared away and was Cloudy without rain

22nd   rained all day   wind violent from the S E¹¹

23rd   rained all last night to day Cloudy

24th   rained moderately for a Short time this morning

25th   Some Showers of rain last night

26th   rained all day with Some hard Showers.   the wind not so violent as it has been for Sevral days past.¹²

November 22, 1805 – January 6, 1806

27th   violent wind and hard rain all day. Campd. at Pt. William [13]

28th   a tremendious Storm from the N W. in the after part of the day. rained all last night and to daye. [14]

29th   rained all last night hard, and to day moderately I decend with 5 men in a canoe to examine the Country.

30th   rained and hailed with short intervales throughout the last night, Some thunder and lightninge. 3 large Hawks killed, which we thought delicious food

   1. Lewis's weather table and remarks appear in Voorhis No. 4 and Clark's in Codex I. This table follows Lewis. Significant variations are noted.
   2. Clark has "r a r. fog."
   3. Lewis's remarks in Voorhis No. 4 are in the margin of his weather table; Clark's in Codex I are separate. Lewis's remarks are followed here, with significant differences in Clark's remarks noted.
   4. Clark has also, "passed the enterance of quick Sand river."
   5. Clark has "Striped" instead of "Garter." In the daily entry he gives the number of seventeen. It may be the Pacific red-sided garter snake, *Thamnophis sirtalis concinnus*.
   6. Clark has "about 2 hours" instead of "meridian."
   7. Clark adds, "the rain has been pretty generally falling Since the 7th inst."
   8. Clark says the "12th instant," and adds, "and no rain. move our encampment."
   9. Clark adds, "I proceed to the Ocean."
   10. Clark adds, "on the 20th untill 1 P. M. the 21st after which it become Cloudy without rain."
   11. Clark says, "The wind violent from the S. S. E. throwing the water of the R over our Camp and rain continued all day."
   12. Clark adds, "Some rain on the morning of the 23d and night of the 24 instant."
   13. Clark writes, "rained moderately all day a hard wind from the S W which compelled us to lie by on the isthmus of point William on the South Side."
   14. Clark has, "The wind which was from the S W. Shifted in the after part of the day to the N W. and blew a Storm which was tremendious. rained all the last night and to day without intermission."

[Lewis]   *December 1st 1805* [1]

Cloudy morning wind from the S. E. sent out the men to hunt and examin the country, they soon returned all except Drewyer and informed me that the wood was so thick it was almost impenetrable and that there was but little appearance of game; they had seen the track of one deer only and a few small grey squirrels.[2] ⟨with yellow th⟩ these suirrels are

At Fort Clatsop

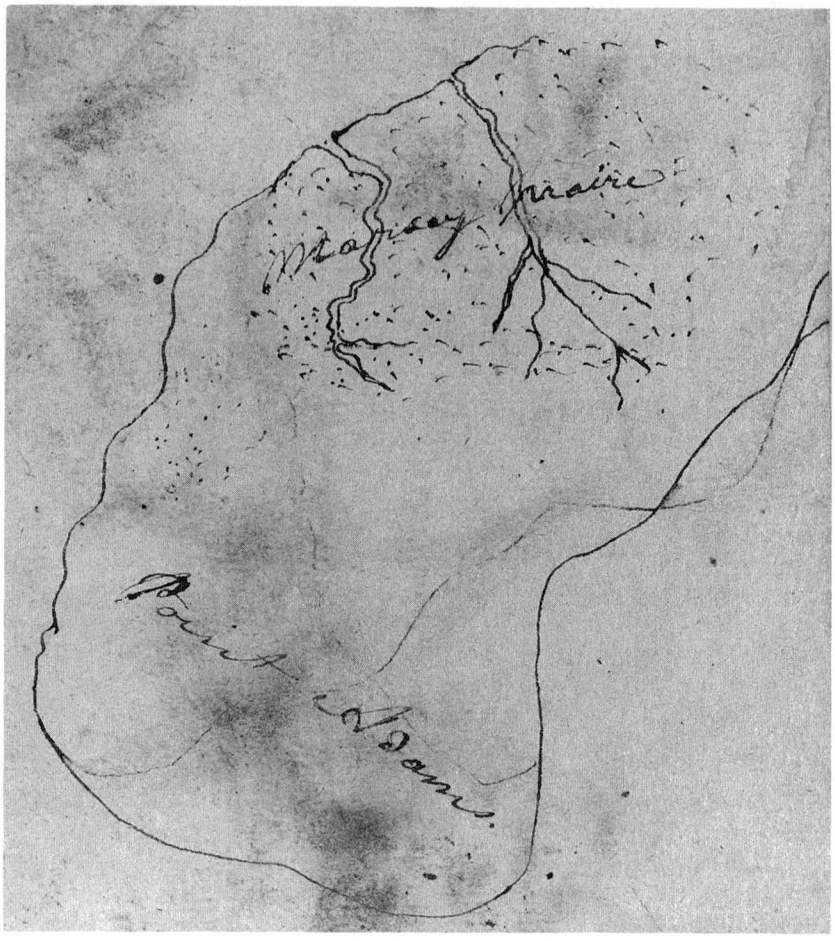

5. Point Adams, Oregon,
ca. December 1, 1805, Codex Ia, p. 7

about the size of the red squirrel of the lakes and eastern Atlantic States, their bellies are of a redish yellow, or tanners ooze[3] colour the tale flat and as long as the body eyes black and moderately large back and sides of a greyish brown[4]   the brier[5] with a brown bark and three laves which put forth at the extremety of the twigs like the leaves of the blackbury brier, tho' is a kind of shrub and rises sometimes to the hight of 10 fe[et]   the green brier yet in leaf;[6] the ash with a remarkable large leaf;[7] the large black alder.[8] the large elder with skey blue buries.[9] the broad leave shrub[10] which grows something like the quill wood but has no joints, the leaf broad and deeply indented   the bark p[e]als hangs on the stem and is of a yelowish brown ⟨yellow⟩ colour.   the seven bark is also found here as is the common low cramburry—there is a wild crab apple which the natives eat   this growth differs but little in appearance from that of the wild crab of the Atlantic States.   but the fruit[11] consists of little oval burries which grow in clusters at the extremities of the twigs like the black haws.   the fruit is of a brown colour, oval form and about double as large as the black haw; the rind is smoth and tough somewhat hard; the seed is like that of the wild crab and nearly as large; the pulp is soft of a pale yellow coulour; and when the fruit has been touched by the frost is not unpleasant, being an agreeable assed.   the tree which bears a red burry in clusters of a round form and size of a red haw.[12]   the leaf like that of the small magnolia, and brark smoth and of a brickdust red coulour   it appears to be of the evergreen kind.—   half after one oclock Drewyer not yet arrived.   heard him shoot 5 times just above us and am in hopes he has fallen in with a gang of elk.—

[Clark] *December 1st Sunday 1805*

    Cloudy windey morning wind from the East, Sent out 2 hunters in the woods, I intended to take 5 men in a Canoe and hunt the marshey Islands above, found the wind too high & returned to partake of the dried fish, The day Some what Cooler than usial, but Scercely perceveable.   began to rain at Sun Set and Continued ⟨untill⟩ half the ⟨oClock⟩ night.   my hunters returned without any thing ⟨except⟩ Saw 2 gang of *Elk*   a disagreeable Situation, men all employed in mending their leather Clothes, Socks &c. and Dressing Some Leather. The Sea which is imedeately in front roars like a repeeted roling thunder and have rored in that way ever Since our arrival in its borders which is now 24 Days Since we arived in Sight of the Great Western Ocian, I cant Say Pasific as Since I have Seen it, it has been the reverse. Elegant Canoes

At Fort Clatsop

[Clark] Sunday December 1st 1805

A cloudy windey morning wind from the East, dispatched two hunters, I deturmined to take a Canoe & a fiew men and hunt the marshey Islands above Point William, the Wind rose So high that I could not proceed, and returned to partake the dried fish, which is our Standing friend, began to rain hard at Sun Set and Continud.   my hunters returned without any thing haveing Seen 2 parcels of elk   men all employed to day in mending their leather Clothes, Shoes &c. and Dressing leather.

The emence Seas and waves which breake on the rocks & Coasts to the S W. & N W roars like an emence fall at a distance, and this roaring has continued ever Since our arrival in the neighbourhood of the Sea Coast which has been 24 days Since we arrived in Sight of the Great Western; (for I cannot Say Pacific) Ocian as I have not Seen one pacific day Since my arrival in its vicinity, and its waters are forming and petially [perpetually] breake with emenc waves on the Sands and rockey Coasts, tempestous and horiable.   I have no account of Capt. Lewis Since he left me.

   1. On the last page of Codex Ia is the following in Clark's hand: "Capt. Lewis rough notes when he left Capt. Clark near the mouth of Columbia for a few days to examine the S. W. side."
   2. Probably Richardson's red squirrel, *Tamiasciurus hudsonicus richardsoni*, a new species; see also February 24 and 25, 1806. Burroughs, 98–99; Cutright (LCPN), 274, 446.
   3. A decoction of vegetable material used in tanning.
   4. Here in Codex Ia, p. 7, is a sketch of Point Adams; see fig. 5.
   5. Salmonberry, *Rubus spectabilis* Pursh, with its characteristic brown, shredding bark, terminal leaves, and upright, shrubby habit. Its edible uses were important to local natives. Hitchcock et al., 3:182; Gunther (EWW), 35. See also February 11, 1806.
   6. Pacific blackberry, as noted earlier. See also February 11, 1806.
   7. Probably bigleaf maple.
   8. The red alder as before.
   9. Probably the red elderberry, *Sambucus racemosa* L. var. *arborescens* (T. & G.) Gray, common to the Fort Clatsop area and an important understory shrub of the Sitka spruce vegetation zone. Lewis may be confusing the plant with the blue elderberry, *S. cerulea* Raf. (formerly *S. glauca* Nutt.), because of the lack of fruit at this season, thus giving the two species a similar appearance. The blue elderberry is the one observed in the Rocky Mountains and noted on February 7, 1806. Hitchcock et al., 4:462–63; Franklin & Dyrness, 61; Little (MWH), 185-NW; cf. Cutright (LCPN), 260, 419.
   10. Ninebark, *Physocarpa capitatus* (Pursh) Kuntze. The "seven bark" is not a separate plant in this instance, but a further reference to ninebark; it relates to the common ninebark in the East, *P. opulifolius* Maxim. Hitchcock et al., 3:125–26; Bailey, 499.

11. Lewis gives here an excellent botanical description of the fruit of the previously noted Oregon crabapple.

12. This is the first diagnostic description of the Pacific madrone, *Arbutus menziesii* Pursh, which indeed has clusters of round berries, with evergreen leaves like a magnolia and a smooth, brick-red bark. It has some ethnobotanical and medicinal uses. Little (CIH), 100-W; Hitchcock et al., 4:4; Gunther (EWW), 44; Cutright (LCPN), 244, 402–3.

[Clark] *December 2nd Monday 1805*

Cloudy and Some little rain this morning I despatched 3 men[1] to hunt and 2 and my Servent in a Canoe to a Creek above to try & Catch Some fish— I am verry unwell the drid fish which is my only diet does not agree with me and Several of the men Complain of a lax, and weakness— I expect Capt. Lewis will return to day with the hunters and let us know if Elk or deer Can be found Sufficent for us to winter on, If he does not come I Shall move from this place, to one of better prospects for game &c. Joseph Fields came home with the marrow bones of an Elk which he had killed 6 miles distant, I sent out 6 men in a canoe for the meat, the evening being late they did not return this night, which proved fair moon Shineing night— This is the first Elk we have killed on this Side the rockey mounts a great deal of Elk Sign in the neighbourhood—

[Clark] *Monday 2nd December 1805*

Cloudy with Some rain this morning I Send out three men to hunt & 2 & my man york in a Canoe up the *Ke-ke-mar-que* Creek in Serch of fish and fowl— I feel verry unwell, and have entirely lost my appetite for the Dried pounded fish which is in fact the cause of my disorder at present— The men are generally Complaining of a lax and gripeing— In the evening Joseph Field came in with the Marrow bones of a elk which he killed at 6 miles distant, this welcome news to us. I dispatched Six men in a empty Canoe with Jo: mediately for the elk which he Said was about 3 miles from the water this is the first Elk which has been killd. on this Side of the rockey mountains— Jo Fields givs me an account of a great deel of Elk Sign & Says he Saw 2 Gangs of those Animals in his rout, but it rained So hard that he could not Shoot them— The party up the Creek returned without any thing and informs me they could not See any fish in the Creek to kill and the fowls were too wild to be killed, this must be owing to their being much hunted and pursued by the Indians in their Canoes.

1. Joseph Field, Pryor, and Gibson.

[Clark] December 3rd Tuesday 1805

a fair windey morning wind from the East, the men Sent after an Elk yesterday returnd. with an Elk which revived the Sperits of my men verry much, I am unwell and cannot Eate, the flesh   O! how disagreeable my Situation, a plenty of meat and incaple of eateing any—   an Indian Canoe Came down with 8 Indians in it from the upper village, I gave a fish hook for a fiew *Wap-e-to* roots, which I eate in a little Elk Supe, The Indians proceeded on down.   wind Contines to blow, and Serjt. Pryor & Gibson who went to hunt yesterday has not returnd. as yet   I marked my name & the day of the month and year on a large Pine tree on this Peninsella & by land "Capt William Clark ⟨November⟩ December 3rd 1805.   By Land. U States in 1804 & 1805"—[1]   The Squar Broke the two Shank bones of the Elk after the marrow was taken out, boiled them & extracted a Pint of Greese or tallow from them—   Serjt. Pryor & Gibson returned after night and informed me they had been lost the greater part of the time they were out, and had killed 6 Elk which they left lying haveing taken out their interals. Some rain this afternoon

[Clark] Tuesday 3d December 1805

a fair windey morning wind from the East   the men returned with the Elk which revived the Spirits of my party verry much   I am Still unwell and Can't eate even the flesh of the Elk.   an Indian Canoe of 8 Indians Came too, those Inds. are on their way down to the *Clât Sops* with *Wap pa to* to barter with that nation, I purchasd. a fiew of those roots for which I gave Small fish hooks, those roots I eate with a little Elks Soupe which I found gave me great relief   I found the roots both nurishing and as a check to my disorder.   The Indians proceeded on down through emence high waves maney times their Canoe was entirely out of Sight before they were ½ a mile distance. Serjt. Pryor & Gibson who went hunting yesterday has not returned untill after night, they informed me that they had killed 6 Elk at a great distance which they left lying, haveing taken out their interals that they had been lost and in their ramble saw a great deel of Elk Sign. after eateing the marrow out of two Shank bones of an Elk, the Squar choped the bones fine boiled them and extracted a pint of Grease, which is Superior to the tallow of the animal. Some rain this evening

I marked my name on a large pine tree imediately on the isthmus William Clark December 3rd 1805. By Land from the U. States in 1804 & 1805.—

   1. Clark probably modeled his inscription after that of Alexander Mackenzie, written on a rock at the end of his journey to the Pacific: "Alexander Mackenzie, from Canada, by land, the twenty second of July, one thousand seven hundred and ninety-three." DeVoto, 355.

[Clark]   *December 4th Wednesday 180[5]*

Some little rain all the last night and this morning after day the rain increased and Continued

I despatched Serjt. Pryer & 6 men to the Elk which he had killed yesterday, with directions to Save the meet and take loads to the River below in the next great bend— a Spring tide which rose 2 feet higher than Common flud tides, and high water at 11 oClock to day— wind from the S. E in the after noon hard wind from South— rained all day, moderately the Swells too high for me to proceed down, as I intended, I feel my self Something better and have an appetite to eate Something

[Clark]   *Wednesday 4th December 1805*

Some rain all the last night, this morning it increased with the wind from the S. E. I Set out Sergiant Pryor and 6 men to the Elk he had killed with directions to Carry the meat to a bay which he informed me was below and as he believed at no great distance from the Elk, and I Should proceed on to that bay as Soon as the wind would lay a little and the tide went out in the evening— the Smoke is exceedingly disagreeable and painfull to my eyes, my appetite has returned and I feel much better of my late complaint— a Spring tide to day rose 2 feet higher than Common flood tides and high water at 11 oClock— Hard wind from the South this evening, rained ⟨hard⟩ moderately all day and the waves too high for me to proceed in Safty to the bay as I intended, in Some part of which I expected would be convenient for us to make winter quarters, the reports of seven huntes agreeing that elke were in great abundance about the Bay below. no account of Capt. Lewis. I fear Some accident has taken place in his craft or party

[Clark] *December 5th Thursday 1805*[1]

Som ⟨Showers of⟩ hard Showers of rain last night, this morn Cloudy and drisley rain, in the bay above the Showers appear harder. High water to day at 12 oClock this tide is 2 Ins. higher than that of yesterday all our Stores again wet by the hard Showers of last night Capt Lewis's long delay below has been the cause of no little uneasiness on my part for him, a 1000 conjectures has crouded into my mind respecting his probable Situation & Safty—. rained hard. Capt Lewis returned haveing found a good Situation and Elk Suffient to winter on, his party killed 6 Elk & 5 Deer in their absence in Serch of a Situation and game

Rain continued all the after pt. of the day accompanied with hard wind from the S W. which provents our moveing from this Camp.

[Clark] *Thursday 5th of December 1805*

Some hard Showers of rain last night, this morning Cloudy and drisley at Some little distanc above the isthmus the rain is much harder. high water to day at 12 this tide is 2 inches higher than that of yesterday. all our Stores and bedding are again wet by the hard rain of last night. Capt. Lewis's long delay below, has been the Sorce of no little uneasness on my part of his probable Situation and Safty, the repeeted rains and hard winds which blows from the S, W. renders it impossible for me to move with loaded Canoes along an unknown Coast we are all wet & disagreeable; the party much better of indispositions—. Capt. Lewis returned with 3 men in the Canoe and informs me that he thinks that a Sufficient number of Elk may be prcured Convenient to a Situation on a Small river which falls into a Small bay a Short distance below, that his party had Killed 6 Elk & 5 Deer in his rout, two men of his party left behind to Secure the Elk

this was verry Satisfactory information to all the party. we accordingly deturmined to proceed on to the Situation which Capt. Lewis had

Viewed as Soon as the wind and weather Should permit and Comence building huts &c.

1. The purpose of the two asterisks near the end of this line is not known.

[Clark] December 6th Friday 1805

Wind blew hard all the last night, and a moderate rain, the waves verry high, This morning the wind which is Still from the S W increased and rained Continued all day, at Dusk wind Shifted to the North and it Cleared up and became fare, High water to day at 12 oClock & 13 Inches higher than yesterday. we were obliged to move our Camp out of the Water on high grown   all wet.

[Clark] Friday 6th of December 1805

The wind blew hard all the last night with a moderate rain, the waves verry high, the wind increased & from the S. W. and the rain Continued all day, about Dark the wind Shifted to the North cleared away and became fair weather.

The high tide of today is 13 inches higher than yesterday, and obliged us to move our Camp which was in a low Situation, on higher ground Smoke exceedingly disagreeable.

[Clark] December 7th Saturday 1805[1]

Some rain from 10 to 12 last night this morning fair, we Set out at 8 oClock down to the place Capt Lewis pitched on for winter quarters, when he was down   proceeded on against the tide   at the point No. 2 we met our men Sent down after meet

To point Adams is *West*

To pt. Disapointment N 75 W

They informed me that they found the Elk after being lost in the woods for one Day and part of another, the most of the meat was Spoiled, they distance was So great and uncertain and the way bad, they brought only the Skins, york was left behind by Some accident which detained us Some time eer he Came up   after passing round the pt. No. 2 in verry high swells, we Stopd & Dined in the commencement of a bay,[2] after which proceeded on around the bay to S E. & assended a Creek[3] 8 miles

6. Plan of Fort Clatsop Drawn over Area of Youngs Bay,
ca. December 7, 1805, Elkskin-bound Journal

7. Plan of Fort Clatsop, ca. December 7, 1805,
Elkskin-bound Journal

At Fort Clatsop

to a high pt. & Camped[4] haveing passed arm[5] makeing up to our left into the countrey

Mt. *St. Helens* is the mountain we mistook for Mt. *Reeaneer*[6]

receved 2 Small Brooks on the East, extencive marshes at this place of Encampment[7] We propose to build & pass the winter, The situation is in the Center of as we conceve a hunting Countrey— This day is fair except about 12 oClock at which time Some rain and a hard wind imedeately after we passed the point from the N. E which Continued for a about 2 hours and Cleared up.   no meat

Wolomped river[8]

Kil-la-mux nation[9] reside to the South of the Columbia and in noumerous 3 V.

Clatt Shop nation on an Island and South Side   Small nation.— *Quan ni o* Chief[10]

made a Chief by name *Tow-wâll*

From *Timm* or long narrows to the first village Std. Side	14	14
To friendly village	6	
To Pilgrim rocks	7	13
To Catteract River 2 Vilg:	11	
To a Village on Std. 3 hous Comsmt. of Mountain	9	
To [blank] River 60 yds Std. Sd.[11]	12	
To the great Shute	6	38
To the last rapid	6	44
To Quik Sand River on the West Side of Mountn.	26	26
To Tomahawk Village S.	16	
To a Vilg on Lard. Side at which place Mt. Rainer may be Seen	20	
To pt. opsd. a large Village behd. an Island	12	
To the narrows of a low mountain	11	59
To a village or 2 Houses Lard. Side	16	
To a village North of Some low marshey Islands Std. S.	33	
To 4 houses under a Std. Hill	15	
To Shallow Bay	16	
To [blank] Inlet	8	88
To Point open Slope blow the Station Camp 1805	3	

November 22, 1805–January 6, 1806

To Chinn nook R. Haleys bay	12	
To Point Disapt.	13	28
	147	

Frow[12]
malet
Beeds
Bells
Thimbles
B. Clothe
Salt
20 lb. Lead
Glass
1 Kittle
2 guns
looking glasses
Sugar
Coffee
Bread
Tobacco
Pork
axes

From the m. of the Creek No 1 40 poles below Pt to a point up the River on the opposit Side No 1 is	S. 88° E.[13]
To the nearest pincial of the mountain is	S. 44° E.
To point No. 2, is	S 30° E
To Lower point No. 3 is	S. 50° W.
To a Stake is	S. 71° W. 82 poles
to a 2d Stake is	S. 75° W. 112 poles
at a vilg. of 26 Houses, thence to a Stake is at [*one word illegible*]	S. 84 W. 68 poles
To the Stake at Camp	N 89° West 94 Poles—
From Camp	
To the pt No. 1 is	East
To the Mountain is	S. 49 E
To point No. 2	S. 47° E.
To point No. 3	S. 41° W.
To Cape Disapt.	S. 88 W
Down the river	N. 77° W 134 poles
To a Creek and	(N. 5 West in a bend)

To the mountain & Point No. 2 in Same cove	S. 49° E
To Point No. 3	S. 35° W.
To Cape Disapt. is	S. 87° W.
To a Point beow me about 1 mile	N 80 West
To point Adams is	S. 8 E. pore Camp

[Clark]   *Saturday 7th of December 1805*

    Some rain from 10 to 12 last night, this morning fair, have every thing put on board the Canoes and Set out to the place Capt Lewis had viewed and thought well Situated for winter quarters— we proceeded on against the tide to a point about [*blank*] miles here we met Sergt Pryor and his party returning to the Camp we had left without any meat, the waves verry verry high, as much as our Canoes Could bear rendered it impossible to land for the party, we proceeded on around the point into the bay and landed to take brackfast on 2 Deer which had been killed & hung up, one of which we found the other had been taken off by [s]ome wild animal probably Panthors or the Wild [cat?] of this Countrey here all the party of Serjt Pryors joined us except my man york, who had Stoped to rite his load and missed his way, Sergt Pryor informed us that he had found the Elk, which was much further from the bay than he expected, that they missed the way for one day and a half, & when he found the Elk they were mostly Spoiled, and they only brought the Skins of 4 of the Elk after brackfast I delayed about half an hour before York Came up, and then proceeded around this Bay which I have taken the liberty of calling Meriwethers Bay the Cristian name of Capt. Lewis who no doubt was the 1st white man who ever Surveyed this Bay,[14] we assended a river which falls in on the South Side of this Bay 3 miles to the first point of high land on the West Side, the place Capt. Lewis had viewed and formed in a thick groth of pine about 200 yards from the river, this situation is on a rise about 30 feet higher than the high tides leavel and thickly Covered with lofty pine. this is certainly the most eligable Situation for our purposes of any in its neighbourhood.

    Meriwethers Bay is about 4 miles across deep & receves 2 rivers the *Kil how-â-nah-kle* and the *Ne tul* and Several Small Creeks— we had a hard wind from the N. E. and Some rain about 12 oClock to day which lasted

2 hours and Cleared away. From the Point above Meriwethers Bay to Point Adams is *West*

to point Disapointment is N. 75° W.—

[*NB: camped on the Ne tul*]

1. Under this entry in the Elkskin-bound Journal appears a floor plan of Fort Clatsop, the party's winter quarters in Clatsop County, Oregon, superimposed on a map of the eastern Youngs Bay area (fig. 6). A similar plan of the fort appears on the inside back cover of this journal (fig. 7).
2. Youngs Bay, Clatsop County. *Atlas* map 82.
3. Lewis and Clark River, Clatsop County. *Atlas* map 82.
4. Near the later site of Fort Clatsop.
5. Youngs River.
6. This sentence is at the top of a page in the Elkskin-bound Journal and was probably inserted later; it interrupts the previous sentence and has been moved for ease of reading.
7. The site of Fort Clatsop (*Atlas* map 84), where the party would remain until March 1806, is about five miles southeast of Astoria, Clatsop County, just south of U.S. Highway 101. Remnants of the fort, on the west side of the Lewis and Clark River, were still visible into the early 1870s and it was relocated through archaeological excavations. The site is now a national memorial containing a reconstruction of the fort. Gibbs (TWO), 238; Caywood; Coues (HLC), 3:904–5 n. 3; Appleman (LC), 345–49. Archaeological excavations at a small Indian campsite across the Lewis and Clark River from Fort Clatsop encountered evidence of occupation during the early historic period. Minor (ASCR).
8. This material (to "made a Chief") appears at the bottom of a page with this entry of December 7 in the Elkskin-bound Journal, upside down to the rest of the material. The river may be the "Wo lump ked R" of *Atlas* map 90, perhaps Youngs River or Lewis and Clark River, which the party viewed from the north side from their Chinook Point camp (November 15–25). The term (meaning unknown) is Chinookan *walámt*. This was apparently written at that time when the men considered Point Adams as an island, before Lewis's reconnaisance of the area on November 30. "Wo-lump-ed R" also appears on fig. 6, but with no clear geographic reference.
9. Tillamook Indians; see below, January 8, 1806.
10. Apparently another name for Coboway. See Clark's entry of March 22, 1806.
11. Probably present Wind (Crusatte's) River. *Atlas* map 78.
12. A list of supplies at this point in the Elkskin-bound Journal. A frow, or froe, is a wedge-shaped tool used for cleaving staves. Criswell, 41. In the corner across from the list appears: "50° 36' 15" Nov. 17 Satdy 1805."
13. This set of bearings appears on the same page as the preceding list of supplies, but upside down to it. Apparently the bearings were taken on the north side of the Columbia estuary in Washington.
14. In fact, the first white man to survey the bay was Broughton of Vancouver's expedition in 1792. He named it Young's (now Youngs) Bay, its present name, after Sir George Young of the British Navy. Barry (BOC), 398.

At Fort Clatsop

[Clark]   *December 8th Sunday 1805*

a Cloudy morning, I took 5 men[1] and Set out to the *Sea* to find the nearest place & make a way, to prevent our men getting lost and find a place to make Salt, Steered S 62° W   at 2 miles passed the head of a Brook running to the right, the lands good roleing much falling timber, lofty Pine of the Spruce kind, & Some fur, passed over a high hill & to a Creek which we kept down 1½ miles and left it to our right, Saw fish in this Creek & Elk & Bear tracks on it, passed over a ridge to a low marshey bottom which we Crossed thro   water & thick brush for ½ a mile to the Comencement of a Prarie which wavers, Covered with grass & Sackay Commis, at ½ Crossed a marsh 200 yds wide, boggey and arrived at a Creek[2] which runs to the right. Saw a gange of Elk on the opposit Side below, rafted the Creek, with much dificulty & followed the Elk thro, emence bogs, & over 4 Small Knobs in the bogs about 4 miles to the South & Killed an Elk, and formed a Camp,[3] Covered our Selves with the Elk Skins.   the left of us Bogs & a lake or pond   those bogs Shake, ⟨the moss⟩ much Cramberry growing amongst the moss. Some rain this evening we made a harty Supper of the Elk & hung up the bals.[4]

[Clark]   *Sunday December 8th 1805 Fort Clatsop*

We haveing fixed on this Situation as the one best Calculated for our Winter quarters I deturmin'd to go as direct a Course as I could to the Sea Coast which we Could here roar and appeared to be at no great distance from us, my principal object is to look out a place to make Salt, blaze the road or rout that they men out hunting might find the direction to the fort if they Should get lost in cloudy weather—and See the probibillity of game in that direction, for the Support of the Men, we Shall Send to make Salt, I took with me five men and Set out on a Course S 60 W   proceeded on a dividing ridge through lofty piney land much falling timber.   passed the heads of 2 brooks one of them had wide bottoms which was over flown & we waded to our knees crossed 2 Slashes [*NB: Swamps*] and arrived at a Creek in a open ridgey prarie covered with Sackacomma [*NB: Sac de Commis*]   this Creek we were obliged to raft, which is about 60 yards over and runs in a direction to Point adams, we discovered a large gange of Elk in the open lands, and we prosued them through verry bad Slashes and Small ponds about 3 miles, Killed one and camped on a Spot Scercely large enough to lie Clear of the Water. it is almost incredeable to assurt the bogs which those animals Can pass through, I prosue'd this gang of Elk through bogs which the wate of a man would Shake for ½ an Acre, and maney places I Sunk into the mud and water up to my hips without finding any bottom on the trale of those Elk. Those bogs are Covered with a kind of moss among' which I observe an ebundance of Cramberries. in those Slashes Small Knobs are promisquisly Scattered about which are Steep and thickly Covered with pine Common to the Countrey & Lorel. we made a Camp of the Elk Skin to keep off the rain which Continued to fall, the Small Knob on which we Camped did not afford a Sufficiency of dry wood for our fire, we collected what dry wood we Could and what Sticks we Could Cut down with the Tomahawks, which made us a tolerable fire.

1. Including Drouillard and Shannon; see below, December 9, 1805.
2. Probably present Skipanon River or one of its tributaries, in Clatsop County, Oregon.
3. In Clatsop County, not far from the coast and north of present Seaside. Not marked on *Atlas* map 84. See Clark's entries for his other trip through this region on January 6, 1806.
4. Clark started to write a new entry with the word "Decem" but left the remaining one-quarter of the page blank and started the next entry at the top of a new page.

[Clark]   December 9th Monday 1805

rained all the last night we are all wet, Send 2 men in pursute of the Elk & with the other 3 I Set out with a view to find the Ocian in our first direction, which Can be at no great Distance, I crossed 3 Slashes by wadeing to my knees & was prevented proceeding by the 4th which was a pond of 200 yds. we. I went around, and was Stoped by a 5th which apd. to be a rung Stream to the right. I then returned to the raft and recrossd. & proceeded down the Stream I first Struck about 2 miles & met 3 Indians, who informed me they lived on the See cost at a Short distance, I determd. to accompany them to their vilg. & we Set out, crossed the Stream, and 2 of the Indians took the Canoe over the wavering open rich plains for ½ a mile and we Crossed the same stream which run to the left, we then left the canoe and proceeded to the Same Stream which runs to the right and empties its Self into the See here I found their vilg.[1] 4 Lodges on the west bank of this little river which is here 70 yards wide, Crossed in a Canoe & was invited to a lodge by a young Chief was treated great Politeness, we had new mats to Set on, and himself and wife produced for us to eate, fish, Lickorish, & black roots, on neet Small mats, and Cramberries & Sackacomey berris, in bowls made of horn, Supe made of a kind of bread made of berries common to this Countrey which they gave me in a neet wooden trencher, with a Cockle Shell to eate it with It began to rain and with a tremendious storm from the S. W. which lasted untill 10 oClock P M— when I was disposd to go to Sleep 2 neet mats was produced & I lay on them but the flees were So troublesom that I Slept but little Those people has 2 plays which they are fond of one is with a Been which they pass from one hand into the other, and the oponent guess on this game the resquist nubr of the white Beeds which is the principal property— they other game is with round Pieces of wood much the Shape of the [blank] Backgammon which they role thro between 2 pins.[2]

[Clark] *Monday 9th December 1805*

rained all the last night we are all wet, I directed 2 hunters Drewyer & Shannon to go in pursute of the Elk, with the other 3 men I deturmined to proceed on to the Ocian, & Set out on a Westerley direction Crossed 3 Slashes and arived at a Creek which I could not Cross as it was deep and no wood to make a raft, I proceeded down this Creek a Short distance and found that I was in a fork of the Creek, I then returned to [NB?: the] raft on which we had Crossed the day [NB?: before]. crossed and kept down about one mile and met 3 Indians loaded with fresh Salmon which they had Giged in the Creek I crossed yesterday in the hills, those indians made Signs that they had a town on the Seacoast at no great distance, and envited me to go to their town which envitation I axcepted and accompand. them, they had a Canoe hid in the Creek which I had just before rafted which I had not observed, we crossed in this little Canoe just large enough to carry 3 men an their loads after Crossing 2 of the Indians took the Canoe on theire Sholders and Carried it across to the other Creek about ¼ of a mile, we Crossed the 2d Creek and proceeded on to the mouth of the Creek which makes a great bend above the mouth of this Creek or to the S. is 3 houses and about 12 families of the Clat Sop Nation, we cross to those houses, which were built on the S. exposur of the hill, Sunk into the ground about 4 feet the walls roof & gable ends are of Split pine boards, the dores Small with a ladder to decend to the iner part of the house, the fires are 2 in the middle of the house their beads ar all around raised about 2½ feet from the bottom flore all covered with mats and under those beads was Stored their bags baskets and useless mats, those people treated me with extrodeanary friendship, one man attached himself to me as Soon as I entered the hut, Spred down new mats for me to Set on, gave me fish berries rutes &c. on Small neet platteers of rushes to eate which was repeated, all the Men of the other houses Came and Smoked with me Those people appeared much neeter in their diat than Indians are Comonly, and frequently wash theer faces and hands— in the eveng an old woman presented a bowl made of a light Coloured horn a kind of Surup made of Dried berries which is common to this Countrey which the natives Call *Shele wele* [*NB: Shel-well*]³ this Surup I though was pleasent, they Gave me Cockle Shells⁴ to eate a kind of Seuip [*NB: Soup*] made of bread of the *Shele well* berries mixed with roots in which they presented in neet trenchers made of wood. a flock of Brant lit in the Creek which was 70 yds wide I took up my Small rifle and Shot one which astonished those people verry much, they plunged into the Creek and brought the brant on Shore— in the evening it began to rain and Continud accompanied with a Violent wind from the S. W. untill 10 oClock P. M. those people have a Singular game which they are verry fond of and is performed with Something [*NB: a piece of bone*] about the Size of a large been [*NB: bean*] which they pass from, one hand into the other with great dexterity dureing which time they Sing, and ocasionally, hold out their hands for those who Chuse to risque their property to guess which hand the been is in—;⁵ the individual who has the been is a banker & opposed to all in the room. on this game they risque their beeds & other parts of their most valuable effects— this amusement has occupied about 3 hours of this evening, Several of the lodge in which I am in have lost all the beeds which they had about them— they have one other game which a man attempted to Show me, I do not properly understand it, they make use of maney peces about the Shape and size of Backgammon Pices [*NB: Men*] which they role [*NB: on the floor*] through between two pins Stuck up at certain distancies &.— when I was Disposed to go to Sleep the man who' had been most attentive named *Cus-ka-lah*[6] producd 2 new mats and Spred them near the fire, and derected his wife to go to his bead which was the Signal for all to retire which they did emediately. I had not been long on my mats before I was attacked most violently by the flees and they kept up a close Siege dureing the night

    1. The site of present Seaside, Clatsop County, Oregon, at the mouth of the Necanicum River. The Clatsop village is shown on *Atlas* map 84 and on figs. 9 and 13.
    2. Biddle provides a diagram of the game and some explanation. Biddle Notes [ca. April 1810], Jackson (LLC), 2:541. Clark has additional information in his entry on this day. See also entry of February 2, 1806; Culin, 281–82, 782.
    3. Salal, *Gaultheria shallon* Pursh. Clark's term is from Chinookan *sálal*, giving rise to its present common name. See Lewis's description on February 8, 1806. The species has extensive ethnobotanical use as food, medicine, and for smoking. Gibbs (AVC), 17; Gunther (EWW), 43; Cutright (LCPN), 265–66.
    4. Coues (HLC), 2:731 n. 18, proposes some species of mussel. The fact that Lewis mentions cockles and mussels as two entities on March 12, 1806, suggests otherwise. The cockle is probably from the family Cardiidae.
    5. A vertical line is drawn through this passage about the game, perhaps by Biddle.
    6. The name is Chinookan *Čuskala*, meaning unknown.

[Clark]   *December 10th 1805 Tusday*

A Cloudey rainy morning those people was Some what astonished, at three Shot I made with my little riffle [rifle] to day, a gangu of Brant Set in the little river, I Killd. 2 of them as they Set, and on my return Saw a Duck which I took the head off of, the men plunged into the water like Spaniards Dogs[1] after those fowls, after eateing a brackfast which was Similar to my Suppar, I attempted to purchase Some fiew roots which I offered red beeds for, they would give Scercely any thing for Beeds of that Colour, I then offered Small fish hooks which they were fond of and gave me Some roots for them, I then Set out on my return by the Same road I had went out accompd. by my young Chief by name *Cus-ca-lar* who Crossed me over the 3 Creek, and returned I proceeded on to my Camp thro a heavy Cold rain, Saw no game— at the Sea Cost near those Indins I found various kinds of Shells, a kind of Bay opsd. those people with a high pt.[2] about 4 miles below, out from which at Some dists I Saw large rocks, as the day was Cloudy I could not See distinctly— found

November 22, 1805–January 6, 1806

Capt Lewis with all hands felling trees, to build with, rained nearly all day, in my absence they men had bt. in the 6 Elk which was Killed Some days past   4 men complaining of being unwell from various causes

[Clark] *Tuesday 10th December 1805*
  a Cloudy rainey morning   verry early I rose and walked on the Shore of the Sea coast and picked up Several Curious Shells.   I Saw Indians walking up and down the beech which I did not at first understand the Cause of, one man came to where I was and told me that he was in Serch of fish which is frequently thrown up on Shore and left by the tide, and told me [*NB: in English*] the "Sturgion was verry good" and that the water when it retired left fish which they eate   this was Conclusive evedance to me that this Small band depended in Some Measure for their winters Subsistance on the fish which is thrown on Shore and left by the tide—   after amuseing my Self for about an hour on the edge of the rageing Seas I returned to the houses, one of the Indians pointed to a flock of Brant Sitting in the creek at Short distance below and requested me to Shute one, I walked down with my Small rifle and killed two at about 40 yds distance, on my return to the houses two Small ducks Set at about 30 Steps from me   the Indians pointed at the ducks they were near together, I Shot at the ducks and accidently Shot the head of one off, this Duck and brant was Carried to the house and every man Came around examined the Duck looked at the gun the Size of the ball which was 100 to the pound and Said in their own language *Clouch Musket*, [*NB: English word Musket*] *wake, com ma-tax Musket* which is, a good Musket do not under Stand this kind of Musket &c.³ I entered the Same house I Slept in, they imediately Set before me their best roots, fish and Surup—, I attempted to purchase a Small Sea otter Skin for read beeds which I had in my pockets, they would not trade for those beeds not priseing any other Colour than Blue or White, I purchased a little of the berry bread and a fiew of their roots for which I gave Small fish hooks, which they appeared fond of—   I then Set out on my return by the Same rout I had Come out accompanied by *Cus-ka lah* and his brother as far as the ⟨Second⟩ 3d Creek, for the purpose of Setting me across, from which place they returned, and I proceeded on through a heavy rain to

the Camp at our intended fort, Saw a bears track & the tracks of 2 Elk in the thick woods— found Capt Lewis with all the men out Cutting down trees for our huts &c. in my absence the Men brought in the Six Elk which was killed Several days ago—. 4 men Complaining of violent Coalds. three Indians in a Canoe Came up from the *Clat Sop* Village yesterday and returned to day. The Sea Coast is about 7 miles distant Nearly West about 5 miles of the distance through a thick wood with reveens hills and Swamps the land, rich black moald 2 miles in a open wavering Sandy prarie, ridge runing parrelal to the river, Covered with Green Grass.

   1. Spaniels according to Criswell, 80.
   2. Tillamook Head, Clatsop County, Oregon. *Atlas* map 84.
   3. The sentence is in the Chinook jargon: ƛuš musket, wek kəmtəks musket, "[it is a] good musket, [I do] not understand [this] musket."

[Clark]   *December 11th Wednesday*

   rained all last night moderately, we are all employed putting up the huts, rained at intervales all day moderately employed in putting up Cabins for our winter quarters, one man with Tumers, one with a Strained Knee, one Sick with Disentary & Serjt. Pryor unwell from haveing his Sholder out of place

[Clark]   *Wednesday 11th December 1805*

   rained all the last night moderately we are all employed putting up huts or Cabins for our winters quarters. Sergeant Pryor unwell from a dislocation of his Sholder, Gibson with the disentary, Jo. Fields with biles on his legs, & Werner with a Strained Knee. The rained Continued moderately all day.

[Clark]   *December 12th Thursday 1805* [1]

   Some moderate Showers last night and this morning all hands who are well employed in building Cabins, despatched 2 men to get board timber, The flees so bad last night that, I made but a broken nights rest we can't get them out of our robes & Skins, which we are obliged to make use of for bedding Some rain to day at Intervales— all at work, in the evening 2 Canoe of Indians Came from the 2 villages of ⟨Clopstots⟩

Clotsop below, & brought Wapitoo roots a black root they call *Si-ni-tor*[2] and a Small Sea orter Skin all of which we purchased for a fiew fishing hooks & Some Snake Indian Tobacco. Those Indians appeare well disposed, I made a Chief of one & gave him a Small medel, his name is *Con-year*[3] we treated those people well— they are tite Deelers, value Blu & white beeds verry highly, and Sell their roots also highly as they purchase them from the Indians abov for a high price

[Clark] *Thursday 12th December 1805*

All hands that are well employ'd in Cutting logs and raising our winter Cabins, detached two men to Split boards— Some rain at intervales all last night and to day— The flees were So troublesom last night that I made but a broken nights rest, we find great dificuelty in getting those trouble insects out of our robes and blankets— in the evening two Canoes of *Clât Sops* Visit us they brought with them *Wap pa to*, a black Sweet root they Call *Sha-na toe qua*, and a Small Sea Otter Skin, all of which we purchased for a fiew fishing hooks and a Small Sack of Indian tobacco which was given by the Snake Inds.

Those Indians appear well disposed we gave a Medal to the principal Chief named *Con-ny-au* or *Com mo-wol* and treated those with him with as much attention as we could— I can readily discover that they are Close deelers, & Stickle for a verry little, never close a bargin except they think they have the advantage Value Blue beeds highly, white they also prise but no other Colour do they Value in the least— the *Wap pa to* they Sell high, this root the purchase at a high price from the nativs above.

    1. An asterisk appears at the end of this line; its purpose is not known.

    2. A variation for the edible thistle noted earlier (November 21, 1805). Lewis's detailed discussion of the plant is on January 21, 1806.

    3. More correctly, Coboway, a Clatsop leader. The captains made him a gift of Fort Clatsop when they left the following spring, and he apparently occupied the structure for several years. His grandson, Silas B. Smith, assisted Olin D. Wheeler in locating the fort site in 1899. His name is not identifiable linguistically. Wheeler, 2:196–98; Ruby & Brown (CITC), 99–101, 107, 107n, 145; Ronda (LCAI), 194, 210–13.

[Clark] *December 13th Friday 1805*

The Indians left us to day after brackfast, haveing Sold us 2 of the robes of a Small animal for which I intend makeing a Capot, and Sold

At Fort Clatsop

Capt Lewis 2 Loucirvia[1] Skins for the Same purpose. Drewyer & Shannon returned from hunting havg. killed 18 Elk and butchered all except 2 which they Could not get as night provented ther finding them & they Spoild.

3 Indians in a Canoe Came and offered us for Sale *Sinutor* roots, fish & 2 Sea otter Skins for Sale none of which we Could purchase. Some rain last night and this day at Several times, light Showers. we Continue building our houses of the Streightest & [*one word illegible*] logs, Sent out 2 men to Split timber to Cover the Cabins, and I am glad to find the timber Splits butifully, and of any width—

[Clark]   *Friday 13th December 1805*

The *Clatsops* leave us to day after a brackfast on Elk which they appeared to be very fond of   before they left us they Sold me two robes of the Skins of a Small animal about the Size of a Cat, and to Captain Lewis 2 Cat or Loucirva Skins for the purpose of makeing a Coat.   Drewyer & Shannon returned from hunting, haveing killed 18 Elk & left them boochered in the woods near the right fork of the river about 6 miles above this place—   in the evining 3 Indians came in a Canoe, and offered to us for Sale roots & 2 Sea otter Skins, neither of which we Could purchase this evening.   Some Showers of rain last night, and to day Several verry hard Showers—   we Continue to put up the Streight butifull balsom pine[2] on our houses—and we are much pleased to find that the timber Splits most butifully and to the width of 2 feet or more.

    1. The French term *loup cervier* denotes the Canada lynx, *Lynx canadensis*. Burroughs, 92. In the second entry Clark notes that the small animal mentioned first was about the "Size of a Cat," by which he probably means the Oregon bobcat.

    2. Opinions differ as to whether this tree was Douglas fir, grand fir, or Sitka spruce. Cutright (LCPN), 248. The best opinion suggests the grand fir. "Balsam" refers to the blisters of fragrant pitch, characteristically found on the smooth bark of the younger trees and injured older trees of the grand fir. The favorably splitting timber also strongly suggests the grand fir. See Lewis's description of the grand fir at February 6, 1806.

[Clark]   *December 14th Saturday 1805*

a cloudy day & rained moderately all day   we finish the log works of our building, the Indians leave us to day after Selling a Small Sea otter

Skin and a roabe, Send 4 men to Stay at the Elk which is out in the woods &c.

[Clark] Saturday 14th December 1805

The Day Cloudy and rained moderately all day we finish the log work of our building, the Indians leave us to day after Selling a Small Sea otter Skin and a roab, dispatch 4 men to the Elk out in the woods with derections to delay untill the party ⟨went⟩ goes up tomorrow. all employd in finishing a house to put meat into. all our last Supply of Elk has Spoiled in the repeeted rains which has been fallen ever Since our arrival at this place, and for a long time before, Scerce one man in Camp Can bost of being one day dry Since we landed at this point, the Sick getting better, my man York Sick with Cholick & gripeing

[Clark] December 15th Sunday 1805

I Set out with 16 men in 3 Canoes for the Elk proced up the 1st right hand fork 4 miles[1] & pack the meat from the woods to the Cano from 4 mile to 3 miles distance all hands pack not one man exempted from this labour I also pack my Self Some of this meat, and Cook for those out in packing Some rain in the evening Cloudy all day, the last load of meat all the party got out of the road or Direction and did not get to the Canoe untill after night, 5 did not join to night

[Clark] Sunday the 15th December 1805.

I Set out early with 16 men and 3 Canoes for the Elk, proceed up the River three miles and thence up a large Creek from the right about 3 miles the hite of the tide water drew up the Canoes and all hands went out in three different parties and brought in to the Canoe each Man a quarter of Elk, I Sent them out for a Second load and had Some of the first Cooked against their return, after eateing a harty diner dispatched the party for a third and last load, about half the men missed their way and did not get to the Canoes untill after Dark, and Serjt. Ordway Colter, Colins Whitehouse & McNeal Staid out all night without fire and in the rain— Cloudy all day Some rain in the evening.

1. Perhaps Johnson Slough, Clatsop County, Oregon; presumably the stream labeled "Kil la malk-ka C" on *Atlas* map 84.

[Clark]   *December 16th Monday 1805*

rained all the last night we Covered our Selves as well as we Could with Elk Skins, & Set up the greater part of the night, all wet I lay in the water verry Cold, the 5 men who Stayed out all night joined me this morning Cold & wet, Ordway Colter Collens, Jo Whitehouse J McNeal, I had the two Canoes loaded with the 11 Elk which was brought to the Canoes, despatched 12 men to meet me below with 2 Elk, The rain Contines, with Tremendious gusts of wind, which is Tremds. I proceeded on and took in the 2 Elk which was brought to the Creek, & Send back 7 men to Carrey to the Canoe & take down to Camp 3 Elk which was left in the woods, and I proceeded on to Camp thro the Same Chanel I had assd. The winds violent Trees falling in every derection, whorl winds, with gusts of rain Hail & Thunder, this kind of weather lasted all day, Certainly one of the worst days that ever was! I found 3 Indeans with Capt Lewis in camp they had brought fish to Sell, we had a house Covered with Punchen & our meat hung up. Several men Complaining of hurting themselves Carry meet, &c.

[Clark]   *Monday 16th December 1805*

I as also the party with me experiencd a most dreadfull night rain and wet without any Couvering, indeed we Set up the greater part of the Night, when we lay down the water Soon Came under us and obliged us to rise. the five men who Stayed out all night joind me this morning wet and Cold, haveing Stayed out without fire or Shelter and the rain poreing down upon them all night their appearance was truly distressing— they had left all their loads near the place they Spent the night— I dispatched 12 men for 2 Elk which was reather below on the opposit Side of the Creak, with directions to meet me at the 2d bend in the Creek below, had all the meat which had been brought in yesterday put into 2 Canoes and proceeded down to the 2d bend where I met the 12 men with the 2 Elk, dispatchd 6 men with one of those who Staid out last night for the meet left in the woods & the remainder an elk at Some distance and proceeded on my Self with 3 Canoes to the fort. wind violent from the S E trees falling, rain and hail, we with Some risque proceeded on thro the high waves in the river, a tempestious disagreeable day.

I found 3 indians at our Camp, they brought fish to Sell which were pore & not fit for use, had the meet house coverd and the meat all hung up, Several men complain of haveing hurt themselves heavy loads of meat.

[Clark]   *December 17th Tuesday 1805*[1]

rained Some last night and this morning, all hands at work about the huts Chinking them, The 7 men left to bring in the Elk left in the woods Come with 2   the 3rd they Could not find, as it was that left by the party that got lost night before last

The after part of the Day fair & Cool, fore part of the Day rain hailed & blew hard, The mountain[2] which lies S. E of this is covered with Snow to day   we fleece[3] all the meat and hang it up over a Small Smoke   The trees are hard to Split for Punchens to Cover our houses &c.[4]

[Clark]   *Tuesday 17th of December 1805*

Some rain last night and a continuation of it this morning. all the men at work about the houses, Some Chinking, Dobbing Cutting out dores &c. &c. The 7 men left to bring in the Elk arrived and informed that they Could not find the meat that the party who Stayed out all night had left— the forepart of this day rained hailed and blew hard, the after part is fair and Cool— a Mountain which is S. [*blank*]° E. about 10 miles distant has got Snow on its top which is ruged and uneavin

Cause a Small fire & Smoke to be made under the meat which is hung up in Small peaces: The trees which our men have fallen latterly Split verry badly into boards. The most of our Stores are wet. our Leather Lodge has become So rotten that the Smallest thing tares it into holes and it is now Scrcely Sufficent to keep off the rain off a Spot Sufficiently large for our bead.

   1. Under this entry in the Elkskin-bound Journal is a sketch map (fig. 8) which appears to show the area between Fort Clatsop and the Pacific Coast, in Clatsop County, Oregon. Opposite this entry is a sketch map (fig. 9) of the area about the site of the expedition's salt works. See December 28, 1805, and *Atlas* map 84.

   2. Perhaps Saddle Mountain, Clatsop County. Coues (HLC), 2:735.

   3. Criswell, 39, derives this verb from the definition of "fleece" as the meat taken from

December 17th Tuesday 1805

rained some last night
and this morning all hands
at work about the huts
Chinking them. The 7 men left
to bring in the Elk left in the woods
Came with 2 the 3rd they could
not find, as it was that left by
the party that got lost the night
before last

✗ Fort   S. 60 W. 7 miles

The after part of the Day fair &
Cool, fore part of the Day rained
hailed & blew hard, The
mountain which lies S. E. of this
is covered with snow to day
we flued all the meat and
hong it up over a small
smoke. The trees are hard to
split for Punchins to cover our
houses &c.

8. Location of Fort Clatsop, ca. December 17, 1805,
Elkskin-bound Journal

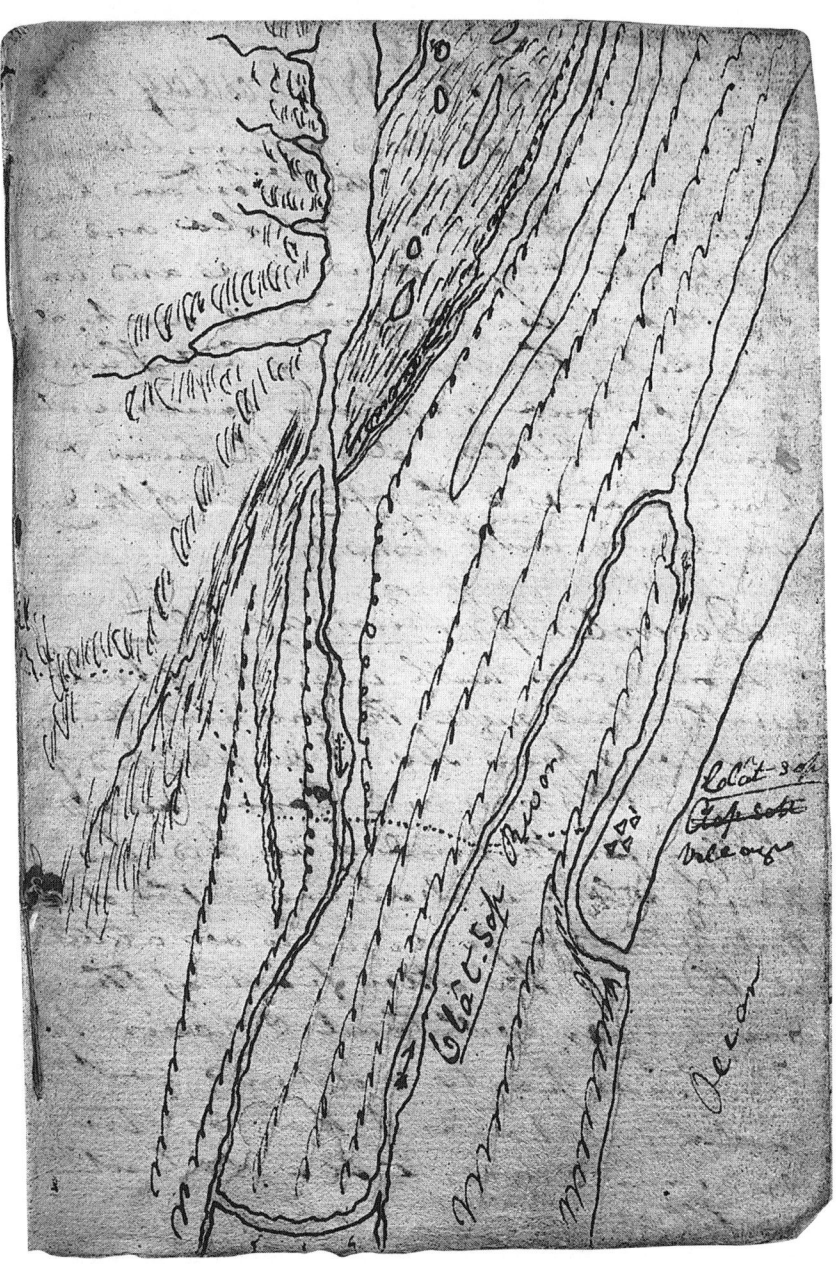

9. Necanicum River, Oregon, ca. December 17, 1805,
Elkskin-bound Journal

the sides of the hump of the bison. As the entry in Codex I indicates below, Clark is clearly referring to cutting the meat into small pieces for smoking.

4. Perhaps in disagreement with his own comment of December 13, and that of Gass on December 14, who said that the timber "splits freely and makes the finest puncheons I have ever seen."

[Clark] *December 18th Wednesday 1805*

rained and Snowed alturnitely all the last night and the gusts of Snow and hail continue untill 12 oClock, Cold and a dreadfull day wind hard and unsettled, we continue at work at our huts, the men being but thinly dressed, and no Shoes causes us to doe but little— at 12 the Snow & hail Seased & the after part of the day was Cloudy with Some rain.

[Clark] *Wednesday 18th December 1805*

rained and Snowed alternetly all the last night, and Spurts of Snow and Hail Continued untill 12 oClock, which has chilled the air which is Cool and disagreeable, the wind hard & unsettled— The men being thinly Dressed and mockersons wıthout Socks is the reason that but little can be done at the Houses to day— at 12 the Hail & Snow Seased, and rain Suckceeded for the latter part of the day

[Lewis] *Fort Clatsop, December 18th 1805.*[1]

This day one of the men shot a bird of the Corvus genus, which was feeding on some fragments of meat near the camp. this bird is about the size of the kingbird or *bee martin,* and not unlike that bird in form. the beak is ¾ of an inch long, wide at the base, of a convex, and cultrated figure, beset with some small black hairs near it's base. the chaps are of nearly equal lengths tho' the upper exceeds the under one a little, and has a small nich in the upper chap near the extremity ⟨srcely⟩ perceptable only by close examineation. the colour of the beak is black. the eye is large and prominent, the puple black, and iris of a dark yellowish brown. the legs and feet are black and imbricated. has four toes on each foot armed with long sharp tallons; the hinder toe is nearly as long as the middle toe in front and longer than the two remaining toes. the tale is composed of twelve fathers the longest of which are five inches, being six in number placed in the center. the remaining six are placed 3 on either side and graduly deminish to four inches which is the shortest

November 22, 1805–January 6, 1806

and outer feathers. the tail is half the length of the bird, the wh[ol]e length from the extremity of the beak to the extremity of the tale being 10 Inches. the head from it's joining the nect forward as far as the eyes nearly to the base of the beak and on each side as low as the center of the eye is black. arround the base of the beak the throat jaws, neck, brest and belley are of a pale bluish white. the wings back and tale are of a bluish black with a small shade of brown. this bird is common to this piny country are also found in the rockey mountains on the waters of the columbia river or woody side of those mountains, appear to frequent the highest sumits of those mountains as far as they are covered with timber. their note is *que,* quit-it, que-hoo; and tâh, tâh, &— there is another bird of reather larger size which I saw on the woddy parts of the rockey mountains and on the waters of the Missouri, this bird I could never kill tho' I made several attempts, the ⟨colour⟩ predominate colour is a dark blue the tale is long and they are not crested; I believe them to be of the corvus genus also. their note is *châr, châr, char-ar,* char; the large blue crested corvus of the Columbia river is also

1. Lewis's note from Codex R, covering zoology rather than the customary botany. The bird is the gray jay, *Perisoreus canadensis* [AOU, 484], a new species. Burroughs, 250–51; Holmgren, 29; Cutright (LCPN), 274, 436. The kingbird used for comparison is *Tyrannus tyrannus* [AOU, 444]. The bird of the woody parts of the Rockies that Lewis mentions near the end of this passage may be the pinyon jay, *Gymnorhinus cyanocephalus* [AOU, 492], first noticed by him on August 1, 1805. Holmgren, 28, identifies it as possibly the mountain bluebird, *Sialia currucoides* [AOU, 768]. The "large blue crested corvus" is Steller's jay, described more fully in the next immediate entry. This is the last of Lewis's original notes in this journal (except for a few lines mentioned below). The remainder of the journal is filled with material copied from other journals by an unknown person. See Introduction and Appendix C, vol. 2. Lewis may have been referring to this passage or the next one, when he noted on March 4, 1806, that he had already described the bird. Another reference to the bird is on the endleaf of this notebook, in Lewis's hand: "note of the corvus bird killed at Fort Clatsop. que-quit it; que hoo repeated, & chat, chat, chat." The note is labeled "Mineralogy" by Lewis; he probably intended that label for the preceding page which has a note on lava, dated September 20, 1804.

[Lewis] [*undated*]¹

Discription of the [⟨male⟩?] blue Crested corvus bird [*EC: Cyanocitta stelleri*] common to the woody and western side of the Rockey mountains, and all the woody country from thence to the Pacific Ocean It's beak is black convex, cultrated, wide at its base where it is beset with hairs, and is 1¼ inches from the opening of the chaps to their extremity, and from the joining of the head to the extremity of the upper chap 1⅛ Inches, the upper exceeds the under chap a little; the nostrils are small round unconnected and placed near the base of the beak where they lye concealed by the hairs or hairy feathers which cover the base of the ⟨beak⟩ upper chap. the eye reather large and full but not prominent and of a deep blueish black, there being no difference in the colour of the puple and the iris. the crest is very full the feathers from 1 ⟨Inch⟩ to 1½ Inches long and occupye the whole crown of the head. the head neck, the whole of the body including the coverts of the wings, the upper disk of the tail and wings are of a fine gossey bright indigo blue Colour the ⟨upper and⟩ under disk of the tail and wings are of a dark brown nearly black. the leg and first joint of the tye are 4¼ In. long, the legs and feet are black and the front covered with 6 scales the hinder part smothe, the toes are also imbrecated, four in number long and armed with long sharp black tallons. the upper ⟨side⟩ disk of the first four or five feathers ⟨next⟩ of the wing next to the boddy, are marked with small transverse stripes of black as are also the upper side of the two center feathers of the tail; the tail is five inches long & is composed of twelve feathers of equal length ⟨each five inches long⟩. the tail 1 & ½ as long as the boddy. the whole length from the point of the beak to extremity of the tail 1 Foot 1 Inch; from the tip of one to the tip of the other wing 1 Foot 5½ Inches. the Conta. the size & the whole Contour of this bird resembles very much the *blue jay* or *jaybird* as they are called in the U' States. like them also they seldom rest in one place long but are in constant motion hoping from spra to spray. what has been said is more immediately applicable to the male, the colours of the female are somewhat different in her the head crest neck half the back downwards and the converts of the wings are of a dark brown, but sometimes there is a little touch of the Indigo on the short feathers on the head at the base of the upper chap. this bird feeds on flesh when they can procure it, also on bugs flies and buries. I do not know whether they distroy little birds but their tallons indicate their ⟨powers⟩ capacity to do so if nature, has directed it. their note is loud and frequently repeated châ' -â' châ' -â' &c.— also twat twat twat, very quick

November 22, 1805–January 6, 1806

1. Lewis's zoological note from Codex Q; the bird is Steller's jay. The blue jay used for comparison is *Cyanocitta cristata* [AOU, 477]. This is the last of such original notes in this journal, the remainder being filled with material copied from other journals by an unknown person. See Introduction and Appendix C, vol. 2. This is an undated passage which Thwaites combined with a preceding zoological note of May 26, 1805, but this material clearly comes from a later date. Thwaites (LC), 6:134–35. It was probably written at Fort Clatsop when Lewis was writing up his natural history material, mostly in Codex J. We place it here with the dated entry from Codex R describing similar species.

[Clark]   *December 19th Thursday 1805*

Some rain with intervales of fair weather last night, The morning Clear and wind from S W. I despatched Sjt. Pryer with 8 men in 2 Canoes across the bay¹ for the boads of an Indian house which is abandoned, the other part of the men continue to doe a little at the huts, the after part of the day Cloudy with hail & rain, Sgt. Pryer and party returned with 2 Canoe loads of Boards, two Indians Came & Stayed but a Short time

[Clark]   *Thursday 19th December 1805*

Some rain with intervales of fair weather last night, this morning Clear & the wind from the S, W. we dispatched Sjt. Pryor with 8 men in 2 Canoes across Meriwethers Bay for the boards of an old Indian house which is vacant, the residue of the men at work at their huts— the after part of the Day Cloudy with Hail and rain, Serjt. Pryor & party returned in the evening with a load of old boards which was found to be verry indifferent 2 Indians Cam and Stayed a Short time to day

1. Youngs (Meriwether's) Bay. As far as *Atlas* map 82 indicates, the abandoned house could have been near Point Adams.

[Clark]   *December 20th Friday 1805*

Some rain and hail last night and this morning it rained hard untill 10 oClock, men all employd Carrying Punchens and Covering Cabins 4 of which we had Covered, & Set Some to Dobing— the after part of the day Cloudy and Some Showers of rain. 3 Indians came with Lickorish Sackacomie berries & mats to Sell, for which they asked Such high prices that we did not purchase any of them,— Those people ask double &

tribble the value of everry thing they have to Sell, and never take less than the full value of any thing, they prise only Blue & white beeds, files fish hooks and Tobacco—   Tobacco and Blue beeds principally

[Clark]   *Friday 20th of December 1805*

Some rain and hail last night and the rained Continued untill 10 oClock a,m, Men all employd in Carrying punchens or boards & Covering the houses, 4 of which were Covered to day, the after part of the day Cloudy with Several Showers of rain   3 Indians arrive in a Canoe. they brought with them mats, roots & Sackacome [*NB: Sac à Commis*] berries to Sell for which they asked Such high prices that we did not purchase any of them.   Those people ask generally double and tribble the value of what they have to Sell, and never take less than the real value of the article in Such things as is calculated to do them Service. Such as Blue & white beeds, with which they trade with the nativs above; files which they make use of to Sharpen their tools, fish hooks of different Sises and tobacco—   Tobacco and blue beeds they do prefur to every thing.

[Clark]   *December 21st Saturday 1805*

rain as usial last night and all day to day moderately.   we Continued at the Cabins dobbing & Shinking[1] of them, fall Several trees which would not Split into punchins—   the Indians were detected in Stealing a Spoon & a Bone, and left us, our Sackey Commy out   Send 2 men to gather Some at the ocian, Saw Elk Sign

[Clark]   *Saturday 21st December 1805*

rained as useal all the last night, and contd. moderately all day to day without any intermition, men employd at the houses.   one of the indians was detected Stealing a horn Spoon, and leave [*NB: turned from*] the Camp.   dispatched two men to the open lands near the Ocian for Sackacome, which we make use of to mix with our tobacco to Smoke which has an agreeable flavour.

1. Either "chinking," filling up the chinks between the logs with mud or some other substance, or "shingling," as Thwaites (LC), 3:287, seems to think. See above, December 17, 1805. Criswell, 23.

November 22, 1805–January 6, 1806

[Clark] December 22nd Sunday 1805

rained all the last night & to day without much intermition   we finish dobbig 4 huts which is all we have Covered, the Punchin floor & Bunks finished   Drewyer go out to trap—   Sjt. J. Ordway, Gibson & my Servent Sick Several with Biles on them & bruses of different kinds, much of our meat Spoiled.

[Clark] Sunday 22nd December 1805

rained Continued all the last night and to day without much intermition, men employd doeing what they can at the houses. Drewyer Set out up the Creek to Set his traps for beaver, Sergt. ordway, Gibson & my Servent Sick, Several men Complain of biles and bruses of differant kinds.

We discover that part of our last Supply of meat is Spoiling from the womph [warmth] of the weather not withstanding a constant Smoke kept under it day and night.

[Clark] December 23rd Monday 18[05]

rained without intermition all last night, and this day   much Thunder in the morning and evening with rain and Some hail to day, we are all employd about our huts have ours Covered and Dobed & we move into it, 2 Canoes of Indians Came up to day.   I purchased 3 mats verry neetly made, 2 bags made with Flags verry neetly made, those the *Clotsops* Carry ther fish in.   also a Panthor[1] Skin and Some Lickorish roots, for which I gave a worn out file, 6 fish hooks & Some Pounded fish which to us was Spoiled, but those people were fond of—   in the evining those people left us   I also gave a String of wompom to a Chief, and Sent a Small pice of Simimon to a Sick Indian in the Town who had attached himself to me

[Clark] Monday 23rd December 1805

Rained without intermition all the last night and to day with Thunder and Hail the fore and after part of this day   Capt Lewis and my Self move into our hut to day unfinished—   two Canoes with Indians of the *Clât Sop* nation Came up to day. I purchased 3 mats and bags all neetly made of flags and rushes, those bags are nearly Square of different size's open on one Side, I also purchased a panthor Skin 7½ feet long including the tail, all of which I gave 6 Small fish hooks, a Small worn out file & Some pounded fish which we Could not use as it was So long wet that it was Soft and molded, the Indians of this neighbourhood prize the pound'd fish verry highly, I have not observed this method of Secureing fish on any other part of the Columbian waters then that about the Great falls. I gave a 2d Chief a String of wampom, and Sent a little pounded fish to *Cus-ca-lah* who was Sick in the village & could not come to See us.

1. Mountain lion or cougar, *Felis concolor*.

[Clark]   *December 24th Tuesday*—5[1]

Some hard rain at different times last night, and moderately this morning without intermition all hands employed in Carrying Punchens & finishing Covering the huts, and the greater part of the men move into them a hard rain in the evening.

Cuscalar the young *Clot Sop* Chief Came with a young brother and 2 young Squar, they gave or laid before Capt Lewis and my Self a mat and each a large Parsel of roots, Some time after he demanded 2 files for his Present we returned the present as we had no files to Speare which displeased them a little they then offered a woman to each which we also declined axcpting which also displeased them.[2] Jo Fields finish for Capt Lewis and my Self each a wide Slab hued to write on, I gave a handkerchief &c

[Clark]   *Tuesday 24th December 1805*

hard rain at Different times last night and all this day without intermition. men all employd in finishing their huts and moveing into them.

Cuscalah the Indian who had treated me So politely when I was at the Clâtsops village, come up in a Canoe with his young brother & 2 Squars he laid before Capt Lewis and my Self each a mat and a parcel of roots— Some time in the evening two files was demanded for the presents of mats and roots, as we had no files to part with, we each returned the present which we had received, which displeased Cuscalah a little. he then offered a woman to each of us which we also declined axcepting of, which displeased the whole party verry much— the female part appeared to be highly disgusted at our refuseing to axcept of their favours &c.

November 22, 1805 – January 6, 1806

our Store of Meat entirely Spoiled, we are obliged to make use of it as we have nothing else except a little pounded fish, the remains of what we purchased near the great falls of the Columbia, and which we have ever found to be a convenient resort, and a portable method of curing fish

1. An asterisk is near the end of this line; its purpose is not known.
2. On another occasion Clark was offered the sister of a Clatsop man who had received medical treatment; Clark declined. Biddle Notes [ca. April 1810], Jackson (LLC), 2:503.

[Clark]   *December 25th Christmas 1805 Wednesday*

Some rain at different times last night and Showers of hail with intervales of fair Starr light, This morning at day we were Saluted by all our party under our winders, a Shout and a Song— after brackfast we divided our tobacco which amounted to 2 Carrots, one half we gave to the party who used Tobacco those who did not we gave a Handkerchief as a present, The day proved Showery all day, the Inds. left us this evening— all our party moved into their huts. we dried Some of our wet goods. I rcved a present of a Fleeshe Hoserey[1] vest draws & Socks of Capt Lewis, pr. Mockerson of Whitehouse, a Small Indian basket of Guterich, & 2 Doz weasels tales[2] of the Squar of Shabono, & Some black roots of the Indians   G. D. Saw a Snake passing across the parth

Our Diner to day Consisted of pore Elk boiled, Spilt [spoiled] fish & Some roots, a bad Christmass diner   worm Day

[Clark]   *Christmas Wednesday 25th December 1805*

at day light this morning we we[re] awoke by the discharge of the fire arm of all our party & a Selute, Shoute and a Song which the whole party joined in under our windows, after which they retired to their rooms were Chearfull all the morning— after brackfast we divided our Tobacco which amounted to 12 carrots one half of which we gave to the men of the party who used tobacco, and to those who doe not use it we make a present of a handkerchief, The Indians leave us in the evening all the party Snugly fixed in their huts— I recved a presnt of Capt L. of a fleece hosrie Shirt Draws and Socks—, a pr. mockersons of Whitehouse a Small Indian basket of Gutherich, two Dozen white weazils tails of the Indian woman, & Some black root of the Indians before their departure— Drewyer informs me that he Saw a Snake pass across the parth to day. The day proved Showerey wet and disagreeable.

we would have Spent this day the nativity of Christ in feasting, had we any thing either to raise our Sperits or even gratify our appetites, our Diner concisted of pore Elk, So much Spoiled that we eate it thro' mear necessity, Some Spoiled pounded fish and a fiew roots.

1. "Fleece hosiery"; woolen, made of fleece, or perhaps fleece-lined.
2. Presumably the long-tailed weasel, *Mustela frenata*. Hall, 2:993–99.

[Clark]   *December 26th Thursday 1805*

rained and blew hard last night Some hard Thunder, The rain continued as usial all day and wind blew hard from the S. E, Joseph Fields finish a Table & 2 Seats for us. we dry our wet articles and have the blankets fleed, The flees are So troublesom that I have Slept but little for 2 nights past and we have regularly to kill them out of our blankets every day for Several past— maney of the men have ther Powder wet by the horns being repeetdly wet, hut Smoke verry bad.

[Clark]   *Thursday 26th December 1805*

rained and blew with great Violence S E all the last night, Some hard Claps of Thunder, the rain as usial Continued all day— we dry our wet articles before the fire, and have our blankets fleed, great numbers were Caught out of the blankets, those trouble insects are So abundant that we have to have them killd. out of our blankets every day or get no Sleep at night— The powder in maney of the mens horns are wet from their being so long exposed to the rain &c.

[Clark]   *December 27th Friday 1805.*

rained last night as usial and the greater part of this day, the men Complete Chimneys & Bunks to day, in the evening a Chief and 4 men Come of the *Clotsop* nation, Chief [*another spelling of name blotted out*] Co-ma-wool ⟨We order⟩ we Sent out R. Fields & Collins to hunt and order Drewyer, Shannon & Labiach to Set out early to morrow to hunt,— Jo Fields, Bratten, & Gibson to make Salt at Point Addams,— Willard &

Wiser, to assist them in carrying the Kittles &c to the Ocian, and all the others to finish the Pickets and gates. worm weather I Saw a Musquetor[1] which I Showed Capt. Lewis— Those Indians gave is, a black root they Call ⟨Shan-nâ-tock-we⟩ Shan-na-tah que a kind of Licquerish which they rost in embers and Call *Cul ho-mo*, a black berry the Size of a Cherry & Dried which they call *Shel-well*,— all of which they prise highly and make use of as food to live on, ⟨tho⟩ for which Capt Lewis gave the chief a Cap of Sheep Skin and I his Son, ear bobs, Piece of riben, a pice of brass, and 2 Small fishing hooks, of which they were much pleased— Those roots & berres, are greatfull to our Stomcks as we have nothing to eate but Pore Elk meet, nearly Spoiled; & this accident of Spoiled meet, is owing to wormth & the repeeted rains, which cause the meet to tante before we Can get it from the woods Musquetors troublesom

[Clark]   *Friday 27th December 1805*

rained last night as usial and the greater part of this day. In the evening *Co-mo wool* the Chief and 4 men of the *Clat Sop* nation the[y] presented us a root[2] which resembles the licquirish in Size and taste, which they roste like a potato which they Call *Cul ho-mo*, also a black root which is cured in a kill like the *pash-a-co* above; this root has a Sweet taste and the natives are verry fond of it— they Call this root *Shaw-na-tâh-que*. also a dried berry about the size of a Chery which they Call *Shele well* all those roots those Indians value highly and give them verry Spearingly. in return for the above roots Capt Lewis gave the Chief a Small piece of Sheap Skin to Ware on his head, I gave his Son a par of ear bobs and a pece of ribon, and a Small piece of brass for which they were much pleased.

Those roots and berries are timely and extreamly greatfull to our Stomachs, as we have nothing to eate but Spoiled Elk meat, I Showed Capt L. 2 Musquetors to day, or an insect So much the Size Shape and appearance of a Musquetor that we Could observe no kind of differance.

    1. Perhaps crane flies, family Tipulidae.
    2. A line is drawn through this passage about roots. The "*pash-a-co*" mentioned here is camas, *Camassia quamash* (Pursh) Greene. See above, September 20, 1805, for linguistic information.

[Clark] *December 28th Saturday 1805*

rained as usial, a great part of the last night, and this morning rained and the wind blew hard from the S. E. Sent out the hunters and Salt makers,[1] & employd the baleanc of the men Carrying the Pickets &c. &c. ⟨The 2⟩ hunters Sent out yesterday returned, haveing killed one deer near the Sea cost, my boy york verry unwell from violent Colds & Strains Carrying in meet and lifting logs on the huts to build them, This day is worm, and rained all day moderately without intermition.

[Clark] *Saturday the 28th December 1805*

rained as usial the greater part of the last night and a continuation this morning accompanied with wind from the S East Derected Drewyer, Shannon, Labeash, Reuben Field, and Collins to hunt; Jos. Fields, Bratten, Gibson to proceed to the Ocean at Some Convenient place form a Camp and Commence makeing Salt with 5 of the largest Kittles, and Willard and Wiser to assist them in Carrying the Kittles to the Sea Coast— all the other men to be employed about putting up pickets & makeing the gates of the *fort*. my man Y. [York] verry unwell from a violent Coald and Strain by Carrying meet from the woods and lifting the heavy logs on the works &c. rained all Day without intermition. the Weather verry worm.

1. The saltmaking camp was established at present Seaside, Clatsop County, Oregon. It operated until February 21, 1806, and produced about three or four bushels of salt. The personnel varied at the site, but usually about three men were present. Appleman (LC), 196–97, 349, 351; *Atlas* map 84. Clatsop Indians inhabited winter villages at Seaside, moving from their summer villages around Point Adams to this area in the fall. Archaeological investigations in the Seaside area have mainly been conducted at two villages. The Palmrose site was inhabited from approximately 2,700 to 1,700 years ago; occupation apparently then shifted to the nearby Par-tee site which was inhabited from approximately 1,700 to 1,000 years ago. Both sites contained abundant artifacts and faunal remains reflecting the littoral adaptation of the prehistoric inhabitants of the northern Oregon coast. Minor (ASCR), 59; Phebus & Drucker.

[Clark] *December 29th Sunday 1805*

rained last night as usial, this morning ⟨fair⟩ Cloudy without rain a hard wind from the S. E. The Inds. left us this morning and returned to their village, after begging for maney things which they did not secure as

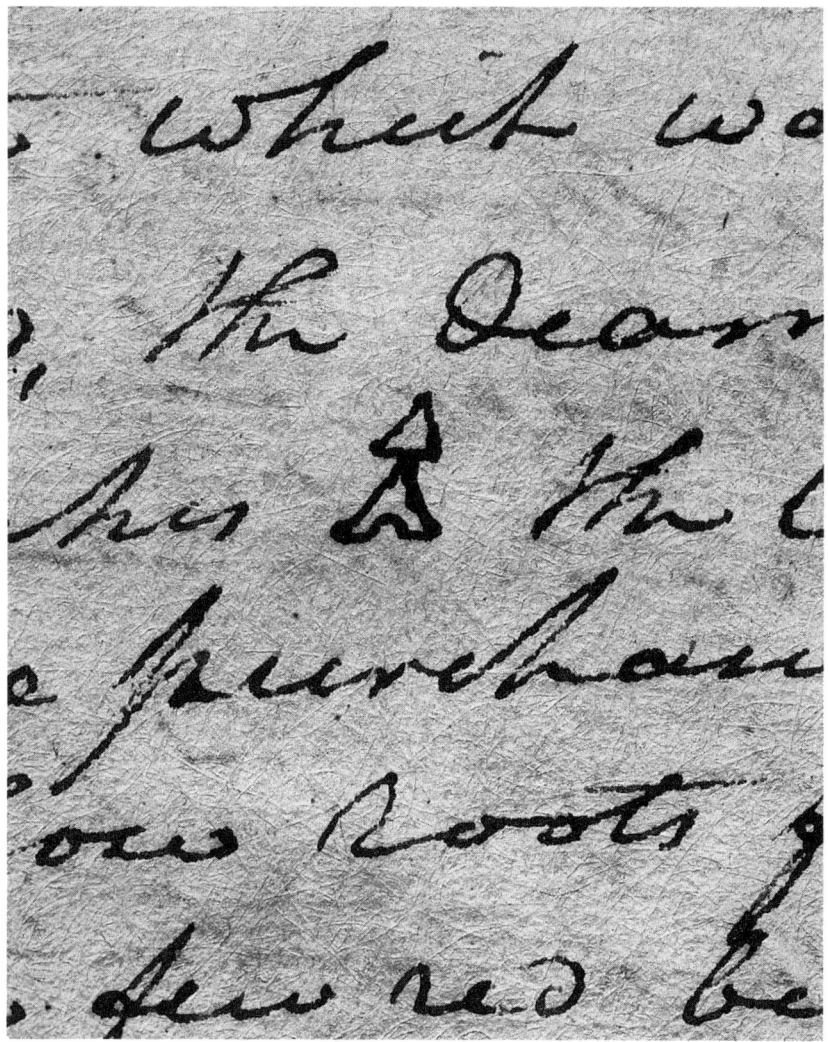

10. Conic Hat, December 29, 1805,
Elkskin-bound Journal

we Could not Spare them   I gave the Chief *Canio*[1] a Razor, Sent out 3 men across the river to hunt, all others employd putting up pickets   Pete Crusat Sick with a violent Cold   My Servent better—   we are told by the Indians that a whale has foundered on the Coast to the N. W[2] and their nations is collecting fat of him, the wind is too high for us to See it, Capt Lewis is been in readiness 2 days to go and Collect Some of the whale oyle   the wind has proved too high as yet for him to Set out in Safty   In the evening a young Chief 4 men and 2 womin of the War-ci-a-cum tribe came in a large canoe with *Wapto* roots, Dressed Elk Skins &c. to Sell, the Chief made me a present of about a half a bushel of those roots—   we gave him a medal of a Small Size and a piece of red ribin to tie around the top of his Hat which was made with a double Cone, the diameter of the upper about 3 Inches[3] the lower a about 1 foot

We purchased about 1 ½ bushels of those roots for which we gave Some few red beeds, Small pices of brass wire and old Check—[4]   those roots proved greatfull to us as we are now liveing on Spoiled Elk which is extreamly disagreeable to the Smel. as well as the taste,

I can plainly discover that a considerable exchange of property is Continually Carried on between the Tribes and villages of those people   they all dress litely   ware nothing ⟨on the⟩ below the waste, a pice of fur abt. around the body, and a Short robe which Composes the total of their dress, except a few Split hats, and beeds around ther necks wrists and anckles, and a few in their ears. They are small and ⟨homely⟩ not handsom generally Speaking women perticularly.

The *Chin nook* womin are lude and Carry on Sport publickly   the Clotsop and others appear deffidend, and reserved

The flees are So noumerous in this Countrey and difficult to get Cleare of that the Indians have difft. houses & villages to which they remove frequently to get rid of them, and not withstanding all their precautions, they never Step into our hut without leaveing Sworms of those troublesom insects.   Indeed I Scercely get to Sleep half the night Clear of the torments of those flees, with the precaution of haveing my blankets Serched and the flees killed every day—   The 1s of those insects we Saw on the Collumbia River was at the 1s Great falls—   I have the Satisfaction to Say that we had but little rain in the Course of this day, ⟨only⟩ not as much as would wet a person.   but hard wind and Cloudy all day.

[Clark]   *Sunday 29th December 1805*

rained all the last night a usial, this morning Cloudy without rain, a hard wind from the S. E   I gave the Cheif a razor, and himself and party left us after begging us for maney articles none of which they recvied as we Could not Spare the articles they were most in want of. Peter Crusat

November 22, 1805 – January 6, 1806

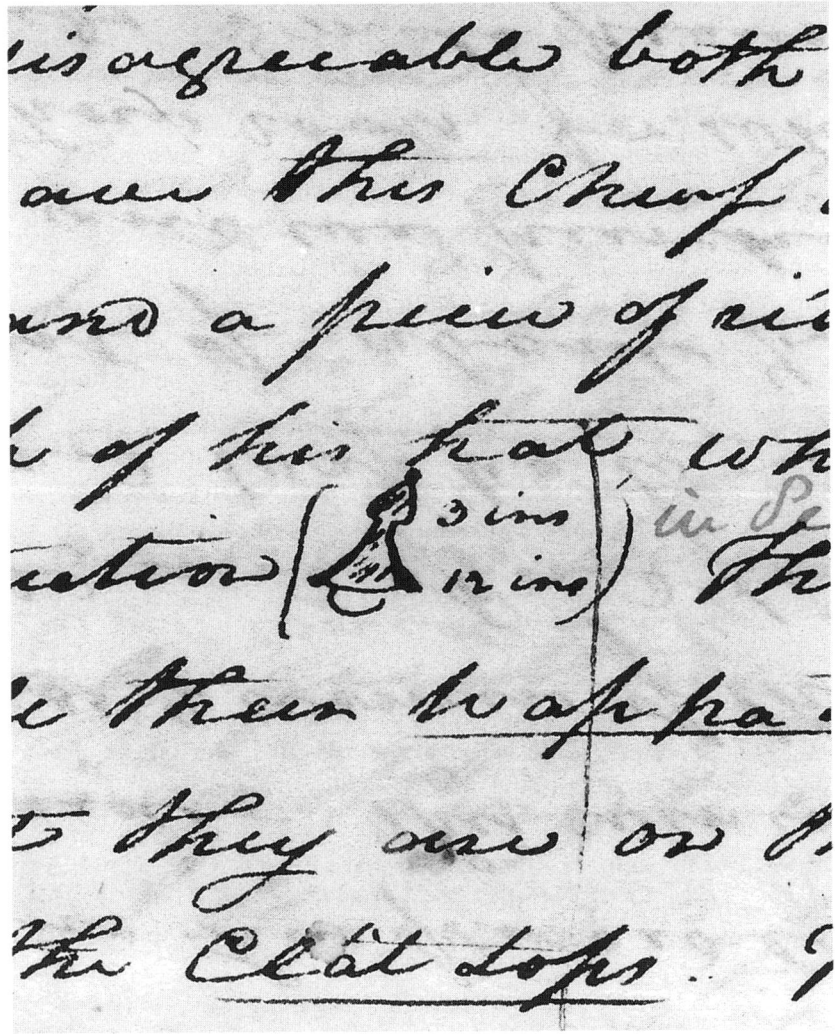

11. Conic Hat, December 29, 1805, Codex I, p. 80

Sick with a violent Cold, my man Y. [York] better. all hands employed about the Pickets & gates of the fort. we were informed day before yesterday that a whale had foundered on the coast to the S. W. near the *Kil a mox* N. and that the greater part of the *Clat Sops* were gorn for the oile & blubber, the wind proves too high for us to proceed by water to See this monster, Capt Lewis has been in readiness Since we first heard of the whale to go and see it and collect Some of its Oil, the wind has proved too high as yet for him to proceed— this evining a young Chief 4 Men and 2 womin of the *War ci a cum* Nation arrived, and offered for Sale Dressed Elk Skins and *Wap pa to*, the Chief made us a preasent of about ½ a bushel of those roots. and we purchased about 1½ bushels of those roots for which we gave Some fiew red beeds Small peaces of brass wire & old Check those roots proved a greatfull addition to our Spoiled Elk, which has become verry disagreeable both to the taste & Smell we gave this Chief a Medal of a Small Size and a piece of red riben to tie around the top of his hat which was of a Singular Construction[5] [*NB: in Peales Museum*][6] Those people will not Sell all their *Wap pa to* to us they inform us that they are on their way to trade with the *Clât Sops*. The nations above Carry on a verry Considerable interchange of property with those in this neighbourhood. they pass altogether by water, they have no roads or pathes through the Countrey which we have observed, except across portages from one Creek to another, all go litely dressed ware nothing below the waste in the Coaldest of weather, a piece of fur around their bodies and a Short roabe Composes the Sum total of their dress, except a few hats, and beeds about their necks arms and legs Small badly made and homely generally. The flees are So noumerous and hard to get rid of; that the Indians have different houses which they resort to occasionally, not withstanding all their precautions they never Step into our house without leaveing Sworms of those tormenting insects; and they torment us in Such a manner as to deprive us of half the nights Sleep frequently— the first of those insects which we saw on the Columbian waters was at the Canoe portage at the great falls. Hard winds & Cloudy all day but verry little rain to day.

1. Probably Coboway. See above, December 12, 1805.
2. "S. W." in the Codex I entry, which is correct, since that was the direction of the "Kil a mox" (Tillamook) people, to which Clark journeyed on January 6, 1806, to see the whale.
3. Here appears a sketch of the hat described (fig. 10). Such hats were typical of the Northwest Coast, and were woven of split cedar bark, sedge, and beargrass. See also below, January 29 and 30, 1806. Gunther (ILNC), 29, 48, 49, 68, 253.
4. Perhaps checked cloth.
5. Here appears another sketch of the conical Indian hat, with dimensions (fig. 11). From this point to the words "homely generally," a vertical line runs through the writing.

6. For Peale and his museum, see above, September 10, 1803. Biddle's note must have been added after the expedition's specimens had gone to the museum.

[Clark] *December 30th Monday 1805*

Hard wind and Some rain last night, this morning fair and the Sun Shown for a Short time   4 Indians Came from the upper Villages   they offered us roots which we did not Chuse to axcept of, as their expectations for those presents of a fiew roots is 3 or 4 times their real worth, those Indians with those of yesterday Continued all day. Drewyer & party of hunters returned and informed they had killed 4 Elk, a party of 6 men was imediately Sent for the meet, they returned at Dusk, with the 4 Elk, of which we had a Sumptious Supper of Elk Tongues & marrow bones which was truly gratifying.

The fort was Completed this evening and at Sun Set we let The Indians know that, our Custom will be to Shut the gates at Sun Set, at which time, they must all go out of the fort   those people who are verry foward and disegreeable, left the huts with reluctiance—   This day proved the best we have had Since at this place, only 3 Showers of rain to day, Cloudy nearly all day, in the evening the wind luled[1] and the fore part of the night fair and clear. I Saw flies & different kinds of insects in motion to day   Snakes are yet to be seen, and Snales without Cover is Common and large,[2] fowls of every kind Common to this quarter abound in the Creek & Bay near us

[Clark] *Monday 30th December 1805*

Hard wind and Some rain last night.   this morning the Sun Shown for a Short time—   four Indians came down from the *War cia cum* Village, they offered us roots which we did not think proper to accept of as in return they expect 3 or 4 times as much as the roots as we Could purchase the Roots for, and are never Satisfied with what they receive, those 4 Indians & these that Came yesterday Stayed all day. Drewyer returned and informed that he had killed 4 Elk at no great distance off, a party of 6 men was imediately dispatched for the meat, and returned at Dusk with the 4 Elk—   we had a Sumptious Supper of Elks tongues & marrow bones which was truly gratifying—   our fortification is Completed this evening—and at Sun Set we let the nativs know that our Custom will be in future, to Shut the gates at Sun Set at which time all Indians must go out of the fort and not return into it untill next morning after Sunrise at which time the gates will be opened, those of the *War ci a cum* Nation who are very foward left the houses with reluctianc this day proved to be the fairest and best which we have had since our arrival at this place, only three Showers dureing this whole day, wind the fore part of the day.

    1. The remainder of this day's entry in the Elkskin-bound Journal comes after the December 31 entry, the link being indicated by the repetition of "luled."
    2. Pacific (or Columbia) woods slug, *Ariolimax columbianus.*

[Clark]   *December 31st Tuesday 1805*[1]
⟨a fair night⟩ A Cloudy night & Some rain, this day proved Cloudy and Some Showers of rain to day all the Indians Continued at their Camp near us, 2 others Canoes Came one from the War-ci-a-cum Village, with three Indians, and the other from higher up the river of the *Skil-lute* nation with three men and a Squar; Those people brought with them Some *Wapto* roots, mats made of flags, & rushes, dried fish and Some fiew *She-ne-tock-we* (or black) roots & Dressed Elk Skins, all of which they asked enormous prices for, particularly the Dressed Elk Skins; I purchased of those people Some *Wapto* roots, two mats and a Small pouch of Tobacco of their own manufactory— for which I gave large fish hooks, which they were verry fond, those Indians are much more reserved and better behaved to day than yesterday— the Sight of our Sentinal who walks on his post, has made this reform in those people who but yesterday was verry impertenant and disagreeable to all— This evening they all Cleared out before the time to Shut the gates, without being derected to doe So— I derected Sinks to be dug and a Sentinal Box which was accomplished
    one of those Indeans brought a Musquet to be repared, which only wanted a Screw flattened, for which he gave me a Peck of Wapto roots, I gave him a flint and a pice of Sheep Skin of which he was pleased—
    January 1st Wednesday *1806* in another book

[Clark]   *Tuesday 31st December 1805*

last night was Cloudy and Some rain, this day prove Cloudy and Showerry all day, all the Indians Continue at their Camp near us, two other Canoes arrived, one from the *War ci â cum* Village with 3 indians and the other of 3 men & a Squar from higher up the river and are of the *Skil-lute* nation, those people brought with them Some *Wappato* roots, mats made of flags and rushes dried fish, and a fiew *Shaw-na tâh-que* and Dressed Elk Skins, all of which they asked enormous prices for, perticularly the dressed Elk Skins, I purchased of those people Some *Wap pa to* two mats and about 3 pipes of their tobacco in a neet little bag made of rushes— This tobacco was much like what we had Seen before with the *So So ne* or Snake indians, for those articles I gave a large fishing hook and Several other Small articles, the fishinghooks they were verry fond of. Those *Skil lutes* are much better behaved than the *War ci a cum* indeed we found a great alteration in the Conduct of them all this morning, the Sight of our Sentinal on his post at the gate, together with our deturmined proseedure of putting all out at Sun Set has made this reform in those *War ci a coms* who is foward impertinant an thieveish.

The nativs all leave us the fort this evening before Sun Set without being told or desired to do So— we had Sinks dug & a Sentinal box made— a *Skil lute* brought a gun which he requested me to have repared, it only wanted a Screw flattened So as to Catch, I put a flint into his gun & he presented me in return a peck of *Wappato* for payment, I gave him piece [*NB: piece*] of a Sheap Skin and a Small piece of blue Cloth to Cover his lock for which he was much pleased and gave me in return Some roots &c.

I Saw flies and different kinds of insects in motion to day— Snakes are yet to be Seen and Snales without Covers is Common and verry large water fowls of various kinds are in great numbers in the rivers and Creeks and the sides of Meriwethers Bay near us but excessively wild—[2] the fore part of this night fair and Clear

With the party of *Clât Sops* who visited us last was a man of much lighter Coloured than the nativs are generaly,[3] he was freckled with long duskey red hair, about 25 years of age, and must Certainly be half white at least, this man appeared to understand more of the English language than the others of his party, but did not Speak a word of English, he possessed all the habits of the indians [4]

1. This is the last daily entry in the Elkskin-bound Journal. Other undated and miscellaneous material from the journal may be found elsewhere in this edition. Clark apparently decided to stop keeping this journal at the end of 1805, later binding the sheets in an elkskin cover. See the Introduction and Appendix C, vol. 2. Four pages follow this entry. The first is blank, the next has some writing in pencil, too faded to decipher but clearly postexpeditionary and in an unknown hand, another blank page, and then the following material in Clark's hand: "To-mar-lar—Grand Chief *Wla lar war lar,* Yel lep pet Chief made a Cheif an gave a Small medal by name of *Ar-lo-quat*—of the Chopunnish Nation—." Yelleppit was chief of the Walulas (Walla Wallas); see above, October 19, 1805. The Nez Perce chief Ar-lo-quat's name is *'álik̄at,* "male mountain goat." The following five words are superimposed over the material above: "Prostitution Carnally Sensuality Lustful Sensual." The exact purpose is unclear, but Clark was presumably thinking about the behavior of the Chinook and Clatsop women and the men of the party. Following that in blue ink is a note obviously added much later: "Presented to J. J. Audubon at St. Louis April 19th 1843—by D. D. Mitchell—Supt—Indian Affairs." See Appendix C, vol. 2.

2. A red vertical line runs through this paragraph to about here, perhaps added by Biddle.

3. Probably the man known to the Astorians as Jack Ramsay, because that name was tattooed on his left arm. His father had deserted or was shipwrecked from a British trading vessel—a very early one, judging from the man's apparent age. An Indian with red hair would have to have inherited genes for the trait from both parents. There are legends, apparently with some basis in fact, that a Spanish ship was shipwrecked in the area, perhaps in 1707, the survivors leaving both red-haired and black descendents, one of whom called himself Soto. Thus the redheaded man Lewis and Clark saw could have had European ancestry on both sides. Cox, 170–71; Franchère (AA), 51; Franchère (JV), 83; Coues (NLEH), 2:768 and n. 33; Ruby & Brown (CITC), 29; Cook, 31–40.

4. About one-quarter of the remainder of the page is blank.

[Lewis and Clark] [*Weather, December 1805*] [1]

Day of the Month	Winds	State of the Weather
1st	E	c. a. r
2nd	S W.	c. a. r
3rd	E	f. a r
4th	S E	r
5th	S W	r
6th	S W.	r
7th	N E	f. a. r

November 22, 1805 – January 6, 1806

8th	N E	C a r²
9th	N E	C. r.
10th	N E	r
11th	S W.	r
12th	S W.	r
13th	S W.	r
14th	S W.	r.
15th	S W.	C. a. r
16th	S W	r.
17th	S W.	f a r. & h
18th	S E	C. a r. s h.
20th	S. W.	f. a r. H.
21st	S W.	r
22nd	S W.	r.
23rd	S W.	r h & L
24th	S. W.	r.
25th	S W.	C. r.
26th	S W.	r. a. t & L
27th	S W.	r
28th	S E	r
29th	S E	c. a r
30th	S E.	f. a. r
31st	S W.	r.

[Remarks]³

1st rained last night and Some this morning.

2nd rained all the last night and untill meridian cloudy the remainder of the day

3rd rained all the last night & to day untill meridan and became fair &c.⁴

4th rained all day

5th rained all last night and today I return to Capt Clark⁵

6th rained last night and all day to day wind not violent in the after part of the day fair in the eving.⁶

7th rained from 10 to 12⁷ and at 2 P M. leave Pt. William

8th Cloudy after a moderate rain last night.

At Fort Clatsop

9th   cloudy and rained moderately untill 3 P M.

10th   a violent wind last night 6 to 9 P M.   river fast with rain. rained all day[8]

11th   rained moderately all last night and to day

12th   do   do   do   do

13th   do   do   do   do

14th   do   do   do   do

15th   rained all last night and untill 8 A. M to day after which it was Cloudy all day.[9]

16th   rained all the last night.   air Cold wind violent from the S W. accompanied with rain.—[10]

17th   rained all last night and to day untill 9 A M when we had a Shower of hail for an hour and Cleared off.

18th   rained Snowed and hailed at intervales all the last night and to day untill meridian.

19th   rained ⟨and hailed⟩ last night and Several Showers of Hail and rain to day.   the air Cool.

20th   Some rain and hail last Night   the rain Contd. untill 10 a. m

21st   rained last night and to day

22nd   do   do   do

23d   rained all last night and moderately to day with Several Showers of Hail accompanied with hard Claps of Thunder and Sharp Lightning.[11]

24th   rained at intervales last night and to day.

25th   do   do   do   do[12]

26th   raind with violent wind all last night and to day with Hard Claps of thunder & Sharp Lightning.

27th   rained moderately last night and to day

28th   do   do   do   do

29th   do   do   do   do untill 7 a.m. after Cloudy the remained of the day   wind hard from the S E.[13]

30th   Hard wind & rain last night.   to day tolerably fair.

31st   rained last night and moderately all day to day.

1. Lewis's weather table and remarks are in Voorhis No. 4; Clark's are in Codex I. This table follows Lewis.
2. Clark has "C."
3. Lewis's remarks in Voorhis No. 4 are in the margin of his weather table; Clark's are separate. Lewis's remarks are followed here, with significant differences in Clark's remarks noted.
4. Clark writes, "fair from 12 to 2 P M. rained all the last night & this morning. rained the night of the 1st and morning of the 2 and Cloudy the remainder of the day. rained at intervals the night of the 2d instant with constant hard and Sometimes violent winds."
5. Clark writes, "rained yesterday, last night, and moderately to day; all day wind violent in the after part of the day. Capt Lewis joined me from below." Some of the punctuation may be a later addition.
6. Clark writes, "rained all last night and to day untill 6 oClock at which time it Clear'd away and became far. the winds also Seased to blow violent."
7. From here Clark has, "last night fair day leave Point William a hard wind from the N W. and a Shower of rain at 2 P M."
8. Clark says, "rained all day and the air cool I return from the Ocean a violent wind last night from the S W. rained the greater part of the night of the 8th and all day the 9th int."
9. Clark says, "rained a[t] Short intervals from the 10th instant untill 8 A. M. to day I with 16 men Set out after meat."
10. Clark adds, "return with 16 Elk."
11. Clark adds, "rained 21 & 22 all day & night."
12. Clark repeats the words from the previous day and has also "(in our Huts)."
13. Clark writes, "rained moderately without much intermittion from the 26th untill 7 a m. this morning hard wind from the S. E."

Fort Clatsop 1806.

[Lewis]   *January 1st Tuesday.* [Wednesday]¹

This morning I was awoke at an early hour by the discharge of a volley of small arms, which were fired by our party in front of our quarters to usher in the new year; this was the only mark of rispect which we had it in our power to pay this celebrated day. our repast of this day tho' better than that of Christmass, consisted principally in the anticipation of the 1st day of January 1807, when in the bosom of our friends we hope to participate in the mirth and hilarity of the day, and when with the zest

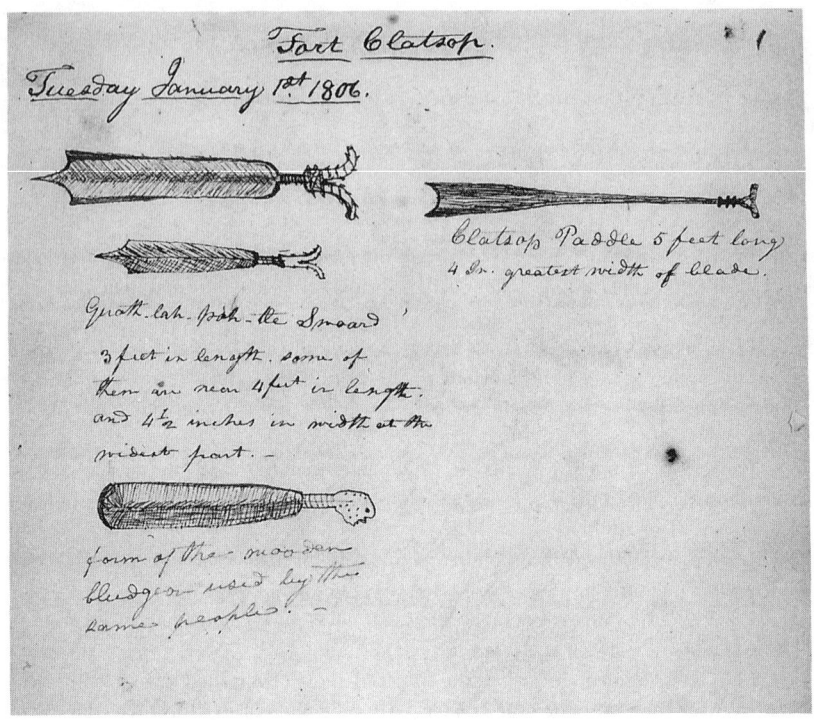

12. Two Swords, a Bludgeon, and a Paddle,
January 1, 1806, Codex J, p. 1

given by the recollection of the present, we shall completely, both mentally and corporally, enjoy the repast which the hand of civilization has prepared for us. at present we were content with eating our boiled Elk and wappetoe, and solacing our thirst with our only beverage *pure water*. two of our hunters who set out this morning reterned in the evening having killed two bucks elk; they presented Capt. Clark and myself each a marrow-bone and tonge, ⟨each⟩ on which we suped. visited today by a few of the Clotsops who brought some roots and burries for the purpose of trading with us. we were uneasy with rispect to two of our men, Willard and Wiser, who were dispatched on the 28th ulto. with the saltmakers, and were directed to return immediately; their not having returned induces us to believe it probable that they have missed their way.— our fourtification being now completed we issued an order for the more exact and uniform dicipline and government of the garrison. (see orderly book 1st January 1806).—

[Clark] *January 1st Wednesday 1806*[2]

This morning proved cloudy with moderate rain, after a pleasent worm night during which there fell but little rain— This morning at Day we wer Saluted from the party without, wishing us a "hapy new year" a Shout and discharge of their arms— no Indians to be Seen this morning— they left the place of their encampment dureing the last night— The work of our houses and fort being now Complete, we Ishued an order in which we pointed out the rules & regulations for the government of the Party in respect to the Indians as also for the Safty and protection of our Selves &c.

two Clotsops Came with a mat and Some fiew roots of Cut wha mo, for which they asked a file they did not trade but Continued all night

Sent out 2 hunters this morning who returned, haveing killed 2 Elk about 3 miles distant, Some fiew Showers of rain in the Course of this day. Cloudy all the day.

Fort Clatsop 1806
[Clark] *Wednesday the 1st of January*

This morning I was awoke at an early hour by the discharge of a Volley of Small arms, which were fired by our party in front of our quarters to usher in the new year, this was the only mark of respect which we had it in our power to pay this Selibrated day. our repast of this day tho' better than that of Christmas Consisted principally in the anticipation of the 1st day of January 1807, when in the bosom of our friends we hope to participate in the mirth and hilarity of the day, and when with the relish given by the recollection of the present, we Shall Completely, both mentally and Corparally, the repast which the hand of Civilization has produced for us. at present we were Content with eating our boiled Elk and *Wappato*, and Solacing our thirst with our only beverage *pure water*. two of our hunters who Set out this morning returned in the evening haveing killed two Buck Elks; they presented Capt. Lewis and my Self each a marrow bone and tongue on which we Suped— we are visited to day by a fiew of the Clatsops by water they brought some roots and berries for the purpose of tradeing with us. our fortification being now Complete we issue an order for the more exact and uniform dicipline and government of the garrison. (See orderly book Jany 2d 1806)[3]

At Fort Clatsop

[Clark]   [*undated, December 1805–January 1806*]⁴

A List of the Tribes near the mouth of the Columbia river as given by the Indians, the Places they reside, the names of the Tribes and principal Chiefs of each all of which speak the same language⁵

1st *Clot-sop* Tribe in Several Small villages on the Sea Cost to the S. E. of the Mouth & on the S. E. bank of the Columbia river—not noumerous

  1st Chief *Con-ni a* Co-mo-wool

  2 do *Sha-no-ma*

  3 do *War-ho-lote*

2nd *Chin-nook* Tribe reside opposit on the N. W. Side & in Small villages & Single houses made of Split boards on a Creek of Haleys bay, and on Small lakes or ponds, at no great distance from the river or bay. Tolerably noumerous—so said

☞ Chinnook

  1st Chief is *Stock-home*

  2d do *Com-com-mo-ley*

  3 do *Shil-lar-la-wit*

  4 do *Nor-car-te*

  5 do *Chin-ni-ni*

3rd *Chiltch* Tribe reside ⟨on⟩ near the Sea Coast & north of the *Chinnooks* live in houses and is said to be noumerous Speak same Language

  1st Chief *Mar-lock-ke*

  2d do *Col-chote*

  3rd do *Ci-in-twar*

4th *Ca-la-mox* Tribe reside on the Sea coast to the S. E of the Columbia River and on a Small river,⁶ and as I am informed by the *Clot-sops* inhabit 10 Villages 6 of them on the ocian & 4 on the Little river, those Ca-la-mox are said not to be noumerous Speake the Clotsop language

  1st Chief *O-co-no*

5th *Calt-har-mar* Tribe reside in one village of large Houses built of Split boards and neetly made, on the S. E. Side of the Columbia River, behind a Island in a Deep bend of the River to the S. E. they are not noumerous, and live as the others do on fish, black roots Lickuerish berries, and *Wap-pe-to* roots, and is as low as those Wapeto roots grow, which is about 15 miles on a Direct line from the Sea.

    1st Chief *Clax-ter* at war against the
    Snake Inds. to the S of the falls
    2d   do   *Cul-te-ell*
    3   do   [blank] at war   Do.

6th *Clax-ter* Nation[7]   This nation reside on [blank] Side of the Columbia River in [blank] villages above about [blank] and are ⟨said to be⟩ noumerous   they latterly ⟨resided⟩ floged the Chinnooks, and are a Dasterly Set
            1st and Great Chief *Qui oo*

7th ⟨Scum as qua up⟩ *War-ci-a-cum* Tribe reside on the N W. Side of the Columbia in the great bend behind Some Islands   this tribe is not noumerous   reside in 2 village of Houses
            The Chief *Scum ar-qua-up*

[Clark]   *January 1st 1806*[8]

A List of the names of Sundery persons, who visit this part of the Coast for the purpose of trade &c. &c. in large Vestles; all of which Speake the English language &c.—as the Indians inform us

Moore[9]	☞	Visit them in a large 4 masted Ship, they expect him in 2 moons to trade.—
1 Eyd. *Skellie*	☞	in a large Shit, long time gorn.—
Youin[10]	☞	In a large Ship, and they expect him in 1 moon to trade with them.—
Swepeton	☞	In a Ship, they expect him in 3 month back to trade—
Mackey[11]	☞	In a Ship, they expect him back in 1 or 2 moons to trade with them.—
Meship[12]	☞	In a Ship, the[y] expect him 2 moons to trade.—
Jackson	☞	Visit them in a Ship and they expect him back in 3 months to trade.—
Balch[13]	☞	In a Ship and they expect him in 3 months to trade.—
Mr. *Haley*[14]		Visits them in a Ship & they expect him back to trade with them in 3 moons to trade— he is the favourite of the Indians (from the number of Presents he givs) and has the trade principaly with all the tribes,—
Washilton[15]		In a Skooner, they expect him in 3 months to return and trade with them— a favourite.—

Lemon	In a Slupe, and they expect him in 3 moons to trade with them.—
Davidson[16]	Visits this part of the Coast and river in a Brig for the purpose of Hunting the Elk returns when he pleases he does not trade any, Kills a great maney Elk &c &—.
⟨*Washilton*⟩ *Fallawan*[17]	In a Ship with guns he fired on & killed Several Indians, he does not trade now and they doe not know when he will return, well done

A List of the Names as given by the Indias of the Traders Names and the quallity of their Vessels which they Say visit the mouth of the Columbia 2 [times] a year for the purpose of Tradeing with the nativs, and from their accounts Spring and autumn—

Mr. Haley	their favourite Trader visits them in a 3 masted vessel			
Youens	visits in a 3 Masted vessle—			
Tallamon	do	3	do	no trade
Swipton	do	3	do	Trader
Moore	do	4	do	do
Mackey	do	3	do	do
Washington	do	3	do	do
Meship	do	3	do	do
Davidson	do	2	do	Hunts Elk
Jackson	do	3	do	Trader
Bolch	do	3	do	do
Skelley	has been along time gorn—			one Eye
Callallamet	do	3		Trader has a wooden Leg.

[Lewis]   *Fort Clatsop, January 1st 1806*[18]

The fort being now completed, the Commanding officers think proper to direct: that the guard shall as usual consist of one Sergeant and three privates, and that the same be regularly relieved each morning at sunrise.   The post of the new guard shall be in the room of the Sergeants rispectivly commanding the same.   the centinel shall be posted, both day and night, on the parade in front of the commanding offercers quarters; tho' should he at any time think proper to remove himself to any other part of the fort, in order the better to inform himself of the desighns or approach of any party of savages, he is not only at liberty, but is hereby required to do so. It shall be the duty of the centinel also to announce the arrival of all parties of Indians to the Sergeant of the Guard, who shall immediately report the same to the Commanding officers.

The Commanding Officers require and charge the Garrison to treat the natives in a friendly manner; nor will they be permitted at any time, to abuse, assault or strike them; unless such abuse assault or stroke be first given by the natives. nevertheless it shall be right for any individual, in a peaceable manner, to refuse admittance to, or put out of his room, any native who may become troublesome to him; and should such native refuse to go when requested, or attempt to enter their rooms after being forbidden to do so; it shall be the duty of the Sergeant of the guard on information of the same, to put such native out of the fort and see that he is not again admitted during that day unless specially permitted; and the Sergeant of the guard may for this purpose imploy such coercive measures (not extending to the taking of life) as shall at his discretion be deemed necessary to effect the same.

When any native shall be detected in theft, the Sergt. of the guard shall immediately inform the Commanding offercers of the same, to the end that such measures may be pursued with rispect to the culprit as they shall think most expedient.

At sunset on each day, the Sergt. attended by the interpreter Charbono and two of his guard, will collect and put out of the fort, all Indians except such as may specially be permitted to remain by the Commanding offercers, nor shall they be again admitted untill the main gate be opened the ensuing morning.

At Sunset, or immediately after the Indians have been dismissed, both gates shall be shut, and secured, and the main gate locked and continue so untill sunrise the next morning: the water-gate may be used freely by the Garrison for the purpose of passing and repassing at all times, tho' from sunset, untill sunrise, it shall be the duty of the centinel, to open the gate for, and shut it after all persons passing and repassing, suffering the same never to remain unfixed long than is absolutely necessary.

It shall be the duty of the Sergt. of the guard to keep the kee of the Meat house, and to cause the guard to keep regular fires therein when the same may be necessary; and also once at least in 24 hours to visit the canoes and see that they are safely secured; and shall further on each morning after he is relieved, make his report verbally to the Commandg officers.—

Each of the old guard will every morning after being relieved furnish two loads of wood ⟨each⟩ for the commanding offercers fire.

No man is to be particularly exempt from the duty of bringing meat from the woods, nor none except the Cooks and Interpreters from that of mounting guard.

Each mess being furnished with an ax, they are directed to deposit in the room of the commanding offercers all other public tools of which they are possessed; nor ⟨are⟩ shall the same at any time hereafter be taken from the said deposit without the knoledge and permission of the commanding officers; and any individual so borrowing the tools are strictly required to bring the same back the moment he has ceased to use them, and no case shall they be permited to keep them out all night.

Any individual selling or disposing of any tool or iron or steel instrument, arms, accoutrements or ammunicion, shall be deemed guilty of a breach of this order, and shall be tryed and punished accordingly.— the tools loaned to John Shields are excepted from the restrictions of this order.

Meriwether Lewis
Capt. 1st U. S. Regt.
Wm. Clark Capt. &c

1. Here begins Lewis's notebook Codex J; on p. 1 before this date are sketches of various Indian implements with captions (fig. 12), p. 2 is blank, then follows the January 1 entry on p. 3. This journal runs to March 20, 1806, covering most of the period at Fort Clatsop, and is one of the richest in natural history and ethnographical data. Clark's Codex I from this point copies Lewis almost verbatim, though not always under the same date. See the Introduction and Appendix C, vol. 2.

2. Clark has additional short entries for January 1, 2, and 3, 1806, in Codex I, pp. 145–46, reading backwards, and following the final entry of January 29. These were probably first drafts before he gave up keeping this journal until some time later when he took up copying Lewis. See the Introduction and Appendix C, vol. 2, and note at January 29, 1806.

3. There is no entry in the Orderly Book for January 2. The last entry in the notebook is on January 1 (see below) and deals with the matters mentioned here. It was apparently Biddle who underlined this passage in red ink.

4. This undated list is found in the Elkskin-bound Journal between the entries of De-

cember 7–8, 1805. Since it is more in the nature of the list of trading captains which follows it in the field book and here, and since that item is dated January 1, 1806, we have placed this tribal material here.

5. After this paragraph are the following numbers, written upside down.

$$\begin{array}{r} 82 \\ 122 \\ 68 \\ \underline{29} \\ [321?] \end{array}$$

Some of these Indians' names may be identified linguistically (all are in the Chinook language):

Clot-sop (Clatsops, see note at November 21, 1805)
    Sha-no-ma, *Šanuma*
    War-ho-lote, *Waxalut*

Chin-nook (Chinooks, see note at November 15, 1805)
    Stock-home, *Ṫawkum*
    Com-com-mo-ley, *Qanqṁli*
    Shil-lar-la-wit, *Šilalawit*
    Nor-car-te, *Nuxkati[x]*
    Chin-ni-ni, *Činini*

Chiltch (Chehalis, see note at November 21, 1805)
    The chiefs' names are unidentifiable.

Ca-la-mox (Tillamooks, see note at January 8, 1806)
    The chief's name is unidentifiable.

Calt-har-mar (Cathlamets, see note at November 11, 1805)
    Clax-ter (see note under tribal name in this entry)
    Cul-te-ell, *Q̇lti il(x)*

Clax-ter (see note under tribal name in this entry)
    Quioo, *K^{w}iu*

War-ci-a-cum (Wahkiakums, see note at November 7, 1805)
    Scumar-qua-up, *Sqamuk^{w}ia*

6. The Necanicum River in southwest Clatsop County, Oregon, "⟨Kilamox River⟩" and "Clatsop River" on *Atlas* map 84.

7. The identity of the Claxter Indians, or more commonly Claxstar, is not completely clear. They are generally considered to have been the Athapascan-speaking Clatskanies. Berreman, 17; Hajda, 106–7, 113–14. In fact, the name may not refer to a tribal designation at all but to the Chinookan term *[t]ła'aqštaq*, which means "round heads," and which is a derisive term applied to slaves and others who were not permitted to deform their heads in the Chinookan manner. Lewis and Clark seemed to have misconstrued the word as a village or tribal name here and as a personal name for a Cathlamet chief at another place in this entry.

8. This list of trading captains and their ships in the Elkskin-bound Journal appears between the entries of December 7 and 8 and is placed by date. The following less de-

tailed list appears in Codex I, p. 156, reading backwards, and is brought together with the other. The list from Codex I is nearly identical to one by Lewis on March 16, 1806. (See note at January 29, 1806.) Both lists here are in Clark's hand. Obviously the captains gathered this information from the Indians at the mouth of the Columbia. We have made an attempt to identify these men from what information is available about early trading ventures in the area. Lewis and Clark evidently understood that these skippers had been at the mouth of the Columbia recently, which is not the case, so far as the record shows, with some of the men referred to in these notes. Some of them may have made other voyages which are not in the records, or the language barrier may have confused the information, although many of the Indians had some English. The principal source is the researches of Frederick W. Howay.

9. Captain Hugh Moore of the British barque *Phoenix*, out of Bengal, was on the Northwest Coast in 1792 and 1794. He was an exceedingly mysterious character, and may have continued in the trade. See also below, February 13, 1806. Ruby & Brown (CITC), 66, 107; Howay (1930), 120–21, 127, 133.

10. In 1792 Vancouver encountered a number of ships trading on the coast, among them the British schooner *Prince William Henry*. Her captain was Ewens, or Ewen, described as a master in the British navy, presumably not in service in peacetime. He may have returned to the coast on unrecorded occasions. Menzies, 124–25, 129; Howay (1930), 127.

11. Vancouver also encountered the American ship *Margaret*, out of Boston, commanded by McGee, or Magee. Menzies, 124–25; Howay (1930), 127.

12. Captain Charles Winship's brigantine *Betsy*, of Boston, was on the Northwest Coast in 1800. Since Winship was arrested by the Spanish in San Diego and died in Mexico that same year, he could not have been one of the traders who regularly returned to the Columbia; there may have been a language problem at this point. However, there were several Winships engaged in the trade. Jonathan Winship, one of the owners of the ship *O'Cain*, of New York, was on board during her trading and sea otter hunting ventures, ranging from California to Alaska, in 1803–4. He very likely conducted trading operations, rather than Captain Joseph O'Cain. Howay (1931), 133, 147, 149; Howay (1932), 54.

13. Perhaps Captain William Bowles of the ship *Mary*, of Boston, who was trading on the coast in 1802–3. Howay (1931), 146–67.

14. For Haley, see above, November 6, 1805.

15. The Indians seem to have remembered the names of captains, not of ships. However, the *Lady Washington*, of Boston, a small sloop of ninety tons, was a companion of Robert Gray's *Columbia Rediviva* (and for a time commanded by Gray) and was on the coast in 1788, 1789, 1791, and 1792. Why Gray's name was never mentioned to Lewis and Clark is impossible to say. Howay (1930), 117–19, 122; Menzies, 125.

16. The only Davidson known to have been in the Northwest Coast trade was the commander of the schooner *Rover* of Boston, which sailed for the coast in 1799 and is thought to have been lost at sea, perhaps in June 1801. He could not have been returning regularly to the Columbia, but here again there may have been a language problem. Howay (1931), 134.

17. Probably the "Tallamon" of the second list. He could be the "Callamon" later re-

ported trading with the Makah at Cape Flattery (see below, March 14, 1806); if so, the latter would not be the wooden-legged "Callalamet."

18. The last detachment order in the Orderly Book.

[Lewis]   *Thursday, January 2nd 1806*

Sent out a party of men and brought in the two Elk which were killed yesterday. Willard and Wiser have not yet returned nor have a party of hunters returned who set out on the 26th Ulto. the Indians who visited yesterday left us at 1 P M today after having disposed of their roots and berries for a few fishinghooks and some other small articles. we are infested with swarms of flees already in our new habitations; the presumption is therefore strong that we shall not devest ourselves of this intolerably troublesome vermin during our residence here. The large, and small or whistling swan, sand hill Crane, large and small gees, brown and white brant, Cormorant, duckan mallard, Canvisback duck, and several other species of ducks, still remain with us; tho' I do not think that they are as plenty as on our first arrival in the neighbourhood. Drewyer visited his traps and took an otter.¹ the fur of both the beaver and otter in this country are extreemly good; those annamals are tolerably plenty near the sea coast, and on the small Creeks and rivers as high as the grand rappids, but are by no means as much so as on the upper part of the Missouri.

[Clark]   *January 2nd Thursday 1806.*

A Cloudy rainey morning after a wet night. dispatched 12 Men for the two Elk Killed yesterday which they brought in at 11 oClock. the day proved Cloudy and wet, the Indians left us at 1 oClock P. M, Drewyer visited his traps which had one otter in one of them. The flees are verry troublesom, our huts have alreadey Sworms of those disagreeable insects in them, and I fear we Shall not get rid of them dureing our delay at this place.

[Clark]   *Thursday 2nd of January 1806.*

Sent out a party of men and brought in the two Elk which was killed yesterday. Willard & Wiser have not yet returned nor have a party of hunters who Set out on the 26th ulto: the Indians who visited us yesterday left us at 1 P. M to day after haveing disposed of their roots and berries for a fiew fishing hooks and Some other Small articles. we are infestd. with Sworms of flees already in our new habatations; the presumption is therefore Strong that we Shall not devest our Selves of this intolerably troublesom vermin dureing our residence here. The large, & Small or whistling Swan, Sand hill crane, large & Small Gees, brown and white brant, Comorant, Duckanmallard, canvis back duck, and Several other Species of Ducks Still remain with us;[2] tho' I doe not think they are as plenty as on our first arrival in the neighbourhood. Drewyer visit his traps at took out an otter. the fur of both the beaver and otter as also the rackoon in this countrey are extreemly good; those animals are tolerably plenty near the Sea coast, on the Small creeks and rivers as high as the grand Rapids.—

1. Otter, *Lutra canadensis*. Burroughs, 75–76.
2. A red vertical line is drawn through this passage about birds, perhaps by Biddle.

[Lewis] *Friday January 3d 1806.*

At 11 A. M. we were visited by our near neighbours, Chief or Tiá,[1] Co-mo-wool; alias Conia and six Clatsops. the[y] brought for sale some roots buries and three dogs also a small quantity of fresh blubber. this blubber they informed us they had obtained from their neighbours the Callamucks[2] who inhabit the coast to the S. E. near whose vilage a whale had recently perished. this blubber the Indians eat and esteeme it excellent food. our party from necessaty having been obliged to subsist some lenth of time on dogs have now become extreemly fond of their flesh; it is worthy of remark that while we lived principally on the flesh of this anamal we were much more healthy strong and more fleshey than we had been since we left the Buffaloe country. for my own part I have become so perfectly reconciled to the dog that I think it an agreeable food and would prefer it vastly to lean Venison or Elk. a small Crow,[3] the blue crested Corvus and the smaller corvus with a white brest,[4] the little brown ren,[5] a large brown sparrow,[6] the bald Eagle and the beatifull Buzzard of the columbia still continue with us.— Sent Sergt. Gass and George shannon to the saltmakers who are somewhere on the coast to the S. W. of us, to enquire after Willard and Wiser who have not yet returned. Reubin Fields Collins and Pots the hunters who set out on the 26th [*EC?:*

28] Ulto. returned this evening after dark. they reported that they had been about 15 Miles up the river at the head of the bay just below us and had hunted the country from thence down on the East side of the river, even to a considerable distance from it and had proved unsuccessfull having killed one deer and a few fowls, barely as much as subsisted them. this reminded us of the necessity of taking time by the forelock,[7] and keep out several parties while we have yet a little meat beforehand.— I gave the Chief Comowooll a pare of sattin breechies with which he appeared much pleased.—

[Clark] *January 3rd Friday 1806*

The Sun rose fair this morning for the first time for Six weeks past, the Clouds Soon obscure it from our view, and a Shower of rain Suckceeded— last night we had Sharp lightening a hard thunder Suckceeded with heavy Showers of hail, and rain, which Continud with intervales of fair moon Shine dureing the night. Sent out Sergt. Gass & 2 men to the Salt makers with a vew to know what is the Cause of the delay of 2 of our party *Willard* & *Wiser* who we are uneasy about, as they were to have been back 6 days ago.

[Clark] *Friday the 3rd January 1806*

At 11 A. m. we were visited by our near neighbour Chief (or *Tiá*)[8] *Co mo wool* alias *Conia* [NB: *Coônê*] and Six Clat sops. they brought for Sale Some roots berries and 3 Dogs also a Small quantity of fresh blubber. this blubber they informed us they had obtained from their neighbours the *Cal lá mox* who inhabit the coast to the S. E near one of their Villages a Whale had recently perished. this blubber the Indians eat and esteem it excellent food. our party from necescity have been obliged to Subsist Some length of time on dogs have now become extreamly fond of their flesh; it is worthey of remark that while we lived principally on the flesh of this animal we wer much more helthy Strong and more fleshey then we have been Sence we left the Buffalow Country. as for my own part I have not become reconsiled to the taste of this animal as yet. a Small Crow, the blue Crested Corvus and the Smaller Corvus with a white breast, the little brown ren, and a large brown Sparrow, the bald Eagle, and the butifull Buzzard of the Columbia Still Continue with us,[9] Send

Sarjt. Gass and G. Shannon to the Salt makers who are on the Sea Coast to the S, W. of us, to enquire after Willard & Wiser who have not yet returned. R. Field, potts & Collins the hunters who Set out on the 28th ulto. returned this evening after dark. they reported that they had been about 15 miles up the river which falls into Meriwethers Bay to the East of us,[10] and had hunted the Country a considerable distance to East, and had proved unsucksesfull haveing killed one Deer and a fiew fowls, bearly as much as Subsisted them. this reminded us of the necessity of takeing time by the forelock, and keep out Several parties while we have yet a little meat beforehand. Capt Lewis gave the Cheif Cania a par of Sattin breechies with which he appeared much pleased.—

1. In Chinookan the term is *tia*. In the Chinook jargon it is *táyi*, which is borrowed from the Nootkan word *ta·yi·*; all mean "chief."
2. The Tillamooks; the direction should be southwest.
3. Probably the northwestern crow, *Corvus caurinus* [AOU, 489], a new species. See also March 3, 1806. Cutright (LCPN), 273, 432; Holmgren, 29. Perhaps it was Biddle who drew a red vertical line through this passage about birds.
4. Probably the gray jay; see above, December 18, 1805.
5. Perhaps the winter wren.
6. Possibly the golden-crowned sparrow, *Zonotrichia atricapilla* [AOU, 557]. Burroughs, 258. The fox sparrow, *Passerella iliaca* [AOU, 585], has also been suggested. Holmgren, 33.
7. In Roman mythology Opportunity, or Time (Saturn), was represented as having hair on the front of the head, but being bald behind. The expression has been used by Rabelais, Spenser, and Shakespeare.
8. Perhaps it was Biddle who added the red-inked parentheses around "or Tiá."
9. Biddle may have drawn the red vertical line through this passage about birds.
10. Youngs River, Clatsop County, Oregon. *Atlas* map 82.

[Lewis] *Saturday January 4th 1806.*

Comowooll and the Clatsops who visited us yesterday left us in the evening. These people the Chinnooks and others residing in this neighbourhood and speaking the same language have been very friendly to us; they appear to be a mild inoffensive people but will pilfer if they have an opportuny to do so where they conceive themselves not liable to detection. they are great higlers in trade and if they conceive you anxious to purchase will be a whole day bargaining for a handfull of roots; this I should have thought proceeded from their want of knowledge of the comparitive value of articles of merchandize and the fear of being cheated, did I not find that they invariably refuse the price first offered them and afterwards very frequently accept a smaller quantity of the same article; in order to satisfy myself on this subject I once offered a Chinnook my watch two knives and a considerable quantity of beads for a small inferior sea Otter's[1] skin which I did not much want, he immediately conceived it of great value, and refused to barter except I would double the quantity of beads; the next day with a great deal of importunity on his part I received the skin in exchange for a few strans of the same beads he had refused the day before. I therefore believe this trait in their character proceeds from an avaricious all grasping disposition.   in this rispect they differ from all Indians I ever became acquainted with, for their dispositions invariably lead them to give whatever they are possessed off no matter how usefull or valuable, for a bauble which pleases their fancy, without consulting it's usefullness or value.   nothing interesting occurred today, or more so, than our wappetoe being all exhausted.

[Clark]   Saturday 4th January 1806

Comowool and the Clatsops who visited us yesterday left us in the morning. Those people the *Chinnook* and others resideing in this neighbourhood and Speaking the Same language have been very friendly to us; they appear to be a mild inoffensive people but will pilfer if they have an oppertunity to do So when they Conceive themselves not liable to detection.   they are great higlers in trade and if they Conceive you anxious to purchase will be a whole day bargaining for a hand full of roots; this I Should have thought proceeded from their want of Knowledge of the Comparitive value of articles of merchindize and the fear of being Cheated, did I not find that they invariably refuse the price first offered them and afterwards very frequently accept a Smaller quantity of the Same article; in order to Satisfy myself on this point, I onc[e] offered a Clatsop man my watch a knife, a Dollar of the Coin of U State and hand full of beads, for a Small Sea otter Skin, which I did not much want, he immediately Conceived it of great value, and refused to Sell unless I would give as maney more ⟨blue⟩ beads; the next day with a great deel of importunity on his part we receved the Skin in exchange for a fiew Strans of the Same beeds he had refused the day before.   I therefore beleive this treat in their Charector proceeds from an avcricious all grasping disposition. in this respect they differ from all Indians I ever became acquainted with, for their dispositions invariably lead them to give what ever they are possessed off no matter how usefull or valueable, for a bauble which pleases their fancy, without Consulting its usefullness or value. nothing occured to day, or more So, than our *wappato* being all exhausted.

1. The sea otter, *Enhydra lutris*.

[Lewis] *Sunday January 5th 1806.*

At 5 P. M. Willard and Wiser returned, they had not been lost as we apprehended. they informed us that it was not untill the fifth day after leaving the Fort that they could find a convenient place for making salt; that they had at length established themselves on the coast about 15 Miles S. W. from this, near the lodge of some Killamuck families; that the Indians were very friendly and had given them a considerable quantity of the blubber of a whale which perished on the coast some distance S. E. of them; part of this blubber they brought with them, it was white & not unlike the fat of Poark, tho' the texture was more spongey and somewhat coarser. I had a part of it cooked and found it very pallitable and tender, it resembled the beaver or the dog in flavour. it may appear somewhat extraordinary tho' it is a fact that the flesh of the beaver and dog possess a very great affinity in point of flavour. These lads also informed us that J. Fields, Bratton and Gibson (the Salt makers) had with their assistance erected a comfortable camp killed an Elk and several deer and secured a good stock of meat; they commenced the making of salt and found that they could obtain from 3 quarts to a gallon a day; they brought with them a specemine of the salt of about a gallon, we found it excellent, fine, strong, & white; ⟨salt;⟩ this was a great treat to myself and most of the party, having not had any since the 20th ultmo.; I say most of the party, for my friend Capt. Clark declares it to be a mear matter of indifference with him whether he uses it or not; for myself I must confess I felt a considerable inconvenience from the want of it; the want of bread I consider as trivial provided, I get fat meat, for as to the species of meat I am not very particular, the flesh of the dog the horse and the wolf, having from habit become equally formiliar with any other, and I have learned to think that if the chord be sufficiently strong, which binds the soul and boddy together, it dose not so much matter about the materials which compose it. Colter also returned this evening unsuccessfull from the chase, having been absent since the 1st Inst.— Capt. Clark determined this evening to set out early tomorrow with two canoes and 12 men[1] in quest of the whale, or at all events to purchase from the Indians a parcel of the blubber, for this purpose he prepared a small assortment of merchandize to take with him.

[Clark] *Sunday 5th of January 1806*

At 5 p. m. Willard and Wiser returned, they had not been lost as we expected. they informd us that it was not untill the 5th day after leaveing the fort, that they Could find a Convenient place for makeing Salt; that they had at length established themselves on the Sea Coast about 15 miles S. W. from this, near the houses of Some Clat Sop & Kil a mox families; that the Indians were very friendly and had given them a considerable quantity of the blubber of the whale which perished on the Coast Some distance S. E. of them, it was white and not unlike the fat of Pork, tho' the texture was more Spungey and Somewhat Coarser. we had part of it Cooked and found it very pallitable and tender, it resembles the beaver in flavour. those men also informed us that the Salt makers with their assistance had erected a Comfortable Camp, had killed an Elk and Several Deer and Secured a good Stock of Meat; they Commenced the makeing of Salt and found that they Could make from 3 quarts to a gallon a day; they brought with them a Specimen of the Salt, of about a gallon, we found it excellent white & fine, but not So Strong as the rock Salt or that made in Kentucky or the Western parts of the U, States— this Salt was a great treat to most of the party, haveing not had any Since the 20th ulto. as to my Self I care but little whether I have any with my meat or not; provided the meat fat, haveing from habit become entirely cearless about my diat, and I have learned to think that if the Cord be Sufficiently Strong which binds the Soul and boddy together, it does not So much matter about the materials which Compose it.

Colter returned this evening unsecksessfull from the Chase, haveing been absent since the 1st inst.

I determine to Set out early tomorrow with two canoes & 12 men in quest of the whale, or at all events to purchase from the indians a parcel of the blubber, for this purpose I made up a Small assortment of merchindize, and directed the men to hold themselves in readiness &c.

1. See next entry for possible members of this party.

[Lewis] *Monday January 6th 1806.*

Capt Clark set out after an early breakfast with the party in two canoes as had been concerted the last evening; Charbono and his Indian woman were also of the party; the Indian woman was very impotunate to be permited to go, and was therefore indulged; she observed that she had traveled a long way with us to see the great waters, and that now that monstrous fish was also to be seen, she thought it very hard she could not be permitted to see either (she had never yet been to the Ocean).

The Clatsops, Chinnooks, Killamucks &c. are very loquacious and inquisitive; they possess good memories and have repeated to us the names capasities of the vessels &c of many traders and others who have visited the mouth of this river; they are generally low in stature, proportionably small, reather lighter complected and much more illy formed than the Indians of the Missouri and those of our frontier; they are generally cheerfull but never gay. with us their conversation generally turns upon the subjects of trade, smoking, eating or their women; about the latter they speak without reserve in their presents, of their every part, and of the most formiliar connection. they do not hold the virtue of their women in high estimation, and will even prostitute their wives and daughters for a fishinghook or a stran of beads. in common with other savage nations they make their women perform every species of domestic drudgery. but in almost every species of this drudgery the men also participate. their women are also compelled to geather roots, and assist them in taking fish, which articles form much the greatest part of their subsistance; notwithstanding the survile manner in which they treat their women they pay much more rispect to their judgment and oppinions in many rispects than most indian nations; their women are permitted to speak freely before them, and sometimes appear to command with a tone of authority; they generally consult them in their traffic and act in conformity to their opinions. I think it may be established as a general maxim that those nations treat their old people and women with most differrence [deference] and rispect where they subsist principally on such articles that these can participate with the men in obtaining them; and that, that part of the community are treated with least attention, when the act of procuring subsistence devolves intirely on the men in the vigor of life. It appears to me that nature has been much more deficient in her filial tie than in any other of the strong affections of the human heart, and therefore think, our old men equally with our women indebted to civilization for their ease and comfort. Among the Siouxs, Assinniboins and others on the Missouri who subsist by hunting it is a custom when a person of either sex becomes so old and infurm that they are unable to travel on foot from camp to camp as they rome in surch of subsistance, for the children or near relations of such person to leave them without compunction or remose; on those occasions they usually place within their reach a small peace of meat and a platter of water, telling the poor old superannuated wretch for his consolation, that he or she had lived long enough, that it was time they should dye and go to their relations who can afford to take care of them much better than they could. I am informed that this custom prevails even among the Minetares Arwerharmays and Recares[1] when attended by their old people on their hunting excursions; but in justice to these people I must observe that it appeared to me at their vilages, that they provided tolerably well for their aged persons, and several of their feasts appear to have principally for their object a contribution for their aged and infirm persons.[2]

This day I overhalled our merchandize and dryed it by the fire, found it all damp; we have not been able to keep anything dry for many days together since we arrived in this neighbourhood, the humidity of the air has been so excessively great. our merchandize is reduced to a mear handfull, and our comfort during our return the next year much depends on it, it is therefore almost unnecessary to add that we much regret the reduced state of this fund.—[3]

[Clark] 2 3 4 5 & all Day[4]

6t of January 1805 all last night rained without intermition, & the morning. I sat out with 12 men[5] in 2 Canoes to around thro: the bay and up a Creek to an old landing at which place the Indians have a roade

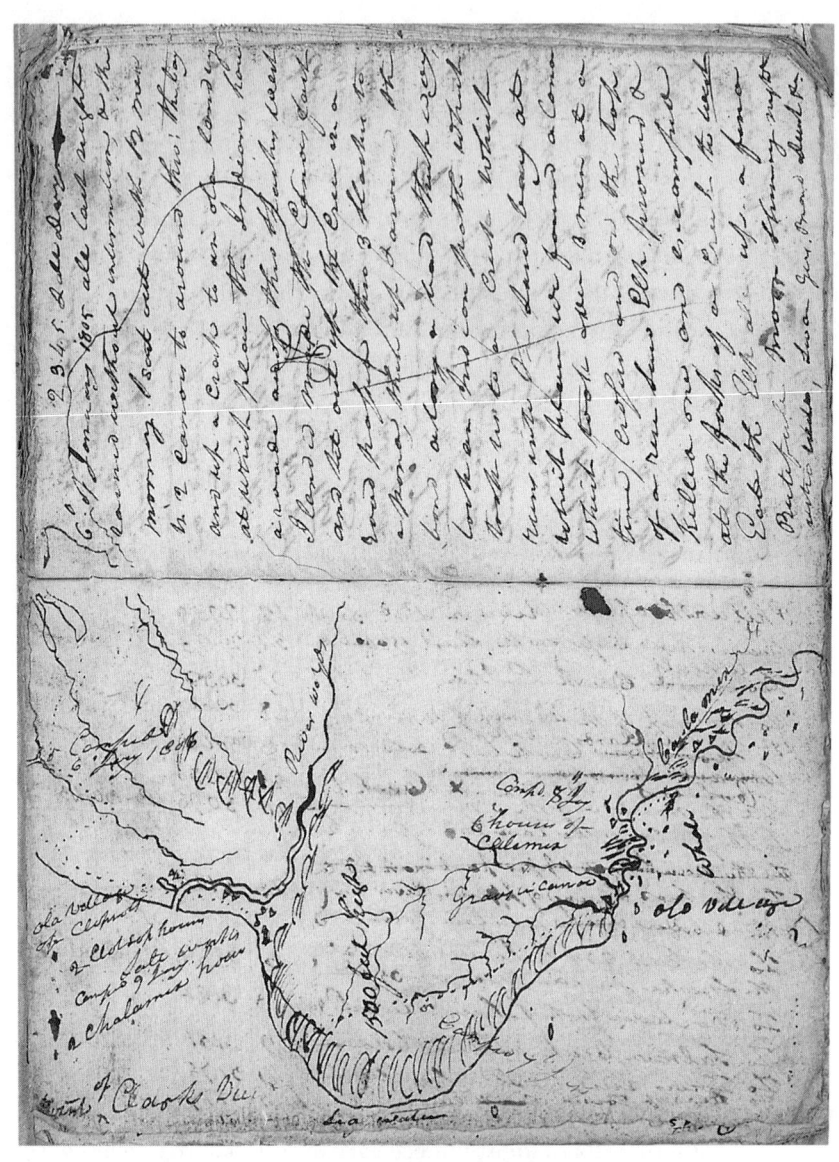

13. Route to the Whale Site,
ca. January 6–10, 1806, Clark's First Draft

across thro Shashes West   I landed made the Canoes fast and Set out up the Cree on a road   passed thro 3 Stashes to a pond, then up & around th bend along a bad thick way, took an Indian path which took us to a Creek which runs into the Sand bay at which place we found a Canoe which took over 3 men at a time   crossed and on the top of a rise Saw Elk   prosued & Killed one and encamped at the forks of a Creek[6]   the *West*   Eate th Elk all up.   a fine Butifull moon Shining night unto [*one word illegible*], Swan Geese, Brand [Duck?] &c.

[Clark]   Monday 6th of January 1806

The last evening Shabono and his Indian woman was very impatient to be permitted to go with me, and was therefore indulged; She observed that She had traveled a long way with us to See the great waters, and that now that monstrous fish was also to be Seen, She thought it verry hard that She Could not be permitted to See either (She had never yet been to the Ocian).   after an early brackfast I Set out with two Canoes down the *Ne tel* R into Meriwether Bay with a view to proced on to the Clatsop town, and hire a guide to conduct me through the Creeks which I had every reason to beleeve Comunicated both with the Bay and a Small river near to which our men were making Salt.   Soon after I arrived in the Bay the wind Sprung up from the N. W and blew So hard and raised the waves so high that we were obliged to put into a Small Creek Short of the Village.   finding I could not proceed on to the Village in Safty, I deturmined to assend this Creek as high as the Canoes would go; which from its directions must be near the open lands in which I had been on the 10th ulto., and leave the Canoes and proceed on by land.   at the distance of about 3 miles up this Creek I observed Some high open land, at which place a road Set out and had every appearance of a portage, here I landed drew up the Canoes and Set out by land, proceeded on through 3 deep Slashes to a pond about a mile in length and 200 yards wide, kept up this pond leaving it to the right, and passing the head to a Creek which we Could not Cross, this Creek is the one which I rafted on the 8th & 9 ultimo: and at no great distance from where I crossed in *Cus ca lars* Canoe on the 10th ulto. to which place I expected a find a canoe, we proceeded on and found a Small Canoe at the place I expected, calculated to Carry 3 men, we crossed and from the top of a ridge in the Prarie we Saw a large gange of Elk feeding about 2 miles below on our direction. I divided the party So as to be Certain of an elk, Several Shot were fired only one Elk fell, I had this Elk butchered and carried to a Creak in advance at which place I intended to encamp, two other Elk were badly Shot, but as it was nearly dark we Could not pursue them, we proceeded on to the forks of the Creek which we had just Crossed turning around to the S W. and meeting one of equal Size from the South, the two makeing a little river 70 yards wide which falls into the Ocian near the 3 Clat Sop houses which I visited on the 9th ulto. in the forks of this Creek we found Some drift pine which had been left on the Shore by the tide of which we made fires. the evening a butifull Clear moon Shiney night, and the 1st fair night which we have had for 2 months

1. The Hidatsas, Awaxawi Hidatsas, and the Arikaras.

2. Biddle elaborates some on the Indians' treatment of women and the elderly, perhaps from conversations with Clark in 1810. Biddle Notes [ca. April 1810], Jackson (LLC), 2:504–6.

3. The middle portion of this paragraph has a vertical line through it, drawn in dark ink.

4. Here begins a journal fragment (First Draft) found in the American Philosophical Society, containing Clark's entries for January 6–10, 1806 (misdated 1805), covering his trip to see the whale. Each page of daily entry material has a large "x" across it. Clark's entries for those days in Codex I were presumably composed later, perhaps from these notes. Additional material from this journal is found elsewhere in the edition. See Introduction and Appendix C, vol. 2; Moulton (SJ), 198–99. Opposite and partially under this entry is a sketch map (fig. 13) showing Clark's route to the site and the location of Fort Clatsop. The relative positions of the two are somewhat distorted.

5. From references in Clark's entries we know that the following members of the party were with him: Charbonneau, Sacagawea, Pryor, Frazer, McNeal, and Werner. He met Joseph Field, Bratton, Gibson, Gass, and Shannon at the salt works. And Lewis mentions that Drouillard and Collins were hunting away from Fort Clatsop. On the front cover of this draft is a list of men's names in Clark's hand. Since Charbonneau's and the four soldiers' names are included, we may suppose that this is a list of the persons who made the trip, excluding Sacagawea's name and that of her child, Jean Baptiste, who surely went along. The list names thirteen rather than twelve persons, but Charbonneau may have been thought of as a supernumerary when Clark wrote twelve in the text. The column of names reads: "Serjt Pryor, Peter [*either Cruzatte or Weiser*], Frasure, Colter, Werner, Battiest [*i.e., Lepage*], R. Fields, Potts, McNeal, Labiech, Windsor, Shabono, and Shield." Another column of words is opposite the names but apparently unrelated to them. The reason for the plus marks is not known, but may have been a further inventory check: "Meadle +, Dollar +, Bags, Beeds +, Wampom +, Knives +, F. Hooks +, Paint +, Ribin

November 22, 1805 – January 6, 1806

+, Wire +, arm bands, a red flag +, 3 files +, needles +, Thread, Paper & Ink pen &c." Except for the last, these may have been items taken along as Indian presents or for trade. Finally two columns of figures and these random jottings appear on the cover: "Boate, Beautiful, Elegant, neat, 15–4."

```
3560      154
 428      165
————     ————
3988      319
 144     3560
————     ————
4132      889
```

6. Clark camped at the forks of his "Ne-er ca wen a ca" River, probably today's Neacoxic Creek, but not quite like Clark's geographic description. *Atlas* map 84; fig. 13.

Chapter Twenty-Seven

At Fort Clatsop

January 7–20, 1806

[Lewis] *Monday [NB: Tuesday] January 7th 1806.*

Last evening Drewyer visited his traps and caught a beaver and an otter; the beaver was large and fat we have therefore fared sumptuously today; this we consider a great prize for another reason, it being a full grown beaver was well supplyed with the materials for making bate with which to catch others. this bate when properly prepared will intice the beaver to visit it as far as he can smell it, and this I think may be safely stated at a mile, their sense of smelling being very accute. To prepare beaver bate, the castor[1] or bark stone is taken as the base, this is gently pressed out of the bladderlike bag which contains it, into a phiol of 4 ounces with a wide mouth; if you have them you will put from four to six stone in a phiol of that capacity, to this you will add half a nutmeg, a douzen or 15 grains of cloves and thirty grains of cinimon finely pulverized, stir them well together and then add as much ardent sperits to the composition as will reduce it the consistency mustard prepared for the table; when thus prepared it resembles mustard precisely to all appearance. when you cannot procure a phiol a bottle made of horn or a tight earthen vessel will answer, in all cases it must be excluded from the air or it will soon loose it's virtue; it is fit for uce immediately it is prepared but becomes much stronger and better in about four or five days and will keep for months provided it be perfectly secluded from the air. when cloves are not to be had use double the quantity of Allspice, and when no spice can be obtained use the bark of the root of sausafras; when sperits can not be had use oil stone of the beaver adding mearly a sufficient quantity to moisten the other materials, or reduce it to a stif past. it appears to me that the principal uce of the spices is only to give a variety to the scent of the bark stone and if so the mace[2] vineller[3] and other sweetsmelling spices might be employed with equal advantage. The male beaver has six stones, two which contain a substance much like finely pulvarized bark of a pale yellow colour and not unlike tanner's ooz in smell, these are called the *bark stones* or castors; two others, which like the bark stone resemble small bladders, contain a pure oil of a strong rank disagreeable smell, and not unlike *train oil*,[4] these are called the *oil stones;* and 2 others of generation. the Barkstones are about two inc[h]es in length, the others somewhat smaller all are of a long oval form; and lye in a bunch together between the skin and the root of the tail, beneath or behind the fundament with which they are closely connected and seem to communicate. the pride[5] of the female lyes on the inner side much like those of the hog. they have no further parts of generation that I can perceive and therefore beleive that like the birds they copulate with the extremity of the gut. The female have from two to four young ones at a birth and bring fourth once a year only, which usually happens about the latter end of may and begining of June. at this stage she is said to drive the male from the lodge, who would otherwise destroy the young.— dryed our lodge and had it put away under shelter; this is the first day during which we have had no rain since we arrived at this place. nothing extraordinary happened today.—

[Clark] *Jany 7th Tuesday 1805* [1806]

Set out at Day light, porceded up the Creek about 2 mile and crossed on a tree trunk the Salt makers have ⟨made⟩ fallen across, then proceeded on to the Ocean ¾ mile & proceded up 3 miles to the mouth of Colimex River[6] about 80 or 100 yds wide verry rapid & Cuts its banks, here we found an old Village of 3 houses, one only inhabited by one familey, I gave the man a fish hook to put the party across, on the bank found a *Skeet* fish [X: *Skaite*][7] which had been lef by the tide proceded on 2 miles on the bank opposit a kind of bay the river Cross to the Sea Cost to 2 Inds Indians Lodges at which place I found our Salt makers near the

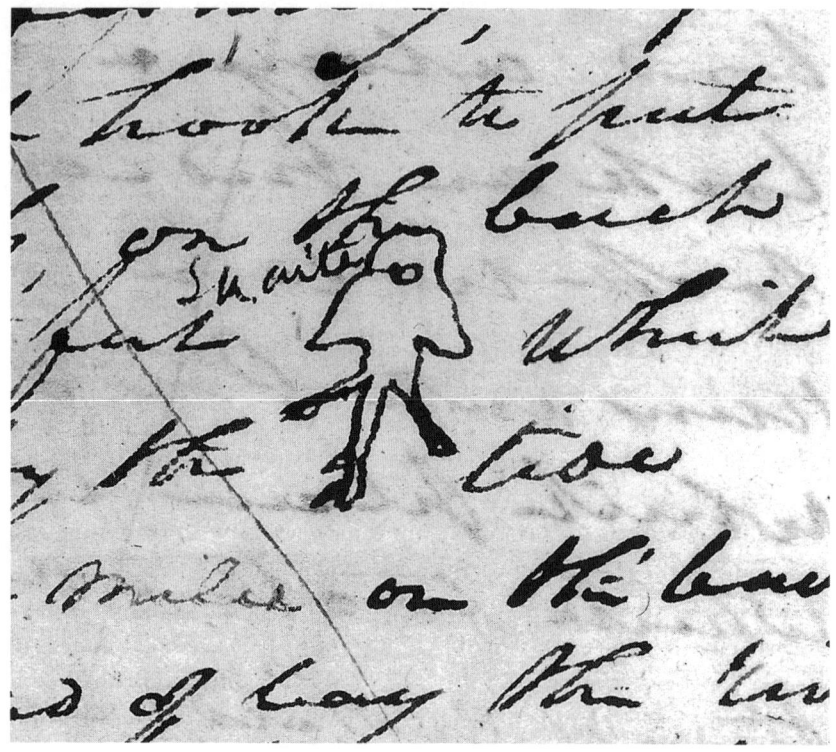

14. Skate (big skate, *Raja binoculata*),
January 7, 1806, Clark's First Draft

foot of a mountain which form the Shore.   Brackfast and hirired an Indian to pilot me to the *Ca le mix* nation where the whale is for which I gave a file, we proceded on the Stone under a high hill on our right bluff. Soft Stone Sees verry high, Several parts of this hill recently Sliped in, about ¾ of a mile abov the Houses Saw a Canoe in which the Dead was buried   at 2½ miles assended a Steep mountain,[8] as Steep at it is possible places for 1500 [*two letters smudged, illegible*] feet   we hauled our Selves up by the assistence of the bushes   if one had Given way we must have fallen a great distanc   the Steepest worst & highest mountain I ever assended I think it at least 1500 feet highr than the Sea imidiately under on the riht.   we met 14 Indians loaded with blubber   proceded on thro an unusual bad way falling timber bendig under logs &c. and encamped on a Creek[9] which runs to my left   find Day and night, the timber Spruc White Cedar & &.

January 7–20, 1806

[Clark]   *Tuesday 7th of January 1805* [1806]

    Some frost this morning. I[t] may appear Somewhat incrediable, but So it is that the Elk which was killed last evening was eaten except about 8 pounds, which I directed to be taken along with the Skin, I proceded up the South fork of the Creek about 2 miles and crossed on a pine tree which had been fallen by the Saltmakers on their first going out, on this tree we crossed the deepest of the water and waded on the opposit Side for 30 yards, from thence to the ocian ¾ of a mile through a Continuation of open ridgey Prarie, here the Coast is Sandy, we proceeded on the Sandy beech nearly South for 3 miles to the mouth of butifull river with bold and rapid Current of 85 yards wide and 3 feet deep in the Shallowest place, a Short distance up this river on the N E Side is the remains of an old village of Clatsops. I entered a house where I found a Man 2 Womn & 3 Children, they appeared retchedly pore & dirty, I hired the man to Set us across the River which I call after the Nation *Clat Sop* river for which I gave 2 fishing hooks— at this place the Creek over which I crossed on a tree passes within 100 yards of the *Clat Sop* river over which the nativs have a portage which affords them an easy Communication with the villages near point adams, and at the mouth of the Creek, on which we lay last night. in walking on the Sand after crossing the river I Saw a Singular Species of fish which I had never before Seen one of the men Call this fish a Skaite,[10] it is properly a Thornback. I proceeded on about 2 miles to near the base of high Mountain where I found our Salt makers, and with them Sergt. Gass, Geo. Shannon was out in the woods assisting Jo Field and gibson to kill Some meat, the Salt makers had made a neet Close Camp, Convenient to wood Salt water and the fresh water of the Clât Sop river which at this place was within 100 paces of the Ocian they wer also Situated near 4 houses of Clatsops & Killamox, who they informed me had been verry kind and attentive to them. I hired a young Indian to pilot me to the whale for which Service I gave him a file in hand and promised Several other Small articles on my return, left Sergt. Gass and one man of my party Werner to make Salt & permited Bratten to accompany me, we proceeded on the round Slipery Stones under a high hill which projected into the ocian about 4 miles further than the direction of the Coast. after walking for 2½ miles on the Stones my guide made a Sudin halt, pointed to the top of the mountain and uttered the word *Pe Shack* which means bad [*NB: bad*],[11] and made Signs that we could not proceed any further on the rocks, but must pass over that mountain, I hesitated a moment & view this emence mountain the top of which ⟨apd⟩ was obscured in the clouds, and the assent appeard. to be almost perpindecular; as the Small Indian parth allong which they had brought emence loads but a fiew hours before, led up this mountain and appeared to assend in a Sideling direction, I thought more than probable that the assent might be torerably easy and therefore proceeded on, I soon found that the [*blank*] become much worst as I assended, and at one place we were obliged to Support and draw our Selves up by the bushes & roots for near 100 feet, and after about 2 hours labour and fatigue we reached the top of this high mountain, from the top of which I looked down with estonishment to behold the hight which we had assended, which appeared to be 10 or 12 hundred feet up a mountain which appeared to be almost perpindicular, here we met 14 Indians men and women loaded with the oil & Blubber of the whale. In the face of this tremendeous precipic imediately below us, there is a Strater of white earth[12] (which my guide informed me) the neighbouring indians use to paint themselves, and which appears to me to resemble the earth of which the French Porcelain is made; I am confident that this earth Contains argill, but whether it also Contains Silex or magnesia, or either of those earths in a proper perpotion I am unable to deturmine. we left the top of the precipice and proceeded on a bad road and encamped on a Small run passing to the left. all much fatiagued

    1. Castoreum, obtained from the perineal glands of the beaver.
    2. A spice consisting of the dried arillode of the nutmeg, *Myristica fragrans* Houtt. Bailey, 420–21.
    3. Common vanilla, *Vanilla fragrans* Ames. Ibid., 301.
    4. Whale oil.
    5. The female genitals. Criswell, 68.
    6. Necanicum River, Clatsop County, Oregon. *Atlas* map 84; fig. 13.
    7. Most likely a numerous species from shallow water, probably the big skate, *Raja binoculata*. At this point in Clark's First Draft appears a sketch of the skate, fig. 14. Burroughs, 260.
    8. Tillamook Head, Clatsop County, whose highest point is 1,136 feet above sea level (and given variously in expedition journals and maps); "Point of Clarks view" on *Atlas* map 84.
    9. Perhaps on Canyon Creek of Tillamook Head. *Atlas* map 84; fig. 13.

10. A vertical line is drawn through this passage about the fish, to about this point.
11. The word is in Chinook jargon (borrowed from Nootkan), *pišak*, "bad."
12. Tillamook Head is probably an intracanyon flow in the valley of an ancestral Columbia River. It is of lava of Miocene age that invaded slightly older sandstones and mudstones of the Cannon Beach Member of the Astoria Formation. The stratum of white earth may be clay formed by the alteration of a layer of mudstone during the intrusion of the molten basalt sill. Clark's silex is either quartz or basalt silica. A red vertical line is drawn through this passage from "In the face" to "unable to deturmine," perhaps the work of Biddle.

[Lewis] *Tuesday [NB: Wednesday] January 8th 1806.*

Our meat is begining to become scarse; sent Drewyer and Collins to hunt this morning. the guard duty being hard on the men who now remain in the fort I have for their relief since the departure of Capt. Clark made the Cooks mount guard. Sergt. Gass and Shannon have not yet returned, nor can I immajen what is the cause of their detention. In consequence of the clouds this evening I lost my P. M. observation for Equal Altitudes,[1] and from the same cause have not been able to take a single observation since we have been at this place. nothing extraordinary happened today.

The Clatsops Chinnooks and others inhabiting the coast and country in this neighbourhood, are excessively fond of smoking tobacco. in the act of smoking they appear to swallow it as they dran it from the pipe, and for many draughts together you will not perceive the smoke which they take from the pipe; in the same manner also they inhale it in their lungs untill they become surcharged with this vapour when they puff it out to a great distance through their nostils and mouth; I have no doubt the smoke of the tobacco in this manner becomes much more intoxicating and that they do possess themselves of all it's virtues in their fullest extent; they freequently give us sounding proofs of it's creating a dismorallity of order in the abdomen, nor are those light matters thought indelicate in either sex, but all take the liberty of obeying the dictates of nature without reserve. these people do not appear to know the uce of sperituous liquors, they never having once asked us for it; I presume therefore that the traders who visit them have never indulged them with the uce of it; from what ever cause this may proceede, it is a very fortunate occurrence, as well for the natives themselves, as for the quiet and safety of thos whites who visit them.

[Clark] *Jany 8 Wedned*

Set out at Day a fine morning wind hard from S. E at 1½ miles arived at a Open where I had a view of the Seas Coast for a long Distance rocks in every direction. Struck a branch and come down to the Sea at which place an old village between 2 Creeks of the Colemix Nation[2] which inhabits this Coast, grave yard deposed of in Canoes in which the bodies are laid in boxes in the Canoe, Paddles &c thos poople must use thos Canoes in the higher Seas of which then ever I Saw on a Cost ruding Countrey Crossed ⟨great⟩ 3 points rocks great Distanc in the Sea, hill Sides Sliping from emins ravins which appears to [illegible] the [blank] proceeded on to the mouth of a Creek[3] about 80 yards wide at which Place I saw 5 Lodges of Indian of the *Ca la mix* nation,[4] boiling whale in a trough of about 20 gallons with hot Stones, and the oyle they put into a Canoe I proceded on a Short distance to the whale[5] which was nothing more than the Sceleton, of 105 feet long, we took out a few bones and returned to the Cabins at the mouth of the Creek, and attempted to trade with thos people who I found Close and Capricious, would not trade the Smallest piece except they thought they got an advantage of the bargain, their disposition is averitious, & independant in trade, they offered to trade for Elk of which we had not I purchased some oile and about 120 w of ⟨fish⟩ Blubber after rendered, finding they would not trade I Deturmined to return home with what we have The Houses of these people appear temporary a ridge pole on 2 forks Supported a Certain number of Split boards of the red Cedar & pine, Set on the end the gable ends of the Same materials and Calculated for 2 families first, The Dress and appearenc of the nativs as also the language is procisely that of the Clopsots & *Chinnooks,* those people Save their oile in bladder Guts &c.

Their food is principally fish that is thrown on the Shores by the Seas & left by the tide,

This Cost is rockey, the mountains high & rugged, They inform me that their nation lives in 5 villages to the S E of this place at the mouths of Creek in which they catch Samn. in the Season, I got of those people a few roots Some Sturgeon whale—[blank] &. They Call a whale *E cu-la* a Creek *Shu man,*[6] they have Some fiew Sea ortter for which they ask Such prices I could not purchase any of them

Th party much fatigued in crossing 1 mountain & 4 high Points Steep & Slipery, also Stony Beach Slippery and tiresom

The high tide obliged me to delay untill late before the tide put out, I Shot a raven & a gul with my Small riffle which Suppised these people a little   They are fond of blue & white large beed only, files & fish Hooks which are large— after Diner we Set out Crossed the Creek in a Small Canoe   The tide out and Encamped on the opposit Side,[7] I was asked for ferrage and paid a pin, one hut on the Side in which I Camped & Village a Short distance above which I did not See last night, all the men came over & Smoked with me, about bed time I herd a hollowing on the opposit Side of the river which allarmed all the Indian men about me, they run across the Creek, I Suspected perhaps Some of my party was over after the Squars, by exemening found that *McNeal* was not in Camp, ⟨I was⟩ my guide who Staid with me told me Some body throat was Cut. I emediately Sent Serjt Pryor & ⟨4⟩ 2 men across for *McNeal*, they Soon returned haveing met the person   I was anxious to find out the Cause of the allarm, McNeal Said that a man envited him to go across and get Some fish, locked arms of which he Contd to hold   he took him into a lodge and the woman gave him a Small piec   the man then invited him to another, the woman of the lodge puled his blanket, & Sent out a Squar to hollow across, to inform of Something which ald. [alarmed?] McNeal I Sent over Sergt. Pryor to Know the Cause of the allarm which he was informed that a Plot was laid to *kill* McNeal for his Blanket & Clothes by this Indian who was from another Villg at Some distance, and that She had attempted to Stop McNeal & findeing She Could not that She then allarmed the men, Several of the mans Band was with me who imedeately Cleared out, 2 men Came over & Slept at my feet. I kept a guard & Sentinel all night   a fair night wind blew from S. E.   during the evening I acquired all the information possiable respecting the Coast to the S. E. got the name of many nations & the Nos. of their houses, a map of the Coast in their way. I am very pore & weak for want of Sufficient food and fear much that I shall require more assistance to get back than I had to get to this place.   a deturmined [purcistance?] will as it has done carry me through

[Clark]   *Wednesday 8th January 1805* [1806]

The last night proved fair and Cold wind hard from the S. E. we Set out early and proceeded to the top of the mountain next to the which is much the highest part and that part faceing the Sea is open, from this point I beheld the grandest and most pleasing prospects which my eyes ever surveyed, in my frount a boundless Ocean; to the N. and N. E. the coast as as far as my sight Could be extended, the Seas rageing with emence wave and brakeing with great force from the rocks of Cape Disapointment as far as I could See to the N. W. The Clatsops Chinnooks and other villagers on each Side of the Columbia river and in the Praries below me, the meanderings of 3 handsom Streams heading in Small lakes at the foot the high Country; The Columbia River for a ⟨long⟩ Some distance up, with its Bays and Small rivers and on the other Side I have a view of the Coast for an emence distance to the S. E. by S. the nitches and points of high land which forms this Corse for a long ways aded to the inoumerable rocks of emence Sise out at a great distance from the Shore and against which the Seas brak with great force gives this Coast a most romantic appearance.[8] from this point of View my guide pointed to a village at the mouth of a Small river near which place he Said the whale was, he also pointed to 4 other places where the princpal Villages of the *Kil la mox* were Situated, I could plainly See the houses of 2 of those Villeges & the Smoke of a 3rd which was two far of for me to disern with my naked eye—[9] after taking the Courses and computed the Distances in my own mind, I proceeded on down a Steep decent to a Single house the remains of an old *Kil a mox* Town[10] in a nitch imediately on the Sea Coast, at which place great no. of eregular rocks are out and the waves comes in with great force. Near this old Town I observed large Canoes of the neetest kind on the ground Some of which appeared nearly decayed others quit Sound, I examoned those Canoes and found they were the repository of the dead— This Custom of Secureing the Dead differs a little from the Chinnooks. the Kil a mox Secure the dead bodies in an oblong box of Plank, which is placed in an open Canoe resting on the ground, in which is put a paddle and Sundery other articles the property of the disceased.[11] The Coast in the neighbourhood of this old village is slipping from the Sides of the high hills, in emence masses; fifty or a hundred acres at a time give way and a great proportion of an instant precipitated into the Ocean. those hills and mountains are principally composed of a yellow Clay; their Slipping off or Spliting assunder at this time is no doubt Caused by the incessant rains which has fallen within the last two months.[12] the mountans Covered with a verry heavy Croth of pine & furr, also the white Cedar or *arbor vita* and a Small proportion of the black alder, this alder grows to the hight of Sixty or Seventy feet and from 2 to 3 feet in diamiter. Some Species of pine [*NB: or fur*] on the top of the Point of View rise to the emmence hight of 210 feet and from 8 to 12 feet in diameter, and are perfectly Sound and Solid.[13] Wind hard from the S. E and See looked [*blank*] in the after part of the Day breaking with great force against the Scattering rocks at Some distance from Shore, and the ruged rockey points under which we wer obleged to pass and if we had unfortunately made one false Stet we Should eneviateably have fallen into the Sea and dashed against the rocks in an instant, fortunately we passed over 3 of those dismal points and arived on a butifull Sand Shore on which we Continued for 2 miles, Crossed a Creek 80 yards near 5 Cabins, and proceeded to the place the whale had perished, found only the Skelleton of this monster on the Sand between 2 of [*NB: 2 of*] the villages of the *Kil a mox* nation; the Whale was already pillaged of every valuable part by the Kil a mox Inds. in the vecinity of whose village's it lay on the Strand where the waves and tide had driven up & left it. this Skeleton [*NB: of the Whale Capt. Clark*] measured 105 feet.[14] I returned to the village of 5 Cabins on the Creek which I shall call *E co-la* or whale Creek, found the nativs busily engaged boiling the blubber, which they performed in a large Squar wooden trought by means of hot Stones; the oil when extracted was Secured in bladders and the Guts of the whale; the blubber from which the oil was only partially extracted by this process, was laid by in their Cabins in large flickes[15] for use; those flickes they usially expose to the fire on a wooden Spit untill it is prutty well wormed through and then eate it either alone or with roots of the rush, *Shaw na tâk we* or diped in the oil. The *Kil a mox* although they possessed large quantities of this blubber and oil were so prenurious that they disposed of it with great reluctiance and in Small quantities only; insomuch that my utmost exertion aided by the party with the Small Stock of merchindize I had taken with me were not able to precure more blubber than about 300 wt. and a fiew gallons of oil; Small as this Stock is I prise it highly; and thank providence for directing the whale to us; and think him much more kind to us than he was to jonah, having Sent this monster to be *Swallowed by us* in Sted of *Swallowing of us* as jonah's did. I recrossed *E co la* Creek and Encamped on the bank at which place we observed an ebundance of fine wood the Indian men followed me for the purpose of Smokeing. I enquired of those people as well as I could by Signs the Situation, mode of liveing & Strength of their nation They informed me that the bulk of their nation lived in 3 large villages Still further along the Sea coast to the S, S, W. at the enterence of 3 Creek which fell into a bay,[16] and that other houses were Scattered about on the Coast, Bay and on a Small river which fell into the Bay in which they Cought Salmon, and from this Creek (which I call *Kil a mox* River)[17] they crossed over to the *Wappato I.* on the *Shock-ah-lil com* [*NB?: lil com*] (which is the Indian name for the Columbia river)[18] and purchased Wappato &c. that the nation was once verry large and that they had a great maney houses, In Salmon Season they Cought great numbers of that fish in the Small Creeks, when the Salmon was Scerce they found Sturgion and a variety of other fish thrown up by the waves and left by the tide which was verry fine, Elk was plenty in the mountains, but they Could not Kill maney of them with their arrows. The *Kil â mox* in their habits Customs manners dress & language[19] differ but little from the Clatsops, Chinnooks and others in this neighbourhood are of the Same form of those of the Clatsops with a Dore at each end & two fire places i, e the house is double as long as wide and divided into 2 equal parts with a post in the middle Supporting the ridge pole, and in the middle of each of those divisions they make their fires, dores Small & houses Sunk 5 feet

    1. A partial observation for the morning may be in another journal. See below, part 3 of Chapter 30.
    2. The Tillamooks lived below the Clatsop in southern Clatsop and Tillamook counties, and northern Lincoln County on the northern Oregon coast. *Atlas* maps 84, 85. Tillamook Head and Tillamook Bay also commemorate them. Their name is from Chinookan *(i)t'ilimukš*. Their northernmost settlement was at the mouth of Necanicum Creek at modern Seaside, Tillamook County, and was apparently shared with the Clatsop. They belonged to the coastal branch of the Salishan-language family. As noted by Lewis and Clark, the Tillamooks shared a number of outward cultural traits with the neighboring Clatsops, in spite of the language difference. Hodge, 2:750–51; Suphan; Taylor (TI); Ronda (LCAI), 186, 206.

3. Present Ecola (formerly Elk) Creek, Clatsop County, "*E-cu-lah* or Whale Creek" on *Atlas* map 84, and unnamed on fig. 13. See note below for linguistic information.

4. At the present city of Cannon Beach, Clatsop County. *Atlas* map 84.

5. Only the blue whale, *Balaenoptera musculus*, the largest of all living animals, is known to attain the length given by Clark. Conditions may not have been conducive to exact measurement. Cutright (LCPN), 253.

6. The Lower Chinookan term for "whale," *íkuli*. Gibbs (AVC), 20; Boas (Ch), 608. Clark's "Shu man" is Chinookan *šux̣mn*, for the creek's name rather than the word for creek; its meaning is not known, nor is the creek to which the natives may have been referring.

7. On the north side of Ecola Creek, in the north part of Cannon Beach. *Atlas* map 84; fig. 13.

8. Clark was probably seeing formations such as Haystack Rock and The Needles southwest of Cannon Beach.

9. A vertical line runs through this passage, from "the whale was" to "my naked eye."

10. This Tillamook village corresponds with a known archaeological site. Minor (EAS), 13–16. One of the Tillamook villages that the captain observed from a distance was almost certainly at Cronin Point on the north shore of Nehalem Bay. Archaeological work indicates that occupation of this village began at least 400 years ago and continued into the early historic period. Woodward (PSOC). A similar span of occupation has been documented at a site on Netarts Bay. Newman. Farther south in Tillamook territory, excavations at the Three Rox site in the Salmon River estuary encountered slightly earlier evidence of occupation extending back to about 900 years ago. Murray & Marrant. The burial canoes observed by Clark represent a variation on this common Northwest Coast mortuary custom.

11. A vertical line begins at "This custom" and runs to about here.

12. Most of the hills in this area are formed of sandstone and mudstone of the Miocene-age Cannon Beach Member of the Astoria Formation. Landslides often result when excess water (generally winter precipitation) saturates these soft rocks or the deep soil formed from them. Wave action is responsible for many of the landslides adjacent to the shore. The erosive action continues today in the Ecola State Park area.

13. Again a vertical line beginning at "this alder" and running to about here, done in red ink, perhaps by Biddle.

14. This sentence and a part of the preceding one is marked out with a red vertical line, perhaps by Biddle.

15. A form of "flitches," the side of an animal, later used only of a hog; here perhaps meaning strips. Criswell, 40.

16. Tillamook Bay, in Tillamook County, into which flow Kilchis, Wilson, and Trask rivers. *Atlas* map 85.

17. Perhaps Wilson River. *Atlas* map 85.

18. Silas B. Smith, grandson of Chief Coboway, declared that Clark misunderstood the Indians, who did not give distinguishing names to rivers. Shocatilicum was the name of the chief of the Cathlamets, who lived in the direction from which they obtained the wapato. Wheeler, 2:224. On the other hand, linguistic analysis has the phrase in Chi-

nookan as *šax̣al ilx̣am*, "upriver country" suggesting that the speaker was pointing upriver and not giving a proper name at all. For Wapato Island (present Sauvie's Island), see *Atlas* map 80. The word "Wappato" was apparently substituted for an erased word. "Shock-ah-lil com" appears to have been added to a blank space. Wheeler, 2:224.

19. Perhaps the Tillamooks (Salishan speakers) were speaking Chinook trade jargon to Clark.

[Lewis]   *Friday [NB: Thursday] January 9th 1806.*

Our men are now very much engaged in dressing Elk and Deer skins for mockersons and cloathing. the deer are extreemly scarce in this neighbourhood, some are to be found near the praries and open grounds along the coast. this evening we heard seven guns in quick succession after each other, they appeared to be on the Creek to the South of us and several miles distant; I expect that the hunters Drewyer and Collins have fallen in with a gang of Elk. some marrow bones and a little fresh meat would be exceptable; I have been living for two days past on poor dryed Elk, or *jurk* as the hunters term it.

The Clatsops Chinnooks &c. bury their dead in their canoes. for this purpose four pieces of split timber are set erect on end, and sunk a few feet in the grown, each brace having their flat sides opposite to each other and sufficiently far assunder to admit the width of the canoes in which the dead are to be deposited; through each of these perpendicular posts, at the hight of six feet a mortice is cut, through which two bars of wood are incerted; on these cross bars a small canoe is placed in which the body is laid after being carefully roled in a robe of some dressed skins; a paddle is also deposited with them; a larger canoe is now reversed, overlaying and imbracing the small one, and resting with it's gunwals on the cross bars; one or more large mats of rushes or flags are then roled around the canoes and the whole securely lashed with a long cord, usually made of the bark of the *Arbor vita* or white cedar. on the cross bars which support the canoes is frequently hung or laid various articles of cloathing culinary eutensels &c. I cannot understand them sufficiently to make any enquiries relitive to their relegeous opinions, but presume from their depositing various articles with their dead, that they believe in a state of future existence.

The persons who usually visit the entrance of this river for the purpose of traffic or hunting I believe are either English or Americans; the Indians inform us that they speak the same language with ourselves, and give us proofs of their varacity by repeating many words of English, as musquit, powder, shot, nife, file, damned rascal, sun of a bitch &c. whether these traders are from Nootka sound, from some other late establishment on this coast, or immediately from the U' States or Great Brittain, I am at a loss to determine, nor can the Indians inform us. the Indians whom I have asked in what direction the traders go when they depart from hence, or arrive here, always point to the S. W. from which it is presumeable that Nootka cannot be their destination; and as from Indian information a majority of these traders annually visit them about the beginning of April and remain with them six or seven Months, they cannot come immediately from Great Britain or the U' States, the distance being too great for them to go and return in the ballance of the year. from this circumstance I am sometimes induced to believe that there is some other establishment on the coast of America south West of this place of which little is but yet known to the world, or it may be perhaps on some Island in the pacific ocean between the Continents of Asia and America to the South West of us.[1] This traffic on the part of the whites consists in vending, guns, (principally old british or American musquits) powder, balls and Shot, Copper and brass kettles, brass teakettles and coffee pots, blankets from two to three point,[2] scarlet and blue Cloth (coarse), plates and strips of sheet copper and brass, large brass wire, knives, beads and tobacco with fishinghooks buttons and some other small articles; also a considerable quantity of Sailor's cloaths, as hats coats, trowsers and shirts. for these they receive in return from the natives, dressed and undressed Elkskins, skins of the sea Otter, common Otter, beaver, common fox,[3] spuck,[4] and tiger cat;[5] also dryed and pounded sammon in baskets, and a kind of buisquit, which the natives make of roots called by them shappelell.[6] The natives are extravegantly fond of the most common cheap blue and white beads, of moderate size, or such that from 50 to 70 will weigh one penneyweight.[7] the blue is usually pefered to the white; these beads constitute the principal circulating medium with all the indian tribes on this river; for these beads they will dispose any article they possess.— the beads are strung on strans of a fathom in length and in that manner sold by the bredth or yard.—

[Clark]   January 9th Thursday 180[5?]

a fine morning wind N E   Set out at day lighte every man Some meat of the whale and a little oile   proceded on the track   we Came out to a house at a branch where we halted ½ an hour to rest   this house is at at place an old village has formerly been, on the Coast at the Comencment [*blank*] 27 foot wide 35 feet long Sunk in the ground 5 feet 2 Dores & 2 fire places dores 29 Ins. high & 14¼ wide handsom Steps to decend down a post in the middle Coverede with boards Split thin an 2 feet wide, old grave in Canoes of 3 feet 8 Inches wide & 5 feet long neetly made high at bow   proceded on to the top of the hill Passing 3 bad points rockey &.   from the Point Clarks Point of view Cape Disapt. bears S. 12° E passing a Great point at 15 miles one at 40 miles rocks out to the 1st large point from the Creek 4 points, between the 1st large Point and 2d a point of many large rocks, Day Clouded up, I can See a point Bearing N 5° East a long way just in Sight.   from Clarks ⟨lookout⟩ View Point to Cape Disapointment is N 20° W.   To point *adams* & the open Slope point is North and a Sharp point, met a party of Chinnooks going to get whale blubber to eate & oile each of which they eate together, we also over took Several parties of the Clot Sops loaded with imence laods of the blubber and *oile* maney of those loads I with difficuelty raised, Estonishing what custom will [do?]   at 2 oClock we arrived at the Camp of our Salt makers verry much fatigued, more So than I ever was before, the Indians all proceeded on, I concluded to Stay all night,[8] as the party was much fatigued, and Send out 2 men which I had left here to hunt Ducks up the little river, Jo. Fields had killed an Elk and brought in a quarter on which we Dined   he also had killed & brought in a *Deer*. The Indians with the oile & bluber tole me they had to purchase of the *Ca-le nixx*[9] and would Come to the *fort* & Sell to us in 3 Days time, this I incouraged, as I expect to purchase at the fort as cheep as at the village at which I was, day proved fine.   rained the greater part of the night   I went into an Indian Lodge they were pore Durty and the house full of flees.   he offered me roots which they geather on the Sea Cost a kind of rush, of which they offered me to eate,

[Clark]   *Thursday 9th of January 1805* [1806]
   a fine morning wind from the N. E.   last night about 10 oClock while Smokeing with the nativ's I was alarmed by a loud Srile voice from the Cabins on the opposite Side, the Indians all run immediately across to the village, my guide who Continued with me made Signs that Some one's throat was Cut, by enquiry I found that one man McNeal was absent, I imediately Sent off Sergt. N. Pryor & 4 men in quest of McNeal who' they met comeing across the Creak in great hast, and informed me that the people were alarmed on the opposit Side at Something but what he could not tell, a man had verry friendly envited him to go and eate in his lodge, that the Indian had locked armes with him and went to a lodge in which a woman gave him Some blubber, that the man envited him to another lodge to get Something better, and the woman [*NB: knowing his design*] held him [*NB: McNeal*] by the blanket which he had around him   [*NB: He not knowing her object freed himself & was going off, when this woman a Chinnook an old friend of McNeals*] ⟨and⟩ another ran out and hollow'd and his pretended friend disapeared—   I emediately ordered every man to hold themselves in a State of rediness and Sent Sergt. Pryor & 4 men to know the cause of the alarm which was found to be a premeditated plan of the pretended friend of McNeal to assanate for his Blanket and what fiew articles he had about him, which was found out by a Chin nook woman who allarmed the men of the village who were with me in time to prevent the horred act.   this man was of another band at Some distance and ran off as Soon as he was discovered.   we have now to look back and Shudder at the dreadfull road on which we have to return of 45 miles S E of Point adams & 35 miles from Fort *Clatsop*.   I had the blubber & oil divided among' the party and Set out about Sunrise and returned by the Same rout we had went out, met Several parties of men & womin of the Chinnook and Clatsops nations, on their way to trade with the *Kil a mox* for blubber and oil; on the Steep decent of the Mountain I overtook five men and Six womin with emence loads of the Oil and blubber of the Whale, those Indians had passed by Some rout by which we missed them as we went out yesterday; one of the women in the act of getting down a Steep part of the mountain her load by Some means had Sliped off her back, and She was holding the load by a Strap which was fastened to the

mat bag in which it was in, in one hand and holding a bush by the other, as I was in front of my party, I endeavored to relieve this woman by takeing her load untill She Could get to a better place a little below, & to my estonishment found the load as much as I Could lift and must exceed 100 wt. the husband of this woman who was below Soon came to her releif, those people proceeded on with us to the Salt works, at which place we arrived late in the evening, found them without meat, and 3 of the Party J. Field Gibson & Shannon out hunting. as I was excessively fatigued and my party appeared verry much so, I deturmined to Stay untill the morning and rest our Selves a little. The Clatsops proceeded on with their lodes— The Clatsops, Chin nooks Kil á mox &c. are verry loquacious and inquisitive; they possess good memories and have repeeted to us the names capasities of the Vessels &c of maney traders and others who have visited the mouth of this river; they are generally low in Statue, proportionably Small, reather lighter complected and much more illy formed than the Indians of the Missouri and those of our fronteers; they are generally Chearfull but never gay. with us their Conversation generally turns upon the subject of trade, Smokeing, eating or their womin; about the latter, they Speak without reserve in their presence, of their every part, and of the most farmiliar Connection. they do not hold the virtue of their womin in high estimation, and will even prostitute their wives and Daughters for a fishing hook or a Stran of beeds. in Common with other Savage nations they make their womin perform every Species of domestic drugery; but in almost every Species of this drugery the men also participate. their woman are compelled to gather roots, and assist them in takeing fish; which articles form much the greater part of their Subsistance; notwithstanding the Survile manner in which they treat their womin they pay much more respect to their judgement and oppinion in maney respects than most indian nations; their womin are permited to Speak freely before them, and Sometimes appear to command with a tone of authority; they generally consult them in their traffic and act conformably to their opinions.

I think it may be established as a general maxim that those nations treat their old people and women with most defference and respect where they Subsist principally on Such articles that these can participate with the men in obtaining them; and that, that part of the Community are treated with least attention, when the act of precureing subsistance devolves intirely on the men in the vigor of life. It appears to me that nature has been much more deficient in her filial ties than in any others of the Strong effections of the humane heart, and therefore think our old men equally with our woman indebted to Sivilization for their ease and Comfort. I am told among the Sioux's, Assinniboins and others on the Missouri who Subsist by hunting it is a Custom when a person of either Sex becoms So old and infirm that they are unable to travel on foot, from Camp to Camp as they rove in serch of Subsistance, for the Children or near relations of Such person to leave them without Compunction or remorse; on those occasions they usially place within their reach a Small piece of meat and a platter of water, telling the poor old Superannuated retch for their Consolation, that he or She had lived long enough, and that it was time they Should die and go to their relations who Can afford to take Care of them, much better than they Could. I am informed that the Me ne tar es Ar war har mays and Ricares when attended by their old people on their hunting expedition prosued the Same Custom; but in justice to those people I must observe that it appeared to me at their villages, that they provided tolerably well for their aged persons, and Several of their *feasts* appear to have principally for their object a contribution for their aged and infirm persons. In one of the Mandan villages I Saw an old man to whome I gave a knife and enquired his age, he Said he had Seen more than 100 winters, and that he Should Soon go down the river to their old village— he requested I would give him Something to prevent the pain in his back his grand Son a Young man rebuked the old man and Said it was not worth while, that it was time for the old man to die. the old man occupied one Side of the fire and was furnished with plenty of Covouring and food, and every attention appeared to be paid him &c. Jo. Field in my absence had killed an Elk and a Deer, brought in the Deer and half of the Elk on a part of which we Suped, Some rain a little after dark. I visited a house near the Salt boilers found it inhabited by 2 families, they were pore dirty and their house Sworming with flees.—

1. In 1788 the British sea captain John Meares established a trading base on Nootka Sound, Vancouver Island. A few years later American traders were using Clayoquot Sound on the same island as a base. Neither of these was a permanent settlement. The conjecture about a Pacific island was also correct, for most of these traders were operating

out of the Hawaiian Islands. Thwaites (LC), 3:327 n. 1; Gibson (BMNC); Gough; Ruby & Brown (CITC), 40–90.

2. Referring to a system for measuring trade blankets by size and weight. See above, August 20, 1805.

3. Probably the red fox, *Vulpes vulpes*.

4. See below, February 23, 1806.

5. The men's term for the Oregon bobcat. Burroughs, 92–93.

6. Cous, *Lomatium cous* (Wats.) Coult. & Rose. Hitchcock et al., 3:548–49. See above, November 1, 1805.

7. A troy weight of twenty-four grains, one-twentieth of a troy ounce.

8. At the salt works camp at Seaside, Clatsop County, Oregon. *Atlas* map 84; fig. 13.

9. Presumably the Tillamooks.

[Lewis]   Saturday [NB: Friday] *January 10th 1806.*

About 10 A. M. I was visited by Tia *Shâh-hâr-wâr-cap*[1] and eleven of his nation in one large canoe; these are the Cuth'-lah-mah' nation who reside first above us on the South side of the Columbia river; this is the first time that I have seen the Chief, he was hunting when we past his vilage on our way to this place. I gave him a medal of the smallest size;[2] he presented me with some indian tobacco and a basquit of wappetoe, in return for which I gave him some thread for making a skiming net and a small piece of tobacco.   these people speak the same language with the Chinnooks and Catsops whom they also resemble in their dress customs manners &c.   they brought some dryed salmon, wappetoe, dogs, and mats made of rushes and flags, to barter; their dogs and a part of their wappetoe they disposed off, an remained all night near the fort. This morning Drewyer and Collins returned having killed two Elk only, and one of those had died in their view over a small lake which they had not the means of passing it being late in the evening and has of course spoiled, as it laid with the ⟨guts⟩ entrals in it all night; as the tide was going out we could not send for the elk today, therefore ordered a party to go for it early in the morning and George and Collins to continue their hunt; meat has now become scarce with us.—

Capt Clark returned at 10 P. M. this evening with the majority of the party who accompanyed him; having left some men to assist the saltmakers to bring in the meat of two Elk which they had killed, and sent 2 others through by land to hunt. Capt. Clark found the whale on the Coast about 45 Miles S. E. of Point ⟨Adams⟩ [X: Round], and about 35 Miles from Fort Clatsop by the rout he took; The whale was already pillaged of every valuable part by the Killamucks, in the vicinity of one of whose villages it lay on the strand where the waves and tide had driven up and left it. this skelleton measured one hundred and five feet. Capt. C. found the natives busily engaged in boiling the blubber, which they performed in a large wooden trought by means of hot stones; the oil when extracted was secured in bladders and the guts of the whale; the blubber, from which the oil was only partially extracted by this process, was laid by in their lodges in large fliches for uce; this they usually expose to the fire on a wooden spit untill it is pretty well warmed through and then eat it either alone or with the roots of the rush, squawmash, fern wappetoe &c. The natives although they possessed large quantities of this blubber and oil were so penurious that they disposed of it with great reluctance and in small quantities only; insomuch that the utmost exertions of Capt. C. and the whole party aided by the little stock of merchandize he had taken with him and some small articles which the men had, were not able to procure more blubber than about 300 lb. and a few gallons of the oil; this they have brought with them, and small as the store is, we prize it highly, and thank ⟨the hand of⟩ providence ⟨which had⟩ for directing the whale to us, and think him much more kind to us than he was to jonah, having sent this monster to be *swallowed by us* in stead of *swallowing of us* as jona's did. Capt. C. found the road along the coast extreemly difficult of axcess, lying over some high rough and stoney hills, one of which he discribes as being much higher than the others, having it's base washed by the Ocea[n] over which it rares it's towering summit perpendicularly to the hight of 1500 feet; from this summit Capt. C. informed me that there was a delightfull and most extensive view of the Ocean, the coast and adjacent country; this Mout. I have taken the liberty of naming *Clark's Mountain and point of view;* it is situated about 30 M. S. E. of Point ⟨Adams⟩ [*NB?: Disapointment*] and projects about 2½ miles into the Ocean; *Killamucks* [*NB: Qu. Clatsop*] river falls in a little to the N. W. of this mountain; in the face of this tremendous precepice there is a stra of white earth (see specimen No. [*blank*]) which the neighbouring Indians use to paint themselves, and which appears to me to resemble the earth of which the French Porcelain is made; I am confident this earth contains Argill, but wether it also contains Silex or magnesia, or either of those earths in a

At Fort Clatsop

proper proportion I am unable to determine.— Shannon and Gass were found with the Salt makers and ordered to return McNeal was near being assassinated by a Killamuck Indian, but fortunately escaped in consequence of a Chinnook woman giving information to Capt. C., the party and Indians with them before the villain had prepaired himself to execute his purposes. The party returned excessively fortiegued and tired of their jaunt. Killamucks [*NB: Clatsop*] river is 85 yards wide, rappid and 3 feet deep in the shallowest part. The Killamucks in their habits customs manners dress and language differ but little from the Clatsops & Chinnooks. they place their dead in canoes resting on the ground uncovered, having previously secured the dead bodies in an oblong box of plank.

The coast in the neighbourhood of Clarks Mountain is sliping off & falling into the Ocean in immence masses; fifty or a hundred Acres at a time give way and a great proportion in an instant precipitated into the Ocean. these hills and mountains are principally composed of a yellow clay; there sliping off or spliting assunder at this time is no doubt caused by the incessant rains which have fallen within the last two months. the country in general as about Fort Clatsop is covered with a very heavy growth of several species of pine & furr, also the arbor vita or white cedar and a small proportion of the black Alder which last sometimes grows to the hight of sixty or seventy feet, and from two to four feet in diameter. some species of the pine rise to the immence hight of 210 feet and are from 7 to 12 feet in diameter, and are perfectly sound and solid.—

[Clark]   *Jany 10 Friday 1805* [1806][3]

I left Sergt. Gass here and Set out at Sun rise, Crossed the little river[4] which I waded 85 yards wide & 3 feet Deep Swift, at which place I Saw Several Indians one of which had 2 butifull Sea orter Skins on as a roabe, ⟨I proceeded on⟩ here the Creek which I crossed at a tree and on which I camped the 6th inst. came within [*illegible interlineation of three letters*] 200 yds of the river & they Inds. make a portage here, Continued on a place 3 miles Crossed this Creek in a Small Canoe. here I expected to find Shannon and gibson with meet to furnish the Salt makers, but did not, divided the party Sent 2 men to my right to try and kill Elk, Soon after met Gibson & Shannon with meat, they had killed 2 Elk 2 miles to my right, ⟨we⟩ I divided the meat between the party, and the load of 3 men whome I Send with gibson & Shannon to help Carrey the 2 Elk to the Salt makers, and I my Self and the party returned by the Same rout we went out to the Canoes   Rd. Frasure behaved very badly, and mutonous—[5] he also lost his ⟨big⟩ large Knife. I Sent him back to look for his knife, with Directions to return with the party of Serjt Gass, I proceeded on, here is a portage of ¼ of a mile from this Creek to a branch which falls into the Bay, we proceeded on a much bette road than we went out across a Deep Slash and found our Canoes Safe, and Set out at Sunset, and arived at the foart, wet and Cold at 9 oClock P. M.   found a Cheif & number of Indians both Encamped on the Shore, and at the fort of the ⟨Cha⟩ *Cath la-hur* Tribe which lives at no great distance above this back of an Island Close under the South Side of the Columbia River

Those people Speake the Same Language of the *Clotsops* dress nearly alike   the men of both Cut their hair in the neck.   use blankets of ⟨this⟩ the manifactory of the nativs near the falls of the *Sheep* Wool—fond of brass arm bands and Check, They bring *Wap-pa-to* root (which is Sagittifolia or the Common *arrow head* which is Cultivated by the Chinees) to Sell.[6]

[Clark] *Friday the 10th of January 1806*

I derected Serjt. Gass to Continue with the Salt makers untill Shannon return from hunting, and then himself and Shannon to return to the Fort, I Set out at Sunrise with the party waded the Clat Sop river which I found to be 85 Steps across and 3 feet deep, on the opposite Side a Kil a mox Indian Came to and offered to Sell Some roots of which I did not want, he had a robe made of 2 large Sea otter Skins which I offered to purchase, but he would not part with them, we returned by nearly the Same rout which I had Come out, at four miles, I met Gibson & Shannon each with a load of meat, they informed me that they had killed Elk about 2 miles off, I directed 3 men to go with the hunters and help them pack the meat to the place they were makeing Salt, and return to the fort with Serjt. Gass, the balance of the party took the load of the 3 men, after crossing the 2d Creek frasure informed me that he had lost his big knife, here we Dined, I put frasurs load on my guide who is yet with me, and Sent him back in Serch of his knife with directions to join the other men who were out packing meat & return to the fort all together. I arrived at

At Fort Clatsop

the Canoes about Sunset, the tides was Comeing in   I thought it a favourable time to go on to the fort at which place we arrived at 10 oClock P M, found Several inidians of the Cath'-lâh-mâh nation the great Chief *Shâh-hâr-wâh cop* who reside not far above us on the South Side of the Columbia River, this is the first time I have Seen the Chief, he was hunting when we passed his village on our way to this place, we gave him a medal of the Smallest Size, he presented me with a basquet of Wappato, in return for which I gave him a fish hook of a large Size and Some wire, those people Speak the Same language with the Chinnooks and Clatsops, whome they all resemble in Dress, Custom, manners &c.   they brought Some Dried Salmon, Wappato, Dogs, and mats made of rushes & flags to barter; their Dogs and part of their wappato they disposed of, and remained in their Camp near the fort all night.

In my absence the hunters from the fort killed only two Elk which is yet out in the woods. Capt. Lewis examined our Small Stock of merchendize found Some of it wet and Dried it by the fire. Our merchindize is reduced to a mear handfull, and our Comfort, dureing our return next year, much depends on it, it is therefore almost unnecessary to add that it is much reduced   T[he] nativs in this neighbourhood are excessively fond of Smokeing tobacco.   in the act of Smokeing they appear to Swallow it as they draw it from the pipe, and for maney draughts together you will not perceive the Smoke they take from the pipe, in the Same manner they inhale it in their longs untill they become Surcharged with the vapour when they puff it out to a great distance through their norstils and mouth; I have no doubt that tobacco Smoked in this manner becomes much more intoxicating, and that they do possess themselves of all its virtues to the fullest extent; they frequently give us Sounding proofs of its createing a dismorallity of order in the abdomen, nor are those light matters thought indelicate in either Sex, but all take the liberty of obeying the dicktates of nature without reserve. Those people do not appear to know the use of Speritious licquors, they never haveing once asked us for it; I prosume therefore that the traders who visit them have never indulged them with the use of it; of whatever Cause this may proceed, it is a verry fortunate occurrence, as well for the nativs themselves, as for the quiet and Safty of those whites who visit them. George Drewyer visited this traps in my absence and caught a Beaver & a otter; the beaver was large and fat, and Capt. L. has feested Sumptiously on it yesterday; this we Consider as a great prize, it being a full grown beaver was well Supplyed with the materials for makeing bate with which to Catch others. this bate when properly prepared will entice the beaver to visit it as far as he can Smell it, and this I think may be Safely Stated at ½ a mile, their Sence of Smelling being verry accute. To prepare beaver bate,[7] the Caster or bark Stone is taken as the base, this is generally pressed out of the bladder like bag which Contains it, into a phiol of 4 ounces with a wide mouth; if you have them you will put from 4 to 6 Stone in a phial of that Capacity, to this you will add half a nutmeg, a Dozen or 15 grains of Cloves and 30 grains of Sinimon finely pulverised, Stur them well together, and then add as much ardent Sperits to the Composition as will reduce it to the Consistancey of mustard prepared for the table, when thus prepared it resembles mustard precisely to all appearance. When you cannot precure a phial a bottle made of horn or a light earthern vessel will answer, in all Cases it must be excluded from the air or it will Soon lose its Virtue; it is fit for use imediately ⟨as So⟩ it is prepared but becoms much Stronger and better in 4 or 5 days and will keep for months provided it be purfectly Secluded from the air. when Cloves are not to be had use double the quantity of allspice, and when no Spices can be obtained use the bark of the root of the Sausafras; when Sperits cannot be had use oil Stone of the beaver adding mearly a Sufficent quantity to moisten the other materials, or reduce it to a Stiff paste. it appears to me that the principal use of the Spices is only to give a variety to the Scent of the bark Stone and if So the mace vineller, and other Sweet Smelling Spices might be employd with equal advantage. The Male Beaver has Six stones, two which Contanes a Substance much like finely pulverised bark of a pale yellow Colour and not unlike tanner's ooz in Smell, these are Called the *bark Stones* or castors; two others, which like the bark stone resemble Small blatters, contain a pure oil of a Strong rank disagreable Smell, and not unlike train Oil, these are Called the *Oil Stones,* and two others of Generation. The bark stones are about 2 inches in length, the others Somewhat Smaller, all are of a long Oval form, and lye in a bunch together between the skin and the root of the tail beneath or behind the fundiment with which they are Closely Connected and Seam to Communicate, the pride of the female lye on the inner Side much like those of the hog they have no further parts of Generation that I can proceive, and therefore believe that like the birds they Coperate with the extremity of the gut. The female have from 2 to 4 young ones at a birth and bring forth once a year only which usially happins about the Latter end of May and beginning of June.   at this Stage She is Said to drive the Mail from the lodge, who would otherwise distroy the young—.

    1. The term is Chinookan *Tia*, "chief," *Šaxawaq̓ap*, meaning unknown.

    2. Probably the 55 mm Jefferson medal, the smallest of the three presidential sizes. However, it may be the somewhat mysterious "5th Sise" of medal, referred to in the Baling Invoices of the Fort Mandan Miscellany, vol. 3, p. 496. Prucha speculates that this fifth size could be an American silver dollar pierced for suspension as a medal, as mentioned above, October 29, 1804. Prucha (IPM), 17, 93, 94; Cutright (LCIPM), 162–63.

    3. This ends daily entries in the draft for Clark's excursion to the whale site. Then follows a number of tables and summaries that will be found in appropriate places in this edition (many in Chapter 30 of this volume).

    4. Necanicum River, Clatsop County, Oregon. *Atlas* map 84; fig. 13.

    5. The Codex I reference to Frazer for the day mentions only his being sent back for his knife, saying nothing about mutinous behavior. Neither the Orderly Book nor any other journal says anything about a trial or punishment for mutiny. Evidently Clark, perhaps after consultation with Lewis, decided that Frazer's behavior during the difficult and trying trip to and from the whale site was not serious enough to warrant disciplinary action.

    6. Under this paragraph, apparently in Clark's hand, are several indeterminable words and letters in red ink. One word appears to be "Dawson."

    7. Beginning with this sentence a red vertical line runs to the end of this entry, perhaps done by Biddle.

[Lewis] *Sunday [NB: Saturday] January 11th 1806.*

Sent a party[1] early this morning for the Elk which was killed on the 9th.   they returned with it in the evening; Drewyer and Collins also returned without having killed anything.   this morning the Sergt. of the guard reported the absence of our Indian Canoe, on enquiry we found that those who came in it last evening had been negligent in securing her and the tide in the course of the night had taken her off; we sent a party down to the bay in surch of her, they returned unsuccessfull, the party also who went up the river and Creek in quest of the meat were ordered to lookout for her but were equally unsuccessfull; we ordered a party to resume their resurches for her early tomorrow; this will be a very considerable loss to us if we do not recover her; she is so light that four men can carry her on their sholders a mile or more without resting; and will carry three men and from 12 to 15 hundred lbs. the Cuthlâhmâhs left us this evening on their way to the Catsops, to whom they purpose bartering their wappetoe for the blubber and oil of the whale, which the latter purchased for beads &c. from the Killamucks; in this manner there is a trade continually carryed on by the natives of the river each trading some article or other with their neighbours above and below them; and thus articles which are vended by the whites at the entrance of this river, find their way to the most distant nations enhabiting it's waters.

[Clark] *Saturday 11th of January 1806*

Sent a party early this morning for the Elk which was killed on the 9th they returned with it in the evining; This morning the Serjt. of the guard reported that our Indian Canoe had gone a Drift, on enquiry we found that those who Came in it last evening had been negligent in Secureing her, and the tide in Corse of the night had taken her off; we Sent a party down to the bay in Serch of her, they returned unsecksessfull, the party who went up the river and Creek after meat were derected to look out for her but were equally unsecksessfull; this will be a verry considerable loss to us if we do not recover her, She is so light that 4 men Can Carry her on their Sholders a mile or more without resting, and will Carry four men and from 10 to 12 hundred pounds. The Cath lâ mâhs left us this evening on their way to the Clatsops, to whome they perpose bartering their wappato for the blubber & Oil of the whale, which the latter purchased for Beeds &c. from the Kil á mox; in this manner there is a trade Continually Carried on by the nativs of the river each tradeing Some articles or other with their neighbours above and below them, and those articles which are Vended by the whites at their enterance of this river, find their way to the most distant nations inhabiting its waters.

1. Including Sergeant Ordway.

[Lewis] *Monday [NB: Sunday] January 12th 1806.*

The men who were sent in surch of the canoe returned without being able to find her, we therefore give her over as lost. This morning sent out Drewyer and one man to hunt, they returned in the evening, Drewyer having killed seven Elk; I scarcely know how we should subsist were it not for the exertions of this excellet hunter. At 2 P. M. the ballance of the party who had been left by Capt. C. arrived; about the same time the two hunters also arrived who had been dispatched by Capt C. for the purpose of hunting on the 9th inst.; they had killed nothing. We have heretofore usually divided the meat when first killed among the four messes into which we have divided our party leaving to each the care of preserving and the discretion of using it, but we find that they make such prodigal use of it when they hapen to have a tolerable stock on hand that we have determined to adapt a different system with our present stock of seven Elk; this is to jerk it & issue it to them in small quantities.—

[Clark] *Sunday the 12th January 1806*

This morning Sent out Drewyer and one man to hunt, they returned in the evening Drewyer haveing killed 7 Elk; I scercely know how we Should Subsist, I beleive but badly if it was not for the exertions of this excellent hunter; maney others also exert themselves, but not being accquainted with the best method of finding and killing the elk and no other wild animals is to be found in this quarter, they are unsucksessfull in their exertions.   at 2 P. M Serjt. Gass and the men I left to assist the Salt makers in Carrying in their meat arrived also the hunters which I directed to hunt in the point, they killed nothing—.   We have heretofore devided the meat when first killed among the four messes, into which we have divided our party, leaveing to each the Care of preserving and distribution of useing it; but we find that they make such prodigal use of it when they happen to have a tolerable Stock on hand, that we are determined to adapt a Different System with our present stock of Seven Elk; this is to jurk it and issue it to them in Small quantities—.

[Lewis] *Tuesday [NB: Monday] January 13th 1806.*

This morning I took all the men who could be spared from the Fort and set out in quest of the flesh of the seven Elk that were killed yesterday, we found it in good order being untouched by the wolves, of which indeed there are but few in this country; at 1 P. M. we returned having gotten all the meat to the fort.   this evening we exhausted the last of our candles, but fortunately had taken the precaution to bring with us moulds and wick, by means of which and some Elk's tallow in our possession we do not yet consider ourselves destitute of this necessary article; the Elk we have killed have a very small portion of tallow.

The traders usually arrive in this quarter, as has been before observed, in the month of April, and remain untill October; when here they lay at anchor in a bay within Cape Disappointment[1] on the N. side of the river; here they are visited by the natives in their canoes who run along side and barter their comodities with them, their being no houses or fortification on shore for that purpose. the nations who repare thither are fist, those of the sea coast S. E. of the entrance of the river, who reside in the order in which their names are mentioned, begining at the entrance of the river (viz) The Clatsop, Killamuck,[2] Ne-cost, Nat-ti, Nat-chies, Tarl-che, E-slitch, You-cone and So-see. secondly those inhabiting the N. W. coast begining at the entrance of the river and mentioned in the same order; the Chinnook and Chiltch the latter very numerous; and thirdly the Cath-lâh-mah, and Skil-lutes, the latter numerous and inhabiting the river from a few miles above the marshey Islands, where the Cuth-lâh-mâhs cease, to the grand rappids. These last may be esteemed the principal carryers or intermediate traders betwen the whites and the Indians of the Sea Coast, and the E-ne-shurs, the E-chee-lutes, and the Chil-luck-kit-te quaws, who inhabit the river above, to the grand falls inclusive, and who prepare most of the pounded fish which is brought to market. The bay in which this trade is carried on is spacious and commodious, and perfectly secure from all except the S. and S. E. winds, these however are the most prevalent and strong winds in the Winter season.[3] fresh water and wood are very convenient and excellent timber for refiting and reparing vessels.—

[Clark] Monday 13th January 1806

Capt. Lewis took all the men which Could be Speared from the Fort and Set out in quest of the flesh of the Seven Elk which were killed yesterday they found the meat all Secure untouched by the Wolves, of which indeed there are but fiew in this Countrey; at 1 P. M. the party returned with the 2d and Last load of meat to the fort. this evening we finished all last of our Candles, we brought with us, but fortunately had taken the precaution to bring with us moulds and wick, by means of which and

Some Elk tallow in our possession we do not think our Selves distitute of this necessary article, the Elk which have been killed have a verry Small portion of tallow. The Traders usially arrive in this quarter, in the month of april, and remain until October; when here they lay at anchor in a Bay within Cape Disapointment on the N. Side of the river; here they are visited by the nativs in their Canoes who run along Side and barter their Comodities with them, their being no houses or fortification on Shore for that purpose.

The nations who repare thither ar first those of the Sea Coast S. E & N W of the enterance of the river, who reside in the order in which their names are mentioned to the S E. the Clat Sops, Kil-á-mox, and those to the N W. the Chin nooks, and Chiltch [*NB?: Ch. on the coast to the N. W*]; and Secondly the Cath-lâh-mâh, War-ki-a-cum, and Skil-lutes, the latter noumerous and inhabiting [*NB: the river Coweliskee.*][4] those last may be considered or intermedeate traders between the whites and nations on the Sea Coast, and the E-ne-churs, the E-chee-lutes, and the Chil-luck-kit-te-quaws, who inhabit the river up to the great falls inclusive, and who prepare most of the pounded fish which is brought to Market.

The Bay in which the trade is Carried on is Spacious and Commodious, and perfectly Secure from all except the S. & S E Winds and those blow but Seldom   the most prevalent & Strong winds are from the S W & N W in the Winter Season.   fish water and wood are very Convenient and excellent timber for refitting and repareing vessels.—.

1. Baker Bay, Pacific County, Washington. *Atlas* map 82.
2. In his subsequent entry for January 25, Lewis corrected himself to say that these groups named after the Tillamooks (Killamucks) were actually different bands of the Tillamook Indians (see also the Estimate of Western Indians, Chapter 30). However, most of these names refer to villages of the Alsea and Yaquina Indians, speakers of the Alsean language, who resided below the Tillamooks on the north-central Oregon coast. Dorsey (ST); Hodge, 1:665, 738–39, 2:982, 992–93; Hajda, 97–98; *Atlas* maps 84, 93. Some of the terms may be identified linguistically. "E-slitch" is from the Tillamook language, nšlǽtš,' "Siletz (River)." "You-cone" and "So-see" are both from the Alsea language, yaqó·n, "Yaquina," and possibly wusí·, for "Alsea." Cf. Frachtenburg, 288, 304.
3. Note the discrepancy with Clark's statement on the winds in his entry for this date, below.
4. Biddle's insertion was added to a large blank space.

[Lewis]   *Wednesday [NB: Tuesday] January 14th 1806.*

    This morning the Sergt. of the Guard reported the absence of one of the large perogues, it had broken the chord by which it was attatched and the tide had taken it off; we sent a party immediately in surch of her, they returned in about 3 hours having fortunately found her. we now directed three of the perogues to be drawn up out of reach of the tide and the fourth to be mored in the small branch just above the landing and confined with a strong rope of Elk-skin. had we lost this perogue also we should have been obliged to make three small ones, which with the few tools we have now left would be a serious undertaking. a fatiegue of 6 men employed in jerking the Elk beaf.

    From the best estimate we were enabled to make as we dscended the Columbia we conceived that the natives inhabiting that noble stream, for some miles above the great falls to the grand rappids inclusive annually prepare about 30,000 lbs. of pounded sammon for market. but whether this fish is an article of commerce with the whites or is exclusively sold to and consumed by the natives of the sea Coast, we are at a loss to determine. the first of those positions I am disposed to credit most, but, still I must confess that I cannot imagine what the white merchant's object can be in purchasing this fish, or where they dispose of it. and on the other hand the Indians in this neighbourhood as well as the Skillutes have an abundance of dryed sammon which they take in the creeks and inlets, and I have never seen any of this pounded fish in their lodges, which I pesume would have been the case if they purchased this pounded fish for their own consumption. the Indians who prepared this dryed and pounded fish, informed us that it was to trade with the whites, and shewed us many articles of European manufacture which they obtained for it. it is true they obtain those articles principally for their fish but they trade with the Skillutes for them and not immediately with the whites; the intermediate merchants and carryers, the Skillutes, may possibly consume a part of this fish themselves and dispose of the ballance of it the natives of the sea coast, and from them obtain such articles as they again trade with the whites.[1]

At Fort Clatsop

[Clark] *Tuesday 14th January 1806*

This morning the Serjt. of the guard reported the absence of one of our Canoes it had broken the Cord by which it was attached and the tide had taken her off; we Sent a party imediately in Serch of her, they returned in about 3 hours haveing fortunately found her. we now derect that 3 of the [canoes] be drawed up out of reach of the tide and the 4th to be tied with a long Strong Cord of Elk Skins, ready for use. had we lost this large Canoe we Should have been obliged to make 3 other Small ones, which with the fiew tools we have now left would be a Serious undertakeing. a fatiege of Six men employd in jurking the Elk beef. From the best estermate we were enabled to make as we decended the Columbia we Conceived that the nativs inhabiting that noble Stream (from the enterance of Lewis's river to the neighbourhood of the falls the nativs Consume all the fish they Catch either for food or fuel) From Tow ar ne hi ooks[2] River or a fiew mils above the Great falls to the grand rapids inclusive anually prepare about 30,000 lbs of pounded fish (Chiefly Salmon) for market, but whether this fish is an article of Commerce with their neighbours or is exclusively Sold to, and Consumed by the nativs of the Sea coast, we are at a loss to determine   the latter of those positions I am dispose to credit most, as I cannot imagine what the white merchents objet Could be in purchaseing fish, or where they Could dispose of it. on the other hand the Indians in this neighbourhood as well as the Skillutes and those above have an abundance of Dryed Salmon which they take in the Creeks and inlets.   they are excessively fond of the pounded fish haveing frequently asked us for Some of it—.   the Indians who prepared this pounded fish made Signs that they traded it with people below them for Beeds and trinkets &c and Showed us maney articles of European manufacture which they obtained for it; The Skillutes and Indians about the great rapids are the intermediate merchants and Carryers, and no doubt Consume a part of this fish themselves and dispose of the ballance of it to the nativs of the Sea coast, and from this obtain Such articles as they again trade with the whites.

The persons who usially visit the enterence of this river for the purpose of traffic or hunting, I believe is either English or Americans; the Indians inform us that they Speak the Same language with our Selves, and gave us proofs of their varacity by repeating maney words of English,

Sun of a pitch &c. [NB: heave the lead³ & maney blackguard phrases] whether those traders are from Nootka Sound, from Some other late establishment on this Coast, or imediately from the U States or Great Brittain, I am at a loss to determine, nor Can the Indians inform us. the Indians whome I have asked in what direction the traders go when they depart from hence, allways point to the S. W. from which it is prosumeable that Nootka cannot be their distination, and from Indian information a majority of those traders annually visit them about the beginning of April and remain Some time and either remain or revisit them in the fall of which I cannot properly understand, from this Circumstance they Cannot Come directly from the U States or Great Brittain, the distance being to great for them to go and return in the ballance of a year. I am Sometimes induced to believe that there is Some other Establishment on the Coast of America *South* of this place of which little is but yet known to the world, or it may be perhaps on Some Island in the Pacific Ocian between the Continant of America & Asia to the S. W. of us. This traffic on the part of the whites Consist in vending, guns, principally old British or American Musquets, powder, balls and Shote, ⟨Copper and brass Kettles,⟩ brass tea kettles, Blankets from two to three points, Scarlet and blue Cloth (Coarse), plates and Strips of Sheet Copper and brass, large brass wire Knives Beeds & Tobacco with fishing hooks, buttons and Some other Small articles; also a considerable quantity of Salors Clothes, as hats, Coats, Trouses and Shirts. for those they receive in return from the nativs Dressed and undressed Elk Skins, Skins of the Sea otter, Common Otter, beaver, common fox, ⟨Speck, and⟩ [NB: *Spotted or*] tiger Cat, also Some Salmon dried or pounded and a kind of buisket, [NB: *the native dispose of some of these biscuits   not a great article of trade*] which the nativs make of roots called by them Shappelell. The nativs are extravigantly fond of the most Common Cheap Blue and white beeds, of moderate Size, or Such that from 50 to 70 will way one pennyweight, the blue is usially prefured to the white; those beeds Constitute the principal Circulating medium with all the Indian tribes on this river; for those beeds they will dispose of any article they possess—. the beeds are Strung on Strans of a fathom in length & in that manner Sold by the breth [NB: *arms length or double arms length*] or yard—.

1. Under this date Biddle has additional information on trade with Americans, probably from conversations with Clark in 1810. Biddle Notes [ca. April 1810], Jackson, (LLC), 2:541.
2. The term appears to have been placed into a previously blank space.
3. To throw a weighted line from a ship to determine the water's depth.

[Lewis]   *Thursday [NB: Wednesday] January 15th 1806.*

Had a large coat completed out of the skins of the Tiger Cat and those also of a small animal[1] about the size of a squirrel not known to me; these skins I procured from the Indians who had previously dressed them and formed them into robes; it took seven of these robes to complete the coat. we had determined to send out two hunting parties today but it rained so incessantly that we posponed it. no occurrence worthy of relation took place today.—

The implyments used by the Chinnooks Clatsops Cuthlahmahs &c in hunting are the gun the bow & arrow, deadfalls,[2] pitts, snares, and spears or gigs; their guns are usually of an inferior quality being oald refuse American & brittish Musquits which have been repared for this trade. there are some very good peices among them, but they are invariably in bad order; they apear not to have been long enouh accustomed to fire arms to understand the management of them. they have no rifles. Their guns and amunition they reserve for the Elk, deer and bear, of the two last however there are but few in their neighbourhood. they keep their powder in small japaned[3] tin flasks which they obtain with their amunition from the traders; when they happen to have no ball or shot, they substitute gravel or peices of potmettal, and are insensible of the damage done thereby to their guns. The bow and arrow is the most common instrument among them, every man being furnished with them whether he has a gun or not; this instrument is imployed indiscriminately in hunting every species of anamal on which they subsist. Their bows are extreamly neat and very elastic, they are about two and a half feet in length, and two inches in width in the center, thence tapering graduly to the extremities where they are half an inch wide they are very flat and thin, formed of the heart of the arbor vita or white cedar, the back of the bow being thickly covered with sinews of the Elk laid on with a gleue which they make from the sturgeon; the string is made of sinues of the

January 7–20, 1806

15. Arrow, January 15, 1806, Codex J, p. 25

Elk also. the arrow is formed of two parts usually tho' sometime entire; those formed of two parts are unequally divided that part on which the feathers are placed occupyes four fifths of it's length and is formed of light white pine reather larger than a swan's quill, in the lower extremity of this is a circular mortice secured by sinues roled arround it; this mortice receives the one end of the 2nd part which is of a smaller size than the first and about five inches long, in the end of this the barb is fixed and confined with sinue, this barb is either stone, iron or copper, if metal in this form[4] forming at it's point a greater angle than those of any other Indians I have observed. the shorter part of the arrow is of hearder wood as are also the whole of the arrow when it is of one piece only. as these people live in a country abounding in ponds lakes &c and frequently hunt in their canoes and shoot at fowl and other anamals where the arrow missing its object would be lost in the water they are constructed in the manner just discribed in order to make them float should they fall in the water, and consequently can again be recovered by the hunter; the quiver is usually the skin of a young bear or that of a wolf invariably open at the side in stead of the end as the quivers of other Indians generally are; this construction appears to answer better for the canoe than if they were open at the end only. maney of the Elk we have killed since we have been here, have been wounded with these arrows, the short piece with the barb remaining in the animal and grown up in the flesh.— the deadfalls and snares are employed in taking the wolf[5] the raccoon[6] and fox of which there are a few only. the spear or gig is used to take the sea otter, the common otter, spuck, and beaver. their gig consists of two points or barbs and are the same in their construction as those discribed before as being common among the Indians on the upper part of this river. their pits are employed in taking the Elk, and of course are large and deep, some of them a cube of 12 or 14 feet. these are usually placed by the side of a large fallen tree which as well as the pit lye across the toads frequented by the Elk. these pitts are disguised with the slender boughs of trees and moss; the unwary Elk in passing the tree precipitates himself into the pitt which is sufficiently deep to prevent his escape, and is thus taken.—

[Clark] *Friday* [Wednesday] *15th of January 1806*

Capt. Lewis had a large Coat finished made of the Skins of the tiger Cat, and those of the Small animal about the Size of Small Cat not known to me; those Skins were precured from the Indians who had previously dressed them and formed them into robes; it took Seven of those robes to Complete the Coat. no occurrence worthey of remark took place. rained hard all day. The imployments used by the Chinnooks Clatsops, Cath lah mahs Kil a mox &c. in hunting are the gun the bow & arrow, dead falls, Pitts, Snares, and Spears or gigs; their guns are usially of an inferior quallity being old refuse american or brittish muskets which have been repared for this trade there are Some verry good pieces among them, but they are invariably in bad order they appear not to be long enough acquainted with fire arms to understand the management of them. They have no rifles. Their guns and amunition they reserve for the Elk, Deer, and Bear, of the two last however there are but fiew in their neighbourhoods. they keep their powder in Small japaned tin flasks which they obtain with their amunition from the traders; when

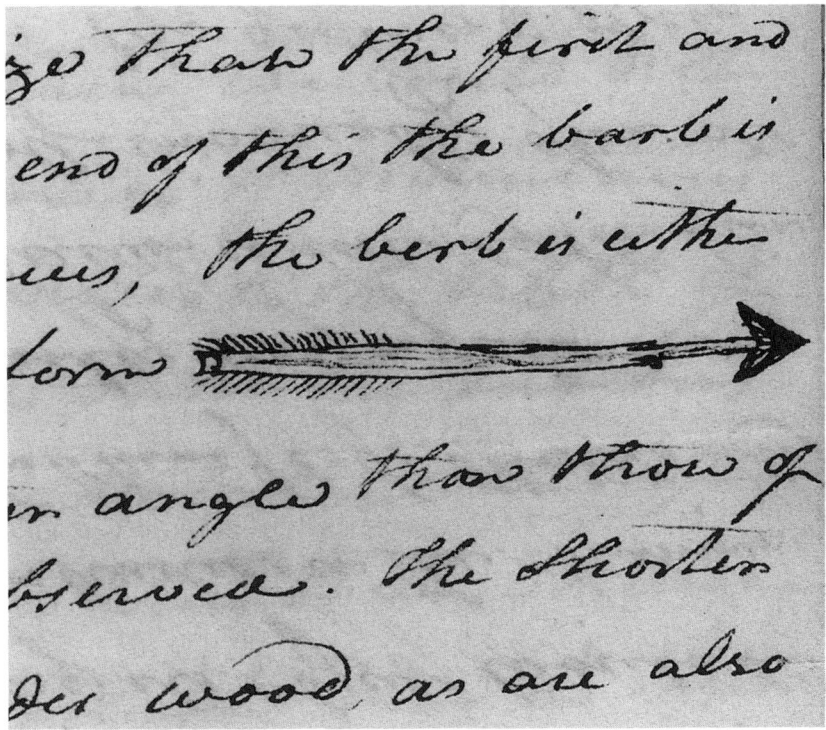

16. Arrow, January 15, 1806, Codex I, p. 119

they happen to have no Ball or Shot they Substitute Gravel and are insenceable of the dammage done thereby to their Guns.

    The Bow and arrow is the most common instrement among them, every man being furnished with them whether he has a gun or not, this instrement is imployed indiscreminately in hunting every Species of animal on which they Subsist, Their bows are extreemly meet [neat] and very elastic, they are about two feet Six inches long and two inches wide in the Center, thence tapering gradually to the extremities, where they ar ¾ of an Inch wide, they are very flat and thin, formed of the heart of the arbor vita or white Cedar, the back of the Bow being thickly Covered with Sinues of the Elk laid on with a Gleue which they make from the Sturgeon; the String is made of the Sinues of the Elk also, the arrow is formed of two parts usually tho' Sometimes entire; those formed of 2 parts are uneaquilly devided, the part on which the feathers are placed occupie ⅕ of it's length and is formed of light white pine rather larger than a Swans quill, in the lower extremity of this is a Circular mortice Secured by Sinues raped around it; this mortice recives the one end of the 2d part which is of Smaller Size than the first and about five inches long, in the end of this the barb is fixed and Confined with Sinues, the berb is either Iron Copper or Stone— in this form[7] forming at its point a greater angle than those of any other Indians I have observed. The Shorter part of the arrow is of harder wood, as are also the whole of the arrow where it is of one piece only. as these people live in a Countrey abounding in Ponds lakes &c. and frequently hunt in their Canoes and Shoot at fowls and other animals where the arrow missing its object would be lost in the water they are constructed in the Manner just discribed in order to make them flote Should they fall in the water, and Consequently Can again be recovered by the hunter; the quiver is useally the Skin of a young bear or that of a wolf invariably open at the Side in Sted of the end, as the quiver of other Indians generally are, this Construction appears to answer better for the Canoe, than if they were open at the end only. maney of the Elk which our hunters have killd. Sence we have been here have been wounded with those arrows, the Short piece with the barbe remaining in the Animal and grown up in the flesh.— the Deadfalls & Snares are employd in takeing the Wolf, the racoon and fox of which there are a fiew. the Spear or gig is used to take the Sea otter, [*NB?: or*] *Spuck*, [*NB?: Ind. name*] & Beaver. The gig consists of two points or birbs and are the Same in their Construction as those which are Common among the Indians on the upper part of this river and before discribed. Their pitts are employed in takeing the Elk, and of Course are large and Deep, Some of them a Cube of 12 or 14 feet, those ar commonly placed by the Side of a large fallen tree which as well as the pitt lie across the roads frequented by the Elk, these pitts are disguised with the Slender bows of trees & moss: the unwarry Elk in passing the tree precipates himself into the pitt which is Sufficiently deep to prevent his escape.—

1. Perhaps the mountain beaver, a gopherlike rodent. See below, February 26, 1806.
2. A trap constructed so that a weight falls on the animal and kills or disables it.
3. Covered with a hard, brilliant varnish.
4. Here a drawing of the arrow (fig. 15) in Lewis's Codex J, p. 25.
5. Gray wolf, *Canis lupus*.

6. Raccoon, *Procyon lotor*.
7. Another drawing of the arrow (fig. 16) in Clark's Codex I, p. 119.

[Lewis]   Friday [NB: Thursday] January 16th 1806.

This evening we finished curing the meat. no occurrence worthy of relation took place today. we have plenty of Elk beef for the present and a little salt, our houses dry and comfortable, and having made up our minds to remain until the 1st of April, every one appears content with his situation and his fare. it is true that we could even travel now on our return as far as the timbered country reaches, or to the falls of the river; but further it would be madness for us to attempt to proceede untill April, as the indians inform us that the snows lye knee deep in the plains of Columbia during the winter, and in these plains we could scarcely get as much fuel of any kind as would cook our provision as we descended the river; and even were we happyly over these plains and again in the woody country at the foot of the Rocky Mountains we could not possibly pass that immence barrier of mountains on which the snows ly in winter to the debth in many places of 20 feet; in short the Indians inform us that they are impracticable untill about the 1st of June, at which time even there is an abundance of snow but a scanty subsistence may be obtained for the horses.— we should not therefore forward ourselves on our homeward journey by reaching the rocky mountains early than the 1st of June, which we can easily effect by seting out from hence on the 1st of April.—

The Clatsops Chinnooks &c. in fishing employ the common streight net, the scooping or diping net with a long handle, the gig, and the hook and line. the common net is of different lengths and debths usually employed in taking the sammon, Carr and trout in the inlets among the marshey grounds and the mouths of deep creeks. the skiming or [s]cooping net to take small fish in the spring and summer season; the gig and hook are employed indiscriminately at all seasons in taking such fish as they can procure by their means. their nets and fishing lines are made of the silk-grass or white cedar bark; and their hooks are generally of European manufactary, tho' before the whites visited them they made hooks of bone and other substances formed in the following manner[1] A C, and

17. Bone Fishhook and Line,
January 16, 1806, Codex J, p. 28

C. B. are two small pieces of bone about the size of a strong twine, these are flattened and leveled off of their extremities near C. where they are firmly attatched together with sinues and covered with rosin. C A. is reduced to a sharp point at A where it is also bent in a little; C B. is attatched to the line, for about half it's length at the upper extremity B. the whole forming two sides of an accute angled triangle.

[Clark] *Saturday* [Thursday] *16th January 1806*
    This evening we finished cureing the meat. no occurrence worthey of relation took place to day. we have a plenty of Elk beef for the present and a little Salt, our houses dry and Comfortable, haveing made up our minds to Stay untill the 1st of April every one appears contented with his Situation, and his fair. it is true we Could travel even now on our return as far as the timbered Country reaches, or to the falls of the river, but further it would be madness for us to attempt to proceed untill april, as

the indians inform us that the Snows lyes knee deep in the Columbian Plains dureing the winter, and in those planes we could not git as much wood as would Cook our provisions untill the drift wood comes down in the Spring and lodges on the Shore &c.   and even were we happily over those plains and in the woodey countrey at the foot of the *rockey mountains*, we could not possibly pass that emence bearier of mountains on which the Snow lyes in winter to the debth in maney placs of 20 feet; in Short the Indians tell us they impassable untill about the 1s of June, at which time even then is an abundance of snow but a Scanty Subsistance may be had for the horses—   we Should [not] foward our homeward journey any by reaching the Rocky mountains earlier than the 1st of June which we can effect by Setting out from hence by the 1st of April—

The Clatsops, Chinnooks &c. in fishing employ the Common Streight net, the Scooping or dipping net with a long handle, the gig, and the hook and line.   the Common nets are of different lengths and debths

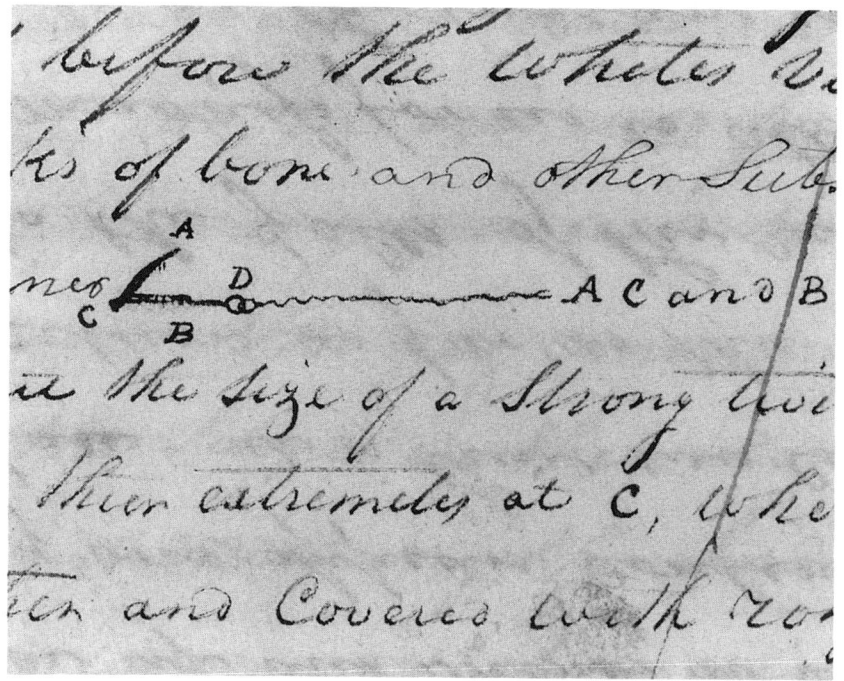

18. Bone Fishhook and Line,
January 16, 1806, Codex I, p. 122

usually employd in takeing the Salmon, Carr and trout in the inlets among the marshey grounds and the mouths of deep Creeks,— the Skiming or [s]cooping nets to take Smaller fish in the Spring and Summer Season; the gig and hook are employed indiscreminately at all Seasons in takeing Such fish as they Can precure by these means. their nets and fishing lines are made of the Silk Grass or white Cedar bark; and their hooks are generally of European manufactory, tho' before the whites visited them they made their Hooks of bone and other Substances formed in the following manner[2] A C and B C are two Small pieces of bone about the Size of a Strong twine, these are flattened & beaveled off to their extremites at C, where they are firmley attached together and Covered with rozin   C A is reduced to a Sharp point at A where it is also bent in a little; C B is attached to the line, at the upper extremity B. the whole forming two Sides of an accute angled triangle. the [line] has a loop at D which it is anexed to a longer line and taken off at pleasure.[3] Those Hooks are yet common among' the nativs on the upper parts of the Columbia river for to Catch fish in Deep places.

   1. Here a diagram of the fishhook (fig. 17) in Lewis's Codex J, p. 28.
   2. Another diagram of the fishhook (fig. 18) in Clark's Codex I, p. 122.
   3. A red vertical line runs through this paragraph to about this point, drawn perhaps by Biddle.

[Lewis]   *Saturday [NB: Friday] January 17th 1806*

This morning we were visited by Comowool and 7 of the Clatsops our nearest neighbours, who left us again in the evening. They brought with them some roots and buries for sale, of which however they disposed of but very few as they asked for them such prices as our stock in trade would not license us in giving. the Chief Comowool gave us some roots and buries for which we gave him in return a mockerson awl and some thread; the latter he wished for the purpose of making a skiming net. one of the party was dressed in t[h]ree very elegant Sea Otter skins which we much wanted; for these we offered him many articles but he would not dispose of them for any other consideration but blue beads, of these we had only six fathoms left, which being 4 less than his price for each skin he would not exchange nor would a knife or an equivalent in beads[1] of any other colour answer his purposes, these coarse blue beads are their f[av]orite merchandiz, and are called by them *tia Commáshuck'* or Chiefs beads. the best wampum is not so much esteemed by them as the most inferior beads. Sent Coalter out to hunt this morning, he shortly after returned with a deer, venison is a rarity with us we have had none for some weeks. Drewyer also set out on a hunting excertion and took one man[2] with him. he intends both to hunt the Elk and trap the beaver.

The Culinary articles of the Indians in our neighbourhood consist of wooden bowls or throughs, baskets, wooden spoons and woden scures or spits. Their wooden bowls and troughs are of different forms and sizes, and most generally dug out of a solid piece; they are ither round or simi globular, in the form of a canoe, cubic, and cubic at top terminating in a globe at bottom; these are extreemly well executed and many of them neatly carved the larger vessels with hand-holes to them; in these vessels they boil their fish or flesh by means of hot stones which they immerce in the water with the article to be boiled. they also render the oil of fish or other anamals in the same manner. their baskets are formed of cedar bark and beargrass so closely interwoven with the fingers that they are watertight without the aid of gum or rosin; some of these are highly ornamented with strans of beargrass which they dye of several colours and interweave in a great variety of figures; this serves them the double perpose of holding their water or wearing on their heads; and are of different capacites from that of the smallest cup to five or six gallons; they are generally of a conic form or reather the segment of a cone of which the smaller end forms the base or bottom of the basket. these they make very expediciously and dispose off for a mear trifle. it is for the construction of these baskets that the beargrass becomes an article of traffic among the natives this grass grows only on their high mountains near the snowey region; the blade is about ⅜ of an inch wide and 2 feet long smoth pliant and strong; the young blades which are white from not being exposed to the sun or air, are those most commonly employed, particularly in their neatest work. Their spoons are not remarkable nor abundant, they are generally large and the bole brawd. their meat is roasted with a sharp scure, one end of which is incerted in the meat with the other is set erect in the ground. the spit for roasting fish has it's upper extremity split, and between it's limbs the center of the fish is inscerted with it's head downwards and the tale and extremities of the scure secured with a string, the sides of the fish, which was in the first instance split on the back, are expanded by means of small splinters of wood which extend crosswise the fish. a small mat of rushes or flags is the usual plate or dish on which their fish, flesh, roots or burries are served. they make a number of bags and baskets not watertight of cedar bark, silk-grass, rushes, flags and common coarse sedge.[3] in these they secure their dryed fish, rooots, buries, &c.—

[Clark] *Sunday* [Friday] *17th January 1806*

 This morning we were visited by Comowool and 7 of the Clatsops our nearest neighbours, who left us again in the evening. They brought with them Some roots and beries for Sale, of which however they disposed of very fiew as they asked for them Such prices as our Stock in trade would not licence us in giveing. The Chief Comowool gave us Some roots and berries, for which we gave him in return a mockerson awl and Some thread; the latter he wished for the purpose of makeing a Skiming Net. one of the party was dressed in three verry elegant Sea otter Skins which we much wanted; for these we offered him maney articles but he would not dispose of them for aney other Consideration but Blue beeds, of those we had only Six fathoms left, which being 4 less than his price for each Skin he would not exchange nor would a Knife or any other equivolent in beeds of aney other Colour answer his purpose; these Coarse blue beeds are their favourite merchandize and are Called by them *Tia com ma shuck* or Chief beeds, the best Wampom is not as much esteemed by them as the most indifferent beeds. Sent Colter out to hunt he Shortly after returned with a Deer, Venison is a rarity with us we have had none for Some weeks. Drewyer Set out on a hunting expedition one man went with him. he intends to hunt the Elk and trap the beaver.

 The Culinary articles of the Indians in our neighbourhood Consists of wooden bowls or troughs, Baskets, Shell and wooden Spoons and wooden Scures or Spits, their wooden Bowles and troughs are of different forms and Sizes, and most generally dug out of Solid piecies; they are either round, Square or in the form of a canoe; those are extreemly well executed and maney of them neetly covered, the larger vessels with handholes to them; in these vessels they boil their fish or flesh by means of hot Stones which they immerce in the water with the articles to be boiled. They also render the Oil of the fish, or other animals in the Same manner. Their baskets are formed of Cedar bark and bargrass So closely interwoven withe hands or fingers that they are watertight without the aid of gum or rozin; Some of those are highly orniments with the Strans of bargrass which they dye of Several Colours and interweave in a great variety of figures; this Serves a double purpose of holding the Water or wareing on their heads; and are of different Capacities, from that of a Smallest Cup to five or Six gallons, they are generally of a Conic form or reather the Segment of a Cone of which the Smaller end forms the base or bottom of the basket. these they make verry expediciously and dispose of for a mear trifle. it is for the Construction of those baskets that Bargrass becoms an article of traffic among the nativs of the Columbia. this grass grows only on their mountains near the Snowey region; the blade is about ⅜ of an inch wide and 2 feet long Smothe plient & Strong; the young blades which are white from not being exposed to the Sun or air, are those which are most Commonly employ'd, particularly in their neatest work. Their wooden Spoons are not remarkable nor abundant, they are large & the bowls broad. their meat is roasted with a Sharp Scure, one end of which is incerted in the meat while the other is Set erect in the ground. The Spit for roasting fish has its upper extremity Split, and between its limbs the Center of the fish is incerted with its head downwards, and the tale and the extremities of the Scure Secured with a String, the Side of the fish, which was in the first instance Split in the back, are expanded by means of Small Splinters of wood which extend Crosswise the fish. a Small mat of rushes or flags is the usual[4] plate, or Dish on which their fish, flesh, roots & berries are Served. they make a number of Bags and Baskets not water tight of Cedar bark Silk Grass, rushes, flags, and common Corse Sedge—. in those they Secure their dried fish, roots berries &.—[5]

   1. Someone has drawn an "x" across a couple of lines about here.
   2. Lepage; see below, January 24, 1806.
   3. Silk grass is probably one of the taller species of dogbane, Indian hemp, *Apocynum* sp., which has long, silky fibers in the outer bark that was extensively used for cordage. The enumeration of all the important textile plants as given here, including the coarse sedge, *Carex* sp., is an important source for ethnobotanical studies. Notably, the fibers from nettles, extensively used by Indians of the region, was not recorded. See Ruby &

Brown (CITC), 15, for a review of textiles, fibers, and basket materials in use by the Lower Chinooks, but without botanical names. Hitchcock et al., 4:78–82; Gunther (EWW), 28; Cutright (LCPN), 267–68, 267 n. 25.

    4. "Usual" is substituted for another, crossed-out word, which is illegible.

    5. About the remaining one-quarter of this page is blank.

[Lewis]   *Sunday [NB: Saturday] January 18th 1806.*

    Two of the Clatsops who were here yesterday returned today for a dog they had left; they remained with us a few hours and departed. no further occurrence worthy of relation took place. the men are still much engaged in dressing skins in order to cloath themselves and prepare for our homeward journey. The Clatsops Chinnooks &c construct their houses of timber altogether.¹ they are from 14 to 20 feet wide and from 20 to 60 feet in length, and acommodate one or more families sometimes three or four families reside in the same room. thes houses a[re] also divided by a partition of boards, but this happens only in the largest houses as the rooms are always large compared with the number of inhabitants. these houses are constructed in the following manner; two or more posts of split timber agreeably to the number of divisions or partitions are furst provided, these are sunk in the ground at one end and rise perpendicularly to the hight of 14 or 18 feet, the tops of them are hollowed in such manner as to receive the ends of a round beam of timber which reaches from one to the other, most commonly the whole length of the building, and forming the upper part of the roof; two other sets of posts and poles are now placed at proper distances on either side of the first, formed in a similar manner and parrallel to it; these last rise to the intended hight of the eves, which is usually about 5 feet. smaller sticks of timber are now provided and are placed by pares in the form of rafters, resting on, and reaching from the lower to the upper horizontal beam, to both of which they are attatched at either end with the cedar bark; two or three ranges of small poles are now placed horizontally on these rafters on each side of the roof and are secured likewise with strings of the Cedar bark. the ends sides and partitions are then formed with one range of wide boards of abut two inches thick, which are sunk in the ground a small distance at their lower ends and stand erect with their upper ends laping on the outside of the eve poles and end rafters to which they are secured by an outer pole lying parallel with the eve poles and rafters being secured to them by chords of cedar bark which pass through wholes made in the boards at certain distances for that purpose; the rough [roof] is then covered with a double range of thin boards, and an aperture of 2 by 3 feet left in the center of the roof to permit the smoke to pass.   these houses are sometimes sunk to the debth of 4 or 5 feet in which cace the eve of the house comes nearly to the surface of the earth.   in the center of each room a space of six by eight feet square is sunk about twelve inches lower than the floor having it's sides secured with four sticks of squar timber, in this space they make their fire, their fuel being generally pine bark.   mats are spread arround the fire on all sides, on these they set in the day and frequently sleep at night.   on the inner side of the hose on two sides and sometimes on three, there is a range of upright peices about 4 feet removed from the wall; these are also sunk in the ground at their lower ends, and secured at top to the rafters, from these other peices ar extended horizontally to the wall and are secured in the usual method by bark to the upright peices which support the eve poles.   on these short horizontal pieces of which there are sometimes two ranges one above the other, boards are laid, which either form ther beads, or shelves on which to put their goods and chattles of almost every discription.   their uncured fish is hung on sticks in the smoke of their fires as is also the flesh of the Elk when they happen to be fortunate enough to procure it which is but seldom.—

[Clark] *Monday* [Saturday] *18th January 1806*

Two of the Clatsops that were here yesterday returned to day for a Dog they had left; they remained with us a fiew hours and departed.   no further accounts worthey of relation took place.   the men are much engaged dressing Skins in order to Cloath themselves and prepare for the homeward journey.[2]

The Clatsops Chinnooks &c. construct their *Houses* of timber altogether.   they are from 14 to 20 feet wide, and from 20 to 60 feet in length, and accomodate one or more families   Sometimes three or four families reside in the Same room.   this house is also devided by petitions of Boards, but this happens only in the largest houses, as the rooms are

At Fort Clatsop

always large Compared with the number of inhabitents. those houses are Constructed in the following manner; two or more posts of Split timber agreeably to the number of devisions or partitions are first provided, these are Sunk in the ground at one end and raised pirpindicular to the hight of 12 or 14 feet, the top of them are hollowed So as to recive the end of a round beem of timber which reaches from one to the other or the entire length of the house; and forming the ridge pole; two other Sets of posts and poles are then placed at proper distances on either Side of the first, formed in a Similar manner and parrelal to it; those last rise to the intended hight of the eves, which is usially about 5 feet,— Smaller Sticks of timber is then previded and are placed by pears in the form of rafters, resting on, and reaching from the lower to the upper horizontial beam, to both of which they are atached at either end with the Cedar bark; two or 3 ranges of Small poles are then placed Horizontially on these rafters on each Side of the roof & are Secured likewise with Cedar bark. the ends, Sides, and partitions are then formed, with one range of wide boards of about 2 inches thick, which are Sunk in the ground a Small distance at their lower ends & Stands erect with their upper ends lapping on the out Side of the eve poles and end rafters to which they are Secured by a outer pole lyeing parrelal with the eve pole and rafters being Secured to them by Cords of Cedar bark which pass through wholes made in the bods at Certain distances for that purpose; the rough [roof] is then Covered with a double range of thin boards, and an aperture of 2 by 3 feet left in the Center of the roof to admit the Smoke to pass. These houses are commonly Sunk to the debth of 4 or 5 feet in which Case the eve of the house comes nearly to the Surface of the earth. in the Center of each room a Space of from 6 by 8 feet is Sunk about 12 inches lower than the floar haveing its Sides Secured by four thick boards or Squar pieces of timber, in this Space they make their fire, their fuel being generally dry pine Split Small which they perform with a peice of an Elks horn Sharpened at one end drove into the wood with a Stone. mats are Spred around the fire on all Sides, on these they Sit in the day and frequently Sleep at night. on the inner Side of the house on two Sides and Sometimes on three, there is a range of upright pieces about 4 feet removed from the wall; these are also Sunk in the ground a[t] their lower end, and Secured at top to the rafters, from those, other pieces are extended horozontially to the wall and are Secured in the usial manner with bark to the upright pieces which Support the eve pole. on these Short horizontial peics of which there are Sometimes two ranges one above the other, boards are laid, which either form their beads, or Shelves on which to put their goods and Chattles, of almost every discription.   their uncured fish is hung on Sticks in the Smoke of their fires as is also the flesh of the Elk when they happen to be fortunate enough to precure it which is but Seldom—.

1. Rectangular plank houses broadly similar to those of the Chinookan peoples were the characteristic form along the Pacific Coast from southern Alaska to northern California. While commonly semi-subterranean, they were sometimes constructed entirely above ground (as among the Wahkiakums, see entry for November 7, 1805). Although varying considerably in terms of construction detail and gross size, the gabled-style Chinookan house was found at least as far north as the Quinaults and as far south as the southern Oregon coast. Olson (TNC), 24–27; Ray (LCEN), 124–26; Hajda, 140–44.

2. A red vertical line begins with the next paragraph and runs nearly to the end of the entry, perhaps placed there by Biddle.

[Lewis]   Monday [NB: Sunday] January 19th 1806.

This morning sent out two parties of hunters, consisting of Collins[1] and Willard whom we sent down the bay towards point Adams, and Labuish and Shannon whom we sent up Fort River;[2] the fist by land and the latter by water. we were visited today by two Clatsop men and a woman who brought for sale some Sea Otter skins of which we purchased one, giving in exchange the remainder of our blue beads consisting of 6 fathoms and about the same quantity of small white beads and a knife. we also purchased a small quantity of train oil for a pair of Brass armbands and a hat for some fishinghooks. these hats are of their own manufactory and are composed of Cedar bark and bear grass interwoven with the fingers and ornimented with various colours and figures, they are nearly waterproof, light, and I am convinced are much more durable than either chip[3] or straw. These hats form a small article of traffic with the Clatsops and Chinnooks who dispose of them to the whites. the form of the hat is that which was in vogue in the Ued States and great Britain in the years 1800 & 1801 with a high crown reather larger at the top than where it joins the brim;[4] the brim narrow or about 2 or 2½ inches.

Several families of these people usually reside together in the same room; they appear to be the father & mother and their sons with their son's wives and children; their provision seems to be in common and the greatest harmoney appears to exist among them. The old man is not always rispected as the head of the family, that duty most commonly devolves on one of the young men. They have seldom more than one wife, yet the plurality of wives is not denyed them by their customs. These families when ascociated form nations or bands of nations each acknoledging the authority of it's own chieftain who dose not appear to be heriditary, nor his power to extend further than a mear repremand for any improper act of an individual; the creation of a chief depends upon the upright deportment of the individual & his ability and disposition to render service to the community; and his authority or the deference paid him is in exact equilibrio with the popularity or voluntary esteem he has acquired among the individuals of his band or nation. Their laws like those of all uncivilized Indians consist of a set of customs which have grown out of their local situations. not being able to speak their language we have not been able to inform ourselves of the existence of any peculiar customs among them.

[Clark] *Tuesday* [Sunday] *19th of January 1806*

This morning Sent out two parties of hunters, one party towards Point adams and the other party up *Ne tel* River by water. we were visited to day by two Clatsop men and a woman who brought for Sale Some Sea otter Skins of which we purchased one gave in exchange the remainder of our blue beeds Consisting of 6 fathoms, and the Same quantity of Small white beids and a knife. we also purchased a Small quantity of train oil for a par of Brass arm bands, and a hat for Som fishinghooks. these hats are of their own manufactory and are Composed of Cedar bark and bear grass interwoven with the fingers and ornimented with various Colours and figures, they are nearly water proof, light, and I am Convinced are much more dureable than either Chip or Straw,— These hats form a article of traffic with Clatsops an Chinnooks who dispose of them to the whites, the form of the Hats is that which was in voge in the U States and Great Britain in 1800 & 1801 with a high Crown rather larger at the top than where it joins the brim, the brim narrow about 2 or 2½ inches.

Several families of those people usially reside together in the Same room; they appear to be the father mother with their Sons and their Sons wives and children; their provisions appears to be in common and the greatest harmoney appears to exist among them. the old man is not always respected as the head of the family that duty generally devolves on one of the young men. They have Sildom more than one wife, yet plurality of wives are not denyed them by their Customs. those families when associated [form] bands of nations each acknowledgeing the authority of its own Chieftains, who does not appear to be herititary, or has power to extend further than a mear repremand for any improper deportment of the indevidual; the Creation of a Chief depends upon the upright Conduct of the individual his abiltity and disposition to render Service to the Comunity, and his authority and the defference paid him is in extent equilibrio with the popolarity or volintary esteem he has acquired among the individuals of his band, or nation. Their Laws like all uncivilized Indians Consist of a Set of customs which has grown out of their local Situations. not being able to Speak their language we have not been able to inform ourselves of the existance of any peculiar Customs among them.

1. Perhaps an error for Colter; Collins seems to have been with the saltmakers on the shore. See below, January 25, 1806.
2. Lewis and Clark River, Clatsop County, Oregon. *Atlas* map 82, 84.
3. Palm leaf, straw, or wood, split into thin pieces for making hats.
4. Not typical of the conical style of native hats, but like the one mentioned in Clark's second entry of November 21, 1805.

[Lewis] *Tuesday [NB: Monday] January 20th 1806.*

Visited this morning by three Clatsops who remained with us all day; the object of their visit is mearly to smoke the pipe. on the morning of the eighteenth we issued 6 lbs. of jirked Elk pr. man, this evening the Sergt. repoted that it was all exhausted; the six lbs. have therefore lasted two days and a half only. at this rate our seven Elk will last us only 3 days longer, yet no one seems much concerned about the state of the stores; so much for habit. we have latterly so frequently had our stock of provisions reduced to a minimum and sometimes taken a small touch of fasting that three days full allowance excites no concern. In those cases our skill as hunters afford us some consolation, for if there is any game of any discription in our neighbourhood we can track it up and kill it. most of the party have become very expert with the rifle. The Indians who visited us today understood us sufficiently to inform us that the whites did not barter for the pounded fish; that it was purchased and consumed by the Clatsops, Chinnooks, Cathlahmah's and Skillutes. The native roots which furnish a considerable proportion of the subsistence of the indians in our neighbourhood are those of a species of Thistle, fern[1] and rush;[2] the Liquorice, and a small celindric root[3] the top of which I have not yet seen, this last resembles the sweet pittatoe very much in it's flavor and consistency.

[Clark]   Wednesday [Monday] 20th January 1806

Visited this morning by three Clapsots who remained with us all day; the object of their visit is mearly to Smoke the pipe. on the morning of the 18 inst. we issued 6 wt. of jurked meat pr. man, this evening the Serjt. reports that is all exhosted; the 6 w. have therefore lasted 2 days and a half only. at this rate our Seven Elk will only last us 3 days longer, yet no one appears much concerned about the State of the Stores; So much for habet. we have latterly so frequently had our Stock of provisions reduced to a minimum and Sometimes taken a Small tuck of fasting that 3 days full allowance exites no concern. In those Cases our Skill as hunters affords us Some Consolation, for if there is any game of any discription in our neighbourhood we can track it up and kill it. most of the party have become very expert with the rifle. The Indians who visit us to day understood us Sufficiently to inform us that the white who visit them did not barter for the pounded fish; that it was purchased and Consumed by the Clatsops, Chin nooks, Cath lâh mâhs and Skil lutes, and Kil a moxs.

The native roots which furnish a considerable proportion of the Subsistance of the indians in our neighbourhoodd are those of a Species of Thistle, fern, and rush; the Licquorice, and a Small celindric root the top of which I have not yet Seen, this last resembles the Sweet potato verry much in its flavour and Consistency.[4]

    1. Western bracken fern, *Pteridium aquilinium* L. var. *pubescens* Underw. See Lewis's detailed description of this species on January 22, 1806. Hitchcock et al., 1:93; Gunther (EWW), 14–15; Ray (LCEN), 120; Cutright (LCPN), 264, 274, 416.

2. Giant horsetail, *Equisetum talmateia* Ehrh. Hitchcock et al., 1:47; Gunther (EWW), 15; Ray (LCEN), 120; Cutright (LCPN), 264.

3. The identity of this species is not clear. It may be one of the roots described by Swan (NC), 88, but its identity is also unknown. The plant is mentioned again on January 24, with reference to this entry.

4. A red vertical line runs through this paragraph, perhaps penned by Biddle.

Chapter Twenty-Eight

At Fort Clatsop

January 21–March 17, 1806

[Lewis] *Wednesday [NB: Tuesday] January 21st 1806.*
 Two of the hunters Shannon & Labuish returned having killed three Elk. Ordered a party to go in quest of the meat early tomorrow morning and the hunters to return and continue the chase. the Indians left us about 12 O'Clk. The root of the thistle,[1] called by the natives *shan-ne-tâh-que* is a perpendicular fusiform and possesses from two to four radicles; is from 9 to 15 Inces in length and about the size a mans thumb; the rhind somewhat rough and of a brown colour; the consistence when first taken from the earth is white and nearly as crisp as a carrot; when prepared for uce by the same process before discribed of the white bulb or *pashshequo quawmash*, it becomes black, and is more shugary than any fuit or root that I have met with in uce among the natives; the sweet is precisely that of the sugar in flavor; this root is sometimes eaten also when first taken from the ground without any preperation; but in this way is vastly inferior. it delights most in a deep rich dry lome which has a good mixture of sand. the stem of this plant is simple ascending celindric and hisped. the root leaves yet possess their virdure and are about half grown of a plale green. the cauline leaf as well as the stem of the last season are now dead, but in rispect to it's form &c. it is simple, crenate, & oblong, reather more obtuse at it's apex than at the base or insertion; it's margin armed with prickles while it's disks are hairy, it's insertion decurrent and position declining. the flower is also dry and mutilad. the pericarp seems much like that of the common thistle. it rises to the hight of from 3 to 4 feet.—

[Clark]   *Thursday [EC: Tuesday] 21st of January 1806*

Two of the hunters Shannon & Labieche returned haveing killed three Elk, ordered a party to go in quest of the meat early tomorrow morning and the hunters to return and continue the chase—. the indians left us about 12 oClock.[2]

The root of the thistle called by the nativs *Chan-ne-tâk-que* is pirpendicular and possesses from two to 4 radicles; is from 9 to 15 inches in length and is Commonly about the Size of a mans thum the rhine Somewhat rough and of a brown Colour; the Consistence when first taken from the earth is white and nearly as Crisp as a Carrot, when prepared for use by the Same process before discribed of the white bulb or *pash she quo, qua-mosh,* it becomes black and is more Sugary than any root I have met with among the nativs; the Sweet is prosisely that of the Sugar in flavor, this root is Sometimes eaten when first taken from the ground without any preperation, in this way it is well tasted but soon weathers and becoms hard and insipped. it delights most in a deep rich moist lome which has a good mixture of Sand— The Stems of this plant is Simple ascending celindric and hisped. the root leaves, posses their virdue and are about half grown of a deep Green. the Cauline leaf as well as the Stem of the last Season are now dead, but in respect to it's form &c. it is Simple Crenated and oblong, rather more obtuce at it's apex than the base or insertion, it's margin armed with prickles while it's disks are hairy, its insertion decurrent and position declineing. the flower is also dry and mutilated the pericarp seems much like that of the Common thistle it rises to the hight of from 3 to 4 feet.

   1. The edible thistle. The "pashshequo quawmash" used for comparison is the camas. See above, September 20, 1805, for linguistic information on the camas, and November 21, 1805, for the thistle. Someone has drawn a vertical line through this passage in pencil.

   2. Beginning with the next paragraph, a red vertical line runs to the end of the entry, perhaps drawn by Biddle.

[Lewis]   *Thursday [NB: Wednesday] January 22nd 1806.*

The party[1] sent for the meat this morning returned with it in the Evening; it was in very inferior order, in short the animals were poor. Reubin Fields also remained with the other hunters Shannon & Labuish our late supply of salt is out.   we have not yet heared a sentence from the other two parties of hunter's[2] who are below us towards Point Adams and the Praries.

There are three species of fern in this neighbourhood the root[3] one of which the natves eat; this grows very abundant in the open uplands and praries where the latter are not sandy and consist of deep loose rich black lome.[4]   the root is horizontal sometimes a little deverging or obliquely descending, frequently dividing itself as it procedes into two equal branches and shooting up a number of stems; it lies about 4 Inces beneath the surface of the earth.   the root is celindric, with few or no radicles and from the size of a goose quill to that of a man's finger; the center of the root is divided into two equal parts by a strong flat & white ligament like a piece of thin tape   on either side of this there is a white substance which when the root is roasted in the embers is much like wheat dough and not very unlike it in flavour, though it has also a pungency which becomes more visible after you have chewed it some little time; this pungency was disagreeable to me, but the natives eat it very voraciously and I have no doubt but it is a very nutricious food.   the bark of the root is black, somewhat rough, thin and brittle, it easily seperates in flakes from the part which is eaten as dose also the internal liggament.   this root perennil.   in rich lands this plant rises to the hight of from 4 to five feet.   the stem is smooth celindric, slightly groved on one side erect about half it's hight on the 2 first branches thence reclining backwards from the grooved side; it puts forth it's branches which are in reallyty long footstalks by pares from one side only and near the edges of the groove, these larger footstalks are also grooved cilindric and gradually tapering towards the extremity, puting forth alternate footstalks on either side of the grove near it's edge; these lesser footstalks the same in form as the first put forth from forty to fifty alternate pinate leaves which are sessile, horizontal, multipartite for half their length from the point of insertion and terminating in a long shaped apex, and are also revolute with the upper disk smoth and the lower slightly cottanny.   these alternate leaves after proceeding half the length of the footstalk cease to be partite and assume the tongue like form altogether.   this plant produces no flower or fruit whatever, is of a fine green colour in summer and a beautifull plant.   the top is annual and is of course dead at present.—

[Clark] Friday [EC: Wednes] 22nd January 1806

The party Sent for the meat this morning returned with it in the evening; it was in verry inferior order, in Short the animals were pore. Rieuben Field Shannon and Labiech remained in the woods to hunt. our late Supply of Salt is out. we have not heard a word of the other hunters who are below us towards point adams and the Praries. Some rain this day at intervales—

There are three Species of fern in this neighbourhood the root one of which the nativs eate; that of which the nativs eate produce no flowers whatever or fruit of a fine green Colour and the top is annual, and in Course dead at present.[5]

I observe no difference between the licorice[6] of this Countrey and that Common to maney parts of the United States where it is sometimes Cultivated in our gardins—. this plant delights in a deep lose Sandy Soil; here it grows verry abundant and large; the nativs roste it in the embers and pound it Slightly with a Small Stick in order to make it Seperate more readily from the Strong liggaments which forms the center of the root; this they discard and chew and Swallow the ballance of the root; this last is filled with a number of thin membrencies like network, too tough to be masticated and which I find it necessary also to discard. This root when roasted possesses an agreeable flavour not unlike the Sweet potato. The root of the thistle (described yesterday) after undergoing the process of Sweting or bakeing in a *kiln* is Sometimes eaten with the train oil also, at other times pounded fine and mixed with Cold water, untill reduced to the Consistancy of Gruel; in this way I think it verry agreeable. but the most valuable of all their roots is foreign to this neighbourhood I mean the *Wappetoe.*

The *Wappetoe,* or bulb of the Sagitifolia or common arrow head, which grows in great abundance in the marshey grounds of that butifull and fertile vally on the Columbia commenceing just above the quick Sand River and extending downwards for about 70 miles. this *bulb* forms a principal article of trafic between the inhabitents of the vally and those of their neighbourhood or Sea coast.

1. Sergeant Ordway says he was with this party.
2. Apparently Colter and Willard made up one of these parties, Drouillard and Lepage the other. See below, January 24, 1806.

3. Western bracken fern.

4. Quaternary terrace deposits of sand and gravel underlie much of the Lewis and Clark River valley. Away from the river bluffs these deposits are commonly overlain by terrace deposits consisting mainly of silt and clay.

5. In the next two paragraphs red vertical lines cross out portions of the botanical descriptions, perhaps done by Biddle.

6. Clark is here borrowing from Lewis's entry of January 24 and describing the seashore lupine. By the liquorice of the country he means the wild liquorice, *Glycyrrhiza lepidota* (Nutt.) Pursh (as noted on May 8, 1805), and in comparison to the cultivated liquorice, *G. glabra* L. Lewis is mistaken in the lupine being large; it is actually a prostrate plant. He may have been seeing only the root at this point with additional information coming from the natives. Cutright (LCPN), 265, discusses the question of identifying the plant. See also the entries of November 17 and December 27, 1805.

[Lewis]   *Friday [NB: Thursday] January 23rd 1806.*

This morning dispatched Howard and Warner to the Camp of the Saltmakes for a supply of salt. The men of the garison are still busily employed in dressing Elk's skins for cloathing, they find great difficulty for the want of branes;[1] we have not soap to supply the deficiency, nor can we procure ashes to make the lye; none of the pines which we use for fuel affords any ashes; extrawdinary as it may seem, the greene wood is consoomed without leaving the residium of a particle of ashes.—

The root of the rush[2] used by the natives is a sollid bulb about one inch in length and usually as thick as a man's thumb, of an ovate form depressed on two or more sides, covered with a thin smothe black rind. the pulp is white brittle and easily masticated either raw or roasted   the latter is the way in which it is most usually prepared for uce.   this root is reather insipid in point of flavour, it grows in greatest abundance along the sea coast in the sandy grounds and is most used by the Killamucks and those inhabiting the coast.   each root sends up one stock only which is annual, the root being perenniel.   the bulb is attatched to the bottom of the caulis or stem by a firm small and strong radicle of about one Inch long; this radicle is mearly the prolongation of the caulis and decends perpendicilarly; a little above the junction of this radicle with the caulis, the latter is surrounded in a whorl with a set of small radicles from 6 to 9 inches long which are obliquely descending.   the caulis is celindric erect hollow and jointed, and is about the size or reather larger than the largest quill.   it rises to the hight of 3 or 4 feet, not branching nor dose it either bear flower or seed that I can discover tho' I am far from denying that it dose so sometimes, but I have not been able to discover it. the stem is rough like the sand rush and is much like it when green or in it's succulent state. at each joint it puts out from twenty to thirty long lineal stellate or radiate & horizontal leaves which surround the stem. above each joint about half an inch the stem is sheathed like the sand rush.

[Clark]   *Saturday [EC: Thurs.] 23rd of January 1806*

This morning dispatched Howard & Werner to the Camp of the Salt makers for a Supply of Salt. the men of the garrison are Still busily employed in dressing Elk Skins for cloathing, they fine great dificuelty for the want of branes; we have not Soap to Supply the deficiency, nor can we precure ashes to make the lye; none of the pine which we use for fuel afford any ashes; extrawdinary as it may seem, the green wood is cosumed without leaveing the risideum of a particle of ashes.—[3]

The root of the rush used by the nativs is a Solid bulb about one inch in length and usially as thick as a mans thumb, of an ovel form depressed on two or more Sides, covered with a thin black rine. the pulp is white brittle and easily masticated either raw or rosted, the latter is the way it is most commonly prepared for use. this root is reather insippid in point of flavour, it grows in the Greatest abundance along the Sea coast in the wet Sandy grounds and is most used by the Kil á mox and those inhabiting the Sea coast. each root Sends up its Stalk which is annual, the root being perennial. the bulb is atached to the bottom of the Stem by a firm Small and Strong radicle which is mearly the prolongation of the Stem which is hollow and jointed and is rather larger than the largest quill. it rises to the hight of 3 or 4 feet, not branching no does it either bear flower or Seed that I could discover tho I am far from denying that it does So Sometimes, and perhaps every year, but I have not been able to discover it, the Stem is rough like the Sand rush, and it's much like it when green, at each joint it puts out from 20 to 30 radiate & horizontal leaves which Surrounds the Stem. above each joint about half an inch the Stem is Shethed like the Sand rush.

The instruments used by the nativs in digging their roots is a Strong Stick of three feet and a half long Sharpened at the lower end and its upper inserted into a part of an Elks or buck's horn which Serves as a

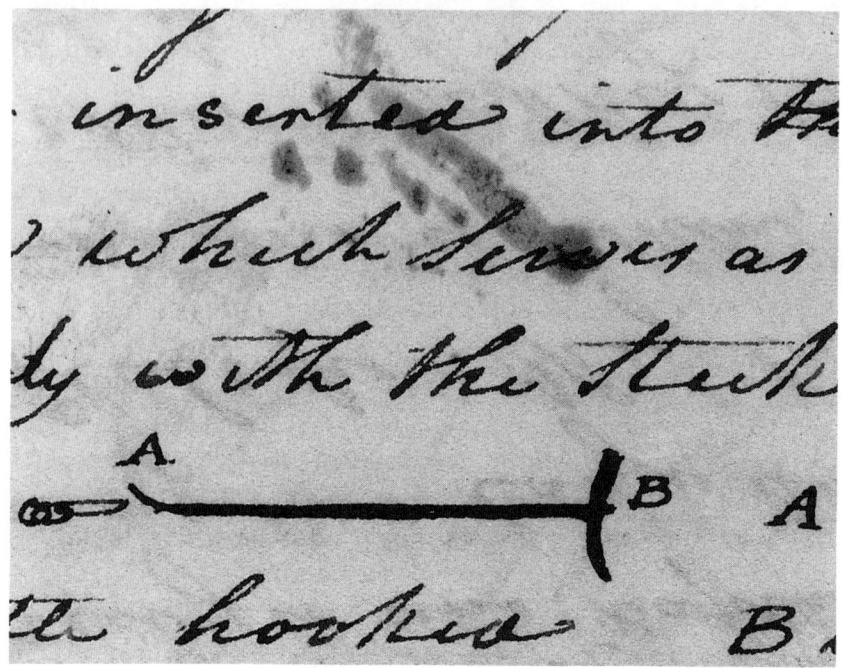

19. Digging Instrument,
January 23, 1806, Codex I, p. 135

handle; Standing transvirsely in the Stick— or it is in this form as thus[4] A is the lower part which is a little hooked B is the upper part or handle of Horn.—

    1. Animal brains were employed in tanning leather; it is to this that Lewis refers, rather than to any lack of intelligence on the part of the men.
    2. Giant horsetail. A dark line runs through the preceding paragraph and the first few lines of this paragraph, perhaps done by Biddle.
    3. The first few lines of the next two paragraphs have red vertical lines running through them, perhaps drawn by Biddle.
    4. At this point in Codex I (p. 135) appears a diagram of the digging instrument described (fig. 19). A similar drawing appears in Codex P, p. 92, probably copied from Codex I or Codex J (see next entry) by an unknown person at a later date. Moulton (SJ).

[Lewis]   *Saturday [NB: Friday] January 24th 1806.*
    Drewyer and Baptiest La Paage returned this morning in a large Canoe with Comowooll and six Clatsops. they brought two deer and the flesh of three Elk & one Elk's skin, having given the flesh of one other Elk

January 21–March 17, 1806

which they killed and three Elk's skins to the Indians as the price of their assistance in transporting the ballance of the meat to the Fort; these Elk and deer were killed near point Adams and the Indians carryed them on their backs about six miles, before the waves were sufficiently low to permit their being taken on board their canoes. the Indians remained with us all day. The Indians witnissed Drewyer's shooting some of those Elk, which has given them a very exalted opinion of us as marksmen and the superior excellence of our rifles compared with their guns; this may probably be of service to us, as it will deter them from any acts of hostility if they have ever meditated any such. My Air-gun also astonishes them very much, they cannot comprehend it's shooting so often and without powder; and think that it is *great medicine* which comprehends every thing that is to them incomprehensible.—

I observe no difference between the liquorice of this country and that common to many parts of the United states where it is also sometimes cultivated in our gardens. this plant delights in a deep loose sandy soil; here it grows very abundant and large; the natives roast it in the embers and pound it slightly with a small stick in order to make it seperate more readily from the strong liggament which forms the center of the root; this the natives discard and chew and swallow the ballance of the root; this last is filled with a number of thin membrenacious lamela like net work, too tough to be masticated and which I find it necessary also to discard. this root when roasted possesses an agreeable flavour not unlike the sweet pittaitoe. beside the small celindric root mentioned on the 20th inst., they have also another about the same form size and appearance which they use much with the train oil, this root is usually boiled; to me it possesses a disagreeable bitterness. the top of this plant I have never yet seen. The root of the thistle after undergoing the prossess of sweating or baking in a kiln is sometimes eaten with the train oil also, and at other times pounded fine and mixed with could water untill reduced to the consistency of sagamity[1] or indian mush; in this way I think it very agreeable. but the most valuable of all their roots is foreign to this neighbourhood I mean the *Wappetoe,* or the bulb of the Sagitifolia or common arrow head, which grows in great abundance in the marshey grounds of that beatifull and firtile valley on the Columbia commencing just above the entrance of Quicksand River, and extending downwards for about 70

At Fort Clatsop

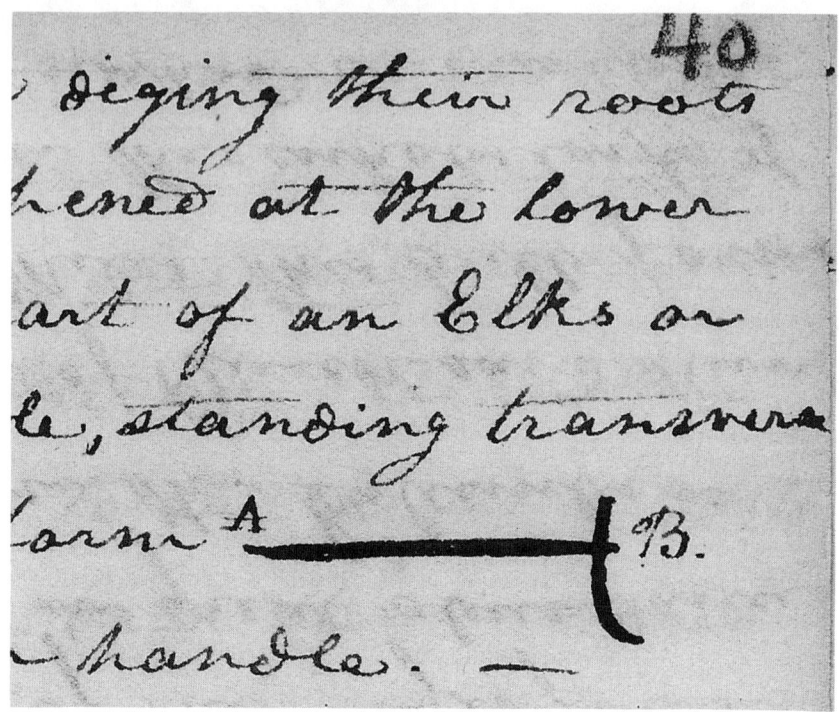

20. Digging Instrument,
January 24, 1806, Codex J, p. 40

Miles. this bulb forms a principal article of traffic between the inhabitants of the valley and those of this neighbourhood or sea coast. The instrument used by the natives in diging their roots is a strong stick of 3½ feet long sharpened at the lower end and it's upper inscerted into a part of an Elks or buck's horn which serves as a handle, standing transversely with the stick or it is in this form[2]   A the lower point, B the upper part or handle.—

[Clark] *Sunday [EC: Friday] 24th of January 1806*[3]

Drewyer and Bapteist laPage returned this morning in a large Canoe with Commowol and six Clatsops.   they brought two Deer and three Elk and one elk Skin, haveing given the flesh of one other Elk they killed and three Elk skins to the Indians as the price of their assistance in transporting the ballance of the meat to the Fort; these Deer and Elk were killed near pt. Adams and those Indians Carried them on their Backs near 4 miles, before the waves were Sufficiently low to permit their being taken on board their Canoes. The indians remain'd with us all day. The Clapsots witnessed Drewyers Shooting Some of those Elk, which has given them a very exolted opinion of us as marksmen and the Superior excellency of our rifles Compared with their guns; this may probably be of service to us, as it will deter them from any acts of hostility if they have ever meditated any such.

our air gun also astonishes them very much, they Cannot Comprehend its Shooting So often and without powder, and think that it is *great medison* which Comprehends every thing that is to them incomprehensible.[4]

The nativs of this neighbourhood ware no further Covering than a light roabe, their feet legs & every other part exposed to the frost Snow & ice &c.

   1. Corn mush, or a gruel or porridge made from coarse hominy. Criswell, 74. The word apparently comes from Cree *kiisaakamitew*, "it is hot [a liquid]."
   2. Here in Codex J, p. 40, appears a diagram of the digging instrument (fig. 20).
   3. In the upper right-hand corner of this page (136) of Codex I are the words, "[India?] Chief Wanner shi a," faintly penned, apparently by Clark.
   4. The next paragraph has a red vertical line through it, perhaps placed there by Biddle.

[Lewis] *Sunday [NB: Saturday] January 25th 1806.*

Commowooll and the Clatsops departed early this morning. At meridian Colter returned and repoted that his comrade hunter Willard had continued his hunt from point Adams towards the salt makers; and that they had killed only those two deer which the Indians brought yesterday. In the evening Collins one of the saltmakers returned and reported that they had mad about one bushel of salt & that himself and two others had hunted from the salt camp for five days without killing any thing and they had been obliged to subsist on some whale which they procured from the natives.

The native fruits and buries in uce among the Indians of this neighbourhood are a deep purple burry about the size of a small cherry called by them *Shal-lun,*[1] a small pale red bury called *Sol'-me;*[2] the vineing or low Crambury,[3] a light brown bury reather larger and much the shape of the black haw;[4] and a scarlet bury about the size of a small cherry the plant called by the Canadin Engages of the N. W. *sac a commis* produces this bury;[5] this plant is so called from the circumstance of the Clerks of those trading companies carrying the leaves of this plant in a small bag for the purpose of smokeing of which they are excessively fond. the Indians call this bury [blank]

I have lately learned that the natives whome I have heretofore named as distinct nations, living on the sea coast S. E. of the Killamucks, are only bands of that numerous nation, which continues to extend itself much further on that coast than I have enumerated them, but of the particular appellations of those distant bands I have not yet been enabled to inform myself; their language also is somewhat different from the Clatsops Chinnooks and Cathlâhmâhs; but I have not yet obtaind a vocabulary which I shall do the first oportunity which offers.[6]

[Clark] Monday [EC: Satur] *25th of January 1806*

Commowol and the Clatsops departed early this morning. Colter returned and reported that his comrade hunter Willard had Continued his hunt from Point Adams towards the Saltmakers; and that they had killed only those two deer which the indians brought yesterday; in the evening Collins one of the Saltmakers returned and reported that they had made about one bushel of Salt and that himself and two others had hunted from the Salt Camp for five days without killing any thing and they had been obliged to Subsist on Some whale which they purchased from the nativs—.[7]

The native fruits and berries in use among the Indians of this neighbourhood are a Deep purple about the Size of a Small cherry called by them *Shal lun,* a Small pale red berry called *Sol me;* the vineing or low brown berry, a light brown berry rather larger and much the Shape of a black haw; and a Scarlet berry about the Size of a Small Chirry the plant Called by the Canadian Engages of the N. W. *Sac a commis* produces this berry; this plant is So Called from the circumstances of the Clerks of these tradeing Companies Carrying the leaves of this plant in a Small bag for the purpose of Smokeing of which they are excessively fond the Indians Call this berry [blank]

1. Salal; see Lewis's description, February 8, 1806.
2. See above, November 13, 1805, and below, January 27, 1806.
3. Wild cranberry.
4. Oregon crabapple; see January 28, 1806.
5. Bearberry or kinnikinnick, *Arcostaphylos uva-ursi* (L.) Spreng. Lewis's etymology for the term saccacommis is incorrect, see notes above at February 28, 1805. Lewis's detailed discussion of the plant is at January 29, 1806.
6. The Tillamooks belonged to the coastal division of the Salishan-language family. South of them along the coast were some small groups belonging to the Alsean, Siuslawan, and Coosan-language families: the Alseas and the Yaquinas, the Siuslaws, the Coos, and the Umpquas. Thompson (NW).
7. The first few lines of the next paragraph have a red vertical line running through, perhaps set there by Biddle.

[Lewis] *Monday [NB: Sunday] January 26th 1806.*

Werner and Howard who were sent for salt on the 23rd have not yet returned, we are apprehensive that they have missed their way; neither of them are very good woodsmen, and this thick heavy timbered pine country added to the constant cloudy weather makes it difficult for even a good woodsman to steer for any considerable distance the course he wishes. we ordered Collins to return early in the morning and rejoin the salt makers, and gave him some small articles of merchandize to purchase provisions from the Indians, in the event of their still being unfortunate in the chase. The Shallun [*NB: See Febry. 8 1806*][1] or deep purple berry is in form much like the huckkleberry and terminates bluntly with a kind of cap or cover at the end like that fruit; they are attatched seperately to the sides of the boughs of the shrub by a very short stem hanging underneath the same and are frequently placed very near each other on the same bough; it is a full bearer. the berry is easily geathered as it seperates from the bough readily, while the leaf is strongly affixed. the shrub which produces this fruit rises to the hight of 6 or 8 feet sometimes grows on the high lands but moste generally in the swampy or marshey grounds; it is an evergreen. the stem or trunk is from three to 10 Inches in circumference irregularly and much branched, seldom more than one steem proceding from the same root, tho' they are frequently associated very thickly. the bark is somewhat rough and of a redish brown colour. the wood is very firm and hard. the leaves are alternate declining and attatched by a short fotstalk to the two horizontal sides of the boughs; the form is a long oval, reather more accute towards its apex than at the point of insertion; it's margin slightly serrate, it's sides colapsing or partially foalding upwards or channelled; it is also thick firm [s]mothe and glossey, the upper surface of a fine deep green, while the under disk is of a pale or whiteish green. this shrub retains it's virdure very perfectly during the winter and is a beautifull shrub.— the natives either eat these berrys when ripe immediately from the bushes or dryed in the sun or by means of their sw[e]ating kilns; very frequently they pound them and bake then in large loaves of 10 or fifteen pounds; this bread keeps very well during one season and retains the moist jeucies of the fruit much better than by any other method of preservation. this bread is broken and stired in could water until it be sufficiently thick and then eaten; in this way the natives most generally use it.—

[Clark] *Tuesday [EC: Sun] 26th of January 1806*

We order Collins to return early in the morning and join the Salt makers, and gave him Some Small articles of merchendize to purchase Some provisions from the indians in the event of their Still being unfortunate in the chase.

The [NB: *Shal-lun*][2] or deep purple berry is in form much like the huckleberry and termonate bluntly with a kind of Cap or cover at the end like that fruit; they are attached Seperately to the Sides of the boughes of the shrub by a very Short Stem ganging under neath the Same, and are frequently placed verry near each other on the Same bough it is a full bearer; the berry is easily gathered as it Seperates from the bough, readily, while the leaf is Strongly affixed. the Shrub which produces this fruit rises to the hight of 6 or 8 feet Sometimes grows on high lands but most frequently in Swampy or marshey grounds; it is an ever green. the Stem or trunk is from 3 to 10 inches in circumferance irrigularly and much branched, Seldom more than one Stem proceeding from the Same root, tho they are frequently associated very thickly. the bark is Somewhat rough and of a redish brown Colour. the wood is very firm and hard. the leaves are alternate declining and attachd by a Short fotstalk to the two horozontal Sides of the bough's; the form is a long oval, reather more accute towards its apex that at the point of insertion; it's Sides partially folding upwards; or Channeled, it is also thick ⟨firm and⟩ Smothe and glossy, the upper Surfice of a fine deep green, while the under disk is of a pale or whiteish green.   this Shrub retains its verdure verry perfectly dureing the winter and is a butifull Shrub—.   the nativs either eate those berries ripe imediately from the bushes, or dried in the Sun or by means of the Swetting kiln; verry frequently they pound them and bake them in large loaves 10 or 15 pounds weight; this bread keeps verry well dureing one Season and retains the moist jouicies of the frute much better than any other method of preperation. The bread is broken and Stured in Coald water untill it be Sufficiently thick and then eaten, in this way the nativ's most generally use it—.—.

   1. As Biddle notes in the emendation, Lewis describes the true "shullon," or salal, on February 8, 1806. The plant described here is evergreen huckleberry, *Vaccinium ovatum* Pursh, another species discovered by the expedition. Hitchcock et al., 4:34; Gunther (EWW), 44; Cutright (LCPN), 261 n. 19, 274–75, 422.
   2. The original word here has been replaced by Biddle's red-inked emendation. The first few lines of the paragraph have a red vertical line drawn through, perhaps Biddle's work.

[Lewis] *Tuesday [NB: Monday] January 27th 1806.*
   This morning Collins set out for the Salt works.   in the evening Shannon returned and reported that himself and party had killed ten Elk. he left Labuche and R. fields with the Elk.   two of those Elk he informed us were at the distance of nine miles from this place near the top of a mountain, that the rout by which they mus be brought was at least four miles by land through a country almost inaccessible from the fallen timber, brush and sink-holes, which were now disgused by the snow; we therefore concluded to relinquish those two Elk for the present, and ordered every man who could be speared from the fort to go early in the morning in surch of the other eight.
   Goodrich has recovered from the Louis veneri which he contracted from an amorous contact with a Chinnook damsel. I cured him as I did Gibson last winter by the uce of murcury.[1] I cannot learn that the Indians have any simples which are sovereign specifics in the cure of this disease; and indeed I doubt very much wheter any of them have any means of effecting a perfect cure.   when once this disorder is contracted by them it continues with them during life; but always ends in decipitude, death,

or premature old age; tho' from the uce of certain simples together with their diet, they support this disorder with but little inconvenience for many years, and even enjoy a tolerable share of health; particularly so among the Chippeways who I believe to be better skilled in the uce of those simples than any nation of Savages in North America. The Chippeways use a decoction of the root of the Lobelia,[2] and that of a species of sumac[3] common to the Atlantic states and to this country near and on the Western side of the Rocky Mountains. this is the smallest species of the sumac, readily distinguished by it's winged rib, or common footstalk, which supports it's oppositely pinnate leaves. these decoctions are drank freely and without limitation. the same decoctions are used in cases of the gonnaerea and are effecatious and sovereign. notwithstanding that this disorder dose exist among the Indians on the Columbia yet it is witnessed in but few individuals, at least the males who are always sufficiently exposed to the observations or inspection of the phisician. in my whole rout down this river I did not see more than two or three with the gonnaerea and about double that number with the pox.—

The beary which the natives call *solme*[4] is the production of a plant about the size and much the shape of that common to the atlantic states which produces the berry commonly called *Solloman's seal berry*. this berry also is attatched to the top of the stem in the same manner; and is of a globelar form, consisting of a thin soft pellecle which encloses a soft pulp inveloping from three to four seeds, white, firm, smothe, and in the form of a third or quarter of a globe, and large in proportion to the fruit or about the size of the seed of the common small grape. this berry when grown and unripe is not speckled as that of the Solomon's seal berry is; this last has only one globular smoth white firm seed in each berry.— the Solme grows in the woodlands among the moss and is an annual plant to all appearance.—

[Clark] *Wednesday [EC: Mon] 27th January 1806*

This morning Collins Set out to the Saltmakers Shannon returned and reported that himself and party had killed 10 Elk. he lef Labiech & R Field with the Elk, two of those Elk he informed us was at the distance of 9 miles from this place near the top of a mountain, that the rout by which they must be brought was at least 5 miles by land thro' a Countrey

January 21–March 17, 1806

almost inexcessable, from the fallen timber brush, and Sink holes, which were now disguised by the Snow; we therefore Concluded to relinquish those two Elks for the present, and ordered every man that Could be Speared from the Fort to go early in the morning in Serch of the other Eight, which is at no great distance from the *Netul* river, on which we are. Goudrich has recoverd from the louis veneri which he contracted from a amorous Contact with a Chinnook damsel. he was Cured as Gibson was with murcury by [*blank*][5] I cannot lern that the Indians have any Simples Sovereign Specifics in the cure of this disease; indeed I doubt verry much whether any of them have any means of effecting a perfect cure. when once this disorder is contracted by them it Continues with them dureing life; but always ends in decepitude, death; or premature old age; tho' from the use of certain Simples together with their diet, they Support this disorder with but little inconveniance for maney years, and even enjoy a tolerable Share of health; particularly So among the Chippeways who I beleive to be better Skilled in the use of those Simples than any nation of Indians in North America. The Chippaways use a decoction of the root of the *Labelia,* and that of a Species of Sumac Common to the Atlantic States[6] and to this countrey near and on the western Side of the Rocky mountains. This is the Smallest Specis of Sumake, readily distinguished by it's winged rib, or common footstalk, which Supports it's oppositly pinnate leaves. these decoctions are drank freely and without limatation. the Same decoctions are used also in cases of the gonnarea and are effecatious and sovereign. notwithstanding that this disorder does exist among the indians on the Columbia yet it is witnessed in but fiew individuals high up the river, or at least the males who are always Sufficiently exposed to the observation or inspection of the phisician. in my whole rout down this river I did not See more than two or three with Gonnarea and about double that number with the Pox.—

The berry which the nativs Call *Sol me* is the production of a plant about the Size and much the Shape of that Common to the atlantic States which produces the berry Commonly Called *Sollomons Seal berry*[7] this berry is also attached to the top of the Stem in the Same manner; and is of a globular form Consisting of a thin Soft Pellicle rine which encloses a Soft Pellicle pulp inveloping from 3 to 4 Seed, white firm, Smothe, and in the form of a third or a quarter of a Globe, and large in perportion to the fruit, or about the Size of the Seed of the Common Small grape. the berry when grown and unripe is not Specked as the Solomon's seal Berry is; this last haveing only one Globaler Smothe, ferm, white Seed in each berry—. the *Sol me* grows in the wood lands amonge the moss and on the high ridges. and is an annual plant to all appearance.—.

   1. There is apparently some question whether Lewis could be said to have cured syphilis by using mercury. Six months later (see Lewis's entry for July 2, 1806), Goodrich and McNeal were exhibiting symptoms of the secondary stage of the disease. Goodrich, McNeal, and Gibson were among the expedition members Clark listed as dead some twenty years later, but since some fifteen had died in all, it seems unwise to make any conclusions about the unrecorded causes of the deaths of the three. Cutright (LCPN), 254–56; Chuinard (OOMD), 264–65; Clark's List (ca. 1825–28), Jackson (LLC), 2:638–39. The "Louis veneri" is *lues venerea*, Latin for syphilis.
   2. Blue cardinal-flower, *Lobelia siphilitica* L., Fernald, 1355.
   3. Dwarf sumac, *Rhus copallina* L., an eastern species that reaches its western limit in eastern Kansas and southeast Nebraska. Barkley, 223; Fernald, 977.
   4. It is either *Smilacina stellata* (L.) Desf. (Coues's *S. sessilifolia*), with dark blue or green berries and blue stripes, or *S. racemosa* (L.) Desf., having red berries with small purple spots, both called false Solomon's seal. The plant is compared to Solomon's seal, *Polygonatum biflorum* Ell., a species in the East. Hitchcock et al., 1:800–801; Bailey, 212–13; Coues (HLC), 3:826 n. 12. See above, November 13, 1805, for a discussion of the term "solme."
   5. The lines about Goodrich have a red vertical line through them, perhaps drawn by Biddle.
   6. Again a red vertical line from "The Chippaways" to about here.
   7. Another red vertical line from the beginning of this paragraph to about here.

[Lewis] *Wednesday [NB: Tuesday] January 28th 1806.*

Drewyer and Baptiest La Page set out this morning on a hunting excursion. about noon Howard and Werner returned with a supply of salt; the badness of the weather and the difficulty of the road had caused their delay. they inform us that the salt makers are still much straitened for provision, having killed two deer only in the last six days; and that there are no Elk in their neighbourhood. The party[1] that were sent this morning up Netul[2] river for the Elk returned in the even ing with three of them only; the Elk had been killed just before the snow fell which had covered them and so altered the apparent face of the country that the hunters could not find the Elk which they had killed. the river on which

Fort Clatsop stands we now call Ne-tul, this being the name by which the Clatsops call it.

The Cranbury of this neighbourhood is precisely the same common to the U' States, and is the production of marshey or boggy grounds. The light brown berry,[3] is the fruit of a tree about the size shape and appearance in every rispect with that in the U. States called the wild crab apple; the leaf is also precisely the same as is also the bark in texture and colour. the berrys grow in clumps at the end of the small branches; each berry supported by a seperate stem, and as many as from 3 to 18 or 20 in a clump. the berry is ovate with one of it's extremities attatched to the peduncle, where it is in a small degre concave like the insertion of the stem of the crab apple. I know not whether this fruit can properly be denominated a berry, it is a pulpy pericarp, the outer coat of which is in a thin smoth, tho' firm tough pillecle; the pericarp containing a membranous capsule with from three to four cells, each containing a seperate single seed in form and colour like that of the wild crab. The wood of this tree is excessively hard when seasoned. the natives make great uce of it to form their wedges with which they split their boards of pine for the purpose of building houses. these wedges they also employ in splitting their fire-wood and in hollowing out their canoes. I have seen the natives drive the wedges of this wood into solid dry pine which it cleft without fracturing or injuring the wedg in the smallest degree. we have also found this wood usefull to us for ax handles as well as glutts[4] or wedges. the native also have wedges made of the beams of the Elk's horns which appear to answer extremely well. this fruit is exceedingly assid, and resembles the flavor of the wild crab.

[Clark] *Thursday [EC: Tue] 28th January 1806*

Drewyer and Baptiest Lapage Set out this morning on a hunting excursion. about noon Howard & Werner returned with a Supply of Salt; the badness of the weather and the dificuelty of the road had detained them. they informed us that the Salt makers are Still much Stratened for provisions ⟨that⟩ haveing killed two deer only in the last Six days; and that there are no Elk in their neighbourhood.

The party that was Sent up the Netul river for the Elk returned this evening with three of them only; The Elk had been killed just before the Snow fell which had Covered them and So altered the apparant face of the Countrey that the hunters Could not find them. The River on which Fort *Clat Sop* Stands we now call Netul, this being the name by which the Clatsops Call it.

The Cranberry of this neighbourhood is precisely the Same Common to the united States, and is the production of boggy or mashey grounds.—.[5]

The *light-brown berry,* is the fruit of a tree, about the Size Shape and appearance in every respect with that in the united States called the *wild Crab apple;* the leaf is also presisely the Same as is also the bark in textue and colour. the berry grows in Clumps at the ends of the Smaller branches; each berry Supported by a Stem, and as maney as from 3 to 18 or 20 in a Clump. the berry is oval with one of its extremitis attatched to the peduncle, where it is in a Small degree Concave like the insersion of the Stem of the Crab apple. I know not whether this fruit Can properly be denomonated a berry, it is a pulpy pericarp, the outer coat of which is a thin Smothe, capsule with from three to four Cells, each containing a Seperate Single Seed in form and Colour like that of the wild Crab apple The wood of this tree is excessively hard when Seasoned. The nativs make great use of it to form their wedges of which they Split their boards of Pine for the purpose of building houses. those wedges they employ in common with those formed of the Elks horn, in Splitting their fire wood and in hollowing out their Canoes. I have Seen the nativs drive the wedges of this wood into a solid dry pine which it cleft without fractureing injuring the wedge in the Smallest degree. we have also found this wood usefull to us for ax handles, as well as glutt or wedges. The bark of this tree is chewed by our party in place of tobacco.

The fruit is exceedingly ascid and resembles the flavor of the wild Crab.

1. According to Ordway, Shannon was one of the hunters and presumably went with the party to locate the animals.
2. This word was added in place of an erased word.
3. Oregon crabapple, first noted on November 4, 1805.
4. A glut is a block of metal or wood used as a wedge.
5. A red vertical line runs through this paragraph and the first few lines of the next, perhaps penned by Biddle.

January 21–March 17, 1806

[Lewis] *Thursday* [*NB: Wednesday*] *January 29th 1806.*

Nothing worthy of notice occurred today. our fare is the flesh of lean elk boiled with pure water, and a little salt. the whale blubber which we have used very sparingly is now exhausted. on this food I do not feel strong, but enjoy the most perfect health;— a keen appetite supplys in a great degree the want of more luxurious sauses or dishes, and still render my ordinary meals not uninteresting to me, for I find myself sometimes enquiring of the cook whether dinner or breakfast is ready.—[1]

The *Sac a commis* is the growth of high dry situations, and invariably in a piney country or on it's borders. it is generally found in the open piney woodland as on the Western side of the Rocky mountain but in this neighbourhood we find it only in the praries or on their borders in the more open wood lands; a very rich soil is not absolutely necessary, as a meager one frequently produces it abundantly. the natives on this side of the Rockey mountains who can procure this berry invariably use it; to me it is a very tasteless and insippid fruit. this shrub is an evergreen, the leaves retain their virdure most perfectly through the winter even in the most rigid climate as on lake Winnipic.[2] the root of this shrub puts forth a great number of stems which seperate near the surface of the ground; each stem from the size of a small quill to that of a man's finger; these are much branched the branches forming an accute angle with the stem, and all more poperly pocumbent than creeping, for altho' it sometimes puts forth radicles from the stem and branches which strike obliquely into the ground, these radicles are by no means general, equable in their distances from each other nor do they appear to be calculated to furnish nutriment to the plant but reather to hold the stem or branch in it's place. the bark is formed of several thin layers of a smoth thin brittle substance of a dark or redish brown colour easily seperated from the woody stem in flakes. the leaves with rispect to their position are scatered yet closely arranged near the extremities of the twigs particularly. the leaf is about ¾ of an inch in length and about half that in width, is oval but obtusely pointed, absolutely entire, thick, smoth, firm, a deep green and slightly grooved. the leaf is supported by a small footstalk of proportionable length. the berry is attatched in an irregular and scattered manner to the small boughs among the leaves, tho' frequently closely arranged, but always supported by seperate short and small peduncles, the insertion of which poduces a slight concavity in the bury while it's opposite side is slightly convex; the form of the berry is a spheroid; the shorter diameter being in a line with the peduncle.— this berry is a pericarp the outer coat of which is a thin firm tough pellicle, the inner part consists of a dry mealy powder of a yellowish white colour invelloping from four to six proportionably large hard light brown seeds each in the form of a section of a spheroid which figure they form when united, and are destitute of any membranous covering.— the colour of this fruit is a fine scarlet. the natives usually eat them without any preperation. the fruit ripens in september and remains on the bushes all winter. the frost appears to take no effect on it. these berries are sometimes geathered and hung in their lodges in bags where they dry without further trouble, for in their most succulent state they appear to be almost as dry as flour.—

[Clark]   *Friday [EC: Wedn] 29th January 1806*[3]

Nothing worthey of notice occured to day. our fare is the flesh of lean Elk boiled with pure water and a little Salt. the whale blubber which we have used very Spearingly is now exhosted. on this food I do not feel Strong, but enjoy tolerable health—. a keen appetite Supplies in a great degree the want of more luxurious Sauses or dishes, and Still renders my ordanary meals not uninteresting to me, for I find myself Sometimes enquireing of the Cook whether dinner Supper or Brackfast is ready.—. indeed my appetite is but Seldom gratified, not even after I have eaten what I conceve a Sufficency.—[4]

Maney of the nativs of the Columbia were hats & most commonly of a conic figure without a brim confined on the head by means of a String which passes under the chin and is attached to the two opposit Sides of a Secondary rim within the hat— the hat at top termonates in a pointed knob of a conic form, or in this Shape.[5] these hats are made of the bark of Cedar and beargrass wrought with the fingers So closely that it Casts the rain most effectually in the Shape which they give them for their own use or that just discribed, on these hats they work various figures of different colours, but most commonly only black and white are employed. these figures are faint representations of the whales, the Canoes, and the harpooners Strikeing them. Sometimes Square dimonds triangle &c. The form of a knife which Seems to be prefured by those people is a

Many of the natives of the Columbia wear hats & most commonly of a conic figure without a brim, confined on the head by means of a string which passes under the chin and is attached to the two opposite sides of a secondary rim within the hat. the hat at top terminates in a pointed knob of a conic form, or in this shape. these hats are made of the bark of cedar and beargrass wrought with the fingers so closely that it casts the rain most effectually in the shape which they give them for their own use or that just discribed. on these hats they work various figures of different colours, but most commonly only black and white are em=ployed. these figures are faint representations of the whales, the Canoes, and the harpooners Strikeing them. Sometimes Square diamonds triangle &c. The form of a knife which seems to be prefered by those people is a double edged and double pointed dagger; the handle being near the middle the blades of unequal length, the longest from 9 to 10 inches and the Shorter one from 3 to 5 inches. those knives they carry with them habitually and most usually in the hand, sometimes exposed, when in company with Strangers under their Robes. with this knife they cut & clense their fish, make their arrows &c. this is the form of the knife ◆ is a small loop of a Strong twine throng through which they Sometimes they insert the Thumb in order to prevent its being wrested from their hand. —

21. Conic Hat and Double-edged Knife,
January 29, 1806, Codex I, p. 144

At Fort Clatsop

double Edged and double pointed dagger the handle being near the middle, the blades of uneaquel length, the longest from 9 to 10 incs. and the Shorter one from 3 to 5 inches. those knives they Carry with them habitually and most usially in the hand, Sometimes exposed, when in Company with Strangers under their Robes with this knife they Cut & Clense their fish make their arrows &c. this is the form of the Knife[6] A is a Small loop of a Strong twine throng through which they Sometimes they incert the thumb in order to prevent it being wrested from their hand.—.

  1. The first few lines of the next paragraph have a dark vertical line through them, perhaps drawn by Biddle.
  2. Lake Winnipeg, in Manitoba.
  3. Here with this entry end the daily entries in Clark's Codex I. At the top of the next page (145) is the note in Clark's hand, "See Book No. 8," his designation for Voorhis No. 2, which takes up his journalizing from here. Reading backwards, that page and the next have Clark's extra entries for January 1, 2, and 3, 1806. Continuing to read backwards comes Lewis's "Estimate of Western Indians" (pp. 148–49), completed by Clark on p. 147, Clark's "Estimate of Western Indians" (pp. 150–51, 153–55), and Clark's "A List of the Names as given by the Indias of the Traders Names . . . " (p. 156). The two versions of the "Estimate" are found in Chapter 30; the list is placed at January 1, 1806. On p. 152 is a map of the mouth of the Columbia showing Cape Disappointment (fig. 1). The end flyleaf has the following figures:

	24	39	
	10	46	
38½	34	7	
46	44½		
	136		
	136		
	17	76	70½
	1513		
	40		
	1553	681½	69½
	198	486½	7
	1751	195	486½

Perhaps Clark intended to start the new year of 1806 writing in this notebook, beginning after some statistical materials he had already entered. Then for some reason he changed his mind and reversed the book, and it now appears as Codex I, with the principal writing coming from the other end of the book. See also Appendix C, vol. 2, and notes at January 1, 1806.

4. The first few lines of the next paragraph and the first lines about the knife have a red vertical line through them, perhaps drawn by Biddle.

5. Here in Clark's Codex I, p. 144, appears a small sketch of the conic hat (fig. 21).

6. Here in Clark's Codex I, p. 144, appears a small sketch of the double-edged knife (fig. 21).

[Lewis] *Friday [NB: Thursday] January 30th 1806.*

Nothing transpired today worthy of notice. we are agreeably disappointed in our fuel which is altogether green pine. we had supposed that it burn but illy, but we have found that by spliting it that it burns very well. The dress of the Clatsops and others in this neighbourhood differs but little from that discribed of the skillutes; they never wear leggins or mockersons which the mildness of this climate I presume has rendered in a great measure unnecessary; and their being obliged to be frequently in the water also renders those articles of dress inconvenient. they wear a hat of a conic figure without a brim confined on the head by means of a stri[n]g which passes under the chin and is attatched to the two opsite sides of a secondary rim within the hat. the hat at top terminates in a pointed knob of a connic form also, or in this shape.[1] these hats are made of the bark of cedar and beargrass wrought with the fingers so closely that it casts the rain most effectually in the shape which they give them for their own uce or that just discribed. on these hats they work various figures of different colours, but most commonly only black and white are employed. these figures are faint representations of whales the canoes and the harpoonneers striking them. sometimes squares dimonds triangles &c. The form of knife which seems to be prefered by these people is a double edged and double pointed daggar; the handle being in the middle, and the blades of unequal lengths, the longest usually from 9 to ten inches ⟨long⟩ and the shorter one from four to five. these knives they carry with them habitually and most usually in the hand, sometimes exposed but most usually particularly when in company with strangers, under their robes with this knife they cut and clense their fish make their arrows &c. this is somewhat the form of the knife—[2] A is a

=quently in the water also renders those articles of dress in=
=convenient. they wear a hat of a conic figure without a
brim confined on the head by means of a string which
passes under the chin and is attatched to the two opsite
sides of a secondary rim within the hat. the hat at top
terminates in a pointed knob of a connic form also or in
this shape. these hats are made of the bark of cedar
and beargrass wrought with the fingers so closely that
it casts the rain most effectually in the shape which they
give them for their own use or that just described. on these
hats they work various figures of different colours, but
most commonly only black and white are employed. these
figures are faint representations of the whales the canoes and
the harpooneers striking them. sometimes squars. dimonds
triangles &c. The form of knife which seems to be prefered
by these people is a double edged and double pointed dag=
=gar; the handle being in the middle, and the blades of
unequal lengths, the longest usualy from 9 to ten inches
long and the shorter one from four to five. these knives
they carry with them habitually and most usually in
the hand, sometimes exposed but most usually particu=
=larly when in company with strangers, under their robes.
with this knife they cut and clense their fish make
their arrows &c. this "somewhat the form of the knife
A is a small loop of a strong twine through which
they sometimes insert the thumb in order to prevent its being
wrested from their hand.

~~Friday~~ Saturday January 31st 1806.

Sent a party of eight men up the river this morning to
renew their surch for the Elk and also to hunt; they proceded
but a few miles before they found the river so obstructed
with ice that they were obliged to return. Joseph Fields
arrived this evening, informs us that he had been hunting

22. Conic Hat and Double-edged Knife,
January 30, 1806, Codex J, p. 48

small loop of a strong twine through which they sometimes insert the thumb in order to prevent it's being wrested from their hand.

Fort Clatsop on the Pacific Ocian
on the South Side of the Columbia River
Thursday 30th January 1806[3]

[Clark]

Nothing transpired to day worthey of notice. we are agreeably disapointed in our fuel which is altogether green pine. we had Supposed that it burned badly, but we have found by Spliting it burns very well.

The dress of the Clatsops and others of the nativs in the neighbourhood differ but little from that described of the Skilutes and *Wau ki a cums;* they never ware ligins or mockersons which the mildness of the Climate I presume has rendered in a great measure unnecessary; and their being obliged to be frequently in the water also renders those articles of dress inconveniant.

The *Sac-a commis* is the groth of high dry Situations, and invariably in a piney Country, or on its borders; it is Generally found in the open piney woodlands as on the Western Side of the Rocky mountains but in this neighbourhood we find it in the praries or on the borders in the more open woodland's; a very rich Soil is not absolutely necessary, as a meager one frequently produces it abundantly. the nativs on the West side of the Rocky mountains who can precure this berry invariably use it; to me it is a very tasteless and insipid frute. This Shrub is an evergreen, the leaves retain their virdue most perfectly throughout the winter even in the most rigid climate as on Lake Winnipic. the root of this shrub puts foth a great number of Stems, which seperate near the surface of the ground; each Stem from the size of a Small quill, to that of a mans finger. These are much branched forming an accute angle with the Stem, and all more properly procumbent than crossing, for altho' it sometimes puts foth radicles from the Stems and branches which Strike obliquely into the ground, those radicles are by no means general, equable in their distances from each other nor do they appear to be calculated to furnish nutriment to the plant but rather to hold the Stem or branch in its place. the bark is formed of several thin layers of a Smothe thin brittle substance of a redish brown colour easily seperated from the woody Stem in flakes. the leaves with respect to their possition are scatter'd yet closely arranged

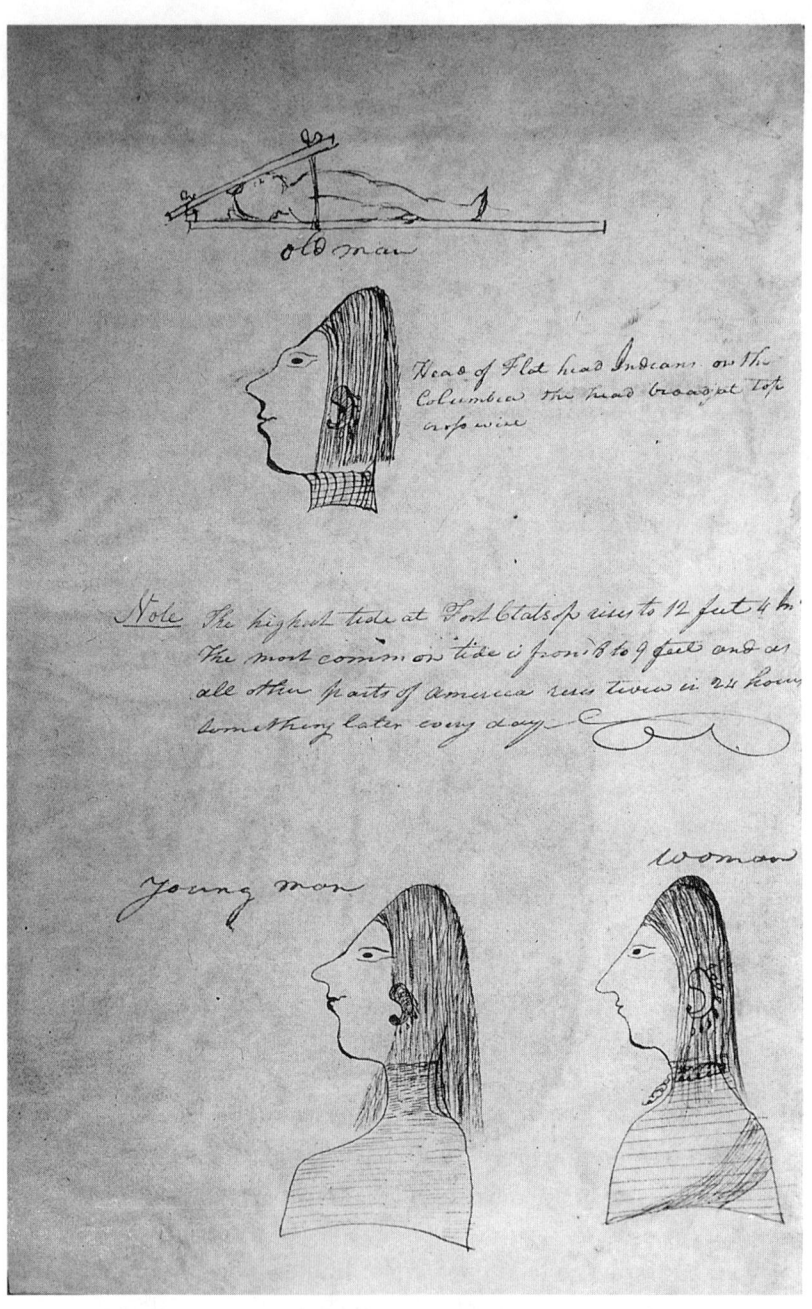

23. Method of Head-flattening and
Adults with Skull Deformation,
ca. January 30, 1806, Voorhis No. 2

near the extremities of the twigs particularly. the leaves are about ¾ of an inch in length and about half that in width, is oval but obtusely pointed, absolutely entire, thick, Smoth, firm, a deep green and slightly grooved. the leaf is Supported by a Small footstalk of preportionable length. the berry is attached in an irregular and Scattered manner to the Small boughs among the leaves, tho' frequently Closely arranged, but always Supported by a Seperate Short and Small peduncles, the incersion of which produces a Small concavity in the berry while its opposit side is Slightly convex; the form of the berry is a Spheroid, the Shorter diameter being in a line with the peduncle or Stem—. this berry is a pericarp the outer Coat of which is a thin firm tough pellicle, the inner part consists of dry mealy powder of a yellowish white colour invelloping from four to six propotionably large hard light brown seeds each in the form of section of a spheroid which figure they form when united, and are distitute of any membranous covering.— the colour of this fruit is a fine scarlet. the nativs usually eat them without any preparation. the fruit ripens in September and remains on the bushes all winter. the frost appears to take no effects on it. these berries are Sometimes gathered and hung in their houses in bags where they dry without further trouble, for in their succulent State they appear to be almost as dry as flour.

1. Here in Lewis's Codex J, p. 48, appears a small sketch of the conic hat (fig. 22).
2. A small sketch of the double-edged knife in Lewis's Codex J, p. 48 (fig. 22).
3. Here begins Clark's notebook journal Voorhis No. 2 going to April 3, 1806. On the first page are sketches relating to the lower Columbia practice of skull deformation, with notes (fig. 23).

[Lewis] *Saturday [NB: Friday] January 31st 1806.*

Sent a party of eight men[1] up the river this morning to renew their surch for the Elk and also to hunt; they proceded but a few miles before they found the river so obstructed with ice that they were obliged to return. Joseph Fields arrived this evening, informed us that he had been hunting in company with Gibson and Willard for the last five days in order to obtain some meat for himself and the other Salt makers, and that he had been unsuccessfull untill yesday evening when he had fortunately killed two Elk, about six miles distant from this place and about 8 from the salt works; he left Gibson and Willard to dry the meat of these

Elk and had come for the assistance of some men to carry the meat to the salt camp; for this purpose we ordered four men to accompany him early in the morning. discovered that McNeal had the pox, gave him medecine. Charbono found a bird[2] dead lying near the fort this morning and brought it to me I immediately recognized it to be of the same kind of that which I had seen in the Rocky mountains on the morning of the 20th of September last. this bird is about the size as near as may be of the robbin. it's contour also is precisely the same with that bird. it measures one foot 3¼ Inches from tip to tip of the wings when extended. 9¼ inches from the extremity of the beak to that of the tail. the tail is 3¾ inches in length, and composed of eleven feathers of the same length. The beak is smoth, black, convex and cultrated; one and ⅛ inches from the point to the opening of the chaps and ¾ only uncovered with feathers; the upper chap exceeds the other a little in length. a few small black hairs garnish the sides of the base of the upper chap. the eye is of a uniform deep sea green or black, moderately large. it's legs feet and tallons are white; the legs are an inch and a ¼ in length and smoth; four toes on each foot, of which that in front is the same length with the leg including the length of the tallon, which is 4 lines;[3] the three remaining toes are ¾ of an inch, each armed with proportionably long tallons. the toes are slightly imbricated. the tallons are curved and sharply pointed. The crown of the head from the beak back to the neck, the back of the neck imbracing reather more than half the circumpherence of the neck, the back and tale, are of bluish dark brown; the two outer feathers of the tale have a little dash of white near their tips not percemtible when the tail is foalded. a fine black forms the ground of the wings; two stripes of the same colour pass on either side of the head from the base of the beak along the side of the head to it's junction with the neck, and imbraces the eye to it's upper edge; a third stripe of the same colour ¾ of an inch in width passes from the sides of the neck just above the butts of the wings across the croop in the form of a gorget.[4] the throat or under part of the neck brest and belly is of a fine yellowish brick red. a narrow stripe of this colour also commences just above the center of each eye, and extends backwards to the neck as far as the black stripe reaches before discribed, to which, it appears to answer as a border. the feathers which form the 1st and second ranges of the coverts of the two joints of the wing next the body, are beautifully tiped with this brick red; as is also each large feather of the wing on the short side of it's plumage for ½ an inch in length commening at the extremity of the feathers which form the first or main covert of the wing. this is a beatifull little bird. I have never heard it's note it appears to be silent.[5] it feeds on berries, and I beleive is a rare bird even in this country, or at least this is the second time only that I have seen it.— between the legs of this bird the feathers are white, and those which form the tuft underneath the tail are a mixture of white and a brick red.—

Observed equal altitudes today with Sextant.

	h	m	s		h	m	s
A. M.	8	55	24	P. M.	1	11	58

Altitude by Sextn. 40° 32′—

	h	m	S
Chronomometer too slow on Mean Equated Solar time.	1	10	26.1

☞ The days of the month for January are right, but the days of the weak as affixed are all wrong, nor did I discover it untill this morning.—[6]

[Clark] *Friday January 31st 1806*

Sent a party of Eight men with the hunters to renew their Serch for the Elk, and also to hunt; they proceeded but a fiew miles before they found the river So obstructed with ice that they were obliged to return. Jo. Field arrives this evening, informs us That he had been hunting in Company with gibson and willard for the last four days in order to obtain some meat for himself and the other Salt-makers, and that he had been unsucksessfull untill yesterday evening when he had fortunately killed two Elk, about six miles distant from this place and about 8 from the Salt works; he left gibson and willard to dry the meat of those Elk, and had come for assistance to carry the meat to the Salt Camp; for this purpose we ordered four men to accompany him early in the morning. discovered that McNeal had the pox, gave him medicine. Chabono found a bird dead lying near the Fort this morning and brought it in, I reconized it to be the Same kind of that which I had Seen in the Rocky Mountains at severl different times. this berd is about the Size as near as may be of the robin. it's contour is also presisely the Same with that bird. it measured one foot ¾ inches from tip to tip of the wings when extended. 9¼ inches from the extremity of the beak to that of the tail. the tail is 3¾ inches in length, and Composed of 11 feathers of the Same length. The beak is Smoth, black, convex and cultrated; 1⅛ inchs from the point to the opening of the Chaps and ¾ only uncovered with feathers, the upper Chap exceeds the other a little in length. a fiew Small black hairs garnish the Side of the upper chap. The Eye is of a uniform deep Sea green or black, moderately large. it's legs feet and tallants are white; the legs are of 1¼ in length and Smoth; four toes on each foot, of which that in front is the Same length of the leg including the tallants, which is 4 lines; the 3 remaining toes are ¾ of an inch, each armed with proportianably large tallons. the toes are Slightly imbricated. the tallons are curved and Sharply pointed. The Crown of the head from the beak back to the neck imbracing rather more than half the circumphrence of the neck, the Back and tail is of a bluish dark brown; the two outer feathers of the tail have a little dash of white near the tips, not proceivable when the tail is foalded. a fine black forms the ground of the wings; two Stripes of the same colour passes on either side of the Head from the base of the Back along the Side of the head to it's junction with the neck, and embraces the eye to its upper edge; a third Stripe of the Same Colour ¾ of an inch in width passes from the Side of the neck just above the buts of the wings across the croop in the form of a gorget. the throat or under part of the neck brest and belly is of a fine Yellowish brick red. a narrow Stripe of this Colour also Commences just above the center of each eye, and extends backwards to the Neck as far as the black Spots reaches before discribed, to which it appears to answer as a border. the feathers which form the 1st and Second range of the coverts of the two joints of the wings next the body are butifully tiped with this Brick red; as is also each large feather of the wing on the Short Side of its plumage for ½ an inch in length Comencing at the extremity of the feather which form the first or main Covert of the wing. This is a butifull little bird. I have never herd its notes it appears to be Silent. it feeds on berries, and I believe is a rare bird even in this country—. between the legs of this bird the feathers are white, and those which form the tuft underneath the tail are a mixture of white and Brick red.

Observed equal altitudes today with Sextant.

	h	m	s		h	m	s
A. M.	8	55	24	P. M.	1	11	58

altd. by Sextt. 40° 32′—

	h	m	S
Chronomometer too Slow on mean Equated Solar time—	1	10	26.20

[Lewis and Clark][7]

Equal altitudes the [blank] Day 31st of January 1806 at Fort *Clat Sop* with Sextant—

h	m	s		h	m.	s	
8	52	28	P. M.	1	9	3	⎫
″	55	24		″	12	13	⎬ altd. 40° 32′ 00″
″	58	21		″	14	53	⎭

	h	m	S.
Chronometer too slow on Mean Equated Solar time—	1	10	26.1
	1	9	3
+ 12 hours—	12		
	13	9	3
- corrisponding observt P. M.	8	58	21
of which take half— 2	4	10	42
= to half interval of obst.	2	5	21
+ forenoon or A. M.—	8	58	21
time that the ☉'s center was on the Meridian as shown by the Chronometer—	11	3	42

1. Including Gass, according to Ordway.

2. The varied thrush, *Ixoreus naevius* [AOU, 763], already known to science. Lewis recalled correctly the date of his first notice of the bird. The robin used for comparison is *Turdus migratorius* [AOU, 761]. Someone has drawn a dark vertical line down to "imbricated"; perhaps it was Biddle.

3. A line here may be one twelfth of an inch.

4. Gorget; see above, March 9, 1805.

5. The thrush is not actually silent.

6. Some of the days of the week in Lewis's journal for January have been corrected, perhaps by Biddle in 1810.

7. This observation appears in the First Draft field book which contains Clark's draft diary of January 6–10, 1806, and several miscellaneous items. It is placed here by date.

At Fort Clatsop

Clark wrote the first part; Lewis takes over beginning with, "Chronometer too slow." At the bottom of the page in red ink are the following words in Clark's hand: "Davidson, Dandridge, Day and Year." Two blank pages then follow.

[Lewis and Clark] [*Weather, January 1806*][1]

Day of the month	aspect of the weather at ☉ rise	Wind at ☉ rise	Weather at 4 OC. P.M.	Wind at 4 OC. P.M.
1st	c a r	S. W.	r a c	S.
2nd	c a r	S W.	r	S. W.
3rd	c. a. r. h. T & L.	S W	c a r h. f	S. W.
4th	c a r & h	S W	r a f & r	S. E
5th	r	S E	r	S. E
6th	c a r	S E	f	E
7th	f	N. E.	c. a. r.[2]	S E
8th	f	N. E	c a f	S. E.
9th	f	S. W.	c a f	S. W
10th	f. a r	S. W.	c a f	S. W
11th	c	S. W.	c a r	S. W.
12th	f a c	N. W.	c	N. W.
13th	r	S. W.	r	S. W.
14th	f a r	N. E.[3]	c a f	S.
15th	r a c & r	S E	r. a r	S
16th	r a r	S. W.	r. a r	S W
17th	c a r	S. W	c	S W
18th	r. a. r.	S. W	c a r	S W
19th	c a r	S.	c a r	S W
20th	r a r	S. W	r a r	S W
21st	c a r	S. W.	c a r	S W
22ed	r a r	S W	c a r	S W
23rd	c a r H T & L[4]	S W	c a f	S. W.
24th	c a r & S	S E	c a r h & S	E
25th	h a r h & S	N. E.	c a r h & S	N E
26th	c a h & s	N. E	c a s	N E
27th	f. a. s	N. E	f	N E
28th	f	N E	f	N. E
29th	f	N E	f	N E
30th	S. a. S.	N.	C a. S	W
31st	f a c	N. E.	f.	N. E

258

[Remarks]⁵

1st   sun visible for a few minutes about 11 A M. the changes of the weather are exceedingly suddon. sometimes tho' seldom the sun is visible for a few moments the next it hails & rains, then ceases, and remains cloudy the wind blows and it again rains; the wind blows by squalls most generally and is almost invariably from S. W. these visicitudes of the weather happen two three or more times half⁶ a day. snake seen 25th Decembr

3d   the sun visible for a few minutes only. The thunder and lightning of the last evening was violent. a Singular occurrence for the time of year. the loss of my Thermometer I most sincerely regret. I am confident that the climate here is much warmer than in the same parallel of Latitude on the Atlantic Ocean tho' how many degrees is now out of my power to determine. Since our arrival in this neighbourhood on the 7th of November, we have experienced one slight white frost only which happened on the morning of the 16th of that month.⁷ we have yet seen no ice, and the weather so warm that we are obliged cure our meat with smoke and fire to save it. we lost two parsels by depending on the air to preserve it, tho' it was cut in very thin slices and sufficiently exposed to the air.

4th   the sun visible about 2 hours

6th   the sun⁸ shown about 5 hours this evening & it continued fare during the night.⁹

7th   it clouded up just about sunset, but shortly after became fare.

8th   lost my P. M. obstn. for Equal Altitudes.

9th   began to rain at 10 P. M. and continued all night.

10th Various flies and insects now alive and in motion.¹⁰

12th cool this morning but no ice nor frost at miday sand flies and insects in motion the wind from any quarter off the land or along the N. W. Coast causes the air to become much cooler. every species of waterfowl common to this country at any season of the year still continue with us.

At Fort Clatsop

14th weather perfectly temperate I never experienced a winter so warm as the present has been.[11]

15th Saw several insects, weather warm, we could do very well without fire, I am satsifyed that the murcury would stand at 55 a. O.

16th wind hard this morning   rained incessently all night.

17th rained incessently all night, insect in motion

18th rained very hard last night

19th rained the greater part of last night.

20th raind greater part of night   wind hard

21st wind hard this morning   contued all day

22ed wind violent last night & this morning

23d the sun shown about 2 h in the fore noon   when the sun is said to shine ore the weather fair it is to be understood that it bearly casts a shaddow, and that the atmosphere is haizy of a milkey white colour.

24th this morning the snow covered the ground and mas cooler than any wether we have had, but no ice

25th the ground covered with snow this morning ½ inch deep   ice on the water in the canoes ¼ of an inch thick.   it is now preceptably coulder than it has been this winter.—

26th at 4 P. M. last evening the snow was one Inch deep ☉ rise this morning 4¼[12] inches deep   icesickles of 18 Inches in length hanging to the eves of the houses. coulder than it has been   the snow this evening is 4¾ inches deep, the icesickles of 18 inches in length continued suspended from the eves of the houses during the day.   it now appears something like winter for the first time this season.

27th the sun shone more bright this morning than it has done since our arrival at this place.   the snow since 4 P. M. yesterday has increased to the debth of 6 Inches, and this morning is perceptibly the couldest that we have had. I suspect the Murcury would stand at about 20° above naught; the breath is perceptible in our room by the fire.[13]

28th last night exposed a vessel of water to the air with a view to discover the debth to which it would freiz in the course of the night, but unfortunately the vessel was only 2 inches deep and it feized the whole thickness; how much more it might have frozen had the vessel been deeper is therefore out of my power to decide. it is the couldest night that we have had, and I suppose the murcury this morning would have stood as low as 15° above o.—

29th not so could, water in a vessel exposed to the [air] during the night freized ⅜ths of an inch only.[14]

30th the weather by no means as could as it has been   snow feell about one inch deep

31st this morning is plesant, the night was clear and cold   notwithstanding the could weather the Swan white Brant geese & ducks still continue with us; the sandhill crain also continues.— the brown or speckled brant are mostly gone some few are still to be seen   the Cormorant loon and a variety of other waterfowls still remain. The Winds from the Land brings us could and clear weather while those obliquely along either coast or off the Oceans bring us warm damp cloudy and rainy weather. the hardest winds are always from the S. W.

The blue crested Corvus bird has already began to build it's nest. their nests are formed of small sticks; usually in a pine tree.—

Great numbers of Ravens, and a Small black Crow are continually about us. The pale yellow Streiked and dove coloured robin is about, also the little brown ren or fly-catsch which is a little larger than the humming bird.[15]

   1. Lewis's weather table and notes are in Codex J; Clark's are in Codex I. This table follows Lewis, with substantial differences noted.
   2. Clark has "c. a. f."
   3. Clark has "N W."
   4. Clark has "C a. r. t. & L."
   5. Lewis in Codex J has remarks both in the margin of his weather table and separately; Clark's remarks in Codex I are also in the margin and separate. These remarks follow Lewis, with substantial differences noted.

6. Clark does not have "half."

7. Clark has "last month," probably an error since he is presumably referring to November.

8. Lewis has omitted the word "sun" which is supplied by Clark in his journal.

9. Clark adds, "I Set out with 12 men to the Kilamox Nation &c."

10. Clark also says, "I returned from visiting the whale at the *Kil a mox* nation 45 m. S S. W."

11. Clark adds, "as yet."

12. Clark says, "4¾."

13. Clark adds, "(The Indians nearly necked nothing but a Slight roab.)"

14. This marginal remark in both Lewis's and Clark's tables appears to be under the twenty-eighth. However, it conflicts so greatly with their separate remarks for that date that it has been placed under the twenty-ninth.

15. This last paragraph is found only in Clark's Codex I. The "pale yellow streiked and dove coloured robin" is presumably one bird, the varied thrush. Lewis describes it this day in his notebook journal. The wren is probably the winter wren, but see Holmgren, 34, for other possibilities.

[Lewis] *Saturday February 1st 1806.*

This morning a party of four men set out with Joseph Fields; Sergt. Gass with a party of five men again set out up the Netul river in surch of the Elk which had been killed some days since, and which could not be found in consequence of the snow. The Canoes of the natives inhabiting the lower portion of the Columbia River make their canoes remarkably neat light and well addapted for riding high waves. I have seen the natives near the coast riding waves in these canoes with safety and apparently without concern where I should have thought it impossible for any vessel of the same size to lived a minute. they are built of whitecedar or Arborvita generally, but sometimes of the firr. they are cut out of a solid stick of timber, the gunwals at the upper edge foald over outwards and are about ⅝ of an inch thick and 4 or five broad, and stand horrizontally forming a kind of rim to the canoe to prevent the water beating into it. they are all furnished with more or less crossbars in proportion to the size of the canoe. these bars are round sticks about half the size of a man's arm, which are incerted through holes ⟨just⟩ made in either side of the canoe just below the rim of the gunwall and are further secured with strings of waytape;[1] these crossbars serve to lift and manage the canoe on land. when the natives land they invariably take their canoes on shore, unless they are heavily laden, and then even, if they remain all night, they discharge their loads and take the canoes on shore. some of the large canoes are upwards of 50 feet long and will carry from 8 to 10 thousand lbs. or from 20 to thirty persons and some of them particularly on the sea coast are waxed painted and orniemented with curious images at bough and Stern; those images sometimes rise to the hight of five feet; the pedestals on which these immages are fixed are sometimes cut out of the solid stick with the canoe, and the imagary is formed of seperate small peices of timber firmly united with tenants and motices without the assistance of a single spike of any kind. when the natives are engaged in navigating their canoes one sets in the stern and steers with a paddle the others set by pears and paddle over the gunwall next them, they all kneel in the bottom of the canoe and set on their feet. their paddles are of a uniform shape of which this is an imitation[2] these paddles are made very thin and the middle of the blade is thick and hollowed out siddonly and made thin at the sides while the center forms a kind of rib. the blade occupys about one third of the length of the paddle which is usually from 4½ to 5 feet. I have observed four forms of canoe only in uce among the nations below the grand chatarac of this river they are as follow. this is the smallest size[3] about 15 feet long and calculated for one or two persons, and are most common among the Cathlahmahs and Wâck ki a cums among the marshey Islands. A the bow; B, the stern; these[4] are from twenty to thirty five feet and from two ½ to 3 feet in the beam and about 2 feet in the hole; this canoe is common to all the nations below the grand rappids. it is here made deeper and shorter in proportion than they really are.— the bowsprit from C, to D is brought to a sharp edge tapering gradually from the sides.

This is the most common form[5] of the canoe in uce among the Indians from; the Chil-luck-kit-te-quaw inclusive to the Ocean and is usually about 30 or 35 feet long, and will carry from ten to twelve persons. 4 men are competent to carry them a considerable distance say a mile without resting. A is the end which they use as the bow, but which on first sight I took to be the stern   C. D. is a comb cut of the sollid stick with the canoe and projects from the center of the end of the canoe being about 1 inch thirck it's sides parallel and edge at C D. sharp. it is from 9 to 11 Inches in length and extends from the underpart of the bowsprit at A to the bottom of the canoe at D.— the stern B. is mearly rounding and images sometimes rise to the hight of five feet; the pedestie on which these immages are fixed are sometimes cut out of the solid stick with the canoe, and the imagary is formed of seperate small peices of timber firmly united with tenons and motices without the ospistance of a single spike of any kind. when the natives are engaged in navigating their canoes one sets in the stern and steers with a paddle the others set by pears and paddle over the gunwall near them, they all kneel in the bottom of the canoe and set on their feet. their paddles are of an uniform shape of which this is an imitation. these paddles are made very thin and the middle of the blade is thick and hollowed out sediomly and made thin on the sides while center forms a kind of rib. the blade occupys about one third of the length of the paddle which is usually from 4½ to 5 feet. I have observed four forms of canoes only in use among the nations below the grand chataract of this river they are as follow. this is the smallest size about 15 feet long and calculated for one or two persons, and are most common among the Cath -lah-mahs, and Wäck ki-a-cums among the marshey Islands. A the bow; B, the stern; these are from twenty to thirty five feet and from two to 3 feet in the beam and about 2 feet in the hole. this canoe is common to all the nations below the grand rapphids. it is here made the bowsprit from C to D is brought to a sharp edge tapering gradually from the sides deeper and shorter in proportion than they really are. This is the most common form of the canoe in use among the Indians from the Chil-luck-kit-te-quaw inclusive to the Ocean and is usually about 30 or 35 feet long, and will carry from ten to twelve persons. 4 men are competent to carry them a considerable distance say a mile without resting. A is the end which they use as the bow, but which on first sight I took to be the stern C. D. is a comb cut of the sollid stick with the canoe and projects from

24. Paddle, Small Canoe, Canoe with High Bow, and Most Common Canoe, February 1, 1806, Codex J, p. 52

graduly ascending. 1 2 3 represents the rim of the gunwalls about 4 Inches wide, reather ascending as they recede from the canoe. 4 5 6 7 8 are the round holes through which the cross bars are inserted.—

This form of canoe[6] we did not meet with untill we reached tidewater or below the grand rappids. from thence down it is common to all the nations but more particularly the Killamucks and others of the coast. these are the largest canoes. B. is the bow and comb. C. the stern and comb. their immages are representations of a great variety of grotesque figures, any of which might be safely worshiped without committing a breach of the commandments.[7]

They have but few axes among them, and the only too usually imployed in felling the trees or forming the canoe, carving &c is a chissel formed of an old file about an Inch or an Inch and a half broad. this chissel has sometimes a large block of wood for a handle; they grasp the chissel just below the block with the right hand holding the edge down while with the left they take hold of the top of the block and strike backhanded against the wood with the edge of the chissel.[8] a person would suppose that the forming of a large canoe with an instrument like this was the work of several years; but these people make them in a few weeks. they prize their canoes very highly; we have been anxious to obtain some of them, for our journey up the river but have not been able to obtain one as yet from the natives in this neighbourhood.— today we opened and examined all our ammunition, which had been secured in leaden canesters. we found twenty seven of the best rifle powder, 4 of common rifle, three of glazed and one of the musqut powder in good order,[9] perfectly as dry as when first put in the canesters, altho' the whole of it from various accedents has been for hours under the water. these cannesters contain four lbs. of powder each and ⟨contain⟩ 8 of lead. had it not have been for that happy expedient which I devised of securing the powder by means of the lead, we should not have had a single charge of powder at this time. three of the canesters which had been accedentally bruized and cracked, one which was carelessly stoped, and a fifth that had been penetrated with a nail, were a little dammaged; these we gave to the men to make ⟨it⟩ dry; however exclusive of those five we have an abundant stock to last us back; and we always take care to put a proportion of it in each canoe, to the end that should one canoe or more be lost we should

25. Canoe with Carved Images,
February 1, 1806, Codex J, p. 53

still not be entirely bereft of ammunition, which is now our only hope for subsistence and defence in a rout of 4000 miles through a country exclusively inhabited by savages.—

[Clark]   *Saturday February 1st 1806*

    This morning a party of four men Set out with Jo. Field; and Sergt. Gass with a party of five men again Set out up the Netul river in Serch of the Elk which had been killed Some days since, and which Could not be found in Consequence of the Snow.

    The Canoes of the nativs inhabitting the lower part of the Columbia River from the Long narrows down make their canoes remarkably neat light and well addapted for rideing high waves. I have Seen the nativs near the Coast rideing waves in these Canoes in Safty and appearantly without Concern when I Should it impossible for any vessel of the Same Size to have lived or kept above water a minute. they are built of Arborvitia or white Cedar generally, but Sometimes of fir. they are cut out of a solid Stick of timber, the gunnals at the upper edge fold over outwards and are about ⅝ of an inch thick and 4 or 5 broad, and Stand out nearly Horizontially forming a kind of rim to the Canoe to prevent the water beating into it. they are all furnished with more or less Cross bars agreeably to thier sizes of the Canoe, those bars are round Sticks about 1 inch and ½ diameter which are atached to the iner Side of the canoes a little below the rim on either Side with throngs of Cedar bark which is incerted through holes and made fast to the ends of the Stick, which is made Smaller than the other part of the Stick to prevent the cord Slipping off these cross bears Serve to Strengthen the canoe, and by which they lift and manage her on land. when the nativs land the[y] invariably take their Canoes on Shore unless they are heavily ladined, and then even, if they remain all night, they discharge their loads and take the Canoe on Shore.

    Some of the large Canoes are upwards of 50 feet long and will Carry from 8 to 12 thousand lbs. or from 20 to 30 persons, and Some of them particularly on the Sea Coast are waxed painted and orminented with curious images on bow and Stern; those images sometimes rise to the hight of five feet; the pedestile on which these images are fixed, are Sometimes cut out of the Solid Stick with the Canoe, and the image is formed of the canoe, and by which they lift and manage her on land. When the natives land they invariably take their canoes on shore unless they are heavily ladened, and then even, if they remain all night, they discharge their loads and take the canoe on shore.

Some of the large canoes are upwards of 50 feet long and will carry from 8 to 12 thousand lbs. or from 20 to 30 persons, and some of them particularly on the sea coast are waxed painted and ornimented with curious images on bow and stern; those images sometimes reach to the heigth of five feet; the pedestile on which these images are fixed, are sometimes cut out of the solid stick with the canoe, and the image is formed of seperate peices of timber firmly united with tenants and mortices, without the appearance of a single spike or nail of any kind. When the natives are engaged in navigateing their canoes. one sits in the stern and steers with a paddle the others set by pars and paddle over their gunnels next them, they all kneel in the bottom of the canoe and set on their feet. their paddles are of an uniform shape which this is an imitation ⟍───⟋ those paddles are made verry thin and the middle of the blade is thick and hollowed out suddenly, and made thin on the sides, the center forming a kind of ridge. the occupies about 1/3 of the length of the paddle which is usually 4 to 4½ feet in length. I have observed five form of canoes only in use among the natives below the Grand Cataract of this river. They are as follows.
⌣─── this is the smallest size about 15 feet long, ───▶ and

26. Paddle, Small Canoe, and Sharp-pointed Paddle,
February 1, 1806, Voorhis No. 2

and Calculated for one two men nearly to cross creeks, take over short portages to navagate the ponds and still water, and is mostly in use amongst the Clat-sops and Chinnooks. ⸻ this is the next smallest and from 16 to 20 feet long and calculated for two or 3 persons and are most common among the Wau-kie-â-cums and Cath-lâh-mâhs among the marshey Islands, near their villages. A the bow; B the Stern; thow are from D 20 to 40 feet in length and from 2½ to 3½ feet in the beam and about 2 feet deep. This Canoe is common to all the nations below the grand Rapids it here made deeper and Shoter in pertotion than the Canoe realy is, the bow sprit from c to D, is brought to a sharp edge tapering gradually from the sides. This is the most common form of the Canoes in use among the indians from the Chil-luck-kit-te-quaw inclusive to the ocean and is commonly from about 30 to 35 feet long, and wile carry from 10 to 12 persons. 4 men are competent to carry them a considerable distance say a mile without resting. A is the end the natives use as the bow, but which on first sight I took to be the stern c.d is a comb cut of the solid wood with the Canoe, and projects from the center of the end of the Canoe being about 1 inch thick, it's sides parallel and edge at c,d, sharp it is from 9. to 11 inches in ditth and extends from the under part of the bow sprit at A to the bottom at ,d,- the Stern B is nearly rounding and gradually assending). 1,2,3, represents the rim of the gunuals about 4 inches wide, eather assending as they recede from the canoe. 4,5,6,7,8. are the holes thro-

27. Another Small Canoe, Canoe with High Bow, and Most Common Canoe, February 1, 1806, Voorhis No. 2

Seperate pieces of timber firmly united with tenants and mortices without the appearance of a Single Spike or nail of any kind. when the nativs are engaged in navigateing their Canoes, one Sets in the Stern and Stears with a paddle the others Set by pars and paddle over their gunnals next them, they all kneel in the bottom of the Canoe and Set on their feet. their paddles are of an uniform shape which this is an imitation[10] those paddles are made verry thin and the middle of the blade is thick and hollowed out Suddenly, and made thin on the Sides, the center forming a kind of ridge. the [handle] occupies about ⅓ of the length of the paddle which is usually 4 to 4½ feet in length. I have observed five forms of Canoes only in use among the nativs below the Grand Cataract of this river. they are as follows.[11] this is the Smallest Size about 15 feet long,[12] and Calculated for one two men mearly to cross creeks, take over Short portages to navagate the ponds and Still water, and is mostly in use amongst the Clatsops and Chinnooks.[13] this is the next Smallest and from 16 to 20 feet long and calculated for two or 3 persons and are most common among the *Wau-ki-á-cums* and *Cath-lâh-mâhs* among the marshey Islands, near their villages.[14] A the bow; B the Stern; those are from 20 to 40 feet in length and from 2½ to 3½ feet in the beam and about 2 feet deep; this Canoe is common to all the nations below the grand Rapids it here made deeper and Shorter in pertotion than the Canoe realy is, the bow sprit from C. to D. is brought to a Sharp edge tapering gradually from the Sides.[15] This is the most common form of the Canoes in use among the indians from the Chil-luck-kit-te quaw inclusive to the ocian and is commonly from about 30 to 35 feet long, and will carry from 10 to 12 persons. 4 men are competent to carry them a considerable distance Say a mile without resting. A is the end the nativs use as the bow, but which on first Sight I took to be the Stern   c. d. is a comb cut of the solid wood with the Canoe, and projects from the Center of the end of the Canoe being about 1 inch thick, it's Sides parallel and edge at c, d, Sharp   it is from 9 to 11 inches in debth and extends from the under part of the bow sprit at A to the bottom at, d,. the Stern B is nearly rounding and gradually assending.   1, 2, 3, represents the rim of the gunnals about 4 inches wide, reather ascending as they recede from the Canoe.   4, 5, 6, 7, 8, are the holes through which the String pass to fasten the round pieces which pass Crosswise the Canoe to Strengthen & lift her.[16] This

January 21–March 17, 1806

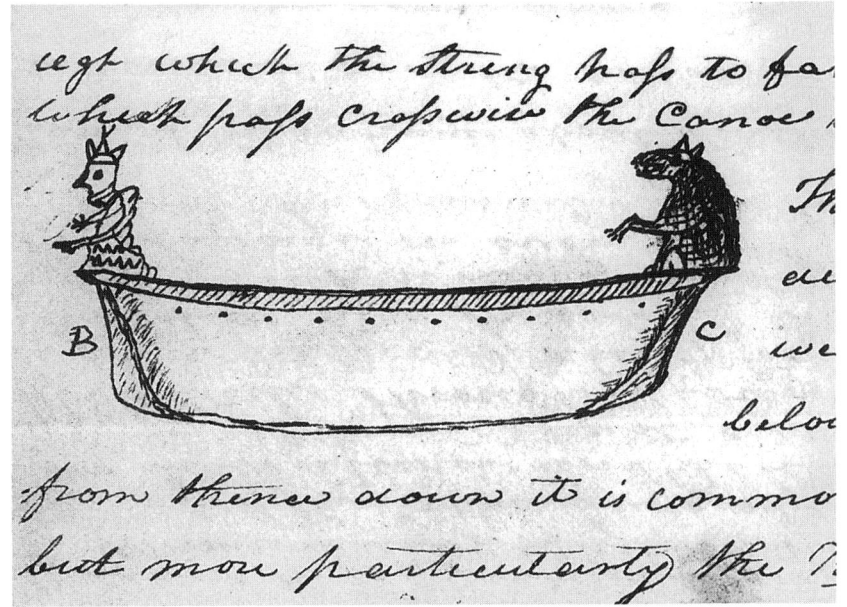

28. Canoe with Carved Images,
February 1, 1806, Voorhis No. 2

form of a canoe we did not meet with untill we reached tide water or below the Great Rapids. from thence down it is common to all the nations but more particularly the *Kil a mox* and others of the Coast. these are the largest Canoes, I measured one at the Kilamox villag S S W of us which was [*blank*] feet long [*blank*] feet wide and [*blank*] feet deep, and they are most Commonly about that Size. B is the bow, and Comb. C, the stern and Comb. Their images are representations of a great variety of grotesque figures, any of which might be Safely worshiped without commiting a breach of the Commandments.

They have but fiew axes among them, and the only tool usially employd in forming the Canoe, carveing &c is a chissel formed of an old file about an inch or 1 ½ inchs broad, this chissel has Sometimes a large block of wood for a handle; they grasp the chissel just below the block with the right hand holding the top of the block, and Strikes backwards against the wood with the edge of the Chissel. a person would Suppose that forming a large Canoe with an enstriment like this was the work of Several years; but those people make them in a fiew weeks. They prize their Canoes very highly; we have been anxious to obtain Some of them, for our journy up the river but have not been able to obtain one as yet from the nativs in this neighbourhood.

To day we opened and examined all our Ammunition, which has been Secured in leaden Canistirs. we found twenty Sevin of the best Rifle powder, 4 of Common rifle, 3 of Glaize and one of Musquet powder in good order, perfectly as dry as when first put in the Canisters, altho the whole of it from various accidince have been for hours under the water. these Cannisters Contain 4 pounds of powder each and 8 of Lead. had it not been for that happy expedient which Capt Lewis devised of Securing the powder by means of the Lead, we Should have found great dificuelty in keeping dry powder untill this time—; those Cannisters which had been accidently brused and cracked, one which was carelessly Stoped, and a fifth which had been penetrated with a nail; were wet and damaged; those we gave to the men to Dry; however exclusive of those 5 we have an abundant Stock to last us back; and we always take Care to put a purpotion of it in each canoe, to the end that Should one Canoe or more be lost we Should Still not be entirely bereft of ammunition, which is now our only hope for Subsistance and defences in the rout of 4,000 miles through a Country exclusively inhabited by Indians—many bands of which are Savage in every Sense of the word—.

  1. Or watap, the stringy roots of trees used in construction, particularly of canoes.
  2. Here in Lewis's Codex J, p. 52, appears a sketch of the paddle (fig. 24).
  3. A sketch of the first (small) type of canoe appears about here in Lewis's Codex J, p. 52 (fig. 24). Probably the so-called shovel-nose canoe of the Chinooks. Ruby & Brown (CITC), 17; Waterman, 10–11; Olson, 19; Waterman & Coffin, plate 2.
  4. About here in Lewis's Codex J, p. 52, appears a sketch of the second (high bow) type of canoe (fig. 24). It appears to be the so-called "Chinook" canoe, actually made by the Nootkas of Vancouver Island, British Columbia, and traded south to the Chinooks; it was considered an excellent, sea-worthy craft. Ruby & Brown (CITC), 18; Waterman, 9–11, 16–19, plate 2, clearly illustrating the same general type; Olson, 19.
  5. A sketch of the third (most common) type of canoe in Lewis's Codex J, p. 52 (fig. 24). Perhaps a so-called freight canoe. Waterman & Coffin, 17–18, plate 1.
  6. A sketch of the fourth (carved images) type of canoe in Lewis's Codex J, p. 53 (fig. 25), apparently less widely distributed than the previous types. Drucker, 76.
  7. One of the rare Biblical references in the journals, citing the injunction against

making or worshipping an image of anything in the heavens, on the earth, or in the waters under the earth. Exodus, 20:4.

8. Olson, 13–14, plate 1, cites this passage.

9. Gunpowder was graded for use according to the fineness of the grains. Rifle powder was finer than musket powder, which was again finer than that used for cannon. "Glazed" powder grains had a hard, smooth surface, making them more resistant to moisture. Russell (GEF), 222.

10. A sketch of the paddle in Clark's Voorhis No. 2 journal (fig. 26).

11. A sketch of the first (small) type of canoe in Clark's Voorhis No. 2 journal (fig. 26).

12. Another paddle with a sharp point is shown here in Clark's Voorhis No. 2 at the bottom of the page; it is not discussed in the text (fig. 26).

13. A sketch of the next (another small) type of canoe in Clark's Voorhis No. 2 journal (fig. 27), not shown or described in Lewis's entry for this date, above.

14. A sketch of the third (high bow) type of canoe in Clark's Voorhis No. 2 journal (fig. 27), Lewis's second type.

15. A sketch of the fourth (most common) type of canoe in Clark's Voorhis No. 2 journal (fig. 27), Lewis's third type.

16. A sketch of the last (carved images) type of canoe in Clark's Voorhis No. 2 journal (fig. 28), Lewis's fourth type.

[Lewis] *Sunday February 2cd 1806.*

Not any occurrence today worthy of notice; but all are pleased, that one month of the time which binds us to Fort Clatsop and which seperates us from our friends has now elapsed. one of the games of amusement and wrisk of the Indians of this neighbourhood like that of the Sosones consists in hiding in the hand some small article about the size of a bean; this they throw from one hand to the other with great dexterity accompanying their opperations with a particular song which seems to have been addapted to the game; when the individul who holds the peice has amused himself sufficiently by exchanging it from one hand to the other, he hold out his hands for his compettitors to guess which hand contains the peice; if they hit on the ha[n]d which contains the peice they win the wager otherwise loose. the individual who holds the peice is a kind of banker and plays for the time being against all the others in the room; when he has lost all the property which he has to venture, or thinks proper at any time, he transfers the peice to some other who then also becoms banker. The Sosone and Minnetares &c have a game of a singular kind but those divide themselves in two parties and play for a common wager to which each individual contributes to form the stock of his party. one of them holdes the peice and some one of the opposite party gesses which hand contains if he hits on the ha[n]d which contains it the peice is transferred to the opposite party and the victor counts one, if he misses the party still retain the peice and score one but the individual tranfers the peice to some other of his own party; the game is set to any number they think proper, and like the natives of this quarter they always accompany their opperations with a particular song. the natives here have also another game which consists in bowling some small round peices about the size of Bacgammon men, between two small upright sticks placed a few inches asunder, but the principals of the game I have not learn not understanding their language sufficiently to obtain an explanation. their boys amuse themselves with their bows and arrows as those do of every Indian nation with which I am acquainted. these people are excessively fond of their games of risk and bet freely every species of property of which they are possessed. They have a smal dog which the[y] make usefull only in hunting the Elk.[1]

[Clark] *Sunday February 2nd 1806*

Not any accurrence to day worthy of notice; but all are pleased, that one month of the time which binds us to fort *Clatsop,* and which Seperates us from our friends, has now alapsed.

The games of amusements of the natives of this neighbourhood are Several, one of which is verry similar to one which the Sosone's & Minatare's are verry fond of and frequently play. they devide themselves into two parties and play for a common wager to which each individual Contributes to form the Stock of his party, one of them holdes the piece which is usually about the Size of a Bean, and Some one of the oposit party gesses which hand Contains, if he hits on the hand which Contains it, the piece is transfired to the opposit party and the victor Counts one, if he misses the party Still retains the piece and scores one, but the individual transfirs the piece to Some one of his own party; the game is Set to any number they think proper. they always accompany their opperations with a particular Song. The amusements of the boys of all nations which I am acquainted with are generally the Bows and arrows.

All nations of Indians with which I am acquainted are excessive fond of their games of risk, and bet away Species of property of which they are possessed.

The nativs of this neighbourhood have a Small Dog which they make usefull only in hunting the Elk.

1. An "x" in dark ink is drawn across this last sentence.

[Lewis] *Monday February 3rd 1806.*

About three o'clock Drewyer and La Page, returned; Drewyer had killed seven Elk in the point below us, several miles distant but can be approached with in ¾ of a mile with canoes by means of a small creek which discharges itself into the bay[1] on this side of the Clatsop village direct Sergt. pryor to go in quest of the meat, the wind was so high that they were unable to set out untill a little before sunset, when they departed; at 10 P. M. they return excessively could and informed us that they could not make land on this side of the bay nor get into the creek in consequence of the tide being out and much lower than usual. we are apprehensive that the Clatsops who know where the meat is will rob us of a part if not the whole of it. at half after 4 P. M. Sergt Gass returned with his party, they brought with them the flesh of four other Elk which the hunters had found, being a part of the ten which were killed up the Netul river the other day. he left R. Fields, Shannon and Labuish to continue the hunt and made an appointment to return to them on Friday. late in the evening the four men who had been sent to assist the saltmakers in transporting meat which they had killed to their camp, also returned, and brought with them all the salt which had been made, consisting of about one busshel only. with the means we have of boiling the salt water we find it a very tedious opperation, that of making salt, notwithstanding we keep the kettles boiling day and night. we calculate on three bushels lasting us from hence to our deposits of that article on the Missouri.

[Clark] *Monday February 3rd 1806*

About 3 oClock Drewyer & Lapage returned, Drewyer had killed Seven Elk in the point below us, Several miles distant, but Can be approached within ¾ of a mile with Canoes by means of a Small Creak which discharges itself into the Bay, on this Sid of the Clatsop Village. Directed Serjt. Pryor to go in quest of the meat, the winds was So high that they were unable to Set out untill a little before Sunset, when they departed; at 10 P. M. they returned excessively Cold and informed us that they could not make land on this Side of the bay or get into the Creek in consequence of the tides being out and much lower than usial. we are apprehensive that the Clatsops knowing where the meat is, will rob us of a part if not the whole of it. at half after 4 P. M Sergt. Gass returned with his party they brought with them the flesh of 4 other Elk which the hunters had found, being part of the 10 which were killed up the Netul river the other day. He left Ro. Field, Shannon & Labiesh to Continue the hunt, and made an appointment to return to them on friday. late in the evening the four men who had been Sent to assist the Saltmakers in transporting meat which they had killed to their Camp also returned, and brought with them all the Salt which had been made, consisting of about one Sushel only. with the means we have of boiling the Salt water we find it a very tegious opperation that of makeing Salt, notwithstanding the Kittles are kept boiling day and night. we Calculate on three bushels lasting us from hiere to our deposit of that article on the Missouri.

1. The point is presumably Point Adams at the mouth of the Columbia in Clatsop County, Oregon. The creek might be Skipanon River; Coues (HLC), 2:797, suggests Alder or Tansey Creek. The bay is Youngs Bay. *Atlas* map 82.

[Lewis] *Tuesday February 4th 1806.*

Sergt. Pryor with a party of five men set out again in quest of the Elk which Drewyer had killed. Drewyer and La Page also returned to continue the chase in the same quarter. the Elk are in much better order in the point near the praries than they are in the woody country arround us or up the Netul. in the praries they feed on grass and rushes, considerable quantities of which are yet green and succulet. in the woody country their food is huckle berry bushes, fern, and an evergreen shrub which resembles the lorel[1] in some measure; the last constitutes the greater part of their food and grows abundantly through all the timbered country, particularly the hillsides and more broken parts of it. There are svral species of fir in this neighbourhood which I shall discribe as well as my slender botanicall skil will enable me and for the convenience of comparison with each other shal number them. (No 1.)[2] a species which grows to immence size; very commonly 27 feet in the girth six feet above the surface of the earth, and in several instances we have found them as much as 36 feet in the girth or 12 feet diameter perfectly solid and entire. they frequently rise to the hight of 230 feet, and one hundred and twenty or 30 of that hight without a limb. this timber is white and soft throughout and rives better than any other species which we have tryed. the bark skales off in irregula rounded flakes and is of a redish brown colour particularly of the younger growth. the stem of this tree is simple branching, ascending, not very defuse, and proliferous. the leaf of this tree is acerose, $1/10$th of an Inh in width, and ¾ of an Inch in length; is firm, stif and accuminate; they are triangular, a little declining, thickly scattered on all sides of the bough, but rispect the three uppersides only and are also sessile growing from little triangular pedestals of soft spungy elastic bark. at the junction of the boughs, the bud-scales continue to incircle their rispective twigs for several yeas; at least three years is common and I have counted as many as the growth of four years beyond these scales. this tree affords but little rosin. it's cone I have not yet had an opportunity to discover altho' I have sought it frequently; the trees of this kind which we have felled have had no cones on them.—

February 4th 1806.[3]

Observed Meridian Altitude of ☉'s U. L. with Sextant by the direct observation 55° 59' 15"

Latitude deduced from this observation N. 46° 10' 16.3"

By the mean of several observations found the error of the Sextant to be Subtractive —° 5' 45"

[Clark] *Tuesday February 4th 1806*

Serjt. Pryor with a party of 5 men Set out again in quest of the Elk which Drewyer had Killed. Drewyer also returned to continue the Chase in the Same quarter. the Elk are in much better order in the point near the praries than they are in the woodey Country around us or up the Netul. in the praries they feed on grass and rushes, which are yet green. in the woddey Countrey their food is huckleberry bushes, fern, and the *Shal-lon* an evergreen Shrub, which resembles the Lorel in Some measure; the last constitutes the greater part of their food and grows abundant through all the timbered Country, particularly the hill Sides and more broken parts of it. There are Several Species of *Fir* in this neighbourhood which I shall discribe as well as my botanicale Skill will enable me, and for the Convenience of Comparrison with each other Shall number them. (No. 1,) a Species which grows to an emence size; verry commonly 27 feet in Surcumferonce at 6 feet above the surface of the earth, and in Several instances we have found them as much a[s] 36 feet in the Girth, or 12 feet Diameter perfectly Solid & entire.   they frequently rise to the hight of 230 feet, and 120 or 130 of that hight without a limb. this timber is white and Soft throughout and rives better than any other Species we have tried   the bark Shales off in arregular rounded flakes and is of a redish brown Colour, particularly of the younger growth, the Stem of this tree is simple branching, assending, not very defuse, and proliferous, the leaf of this tree is accerose ½ a line in width, and ¾ of an inch in length; is firm Stiff and accuminate; they are triangular, little declineing, thickly scattered on all Sides of the Bough, but respect the three upper Sides only Growing from little triangular pedistals of Soft Spungy Elastic bark.   at the junction of these bough's, the bud-scales continue to incircle the respective twigs for several years; at least 3 years is common and I have counted as maney as the groth of 4 years beyond these Scales.   this tree affords but little rozin.   it's cone I have not yet had an oppertunity to discover altho' I have Sought it frequently; the trees of this kind which we have fell'd have had no cones on them.—

1. Salal; see February 8, 1806.
2. Sitka spruce, a species new to science. Cutright (LCPN), 259, 274, 414. It was encountered earlier on November 4, 1805, and called spruce pine. A dark vertical line runs through this passage, perhaps drawn by Biddle.
3. Lewis's astronomical observation, found at the end of the previous day's entry.

[Lewis] *Wednesday February 5th 1806.*

Late this evening one of the hunters fired his gun over the swamp of the Netul opposite to the fort and hooped. I sent sergt. Gass and a party of men over; the tide being in, they took advantage of a little creek which makes up in that direction nearly to the highlands, and in their way fortunately recovered our Indian Canoe, so long lost and much lamented. The Hunter proved to be Reubin Fields, who reported that he had killed

January 21–March 17, 1806

six Elk on the East side of the Netul a little above us; and that yesterday he had heard Shannon and Labuishe fire six or seven shots after he had seperated from them and supposed that they had also killed several other Elk. Filds brought with him a phesant[1] which differed but little from those common to the Atlantic states; it's brown is reather brighter and more of a redish tint. it has eighteen feathers in the tale of about six inches in length. this bird is also booted as low as the toes. the two tufts of long black feathers on each side of the neck most conspicuous in the male of those of the Atlantic states is also observable in every particular with this.— Fir No. 2[2] is next in dignity in point of size. it is much the most common species, it may be sad to constitute at least one half of the timber in this neighbourhood. it appears to be of the spruse kind. it rises to the hight of 160 to 180 feet very commonly and is from 4 to 6 feet in diameter, very streight round and regularly tapering. the bark is thin of a dark colour, and much divided with small longitudinal intersticies; that of the boughs and young trees is somewhat smoth but not so much so as the balsom fir nor that of the white pine of our country. the wood is white throughout and reather soft but very tough, and difficult to rive. The trunk of this tree is a simple branching diffused stem and not proliferous as the pines & firs usially are but like most other trees it puts forth buds from the sides of the small boughs as well as their extremities. the stem usually terminates in a very slender pointed top like the cedar. The leaves are petiolate, the footstalk small short and oppressed; acerose reather more than half a line in width and very unequal in length, the greatest length being little more than half an inch, while others intermixed on every part of the bough are not more than a ¼ in length. flat with a small longitudinal channel in the upper disk which is of a deep green and glossey, while the uder disk is of a whiteish green only; two ranked, obtusely pointed, soft and flexable. this tree affords but little rosin. the cone is remarkably small not larger than the end of a man's thumb soft, flexable and of an ovate form, produced at the ends of the small twigs.

[Clark] *Wednesday February 5th 1806*

Late this evening one of the hunters fired off his gun over the marsh of the Netul opposit to the fort & hhoped. we Sent Sergt. Gass and a party of men over; the tide being in they took advantage of a little Creek which makes up in that direction nearly to the high lands, and in their way fortunately recovered our Indian Canoe So long lost and much lamented. The hunter provd. to be Reubin Field, who reported that he had killed Six Elk on the East Side of the Netul a little above us; and that he had parted with Shannon and Labiesh yesterday after he had herd them fire Six or Seven Shot after he had Seperated from them, and Supposed that they had also killed Several other Elk. Fields brought with him a Pheasant which differs but little from those Common to the United States— Fur No. 2 is next in dignity in point of Size. it is much the most common Species, it may be Said to Constitute one half of the timber of this neighbourhood. it appears to be of the Spruce kind. it rises to the higth of 160 or 180 feet very Commonly and is from 4 to 6 feet in diameter, very Streight round and regularly tapering. the bark is thin of a dark colour, and much divided with Small longitudinal interstices; that of the boughs and young trees are Somewhat Smoth but not So much so as the balsom fir, nor that of the white pine of our Countrey. the wood is white throughout and rather Soft but rather tough and dificuelt to rive. The trunk of this tree is Simple branching, deffused Stem and not proliferous as the pine and fir usially are, but like most other trees it puts foth buds from the Sides of the Small boughes as well as from their extremities. the Stem usially termonate in a very slender pointed top like the Cedar. The leaves are petiolate, the footstalk Small Short and oppressed; acerose reather more than ½ a line in wedth and very uneaqual in length, the greatest length being a little more than half an inch, while others intermixed on every part of the bough are not more than a ¼ of an inch in length. flat with a Small longitudinal channel in the upper disk which is of a Deep green and glossy, while the ⟨upper⟩ under disk is of a whitish green only; two ranked, obtusely pointed, Soft and flexable. this tree affords but little rosin. the Cone is remarkably Small, not larger than the end of a mans thumb Soft, flexable and of an oval form, produced at the end of a Small twig.

 1. Oregon ruffed grouse. See also below, March 3, 1806. Perhaps it was Biddle who drew the red vertical line through this passage and the first several lines about the "fir."
 2. This is neither a fir nor a spruce, but the western hemlock, an important, dominant species of the forests of the Pacific Northwest. Franklin & Dyrness, 70–72.

[Lewis]   *Thursday February 6th 1806.*

    Sent Sergts. Gass and Ordway this morning with R. Fields and a party of men[1] to bring in the Elk which Field had killed. Late in the evening Sergt. Pryor returned with the flesh of about 2 Elk and 4 skins the Indians having purloined the ballance of seven Elk which Drewyer killed the other day. I find that there are 2 vilages of Indians living on the N. side of the Columbia near the Marshy Islands who call themselves Wâck-ki-á-cum. these I have hertofore Considered as Cath-lâh-mâhs. they speak the same language and are the same in every other rispect.

    No. 3[2] A species of fir which one of my men informs me is precisely the same with that called the balsam fir of Canada. it grows here to considerable size, being from 2½ to 4 feet in diameter and rises to the hight of eighty or an hundred feet. it's stem is simple branching, ascending and proliferous. it's leaves are sessile, acerose, one ⅛ of an inch in ¹⁄₁₆th of an inch in width, thickly scattered on all sides of the twigs as far as the growth of four preceeding years and rispect the three undersides only the uper side being neglected and the under side but thinly furnished; gibbous, a little declining, obtusely pointed, soft flexible, and the upper disk longitudinally marked with a slight channel; this disk is of a glossy deep gre[e]n, the under one green tho' paler and not glossy. this tree affords considerable quantities of a fine clear arromatic balsam in appearance and taste like the Canadian balsam. smal pustules filled with this balsam rise with a blister like appearance on the body of the tree and it's branches; the bark which covers these pustules is soft thin smoth and easily punctured. the bark of the tree generally is thin of a dark brown colour and reather smooth tho' not as much so as the white pine of our county. the wood is white and soft.— (No. 4)[3] is a species of fir which in point of size is much that of No. 2. the stem simple branching ascending and proliferous; the bark of a redish dark brown and thicker than that of No. 3. it is divided with small longitudinal interstices, but these are not so much ramifyed as in species No. 2. the leaves with rispect to their position in regard to each other is the same with the balsam fir, as is the leaf in every other rispect except that it not more than ⅔ds the width and little more than half the length of the other, nor is it's upper disk of so deep a green nor so glossey. it affords no balsam and but little rosin. the wood also white soft and reather porus tho' tough.—

No 5.[4] is a species of fir which arrives to the size of Nos. 2 and 4, the stem simple branching, diffuse and proliferous. the bark thin, dark brown, much divided with small longitudinal interstices and sometimes scaleing off in thin rolling flakes. it affords but little rosin and the wood is redish white ⅔ds of the diameter in the center, the ballance white, somewhat porus and tough. the twigs are much longer and more slender than in either of the other species. the leaves are acerose, 1/20th of an inch in width, and an inch in length, sessile, inserted on all sides of the bough, streight, their extremities pointing obliquely toward the extremities of the bough and more thickly placed than in either of the other species; gibbous and flexeable but more stif than any except No. 1 and more blontly pointed than either of the other species; the upper disk has a small longitudinal channel and is of a deep green tho' not so glossy as the balsam fir, the under disk is of a pale green.— No. 6[5] the white pine; or what is usually so called in Virginia. I see no difference between this and that of the mountains in Virginia; unless it be the uncommon length of cone of this found here, which are sometimes 16 or 18 inches in length and about 4 inches in circumpherence. I do not recollect those of virginia perfectly but it strikes me that they are not so long. this species is not common I have only seen it but in one instance since I have been in this neighbourhood which was on the border of Haley's bay[6] on the N. side of the Columbia near the Ocean.

[Clark] *Thursday February 6th 1806*

Sent Serjt. Gass and party this morning with Ru Field to bring in the Elk which Field had killed. late in the evening Serjt. Pryor returned with the flsh of about 2 Elk and four skins the Indians haveing taken the ballance of Seven Elk which Drewyer killed the other day. I find that those people will all Steal.

No. 3 a Species of fir, which one of my men inform me is presisely the Same with that called the balsam fir of Canada. it grows here to considerable Size, being from 2½ to 4 feet in diameeter and rises to the hight of 100 or 120 feet. it's Stem is Simple branching assending and proliferous—. it's leaves are cessile, acerose, ⅛ of an inch in length and 1/16 of an inch in width, thickly scattered on all Sides of the twigs as far as the groth of four proceeding years, and respects the three undersides only, the upper Side being neglected and the under Side but thinly furnished; gibbous a little declineing, obtusely pointed, Soft flexable, and the upper disk longitudinally marked with a Slight Channel; this disk is of a glossy deep green, the under one green tho paler and not glossy. This tree affords a considerable quantity of a fine Clear arromatic Balsom in appearance and taste like the Canadian balsom. Small pustuls filled with the balsom rise with a blister like appearance on the body of the tree and it's branches; the bark which covers these pustules is Soft thin Smothe and easily punctured. the bark of the [tree] is generally thin of a dark brown colour and reather Smooth tho' not as much so as the white pine of the U. States the wood is white and Soft.

No. 4 a Species of *fir* which in point of Size is much that of No 2,—. the Stem Simple branching assending and proliferous; the bark of a redish dark brown and thicker than that of No. 3. it is devided with Small longitudinal interstices, but these are not So much ramefied as in the Specis No. 2. the leaves with respect to their possition in reguard to each other is the Same with the balsam fir, as is the leaf in every other respect than that, it is not more than ⅔ds the width and little more than half the length of the other, nor is it's upper disk of so deep a green nor glossy. it affords no balsam, and but little rosin. the wood also white Soft and reather porus tho' tough—.— No. 5 is a species of *fir* which arives to the Size of No. 2, and No. 4. the Stem Simple branching, diffuse and proliferous. the bark thin dark brown, much divided with Small longitudinal interstices scaleing off in thin rolling flakes. it affords but little rosin and the wood is redish white ⅔ds of the diamieter in the Center the ballance white Somewhat porus and tough. the twigs are much longer and more slender than in either of the other speceies. the leaves are acerose 1/20 of an inch in width, and an inch in length, sessile, inserted on all Sides of the bough, Streight, their extremities pointing obliquely towards the extremities of the bough and more thickly placed than in either of the other Species; gibbous and flexable but more stiff than any except No. 1 and more blontly pointed than either of the other Species; the upper disk has a Small longitudinal Channel and is of a deep green tho' not so Glossy as the balsam fir, the under disk is of a pail green. No. 6 the White pine; or what is usially So Called in Virginia. I see no difference between this and that of the mountains in Virginia; unless it be the uncommon length of the cone of this found here, which are Sometimes 16 or 18 inches in length and about 4 inches in Surcumfrance. I do not recollect those of Virginia, but it Strikes me that they are not So long. this Species is not common I have Seen it only in three instances since I have been in this neighbourhood, I saw a few on Haleys bay on the North Side of the Columbia River, a fiew scattering on the Sea coast to the North on one of which I engraved my name—and Some on the S S E Side of *E co la* Creek near the Kil â mox nation, at which place I Saw the white & red Cedar—

   1. Including Peter Weiser; see below, February 7, 1806.
   2. Grand fir, another new species. Cutright (LCPN), 260, 400.
   3. Based on the description of the needle length compared to the "balsam fir" or grand fir, this may be a depauperate form of grand fir. The only other possibility is Pacific silver fir, *Abies amabilis* (Dougl.) Forbes, which indeed has smaller needles as described, but has a gray to nearly white bark, unlike that described. Pacific silver fir is also found at higher elevations in the Cascade Range, although there is a small coastal population. Hitchcock et al., 1 : 115; Little (CIH), 1-W. The first few lines of this passage have a red vertical line through them, perhaps penned by Biddle.
   4. Douglas fir. This species is an important sub-dominant tree of the Sitka spruce vegetation zone. Franklin & Dyrness, 53–61.
   5. Western white pine, *Pinus monticola* Dougl., a new species and today a valuable lumber tree. It is currently not documented as occurring at the mouth of the Columbia River. Both western white pine and Pacific silver fir occur near sea level in forested swamps in the Sitka spruce zone, together with western redcedar, western hemlock, and red alder. Hitchcock et al., 1 : 129; Little (CIH), 62-W; Franklin & Dyrness, 68; Cutright (LCPN), 274, 414.
   6. Baker Bay, Pacific County, Washington. *Atlas* map 91.

[Lewis] *Friday February 7th 1806.*

This evening Sergt. Ordway and Wiser returned with a part of the meat which R. Fields had killed; the ballance of the party with Sergt. Gass remained in order to bring the ballance of the meat to the river at a point agreed on where the canoe is to meet them again tomorrow morning. This evening we had what I call an excellent supper it consisted of a marrowbone a piece and a brisket of boiled Elk that had the appearance of a little fat on it. this for Fort Clatsop is living in high stile. In this neighbourhood I observe the honeysuckle[1] common in our country I first met with it on the waters of the Kooskooske near the Chopunnish nation, and again below the grand rappids In the Columbian Valley on tidewater. The Elder[2] also common to our country grows in great abundance in the rich woodlands on this side of the rocky Mountains; tho' it differs Here in the colour of it's berry, this being of a pale sky blue while that of the U' States is a deep perple. The seven bark or nine-bark[3] as it is called in the U' States is also common in this quarter. There is a species of huckleberry[4] common to the piny lands from the commencement of the Columbian valley to the seacoast; it rises to the hight of 6 or 8 feet. is a simple branching some what defuse stem; the main body or trunk is cilindric and of a dark brown, while the colateral branches are green smooth, squar, and put forth a number of alternate branches of the same colour and form from the two horizontal sides only. the fruit is a small deep perple berry which the natives inform us is very good. the leaf is thin of a pale green and small being ¾ of an inch in length and ⅜ in width; oval terminateing more accutely at the apex than near the insertion of the footstalk which is at the base; veined, nearly entire, serrate but so slightly so that it is scarcely perceptible; footstalk short and there position with rispect to each other is alternate and two ranked, proceeding from the horizontal sides of the bough only. The small pox has distroyed a great number of the natives in this quarter.[5] it prevailed about 4 years since among the Clatsops and distroy several hundred of them, four of their chiefs fell victyms to it's ravages. those Clatsops are deposited in their canoes on the bay a few miles below us. I think the late ravages of the small pox may well account for the number of remains of vilages which we find deserted on the river and Sea coast in this quarter.—

[Clark] *Friday February 7th 1806*

This evening Serjt Ordway and wiser returned with a part of the meat which R. Field had killed; the balance of the Party with Serjt. Gass remained in order to bring the ballance of the meat to the river at a point agreeed on, where the Canoe is to meet them again tomorrow morning. This evening we had what I call an excellent supper it consisted of a marrowbone, a piece of brisket of boiled Elk that had the appearance of a little fat on it. this for Fort Clatsop is liveing in high Stile, and in fact fiesting—.

In this neighbourhood I observe the honeysuckle common in the U

States, I first met with it on the waters of the Kooskooske near the Chopunnish Nation, and again below the grand rapids in the Columbian Vally on tide water. The Elder also common to our Countrey grows in great abundance in the rich wood land on this Side of the rocky mountains, tho it differs here in the Colour of its berry, this being of a pale Sky blue while that of the U, States is a deep purple. The Seven or nine bark as it is called in the U, States is also Common in this quarter. There is a Species of huckkleberry Common to the piney lands from the Commencement of the Columbian Vally to the Sea coast; it rises to the hight of 6 or 8 feet, is a Simple branching, Somewhat defused Stem; the main body or trunk is cilindric branches are green Smothe squar, and put foth a number of alternet branches of the Same Colour and form from the two horizontal Sides only. the frute is a small deep purple berry which the nativs inform us is very good, the leaf is thin of a ⟨deep⟩ pale green and Small being ¾ of an inch in length and ⅜ in width; oval terminateing more accoutely at the apax, than near the insertion of the footstalk which is at the base vened nearly entire; footstalks Short and their position in respect to each other is alternate and too ranked, proceeding from the horizontal Side of the bough only.

The *Small Pox* had distroyed a great number of the nativs in this quarter. it prouailed about 4 or 5 yrs Sinc among the Clatsops, and distroy'd Several hundreds of them, four of their Chiefs fell a victym to it's ravages. these Clatsops are Deposited in their Canoes on the bay a fiew miles below us. I think the late ravages of the Small Pox, may well account for the number of remains of villages which I Saw on my rout to the Kil a mox in Several places—.

1. Orange honeysuckle, *Lonicera ciliosa* (Pursh) DC., a new species first observed on the Lolo Trail. It has numerous medicinal uses among the tribes of western Washington. Hitchcock et al., 4:458; Gunther (EWW), 48; Cutright (LCPN), 212, 261 n. 19, 410.

2. The blue elderberry; the species used for comparison is the common elderberry, *Sambucus canadensis* L. Fernald, 1342. This passage is struck through with a red vertical line, perhaps placed by Biddle.

3. The ninebark, first mentioned on December 1, 1805.

4. Mountain huckleberry, *Vaccinium membranaceum* Dougl. ex. Hook., a new species. Hitchcock et al., 4:32; Cutright (LCPN), 212, 422.

5. At least two smallpox epidemics occurred among the Chinookan peoples of the Lower Columbia Valley before the arrival of Lewis and Clark. The first, during the 1770s,

was probably particularly devastating, as it presumably took hold upon populations previously unaffected by this disease. Smallpox was then reintroduced in 1800–1801 as Lewis indicates. For an assessment of the effects of disease on the Chinookans and other native Northwest Coast peoples, see Boyd.

[Lewis]   *Saturday February 8th 1806.*

Sent Sergt. Ordway and two men this morning to join the party with Sergt. Gass and bring the ballance of R. Fields's Elk. in the evening they returned with the balance of the flesh of five Elk, that of one of them having become tainted and unfit for uce. late in the evening Sergt. Pryor returned with Shannon Labuish and his party down the Netul. they brought with them the flesh of 4 Elk which those two hunters had killed. we have both dined and suped on Elk's tongues and marrow bones.

I have discovered that the shrub and fruit discribed on the 26th of January is not that which the Indians call the *Shal-lon,* but that is such as is there discribed, and the berry is estemed and used by the natives as there mentioned except that it is not like the shallon, baked in large loaves, but is simply dryed in the sun for winter uce, when they either eat them in thir dryed state or boil them in water. The *Shallon*[1] is the production of a shrub which I have heretofore taken to be a speceis of loral and mentioned as abounding in this neighbourhood and that the Elk fed much on it's leaves. it generally rises to the hight of 3 feet but not unusually attains to that of 5 feet. it grows very thick and is from the size of a goos quill to that of a man's thumb, celindric, the bark of the older or larger part of the stock is of a redish brown colour while that of the younger branches and succulent shoots are red where most exposed to the sun and green elsewhere. the stem is simple branching reclining, and partially fluxouse, or at least the smaler stocks or such parts of them and the boughs ⟨which⟩ as produce the leaves, take a different direction at the insertion of every petiole. the leaf is oval four & ¾ inches in length and 2½ in width. petiolate, the petiole short only ⅜th of an inch in length, celindric with a slight channel on it's upper side where it is generally red; undivided or entire, slightly serrate, the apex termineating in an accute point; the upper disk of a glossey deep green, the under disk of a pale green; veined. the leaves are also alternate and two ranked. the root is horizontal puting forth perpendicular radicles. this shrub is an evergreen. the fruit is a deep perple berry about the size of a buck short or common black cherry, of an ovate form tho reather more bluntly pointed, than at the insertion of the peduncle; at the extremity, the thin coloured membranous pellicle, which forms the surface of the pericarp, is divided into five accute angular points, which meet in the center, and contains a soft pulp of the same colour invelloping a great number of small brown kidney formed seeds. each berry is supported by a seperate celindric peduncle of half an inch in length; these to the number of ten or twelve issue from a common peduncle or footstalk which is fuxouse and forms the termination of the twig of the present years growth; each peduncle supporting a berry is furnished with one oblong bracte placed at it's insertion on the common foots[talk] which when the fruit is ripe withers with the peduncle.—

[Clark] *Saturday February 8th 1806*

Sent Serjt. Ordway and two men this morning to joint the party with Serjt. Gass, and bring the ballance of R. Field's Elk. in the evening they returned with the ballance of the flesh of five Elk, that of one of them having become tainted and unfit for use. late in the evening Serjt. Pryor returned with Shannon Labieshe and his party down the Netul. they brought with them the flesh of 4 Elk which those two hunters had killed.

we have both Dined and Suped on Elks tongues and marrowbones. a great Luxury for Fort Clatsop.

The *Shal lon* is a production of Shrub which I have taken heretofore to be a Species of Loral and mentioned as abounding in this neighbourhood, and that the Elk feed much on its leaves. it generally rises to the hight of 3 feet, and not unusialy attain to that of 5 feet. it grows very thick and is from the size of that of a goose quil to that of a mans thumb, Celendric. the bark of the older or larger part of the Stalk is of a redish brown Colour, whilst that of the younger branches & succulent Shoots are red where most exposed to the Sun and green elsewhere. the Stem is Simple branching, reclineing and partially fuxouse, or at least the Smaller Stalks or Such parts of them and their boughs ⟨as⟩ which produce the leaves, take a different direction at the insertion of every petiole.[2] A, A, the leaves as they grow from the Stalk   B. B. B the Stalk between each leaf.

January 21 – March 17, 1806

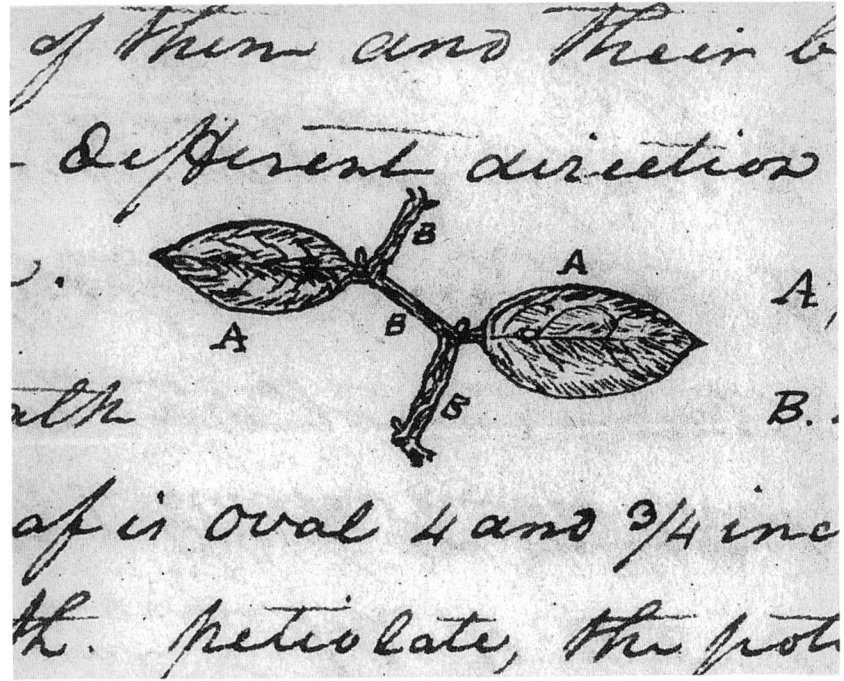

29. Stalk and Leaves of the Shallon (salal, *Gaultheria shallon*),
February 8, 1806, Voorhis No. 2

The leaf is oval 4 and ¾ inches in length, and 2 and a half in width. petiolate, the potiale Short only ⅜ of an inch in length cilindric with a Slight Channel on its upper Side where it is generally red; undevided, or entire, Slightly serrate, the apex termonateing in an accute point; the upper disk of a glossy deep Green, the under disk of a pail Green, veined. the leaves are also alternate and two ranked. the root is horozontal, putting foth pirpendicular radicles. This Shrub is an evergreen. the frute is a deep purple berry about the Size of a buck Shot or common black cherry, of an ovale form, tho' reather more bluntly pointed than at the insertion of the peduncle, at the extremity, the thin coloured membranus pellicle, which forms the Surfice of the paricarp, is divided into 4 anguar points, which meet at the Center, and Contains a Soft pulp of the Same Colour invelloping a great number of Small brown kidney formed Seed—. each berry is Supported by a Seperate celindric peduncle of half an inch in length, these to the number of 10 or 12 issue from a common peduncle of footstalk which forms the termination of the twig of the present years groth; each peduncle Supporting a berry is furnished with one oblong bracte placed at it's insertion on the common footstalk, which when the frute is ripe withers with the peduncle—.

1. The first description of salal. Cutright (LCPN), 274, 409. The text of this paragraph to here is struck through with a red vertical line, done perhaps by Biddle.

2. Here in Clark's notebook Voorhis No. 2 appears a sketch of the leaves of the salal (fig. 29) which is not duplicated in Lewis's Codex J; this may suggest that Clark was the artist for the various plant sketches in the Fort Clatsop journals.

[Lewis] *Sunday February 9th 1806*

This morning Collins and Wiser set out on a hunting excurtion; the[y] took our Indian canoe and passed the Netul a little above us. in the evening Drewyer returned; had killed nothing but one beaver. he saw one black bear,[1] which is the only one which has been seen in this neighbourhood since our arrival; the Indians inform us that they are abundant but are now in their holes.

in the marshy ground frequently overflown by the tides there grows a species of fir which I take to be the same of No. 5[2] which it resembles in every particular except that it is more defusely branched and not so large, being seldom more than 30 feet high and 18 inches or 2 feet in diameter; it's being more defusely branched may proceed from it's open situation seldom growing very close. the cone is 2½ inches in length and 3¾ in it's greatest circumpherence, which is near it's base, and from which it tapers regularly to a point. it is formed of imbricated scales of a bluntly rounded form, thin not very firm and smoth. a thin leaf is inserted into the pith of the cone, which overlays the center of and extends ½ an inch beyond the point of each scale. the form of this leaf is somewhat thus[3] overlaying one of the imbricated scales.

The stem of the black alder[4] of this country before mentioned as arriving to great size, is simply branching and defuse. the bark is smooth of a light colour with wh[i]te coloured spreading spots or blotches, resembling much that of the beech; the leaf fructification &c is precisely that of the common alder of our country. these trees grow seperately from different roots and not in clusters or clumps as those of the Atlantic states. fearing that our meat would spoil we set six men to jurking it.—

January 21–March 17, 1806

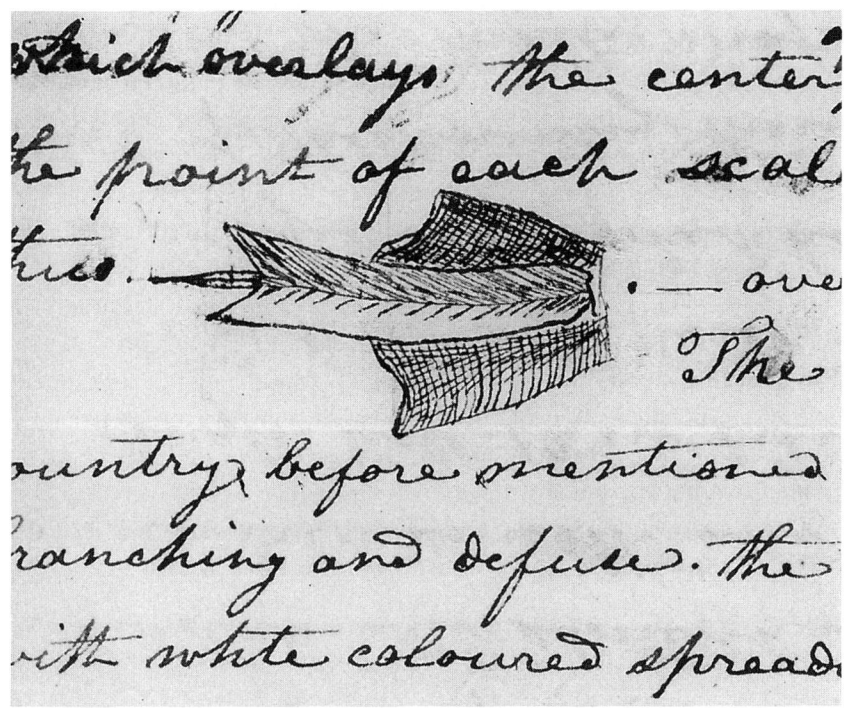

30. Fir Leaf (Douglas fir, *Pseudotsuga taxifolia*),
February 9, 1806, Codex J, p. 65

[Clark] *Sunday February 9th 1806*

This morning Collins & Wiser Set out on a hunting excurtion; in the evening Drewyer returned; had Killed nothing but one Beaver. he Saw one black Bear, which is the only one which has been seen in the neighbourhood Since our arrival. the Indians inform us that they are abundant but are now in their holes.

In the marshey grounds frequently overflown by the tides there grows a Species of *fir* which I took to be the Same of *No. 5*. from examonation I find it a distinct species of fir. it is more perfusely branched. This tree Seldom rises to a greater hight than 35 or 40 feet and is from 2 to 4 feet in Diamieter; the Bark the Same with that of No. 1. only reather more rugid. the leaf is acerose, $2/10$ of an inch in width and $3/4$ in length, they are firm Stiff and Somewhat accuminated, ending in a Short pointed hard tendril, gibbous thickly scattered on all Sides of the bough as respects the 3 upper Sides only; those which have their insertion on the underside incline side- wise with their points upwards giveing the leaf the Shape of a Sythe. the others are perpindicular or pointing upwards, (giveing the leaf) growing as in No. 1 from Small triangular pedestals of a Soft Spungy elastic bark. the under disk of these leaves or that which grows nearest to the Base of the bough is of a dark glossy green, while the upper or opposit side is of a whiteish pale green; in this respect differing from almost all leaves. The boughs retain their leaves as far back as almost to the Sixth year's groth. the peculiarity of the budscales observed in No. 1 is obsd. in this Species. The Cone is 3½ Inches in length, and 3 in circumfranse, of an ovale figure being thickest in the middle and tapering and terminateing in two obtuce points. it composes several flexable, thin, obtusely jointed Smoth and redish brown imbricated scales. each scale Covering two small winged Seed and being itself Covered in the center by a small thin inferior scale accutely pointed. The Cone is Some what of this figure.[5] they proceed from the sides as well as the ex-

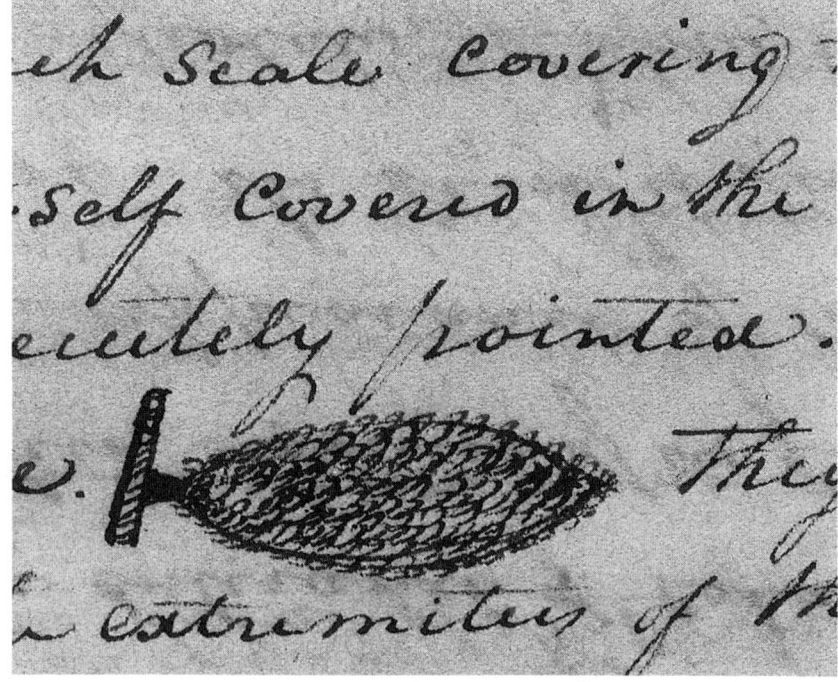

31. Fir Cone (Sitka spruce, *Picea sitchensis*),
February 9, 1806, Voorhis No. 2

tremities of the bough, but in the former case allways at or near the Commencement of Some one years groth which in Some instances are as far back as the third year.—.

The Stem of the Black Alder of this countrey before mentioned as ariveing at great Size, is Simple branching and defuse. the bark is Smoth of a light Colour with white Coloured Spredding Spots or blotches, resembling much that of beech. the leaf is procisely that of the Common alder of the United States or Virginia. those trees grow Seperately from different roots and not in Clusters or Clumps, as those of the atlantic States, casts its folage about the 1st of December.

Fearing that our meat would Spoil we Set Six men to jurking it to day, which they are obliged to perform in a house under shelter from the repeated rains.

1. The familiar, widely-distributed black bear, *Ursus americanus*. The entry to here is crossed through with a dark vertical line.
2. Again the Douglas fir. From here the next several lines are crossed through with a red vertical line, again perhaps the work of Biddle.
3. A sketch of the leaf of the Douglas fir in Lewis's Codex J, p. 65 (fig. 30). The peculiar, toothed, conescale bract is diagnostic of Douglas fir alone, and confirms the earlier identification of this species on February 6, 1806.
4. Red alder. The species has a variety of important ethnobotanical uses and the wood of the alder is, next to western redcedar, the most widely used in Northwest Coast woodworking. Gunther (EWW), 27.
5. A sketch of the cone of the Sitka spruce in Clark's Voorhis No. 2 journal (fig. 31; cf. fig. 40). Clark begins noting the Douglas fir (no. 5) but then describes the Sitka spruce, borrowing from Lewis's entry of February 18.

[Lewis] *Monday February 10th 1806.*

Drewyer visited his traps today but caught no beaver. Collins and Wiser returned had killed no Elk. Willard arrived late in the evening from the Saltworks, had cut his knee very badly with his tommahawk. he had killed four Elk not far from the Salt works the day before yesterday, which he had butched and took a part of the meat to camp, but having cut his knee was unable to be longer ucefull at the works and had returned. he informed us that Bratton was very unwell, and that Gibson was so sick that he could not set up or walk alone and had desired him to ask us to have him brought to the Fort. Coalter also returned this evening. continue the operation of drying our meat.

At Fort Clatsop

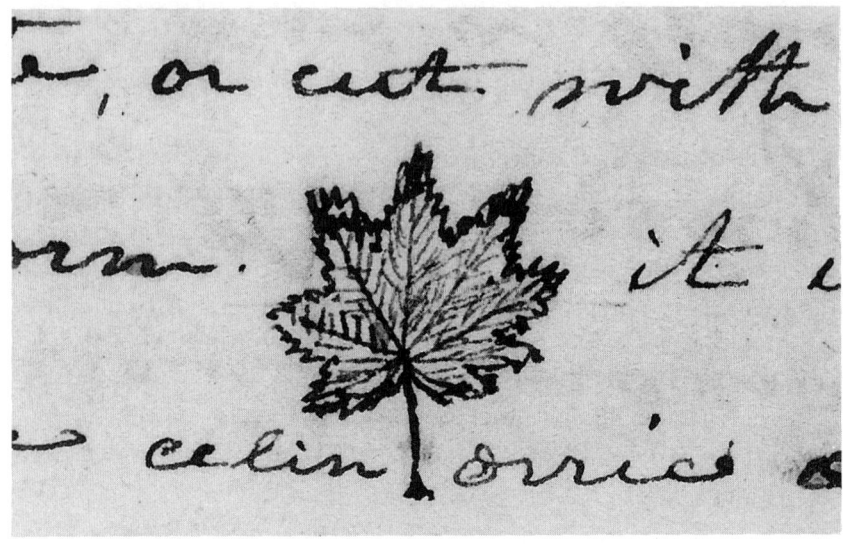

32. Maple Leaf (vine maple, *Acer circinatum*),
February 10, 1806, Codex J, p. 66

There is a tree[1] common to the Columbia river below the entrance of cataract river[2] which in it's appearance when divested of it's foliage, much resembles the white ash; the appearance of the wood and bark is also that of the ash. it's stem is simple branching and diffuse. the leaf is petiolate, plane, scattered, palmate lobate, divided by four deep sinuses; the lobes are repand, or terminate in from 3 to 5 accute angular points, while their margins are indented with irregular and somewhat circular incissures. the petiole is celendric smooth and 7 inches long. the leaf 8 inches in length and 12 in bredth. this tree is frequently 3 feet in diameter and rises to 40 or 50 feet high. the fruit is a winged seed somewhate like the maple. in the same part of the country there is also another growth[3] which resembles the white maple in it's appearance, only that it is by no means so large; seldom being more than from 6 to 9 inches in diamater, and from 15 to 20 feet high; they frequently grow in clusters as if from the same bed of roots spreading and leaning outwards. the twigs are long and slender. the stems simple branching. the bark smooth and in colour resembling that of the white maple. the leaf is petiolate, plane, scattered nearly circular, with it's margin cut with accute angular incissures of an inch in length and from six to 8 in number the accute angular points formed by which incissures are crenate, or cut with small accute angular incissures. or in this form.[4] it is 3 inches in length, and 4 in width. the petiole celindric smooth and one and a ¼ inches long. the fruit or flower not known.

[Clark]   *Monday February 10th 1806*

Collins and Wiser returned without killing any Elk. Willard arrived late this evening from the Salt Camp, he had cut his knee very badly with his tomahawk. he had killed four Elk not far from the Salt Camp, the day before yesterday, which he had butchered and took a part of the meat to the Camp, but haveing Cut his Knee was unable to be longer Servisable at the works & had returned. he informed us that Bratten was very unwell, and that Gibson was So Sick that he could not Set up or walk alone, and had desired him to ask us to have him brought to the Fort. Colter also returnd. this evening. continue the opperation of dryin our meat.

There is a tree common to the Columbia river below the enterance of Cataract River which in its appearance when divested of its folage, much resembles the white ash; the appearance of the wood and bark is also that of the ash. it's Stem is Simple branching and diffuse. the lief is petiolate, plane, scattered palmate lobate, divided by four deep Sinusus; ⟨Scattered⟩ the lobes are repand or terminate in from 3 to 5 accute angular points, while their margins are indented with irregular and Somewhat Circular incissures. the peteole is Celindric Smoth and 7 inches long. the leaf 8 inches in length and 12 in bredth. this tree is frequently 2 & 3 feet in diamieter, and rises to 50 or 60 feet high—the froot is a winged Seed Somewhat like the maple. In the Same part of the countrey there is also another groth, which resembles the white maple in its appearance, only that it is by no means so large, seldom being more than from 6 to 9 inches in diamieter, and from 20 to 30 feet high; they frequently grow in clusters as if from the same bed or root, Spreading and leaning outwards. the twigs are long and Slender. the Stems simple branching. the bark Smoth and in Colour resembles that of the white maple. the leaf is patiolate, plain, scattered nearly circular, with it's margin cut with accute anglar incissures of an inch in length and from 6 to 8 in number, the accute angular points formed, by which incissures, are crenate, or cut with small angular incissures. or in this form.[5] it is 3 inches in length, and 4 in

33. Maple Leaf (vine maple, *Acer circinatum*),
February 10, 1806, Voorhis No. 2

width. the petiole is cilendric smoth and 1 ¼ inches long. the froot or flour I have not as yet found out &c.

1. Bigleaf maple. The confusion with the Oregon white ash in the Columbia gorge on November 4, 1805, is clarified here. The tree's bark was used for rope-making, while the wood was used for smoking salmon and for carving. Gunther (EWW), 39–40. Beginning with this sentence the next several lines have a red vertical line through them, perhaps done by Biddle.
2. Klickitat River, Klickitat County, Washington. *Atlas* map 78.
3. Vine maple, *Acer circinatum* Pursh, another new species. This shrub or small tree was used by the Northwest Coast Indians for open-work carrying baskets, for fish traps, construction, and many other uses. Hitchcock et al., 3:411; Gunther (EWW), 40; Cutright (LCPN), 244, 400.
4. A sketch of the vine maple leaf (fig. 32) in Lewis's Codex J, p. 66.
5. Another sketch of the vine maple leaf (fig. 33) in Clark's Voorhis No. 2.

[Lewis]   *Tuesday February 11th 1806.*

This morning Sergt. Gass Reubin Fields and Thompson passed the Netul opposite to us on a hunting expedition. sent Sergt Pryor with a party of four men to bring Gibson to the fort. also sent Colter and

Wiser to the Salt works to carry on the business with Joseph Fields; as Bratton had been sick we desired him to return to the Fort also if he thought proper; however in the event of his not coming Wiser was directed to return.

There is a shrub[1] which grows commonly in this neighbourhood which is precisely the same with that in Virginia some times called the quill-wood. also another[2] which grows near the water in somewhat moist grounds & rises to the hight of 5 or 6 feet with a large, peteolate spreading plane, crenate and somewhat woolly leaf like the rose raspberry. it is much branched the bark of a redish brown colour and is covered with a number of short hooked thorns which renders it extreemly disagreeable to pass among; it dose not cast it's foliage untill about the 1st of December. this is also the case with the black alder. The[re] is also found in this neighbourhood an evergreen shrub[3] which I take to be another variety of the Shallun and that discribed under that name in mistake on the 26th of January. this shrub rises to the hight of from four to five feet, the stem simple branching, defuse and much branched. the bark is of a redish dark brown, that of the mane stem is somewhat rough while that of the boughs is smooth. the leaves are petiolate the petiole ¹⁄₁₀ of an inch long; oblong, obtuse at the apex and accute angular at the insertion of the petiole; ¾ of an inch in length and ⅜ths in width; convex, somewhat revolute, serrate, smoth and of a paler green than the evergreens usually are; they are also opposite and ascending. the fruit is a small deep perple berry like the common huckleberry of a pleasent flavor. they are s[e]perately scattered & attatched to the small boughs by short peduncles.—. the natives eat this berry when ripe but seldom collect it in such quantities as to dry it for winter uce.—

[Clark] *Tuesday February 11th 1806.*

This Morning Serjt. Gass R. Field and J. Thompson passed the Netul opposit to us on a hunting expedition. Sent Serjeant Natl. Pryor with 4 men in a Canoe to bring gibson to the Fort. also Sent Colter & P. Weser to the Salt works to carry on the business with Jos. Field; as bratten is also Sick we derected that he Should return to the fort if ⟨the⟩ he continued unwell;

There is Shrub which grows Commonly in this neighbourhood which grows on the Steep Sides of the hills and also in low moist grounds, and rise to the hight of 5 or 6 feet with a large peteolate, Spreading plain crenate and Somewhat woolly leaf like the rose raspberry. it is much branched the bark of a redish brown colour and is covered with a number of Short hooked thorns which renders it extreamly disagreeable to pass among, it does not cast its foliage untill about the 1st of December.

There is a Species of *bryor*[4] which is common in this neighbourhood of a green colour which grows most abundant in the rich dry lands near the water courses, but is also found in Small quantities in the piney lands at a distance from the water Courses in the former Situations the Stem is frequently the Size of a mans finger and rise perpendicularly to the hight of 4 or 5 feet when it decends in an arch and becoms procumbent or rests on Some neighbouring plant or Srubs; it is Simple unbranched and celindric; in the latter Situation it is much Smaller, and usially procumbent. the Stem is armed with Sharp and hooked bryors. the leaf is peteolate, ternate and resembles in Shape and appearance that of the purple Raspberry common to the atlantic States. The frute is a berry resembling the Blackberry in every respect and is eaten when ripe and much esteemed by the nativs but is not dryed for winters Consumption. in the Countrey about the enterance of the quick Sand river[5] I first discovered this bryor, it grows So abundantly in the furtile Vally of Columbia and on the Islands in that part of the river, that the Countrey near the river is almost impenitrable in maney places. This green Bryor retains its leaf or foliage and virdue untill late in December. The Briory bush with a wide leaf is also one of its ascociates.[6]

    1. Perhaps the Oregon grape which is given a fuller description the next day. Quill wood may be mountain holly of the next day's entry. Thwaites (LC), 4 : 59 n. 1. Several lines, starting with this paragraph, have a red vertical line through them, perhaps Biddle's work.

    2. Probably the Pacific blackberry.

    3. The evergreen huckleberry of January 26, 1806.

    4. Clark's description (copied from Lewis's entry of February 13), noting the ternate (trifoliate) leaf, abundance, and green color, confirms the identification of Pacific blackberry as given earlier.

    5. Sandy River, Multnomah County, Oregon. *Atlas* map 79.

6. The "Briory bush" is salmonberry, with bush referring to the upright habit of the species; see December 1, 1805.

[Lewis] *Wednesday February 12th 1806.*

This morning we were visited by a Clatsop man who brought with him three dogs as a remuneration for the Elk which him self and nation had stolen from us some little time since, how ever the dogs took the alarm and ran off; we suffered him to remain in the fort all night.

There are two species of ever green shrubs which I first met with at the grand rappids of the Columbia and which I have since found in this neighbourhood also; they grow in rich dry ground not far usually from some watercourse. the roots of both species are creeping and celindric. the stem of the 1st[1] is from a foot to 18 inches high and as large as a goos-qull; it is simple unbranced and erect. it's leaves are cauline, compound and spreading. the leafets are jointed and oppositely pinnate, 3 pare & terminating in one, sessile, widest at the base and tapering to an accuminated point, an inch and a quarter the greatest width, and 3 inches & a ¼ in length. each point of their crenate margins armed with a subulate thorn or spine and are from 13 to 17 in number. they are also veined, glossy, carinated and wrinkled; their points obliquely pointing towards the extremity of the common footstalk.— The stem of the 2nd[2] is procumbent abot the size of the former, jointed and unbranched. it's leaves are cauline, compound and oppositely pinnate; the rib from 14 to 16 inches long celindric and smooth. the leafets 2½ inches long and 1 inch wide. greatest width ½ inch from their base, to which they are regularly rounded, and from the same point tapering to an accute apex, wich is mostly, but not invariably tirminated with a small subulate thorn. they are jointed and oppositely pinnate, consisting of 6 pare and terminating in one, sessile serrate, or like the teeth of a whipsaw, each point terminating in a small subulate spine, being from 25 to 27 in number; veined, smooth, plane and of a deep green, their points tending obliquely towards the extremity of the rib or common footstalk. I do not know the fruit or flower of either. the 1st resembles the plant common to many parts of the U' States called the mountain holley.

At Fort Clatsop

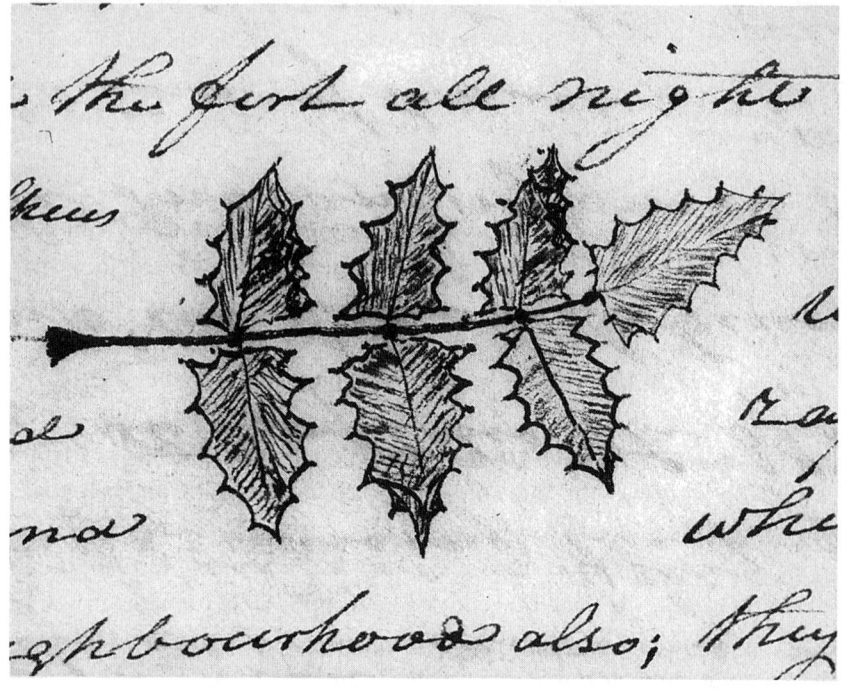

34. Evergreen Shrub Leaf (Oregon grape, *Berberis aquifolium*),
February 12, 1806, Voorhis No. 2

[Clark] *Wednesday February 12th 1806.*

 This morning we were visited by a Clatsop man who brought with him three dogs as a remuneration for the Elk which himself and Nation had Stolen from us Some little time Sence, however the dogs took the alarm and ran off; we suffered him to remain in the fort all night.

 There are two Species of evergreen Shrubs. this is the leaf of one[3] which I first met with at the grand rapids of the Columbia River, and which I have sence found in this neighbourhood also; they usially grow in rich dry ground not far from Some water course. the roots of both Species are creeping and celindric. the Stem of the first (as above) is from a foot to 18 inches high and as large as a Goose quil; it is Simple and erect. its leaves are cauline, and Spredding. the leafits are jointed & oppositly poinnate 3 par and termonateing in one, cessile widest at the base and tapering to an accuminated point, an inch and ¼ the greatest width; & 3¼ inches in length. each point of their crenate margins armed with a thorn or Spine, and are from 13 to 17 in number. they are also veined, glossy, corinated and wrinkled; their points obliquely pointing towards the extremity of the Common footstalk.

The Stem of the 2nd is procumbent about the Size of the former, jointed and umbracated. it's leaves are Cauline, compound and oppositly pointed; the rib from 14 to 16 inches long Celendric and Smooth the leafits 2½ inches long and 1 inch wide. the greatest width ½ inch from their base which they are regularly rounded, and from the Same point tapering to an acute apex, which is mostly but not entirely termonated with a Small Subulate thorn. they are jointed & oppositly pointed consisting of 6 par and termonateing in one (in this form)[4] sessile, Serrate, or like the teeth of a whipsaw, each point terminateing in a small subulate spine, being from 25 to 27 in numbr; veined, Smoth, plane

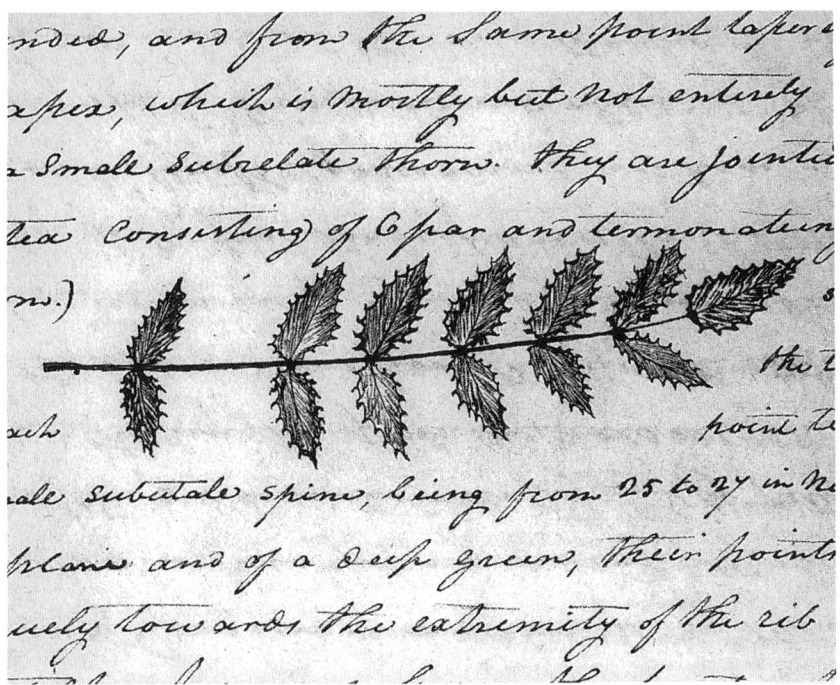

35. Evergreen Shrub Leaf (dull Oregon grape, *Berberis nervosa*), February 12, 1806, Voorhis No. 2

and of a deep green, their points tending obliquely towards the extremity of the rib or common footstalk. I do not know the fruit or flower of either. the 1st resembles a plant Common to maney parts of the United States Called the Mountain Holly—.

    1. Another new species, Oregon grape. It was used for food, dye, and medicine by regional tribes. Hitchcock et al., 2:414; Gunther (EWW), 30; Cutright (LCPN), 258, 288–89, 404. The mountain holly used for comparison is *Ilex montana* T. & G. Fernald, 981. A red vertical line runs through this paragraph to about here, perhaps drawn by Biddle.

    2. The first description of dull Oregon grape. Like the above species, it was used for food, dye, and medicine by the natives. Hitchcock et al., 2:414–15; Gunther (EWW), 30–31; Cutright (LCPN), 244, 404.

    3. A sketch of leaves of the Oregon grape (fig. 34) appearing in Clark's Voorhis No. 2, but not in Lewis's Codex J.

    4. A sketch of leaves of the dull Oregon grape (fig. 35) found in Clark's journal but not in Lewis's.

[Lewis]   *Thursday February 13th 1806.*

    The Clatsop left us this morning at 11 A. M. not any thing transpired during the day worthy of notice. yesterday we completed the operation of drying the meat, and think we have a sufficient stock to last us this month. the Indians inform us that we shall have great abundance of a small fish in March which from their discription must be the herring. these people have also informed us that one *More*[1] who sometimes touches at this place and trades with the natives of this coast, had on board of his vessel three Cows, and that when he left them he continued his course along the N. W. coast. I think this strong circumstancial proof that there is a stettlement of white persons at Nootka sound or some point to the N. W. of us on the coast.[2]

    There is a species of bryer which is common in this neighbourhood of a green colour which grows most abundant in the rich dry lands near the watercourses, but is also found in small quantities in the piny lands at a distance from the watercourses in the former situation the stem is frequently the size of a man's finger and rises perpendicularly to the hight of 4 or 5 feet when it decends in an arch and becomes procumbent or rests on some neighbouring plants or shrubs; it is simple unbranched and celindric; in the latter situation it is much smaller and usually procumbent. the stem is armed with sharp and hooked bryers. the leaf is peteolate ternate and resembles in shape and appearance that of the perple raspberry common to the Atlantic states. the fruit is a berry resembling the black berry in every rispect and is eaten when ripe and much esteemed by the natives but is not dryed for winter consumption. in the country about the entrance of the quicksand river I first discovered this bryer. it groows so abundantly in the fertile valley of Columbia and the Islands in that part of the river that the country near the river is almost impenitrable in many places. the briary bush with a wide leaf is also one of it's ascociates. the green bryer retains it's foliage and verdure untill late in December.— There are also two species of firn which are common to this country beside that formerly discribed of which the natives eat the roots. these from their disparity in point of size I shall designate the large and small firn. both species continue green all winter.— The *large firn*,[3] rises to the [height] of 3 or four feet the stem is a common footstalk or rib which proceedes immediately from the radix wich is somewhat flat on two sides about the size of a man's arm and covered with innumerable black coarce capillary radicles which issue from every pat of it's surface; one of those roots or a collected bed of them will send fourth from twenty to forty of those common footstalks all of which decline or bend outwards from the common center. these ribs are cylindric and marked longitudinally their whole length with a groove or channel on their upper side. on either side of this grove a little below it's edge, the leafets are inserted, being shortly petiolate for about ⅔ds of the length of the middle rib commencing at the bottom and from thence to the extremity sessile. the rib is terminated by a single undivided lanceolate gagged [jagged] leafet. the leafets are lanceolate, from 2 to 4 inches in length gagged and have a small accute angular projection on the upper edge near the base where it is spuar [square] on the side which has the projection and obliquely cut at the base on the other side of the rib of the leafet. or which will give a better idea in this form.[4] the upper surface is Smooth and of a deep green the under disk of a pale green and covered with a brown bubersence of a woolly appearance particularly near the cental fiber or rib. these leafets are alternately pinnate. they are in number from 110 to 140; shortest at the two extremities of the common footstalk and longest in the center, gradualy lengthening and deminishing as they succeed each other.—

36. Fern Leaf (Christmas fern, *Polystichum munitum*),
February 13, 1806, Codex J, p. 71

The *small firn*[5] also rises with a common footstalk from the radix and are from four to eight in number. about 8 inches long; the central rib marked with a slight longitudinal groove throughout it's whole length. the leafets are oppositely pinnate about ⅓rd of the length of the common footstalk from the bottom and thence alternately pinnate; the footstalk terminating in a simple undivided nearly entire lanceolate leafet. the leafets are oblong, obtuse, convex absolutely entire, marked on the upper disk with a slight longitudinal groove in place of the central rib, smooth and of a deep green. near the upper extremity these leafets are decursively pinnate as are also those of the *large firn*. The grasses of this neighbourhood are generally coase harsh and sedge-like, and grow in large tufts.[6] there is none except in the open grounds. near the coast on the tops of some of the untimbered hills there is a finer and softer species which resembles much the green sword.[7] the salt marshes also produce a coarse grass,[8] Bull rushes[9] and the Cattail flagg.[10] the two last the natives make great use in preparing their mats bags &c.—

[Clark]   *Tuesday February 13th 1806.*

 The Clatsop left us this morning at 11 A. M. not anything transpired dureing the day worthy of notice. yesterday we completed the opperation of drying the meat, and think we have a Sufficient Stock to last us this month. the Indians inform us that we shall have great abundance of Small fish in March. which from the discription must be the Herring. Those people have also informed us that one *Moore* who sometimes touches at this place and traded with the nativs of this Coast, had on board his Ship 3 Cows, and that when he left them he continued his course along the N W. Coast. I think this (if those Cows were not Coats [goats]) Strong circumstantial proof that their is a Settlement of white persons at Nootka Sound or Some place to the N W. of us on the coast.

 There are also two Species of *firn* which are common to this Countrey besides that before mentioned of which the nativs eate the roots. these two from their disparity in point of Size I shall distinguish the large and Small firn. both species continue green all winter—.

 The *large fern,* rise to the hight of 3 or 4 feet, the Stem is a Common footstalk or rib which proceeds imediately from the radix which is Somewhat flat on two Sides about the Size of a man's arm and covered with innumerable black coarse capillary radicles which issue from every part of its surface; one of those roots or a collected bead of them will Send forth from 20 to 40 of those Common footstalks all of which decline or bend outwards from the Common center. those ribs are cylindric and marked longitudinally their whole length with a groove or channel on their upper Side. on either Side of this groove a little below it's edge, the leafets are inserted, being partly petiolate for about ⅔ds of the length of the middle rib, commenceing at the bottom and from thence to the extremity Sessile. the rib is termonated by a Single undevided lanceolate gagged leafet. the leafets are lanceolate, from 2 to 4 inches in length gagged and have a Small accute angular projection and obliquely cut at the base on either Side of the rib of the leafet. ⟨on⟩ upper Surface is Smooth and of a deep Green, the under disk of a pale Green and covered

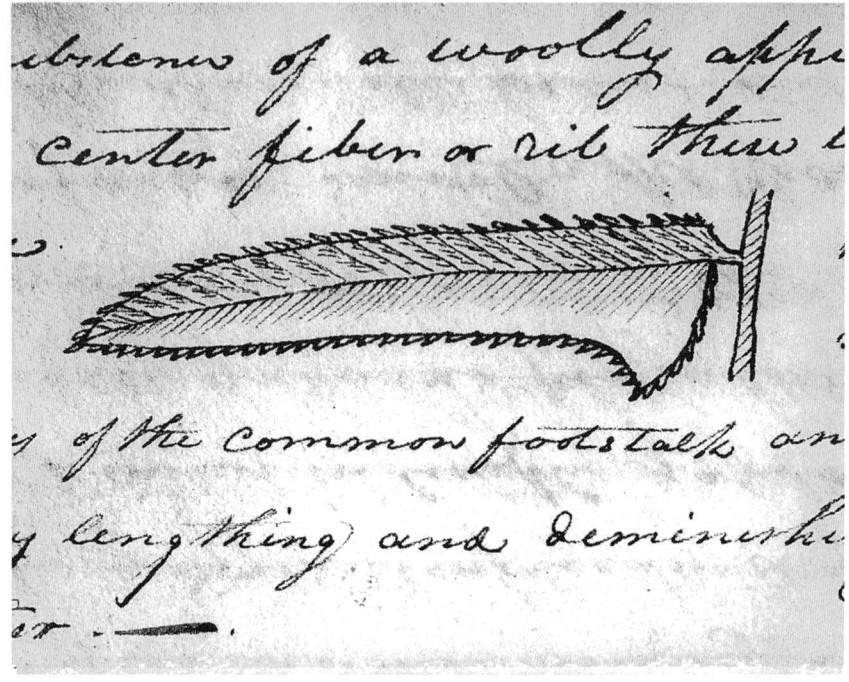

37. Fern Leaf (Christmas fern, *Polystichum munitum*),
February 13, 1806, Voorhis No. 2

with a brown Substance of a woolly appearance particalarly near the center fiber or rib   these leafets are alternately pointed [11]   they are in number from 110 to 140; shortest at the two extremities of the common footstalk and longest in the center, gradually lengthing and diminishing as they Succeeed each other.—.

The *Small firn* also rises with a Common footstalk from the radix and are from 4 to 8 in number, about 8 inches long; the Central rib marked with a Slight longitudinal Groove through out it's whole length.   the leafets are oppositly pinnate about ⅓ of the length of the Common footstalk from the bottom and thence alternately pinnate; the footstalk termonating in a Simple undevided nearly entire lanceolate leafet.   the leafets are oblong, obtuse, convex absolutely entire, marked on the upper disk with a Slight longitudinal grove in place of the central rib, smooth and of a deep green; near the upper extremity those lefets are decurscivily pinnate as are also those of the *larg firn*.

The *Grass's* of this neighbourhood are generally coarse harsh and Sedge like, and grow in large tufts. there is none except in the open grounds. near the Coast on the top of Some of the untimbered hills there is a finer and Softer Species which resembles much the Greensword. the Salt marshes also produce a Corse grass, Bullrushes and the Cattail flaggs. of the two last the nativs make great use in prepareing their mats bags &c. in those bags they Carry their fish Berries roots &c.

1. Possibly Captain Hugh Moore; see above, January 1, 1806.
2. There seems to have been no permanent European settlement between California and Alaska at this time, but trading ships did winter at Nootka Sound, Vancouver Island, British Columbia. Moore's cows, or goats, may have been intended to enhance the comfort of such a stay. A good permanent base for trading vessels was provided by the Sandwich Islands (Hawaii); of this fact Lewis seems to have been ignorant, though he deduced its existence somewhere in the Pacific. Beginning with the next paragraph a red vertical line runs through several lines, perhaps Biddle's doing.
3. Christmas fern, sword fern, *Polystichum munitum* (Kaulf.) Presl, used locally for food, cooking materials, and medicine. Hitchcock et al., 1:89–91; Thwaites (LC), 4:65 n. 1; Gunther (EWW), 13. A red vertical line runs through the first part of this passage about the fern, perhaps placed by Biddle.
4. A sketch of the fern leaf from Lewis's Codex J, p. 71 (fig. 36).
5. Deer fern, *Blechnum spicant* (L.) With. Hitchcock et al., 1:64–65; Thwaites (LC), 4:66 n. 1. Both the Christmas fern and deer fern are characteristic of the moist understory vegetation of the Sitka spruce vegetation zone. Franklin & Dyrness, 59–60.
6. Probably a species of *Carex*.
7. Greensward usually refers to a lush, green meadow rather than to a specific species. A number of grasses in this area could fit Lewis's description as "finer and softer."
8. Probably seashore saltgrass, *Distichlis spicata* (L.) Greene. Hitchcock et al., 1:553; Franklin & Dyrness, 295.
9. Bulrushes are *Scirpus* sp.
10. Common cat-tail, as noted earlier. The ethnobotanical uses for bulrush and cat-tail for coarse baskets and mats were numerous. Gunther (EWW), 21–22.
11. A sketch of the fern leaf (fig. 37) from Clark's Voorhis No. 2.

[Lewis] *Friday February 14th 1806.*

We are very uneasy with rispect to our sick men[1] at the salt works. Sergt. Pryor and party have not yet returned nor can we conceive what causes their delay. Drewyer visited his traps today and caught a very fine fat beaver on which we feasted this evening. on the 11th inst. Capt Clark completed a map of the country through which we have been passing from Fort Mandan to this place.[2] in this map the Missouri Jefferson's river the S. E. branch of the Columbia, Kooskooske³ and Columbia from the entrance of the S. E. fork to the pacific Ocean as well as a part of ⟨Flathead⟩ [*WC?: Clarks*] river⁴ and our tract across the Rocky Mountains are laid down by celestial observation and survey. the rivers are also connected at their sources with other rivers agreeably to the information of the natives and the most probable conjecture arrising from their capacities and the relative positions of their rispective entrances which last have with but few exceptions been established by celestial observation. we now discover that we have found the most practicable and navigable passage across the Continent of North America; it is that which we traveled with the exception of that part of our rout from the neighbourhood of the entrance of Dearborn's River untill we arrived on ⟨the Flat head⟩ [*WC?: Clarks*] Clarks river at the entrance of Traveler's rest creek;⁵ the distance between those two points would be traveled more advantageously by land as the navigation of the Missouri above the river Dearborn is laborious and 420 miles distant by which no advantage is gained as the rout which we are compelled to travel by land from the source of Jefferson's river to the entrance of Travelers rest Creek is 220 miles being further by 500 miles than that from the entrance of Dearborn's river to the last mentioned point and a much *worse* rout if Indian information is to be relyed on; from the same information the Flathead river like that of the S. E. fork of the Columbia which heads with Jefferson's and Maddison's Rivers can not be navigated through the Rocky Mountains in consequence of falls & rappids and as a confermation of this fact, we discovered that there were no salmon in the Flathead river, which is the case in the S. E. branch of the Columbia although it is not navigable. added to this, the Indians further inform us, that the Flathead river runs in the direction of the Rocky Mountains for a great distance to the North before it discharges itself into the Columbia river, which last from the same information from the entrance of the S. E. fork to that of ⟨Flathead⟩ [*WC?: Clarks*] river is obstructed with a great number of difficult and dangerous rappids. considering therefore the danger and difficulties attending the navigation of the Columbia in this part, as well as the circuitous and distant rout formed by itself and the ⟨Flathead⟩ [*WC?: Clarks*] river we conceive that even admitting the ⟨Flathead⟩ [*WC?: Clarks*] river contrary to information to be as navigable as the Columbia river below it's entrance, that the tract by land over the Rocky Mountains usually traveled by the natives from the Entrance of Traveller's-rest Creek to the forks of the Kooskooske is preferable; the same being a distance of 184 Miles. The inferrence therefore deduced from those premices are that the best and most Practicable rout across the Continent is by way of the Missouri [*NB: falls of Missouri*] to the entrance of Dearborn's river or near that place; from thence to ⟨flathead⟩ [*NB: Clarks*] river [*NB: by land to*] at the entrance of Traveller's rest Creek, from thence up Traveller's rest creek to the forks, from whence you pursue a range of mounttains which divides the waters of the two forks of this creek, and which still continuing it's West wardly course divides the waters of the two forks of the Kooskooske river to their junction; from thence to decend this river by water to the S. E. branch of the Columbia, thence down that river to the Columbia and with the latter to the Pacific Ocean.—

[Clark]   *Friday February 14th 1806*

We are very uneasy with respect to our Sick men at the Salt works. Serjt. Pryor and party haveing not yet returneded, nor can we conceive what can be the Cause of their delay. Drewyer visited his traps & to day and Cought a fine fat beaver on which we feasted this evening and thought it a great delecessey.—.

I compleated a *map* of the Countrey through which we have been passing from the Mississippi at the Mouth of Missouri to this place. In the Map the Missouri Jefferson's river the S. E. branch of the Columbia or Lewis's river, Koos-koos-ke and Columbia from the enterance of the S. E fork to the pacific Ocian, as well as a part of Clark's[6] river and our track across the Rocky Mountains are laid down by celestial observations and Survey. the rivers are also conected at their Sources with other rivers agreeably to the information of the nativs and the most probable conjecture arrising from their capacities and the relative positions of their respective enterances which last have with but fiew exceptions been established by celestial observations. We now discover that we have found the most practicable and navigable passage across the Continent of North America; it is that which we have traveled with the exception of that part of our rout from the foot of the *Falls* of the Missouri, or in neighbourhood of the enterance of the Rocky Mountains untill we arive on Clarks river at the enterence of Travelers-rest Creek; the distance between those two points would be traveled more advantagiously by land as the navigation of the Missouri above the *Falls* is crooked laborious and 521 miles distant by which no advantage is gained as the rout which we are compelled to travel by land from the Source of Jeffersons River to the enterance of *Travellers rest* Creek is 220 miles being further by abt. 600 miles than that from the Falls of the Missourie to the last mentioned point (Travellers rest Creek) and a much worse rout if indian information is to be relied on which is from the So so nee or Snake Indians, and the Flatheads of the Columbia west of the rocky mountains. from the Same information Clarks river like that of the S. E. branch of the Columbia which heads with Jefferson's and Maddisons river's can not be navagated thro' the rocky mountains in consequence of falls and rapids, and as a confirmation of the fact we discovered that there were no Salmon in Clark's river, which is not the Case in the S. E. branch of the Columbia altho it is not navagable. added to this, the Indians of different quartes further inform us, that Clark's river runs in the direction of the Rocky Mountains for a great distance to the north before it discharges itself into the Columbia river—. from the Same information the Columbia from the enterance of the S. E. branch to the enterance of Clark's river is obstructed with a great number of dificuelt and dangerous rapids (and the place Clark's river comes out of the Rocky mountains is a tremendious falls &c which there is no possibillity of passing the mountains either by land or water.) Considering therefore the dangers and deficuelties attending the navigation of the Columbia in this part, as well as the circuitous and distant rout formed by itself and that of Clark's River we Conceive that even admitting that Clarks river contrary to information to be as navagable as the Columbia below it's enterance, that the tract by land over the Rocky Mountains usially traveled by the nativs from the enterance of Travellers rest Creek to the Forks of the Kooskooske is preferable; the Same being a distance of 184 miles. The inferrence therefore deduced from these premises are, that the best and most practicable rout across the Continent is by way of the Missouri to the Great *Falls;* thence to *Clarks* river at the enterance of Travellers rest Creek, from thence up travillers rest Creek to the forks, from whence you prosue a range of mountains which divides the waters of the two forks of this Creek, and which still Continues it's westwardly Course on the mountains which divides the waters of the two forks of the Kooskooske river to their junction; from thence to decend this river to the S. E. branch of the Columbia, thence down that river to the Columbia, and down the Latter to the *Pacific Ocian*—. There is a large river which falls into the Columbia on its South Side at what point we could not lern;[7] which passes thro those extencive Columbian Plains from the South East, and as the Indians inform us head in the mountains South of the head of Jeffersons River and at no great distance [*WC:* ☞ *Multnomah*] from the Spanish Settlements, and that that fork which heads with the River Rajhone and waters of the Missouri passes through those extensive plains in which there is no wood, and the river Crowded with rapids & falls many of which are impassable. the other or westerly fork passes near a range of mountains and is the fork which great numbers of Indian Bands of the *So sone* or Snake Indians, this fork most probably heads with North River or the waters of Callifornia. This River may afford a practicable land Communication with New Mexico by means of its western fork. This river cannot be navagable as an unpracticable rapid is within one mile of its enterance into the Columbia, and we are fully purswaded that a rout by this river if practicable at all, would lengthen the distance greatly and incounter the Same dificuelties in passing the Rocky Mountains with the rout by way of Travellers rest Creek & Clarks river.

1. Gibson and Bratton; see above, February 11, 1806.
2. Note the discrepancy between Lewis's description of this map and Clark's description, below. No single map that exactly matches the description has been found, but it was very likely a source for *Atlas* map 123, or that map itself.
3. The "S. E. branch" is the Salmon and the Snake below the confluence with the Salmon; the captains' "Lewis's River." The Kooskooske is the Clearwater.
4. The combination of the Bitterroot and Clark Fork rivers. *Atlas* map 125.
5. Lolo Creek, Missoula County, Montana. *Atlas* map 69.
6. Each "Clark's" in this entry appears to have been written in later over some erasing, after the name was decided upon. Again the Bitterroot-Clark Fork combination. See the Introduction to the *Atlas*.
7. Here Lewis and Clark apparently combined Indian information about the Willamette and the Snake with deductions of their own. When they discovered the Willamette on their return journey, they assumed that the "Multnomah," as they called it, was the great river coming from the southeast. They believed that this river began near the headwaters of the Missouri and the Yellowstone, which is in fact the case with the Snake. Their notion that the Rio Grande (North River, or Rio del Norte) and the "waters of Cali-

fornia" (the Colorado River?) also rose in this same general area (which is true of the Green River, the principal tributary of the Colorado) meant that they still clung to the conception of a height of land which gave rise to all the great rivers of the West. They still did not fully appreciate the extent of territory involved, nor could they know of the existence of the Great Basin. Allen (PG), 327–28; *Atlas* map 125.

[Lewis] *Saturday February 15th 1806.*

Drewyer and Whitehouse set out this morning on a hunting excursion towards the praries of Point Adams. we have heard our hunters over the Netul fire several shot today, but have had no account from them as yet. about 3 P. M. Bratton arrived from the salt works and informed us that Sergt. Pryor and party were on their way with Gibson who is so much reduced that he cannot stand alone and that they are obliged to carry him in a litter. Bratton himself appears much reduced with his late indisposition but is now recovering fast. Bratton informed that the cause of Sergt. Pryor's delay was attributeable to the winds which had been so violent for several days as to render it impossible to get a canoe up the creek[1] to the point where it was necessary to pass with Gibson. the S. W. winds are frequently very violent on the coast when we are but little sensible of them at Fort Clatsop. in consequence of the lofty and thickly timbered fir country which surrounds us on that quarter from the South to the North East.—

after dark Sergt. Pryor arrived with Gibson. we are much pleased in finding him by no means as ill as we had expected. we do no conceive him in danger by any means, tho' he has yet a fever and is much reduced. we beleive his disorder to have orriginated in a violent cold which he contracted in hunting and pursuing Elk and other game through the swams and marshes about the salt works. he is nearly free from pain tho' a gooddeel reduced and very languid. we gave him broken dozes of diluted nitre and made him drink plentifully of sage tea, had his feet bathed in warm water and at 9 P. M. gave him 35 drops of laudanum.[2]

The quadrupeds of this country from the Rocky Mountains to the pacific Ocean are 1st the *domestic animals,* consisting of the horse and the dog only; 2cdly the *native wild animals,*[3] consisting of the Brown white or grizly bear, (which I beleive to be the same family with a mearly accedental difference in point of colour) the black bear, the common red deer, the black tailed fallow deer, the Mule deer, Elk, the large brown wolf, the small woolf of the plains, the large wolf of the plains, the tiger cat, the common red fox, black fox or fisher, silver fox, large red fox of the plains, small fox of the plains or kit fox, Antelope, sheep, beaver, common otter, sea Otter, mink, spuck, seal, racoon, large grey squirrel, small brown squirrel, small grey squirrel, ground squirrel, sewelel, Braro, rat, mouse, mole, Panther, hare, rabbit, and polecat or skunk.   all of which shall be severally noticed in the order in which they occur as well as shuch others as I learn do exist and which not been here recapitulated. The horse is confined principally to the nations inhabiting the great plains of Columbia extending from Latitude 40° to 50° N. and occuping the tract of country lying between the rocky mountains and a range of Mountains which pass the columbia river about the great falls or from Longitude 116 to 121 West.   in this extesive tract of principally untimbered country so far as we have leant the following nations reside (viz) the Sosone or snake Indians, the Chopunnish, sokulks, Cutssahnims, Chymnapums, Ehelutes, Eneshuh & Chilluckkittequaws.   all of whom enjoy the bennefit of that docile, generous and valuable anamal the horse, and all of them except the three last have immence numbers of them. Their horses appear to be of an excellent race; they are lofty eligantly formed active and durable; in short many of them look like the fine English coarsers and would make a figure in any country.   some of those horses are pided [pied] with large spots of white irregularly scattered and intermixed with the black brown bey or some other dark colour,[1] but much the larger portion are of an uniform colour with stars snips and white feet, or in this rispect marked much like our best blooded horses in virginia, which they resemble as well in fleetness and bottom as in form and colours.   the natives suffer them to run at large in the plains, the grass of which furnishes them with their only subsistence their masters taking no trouble to lay in a winters store for them, but they even keep fat if not much used on the dry grass of the plains during the winter.   no rain scarcely ever falls in these plains and the grass is short and but thin. The natives [*WC?: except those near the R. monts*] appear to take no pains in scelecting their male horses from which they breed, in short those of that discription which I have noticed appeared much the most indifferent.   whether the horse was orrigeonally a native of this country or not it is out of my power to determine as we can not understand the language of the natives sufficiently to ask the question. at all events the country and climate appears well adapted to this anamal. horses are said to be found wild in many parts of this extensive plain country. the several tribes of Sosones who reside towards Mexico on the waters of *Clark's* [*NB: Multnomah*]⁵ river or particularly one of them called *Shâ-bo-bó-ah*⁶ have also a great number of mules, which among the Indians I find are much more highly prized than horses. an eligant horse may be purchased of the natives in this country for a lew peads [few beads] or other paltry trinkets which in the U' States would not cost more than one or two dollars. This abundance and cheapness of horses will be extremely advantageous to those who may hereafter attemt the fir trade to the East Indies by way of the Columbia river and the Pacific Ocean.— the mules in the possession of the Indians are principally stolen from the Spaniards of Mexeco;⁷ they appear to be large and fine such as we have seen. Among the Sosones of the upper part of the S. E. fork of the Columbia we saw several horses with spanish brands on them which we supposed had been stolen from the inhabitants of Mexeco.—

[Clark] *Saturday February 15th 1806*

Drewyer and Whitehouse Set out on a hunting excurtion towards the mountains Southwest of us. we have heard our hunters over the Netul fire Several Shot today, but have had no account of them as yet. 3 P. M. Bratten arived from the Saltworks, and informed us that Serjt. Pryor and party were on their way with gibson in a litter. he is verry bad and much reduced with his present indisposition. Wm. Bratten appears much reduced, and is yet verry unwell. he informs that the Cause of Sergt. Pryor's delay was attributiable to the winds which had been so violent for Several days as to render it impossible to get a Canoe up the Creek to the point where it was necessary to pass with Gibson. the S. W. winds are frequently very violent on the coast when we are but little Sensible of them at Fort Clatsop. in Consequence of the lofty and thickly timbered fir country which Surrounds us from that quarter, from the South to the N. East.—. After Dark Sergt. Pryor arrived with Gibson. we are much pleased in findeing him by no means as ill as we had expected. we do not conceive him in danger by any means, tho' he has yet a fever and is much reduced. we believe his disorder to have originated in a violent Cold which he contracted in hunting and prosueing Elk and other game through the Swamps and marshes about the salt works. he is nearly free from pain tho' a good deel reduced and very languid. we gave him double doses of diluted niter and made him drink plentifully of Sage tea, had his feat bathed in worm water and at 9 P. M. gave him 35 drops of laudanum.

The quadrupeds of this countrey from the Rocky Mountains to the Pacific Ocian are *first* the *Domestic Animals,* consisting of the Horses and Dogs only; 2ndly the *Native Wild Animals,* consisting of the White, brown, or Grizly bear (which I believe to be the same family with a mearly accidentail difference in point of Colour) The Black Bear, the Elk, the Common red Deer, the Mule deer, the black tailed fallow Deer, the large brown wolf, the Small wolf of the Plains, the large wolf of the Plains, Panther, the tiger cat, the common red fox, the black fox or fisher, the Silver fox, large red fox of the plains, Small fox of the plains or kit fox, Antelope, Sheep, beaver, Common Otter, Sea Otter, minks, Seals racoons, large Grey Squerril, Small brown Squirrel, Small grey Squirrel, Ground Squirrel, *Sewelel,* Braro, rat, mouse, mole, hare, rabbet, and pole Cat or Skunk. all of which Shall be Severally noticed in the order in which they occur as well as Such others as I learn do exist, and which not been here recapitulated.—

The Horse is principally Confined to the Nations inhabiting the great Plains of Columbia extending from Latitude 40° to 50° N. and occupying the tract of Countrey lying between the Rocky Mountains and a rang of mountains which pass the Columbia River about the Great Falls or from Longitude 116° to 121° West in this extensive tract of Principally untimbered countrey So far as we have lernt the following nations reside (viz) The Sosone, or Snake Indians inhabiting the South fork or [*blank*] River, the Chopunnish, Sokulk's, Cutssahnims, Chym na pum, Ehelutes, Eneshuh & Chilluckkittequaws. all of whome enjoy the benifit of that docile generous and valueable Animal the Horse, and all of them except the three last have emence numbers of them. their horses appear to be of an excellent race; they are lofty eligantly formed active and durable; in Short maney of them look like the fine English coursers and would make a figure in any country. Some of those horses in pided with large spots of white irrigularly scattered and intermixed with black, brown, Bey or Some other dark colour, but much the larger portion are of a uniform

Colour with Stars, snips, and white feet, or in this respect marked much like our best blooded horses in the U, States, which they resemble as well in fleetness and bottom as in form and Colour.   the nativs Suffer them to run at large in the plains, the Grass of which furnish them with their only Subsistance, their owners takeing no trouble to lay in a winters Store for them, but they keep fat if not much used on the dry grass of the plains dureing the winter.   rain scercely ever falls in those plains and the Grass is Short and but thin.   the nativs appear to take no pains in Selecting their male horses from which they bread, in Short those of that discription which I have noticed appear much the most indifferent.   whether the horses was originally a native of this Country or not, it is out of my power to determine as we cannot understand the language of the nativs Sufficiently to ask the question.   at all events the Country and Climate appears well adapted to this Animal. Horses are Said to be found wild in maney parts of this extensive plain Country—. The Several tribes of *Sosones* who reside near Mexico on the waters of Clark's river, or particularly one of them called *Shâ-bo-bó-ah* have also a great number of *Mules*, which among the Inds. I find are much more highly prized than horses. an eligant horse may be purchased of the nativs in this Country for a fiew beeds or other paltry trinkits which in the United States would not cost more than one or two dollars. This abundance and Cheepness of horses will be extremely advantagious to those who may hereafter attempt the fir trade to the East Indies by way of the Columbia and the Pacific Ocian.—. The mules in the possession of the Inds. are principally Stolen from the Spaniards of New Mexico; Such as we have Seen appear to be large with Spanish brands.   among the Sosones of the upper part of Lewis's river we Saw Several horses with Spanish brands on them which the nativs informed us Came from the South most probably from the Settlement in New Mexico, on the heads of the North river or waters of the Bay of California.

   1. Presumably the Skipanon River and its tributary, Cullaby Creek, in Clatsop County, Oregon. *Atlas* maps 82, 84. The next two sentences have a dark vertical line through them, perhaps drawn by Biddle.
   2. "Diluted nitre" is potassium nitrate (saltpeter), used to increase the flow of perspiration and urine and to reduce fevers. Laudanum is tincture of opium, which would help Gibson relax. Cutright (LCPN), 64; Chuinard (OOMD), 156.

3. The following species can be identified as: brown, white, or grizzly bear, *Ursus horribilus;* black bear; common red deer, Columbian white-tailed deer, *Odocoileus virginianus leucura;* black tailed fallow deer, Columbian black-tailed deer; mule deer; elk; large brown wolf, *Canis lupus fuscus;* small wolf of the plains, coyote, *C. latrans;* large wolf of the plains, *C. lupus nubilus;* tiger cat, Oregon bobcat; red fox; black fox or fisher, *Martes pennanti;* silver fox and large red fox of the plains, red fox; small fox of the plains or kit fox, swift fox, *Vulpes velox;* antelope, pronghorn, *Antilocapra americana;* sheep, mountain goat, *Oreamnos americanus;* beaver; otter; sea otter; mink, *Mustela vison;* spuck, young sea otter; harbor seal; raccoon; large gray squirrel, western gray squirrel, *Sciurus griseus;* small brown squirrel, Douglas's squirrel, *Tamiasciurus douglasii;* small gray squirrel, Richardson's red squirrel; ground squirrel, probably Townsend's chipmunk, *Eutamias townsendii;* "sewelel," mountain beaver; "Braro," badger; uncertain rat, mouse, and mole; "Panther," mountain lion; hare, white-tailed jackrabbit, *Lepus townsendii;* rabbit, either eastern cottontail, *Sylvilagus floridanus,* or Nuttall's cottontail, *S. nuttallii;* polecat or striped skunk, *Mephitis mephitis.* Hall, 2:1093, 930–31, 1:446–47, 300–307; Burroughs, 90–92, 168–71, 73–75, 96–98. Many of these species are described in detail elsewhere in this volume. This material has a dark vertical line running through it, perhaps penned by Biddle.

4. The spotted Appaloosa, of which the Nez Perces and some other northwestern tribes were particularly fond.

5. Besides his emendation, Biddle also underscored the word "Clark's" in red ink.

6. Presumably the group given in the captains' Estimate of Western Indians (see Chapter 30) as the "Sho-bar-boo-be-er," said to live "on the S W Side of the Multnomah river high up the Said river," numbering 1,600. Hodge, 2:553, considers them unidentifiable but locates them in the territory of the Mono-Paviotso dialect of the Shoshonean-language family. There were no speakers of this language residing in the upper Willamette (Multnomah) River Valley. Since Lewis and Clark did not have first-hand familiarity with this group, it is likely that they were mistaken about their location. If in place of the Multnomah the Towahnahiooks, that is, the Deschutes River, was meant instead, the reference to a native people with horses and mules could apply to one or more of the Paviotso bands occupying the upper Deschutes watershed at the time of historic contact. The word is Chinookan *šumaxmuix,* but the meaning is unknown and therefore no help in determining the reference.

7. Probably New Mexico.

[Lewis] *Sunday February 16th 1806.*

By several trials made today in order to adjust my Octant and ascertain her error in the direct observation, I found that it was 2° 1' 45" + or additive beyond the fracture; this error was ascertained by a comparison with my sextant the error of which had been previously ascertained. the error of Octant in the direct observation on the broken limb next to 0 or below 55° 20' inclusive is 2° additive only.— Sent Shannon Labuish and Frazier this morning on a hunting excursion up the Kil-haw'-a-nak-kle river¹ which discharges itself into the head of the bay. no tidings yet of Sergt. Gass and party. Bratton is still very weak and complains of a pain in the lower part of the back when he moves which I suppose procedes from dability. I gave him barks.² Gibson's fever still continues obstenate tho' not very high; I gave him a doze of Dr. Rush's³ which in many instances I have found extreemly efficatious in fevers which are in any measure caused by the presence of boil [bile?]. the nitre has produced a profuse perspiration this evening and the pills operated late at night his fever after which abated almost entirely and he had a good night's rest.⁴

The Indian dog is usually small or much more so than the common cur. they are party coloured; black white brown and brindle are the most usual colours. the head is long and nose pointed eyes small, ears erect and pointed like those of the wolf, hair short and smooth except on the tail where it is as long as that of the curdog and streight. the natives do not eat them nor appear to make any other use of them but in hunting the Elk as has been before observed.— The brown white or grizly bear are found in the rocky mountains in the timbered parts of it or Westerly side but rarely; they are more common below the rocky Mountain on the borders of the plains where there are copses of brush and underwood near the watercouses. they are by no means as plenty on this side of the rocky mountains as on the other, nor do I beleive that they are found atall in the woody country, which borders this coast as far in the interior as the range of mountains which, pass the Columbia ⟨river⟩ between the Great Falls and rapids of that river. the black bear differs not any from those common to the United states and are found under the rocky Mountains in the woody country on the borders of the great plains of columbia and also in this tract of woody country which lie between these plains and the Pacific Ocean. their oconimy and habits are also the same with those of the United States.—

[Clark] *Sunday February 16th 1806*

Sent Shannon Labiesh and frazier on a hunting excurtion up the Kilhaw-a-nak-kle river which discharges itself into the head of Meriwethers Bay. no word yet of Sergt. Gass and party. Bratten is verry weak and complains of a pain in the lower part of the back when he moves which I suppose proceeds from debility. I gave him barks and Salt peter. Gibsons

January 21–March 17, 1806

fever Still Continues obstinate tho' not verry high; we gave him a dose of Dr. Rushes pills which in maney instancis I have found extreamly efficasious in fevers which are in any measure Caused by the presence of boil. the niter has produced a perfuse perspiration this evening and the pils opperated late at night his feaver after which abated almost intirely and he had a good nights rest.

The Indian Dogs are usually small or much more so than the common cur. they are party coloured; black white brown and brindle are the more usual colours. the head is long and nose pointed eyes Small, ears erect and pointed like those of the wolf, hair Short and Smooth except on the tail where it is as long as that of the Cur dog and streight. the nativs do not eate them, or make any further use of them than in hunting the Elk as has been before observed. Shannon an Labiesh brought in to us to day a Buzzard or *Vulture* of the Columbia which they had wounded and taken alive. I believe this to be the largest Bird of North America. it was not in good order and yet it wayed 25 lbs had it have been so it might very well have weighed 10 lbs. more or 35 lbs. between the extremities of the wings it measured 9 feet 2 Inches; from the extremity of the beak to that of the toe 3 feet 9 inches and a half. from hip to toe 2 feet, girth of the head 9 inches ¾. Girth of the neck 7½ inches; Girth of the body exclusive of the wings 2 feet 3 inches; girth of the leg 3 inches. the diameter of the eye 4½/10ths of an inch, the iris of a pale scarlet red, the puple of a deep Sea green or black and occupies about one third of the diameter of the eye the head and part of the neck as low as the figures 1 2 is uncovered with feathers except that portion of it represented by dots foward and under the eye. (See likeness on the other Side of this leaf)[5] the tail is Composed of twelve feathers of equal length, each 14 inches. the legs are 4¾ inches in length and of a whiteish colour uncovered with feathers, they are not entirely Smooth but not imbricated; the toes are four in number three of which are foward and that in the center much the longest; the fourth is Short and is inserted near the inner of the three other toes and reather projecting foward. the thye is covered with feathers as low as the Knee. the top or upper part of the toes are imbricated with broad scales lying transversly; the nails are black and in proportion to the Size of the bird comparitively with those of the Hawk or Eagle, Short and bluntly pointed—. the under Side of the wing is Cov-

38. Head of a Vulture (California condor, *Gymnogyps californianus*),
February 16, 1806, Voorhis No. 2

ered with white down and feathers. a white Stripe of about 2 inches in width, also marks the outer part of the wing, imbraceing the lower points of the feathers, which [c]over the joints of the wing through their whole length or width of that part of the wing. all the other feathers of whatever part are of a Glossy Shineing black except the down, which is not glossy, but equally black. the Skin of the beak and head to the joining of the neck is of a pale orrange Yellow, the other part uncovered with feathers is of a light flesh Colour. the Skin is thin and wrinkled except on the beak where it is Smooth. This bird fly's very clumsily. nor do I know whether it ever Seizes it's prey alive, but am induced to believe it does not. we have Seen it feeding on the remains of the whale and other fish which have been thrown up by the waves on the Sea Coast. these I believe constitute their principal food, but I have no doubt but that they also feed on flesh. we did not meet with this bird un[t]ille we had decended the Columbia below the great falls; and have found them more abundant below tide water than above. this is the Same Species of Bird which R. Field killed on the 18th of Novr. last and which is noticed on that day tho' not fully discribed then I thought this of the Buzzard Specis. I now believe that this bird is reather of the Vulture genus than any

January 21–March 17, 1806

other, tho' it wants Some of their characteristics particularly the hair on the neck, and the feathers on the legs. this is a handsom bird at a little distance. it's neck is proportionably longer than those of the Hawks or Eagle. Shannon also brought a Grey Eagle which appeared to be of the Same kind common to the U, States. it weighed 15 pds. and measured 7 feet 7 inches between the extremities of the wings—.

Shannon and Labiesh informed us that when he approached this Vulture after wounding it, that it made a loud noise very much like the barking of a Dog. the tongue is long firm and broad, filling the under Chap and partakeing of its transvirs curvature, or its Sides forming a longitudinal Groove; obtuse at the point, the margin armed with firm cartelagenous prickkles pointed and bending inwards.

1. Youngs River, Clatsop County, Oregon. *Atlas* maps 82, 84.
2. Presumably Peruvian bark (*cinchona*).
3. Rush's pills, a concoction of Benjamin Rush, Lewis's medical advisor, compounded of approximately ten grains of calomel and ten grains of jalap, a powerful physic. Cutright (LCPN), 175; Chuinard (OOMD), 133, 155–56. There is an "x" across the passage at about this point.
4. A dark vertical line runs through the material in the next paragraph, perhaps drawn by Biddle.
5. After the words, "the legs are 4¾ inches" appears a sketch of the California condor's head (fig. 38) in Clark's Voorhis No. 2. See also the sketch on *Atlas* map 68, perhaps a preliminary to this.

[Lewis] *Monday February 17th 1806.*

Collins and Windsor were permited to hunt today towards the praries in Point Adams with a view to obtain some fresh meat for the sick. a little before noon Shannon LaBuishe & Frazier returned with the flesh and hide of an Elk which had been wouded by Sergt. Gass's party and took the water where they pursued it and caught it. they did not see Sergt. Gass or any of his party nor learn what further success they had had. continue the barks with Bratton, and commenced them with Gibson his fever being sufficiently low this morning to permit the uce of them. I think therefore that there is no further danger of his recovery.— at 2 P. M. Joseph Fields arrived from the Salt works and informed us that they had about 2 Kegs of salt on hand which with what we have at this place we suppose will be sufficient to last us to our deposits of that article on the Missouri. we

At Fort Clatsop

there directed a party of six men to go with Fields in the morning in order to bring the salt and kettles to the fort. Shannon ⟨& Labuishe⟩ brought me one of the large carrion Crow or Buzzads of the Columbia which they had wounded and taken alive.¹ I bleive this to be the largest bird of North America. it was not in good order and yet it weighed 25 lbs. had it have been so it might very well have weighed 10 lbs mor or 35 lbs. between the extremities of the wings it measured 9 feet 2 inches; from the extremity of the beak to that of the toe 3 F. 9½ In. from hip to toe 2 feet, girth of head 9¾ In. girth of the neck 7½ Inches; do. of body exclusive of the wings 2 feet 3 Inches; do of leg 3 inches. diameter of the eye 4½/10ths of an inch. the iris of a pale scarlet red, the puple of deep sea green or black and occupied about one third of the diameter of the eye. the head and a part of the neck as low as the figures 1 2 is uncovered with feathers except that portion of it represented by dots (see likeness).² the tail is composed of 12 feathers of equal length, each 14 inches. the legs are 4¾ inches in length and of a white colour un covered with feathers, they are not entirely smooth but not imbricated; the toes are four in number three of which are forward and that in the center much the longes; the fourth is short and is inserted near the inner of the three other toes and reather projecting forward. the thye is covered with feathers as low as the knee. the top or upper part of the toes are imbricated with broad scales lying transversly; the nails are blak and in proportion to the size of the bird comparitively with those of the halk or Eagle, short and bluntly pointed. the under side of the wing is covered with white down and feathers. a white stripe of about two inches in width, also marks the outer part of the wing, imbracing the lower points of the feathers, which cover the joints of the wing through their whole length or width of that part of the wing. all the other feathers of whatever part are glossey shining black except the down which is not glossey but equally black. the skin of the beak and head to the joining of the neck is of a pale orrange yellow the other part uncovered with feathers is of a light flesh colour. the skin is thin and wrinkled except on the beak where it is smooth. this bird flys very clumsily nor do I know whether it ever seizes it's prey alive, but am induced to beleive that it dose not. we have seen it feeding on the remains of the whale & other fish which have been thrown up by the waves on the sea coast. these I beleive constitute their prinsipal food, but I have no doubt but they also feed on flesh; we did

39. Head of a Vulture (California condor, *Gymnogyps californianus*),
February 17, 1806, Codex J, p. 80

not met with this bird untill we had decended the Columbia below the great falls, and have found them more abundant below tide-water than above. I beleive that this bird is reather of the Vulture genus than any other, tho' it wants some of their charactaristics particularly the hair on the neck and feathers on the legs.— this is a handsome bird at a little distance. it's neck is proportionably longer than those of the hawks or Eagle. Shannon also brought me a grey Eagle which appeared to be of the same kind common to the U' States; it weighed 15 lb. and measured 7 Feet 7 Inches between the extremities of the wings.— At 4 P. M. Sergt. Gass and party arrived; they had killed eight Elk. Drewyer and Whitehouse also returned late in the evening, had killed one Elk.— Labuishe informed me that when he approached this vulture, after wounding it, that it made a loud noise very much like the barking of a dog & the tongue is large firm and broad, filling the under chap and partaking of it's transverse curvature, or it's sides colapsing upwards forming a longitudinal groove; obtuse at the point, the margin armed with firm cartelaginous prickkles pointed and bending inwards.

[Clark]   *Monday February 17th 1806*

    Collins and Windser were permited to hunt to day towards the praries in point Adams with a view to obtain Some fresh meat for the Sick. a little before noon Shannon and Labiesh & frazier Came with the flesh and hide of an Elk which had been wounded by Serjt. Gasses party and took the water where they pursued it and cought it. they did not See Sergt. Gass or any of his party or learn what further Sucksess they have had. Continu the barks with Bratten, and Commenced them with gibson his feaver being Sufficiently low this morning to permit the use of them. I think therefore that there is no further danger of his recovery.—. at 2 P. M. Joseph Field arrived from the Salt works and informd us that they had about 2 Kegs of Salt on hand (say 3 bushels) which with what we have at this place we suppose will be Sufficient to last us to our deposit of that article on the Missouri. we directed a party of Six men to go in the morning in order to bring the salt and Kittles to the Fort. at 4 P. M. Serjt. Gass and party arrive; they had killed 8 Elk. Drewyer and Whitehouse also return late in the evening, they had killed one Elk, part of the meat of which they brought in with them.

    The Brown, White, or Grizly *Bear* are found in the rocky mountains in the timbered part of it or Westerly Side but rarely; they are more Common below or on the East Side of the Rocky Mountains on the borders of the plains where there are Copses of bushes and underwood near the water cources. they are by no means as plenty on this Side of the Rocky Mountains as on the other, nor do I believe they are found at all in the woody country which borders this coast as far in the interior as the range of mountains which pass the Columbia between the enterance of Clarks and the Quick sand Rivers[3] or below the Great falls of Columbia.

    The Black *Bear* differs not any from those Common to the U. States, and are found under the Rocky Mountains in the woody country on the borders of the Great Plain's of Columbia and also in this tract of woody country which lie between these plains and the Pacific Ocian. their econimy and habits are also the Same with those of the United States.—.

    1. The first several lines of this material about the condor have a vertical line through them, perhaps placed by Biddle.

    2. A sketch of the California condor's head in Lewis's Codex J, p. 80 (fig. 39).

3. Respectively the Deschutes River, Sherman County, and the Sandy River, Multnomah County, both in Oregon. The mountains are the Cascade Range. Eventually they named the Deschutes the "Towarnahiooks" (variously spelled), giving Clark's name to the present Bitterroot-Clark Fork-Pend Oreille combination of rivers. See Introduction to the *Atlas*, and October 22, 1805.

[Lewis] *Tuesday February 18th 1806.*

This morning we dispatched a party to the Saltworks with Sergt. Ordway and a second with Sergt. Gass after the Elk killed over the Netul. in the evening Sergt. Ordway returned and reported that the waves ran so high in the bay that he could not pass to the entrance of the creek[1] which we had directed him to assend with the canoe. Collins and Winsor returned this evening with one deer which they had killed. the deer are poor and their flesh by no means as good as that of the Elk which is also poor but appears to be geting better than some weeks past.— in the forenoon we were visited by eight Clasops and Chinnooks from whom we purchased a Sea Otter's skin and two hats made of waytape and white ceder bark. they remained untill late in the evening and departed for their village. these people are not readily obstructed by waves in their canoes.— Sergt. Ordway brought me a specemine of a species of pine[2] peculiar to the swamps and marshes frequently overflown by the tide as this is a distinct species I shall call it No. 7. this tree seldom rises to a greater hight than 35 feet and is from 2½ to 4 feet in diameter; the stem is simple branching diffuse and proliferous. the bark the same with that of No. 1 only reather more rugged. the leaf is acerose, $^2/_{10}$ths of an inch in width and ¾ in length. they are firm stif and somewhat accuminated, ending in a short pointed hard tendril, gibbous, thickly scattered on all sides of the bough but rispect the three upper sides only. those which have there insersion on the underside incline sidewise with their points upwards giving the leaf the figure of a sythe. the others are perpendicular or pointing upwards. is sessile growing as in No. 1 from small triangular pedestals of a soft spungy elastic bark. the under disk of these leaves or that which grows nearest towards the base of the bough is a deep glossey green while the upper or opposite side is of a mealy whiteish pale green; in this rispect differing from almost all leaves. the boughs retain their leaves as far back as to the sixth years growth. the peculiarity

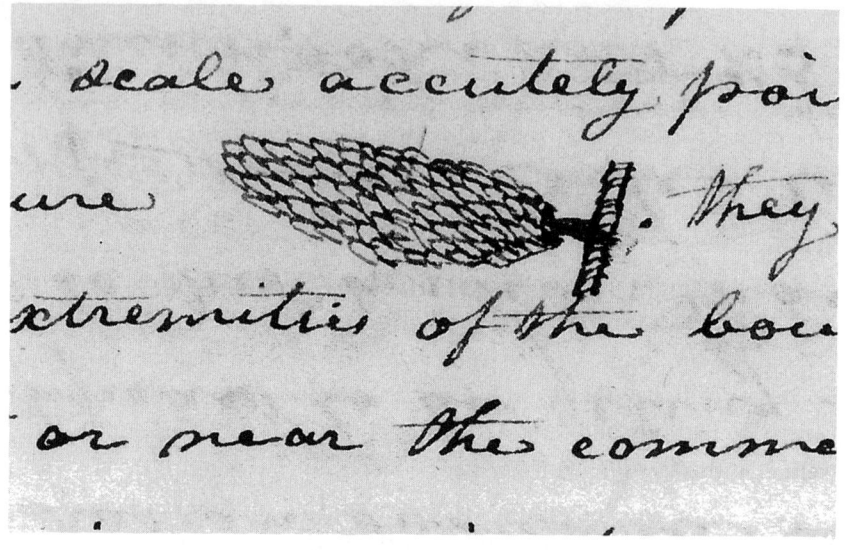

40. Pine Cone (Sitka spruce, *Picea sitchensis*),
February 18, 1806, Codex J, p. 83

of the bud scales observed in No 1 is observed in this species. The cone is 3½ inches in length and 3 in circumherence, of an ovate figure being thickest in the middle and tapering and terminating in two obtuse points. it is composes of small, flexible, thin, obtusely pointed smooth and redish brown imbricated scales. each scale covering two small winged seeds and being itself covered in the center by a small thin inferior scale acutely pointed. the cone is somewhat of this figure.[3] they proceede from the side as well as the extremities of the bough but in the former case always at or near the commencement of some one years growth which is some instances are as far back as the third year.—

[Clark] *Tuesday February 18th 1806*

This morning we dispatched a party to the Salt works with Sergt. Ordway. and a Second party with Sergt. Gass after the Eight Elk killed over the Netul. in the evening Sergt. Ordway returned and reported that the waves ran So high in the Bay that he could not pass to the enterance of a Creek which we had directed him to assend with the Canoe. Collins & Windsir returned this evening with one Deer which they had Killed. the deer are pore and their flesh by no means a[s] good as that of the Elk

January 21–March 17, 1806

which is also poore but appears to be getting better than Some weeks past. in the forenoon we were visited by a Clatsop & Seven Chinnooks from whome I purchased a Sea otter's Skin and two hats made of way tape and Silk grass and white cedar bark. they remained untill late in the evening and departed for their village. those people are not readily obstructed by waves in their Canoes. Since their departure we have discovered that they have Stole an ax.— Whitehouse brought me a roab which he purchased of the Indians formed of three Skins of the *Tiger Cat*,[4] this Cat differs from any which I have ever Seen. it is found on the borders of the plains and the woody Country lying along the Pacific Ocian. this animale is about the Size or reather larger than the wild Cat of our Countrey and is much the Same in form, agility and ferosity. the colour of the back, neck and Sides, is a redish brown irrigular varigated with Small Spots of dark brown the tail is about two inches long nearly white except the extremity which is black; it termonates abruptly as if it had been cut off. the belly is white with Small black spots. butifully varigated. the legs are of the Same Colour with the Sides and back marked with transvers stripes of black the ears are black on the outer Side Covered with fine black hair, Short except at the upper point which is furnished with a pencil of verry fine Streight black hair, ¾ of an inch in length, the fur of this animale is long and fine. much more So than the wild Cat of the U States but less so than the Louserva of the N West.[5] the nativs of this Country make great use of the skins of this Cat, to form the robes which they wear; three whole Skins is the complement usually employed, and Sometimes four in each roab. Those Cats are not marked alike maney of them have but fiew Spots of a darker Colour, particularly on the Back.

    1. Again, probably the Skipanon River, Clatsop County, Oregon. According to Ordway, his party consisted of five men. *Atlas* maps 82, 84.
    2. Sitka spruce, already described by Lewis on February 4, 1805. The small stature, and enhanced, whitish stomatal bands on the upper surface, which led Lewis to believe that this was a new species, probably resulted from the brackish tidal inundation in its marsh habitat as described. All morphological features including the drawing of the pointed conescale bract correspond to those of Sitka spruce. There is a vertical line running through the first several lines of this passage, perhaps set down by Biddle.
    3. A sketch of the Sitka spruce cone (fig. 40; cf. fig. 31) appears here in Lewis's Codex J, p. 83.

4. The first description of the Oregon bobcat.
5. The wild cat is presumably the bobcat, *Lynx rufus*. "Louserva" (*loup cervier*) is the Canada lynx.

[Lewis]   *Wednesday February 19th 1806.*

Sergt. Ordway set out again this morning with a party for the salt works by land. in the evening Sergt. Gass returned with the flesh of eight Elk, and seven skins; having left one skin with Shannon and Labuishe who remained over the netul to continue the chase. we had the Elk skins divided among the messes in order that they might be prepared for covering our baggage when we set out in the spring. our sick are recovering but they appear to strengthen but slowly. The common red deer[1] we found under the rocky mts. in the neighbourhood of the Chopunnish, and about the great falls of the Columbia river and as low down the same as the commencement of tide water. these do not appear to differ essentially from those of our country being about the same size shape and appearance in every rispect except their great length of tail which is more than half as long again as our deer I measured one of them which was 17 inches long. The Black tailed fallow deer[2] are peculiar to this coast and are a distinct species of deer partaking equally of peculiarities of the mule deer and the common deer. their ears are reather larger and their winter coat darker than the common deer; the recepticle of the eye or drane is mor conspicuous; their legs shorter and body thicker and larger than the common deer; their tail is about the length of our deer or from 8 to 10 inches the hair on the underside of which is white, and that of it's sides and top quite black the horns resemble in form and colour those of the mule deer which it also resembles in it's gate; that is bounding with all four feet off the ground at the same time when runing at full speed and not loping as the common deer or antelope do. they are sometimes found in the woodlands but most frequently in the praries and open grounds. they may be said generally to be a size larger than the common deer and that less than the mule deer. they are very seldom found in good order, or fat, even in the season which the common deer are so, and their flesh is inferior to any species of deer which I have ever seen.—

[Clark] Wednesday February 19th 1806.

Sergt. Ordway Set out again with a party to the Salt works by land. in the evening Sergt. Gass returned with the flesh of Eight Elk, and Seven Skins haveing left one Skin with Shannon and Labiche who remained over the Netul to Continue the chase. we devided the Skins between the messes in order that they might be prepared for Covering the baggage when we Set out in the Spring. our Sick appear to Strengthen but Slowly I gave Bratten 6 of Scotts pills[3] which did not work him. he is very weak and Complains of his back.

The *black Fox*[4] or as they are more frequently Called by the N West Trader *Fisher* is found in the woody country on this Coast. how this Animal obtained the name of fisher I know not, but certain it is, that the name is not appropriate, as it does not prey on or Seek it as a prey—. they are extreemly active Strong and made for climbing which they do with great agility, and bound from tree to tree in pursute of the squirel or Rackoon, their natural and most usual food. their Colour is a jut Black except a Small Spot of white on the breast. the body is long, legs Short and formed Something like the turnspit Dog,[5] with a remarkable long tail. it does not differ here from those of the United States.

The *Silver Fox*[6] this animale is very rare even in the Countrey where it exists, I have never Seen more than the Skins of this Animal and those were in the possession of the nativs of the woody Country below the Great falls of the Columbia, from which I think it is most probably they are the inhabitants of the woody country exclusively. from the Skins, it appeard to be about the Size of the large red Fox of the plains and much of its form with a large tail. the legs I think somewhat longer it has a fine long deep fur poil. the poil is of a dark lead colour and the long hairs intermixed with it, are either white or black at the lower part, and white at top, the whole mixture forming a butifull Silver Grey. I think this the handsomest of all the Fox Species, except a Species[7] of which I Saw one running, and Capt Lewis had a good view of another of the Same Species on the Missouri near the *natural walls*.[8] The large red fox of the plains, and the Kit fox[9] are the Same which we met with on the Missouri and are the inhabitants almost exclusively of the open plains, or of the copse of bushes within the plain country. the Common red or grey fox of the United States is also found in the woody country on this coast, nor does it appear to be altered in respect to it's fur colour or any other particular. we have Seen none of the large red fox.[10]

1. The Columbian white-tailed deer, perhaps a new subspecies. Burroughs, 126–27; Cutright (LCPN), 441; Hall, 2:1093. Vertical lines run through much of this passage about the deer, perhaps drawn by Biddle.
2. Columbian black-tailed deer.
3. The first mention of Scott's pills, which are not to be found in the list of drugs brought from Philadelphia. Possibly they were provided by Dr. Hugh Scott who was residing in Pittsburgh when Lewis passed through in 1803. References make it clear they were a physic. Chuinard (OOMD), 349–51; Chuinard (MMFC).
4. The fisher is actually a weasel. Some witnesses say that it does eat fish. Burroughs, 73.
5. A type of small dog of the time, trained to walk on a treadmill to furnish power to a turn-spit.
6. Not a separate species but a color phase of the red fox.
7. The cross fox, another color phase of the red fox. See above, May 31, 1805.
8. The White Cliffs or Stone Walls of the Missouri in Chouteau County, Montana. *Atlas* maps 41, 53, 60.
9. Otherwise the swift fox.
10. Presumably all the red foxes mentioned are *Vulpes vulpes*.

[Lewis] *Thursday February 20th 1806.*

Permited Collins to hunt this morning he returned in the evening unsuccessfull as to the chase but brought with him some cranberries for the sick. Gibson is on the recovery fast; Bratton has an obstenate cough and pain in his back and still appears to be geting weaker. McNeal from his inattention to his disorder has become worse.[1]

This forenoon we were visited by *Tâh-cum*[2] a principal Chief of the Chinnooks and 25 men of his nation. we had never seen this cheif before he is a good looking man of about 50 years of age reather larger in statue than most of his nation; as he came on a friendly visit we gave himself and party some thing to eat and plyed them plentifully with smoke. we gave this cheif a small medal with which he seemed much gratifyed. in the evening at sunset we desired them to depart as is our custom and closed our gates. we never suffer parties of such number to remain within the fort all night; for notwithstanding their apparent friendly disposition, their great averice and hope of plunder might induce them to be treacherous. at all events we determined allways to be on our guard as much as the nature of our situation will permit us, and never place our selves at the mercy of any savages. we well know, that the treachery of the aborigenes of America and the too great confidence of our countrymen in their sincerity and friendship, has caused the distruction of many hundreds of us. so long have our men been accustomed to a friendly intercourse with the natives, that we find it difficult to impress on their minds the necessity of always being on their guard with rispect to them. this confidence on our part, we know to be the effect of a series of uninterupted friendly intercouse, but the well known treachery of the natives by no means entitle them to such confidence, and we must check it's growth in our own minds, as well as those of our men, by recollecting ourselves, and repeating to our men, that our preservation depends on never loosing sight of this trait in their character, and being always prepared to meet it in whatever shape it may present itself.—[3]

The Mule deer are the same with those of the plains of the Missouri so frequently mentioned. we met with them under the Rocky mountains in the Neighbourhood of the Chopunnish nation on the Kooskooske river, but have not seen them since nor do we know whether they exist in the interior of the great plains of Columbia or on their lower border near the mountains which pass the river about the great falls. The Elk is the same with that found in much the greatest portion of North America, they are common to every part of this country, as well the timbered lands as the plains, but are much more abundant in the former than the latter The large brown woolf[4] is like that of the Atlantic States and are found only in the woody country on the Pacific Ocean imbracing the mountains which pass the Columbia between the great falls and rapids of the same. the large and small woolves[5] of the plains are the inhabitants principally of the open country and the woodlands on their borders and resemble in their habits and appearance those of the plains of the Missouri precisely. they are not abundant in the plains of Columbia because there is but little game on which for them to subsist.—

[Clark] *Thursday February 20th 1806.*
Permited Collins to hunt this morning he returned in the evening unsucksessfull as to the chase, but brought with him Some Cramberries

for the Sick. Gibson is on the recovery fast; Bratten has an obstinate Cough and pain in his back and Still appears to be getting weaker. H. McNeal from his inattention to his disorder has become worse. Willard has a high fever and complains of the pain in his head and want of appetite.

The forenoon we were visited by *Tâh-cum* a principal chief of the Chinnooks and 25 men of his nation. we had never Seen this Chief before he is a good looking man of about 50 years of age reather larger in Statue than most of his nation; as he came on a friendly visit we gave himself and party something to eate and plyed them plenty fully with Smoke. we gave this chief a small Medal with which he Seamed much pleased. in the evening at Sunset we desired them to depart as is our custom and Close our gates. we never Suffer parties of Such numbers to remain within the Fort all night; for not withstanding their apparent friendly disposition, their great averis and hope of plunder might induce them to be treacherous. at all events we are determined always to be on our guard, as much as the nature of our Situation will permit us, and never place our selves at the mercy of any Savages. we well know, that the treachery of the Aborigenes of America and the too great confidence of our country men in their friendship and fadility has caused the distruction of maney hundreds of us. so long has our men been accustomed to a friendly intercourse with the nativs, that we find it dificult to impress on their minds the necessity of always being on their Guard with respect to them. this confidence on our part we know to be the effect of a serious of a friendly and unintorupted intercourse. but the well Known treachery of the natives by no means entitle them to Such confidence, and we must check it's groth in our own minds as well as those of our men, by recollecting our selves, and repeating to our men, that our preservation depends on our *never* loseing Sight of this trate in their character, and being always prepared to meet it in whatever Shape it may present itself.—.

The *Mule Deer* are the Same with those of the Plains of the Missouri So frequently mentioned. we met with them under the rocky mountains in the neighbourhood of the Chopunnish Nation on the Koskooske river, but have not Seen them Since nor do we know whether they exist in the interiors of the great Plains of Columbia, or on the lower border near the mountains which pass the river about the great falls. The *Elk* is the Same with that found in much the greater portion of North America, they are common to every part of this Country, as well the timbered lands as the plains. but are much more abundant in the former than the latter

1. Chuinard (OOMD), 350, suggests that Lewis was expecting McNeal to medicate himself for syphilis with mercury ointment, but that the private had either neglected the treatment or had reinfected himself.
2. Tahcum, or Taucum (*Tawkum*), was known to traders by 1794, and was later acquainted with the Astorians and the North West Company. At one time he was at odds with Comcomly and Shelathwel (or Shillarlawit) which might account for his not having visited the fort with those chiefs. Ruby & Brown (CITC), 63, 69–70, 73, 104, 157. He is the chief called "Stock-home" in an undated entry placed at January 1, 1806.
3. The first few lines of the next paragraph have a vertical line running through them, perhaps done by Biddle.
4. A subspecies of the gray wolf.
5. The first is the gray wolf; the second the coyote.

[Lewis] *Friday February 21st 1806.*

Visited this morning by 3 Clatsop who remained with us all day; they are great begers; I gave one of them a few nedles with which he appeared much gratifyed. in the evening late they departed. Drewyer and Collins went in pursuit of some Elk, the tracks of which Collins had discovered yesterday; but it rained so hard that they could not pursue them by their tracks and returned unsuccessfull. Drewyer saw a *fisher* black fox [*EC: Mustela pennanti*] but it escaped from him among the fallen timber. Sergt. Ordway returned with the party from the salt camp which we have now evacuated. they brought with them the salt and eutensils. our stock of salt is now about 20 Gallons; 12 gallons of which we secured in 2 small iron bound kegs and laid by for our voyage. gave Willard and bratton each a doze of Scotts pills; on the former they operated and on the latter they did not. Gibson still continues the barks three times a day and is on the recovery fast.—[1]

The tyger Cat is found on the borders of the plains and in the woody country lying along the Pacific Ocean. this animal is about the size or reather larger than the wild cat of our country and is much the same in form, agility and ferosity. the colour of the back neck and sides is a redish brown irregularly variegated with small spots of dark brown the tail is about two inches long nearly white except the extremity which is black; it terminates abruptly as if it had been cut off. the belly is white with small black spots, beautifully variagated. the legs are of the same colour with the sides and back marked with transverse stripes of black the ears are black on the outer side covered with fine short hair except at the upper point which furnished with a pensil of fine, streight, black hair, ¾ of an inch in length. the fur of this anamal is long and fine, much more so than the wild cat of the United States but less so than that of Louservea of the N. West. the natives in this quarter make great use of the skins of this Cat to form the robes which they wear; four skins is the compliment usuly employed in each robe. the *Black-fox,* or as they most frequently called in the neighbourhood of Detroit, *Fisher* is found in the woody country on this coast. how this animal obtained the name of fisher I know not, but certain it is, that the name is not appropriate, as it dose not prey on fish or seek it as a prey. they are extreemly active strong and prepared for climbing, which they do with great agility, and bound from tree to tree in pursuit of the squirrel or Rackoon their natural and most usual food. their colour is a jut black except a small spot of white on the breast. the body is long, legs short and formed something like the ternspit dog with a remarkable long tail. it dose not differ here from those of the United States. The *Silver fox* this animal is very rare even in the country where it exists; I have never seen more than the Skins of this anamal and those were in the possession of the natives of the woody Country below the great falls of the Columbia from which I think that it is most probably the inhabtant of the woody country exclusively. from the skin it appeared to be about the size of the large red fox of the plains and much of it's form with a large tail. the legs I think somewhat longer. it has a fine long deep fur poil. the poil is of a dark lead colour and the long hairs intermixed with it are either white or black at the lower part and white at the top, the whole mixture forming a beatifull silver grey. I think this the most beautifull of all the Foxes except species of which I saw one only on the Missouri near the *natural walls.* the large red fox of the plains and the Kit fox are the same which we met with on the Missouri and are the inhabitants almost exclusively of the open plains, or of the cops of brush within the pain country. The common red fox of the

United States is also found in the woody country on this coast nor dose it appear to be altered in rispect to it's fur colour or any other particular

[Clark] *Friday February 21st 1806*

Visited this morning by three Clatsops, who remained with us all day; they are great begers; Capt Lewis gave one of them a fiew nedles with which he appeared much gratified, in the evening late they departed.

Drewyer and Collins went in pursute of Some Elk the tracks of which Collins had discovered yesterday; but it rained So hard they Could not pursue them by the tracks, and returned unsucksessfull. Drewyer Saw a fisher but it escaped from him among the fallen timber. Sergt. Ordway returned with the party from the Salt Camp which we have now avacuated. they brought with them the Salt and utensels. our Stock of Salt is now about 20 Gallons; 12 Gallons we had Secured in 2 Small iron bound Kegs and laid by for our voyage. Gave Willard a dose of Scots pills; they opperated very well. Gibson Still Continus the bark 3 times a day and is on the recovery fast.

The *large brown Wolf* is like that of the atlantic States, and are found only in the woody Country on the Pacific Ocean embraceing the mountains which pass the Columbia between the Great Falls an Rapids of the same. The *large* and *Small Wolves* of the inhabitents principally of the open Country and the wood land on their borders, and resemble in their habits those of the plains of Missouri presisely they are not abundant in the Plains of Columbia because there is but little game on which for them to subsist—.—.

1. Vertical lines run through the next passages, perhaps Biddle's work.

[Lewis] *Saturday February 22cd 1806.*

We were visited today by two Clatsop women and two boys who brought a parsel of excellent hats made of Cedar bark and ornamented with beargrass. two of these hats had been made by measures which Capt Clark and myself had given one of the women some time since with a request to make each of us a hat; they fit us very well, and are in the form we desired them. we purchased all their hats and distributed them among the party. the woodwork and sculpture of these people as well as these hats and their waterproof baskets evince an ingenuity by no means common among the Aborigenes of America. in the evening they returned to their village and Drewyer accompanied them in their canoe in order to get the dogs which the Clatsops have agreed to give us in payment for the Elk they stole from us some weeks since. these women informed us that the small fish began to run which we suppose to be herring from their discription. they also informed us that their Chief, Conia or Comowooll, had gone up the Columbia to the valley in order to purchase wappetoe, a part of which he in tended trading with us on his return. one of our canoes brake the cord by which it was attatched and was going off with the tide this evening; we sent Sergt. Pryor and a party after her who recovered and brought her back. our sick consisting of Gibson, Bratton, Sergt. Ordway, Willard and McNeal are all on the recovery. we have not had as may sick at any one time since we left Wood River. the general complaint seams to be bad colds and fevers, something I beleive of the influenza.[1]

The Antelope is found in the great plains of Columbia and are the same of those on the Missouri found in every part of that untimbered country. they are by no means as plenty on this side of the Rocky Mountains as on the other. the natives here make robes of their skins dressed with the hair on them. when the salmon begin to decline in the latter end of the sunme and Autumn the natves leave the river, at least a majority and remove to the plains at some distance for the purpose of hunting the Antelope. they pursue them on horse back and shoot them with their arrows. The sheep[2] is found in various parts of the Rocky mountains, but most commonly in those parts which are timbered and steep. they are also found in greater abundance on the Chain of mountains wich form the commencement of the woody country on this coast and which pass the Columbia between the great falls and rapids we have never met with this anamal ourselves but have seen many of their skins in possession of the natives dressed with the wooll on them and aso seen the blankets which they manufacture of the wooll of this sheep. from the skin the animal appears to be about the size of the common sheep; of a white colour. the wooll is fine on most parts of the body but not so long as that of our domestic sheep. the wooll is also curled and thick. on the back and more particularly on the top of the neck the wooll is intermixed with a considerable proportion of long streight hairs. there is no wooll on a small part of the body behind the sholders on each side of the brisquit which is covered with a short fine hairs as in the domestic sheep. form the signs which the Indians make in discribing this animal they have herect pointed horns, tho' one of our Engages La Page, assures us that he saw them in the black hills where the little Missouri passes them, and that they were in every rispect like the domestic sheep, and like them the males had lunated horns bent backwards and twisted. I should be much pleased at meeting with this animal, but have had too many proofs to admit a doubt of it's existing and in considerable numbers in the mountains near this coast. the Beaver and common Otter have before been mentioned in treating of the occupations of the natives in hunting fishing &c. these do not differ from those of other parts of the Continent.—

[Clark] *Saturday February 22nd 1806*

We were visited to day by two Clatsops women and two boys who brought a parcel of excellent hats made of Cedar bark, and ornemented with bear grass. two of those hats had been made by measure which Capt Lewis and my Self had given a woman Some time Since, with a request to make each of us a hat; they fit us very well, and are in the form we desired them. we purchased the hats and distribeted them among the party. the woodwork and sculpture of these people as well as those hats and the water proof baskits evince an ingenuity by no means common among the Aborigenes of America. in the evining they returned to their village and Drewyer accompanied them in order to get Some dogs &c. These women informed us that the Small fish began to run which we suppose to be herring from their discription. they also informed us that their Chief Conia Comawool, had gorn up the Columbia to the Vally in order to purchase Wappatoe, a part of which he entended tradeing with us on his return. our sick consisting of Gibson, Bratten, Willard McNeal and Baptiest LaPage is Something better Serjt. Ordway is complaining of a Coald & head ake. we have not had as many Sick at one time Since we left the Settlements of the Illinois. the general Complaint appears to be bad colds and fevers, with a violent pain in the head, and back, something I believe of the influenza.

At Fort Clatsop

The *Antelope* is found in the great plains of Columbia and are the Same with those of the Missouri found in every part of that untimbered Country. they are by no means as plenty on this Side of the Rocky Mountains as on the other. the nativs here make robes of their Skins dressed withe the hair on them. when the Salmon begin to decline in the latter end of Summer and autumn, the nativs leave the river, at least a majority and move out into the plains at Some distance for the purpose of hunting the Antelope. they pursue them on hors back and Shute them with their arrows.

The *Sheep* is found in various parts of the Rocky Mountains, but most Commonly on those parts which are timbered and Steep. they are also found in greater abundance on the chain of mountains which forms the Commencement of the woody country on this Coast and which pass the Columbia between the great falls and rapids. we have never met with this animal ourselves but have Seen maney of their Skins in the possession of the nativs dressed with the wool on them and also Seen and have the blankets which they manufacture of the wool of this Sheep. from the Skin the animal appears to be about the Size of the common Sheep; of a white colour. the wool is fine on most parts of the body, but not so long as that of the domestic Sheep; the wool is also Curled and thick. on the back and more particularly on the top of the neck the wool is intermixed with a Considerable proportion of long Streight hair. there is no wool on a Small part of the body behind the Sholders on each Side of the brisquit which is covered with a Short fine hairs as in the domestic Sheep. from the Signs which the Indians make in discribing this animale they have herect pointed horns, tho' one of our Engages Lapage, assures us that he Saw them in the Black hills where the Little Missouri river passes them, and that they were in every respect like our domestic Sheep, and like them the mail had lunated horns bent backwards and twisted. I should be much pleased at meeting with this animal. but have had too maney proofs to admit a doubt of it's existing and in considerable numbers in the mountains on this Coast. The Beaver and Common Otter have before been mentioned in treating of the Occupation of the nativs in hunting, fishing, &c. these do not differ from those of other parts of the Continent—.—.

1. Two vertical lines run through much of this passage about pronghorn and mountain goat, perhaps Biddle's doing.

2. The mountain goat, which the captains never observed at close range. Clark believed he saw one at a distance on August 24, 1805.

[Lewis]   *Sunday February 23rd 1806.*

not anything transpired during this day worthy of particular notice. our sick are all on the recovery, except Sergt. Ordway who is but little wose and not very ill tho' more so than any of the others. the men have provided themselves very amply with mockersons and leather cloathing, much more so indeed than they ever have since they have been on this voige.[1]

The Sea Otter is found on the sea coast and in the salt water. this anamal when fully grown is as large as a common mastive [mastiff] dog. the ears and eyes are remarkaby small, particularly the former which is not an inch in length thick fleshey and pointed covered with short hair. the tail is about 10 inches in length thick where it joins the body and tapering to a very sharp point; in common with the body it is covered with a deep fir particularly on the upper side, on the under part the fur is not so long. the legs are remarkably short and the feet, which have five toes each are broad large and webbed. the legs are covered with fur and the feet with short hair. the body of this animal is long and nearly of the same thickness throughout. from the extremity of the tail to that of the nose they will measure 5 feet or upwards. the colour is a uniform dark brown and when in good order and season perfectly black and glossey. it is the riches and I think the most delicious fur in the world at least I cannot form an idea of any more so. it is deep thick silkey in the extreem and strong. the inner part of the fur when opened is lighter than the surface in it's natural position. there are some fine black and shining hairs intermixed with the fur which are reather longer and add much to it's beauty. the nose, about the eyes ears and forehead in some of these otter is of a lighter colour, sometimes a light brown. those parts in the young sucking Otter of this species is sometimes of a cream coloured white, but always much lighter than the other parts. the fur of the infant Otter is much inferior in point of colour and texture to that of the full grown otter, or even after it has been weaned. there is so great a difference that I have for some time supposed it a different animal; the Indians called the infant Otter *Spuck,* and the full grow or such as had obtained a coat of good fur, *E-luck'-ke*.² this still further confirmed the opinion of their being distinct species; but I have since learned that the Spuck is the young Otter. the colour of the neck, body, legs and tail is a dark lead brown. The mink is found in the woody country on this coast, and dose not differ in any particu from those of the Atlantic coast. the seal³ are found here in great numbers, and as far up the Columbia river as the great falls above which there are none. I have reason to beleive from the information of the men that there are several species of the seal on this coast and in the river but what the difference is I am unable to state not having seen them myself sufficiently near for minute inspection nor obtained the different kinds to make a comparison. the skins of such as I have seen are covered with a short coarse stiff and glossey hair of a redish bey brown colour. tho' the anamal while in the water or as we saw them frequently in the river appear to be black and spoted with white sometimes. when we first saw those animals at the great falls and untill our arrival at this place we conseived they were the Sea Otter. but the indians here have undeceived us.— I am not much acquainted with the Seal but suppose that they are the same common also to the Atlantic Ocean in the same parallel of latitude. the skins I have seen are precisely such as our trunks are frequently covered with.—

[Clark] *Sunday February 23rd 1806.*

Not any thing transpired desering particular notice. our Sick are all on the recovery. the men have provided themselves verry amply with mockersons & leather clothing, much more So indeed than they have ever been Since they have been on the voyage.

The *Sea Otter* is found only on the Sea Coast and in the Salt water. Those animals which I took to be the Sea Otter from the Great Falls of the Columbia to the mouth, proves to be the Phosia or Seal which at a little distance has every appearance of the Sea Otters. The Sea otter when fully grown is as large as the common mastif dog, the ears and Eyes are remarkably Small, particularly the former which is not an inch in length thick fleshey and pointed, Covered with short hair. the tail is about 10 inches in length thick where it joins the body and tapering to a very Sharp point; in common with the body it is covered with a deep fur particularly on the upper Side, on the under part the fur is not So long. the legs are remarkably Short and the feat which have five toes each are broad large and webbed. the legs are covered with fur and the feet with Short hair. the body of this Animal is long and nearly of the Same thickness throughout. from the extremity of the tail to that of the nose they will measure 5 feet or upwards. the colour is of a uniform dark brown, and when in good order and Season perfectly Black and Glossey. it is the richest and I think the most delightfull fur in the world at least I cannot form an idea of any more so. it is deep thick silky in the extream and Strong. the inner part of the fur when open is lighter than the surface in its natural position. there are Some fine black Shineing hairs intermixed with the fur which are reather longer and add much to its beauty. the nose, about the eyes, ears and forehead in Some of those otter is of a light Colour, Sometimes a light brown. those parts in the young Suckling otters of this Species is Sometimes of a creem colour'd white, but alwayes much lighter than the other parts. the fur of the infant otter is much inferior in point of colour, and texture, to that of the full grown otter, or even after it has been weened—. there is so great a difference that I have for Some time Supposed it a different animal; the Indians Call the infant otter *Spuck,* and the full grown or such as had obtained a Coat of good fur, *E luck'ko.* this Still further confirmed the opinion of their being distinct Species; but I have Since lerned that the Spuck is the young otter. the Colour of the neck, body, legs and tail is a dark lead brown. The *Mink* is found in the woody Country on this Coast and does not differ in any particular from those of the Atlantic Coasts.

The Seal or Phoca are found here in great numbers, and as far up the Columbia as the great Falls, above which there are none. I have reasons to believe from the information of the men that there are Several Species of the Phoca on this Coast and in the river, but what the difference is I am unable to State not haveing Seen them myself Sufficiently near for manute inspection nor obtain the different kinds to make a comparison. the Skins of Such as I have Seen are covered with a Short thick Coarse Glossy hair of a redish bey brown Colour. tho' the animal while in the water, or as we saw them frequently in the river appear to be black and Spoted with white sometimes. I am not much acquainted with the Seal, but Suppose that they are the Same common also to the atlantic Ocian in the Same parrelal of Latitude. the Skins, or those which I have Seen are presisely Such as trunks are frequently Covered with. the flesh of this animal is highly prised by the nativs who Swinge the hair off and then roste the flesh on Sticks before the fire.

   1. The first several lines of the next paragraph have a vertical line running through them, perhaps placed there by Biddle.
   2. Spuck is the Chinookan word *špaq*ʷ, "gray"; it is probably a description rather than a specific term for the infant otter. E-luck'-ke is also Chinookan, *iláki*, "otter." Boas (Ch), 609.
   3. The first, brief, description of the harbor seal.

[Lewis]   *Monday February 24th 1806.*

Our sick are still on the recovery. Shannon & Labuishe returned in the forenoon; they had killed no Elk and reported that they beleived the Elk have retired from their former haunts and gone further back in the country to a considerable distance from this place. this is very unwelcome information for poor and inferior as the flesh of this animal is it is our principal dependance for subsistence.

This evening we were visited by Comowooll the Clatsop Chief and 12 men women & children of his nation. Drewyer came a passenger in their canoe, and brought with him two dogs. The chief and his party had brought for sail a Sea Otter skin some hats, stergeon[1] and a [s]pecies of small fish[2] which now begin to run, and are taken in great quantities in the Columbia R. about 40 miles above us by means of skiming or scooping nets. on this page I have drawn the likeness of them as large as life;[3] it as perfect as I can make it with my pen and will serve to give a general idea of the fish. the rays of the fins are boney but not sharp tho' somewhat pointed. the small fin on the back next to the tail has no rays of bone being a thin membranous pellicle. the fins next to the gills have eleven rays each. those of the abdomen have eight each, those of the pinna-ani[4] are 20 and 2 half formed in front. that of the back has eleven rays. all the fins are of a white colour. the back is of a bluish duskey colour and that of the lower part of the sides and belley is of a silvery white. no spots on any part. the first bone of the gills next be-of small fish which now begin to run and are taken in great quantities in the Columbia R. about 40 miles above us by means of skiming or scooping nets. on this page I have drawn the likeness of them as large as life; it as perfect as I can make it with my pen and will serve to give a general idea of the fish. the rays of the fins are boney but not sharp tho' somewhat pointed. the small fin on the back next to the tail has no rays of bone being a membranous pellicle. the fins next to the gills have eleven rays each. those of the abdomen have eight each, those of the pinnæani are 20 and 2 half formed in front. that of the back has eleven rays. all the fins are of a white colour. the back is of a bleuish dusky colour and that of the the lower part of the sides and belley is of a silver= of white. no spots on any part. the first bone of the gills next behind the eye is of a bleuis cast, and the second of a light gould colour nearly white. the pupil of the eye is black and the iris of a silver white. the under jaw exceeds the upper and the mouth opens to great extent, folding like that of the herring. it has no teeth. the abdomen is obtuse and smooth; in this differing from the herring, shad anchovey &c of the Malacapterygious Order & Class Clupea

41. Eulachon (*Thaleichthys pacificus*),
February 24, 1806, Codex J, p. 93

hid the eye is of a bluis cast, and the second of a light goald colour nearly white. the puple of the eye is black and the iris of a silver white. the underjaw exceeds the uper; and the mouth opens to great extent, folding like that of the herring. it has no teeth. the abdomen is obtuse and smooth; in this differing from the herring, shad anchovey &c of the Malacopterygious Order & Class Clupea,[5] to which however I think it more nearly allyed than to any other altho' it has not their accute and serrate abdomen and the under jaw exceeding the upper. the scales of this little fish are so small and thin that without minute inspection you would suppose they had none. they are filled with roes of a pure white colour and have scarcely any perceptable alimentary duct. I find them best when cooked in Indian stile, which is by roasting a number of them together on a wooden spit without any previous preperation whatever. they are so fat they require no additional sauce, and I think them superior to any fish I ever tasted, even more delicate and lussious than the white fish of the lakes[6] which have heretofore formed my standart of excellence among the fishes. I have heard the fresh anchovey[7] much extolled but I hope I shall be pardoned for beleiving this quite as good. the bones are so soft and fine that they form no obstruction in eating this fish. we purchased all the articles which these people brought us; we suffered these people to remain all night as it rained, the wind blew most violently and they had their women and children with them; the latter being a sure pledge of their pacific dispositions. the Sturgeon which they brought us was also good of it's kind. we determine to send a party up the river to procure some of those fish, and another in some direction to hunt Elk as soon as the weather will permit.

[Clark] *Monday February 24th 1806*

Our Sick are Still on the recovery. Shannon and Labiche returned in the forenoon, they had killed no Elk, and reported that they believe the Elk have returned from their former haunts and gorn further back in the mountains to a considerable distance from this place. this is very unwelcom information, for poore and inferior as the flesh of this animale is, it is our principal dependance for Subsistance.

The *Rackoon* is found in the woody Country on the Coast in considerable quantities. the nativs take a fiew of them in Snars, and deadfalls;

tho' appear not to value their Skins much, and but Seldom prepare them for robes. The large Grey Squirel[8] appear to be a native of a narrow tract of Country on the upper Side of the mountains below the Great falls of Columbia which is pritty well covered in maney parts with a Species of white oak. this animal is much larger than the Gray Squirel of our Country, it resembles it much in form and colour. it is as large as the Fox Squirel[9] of the South Atlantic States. the tail is reather larger than the whole of the body and head, the hair of which is long and tho' inserted on all Sides reispect the horozontal one. the eyes are black, whiskers black and long. the back, Sides, head, tale and outer parts of the legs are of a blue lead colour grey. the breast, belly, and inner parts of the legs are of a pure white. the hair is Short as that of the Fox Squirel but is much finer and intermixed with a propotion of fur. the nativs make great use of those Skins in forming their robes. this Squirel Subsists principally on the acorn and filburts,[10] which last also grow abundantly in the Oak Country—. The Small *brown Squirel*[11] is a butifull little animal about the size of the red Squirel of the E. States or Something larger than the ground Squirel of the U States. the tail is as long as the body and neck formed Somewhat flat. the eyes black, whiskers long and black but not abundant. the back, Sides, head, neck and outer parts of the legs are of a redish dark brown. the throat, breast, belly and inner parts of the legs are of a pale brick red. the tail is a mixture of black and fox coloured red in which the black prodomonates in the middle, and the other on the edges and extremity. the hair of the body is about ½ inch long and So fine and soft that it has the appearance of fur. the hair of the tail is coarser and double as long. this animal Subsists principally on the Seeds of various Species of pine and are always found in the piney Country. they are common to the tract of woody country on this coast. they lodge in Clefts of rocks, holes in the Ground, old Stumps of trees and the hollow trunks of falling timber; in this respect resemble the rat always haveing their habitation in or near the earth. The Small *Grey Squirel*[12] Common to every part of the Rocky Mountains which is timbered, differ from the dark brown squirel just discribed only in its colour. it's back, neck, Sides, head, tail and outer Sides of the legs are of brown lead coloured Grey; the tail has a Slight touch of the fox colour near the extremity of some of the hairs. the throat, belly, breast, and inner part of the legs are of the Colour of tanners ooze and have a narrow Stripe of black commencing behing each Sholder and extending longitudinally for about 3 inches between the Colours of the Side & belly.   their habits are also the Same with the dark brown Squirel of this neighbourhood, and like them are extreamly nimble and active. *The Ground Squirel*[13] is found in various parts of the Countrey as well the Praries as wood lands, and is one of the fiew animals which we have Seen in every part of our voyage.   it differs not at all from those of the U, States.

The *Barking Squirel*[14] and handsom Ground Squirel[15] of the Plains on the East Side of the Rocky Mountains are not found in the plains of the Columbia.

This evening we were visited by Comowooll the Clatsop Chief and 14 men women and Children of his nation. Drewyer came a pasinger in their Canoe, and brought with him two dogs.   the Chief and his party had brought for Sale a Sea otter Skin, Some hats, Sturgeon and a Species of fish which now begins to run and are taken in Great quantities in the Columbia River about 40 miles above us by means of Skiming or scooping nets. See likeness on the other Side of this leaf or page.[16] Capt Lewis gave an old Coat and Vest for a Sea otter Skin, we purchased Several hads of the Indian manufactry and distributed them among the party.   we also purchased a fiew of the Small fish which we found deliciously fine.

1. Presumably the white sturgeon, *Acipenser transmontanus*. Lee et al., 42.

2. The first description of the eulachon, or candle fish, *Thaleichthys pacificus*. Burroughs, 266–67; Cutright (LCPN), 251–52, 274, 427; Lee et al., 126. Lewis's statement about the run of the eulachon refers to their presence in the Cowlitz River, where they can be easily scooped up, and not to the Columbia. A vertical line runs through several lines of this passage, perhaps done by Biddle.

3. A sketch of the eulachon (fig. 41), in Lewis's Codex J, p. 93. Beside it someone, probably Coues, has written in pencil: "see Codex R p. 81" at right angles to the main text. That notation refers to a copy of this entry about the eulachon, but done by an unknown person and presumably at a much later date. See Appendix B, vol. 2; Moulton (SJ), 196–98.

4. The Latin *pinna ani* (or *analis*) refers to the fish's anal fin.

5. Another instance of Lewis's use of the Linnaean system. Today the eulachon is not grouped with the herring and other species, though in the past it was considered a related species.

6. Presumably a fish of the Great Lakes, perhaps *Coregonus* sp., whitefish or cisco.

7. From the family Engraulidae.

8. The first description of the western gray squirrel. Burroughs, 97.

9. Fox squirrel, *Sciurus niger*.

10. Hazelnut, filbert, *Corylus cornuta* Marsh. var. *californica* (DC.) Sharp, like the acorns, harvested by birds and squirrels. Hitchcock et al., 2:83.

11. Another new species, Douglas's squirrel or chickaree. The red squirrel and ground squirrel, mentioned for comparison, are probably the red squirrel, *Tamiasciurus hudsonicus*, and perhaps the eastern chipmunk, *Tamias striatus*, a mostly terrestrial squirrel. Cutright (LCPN), 274, 446; Burroughs, 97–98; Hall, 1:337–40.

12. Richardson's red squirrel.

13. Townsend's chipmunk, actually a new species although they did not recognize it as such. Cutright (LCPN), 273, 442; Burroughs, 96; Coues (HLC), 3:859, 859 n. 58.

14. Lewis and Clark's familiar name for the prairie dog, *Cynomys ludovicianus*.

15. Probably the thirteen-lined ground squirrel, *Spermophilus tridecemlineatus*.

16. See Clark's entry for February 25, 1806, below.

[Lewis]   *Tuesday February 25th 1806.*

It continued to rain and blow so violently that there was no movement of the party today. the Indians left us in the morning on their return to their village. Willard somewhat worse the other Invalledes on the ricovery. I am mortifyed at not having it in my power to make more celestial observations since we have been at Fort Clatsop, but such has been the state of the weather that I have found it utterly impracticable.—[1]

The Rackoon is found in the woody country on this coast in considerable quantities. the natives take a few of them in snars and deadfalls; tho' appear not to vallue their skins much, and but seldom prepare them for robes. The large grey squirrel appears to be a native of a narrow tract of country on the upper side of the mountains just below the grand falls of Columbia which is pretty well covered in many parts with a species of white oak. in short I beleive this squirrel to be coextensive with timber only, as we have not seen them in any part of the country where pine forms the majority of the timber, or in which the oak dose not appear. this animal is much larger than the grey squirrel of our country it resembles it much in form and colours. it is as large as the fox squirrel of the Southern Atlantic states. the tail is reather longer than the whole length of the body and head. the hair of which is long and tho' inserted on all sides reispect the horizontal ones only. the eyes are black. whiskers black and long. the back, sides, head, tail and outer part of the legs are of a blue lead coloured grey. the breast belley and inner part of the

At Fort Clatsop

legs are of a pure white. the hair is short as that of the fox-squirrel but is much finer and intermixed with a proportion of fur. the natives make great use of these skins in forming their robes. this squirrel subsists principally on the acorn and filbird which last also grows abundantly in the oak country.— The small brown squirrel is a beautifull little animal about the size and form of the red squirrel of the Eastern Atlantic states and western lakes. the tail is as long as the body and neck, formed like that of the red squirrel or somewhat flat. the eyes black. whiskers long and black but not abundant. the back, sides, head, neck and outer part of the legs are of a redish dark brown. the throat, breast, belley and inner part of the legs are of a pale brick red. the tail is a mixture of black and fox coloured red in which the black ⟨reather⟩ predominates in the midle and the other on the edges and extremity. the hair of the body is about ½ an inch long and so fine and soft that it has the appearance of fur. the hair of the tail is coarser and doubly as long. this animal subsists principally on the seeds of various species of pine, and are always found in the piny country they are common to the tract of wooddy country on this coast. they lodge in clifts of rocks, holes in the ground old stumps of trees and the hollow trunks of fallen timber; in this rispect resembling the rat, always having their habitatin in or near the earth. the small grey squirrel common to every part of the rocky mountain which is timbered, difirs from the dark brown squirrel just discribed only in it's colour. it's back, sides, neck, head tail and outer side of the legs are of a brown lead coloured grey; the tail has a slight touch of the fox colour near the extremity of some of the hairs. the throat, breast, belley, and inner parts of the legs are of the colour of tanner's ooze and have a narrow stripe of black, commencing just behide each shoulder and exten[d]ing longitudinaly for about 3 inches between the colours of the sides and belley. their habids are also the same of the dark brown squirrel of this neighbourhood and like them are extreemly nimble and active. the ground squirrel is found in every part of the country, as well the praries as woodlands, and is one of the few animals which we have seen in every part of our voyage. it differs not at all from those of the U' States. the barking squirrel and handsome ground squirrel of the plains on the East side of the rocky mountains are not found in the plains of Columbia.

January 21–March 17, 1806

[Clark]   *Tuesday February 25th 1806*

It continued to rain and blow So violently that there was no movement of the party to day. the Indians left us in the morning on their return to their village. Willard Somewhat worse the others are on the recovery. we are mortified at not haveing it in our power to make more Celestial observations since we have been at Fort Clatsop, but Such has been the State of the weather that we have found it utterly impracticable—. I purchased of the Clatsops this morning about half a bushel of Small fish which they had cought about 40 miles up the Columbia in their scooping nets. as this is an uncommon fish to me and one which no one of the party has ever Seen. on the next page I have drawn the likeness of them as large as life; it's as perfect as I can make it with my pen and will Serve to give a general idea of the fish. the rays of the fins are boney but not Sharp tho' Somewhat pointed. the Small fin on the back next to the tail has no rays of bone being a thin membranous pellicle. the fins next to the gills have eleven rays each. those of the abdomen have Eight each, those of the pinna ani are 20 and 2 half formed in front. that of the back has eleven rays. all the fins are of a white colour. the back is of a blueish duskey colour and that of the lower part of the Sides and belly is of a Silvery White. no Spots on any part. the first of the gills next behind the eye is of a blueish cast, and the second of a light gold colour nearly white. the puple of the eye is black and the iris of a silver white. the under jaw exceeds the upper; and the mouth opens[2] to great extent, folding like that of the Herring. it has no teeth. the abdomen is obtuse and Smooth; in this differing from the herring, Shad, anchovey &c. of the Malacapterygious Order and Class Clupea, to which however I think it more nearly allyed than to any other altho' it has not their accute and Serrate abdomen and the under jaw exceeding the upper. the scales of this little fish are So small and thin that without manute inspection you would Suppose they had none. they are filled with roes of a pure white Colour and have Scercely any perceptable alimentary duct. I found them best when cooked in Indian Stile, which is by rosting a number of them together on a wooden spit without any previous preperation whatever. they are so fat that they require no aditional sauce, and I think them Superior to any fish I ever tasted, even more dilicate and lussious than the white fish of

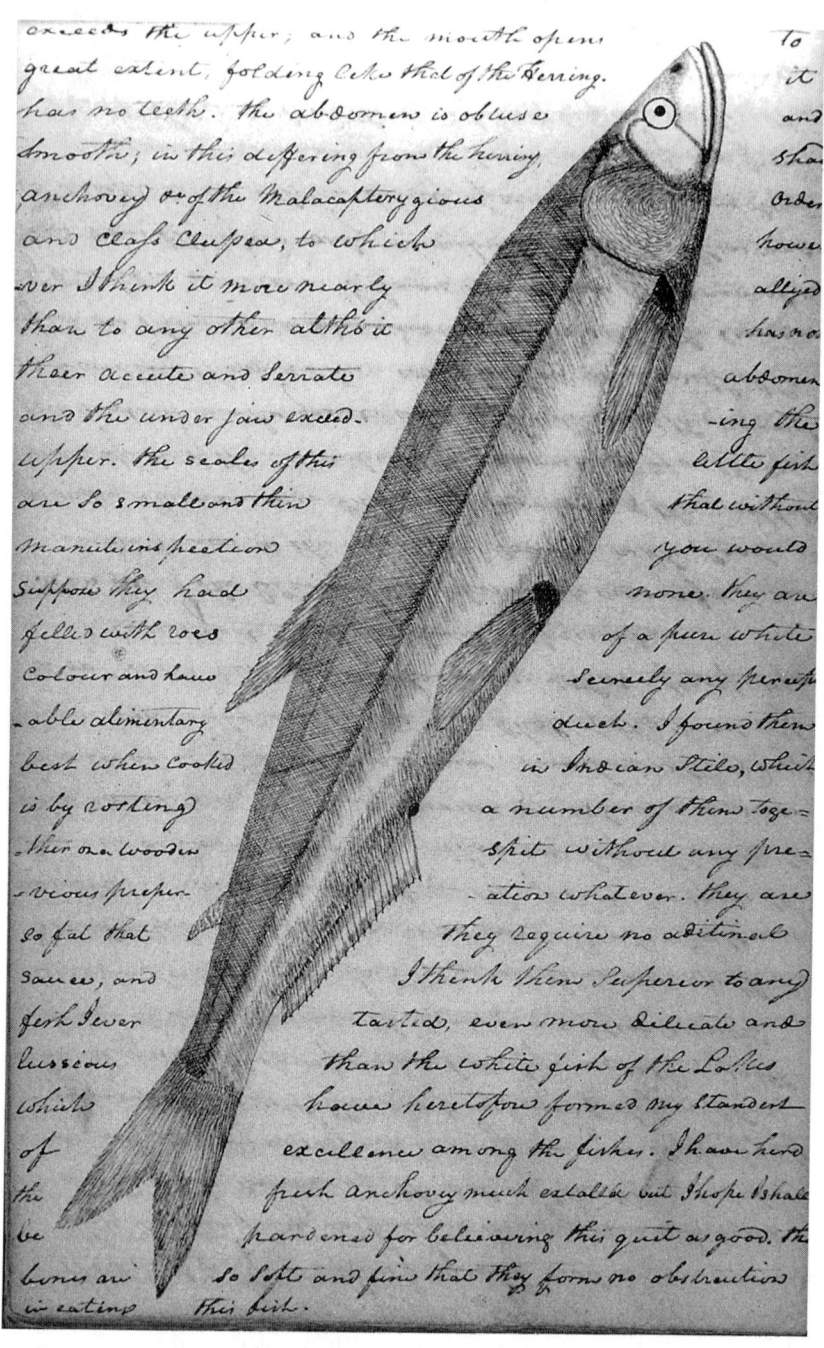

42. Eulachon (*Thaleichthys pacificus*),
February 25, 1806, Voorhis No. 2

the Lakes which have heretofore formed my Standard of excellence among the fishes. I have herd the fresh anchovey much extoll'd but I hope I shall be pardened for believeing this quit as good.   the bones are So Soft and fine that they form no obstruction in eating this fish.

    1. Two light red vertical lines run through the first several lines of the next paragraph and later in the paragraph, perhaps done by Biddle.
    2. At this point in Clark's Voorhis No. 2 appears a sketch of the eulachon (fig. 42).

[Lewis]   *Wednesday February 26th 1806.*

    This morning we dispatched Drewyer and two men in our Indian canoe up the Columbia River to take sturgeon and Anchovey.   or if they were unsuccessfull in fishing we directed them to purchase fish from the natives for which purpose we had furnished them with a few articles such as the natives are pleased with.   we also Sent Shields, Joseph Fields and Shannon up the Netul to hunt Elk.   and directed Reubin Fields and some others to hunt in the point towards the praries of Point Adams.   thus we hope shortly to replenish our stock of provision which is now reduced to a mere minnamum.   we have th[r]ee days provision only in store and that of the most inferior dryed Elk a little tainted.   *a comfortable prospect for good living. Sewelel*[1] is the Chinnook and Clatsop name for a small animal found in the timbered country on this coast.   it is more abundant in the neighbourhood of the great falls and rapids of the Columbia than immediately on the coast.   the natives make great use of the skins of this animal in forming their robes, which they dress with the fur on them and attatch together with sinews of the Elk or deer. I have never seen the animal and can therefore discribe it only from the skin and a slight view which some of our hunters have obtained of the living animal.   the skin when dressed is from 14 to 18 inches in length and from 7 to 9 in width; the tail is always severed from the skin in forming their robes I cannot therefore say what form or length it is.   one of the men informed me that he thought it reather short and flat.   that he saw one of them run up a tree like a squirrel and that it returned and ran into a hole in the ground.   the ears are short thin pointed and covered with short fine hair.   they are of a uniform colour, a redish brown; tho' the base of the long hairs, which exceed the fur but little in length, as well as the fur itself is of a dark colour for at least two thirds of it's length next to the skin. the fur and hair are very fine, short, thickly set and silky. the ends of the fur and tips of the hair being of the redish brown that colour predominates in the ordinary appearance of the animal. I take this animal to be about the size of the barking squirrel of the Missouri. and beleive most probably that it is of the Mustela genus,[2] or perhaps the brown mungo[3] itself. I have indeavoured in many instances to make the indians sensible how anxious I was to obtain one of these animals entire, without being skined, and offered them considerable rewards to furnish me with one, but have not been able to make them comprehend me. I have purchased several of the robes made of these skins to line a coat which I have had made of the skins of the tiger cat. they make a very pleasant light lining. the *Braro*[4] so called by the French engages is an animal of the civit genus and much resembles the common badger. this is an inhabitant of the open plains of the Columbia as they are of those of the Missouri but are sometimes also found in the woody country. they burrow in the hard grounds of the plains with surprising ease and dexterity an will cover themselves in the ground in a very few minutes. they have five long fixed nails on each foot; those of the forefeet are much the longest; and one of those on each hind foot is double like those of the beaver. they weigh from 14 to 18 lbs. the body is reather long in proportion to it's thickness. the forelegs remarkably large and muscular and are formed like the ternspit dog. they are short as are also the hind legs. they are broad across the sholders and brest. the neck short. the head is formed much like the common fist [feist] dog only that the skull is more convex. the mouth is wide and furnished with sharp streight teeth both above and below, with four sharp streight pointed tusks, two in the upper and two in the lower jaw. the eyes are black and small. whiskers are plased in four points on each side near the nose and on the jaws near the opening of the mouth. the ears are very short wide and appressed as if they had ben cut off. the apperture through them to the head is remarkably small. the tail is about 4 inches long; the hair longest on it at it's junction with the body and becoming shorter towards it's extremity where it ends in an accute point. the hairs of the body are much longer on the side and rump than any other part, which gives the body and apparent flatness, particularly when the animal rests on it's belley. this hair is upwards of 3 inches in length particularly on the rump where it extends so far towards the point of the tail that it almost conceals the shape of that part and gives to the whole of the hinder part of the body the figure of an accute angled triangle of which the point of the tail forms the accute angle. the small quantity of coarse fur which is intermixed with the hair is of a redish pale yellow. the hair of the back, sides, upper part of the neck and tail, are of a redish light or pale yellow for about ⅔rds of their length from the skin, next black, and then tiped with white; forming a curious mixture of grey and fox coloured red with a yellowish hue. the belley flanks and breast are of the foxcoloured redish yellow. the legs black. the nails white the head on which the hair is short, is varia gated with black and white. a narrow strip of white commences on the top of the nose about ½ an inch from it's extremity and extends back along the center of the forehead and neck nearly to the sholders— two stripes of black succeed the white on either side imbracing the sides of the nose, the eyes, and extends back as far as the ears. two other spots of black of a ramboidal figure are placed on the side of the head near the ears and between ⟨it⟩ them and the opening of the mouth. two black spots also immediately behind the ears. the other parts of the head white. this animal feeds on flesh, roots, bugs, and wild fruits.— it is very clumsy and runs very slow. I have in two instances out run this animal and caught it. in this rispect they are not much more fleet than the porcupine.

[Clark] *Wednesday February 26th 1806*

This morning we dispatched Drewyer and two men[5] in our indian canoe up the Columbia River to take Sturgion and Anchovey. or if they were unsucksessfull in fishing we directed them to purchase fish from the nativs, for which purpose we had furnished them with a fiew articles Such as the nativs are pleased with. we also Sent Shields Jo. Field and Shannon up the Netul to hunt Elk. and directed Reubin Field and Some other man to hunt in the point towards the Praries & point Adams. thus we hope Shortly to replenish our Stock of provisions which is now reduced to a mear minnamum. we have three days provisions only in Store and that of the most inferior dried Elk a little tainted. *what a prospect for good liveing at Fort Clatsop at present.*

Se we lel is the Clatsop and Chinnook name for a Small animal found in

At Fort Clatsop

the timbered Country on this Coast. it is more abundant in the neighbourhood of the great falls and rapids of the Columbia than imediately on the Coast. the nativs make great use of the Skins of this animal in forming their robes, which they dress with the fur on them and attached together with the sinears of the Elk or Deer. I have never Seen the animale and can therefore only discribe it from the Skin and a Slight view which Some of our party have obtained of the liveing animal. the Skin when dressed is from 14 to 18 inches in length, and from 7 to 9 in width; the tail is always Severed from the body in forming their robes, I cannot therefore Say in what form or length it is. one of the men informed me that he thought it reather Short and flat. that he saw one of them run up a tree like a squirel, and that it returned and ran into a hole in the ground. the ears are Short, thin, pointed and Covered with Short fine hair. they are of uniform Colour, a redish brown; tho the *base* of the long hairs, exceed the fur but little in length, as well as the fur itself is of a Dark colour for at least ⅔ds of it's length next to the Skin. the fur and hair are very fine, Short, thickly Set, and Silky. the ends of the fur and tips of the hair is of a redish brown, that colour prodominates in the ordinary appearance of the Animale. I took this animal to be about the Size of the barking Squirel of the Missouri. and believe most probably that it is of the *Mustela* genus, or perhaps the brown mungo itself I have in maney instances endeavured to make the nativs Sensiable how anxious I was to obtain one of those animals entire, without being Skined, and offered them rewards to furnish me with one, but have not been able to make them Comprehend me. we have purchased Several of the roabs made of those Skins to loin [line] a westcoat of the Sea otter, which I have made and Capt Lewis a Tiger Cat Skin Coat loined with them also, they make a very pleasant light lighting.

The *Rat*[6] in the rocky mountains on its west side are like those on the upper part of the Missouri in and near those Mountains and have the distingushing trait of possessing a tail covered with hair like other parts of the body; one of these we caught at the white bear Islands in the beginning of July last and then partially discribed.

There is rats in this neighbourhood but I have not seen them it is most probable that they are like those of the Atlantic States, or at least the native rat[7] of our country which have no hair on their tail. this Specis we found on the Missouri as far up it as the woody country extended. it is as large as the Common European house rat or reather larger is of a lighter Colour bordering more on the lead or drab colour, the hair longer; and the female has only four tits which are placed far back near the hinder legs. this rat I have Seen in the Southern parts of the State of Kentucky & west of the Miami.

The *Mouse* and *mole*[8] of this neighbourhood are the Same as those native animals with us.

The *Panther*[9] is found indifferently either in the great Plains of Columbia the Western Side of the Rocky Mountains or on this coast in the timbered country. it is precisly the Same animal common to the Atlantic States, and most commonly met with on our frontiers or unsettled parts of the Country. this animal is Scerce in the Country where they exist and are So remarkable Shye and watchfull that it is extreamly dificuelt to kill them.

The *Polecat*[10] is found in every part of the Country. they are very abundant on Some parts of the Columbia, particularly in the neighbourhood of the Great falls & Narrows of that river, where they live in the Clifts along the river & feed on the offal of the Indian fishing Shores. they are the Same as those of other parts of North America.

1. The first description of the mountain beaver. It is a rodent, but not a beaver, and is considered the most primitive of living rodents. Contrary to Lewis's observation about the tail's being severed, it has no apparent tail. The term "sewelel" is from Lower Chinookan *swalál*, "robe of mountain beaver skins," understood as the animal itself. Several light red vertical lines run through these passages about species, perhaps done by Biddle.

2. The Linnaean genus, *Mustela*, includes weasels, ferret, and mink, but not the mountain beaver.

3. Apparently a reference to the mongoose, *Herpestes* sp., which of course is not native to North America.

4. The badger. The *Civet* genus does not apply here and is not used for any North American species. It was apparently a common name for the eastern spotted skunk, *Spilogale putorius*. Criswell, 24; Jones et al., 301–4.

5. Cruzatte and Weiser; see below, March 2, 1806.

6. The newly discovered bushy-tailed woodrat, *Neotoma cinerea;* see above, July 2, 1805. Burroughs, 116–17; Cutright (LCPN), 444.

7. Probably the eastern woodrat, *Neotoma floridana*. Burroughs, 117–18.

8. The mouse may be the meadow mouse or meadow vole, *Microtus pennsylvanicus*, although its distribution does not extend to this limit. The western mole is *Scapanus* sp., while the eastern mole is *Scalopus* sp. Hall, 2:792–96, 1:69–75.

9. The mountain lion.
10. The striped skunk. Burroughs, 80–81.

[Lewis] *Thursday February 27th 1806.*

Reubin Fields returned this evening and had not killed anything. he reports that there are no Elk towards point Adams. C[o]llins who had hunted up the Netul on this side returned in the evening having killed a buck Elk. Willard still continues very unwell the other sick men have nearly recovered. Gutridge and McNeal who have the pox are recovering fast, the former nearly well.[1]

The rat in the Rocky mountain on it's West side are like those on the upper part of the Missouri in and near those mountains and have the distinguishing trait of possessing a tail covered with hair like other parts of the body; one of those we caught at the White bear Islands in the beginning of July last and was then discribed. I have seen the nests of those in this neighbourhood but not the animal. I think it most probable that they are like those of the Atlantic states or at least the native rat of our country which have no hair on the tail. this species we found on the Missouri as far up it as the woody country extended. it is as large as the common European house rat or reather larger, is of a lighter colour bordering more on the lead or drab colour, the hair longer; and the female has only four tits which are placed far back near the hinder legs. this rat I have observed in the Western parts of the State of Georgia and also in Madison's cave in the state of Virginia.[2] the mouse and mole of this neighbourhood are the same as those native animals with us. The Panther is found indifferently either in the Great Plains of Columbia, the Western side of the rocky mountains or on this coast in the timbered country. it is precisely the same animal common to the Atlantic coast, and most commonly met with on our frontiers or unsettled parts of the country. this animal is scarce in the country where they exist and are so remarkable shye and watchfull that it is extreemly difficult to kill them.—

[Clark] *Thursday February 27th 1806*

Reubin Field returned this evening and had not killed anything, he reported that there were no Elk towards point Adams. Collins who had hunted up the Netul on this Side returned in the evening haveing killed a buck Elk. Willard Still Continue very unwell the other Sick men have nearly recovered. Goodrich & McNeal who have the Pox are recovering fast, the former nearly well. La Page complaining.

The *Braro* so called by the French engages is an animal of the Civit genus and much resembles the common badger. this is an enhabitent of the open plains of the Columbia as they are of those of the Missouri, but are Sometimes also found in the woody country. they burrow in the hard Grounds in the Plains with Surprising ease and dexterity and will cover themselves in the Ground in a very fiew minits. they have five long fixed nails on each foot; those of the [f]ore feet are much the longest; and one of those on each hind foot is double like those of the beaver. they weigh from 14 to 20 lbs. the body is reather long in perportion to its thickness. the fore legs remarkably large and muscular and are formed like the turnspit dog. they are Short as also the hind legs. they are broad across the Sholders and breast. the neck Short, the head is formed much like the Common *fist dog* only that the Skull is more Convex, the mouth is wide and furnishid with long Sharp teeth, both above and below, and with four Sharp Streight Pointed tushes, two in the upper and two in the lower jaw. the eyes are black and Small. Whiskers are placed in four points on each Side near the nose and on the jaws near the opening of the mouth. the ears are very Short wide and appressed as if they had been cut off. the appertue through them to the head is remarkably Small; the tail is about 4 inches long; the hair longest on it at it's junction, with the body and becomeing Shorter towards it's extremity where it ends in an accute point. the hairs of the body are much longer on the Sides and rump than any other part, which givs the body an appearent flatness, particularly when the animal rests on it's belly. this hair is upwards of 3 inches in length, particularly on the rump where it extends so far towards the point of the tail, that it almost conceals the Shape of that part and givs to all the hinder part of the body an accute angled triangle, of which the point of the tail forms the accute angle. the Small quantity of fur which is intermixed with the hair is of a redish pale yellow. the hair of the back, Sides upper part of the neck and tail, are of redish light or pale yellow fox about two thirds of their length from the Skin, next black, and then tiped with white; forming a curious mixture of grey and fox coloured. red with a yellowish hue. the belly flanks and breast are of the fox coloured redish yellow. the legs black, the nails white. the head on which the hair is short is varigated with black and white. a narrow Strip of white Commences on the top of the nose about half an inch from its extremity and extends back along the Center of the forehead and neck nearly to the Sholders— two Stripes of black Suckceed the white on either Side, imbraceing the Side of the nose, the eyes, and extends back as far as the ears. two other Spots of black of a romboidal figure are placed on the Side of the head near the ears and between them and the opening of the mouth. two black Spots also imediately behind the ears. the other part of the head white. this animal feeds on flesh, roots, bugs and wild fruits.— it is very clumsy and runs very Slow, depending more on burring to Secure it Self than running. I have in Several instances out run and caught this animal. in this respect they are not much more fleet than the porcupine.

  1. In the next paragraph two light red lines run through the passages about species, perhaps penned by Biddle.
  2. Madisons Cave, about twenty miles northwest of Charlottesville, Virginia, is one of the oldest-discovered and explored caves in the limestone region of the Shenandoah Valley. See Jefferson, 21–23.

[Lewis]   *Friday February 28th 1806.*

    Reubin Fields and Collins set out this morning early on a hunting excurtion. Kuskelar a Clatsop man and his wife visited us today. they brought some Anchovies, Sturgeon, a beaver robe, and some roots for sail tho' they asked so high a price for every article that we purchased nothing but a part of a Sturgeon for which we gave a few fishing hooks. we suffered them to remain all night. Shields Jos. Fields and Shannon returned late this evening having killed five Elk tho' two of them ar on a mountain at a considerable distance. we ordered these hunters to return early in the morning and continue their hunt, and Sergt. Gass to take a party and go in quest of the Elk which they had killed. the hunters inform us that the Elk are tolerable plenty near the mountains about 9 or ten miles distant. Kuskelar brought a dog which Cruzatte had purchased.
    The hare[1] on this side of the Rocky mountains is exclusively the inhabi-

tant of the great Plains of Columbia, as they are of those of the Missouri East of these mountains. they weigh from 7 to eleven pounds. the measure of one which weighed ten lbs. was as follows. from the extremity of the hinder, to that of the fore feet when extended 3 F. length from nose to the extremity of the tail 2 F. 2 I. hight when standing erect 1 F. 3 I. girth of the body 1 F. 4 I. length of tail 6½ I. length of ear 5½ I. width of do 3⅛ I. from the hip to the extremity of toe of the hind foot 1 F. 4¼ I.— the eye is large and prominent. the pupil is circular, of a deep sea green and occupys one third of the diameter of the eye, the iris is of a bright yellowish silver colour. the ears are placed far back on the head and very near each other, they are flexable and the animal moves them with great ease and quickness, and can dilate and throw them forward, or contract and fold them on his back at pleasure. the fold of the front of the ear is of a redish brown colour, the inner folds or those which lie together when the ears are thrown back, and which occupy ⅔rds of the width of the ears are of a pure white except the tips of the ears for about an inch. the hinder folds or those which lie on the back are of a light grey. the head neck, back, sholders, sides, & outer part of the legs and thyes are of a lead coloured grey; the sides as they approach the belley become gradually more white. the belley, brest, and inner part of the legs and thyes are white, with a slight shade of the lead colour. the tail is round and blontly pointed, covered with fine soft white fur not quite as long as on the other parts of the body. the body is covered with a deep fine soft close fur. the colours here discribed are those which the animal assumes from the middle of April to the middle of November, the ballance of the year they are of a pure white, except the black and redish brown of the ears which never changes. a few redish brown spots are sometimes seen intermixed with the white, at this season, on their heads and upper part of the neck and sholders. the body of this animal is smaller and longer in proportion to it's hight than the rabbit. when it runs it carrys it's tail streight behind in the direction of it's body. they appear to run with more ease and bound with greater agility than any animal I ever saw. they are extreemly fleet and never burrow or take sheter in the ground when pursued. it's teeth are like those of the rabbit as is also it's upper lip which is divided as high as the nose. it's food is grass, herbs, and in winter feeds much on the bark of several aromatic shrubs which grow in the plains and the young willow along the rivers and other wartercourses.— I have measured the leaps of this animal and find them commonly from 18 to 21 feet. they are generally found seperate, and never seen to asscociate in any number or more than two or three.— the rabbit[2] are the same of our country and are found indifferently either in the praries or woodlands. they are not very abundant in this country. The Pole-cat is also found in every part of the country. they are very abundant on some parts of the columbia, particularly in the neighbourhood of the great falls and narrows of that river, where the[y] live in the clifts along the river and feed on the offal of the Indian fishing shores. these are the same as those of other parts of North America.—

[Clark]   *Friday February 28th 1806*

Reuben Field and Collins Set out this morning early on a hunting excurtion up the Netul. *Kus ke-lar* a Clatsop man, his wife and a Small boy (a Slave, who he informed me was his Cook, and offerd to Sell him to me for beeds & a gun)[3] visited us to day they brought Some anchovies, Sturgeon, a beaver robe, and Some roots for Sale tho' they asked Such high prices for every article that we purchased nothing but a part of a Sturgeon for which we gave a fiew fishing hooks. we Suffered them to Stay all night. Shields Jos: Field and Shannon returned late this evening haveing killed five Elk tho' two of them are of a mountain at a considerable distance. we ordered these hunters to return early in the morning and continue the hunt, and Sergt. Gass to take a party and go in quest of the Elk which they had killed. the hunters informed us that the Elk is tolerable plenty near the mountains about nine or ten miles distant. Kuskalaw brought a dog which Peter Crusat had purchased with his Capo which this fellow had on.

The *Hare* on this Side of the Rocky Mountains is exclusively the inhabitents of the Great Plains of Columbia, as they are of those of the Missouri East of the mountains. they weigh from 7 to 12 pounds. the measure of one which weighed 10 pounds, was as follows. from the extremity of the hinder, to that of the fore feet when extended 3 Feet. length from nose to the extremity of the tail 2 feet, 2 inches. Hight when Standing erect 1 foot, 3 inches—. Girth of the body 1 foot, 4 inches—. length of tail 6½ inches—. length of ear 5½ inches—. width of ear 3 inches and ⅛—. from the hip to the extremity of toe of the hind foot 1 foot 4¼ inches—. The eye is large and prominent. the pupil is circular, of a deep Sea Green and Occupies one third of the diamiter of the eye, the iris is of a bright yellowish silver colour. The ears are placed far back on the head and very near each other, they are flexable and the animal moves them with great ease and quickness and can dilate and throw them foward, or contract and fold them on his back at pleasure. the fold of the front of the ear is of a redish brown colour, the inner folds are those which lie together when the ears are thrown back, and which occupies ⅔ds of the width of the ears of a pure white except the tips of the ears for about an inch. the hinder folds or those which lie on the back are of a light grey; the Sides as they approach the belly become gradually more white, the belly brest, and inner part of the legs and thyes are white, with a Slight Shade of a lead Colour. The Head, neck, back Sholders, Sides, outer part of the legs and thyes are of a Lead Coloured Grey. the tail is bluntly pointed and round, covered with fine Soft white fur not quite as long as on the other parts of the body. the body is covered with a deep fine Soft close fur. the colours here discribed are those which the Animale assumes from the middle of April to the middle of November, the ballance of the year they are of a pure white, except the black and redish brown of the ears which never changes. a fiew redish brown spots are Sometimes Seen intermixed with the white, at this Season on the heads and upper parts of the neck an Sholders. The body of this animal is Smaller and longer in purpotion to it's hight than the Rabbit. when it runs it carrys its tail Streight behind in the direction of it's body. they appear to run with more ease and bound with greater agility than any animal I ever saw. they are extreemly fleet and never burrow or take Shelter in the grounds when pursued. it's teeth are like those of the rabit, as is also its upper lip which is divided as high as the nose. it's food is Grass, herbs, and in winter feeds much on the bark of Several arematic Shrubs which grow in the plains and the young willows along the rivers and other water courses.— I have measured the leaps of this animal and find them commonly from 18 to 22 feet. they are Generally found Seperate, and never Seen to associate in any number or more than two or three.

1. The white-tailed jackrabbit. A light red line runs through the first few lines of the material, perhaps done by Biddle.
2. Lewis obviously assumed the animal he was seeing to be the eastern cottontail, but it is not found in the region of Fort Clatsop. Coues considers it to be the species now called Nuttall's cottontail. Coues (HLC), 3:866 n. 67. Again a red line for several lines, perhaps Biddle's work.
3. See Clark's entry of March 1, 1806, below.

[Lewis and Clark] [Weather, February 1806][1]

Day of ye Month	aspect of the weather at ☉ rise	Wind at ☉ rise	aspect of the weather at 4 OC₁ P. M.	Wind at 4 O'Clock P. M.
1st	f	N. E.	f	N. E.
2cd	f	N. E.	c a s	S W
3rd	c a s & r	N W	c a f	N. E.
4th	f	N E	f.	N. E.
5th	f	N. E.	f.	N E
6th	f	N. E	c	S. W.[2]
7th	c	S. W.	c	S. W.
8th	c a s r & H	S W	c a f r h & s	S W
9th	c a r & h	S W	c a r & h	S. W.
10th	c a r h & s	N.	c a f & c.	S. W
11th	c a f & c	S W	r a f & r	S W.
12th	r a r & c	S W	r a c & r	S. W
13th	c. a. r	S. W.	c a r	S. W.
14th	c. a f & s	S. W.	r. a. r. f. & r.	S. W.
15th	c. a r & f	S	c a r & f	S. W
16th	r a s & r	S W	r. a. f. & r.	S W
17th	c a r h & s	S W	r a f h s & r	S W
18th	c a r & h	S W	r a r & h	S. W
19th	r a r	S W.	r a r	S. W
20th	c a r	S W	c a r	S. W.
21st	r a c & r	S W	r a c & r	S. W
22cd	f. a. r.	N E	c a f	N E
23rd	f	S. W.	c a f	S W

362

24th	c a f & c	S. W.	r a c & r	S
25th	r a r	S	r a r	S
26th	f a r	N E	c a f & r	S
27th	c a r	S W	r a r	S. W.
28th	r a r	S. W	c a c & f	S. W

[Remarks]³

1st the weather by no means as could as it was tho' it freized last night

2cd the bald Eagle still remains.

3rd the snow fell about half an inch, but the rain which succeded soon melted it   at 9 A. M. the sun shone.   the rain which feel in the latter part of the night freized and formed a slight incrustation on the snow which fell some days past, and also on the boughs of the trees &c. yesterday it continued fair until 11 A. M. when the wind vered about to S. W. and the horizon was immediately overcast with clouds, which uniformly takes place when the wind is from that point.

4th the last night clear and could   the Netul frozen over in several places.   all the waterfowls before innumerated still continue with us.   the bird⁴ which resembles the robbin have now visited us in small numbers   saw two of them yesterday about the fort; they are gentle.

6th very cold last night   think it reather the coldest night that we have had.   cloudy at 9 A M

7th continued cloudy all night   a little snow at 10 A. M.

8th it was principally rain which fell since 4 P. M. yesterday, it has caused the snow to disappear   the rain of the last night has melted down the snow wich has continued to cover the ground since the 24th of January; the feeling of the air and other appearances seem to indicate, that the rigor of the winter have passed; it is so warm that we are apprehensive that our meat will spoil, we therefore cut it in small peices and hang it seperately on sticks. Saw a number of insects flying about.   the small brown flycatch⁵ continues with us.

	this is the smallest of all the American birds except the humming bird.
9th	principally rain which has fallen.
10th	Snow covered the ground this morning disappeared before evening. sun shown 2 hours
12th	it rained the greater part of last night.
13th	Wind very hard last evening and all night
14th	very small quantity of snow fell last night not enough to cover the ground somewhat colder this morning. the sun shown only a few moments.
15th	fair most of last night hard frost this morning. the ground white with it. The robbin returned and were singing which reminded me of spring. some other small birds passed on their flight from the South, but were so high that we would not distinguish of what kind they were. the robbin had left this place before our arrival in November.
16th	but a small quantity of snow nearly all disolved by morning with the succeeding rain. at 11 A. M. it became fair and the insects were flying about. at ½ after 12 O'Ck it again clouded up and began to rain.
17th	the hail and snow covered the ground this morning
18th	wind violent greater part of the day and all night
19th	wind violent all day.
20th	wind violent all night and the greater part of the day.
21st	the wind continues high this morning & untill evening.
22cd	the wind scarcely perceptable
23rd	heavy white frost this morning. at eleven A M it couded up and continued so all day
24th	the wind became hard this evening. much warmer this morning than usual. the aquatic and other birds heretofore enumerated continue with us still. the Sturgeon and a small fish

like the Anchovey begin to run. they are taken in the Columbia about 40 mils. above us.⁶ the anchovey is exquisitely fine.—

25th the wind violent all night and this morning continued untill late in the evening when it ceased.

26th at 9 A. M. it clouded up again

28th it rained constantly during the last night. the sun shown about 9 A. M. partially a few minutes saw a variety of insects in motion this morning some small bugs as well as flies. a brown fly with long legs about half the size of the common house fly was the most common. this has been the first insect that appeared it is generally about the sinks or filth of any kind. the yellow and brown flycatch has returned. it is a very small bird with a tail as long proportiably as a Sparrow.

1. Lewis's weather table and remarks are in Codex J; Clark's are in Voorhis No. 2. This table follows Lewis, with substantial differences noted.
2. Clark has "N. W."
3. Lewis's remarks in Codex J are in the margin of his weather table and separate; Clark's in Voorhis No. 2 are also in the margin of his table and separate. Lewis's remarks are followed here.
4. The varied thrush.
5. Again perhaps the winter wren, but see weather remarks for January 31, 1806.
6. Clark has "about 30 miles."

[Lewis] *Saturday March 1st 1806.*

This morning Sergt. Gass and a party set out in quest of the Elk which had been killed by the hunters the day before yesterday. they returned with the flesh of three of them late in the evening. Thompson was left with the hunters¹ in order to jurk and take care of the flesh of the remaining two. Kuskelar and wife left us about noon. he had a good looking boy of about 10 years of age with him who he informed us was his slave. this boy had been taken prisoner by the Killamucks from some nation on the Coast to the S. East of them at a great distance. like other Indian nations they adopt their slaves in their families and treat them very much as their own children.² Reubin Fields and Collins who have been absent since yesterday morning returned without having killed any game. The birds of the Western side of the Rocky Mountain to the Pacific Ocean, for convenience I shall divide into two classes, which I shal designate from the habits of the birds, *Terrestrial* and *Aquatic*.

The Grouse or Prarie hen³ is peculiarly the inhabitant of the Grait Plains of Columbia   they do not differ from those of the upper portion of the Missouri, the tail of which is pointed or the feathers in it's center much longer than those on the sides.   this Species differs essentially in the construction of this part of their plumage from those of the Illinois⁴ which have their tails composed of fathers of equal length.   in the winter season this bird is booted even to the first joint of it's toes.   the toes are also curiously bordered on their lower edges with narrow hard scales which are placed very close to each other and extend horizontally about ⅛ of an inch on each side of the toes thus adding to the width of the tread which nature seems bountifully to have furnished them at this season for passing over the snow with more ease.   in the summer season those scales fall off. They have four toes on each foot. Their colour is a mixture of dark brown redish and yellowish brown and white confusedly mixed in which the redish brown prevails most on the upper parts of the body wings and tail and the white underneath the belley and lower parts of the breast and tail.   they associate in large flocks in autumn & winter and are frequently found in flocks of from five to six even in summer. They feed on grass, insects, the leaves of various shrubs in the plains and on the seeds of several species of spelts⁵ and wild rye⁶ which grow in the richer parts of the plains.   in winter their food is the buds of the willow & Cottonwood also the most of the native berries furnish them with food.— The Indians of this neighbourhood eat the root of the Cattail or Cooper's flag.⁷   it is pleasantly taisted and appears to be very nutricious.   the inner part of the root which is eaten without any previous preperation is composed of a number of capillary white flexable strong fibers among which is a mealy or starch like substance which readily desolves in the mouth and separate from the fibers which are then rejected.   it appears to me that this substance would make excellent starch; nothing can be of a purer white than it is.—

[Clark]   *Saturday March the 1st 1806*

    This morning we despatched Sergt. Gass with 12 men in two Canoes in quest of the Elk which had been killed by the hunters the day before yesterday. they returned with the flesh of three of them late in the evening. Thompson was left with the hunters in order to jurk and take care of the flesh of the remaining *two*. Kuskalar &c. left us about noon. The boy which this Indian offered to Sell to me is about 10 years of age. this boy had been taken prisoner by the *Kil a mox* from Some Nation on the Coast to the S. East of them at a great distance. like other Indian nations they adopt their Slaves in their famelies and treat them very much like their own Children. Reuben Field and Collins who had been absent Since yesterday morning returned without killing any thing.

    The birds on the western Side of the Rocky Mountain's to the Pacific Ocian for Convenience I Shall devide into from the habit of the birds, *Terrestrial* and *Aquatic.* i e Fowls of the air, and fowls of the water.

    The *Prarie* Hen sometimes called the Grouse is peculiarly the inhabitent of the Great Plains of Columbia. they do not differ from those of the upper portion of the Missouri, the tails of which is pointed or the feathers in its center much longer than those on the Sides. this Species differ assentially in the construction of this part of their plumage from those of the Illinois which have their tail composed of feathers of equal length. in the winter Season this berd is booted even to the first joint of it's toes. the toes are also curiously bordered on their lower edges with narrow hard scales which are placed very close to each other and extend horizontally about ⅛ of an inch on each Side of the toe, thus adding to the width of the tread which nature Seams bountifully to have furnished them with at this Season for passing over the Snow with more ease. in the Summer Season those Scales fall off. they have four toes on each foot. their colour is a mixture of dark brown redish and yellowish brown and white confusedly mixed in which the redish brown prevails most on the upper parts of the body wings and tail. and the white underneath the belley and lower parts of the breast and tail. they associate in large flocks in autumn & winter and are frequently found in flocks of from five to Six even in Summer. They feed on grass, insects, the leaves of various Shrubs in the Praries, and on the Seeds of Several Species of

Spelts and wild rye which grow in the richer parts of the Plains. in the winter their food is the buds of the willow and Cottonwood also the most of the native berries furnish them with food. they cohabit in flock & the Cocks fight verry much at those Seasons.

    1. Shields, Joseph Field, and Shannon; see above, February 28, 1806.

    2. Slaves were one of the most important articles of commerce in the trade networks of the Northwest Coast and interior. The Columbia River was the great artery of this trade, and the Chinooks, the great traders at the river's mouth, were said to have more slaves per capita than any other tribe. Treatment of slaves could be harsher than Lewis indicates; they might be sacrificed at their master's death to accompany him to the next world. Unlike contemporary Anglo-American practices, Northwest slaves sometimes owned their own slaves and might fight at their master's command. Slaves could not deform the heads of their children, a practice reserved for the elite. Ruby & Brown (CITC), 10, 21–22; Ruby & Brown (IPN), 29, 58, 61–62.

    3. A new species, the Columbian sharp-tailed grouse, *Tympanuchus phasianellus columbianus*, a subspecies of those on the upper Missouri, *T. phasianellus* [AOU, 308]. Burroughs, 213; Cutright (LCPN), 81, 244, 387, 436. Beginning with the previous sentence, a red vertical line continues through the first several lines of this paragraph, perhaps done by Biddle.

    4. Perhaps a reference to the greater prairie-chicken, *Tympanuchus cupido* [AOU, 305]. Burroughs, 211.

    5. A term for wheat, *Triticum* sp., which is not native to America. Here the term probably refers to the native species, bluebunch wheatgrass, *Agropyron spicatum* (Pursh) Scribn. & Smith, which is a dominant species in the Columbia basin. Hitchcock et al., 1:459–61; Franklin & Dyrness, 216.

    6. Basin wildrye, *Elymus cinereus* Scribn. & Merrill. Hitchcock et al., 1:561.

    7. Common cat-tail, here called cooper's flag, referring to the plant's long leaves which were placed between barrel staves by coopers to make barrels watertight.

[Lewis] *Sunday March 2cd*

The diet of the sick is so inferior that they recover their strength but slowly. none of them are now sick but all in a state of convalessence with keen appetites and nothing to eat except lean Elk meat. late this evening Drewyer arrived with a most acceptable supply of fat Sturgeon, fresh Anchovies and a bag containing about a bushel of Wappetoe. we feasted on Anchovies and Wappetoe.

The *Cock of the Plains*[1] is found in the plains of Columbia and are in Great abundance from the entrance of the S. E. fork of the Columbia to that of Clark's river. this bird is about ⅔rds the size of a turkey. the

January 21–March 17, 1806

43. Head of Cock of the Plains
(sage grouse, *Centrocercus urophasianus*),
March 2, 1806, Codex J, p. 107

beak is large short curved and convex. the upper exceeding the lower chap. the nostrils are large and the b[e]ak black. the colour is an uniform mixture of dark brown reather bordeing on a dove colour, redish and yellowish brown with some small black specks. in this mixture the dark brown prevails and has a slight cast of the dove colour at a little distance. the wider side of the large feathers of the wings are of a dark brown only. the tail is composed of 19 feathers of which that in the center is the longest, and the remaining 9 on each side deminish by pairs as they receede from the center; that is any one feather is equal in length to one equa distant from the center of the tail on the oposite side. the tail when foalded comes to a very sharp point and appears long in proportion to the body. in the act of flying the tail resembles that of a wild pigeon. tho' the motion of the wings is much that of the pheasant and Grouse. they have four toes on each foot of which the hinder one is short. the leg is covered with feathers about half the distance between the knee and foot. when the wing is expanded there are wide opening between it's feathers the plumeage being so narrow that it dose not extend from one quill to the other. the wings are also proportionably short, reather more so than those of the pheasant or grouse. the habits of this bird are much the same as those of the grouse. only that the food of this fowl is almost entirely that of the leaf and buds of the pulpy leafed thorn;[2] nor do I ever recollect seeing this bird but in the neighbourhood of that shrub. they sometimes feed on the prickley pear. the gizzard of it is large and much less compressed and muscular than in most fowls; in short it resembles a maw quite as much as a gizzard. when they fly they make a cackling noise something like the dunghill fowl. the following is a likeness of the head and beak.[3] the flesh of the cock of the Plains is dark, and only tolerable in point of flavor. I do not think it as good as either the Pheasant or Grouse.— it is invariably found in the plains.— The feathers about it's head are pointed and stif some hairs about the base of the beak. feathers short fine and stif about the ears.

[Clark] *Sunday March 2nd 1806*

The diet of the Sick is So inferior that they recover their Strength but Slowly. none of them are now Sick but all in a State of Covelessence with keen appetites and nothing to eate except lean Elk meat.

The nativs of this neighbourhood eate the root of the Cattail or Cooper's flag. it is pleasantly tasted and appears to be very nutrecious. the inner part of the root which is eaten without any previous preperation is Composed of a number of capellary white flexable Strong fibers among which is a mealy or Starch like Substance which readily disolves in the mouth and Seperates from the fibers which are then rejected. it appears to me that this Substance would make excellent Starch; nothing Can be of a pureer white than it is.—.

This evening late Drewyer, Crusat & Wiser returned with a most acceptable Supply of fat Sturgen, fresh anchoves and a bag Containing about a bushel of *Wappato*. we feasted on the Anchovies and wappatoe.—.

The *Heath Cock* or *cock of the Plains* is found in the Plains of Columbia and are in great abundance from the enterance of Lewis's river to the mountains which pass the Columbia between the Great falls and Rapids of that river. this fowl is about ¾ths the Size of a turkey. the beak is large Short Curved and convex. the upper exceeding the lower chap. the nostrils are large and the back black. the Colour is a uniform mixture of dark brown reather bordering on a dove colour, redish and yellowish brown with Some Small black Specks. in this mixture the dark brown provails and has a Slight cast of the dove colour at a little distance. the wider side of the larger feathers of the wings are of a dark brown only. the tail is composed of 19 feathers of which that in the center is the longest, and the remaining 9 on each Side deminish by pairs as they receede from the Center; that is any one feather is equal in length to one of an equal distance from the Center of the tail on the opposit Side. the tail when folded Comes to a very Sharp point and appears long in perpotion to the body in the act of flying the tail resembles that of a wild pigeon. tho' the motion of the wings is much that of the Pheasant and Grouse. they have four toes on each foot of which the hinder one is Short. the leg is covered with feathers about half the distance between the knee and foot. when the wings is expanded there are wide opening between it's feathers, the plumage being So narrow that it does not extend from one quill to another. the wings are also propotionably Short, reather more So than those of the Pheasant or Grouse. the habits of this bird is much the Same as those of the Prarie hen or Grouse. only that the food of this fowl is almost entirely that of the leaf and buds of the pulpy leafed thorn, nor do I ever recollect Seeing this bird but in the neighbourhood of that Shrub. The gizzard of it is large and much less compressed and muscular than in most fowls, in Short it resembles a maw quite as much as a gizzard. When they fly they make a cackling noise Something like the dunghill fowl. the flesh of this fowl is dark and only tolerable in point of flavour. I do not think it as good as wth the Pheasant or Prarie hen, or Grouse. the feathers above it's head are pointed and Stiff Some hairs about the base of the beak. feathers Short fine and Stiff about the ears, and eye. This is a faint likeness of the *Cock* of the plains or Heath Cock[4] the first of those fowls which we met with was on the Missouri below and in the neighbourhood of the Rocky Mountains and from to the mountain[5] which passes the Columbia between the Great falls and Rapids they go in large gangues or Singularly and hide remarkably close when pursued, make Short flights, &c.

The large Black & White *Pheasant*[6] is peculiar to that portion of the Rocky Mountains watered by the Columbia River. at least we did not See them untill we reached the waters of that river, nor Since we have left

44. Cock of the Plains
(sage grouse, *Centrocercus urophasianus*),
March 2, 1806, Voorhis No. 2

those mountains. they are about the Size of a well grown hen. the contour of the bird is much that of the redish brown Pheasant common to our country. the tail is proportionably as long and is composed of 18 feathers of equal length, of a uniform dark brown tiped with black. the feathers of the body are of a dark brown black and white. the black is that which most prodomonates, and white feathers are irregularly intermixed with those of the black and dark brown on every part but in greater perpotion about the neck breast and belly. this mixture gives it very much the appearance of that kind of dunghill fowl, which the hen-wives of our Countrey Call *dommanicker*.[7] in the brest of Some of those birds the white prodominates most. they are not furnished with tufts of long feathers on the neck as other Pheasants are, but have a Space on each Side of the neck about 2½ inches long and one inch in width on which no feathers grow, tho' it is consealed by the feathers which are inserted on the hinder and front part of the neck, this Space Seams to Serve them to dilate or contract the feathers of the neck with more ease. the eye is dark, the beak black, uncovered Somewhat pointed and the upper exceeds the under chap. they have a narrow Strip of vermillion colour above each eye which consists of a fleshey Substance not protuberant but uneaven, with a number of minute rounded dots. it has four toes on each foot of which three are in front, it is booted to the toes. it feeds on wild fruits, particularly the berry of the *Sac-a-com-mis,* and much also on the Seed of the pine & fir. this fowl is usially found in Small numbers two and three & 4 together on the ground. when Supprised flies up & lights on a tree and is easily Shot their flesh is Superior to most of the Pheasant Species which we have met with. they have a gizzard as other Pheasants &c. feed also on the buds of the Small Huckleberry bushes

1. The sage grouse, *Centrocercus urophasianus* [AOU, 309], a new discovery. Burroughs, 213–15; Cutright (LCPN), 432. The wild pigeon used for comparison is the passenger pigeon, *Ectopistes migratorius* [AOU, 315]. The "dunghill fowl" mentioned later in the entry is the common chicken (see note below). A light red line runs vertically through the first few lines of this paragraph, perhaps done by Biddle.

2. Greasewood, *Sarcobatus vermiculatus* (Hook.) Torr. in Emory. Lewis's remark on the close association between the sage grouse and greasewood may not be entirely correct. Hitchcock et al., 2:213; Franklin & Dyrness, 227; Cutright (LCPN), 137. An interlineation at this point has been erased beyond legibility.

3. A sketch of the head of the sage grouse (fig. 43), in Lewis's Codex J, p. 107.

4. A full-length sketch of the sage grouse (fig. 44), from Clark's Voorhis No. 2.
5. Presumably the Cascade Range. *Atlas* map 78.
6. See notes for Lewis's descriptions of the three "pheasants" in the next entry. Clark's words here were probably copied from that material.
7. A breed of chicken called the dominique, or dominecker, which resembles the Barred Plymouth Rock. Criswell, 33.

[Lewis] Monday March 3rd 1806.

Two of our perogues have been lately injured very much in consequence of the tide leaving them partially on shore. they split by this means with their own weight. we had them drawn out on shore. our convalessents are slowly on the recovery. Lapage is taken sick, gave him a doze of Scots pills which did not operate. no movement of the party today worthy of notice. every thing moves on in the old way and we are counting the days which seperate us from the 1st of April and which bind us to fort Clatsop.— The large black and white pheasant[1] is peculiar to that portion of the Rocky Mountain watered by the Columbia river. at least we did not see them in these mountains until I we reached the waters of that river nor since we have left those mountains. they are about the size of a well grown hen. the contour of the bird is much that of the redish brown pheasant common to our country. the tail is proportionably as long and is composed of eighteen feathers of equal length, of an uniform dark brown tiped with black. the feathers of the body are of a dark brown black and white. the black is that which most predominates, and wh[i]te feathers are irregularly intermixed with those of the black and dark brown on every part, but in greater proportion about the neck breast and belley. this mixture gives it very much the appearance of that kind of dunghill fowl which the hen-wives of our country call *dommanicker*. in the brest of some of these birds the white predominates most. they are not furnished with tufts of long feathers on the neck as our pheasants are, but have a space on each side of the neck about 2½ inches long and 1 In. in width on which no feathers grow, tho' tis concealed by the feathers which are inserted on the hinder and front part of the neck; this space seems to surve them to dilate or contract the feathers of the neck with more ease. the eye is dark, the beak black, curved somewhat pointed and the upper exceeds the under chap. they have a narrow stripe of vermillion colour above each eye which consists of a fleshey substance not protuberant but uneven with a number of minute rounded dots. it has four toes on each foot of which three are in front. it is booted to the toes. it feeds on wild fruits, particularly the berry of the sac-a-commis, and much also on the seed of the pine and fir.—

The small speckled pheasant[2] found in the same country with that above discribed, differs from it only in point of size and somewhat in colour. it is scarcely half the size of the other; ascociates in much larger flocks and is very gentle. the black is more predominant and the dark bron feathers less frequent in this than the larger species. the mixture of white is also more general on every part of this bird. it is considerably smaller than our pheasant and the body reather more round. in other particulars they differ not at all from the large black and white pheasant. this by way of distinction I have called the speckled pheasant. the flesh of both these species of party coloured phesants is of a dark colour and with the means we had of cooking them not very well flavored.

The small brown pheasant[3] is an inhabitant of the same country and is of the size and shape of the specled pheasant which it also resembles in it's economy and habits. the stripe above the eye in this species is scarcely perceptable, and is when closely examined of a yellow or orrange colour instead of the vermillion of the outhers. it's colour is an uniform mixture of dark and yellowish brown with a slight mixture of brownish white on the breast belley and the feathers underneath the tail. the whol compound is not unlike that of the common quail[4] only darker. this is also booted to the toes. the flesh of this is preferable to either of the others and that of the breast is as white as the pheasant of the Atlantic coast.— the redish brown pheasant[5] has been previously discribed.— The Crow raven and Large Blackbird[6] are the same as those of our country only that the crow is here much smaller yet it's note is the same. I observe no difference either between the hawks of this coast and those of the Atlantic.[7] I have observed the large brown hawk, the small or sparrow hawk, and the hawk of an intermediate size with a long tail and blewish coloured wings remarkably swift in flight and very firce. sometimes called in the U' States the hen hawk. these birds seem to be common to every part of this country, and the hawks crows & ravens build their nests in great numbers along the high and inaccessable clifts of the Columbia river and it's S. E. branch where we passed along them.— we also met with the large hooting Owl[s] under the Rocky mountain on the Kooskoskee river. it did not appear to differ materially from those of our country. I think it's colours reather deeper and brighter than with us, particularly the redish brown. it is the same size and form.—

[Clark] Monday March 3rd 1806

Two of our Canoes have been lately injured very much in consequence of the tide leaveing them partially on Shore. they Split by this means with their own weight. we had them drawn out on Shore. our convalessents are Slowly on the recovery. La page is taken Sick. gave him Some of Scotts Pills which did not opperate. no movement of the party to day worthey of notice. every thing moves on in the old way and we are Counting the days which Seperate us from the 1st of April, & which bind us to Fort Clatsop.—.—.

The Small Speckled *Pheasant* found in the Rocky Mountains, and differ from the large black and white pheasant only in point of Size, and Somewhat in colour. it is scercely half the Size of the other; assosiates in much larger flocks and is also very gentle. the black is more predominate and the dark brown feathers less frequent in this than the larger Species. the mixture of white is also more general on every part of this bird. it is considerably Smaller than our Pheasant and the body reather more round. in other particulars they differ not at all, from the large black and white Pheasant. this by way of distinction I have called the Speckled Pheasant. the flesh of both these Species of party coloured Pheasant is of a dark colour, and with the means we had of cooking them were only tolerably flavoured tho' these birds ⟨are⟩ would be fine well cooked.

The small *Brown Pheasant* is an inhabitant of the Same Country and is of the Size and Shape of the Speckled Pheasant, which it also resembles in it's economy and habits, the Stripe above the eye in this Species is scercely preceptable and is when closely examined of a yellow or orrange colour in Sted of the vermillion of the others. it's colour is of a uniform mixture of dark and yellowish brown with a Slight mixture of brownish white on the breast belley and the feathers under the tail. the whole Compound is not unlike that of the Common quaile only darker. this is also booted to the toes. the flesh is tolerable and that of the breast is as white as the Pheasant of the atlantic coast. the redish brown Pheasant has been previously discribed.—.

The *Crow Ravin* and large *Blackbird* are the Same as those of our Country, only that the Crow here is much Smaller, yet its note is the Same. I observe no difference between the Hawk of this Coast and those of the Atlantic. I have observed the large brown Hawk, the Small or Sparrow hawk, and a hawk of an intermediate Size with a long tail and blewish coloured wings, remarkably Swift in flight and very ferce. Sometimes called in the Un. States the hen Hawk. those birds Seam to be common to every part of this Country in greater or smaller numbers, and the Hawks, Crows, and ravins build their nests in great numbers along the high & inaxcessable clifts of the Columbia, and Lewis's rivers when we passd along them. we also met with the large hooting Owl under the Rocky mountains on the Kooskooske R. it's Colour reather deeper than with us, but differ in no other respect from those of the U States.

1. Coues identifies this as the spruce (or Franklin's) grouse, *Dendragapus canadensis* [AOU, 298], specifically an adult male of the species. Burroughs agrees. On the other hand, Holmgren thinks it the ruffed grouse (probably the Oregon subspecies). The former appears more likely as Lewis was familiar with the ruffed grouse of the East and always compared the Oregon variety closely with it. Coues (HLC), 3:870–71, 870–71 nn. 73, 74; Burroughs, 217–18; Holmgren, 32. A red vertical line goes through the first few lines of this passage, perhaps Biddle's work.

2. Uncontestably the spruce grouse, which Coues identifies as either an adult female or young specimen of the bird. Coues (HLC), 3:871–72, 871 n. 75; Burroughs, 217–18; Holmgren, 32. Again the red vertical line.

3. Coues unequivocally identifies this as the Oregon ruffed grouse and Burroughs follows suit but less confidently. Holmgren calls it the blue grouse, *Dendragapus obscurus* [AOU, 297]. The earlier identification seems correct. Lewis and Clark uniformly describe the blue grouse as a large bird of black or dark brown color, while the bird here is noted as yellowish brown, similar to the description of the ruffed grouse given on September 20, 1805. But see n. 5 in this entry. Coues (HLC), 3:872 and n. 76; Burroughs, 218–19; Holmgren, 32.

4. Presumably the northern bobwhite, *Colinus virginianus* [AOU, 289], with which Lewis would have been familiar in the East. Coues (HLC), 3:872.

5. This appears to be the Oregon ruffed grouse since the reference to reddish brown fits with the description of February 5 where the words "redish tint" were used. If that is correct, then identifying the third "pheasant" (see n. 3 here) as the Oregon ruffed grouse may be in error since Lewis states that this fourth bird has been previously described (on February 5 perhaps). If so, then the bird of n. 3 would be the blue grouse of Holmgren. It

may be that a definitive answer is not possible and perhaps Lewis became confused in his writing.

6. The crow is in fact the northwestern crow, a new species. The subspecies of raven in the Fort Clatsop area is *Corvus corax sinuatus;* Lewis would have been familiar with *C. c. principalis* in the East. Both are now combined with the common raven. The blackbird seen in the West would be Brewer's blackbird, *Euphagus cyanocephalus* [AOU, 510], while the bird he had seen in the East would more likely be the rusty blackbird, *E. carolinus* [AOU, 509]. Cutright (LCPN), 434; Burroughs, 248, 255–56. Another red vertical line.

7. Coues suggests that the large brown hawk may be a subspecies of the red-tailed hawk, or Swainson's hawk, *Buteo swainsoni* [AOU, 342]. Holmgren calls it the northern harrier, *Circus cyaneus* [AOU, 331], also called the marsh hawk. The sparrow hawk is *Falco sparverius* [AOU, 360], now known as the American kestrel. The hen hawk Coues identifies as the northern harrier, whereas Holmgren considers it to be Cooper's hawk, *Accipiter cooperii* [AOU, 333]. Coues (HLC), 3:875; Holmgren, 30–31.

8. Burroughs, 208–9, suggests either the Montana horned owl, *Bubo virginianus occidentalis,* or the dusky horned owl, *B. v. saturatus.* Both are now subsumed under the great horned owl, *B. virginianus* [AOU, 375]. See above, April 14 and May 20, 1805.

[Lewis] *Tuesday March 4th 1806.*

Not any occurrence today worthy of notice. we live sumptuously on our wappetoe and Sturgeon. the Anchovey is so delicate that they soon become tainted unless pickled or smoked. the natives run a small stick through their gills and hang them in the smoke of their lodges, or kindle a small fire under them for the purpose of drying them. they need no previous preperation of guting &c and will cure in 24 hours. the natives do not appear to be very scrupelous about eating them when a little feated.—[1] the fresh sturgeon they keep for many days by immersing it in water. they coock their sturgeon by means of vapor or steam. the process is as follows. a brisk fire is kindled on which a parcel of stones are lad. when the fire birns down and the stones are sufficiently heated, the stones are so arranged as to form a tolerable level surface, the sturgeon which had been previously cut into large fletches is now laid on the hot stones; a parsel of small boughs of bushes is next laid on and a second course of the sturgeon thus repating alternate layers of sturgeon and boughs untill the whole is put on which they design to cook. it is next covered closely with matts and water is poared in such manner as to run in among the hot stones and the vapor arrising being confined by the mats, cooks the fish. the whole process is performed in an hour, and the sturgeon thus cooked is much better than either boiled or roasted.

The turtle dove[2] and robbin are the same of our country and are found as well in the plain as open country. the Columbian robbin[3] heretofore discribed seems to be the inhabitant of the woody country exclusively. the Magpy[4] is most commonly found in the open country and are the same with those formerly discribed on the Missouri. the large woodpecker or log cock, the lark woodpecker[5] and the small white woodpecker with a read head[6] are the same with those of the Atlantic states and are found exclusively in the timbered country. The blue crested Corvus and the small white breasted do[7] have been previously discribed and are the natives of a piney country invariably, being found as well on the rocky mountains as on this coast.— the lark[8] is found in the plains only and are the same with those before mentioned on the Missouri, and not very unlike what is called in Virginia the *old field lark*.— The large blueish brown or sandhill Crain are found in the valley of the Rocky mountains in Summer and Autumn where they raise their young, and in the winter and begining of spring on this river below tidewater and on this coast. they are the same as those common to the Southern and Western States where they are most generally known by the name of the Sandhill crain. The vulture[9] has also been discribed. there are two species of the flycatch, a small redish brown species[10] with a short tail, round body, short neck and short pointed beak. they have some fine black specks intermixed with the uniform redish brown. this the same with that which remains all winter in Virginia where it is sometimes called the wren. the second species[11] has lately returned and dose not remain here all winter. it's colours are a yellowish brown on the back head neck wings and tail the breast and belley of a yellowish white; the tail is in proportion as the wren but it is a size smaller than that bird. it's beak is streight pointed convex reather lage at the base and the chaps of equal length. the first species is the smallest, in short it is the smalest bird that I have ever seen in America except the humming bird. both these species are found in the woody country only or at least I have never seen them elsewhere.

[Clark]   *Tuesday March 4th 1806*

Not any accurrance to day worthy of notice. we live Sumptiously on our wappatoe and Sturgeon. the Anchovey is so delicate that they Soon become tainted unless pickled or Smoked. the nativs run a Small Stick through their gills and hang them in the Smoke of their Lodges, or Kindle Small fires under them for the purpose of drying them. they need no previous preperation of gutting &c. and will Cure in 24 hours. the nativs do not appear to be very Scrupilous about eating them a little feated.

the fresh sturgeon they Keep maney days by immersing it in water. they Cook their Sturgeon by means of vapor or Steam. the process is as follows. a brisk fire is kindled on which a parcel of Stones are Sufficiently heated, the Stones are So arranged as to form a tolerable leavel Surface, the Sturgeon which had been previously cut into large flaetches is now laid on the hot Stones; a parcel of Small boughs of bushes is next laid on, and a Second course of the Sturgeon thus repeating alternate layers of Sturgeon & boughs untill the whole is put on which they design to Cook. it is next covered closely with mats and water is poared in Such manner as to run in among the hot Stones, and the vapor arriseing being confind by the mats, cooks the fish. the whole process is performd in an hour and the Sturgeon thus Cooked is much better than either boiled or roasted. in their usial way of boiting of other fish in baskets with hot Stones is not so good.

The *turtle doves* and robin are the Same of those of our countrey and are found as well as the plains as open countrey. the Columbia robin heretofore discribed Seams to be the inhabitent of the woody Country exclusively. the magpye is most commonly found in the open Country and are the Same with those formerly discribed on the Missouri.

The *large wood pecker* or log cock the *lark woodpecker* and the common wood pecker with a red head are the Same with those of the Atlantic States, and are found exclusively in the timbered Country. The Blue crested *Corvus* and the Small white brested *corvus* are the nativs of a piney country invariably, being found as well on the Rocky Mountains as on this coast—. The *lark* is found in the plains only and are the Same with those on the Missouri and the Illinois and not unlike what is Called in Virginia the *old field Lark.*

The large bluish brown or *Sandhill Crain* are found in the Vally's of the Rocky Mountain in Summer and autumn when they raise their young and in the winter and beginning of Spring on this river below tide water and on this coast. they are the Same as those Common to the Southern and West-

January 21–March 17, 1806

ern States where they are most generally known by the name of the Sand hill Crain. The *Vulture* has already been discribed.

There are two Species of fly Catch, a Small redish brown with a Short tail, round body, Short neck, and Short pointed beak, and the Same as that with us sometimes called the Wren. the 2d Species does not remain all winter they have just returned and are of a Yellowish brown Colour.

    1. Perhaps "fetid." A dark "x" covers the first part of this paragraph.
    2. The mourning dove, *Zenaida macroura* [AOU, 316]. A faint red vertical line goes through the first few lines of this paragraph, perhaps Biddle's doing.
    3. The previously described varied thrush; see above, January 31, 1806.
    4. The black-billed magpie, *Pica pica* [AOU, 475].
    5. Respectively, the pileated woodpecker, *Dryocopus pileatus* [AOU, 405], and the northern, or common, flicker, *Colaptes auratus* [AOU, 412], both new species. Logcock was a folk name for the pileated woodpecker, while lark woodpecker was used for flickers. Burroughs, 241–42; Holmgren, 32, 34.
    6. The red-breasted sapsucker, *Sphyrapicus ruber* [AOU, 403]. Burroughs, 241; Holmgren, 34.
    7. Steller's jay and the gray jay. See above, December 18, 1805.
    8. The western meadowlark, *Sturnella neglecta* [AOU, 501.1]. The "old field lark" is the eastern meadowlark, *S. magna* [AOU, 501].
    9. The California condor, described on February 16 and 17, 1806.
    10. The winter wren.
    11. Perhaps Hammond's flycatcher, *Empidonax hammondii* [AOU, 468]. Holmgren, 30. See also Coues (HLC), 3:876 n. 78.

[Lewis]   *Wednesday March 5th 1806.*

    This morning we were visited by two parties of Clatsops. they brought some fish a hat and some skins for sale most of which we purchased. they returned to their village in the evening. late in the evening the hunters returned from the *kil-haw-â-nack-kle* River which discharges itself into the head of the bay. They had neither killed nor seen any Elk. they informed us that the Elk had all gone off to the mountains a considerable distance from us. this is unwelcome information and reather allarming we have only 2 days provision on hand, and that nearly spoiled. we made up a small assortment of articles to trade with the Indians and directed Sergt. Pryor to set out early in the morning in a canoe with 2 men, to ascend the Columbia to the resort of the Indian fishermen and purchase some fish; we also directed two parties of hunters to renew the

Chase tomorrow early. the one up the Netul and the other towards Point Adams. if we find that the Elk have left us, we have determined to ascend the river slowly and indeavour to procure subsistence on the way, consuming the Month of March in the woody country. earlyer than April we conceive it a folly to attempt the open plains where we know there is no fuel except a few small dry shrubs. we shall not leave our quarters at fort Clatsop untill the first of April, as we intended unless the want of subsistence compels us to that measure. The common snipe of the marshes and the small sand snipe are the same of those common to the Atlantic Coast tho' the former are by no means as abundant here.[1] the prarrow[2] of the woody country is also similar to ours but not abundant. those of the plains of Columbia are the same with those of the Missouri, tho' they are by no means so abundant. I have not seen the little singing lark[3] or the large brown Curloo[4] so common to the plains of the Missouri, but I beleive that the latter is an inhabitant of this country during summer from Indian information. I have no doubt but what many species of birds found here in Autumn and Summer had departed before our arrival.

[Clark] *Wednesday March 5th 1806.*

This morning we were visited by two parties of Clatsops they brought Some fish, a hat and Some Skins for Sale most of which we purchased, they returned to their Village in the evening with the returning tide. late in the evening the Hunters returned from the *Kil-haw-â nack-kle* River which discharges itself into the head of the Bay. They had neither killed nor Seen any Elk. they informed us that the Elk had all gorn off to the mountains a considerable distance from us. this is unwelcom information and reather alarming. we have only two days provisions on hand and that nearly Spoiled. we made up a Small assortment of Articles to trade with the Indians, and directed Sergt Natl. Pryor to Set out early in the morning in a canoe with two men, to assend the Columbia to the resort of the Indians fishermen and purchase Some fish; we also derected two parties of hunters to renew the chase tomorrow early. the one up the Netul, and the other towards point Adams. If we find that the Elk have left us, we have determined to assend the river slowly and endeaver to precure Subsistance on the way, Consumeing the month of

March in the woody Country, earlyer than april we conceive it a folly to attempt the Open plains where we know there is no fuel except a fiew Small dry Shrubs. we Shall not leave our quarters at *Fort Clatsop* untill the 1st of April as we intended, unless the want of Subsistance compels us to that measure.

The common *Snipe* of the marshes and the Small sand snipe are the same of those Common to the atlantic coast tho the former are by no means as abundant here.

The Sparrow of the woody country is also Similar to ours but not abundant. those of the plains of Columbia are the Same with those of the Missouri. tho' they are by no means So Abundant. I have not Seen the little Singing lark or the large brown *Curloe* So Common to the Plains of the Missouri. but believe the Curloe is an inhabitent of this Countrey dureing Summer from Indian information and their attemps to mimick the notes of this fowl. I have no doubt but what maney Species of birds found here in autumn and Summer had departed before our arrival.

The *Aquatic Birds* of this country or such as obtain their Subsistence from the water, are the large blue and brown heron, fishing Hawk,[5] blue crested fisher,[6] Gulls of Several Species of the Coast, the large grey Gull of the Columbia,[7] Comorant, loons of two Species,[8] white and the brown brant, Small and large Geese,[9] small and large Swans, the Duckinmallard, canvis back Duck, red headed fishing Duck,[10] black and white duck,[11] little brown Duck,[12] Black Duck, two Species of Divers,[13] blue winged teal,[14] and Some other Species of Ducks, two Species of Plevers.

The hunters who were out last informed me that they discovered a very Considerable fall in the *Kil-haw-â-nack-kle* River[15] on its main western fork at which place it falls abt. 100 feet from the Side of a mountain[16] S. E. about 6 miles from Fort Clatsop and nearly 15 from its enterance into the bay by the Meanderings of this river

a high mountain[17] is Situated S 60° W. about 18 miles from Fort Clatsop on which there has been Snow Since Nov.

1. The common snipe, *Gallinago gallinago* [AOU, 230], and the spotted sandpiper, *Actitis macularia* [AOU, 263]. Holmgren, 33. A dark vertical line through the previous sentence and a red vertical line through this passage may be Biddle's work.

2. Probably the song sparrow, *Melospiza melodia* [AOU, 581]. Ibid.

3. Probably Sprague's pipit, *Anthus spragueii* [AOU, 700]. Ibid., 31.

4. The long-billed curlew, *Numenius americanus* [AOU, 264]. Burroughs, 226–27.
5. The osprey, *Pandion haliaetus* [AOU, 364]. Ibid., 208.
6. The belted kingfisher, *Ceryle alcyon* [AOU, 390]. Ibid., 237–38.
7. Perhaps the western gull, *Larus occidentalis* [AOU, 49]; see below, March 6, 1806. Ibid., 230–31.
8. See below, March 7, 1806.
9. Different subspecies of the Canada goose.
10. Red-breasted merganser, *Mergus serrator* [AOU, 130], or the common merganser, *M. merganser* [AOU, 129]; see above, June 21, 1805.
11. The bufflehead; see below, March 9, 1806.
12. Holmgren, 29, suggests one of several teals, *Anas* sp. See March 10, 1805.
13. See the descriptions and identifications of these birds at March 10, 1806.
14. The blue-winged teal, *Anas discors* [AOU, 140].
15. Youngs River Falls on Youngs River in Clatsop County, Oregon, about ten miles south of Astoria and the bay. The fall (about seventy-five feet) is on the main western fork (Youngs River) as Clark indicates and may be the line crossing the river on *Atlas* map 84. The eastern fork would be today's Klaskanine River. See Thwaites (LC), 4:137 n. 1. Gass reports the discovery of the falls under March 1, 1806, and gets closer to its height, which he gives as sixty feet.
16. Perhaps Lone Ridge in Clatsop County.
17. Identified by Thwaites (LC), 4:137 n. 2, as Saddle Mountain (elevation 3,283 feet), in Clatsop County, but difficult to reconcile with the direction given by Clark, as is any likely peak in the area. If Clark meant east for west, Saddle Mountain would be a possibility. The distance and bearing as given would place one in the Pacific, some miles off the coast.

[Lewis]   *Thursday March 6th 1806.*

This morning the fishing and hunting parties[1] set out agreeably to their instructions given them last evening. at 11 A. M. we were visited by Comowoll and two of his children. he presented us with some Anchovies which had been well cured in their manner. we foud them excellent. they were very acceptable particularly at this moment. we gave the old man some small articles in return. this we have found much the most friendly and decent savage that we have met with in this neighbourhood. Hall had his foot and ankle much injured yesterday by the fall of a large stick of timber; the bones were fortunately not broken and I expect he will be able to walk again shortly. Bratton is now weaker than any of the convalessants, all of whom recover slowly in consequence of the want of proper diet, which we have it not in our power to procure.—[2]

The Aquatic birds of this country, or such as obtain their subsistence from the water, are the large blue and brown heron, fishing hawk, blue crested fisher, gulls of several species of the Coast, the large grey gull of the Columbia, Cormorant, loons of two species, white, and the brown brant, small and large geese, small and large Swan, the Duckinmallard, canvis back duck, red headed fishing duck, black and white duck, little brown duck, black duck, two speceis of divers, blue winged teal, and some other speceis of ducks.

[Clark] *Thursday March 6th 1806*

This morning, the fishing and hunting party's Set out agreeably to their instructions given them last evening. At 11 a. m. we were visited by Commowoll and two boys Sons of his. he presented us with Some Anchovies which had been well Cured in their manner, we found them excellent. they were very acceptable perticularly at this moment. we gave the old mans Sones a twisted wire to ware about his neck, and I gave him a par of old glovs which he was much pleased with. this we have found much the most friendly and decent Indian that we have met with in this neighbourhood.

Hall had his foot and ankle much injured yesterday by the fall of a log which he had on his Sholder; the bones are fortunately not broken, I expect he will be able to walk again Shortly. Bratten is now weaker than any of the convalessants, and complains verry much of his back, all of them recovering Slowly in consequence of the want of proper diet, which we have it not in our power to precure.—

The large Blue and brown *Herons* or crains as they are usialy called in the U States are found below tide water. they are the Same of those of the U, States. The Fishing *Hawk* with the Crown of the head white, and back of a milkey white, and the blue crested or king fisher are found on every part of the Columbia and its water Along which we passed and are the Same with those of the U, States. the fishing hawk is not abundant, particularly in the mountains. There are 4 Species of the larus or gull on this coast and river. 1st a Small Species the Size of a Pegion;[3] white except some black spots about the head and the little bone on the but of the wing. 2d a Species Somewhat larger of a light brown colour, with a mealy coloured back.[4] 3rd the large Grey Gull,[5] or white larus with a greyish brown back, and light grey belly and breast, about the Size of a

45. Head of a White Gull
(northern fulmar, *Fulmarus glacialis*),
March 6, 1806, Voorhis No. 2

well grown pullet, the wings are remarkably long in perpotion to the Size of the body and it's under chap towards the extremity is gibbous and protuberant than in either of the other Species. a *White Gull*[6] about the Size of the Second with a remarkable beak; adjoining the head and on the base of the upper Chap there is an elivated orning of the Same Substance with the beak which forms the nostriels at A; it is Somewhat in this form.[7] the feet are webed and the legs and feet of a yellow colour. the form of the wings body &c are much that of the 2d Species this bird was Seen on Haleys bay.

The large *Grey Gull*[8] is found on the Columbian waters as high as the enterence of the Koos koos ke and in common with the other Species on the coast; the others appear confined to the tidewater, and the 4th Species not So common as either of the others. The Comorant is a large black duck which feeds on fish; I proceive no difference between it & these found in the rivers of the Atlantic Coasts. we met with as high up the river as the enterance of the Chopunnish into the Kooskooske river. they increased in numbers as we decended, and formed much the Greatest portion of waterfowls which we saw on the Columbia untill we reached tidewater, where they also abound but do not bear a Similar proportion to the fowls found in this quarter. we found this bird fat and tolerably flavoured as we decended the Columbia.

1. Including Drouillard, Labiche, and Collins.
2. A red vertical line runs across most of this paragraph, perhaps done by Biddle.
3. Coues identifies it as Bonaparte's gull, *Larus philadelphia* [AOU, 60]; Burroughs says that if so, it must have been a juvenile in its first winter plumage. Coues (HLC), 3:881 n. 84; Burroughs, 230. Holmgren, 30, also gives Bonaparte's gull and adds Forster's tern, *Sterna forsteri* [AOU, 69], as a possibility.
4. According to Coues, a young glaucous-winged gull, *Larus glaucescens* [AOU, 44]. Burroughs appears skeptical of the identification, while Holmgren suggests it could be any of a number of immature gulls. Coues (HLC), 3:881 n. 84; Burroughs, 230; Holmgren, 30.
5. An immature western gull. Coues (HLC), 3:881 n. 84; Burroughs, 230–31. Holmgren, 30, includes the western gull among a number of other species of *Larus* as possibilities.
6. Northern fulmar, *Fulmarus glacialis* [AOU, 86], not a gull. Coues (HLC), 881 n. 84; Burroughs, 179; Holmgren, 30.
7. A sketch of the head of the northern fulmar (fig. 45) in Clark's Voorhis No. 2.
8. The third species of gull, see note above.

[Lewis] *Friday March 7th 1806.*

The wind was so high that Comowol did not leave us untill late this evening. Labuish and Drewyer returned at sunset having killed one Elk only. they report that there are some scattering male Elk in the neighbourhood of the place they killed this one or about 5 miles up the Netul on this side.— Bratton is much wose today, he complains of a violent pain in the small of his back and is unable in consequence to set up. we gave him one of our flanel shirts, applyed a bandage of flannel to the part and bathed and rubed it well with some vollatile linniment which I prepared with sperits of wine,[1] camphor, castile soap[2] and a little laudinum. he felt himself better in the evening.— the large blue and brown herons, or Crains as they are usually called in the U' States are found on this river below tidewater. they are the same with those of the U' States. the fishing hawk with the crown of the head White and back of a mealy white, and the blue crested or King fisher are found on every part of the Columbia and it's waters and are the same with those of the U' States. the fishing hawk[3] is not abundant particularly in the mountains. there are four speceis of larus or gull on this coast and river, 1st a small speceis about the size of a pigeon; white except some black spots about the head and a little brown on the but of the wings, 2nd a speceis somewhat larger of a light brown colour with a whitish or mealy coloured back. 3rd the large grey gull, or white larus with a greyish ⟨black⟩ brown back and a light grey belley and breast, about the size of a well grown pullet or reather larger. the wings are remarkably long in proportion to the size of the body and it's under chap towards the extremity is more gibbous and protuberant than in either of the other speceis. 4th a white gull about the size of the second with a remarkable beak; adjoining the head and at the base of the uper Chap there is an elivated orning of the same substance with the beak which forms the nostrils; it is some what in this form.[4] the feet are webbed and the legs and feet of a yellow colour. the form of the wings body &c are much that of the second species. the large grey gull is found on the river as high as the entrance of the Kooskooske and in common with the other speceis on the coast; the others appear to be confined to tidewater; and the fourth speceis not so common as either of the others. The cormorant is a large black duck which feeds on fish; I perceive no difference between it and those found in the Potomac and other rivers on the Atlantic Coast. tho' I do not recollect seeing those on the atlantic so high up the rivers as those are found here. we first met with them on the Kooskooske at the entrance of Chopunnish river. they increased in quantity as we decended, and formed much the greatest por-

46. Head of a White Gull
(northern fulmar, *Fulmarus glacialis*),
March 7, 1806, Codex J, p. 115

tion of the waterfowl which we saw on the Columbia untill we reached tidewater where they also abound but do not bear a similar proportion to the other fowls found in this quarter.—

There are two speceis of loons. 1st the Speckled loon[5] found on every part of the rivers of this country. they are the same size colours and form with those of the Atlantic coast. the second speceis[6] we first met with at the great falls of the Columbia and from thence down. this bird is not more than half the size of the speckled loon, it's neck is long, slender and white in front. the Colour of the body and back of the neck and head are of a dun or ash colour, the breast and belley are white. the beak is like that of the speckled loon and like them it cannot fly but flutters along on the top of the warter or dives for security when pursued.—

[Clark] *Friday March 7th 1806*

The wind was So high that Comowol did not leave us untill late this evening. Drewyer & Labiesh returned at Sunset haveing killed one Elk only. they report that there are Some Scattering mail Elk in the neighbourhood of the place they killed this one or about 5 miles up the Netul river on the west Side—. Bratten is much worst to day he complains of a violent pain in the Small of his back, and is unable in consequence of it to Set up. we gave him one of our flanel Shirts. I applied a bandage of flanel to the part and rubed it well with Some volatile linniment which was prepared with Sperits of wine, camphire, Sastile Soap, and a little laudinum. he felt himself better in the evening at which time I repeated the linnement and bathed his beet [feet], to restore circulation which he complaind of in that part.

There are two Species of *Loons*. 1st the Speckled loon found on every part of the rivers of this quarter, they are the Same Size Colour and form with those of the Ohio, and atlantic coasts. the 2d Species we first met with at the great falls of the Columbia and from thence down. this bird is not more than half the Size of the Speckled loon, it's neck is long, Slender and white in front. the colour of the body and back of the neck and head are of a dun or ash Colour, the breast and belly are white. the back is like that of the Speckled loon, and like them it cannot fly, but flutters along on the top of the water or Dives for Security when pursued.

John Shields Reubin Fields & Robert frasure measured 2 trees of the fur kind one 37 feet around, appears sound, has but fiew limbs for 200 feet it is East of the Netul abt 280 feet high.

1. Alcohol.
2. Soap made from olive oil and sodium hydroxide.

3. A red vertical starts at "the large blue" and runs to about here, perhaps done by Biddle.

4. A sketch of the northern fulmar's head (fig. 46) in Lewis's Codex J, p. 115.

5. Perhaps the arctic loon, *Gavia arctica* [AOU, 10], specifically the western subspecies, Pacific loon, *G. a. pacifica*. Or it may be the same as "those of the Atlantic coast," that is, the common loon, *G. immer* [AOU, 7]. Burroughs, 177; Coues (HLC), 3:881 n. 85; Holmgren, 32.

6. The western grebe, *Aechmophorus occidentalis* [AOU, 1]. Burroughs, 178–79; Coues (HLC), 3:882 n. 86. Holmgren, 32, considers it to be either the arctic loon or the red-throated loon, *Gavia stellata* [AOU, 11]. With both this and the loon, Lewis was mistaken about their ability to fly.

[Lewis] *Saturday March 8th 1806.*

Bratton is much better today, his back gives him but little pain. Collins returned early in the morning and informed us that he had killed three Elk about five miles distant on the edge of the prarie in Point Adams. one of them fell in a deep pond of water and could not get it, the other two he butcherd and secured. he saw two large herds of Elk in that quarter. we sent Drewyer and Joseph Fields to hunt those Elk. a party were also sent with Labuish for the flesh of the Elk which Drewyer and himself had killed up the netul, they returned with it in the evening. Shields, R. Fields and Frazier returned this evening from the Kilhawanackkle unsuccessfull having seen no Elk. McNeal and Goodrich having recovered from the Louis veneri I directed them to desist from the uce of mercury. The white brant[1] is very common in this country particularly below tidewater where they remain in vast quantities during the winter. they feed like the swan gees &c on the grass roots and seeds which they find in the marshes. this bird is about the size of the brown brant[2] or a third less than the common Canadian or wild goose.[3] the head is proportionably with the goose reather large; the beak also thicker shorter and of much the same form, being of a yellowish white colour except the edges of the chaps, which are frequently of a dark brown. the legs and feet are of the same form of the goose and are of a redish white or pale flesh colour. the tail is composed of sixteen feathers of equal length as those of the geese and brown brant are and bears about the same proportion in point of length. the eye is of a dark colour and nothing remarkable as to size. the wings are rether longer compared with those of the goose but not as much so as in the brown or pided brant. the colour of the plumage of this bird is unifomly a pure white except the large feathers of the extremities of the wings which are black. the large feathers of the 1st joint of the wing next to the body are white. the note of this bird differs essentially from that of the goose; it more resembles that of the brown brant but is somewhat different. it is like the note of young domestic goose which has not perfectly attained it's full note. the flesh of this bird is exceedingly fine, preferable to either the goose or pided brant.— The Brown or pided brant are much the same size and form of the white only that their wings are considerably longer and more pointed. the plumage of the upper part of the body neck head and tail is much the colour of the canadian goose but reather darker in consequence of som dark brown feathers which are distributed and irregularly scattered throughout. they have not the white on the neck and sides of the head as the goose has nor is the neck darker than the body. like the goose there are some white feathers on the rump at the joining of the tail. the beak is dark and the legs and feet also dark with a greenish cast; the breast and belley are of a lighter colour than the back and is also irregularly intermixed with dark brown and black feathers which give it a pided appearance. the flesh of this bird is dark and in my estimation reather better than that of the goose. the habits of this bird are the same nearly with the goose and white brant with this difference that they do not remain in this climate in such numbers during the winter as the others, and that it sets out earlier in the fall season on it's return to the south and arrives later in the spring than the goose. I see no difference between this bird and that called simply the brant, common to the lakes the Ohio and Mississippi &c. The small goose[4] of this country is reather less than the brant; it's head and neck like the brant are reather larger than that of the goose in proportion; their beak is also thicker and shorter. their notes are more like those of our tame gees; in all other rispects they are the same with the large goose with which, they so frequently ascociate that it was some time after I first observed this goose before I could determine whether it was a distinct speceis or not. I have now no hesitation in declaring them a distinct speceis. the large goose is the same of that common on the Atlantic coast, and known by the appellation of the wild, or Canadian goose.

[Clark] Saturday March 8th 1806

Bratten is much better this morning, his back givs him but little pain. Collins returned early in the morning, and informed us that he had killed three Elk about five miles distance on the edge of the prarie in point Adams. one of them fell in a deep pond of water and he could not git to ⟨him⟩ it. the other two he butchered and Saved. he saw two large herds of Elk in that quarter. we Sent Drewyer & Jos: Field to hunt these Elk, a party was also Sent with Labiesh for the flesh of the Elk which Drewyer and himself had killd up the Netul, they returned with it in the evening. Shields, R. Field and Frasure returned this evening from the Kilhawanackkle unsuccessfull haveing Seen no Elk. McNeal and Goodrich haveing recovered from the Louis veneri I derected them to desist from takeing the murcury or useing in future. willard is yet complaining and is low Spirited.

The *White Brant* is very common in this country particularly below tide water where they remain in vast quantities dureing the winter. they feed like the Swan Goose &c. on the grass and roots & Seeds which they find in the marshes this bird is a little larger than the brown brant and a fourth less than the common wild or Canadian goose. the head is proportionably with the goose reather large; the beak thicker Shorter and of the Same form, being of a yellowish white colour except the edges of the Chaps, which are frequently of a dark brown. the legs and feet are of the Same form of the goose and are of a redish white or pail flesh colour. the tail is composed of Sixteen feathers of equal length as those of the geese and brown brant are, and bears about the Same perpotion in point of length. the Eye is of a dark colour and nothing remarkable as to Size. the wings are reather longer compared with those of the goose, but not as much So as is the brown or pieded brant. the colour of the plumage of this bird is uniformly a pure white except the large feathers of the extremities of the wings which are black. The large feathers of the 1st joint of the wing next to the body are white. the note of this bird differs essentially from that of the goose; it more resembles that of the brown brant but is Somewhat different. it is like the note of a young domestic goose which has not perfectly attained its full note. the flesh of this bird is exceedingly fine, prefferable to either the goose or pieded brant. the neck is Shorter in prpotion than that of the goose.

The *Brown* or *pieded brant* are nearly the Size and much the Same form of the white brante only that their wings are considerably longer and more pointed. the plumage of the upper part of the body, neck, head and tail is much the Colour of the Common or Canadian Goose but rather darker in consequence of Some dark brown feathers which are distributed and irregularly scattered throughout. they have not the white on the neck and Sides of the head as the goose has nor is the neck darker than the body. like the goose there are Some white feathers on the rump at the junction of the tail. the beak, legs and feet are dark, with a greenish cast; the breast and belly are of a lighter colour than the back and is also intermixed, irregularly, with dark brown and black feathers which gives it a pieded appearance. the flesh of this bird is dark, and in my estimation reather better than that of the goose. the habits of this bird is nearly the same with the goose and white brant, with this difference that they do not remain in this Climate in Such numbers dureing the winter as the others. I See no difference between this bird and that Called Simpilly the *Brant* Common to the Lakes and frequently Seen on the Ohio and Mississippi in large flocks &c.

The *Small Goose* of this country is reather less than the Brant; it's head and neck like the brant are reather larger than that of the goose in purpotion; their beak is also thicker and Shorter. their notes are more like those of our taim geese, in all other respect they are the Same with the large Goose with which, they So frequently ascoiete, that it was Some time after I first observed this goose before I could whether it was a distinct Speces or not. I have no hesitation now in declareing them a distinct Species. the *large Goose* is the Same as that common to the Ohio, and atlantic coast, and known by the appellation of the wild, or Canadian Goose.

1. Snow goose. A red vertical line runs through much of this passage about the snow goose, perhaps placed by Biddle.
2. Brant.
3. Canada goose.
4. A smaller race of Canada goose; see above, November 2, 1805.

[Lewis] *Sunday March 9th 1806.*

This morning the men set out at daylight to go in qust of the Elk which Collins had killed, they returned with it at eleven A. M. Bratton complains of his back being very painfull to him today; I conceive this pain to be something of the rheumatism. we still apply the linniment and flannel; in the evening he was much better. Drewyer and Joseph Fields returned not having found any Elk. Sergt. Pryor and the fishing party not yet arrived, suppose they are detained by the winds. visited by 3 Clatsop men who brought a dog some fish and a Sea Otter skin for sale. we suffered them to remain all night. we set Shields at work to make some sacks of Elk skin to contain various articles. The large Swan[1] is precisely the same common to the Atlantic States. the small swan[2] differs only from the larger one in size and it's note. it is about one fourth less and it's note entirely different. the latter cannot be justly immetated by the sound of letters nor do I know any sounds with which a comparison would be pertinent. it begins with a kind of whistleing sound and terminates in a round full note which is reather louder than the whistleing, or former part; this note is as loud as that of the large swan. from the peculiar whistleing of the note of this bird I have called it the *whistleing swan* it's habits colour and contour appear to be precisely those of the large Swan. we first saw them below the great narrows of the Columbia near the Chilluckkittequaw nation. They are very abundant in this neighbourhood and have remained with us all winter. in number they are fully five for one of the large speceis. The duckinmallard or common large duck wich resembles the domestic duck are the same here with those of the U' Sts. they are abundant and are found on every part of the river below the mountains. they remain here all winter but I beleive they do not continue during winter far above tidewater. a beautifull duck and one of the most delicious in the world is found in considerable quantities in this neighbourhood during the Autumn and winter. this is the same with that known in the Delliware, Susquehannah, and Potomac by the name of the *Canvisback* and in James River by that of shell-Drake; in the latter river; however I am informed that they have latterly almost entirely disappeared. to the epicure of those parts of the union where this duck abounds nothing need be added in praise of the exquisite flavor of this duck. I have frequently eaten of them in several parts of the Union and I think those of the Columbia equally as delicious. this duck is never found above tide-water; we did not meet with them untill after we reached the marshey Islands;[3] and I beleive that they have already left this neighbourhood, but whether they have gone northwardly or Southwardly I am unable to determin; nor do I know in what part of the Continent they raise their young.— The read headed fishing duck is common to every part of the river and are found as well in the Rocky Mountains as elsewhere; in short this was the only duck we saw on the waters of the Columbia within the mountains. they feed principally on crawfish[4] and are the same in every rispect as those on the rivers in the mountains of the Atlantic Ocean.—

[Clark]   *Sunday Mach 9th 1806*

This morning the men Set out at day light to go in quest of the Elk which Collins had killed, they returned at 11 A. M. Bratten complains of his backs being very painfull to him to day. we Still apply the linnement & flannel; in the evening he was much better. Jos: Field & Drewyer returned not haveing found any Elk. Sergt. Pryor and the fishing party not yet returned, Suppose they are detained by the winds. we are visited by 3 Clatsop men who brought a Dog, Some fish and a Sea otter Skin for Sale. we Suffered them to remain all night. we Set Shields at work to make Some Sacks of Elk Skin to contain my papers, and various articles which we wish kept Dry.

The large *Swan* is precisely the Same Common to the Missouri, Mississippi and the Atlantic States &c. The *Small Swan* differ only from the large one in Size and it's note. it is about ¼th less, and its notes entirely different. the latter cannot be justly immetated by the Sound of letters nor do I know any Sound with which a comparison would be pertinent. it begins with a kind of whistling Sound and terminates in a round full note which is reather louder than the whistling, or former part; this note is as loud as that of the large Swan. from the peculiar whistling of the note of this bird I have Called it the *Whistleing Swan*. it's habits colour and contour appear to be precisely those of the large swan. we first saw them below the great narrows of the Columbia near the Chilluckkittequaw Nation. they are very abundant in this neighbourhood and have remained with us all winter. in number they are fully five for one of the large Species of the Swan's.

The Duckinmallard are the Same here with those of the U, States.

they are abundant and are found on every part of the river below the mountains. they remain here all winter, but I believe they do not remain all winter above tide water.— a butifull Duck and one of the most delicious in the world is found in Considerable quantities in this neighbourhood dureing the Autumn and winter. this is the Same as that known in the Dilliwar, Susquehannah and Potomac by the name of the *Canvisback* and James River by that of Shell-Drake; in the latter river I am informed that they have latterly almost entirely disapeared. the epicures of those parts of the Union where those Ducks abound nothing need be added in prais of the exquisit flavor of this duck. I have eaten of them in Several parts of the Union and I think those of the Columbia equally as delicious. this duck is never found above tide water; we did not meat with them untill after we reached the marshey Islands; and I believe that they have already left this neighbourhood; but whether they are gorn Northerly or Southerly, I am unable to deturmine; nor do I know in what part of the Country they rais their young.—.

The red headed fishing duck is common to every part of the river and are found as well in the Rocky Mountains as elsewhere; in short this was the only duck we Saw within the Mountain on the Columbian waters. they feed principally on Crawfish; and are the Same in every respects as those on the Ohio and rivers in the mountains of the atlantic Ocian.

The *black* and *white* Duck[5] are Small about the Size of the blue-winged teal, or reather larger. the mail is butifully varigated with black and white. the white occupies the Side of the head, breast and back. black the tail, large feathers of the wing, two tufts of feathers which cover the upper part of the wings when folded, the neck and head. the female is darker or has much less white about her. I take this to be the Same Species of duck common to the ohio, as also the atlantic Coast, and Sometimes called the *butter box*. the back is wide and Short, and as well as the legs of a dark Colour. the flesh of this duck is verry well flavored I think Superior to the Duckinmallard.

   1. The trumpeter swan. A red vertical line runs through this material about swans, perhaps done by Biddle.
   2. The tundra, or whistling, swan.
   3. Karlson Island, March Island, and others in Cathlamet Bay, Clatsop County, Oregon. *Atlas* maps 81, 82.

4. A variety of *Astagus,* crayfish.
5. The bufflehead.

[Lewis] Monday March 10th 1806.

About 1 P. M. it became fair and we sent out two parties of hunters on this side of the Netul the one below and the other above. we also directed a party[1] to set out early in the morning and pass the bay and hunt beyond the Kilhowanackklc. from the last we have considerable hope as we have as yet hunted but little in that quarter. it blew hard all day. in the evening the Indians departed. The hunters who were over the Netull the other day informed us that they measured a pine tree, (or fir No 1)[2] which at the hight of a man's breast was 42 feet in the girth about three feet higher, or as high as a tall man could reach, it was 40 feet in the girth which was about the circumpherence for at least 200 feet without a limb, and that it was very lofty above the commencement of the limbs. from the appearance of other trees of this speceis of fir and their account of this tree, I think it may be safely estimated at 300 feet. it had every appearance of being perfectly sound. The black and white duck are small abut the size of the blue-winged teal, or reather larger. the male is beautifully variagated with black and white. the white occupys the sides of the head, breast and back, black, the tail feathers of the wings two tufts of feathers which cover the upper part of the wings when foalded, the neck and head. the female is darker or has much less white about her. I take this to be the same speceis of duck common to the Atlantic coast, and frequently called the butterbox. the beak is wide and short, and as well as the legs, of a dark colour. the flesh of this duck is very well flavored. the brown duck[3] is much in form like the duckinmallard, tho' not much more than half it's size. the colour is an uniform mixture of yellowish and dark brown. there is nothing remarkable in the appearance of this duck it generally resorts the same kind of grassey marshes with the duckinmallard and feeds in a similar manner, on grass seed, and roots. both these ducks are common to the river for some distance above tide water as well as below. The black duck[4] is about the size of the bluewinged teal. their colour is a duskey black the breast and belley somewhat lighter than the other parts, or a dark brown. the legs stand longitudinally with the body, and the bird when on shore stands of cours very

January 21–March 17, 1806

erect. the legs and feet are of a dark brown, the toes are four on each foot, a short one at the heel and three long toes in front, which are unconnected with a web. the webs are attatched to each sides of the several joints of the toe, and divided by deep sinuses at each joint. the web assuming in the intermediate part an eliptical figure. the beak is about two inches long, streight, flated on the sides, and tapering to a sharp point. the upper chap somewhat longest, and bears on it's base at the joining of the head, a little conic protuberance of a cartelagenous substace, being redish brown at the point. the beak is of an ivory white colour. the eye dark. these ducks usually associate in large flocks, and are very noisey; their note being a sharp shrill whistle. they are usually fat and agreeably flavored; and feed principally on moss, and other vegitable productions of the water. we did not meet with them untill we reached tide-water, but I beleive them not exclusively confined to that district at all seasons, as I have noticed the same duck on many parts of the Rivers Ohio and Mississippi. the gizzard and liver are also remarkably large in this fowl. the divers are the same with those of the Atlantic States. the smaller species[5] has some white feathers about the rump with no perceptable tail and is very active and quck in it's motion; the body is of a redish brown. the beak sharp and somewhat curved like that of the pheasant. the toes are not connected but webed like those discribed of the black duck. the larger speceis[6] are about the size of the teal and can flye a short distance which the small one scarcely ever attapts. they have a short tail. their colour is also an uniform brickredish brown, the beak is streight and pointed. the feet are of the same form of the other speceis and the legs are remarkably thin and flat one edge being in front. the food of both speceis is fish, and the flesh unfit for uce. the bluewinged teal are a very excellent duck, and are the same with those of the Atlantic coast.— There are some other speceis of ducks which shall be hereafter discribed as I may hereafter have an opportunity to examine them.—

[Clark] *Monday March 10th 1806*

about 1 P. M. it became fair and we Sent out two parties of hunters on this Side of the Netul, one above and the other below, we also derected a party to Set out early in the morning and pass Meriwethers Bay and hunt beyond the Kilhow anak kle.   from the last we have considerable hope, as we have as yet hunted but little in that quarter.   it blew hard all day, in the evening the Indians departed. The Hunters, S. R. F. & F.[7] who were over the netul the other day informed us that they measured a 2d tree of the fir Speces (No. 1) as high as a man Could reach, was 39 feet in the girth; it tapered but very little for about 200 feet without any Considerable limbs, and that it was a very lofty above the Commmencement of the limbs.   from the appearance of other Species of fir, and their account of this tree, I think it might safely estimated at 300 feet.   it had every appearance of being perfectly Sound in every part—.

The brown Duck is much in form like the Duckinmallard, tho' not much more than half it's Size.   the colour is one uniform mixture of yellowish and dark brown.   there is nothing remarkable in the colour of this duck; it resorts the Same kind of grassy marshes with the Duckinmallard, and feeds in a Similar manner, on grass, Seeds & roots.   both these ducks are common to the river for Some distance above tide water as well as below. The black Duck is about the Size of the bluewinged teel.   their colour is a duskey black the breast and belly Somewhat lighter than the other parts, or a dark brown.   the legs Stand longitudianally with the body, and the Bird when on Shore Stands very erect.   the legs and feet are of a dark brown, the toes are four on each foot, a short one on the heel and three long toes in front which are unconnected with a web.   the web is atached to each Side of the Several joints of the toes, and devided by deep Sinuses at each joint.   the web assumeing in the intermediate part an elipticle figure.   the beak is about two inches long, Streight, flated on the Sides, and tapering to a Sharp point.   the upper chap Somewhat longest and bears on its base at the joining of the head, a little conic protuberance of a cartelagenous Substance, being redish brown.   the beak is of a ivery white colour.   the eye dark.   these ducks usialy associate in large flocks, and are very noisey; their note being a Sharp shrill whistle.   they are usialy fat and tolerably flavoured; and feed on moss and other vegitable productions of the water.   we did not meet with them untill we reached tide water, I have noticed the Same duck on maney parts of the ohio an Mississippi.   the Gizzard and liver are also remarkably large in this fowl—. The Divers are the Same with those of the atlantic States.   the Smaller Species has some white feathers about the rump and no perceptable tail and is very active and quick in its motion; the body is of a redish brown. the beak sharp and Somewhat curved like that of the Pheasant the toes are not connected but webd. like those discribed of the black duck. The large Species are about the Size of the teal &c. the food of both those Species is fish. and their flesh is unfit for use.

The bluewinged teal are a very excellent duck, and are the Same with those of the atlantic coast.— There are some other Species of ducks which Shall be hereafter discribd. as I may hereafter have an oppertunity of exameneing them.

1. Including Drouillard, Joseph Field, and Frazer, as Lewis notes in the next entry.
2. Sitka spruce; see above, February 4, 1806. Two red vertical lines go through several lines about the spruce and bufflehead, perhaps done by Biddle.
3. See March 5, 1806.
4. The American coot. Another red vertical line here.
5. The pied-billed grebe, *Podilymbus podiceps* [AOU, 6]. Burroughs, 178; Holmgren, 29.
6. The red-necked grebe, *Podiceps grisegena* [AOU, 2], or the horned grebe, *P. auritus* [AOU, 3]. Burroughs, 177–78; Holmgren, 29.
7. Shields, Reubin Field, and Frazer.

[Lewis] *Tuesday March 11th 1806.*

Early this morning Sergt. Pryor arrived with a small canoe loaded with fish which he had obtained from the Cathlahmah's for a very small part of the articles he had taken with him. the wind had prevented his going to the fisery on the opposite side of the river above the Wackiacums, and also as we had suspected, prevented his return as early as he would otherwise have been back.— The dogs at the Cathlahmahs had bitten the trong assunder which confined his canoe and she had gone a drift. he borrowed a canoe from the Indians in which he has returned. he found his canoe on the way and secured her, untill we return the Indians their canoe, when she can be brought back. Sent Sergt. Gass and a party in surch of a canoe which was reported to have been sunk in a small creek on the opposite side of the Netul a few miles below us, where she had been left by Shields R. Fields and Frazier when they were lately sent out to hunt over the Netul. They returned and reported that they could not find the canoe she had broken the cord by which she was attatched, and had been carried off by the tide. Drewyer Joseph Fields and Frazier set out by light this morning to pass the bay in order to hunt as they had been directed the last evening. we once more live in *clover*; Anchovies fresh Sturgeon and Wappetoe. the latter Sergt. Pryor had also procured and brought with him. The reptiles of this country are the rattlesnake garter snake and the common brown Lizzard. The season was so far advanced when we arrived on this side of the rocky mountains that but few rattlesnakes were seen I did not remark one particularly myself, nor do I know whether they are of either of the four speceis found in the different parts of the United states, or of that species before mentioned peculiar to the upper parts of the Missouri and it's branches. The garter snake[1] so called in the United States is very common in this country; they are found in great numbers on the open and sometimes marshey grounds in this neighbourhood. they differ not at all from those of the U' States. the black or dark brown lizzard[2] we saw at the rock fort Camp at the commencement of the woody country[3] below the great narrows and falls of the Columbia; they are also the same with those of the United States. The snail[4] is numerous in the woody country on this coast; they are in shape like those of the United States, but are at least five times their bulk. There is a speceis of water lizzard[5] of which I saw one only just above the grand rapids of the Columbia. it is about 9 inches long the body is reather flat and about the size of a mans finger covered with a soft skin of a dark brown colour with an uneven surface covered with little pimples the neck and head are short, the latter terminating in an accute angular point and flat. the fore feet each four toes, the hinder ones five unconnected with a web and destitute of tallons. it's tail was reather longer than the body and in form like that of the Musk-rat, first rising in an arch higher than the back and decending lower than the body at the extremity, and flated perpendicularly. the belley and under part of the neck and head were of a brick red every other part of the colour of the upper part of the body a dark brown. the mouth was smooth, without teeth.

[Clark] *Tuesday March 11th 1806*

Early this morning Sergt. Pryor arrived with a Small Canoe loaded with fish which he had obtained from the *Cath-lah-mah's* for a very Small part of the articles he had taken with him. the wind had prevented his going to the fishery on the opposit Side of the river above the Waukiecum's, and also as we had suspected, prevented his return as early as he otherwise would have been back. The dogs of the Cathlahmah's had bitten the throng assunder which confined his canoe and she had gorn adrift. he borrowed a Canoe from the Indians in which he has returned. he found his canoe on the way and Secured her, untill we return the Indians their Canoe— Sent Sergt. Gass and a party in Serch of one of our Canoes which was reported to have been lost from a hunting party of Shields R. Field & Frazier when they were last out on the opposit Side of the Netul. they returned and reported that they Could not find the Canoe which had broken the Cord with which it was attached, and was caried off by the tide. Drewyer Jo. Field & Frazier Set out by light this morning to pass the bay in order to hunt as they had been directed last evening. we once more live in *Clover;* Anchovies fresh Sturgeon and Wappatoe. the latter Sergt. Pryor had also procured a fiew and brought with him. The Deer of this Coust differ from the Common Deer, fallow Deer or Mule Deer as has beformentiond.

The *Mule Deer*[6] we have never found except in rough Country; they prefer the Open Grounds and are Seldom found in the wood lands near the river; when they are met with in the wood lands or river bottoms and pursued, they imediately run to the hills or open country as the Elk do, the Contrary happens with the common Deer. there are Several differences between the mule and common deer as well as in form as in habits. they are fully a third larger in general, and the male is particularly large; think there is Somewhat greater disparity of Size between the Male and the female of this Species than there is between the male and female fallow Deer; I am Convinced I have Seen a Buck of this Species twice the volume a Buck of the Common Deer. the Ears are peculiarly large, I measured those of a large Buck ⟨of this Species⟩ which I found to be *eleven* inches long and $3\frac{1}{2}$ in width at the widest part; they are not so delicately formed, their hair in winter is thicker longer and of a much darker grey, in Summer the hair is Still coarser longer and of a paler red, more like that of the Elk; in winter they also have a Considerable quantity of very fine wool intermixed with the hair and lying next to the Skin as the Antelope has. the long hair which grows on the outer Side of the first joint of the hind legs, and which in the Common Deer do not usially occupy more than 2 inches in them occupy from 6 to 8; their horns also differ, those in the Common deer consist of two main beams gradually deminishing as the points proceed from it, with the mule deer the horns consist of two beams which at the distance of 4 or 6 inches from the head divide themselves into two equal branches which again either divide into two other equal branches or terminate in a Smaller, and two equal ones; haveing either 2, 4 or 6 points on a beam; the horn is not so rough about the base as the common deer, and are invariably of a much darker Colour. the most Strikeing differance of all, is the white rump and tail. from the root of the tail as a center there is a circular Spot perfectly white of about 3½ inches radius, which occupy a part of the rump and the extremities of buttocks and joins the white of the belley underneath; the tail which is usially from 8 to 9 inches long for the first 4 or 5 inches from its upper extremity is covered with Short white hairs, much Shorter indeed than those hairs of the body; from hence for about one inch further, the hair is Still white but gradually becoms longer; the tail then termonates in a tissue of Black hair of about 3 inches long. from this black hair of the tail they have obtained among the French engages the appelation of the *black tailed Deer,* but this I conceive by no means Characteristic of the Animal as much the larger portion of the tail is white. the Ears and the tail of this Animale when Compared with those of the Common Deer, So well Comported with those of the *Mule* when compared with the Horse, that we have by way of distinction adapted the appellation of the mule Deer[7] which I think much more appropriate. on the inner corner of each eye there is a drane (like the Elk) or large recepticle which Seams to Answer as a drane to the eye which givs it the appearance of weeping, this in the Common Deer of the Atlantic States is scercely proceptable but becoms more Conspicious in the fallow Deer, and Still more So in the Elk; this recepticle in the Elk is larger than any of the Pecora order[8] with which I am acquainted.

  I have Some reasons to believe that the Calumet Eagle[9] is Sometimes found on this Side of the Rocky mountains from the information of the Indians in whose possession I have Seen their plumage. those are the Same with those of the Missouri, and are the most butifull of all the family of the Eagle of America it's colours are black and white with which it is butifully varigated. the feathers of the tail which is so highly prized by the Indians is composed of twelve broad feathers of equal length those are white except about two inches at the extremity which is of a jut black. their wings have each a large circular white Spot in the middle when extended. the body is variously marked with white and black. the form is much that of the Common bald Eagle, but they are reather Smaller and much more fleet. this Eagle is feared by all carnivarous birds, and on his approach all leave the carcase instantly on which they were feeding. it breads in the inaccessable parts of the Mountains where it Spends the Summer, and decends to the plains and low country in the fall and winter when it is usially Sought and taken by the nativs. two tails of this bird is esteemed by Mandans, Minnetares, Ricaras, &c. as the full value of a good horse, or Gun and accoutrements. with the Osage & Kanzas and those nations enhabiting Countrys where this bird is more rare, the price is even double of that mentioned. with these feathers the nativs deckerate the Stems of their Sacred pipes or Calumets; whence the name of Calumet Eagle, which has Generally obtained among the Engages. The Ricaras have domesticated this bird in many instances for the purpose of obtaining its plumage. the nativs in every part of the Continent who can precure those feathers attach them to their own hair and the mains and tail of their favorite horses by way of orniment. they also deckerate their own caps or bonnets with those feathers.[10] The Leather winged bat is found &c.[11]

1. Perhaps the Pacific red-sided garter snake; see below, March 28 and 29, 1806. Two red vertical lines go through the material about reptiles and garter snake, perhaps Biddle's work.

2. Perhaps the western fence lizard, *Sceloporus occidentalis*. Benson (HLCE), 89; Cutright (LCPN), 288, 428–29.

3. At The Dalles, Wasco County, Oregon; see above, October 25, 1806. *Atlas* map 78.

4. Perhaps *Monadenia fidelis*, but more likely *Allogona townsendiana*. Cf. Coues (HLC), 3:898 n. 104.

5. The rough-skinned newt, *Taricha granulosa*. Benson (HLCE), 87. Cf. Burroughs, 280–81; Cutright (LCPN), 244, 429.

6. Columbian black-tailed deer. The "common deer" is *Odocoileus virginianus*, the white-tailed deer.

7. Lewis and Clark devised what remains the common name for this species; see above, May 10, 1805.

8. Equivalent to present order *Artiodactyla* and suborder *Ruminantia*, including elk, deer, and moose.

9. Golden eagle.

10. Coues points out some inaccuracies in this description; see Coues (HLC), 3: 878–79 n. 82.

11. See Lewis's entry for March 12, 1806, below, for the full sentence.

[Lewis]　　　　　　　　　　　　　　　　　　*Wednesday March 12th 1806*

We sent a party[1] again in surch of the perogue but they returned unsuccessfull as yesterday. Sent one hunter out on this side of the Netul, he did not return this evening.[2] I beleive the Callamet Eagle is sometimes found on this side of the rocky mountains from the information of the Indians in whose possession I have seen their plumage. these are the same with those of the Missouri, and are the most beautifull of all the family of the Eagles of America. it's colours are black and white with which it is beautifully variagated. the feathers of the tail which are so highly prized by the Indians is composed of twelve broad feathers of equal length. these are white except about 2 inches at the extremity which is of a jut black. there wings have each a large circular white spot in the middle when extended. the body is variously marked with white and black. the form is much that of the common bald Eagle, but they are reather smaller and much more fleet. this eagle is feared by all carnivorous birds, and on his approach all leave the carcase instantly on which they were feeding. it breads in the inaccessable parts of the mountains where it spends the summer, and decends to the plains and low country in the fall and winter when it is usually sought and taken by the natives. two tails of this bird is esteemed by the Mandans Minetares Ricares, &c as the full value of a good horse, or gun and accoutrements. with the Great and little Osages and those nations inhabiting countries where this bird is more rare the price is even double of that mentioned. with these feathers the natives decorate the stems of their sacred pipes or callamets; whence the name, of Callamet Eagle, which has generally obtained among the Engages. the Ricares have domesticated this bird in many instancies for the purpose of obtaining it's plumage. the natives in every part of the con tinent who can procure these feathers attatch them to their own hair and the mains and tails of their favorite horses by way of ornament. they also decorate their war caps or bonnets with those feathers.— The leather winged batt[3] common to the United States is also found on this side of the Rocky mountains.— Beside the fish of this coast and river already mentioned we have met with the following speceis[4] viz. the Whale, Porpus, Skaite, flounder, Salmon, red charr, two speceis of Salmon trout,[5] mountain or speckled trout,[6] and a speceis similar to one of those noticed on the Missouri within the mountains, called in the Eastern states, bottle-nose.[7] I have no doubt but there are many other speceis of fish, which also exist in this quarter at different seasons of the year, which we have not had an oportunity of seeing.   the shell fish[8] are the Clam, perrewinkle, common mussle, cockle, and a speceis with a circular flat shell. The Whale is sometimes pursued harpooned and taken by the Indians of this coast;[9] tho' I beleive it is much more frequently killed by runing fowl on the rocks of the coast in violent storms and thrown on shore by the wind and tide.   in either case the Indians preseve and eat the blubber and oil as has been before mentioned.[10]   the whale bone they also carefully preserve for sale.— Our party are now furnished with 358 pair of Mockersons exclusive of a good portion of dressed leather.—[11]

[Clark] *Wednesday March 12th 1806*

We Sent a party again in Serch of the Canoe but they returned unsucksessfull as yesterday   Sent one hunter out on this Side of the Netul he did not return this evening. Our party are now furnished with 358 par of Mockersons exclusive of a good portion of Dressed leather, they are also previded with Shirts Overalls Capoes of dressed Elk Skins for the homeward journey.

Besides the fish of this Coast and river already mentioned we have met with the following Species.   viz. the Whale, Porpus, Skaite, flounder, Salmon, red-carr, two Specis of Salmon trout, mountain or Speckled trout, and a Speceis Similar to one of those noticed on the Missouri within the mountains, called in the Eastern States, bottle nose. I have no doubt but there are many other Species of fish which also exist in this quarter at different Seasons of the year, which we have not had an oppertunity of seeing.   the Shell fish are the Clam, perriwinkle, common Muscle, cockle, and a Species with a circular flat Shell.

The Whale is Sometimes pursued harpooned and taken by the Indians of this Coast; tho I believe it is much more frequently killed by running on the rocks of the Coast to S. S. W. in violent Storms, and thrown on different parts of the Coast by the winds and tide—.   in either case the

Indians preserve and eat the blubber and Oil as has been before mentioned. the whale bone they also carefully preserve for Sale.

The Reptiles of this Country are the rattle snake, garter Snake a common brown Lizzard. The Season was so far advanced on this side of the Rocky Mountains that but fiew rattle Snakes were Seen, I did not remark one particularly my Self, nor do I know if they are of either of the four Species found in different parts of the United States, or of that Species before observed only on the upper parts of the Missouri & its branches.

The Garter Snake So Called in the U States is very common in this country, they are found in great numbers on the open and Sometimes marshy grounds in this neighbourhood. they differ not at all from those of the United States. the Black or Dark brown Lizzard we Saw at the long narrows or Commencement of the woody country on the Columbia; they are also the Same with those of the U, States. The Snail is noumerous in the woodey Country on this Coast, they are in Shape like those of the U, States, but are at least five times their bulk. there is a Specis of water Lizzard of which I only Saw one just above the grand rapid of the Columbia. it is about 9 inches long the body is reather flat and about the Size of a mans finger, covered with a Soft Skin of dark brown Colour with an uneaven sufice covered with little pimples, the neck and head are Short, the latter termonateing in an accute angular point and flat. the fore feet each have four toes, the hinder ones five unconnected with a web and destitute of tallons. it's tail was reather longer than the body, and in form like that of the muskrat, first riseing in an arch higher than the back, and decending lower than the body at the extremety, and flated perpindicularly. the belly and under part of the neck and head were of a Brick red every other part of the colour of the upper part of the body are dark brown. the mouth was Smooth without teeth.

The horns of Some of the Elk have not yet fallen off and those of others have Grown to the length of Six inches. the latter are in the best order, from which it would Seem that the pore Elk retain their horns longer.

---

1. Under Sergeant Ordway, according to himself.
2. A red vertical line runs through much of this passage about the eagle, perhaps drawn by Biddle.

3. Thus distinguishing the mammal (here an unknown species) from certain birds referred to as "bats." See above, June 30, 1805.

4. Most of these species are discussed and identified elsewhere in this volume. Biddle (in later years) adds, "Saw no oysters on the Pacific Ocean." Biddle Notes [ca. April 1810], Jackson (LLC), 2:502.

5. Probably the coho (or silver) salmon, *Oncorhynchus kisutch*, called the "white Salmon Trout" on March 16, 1806, and the steelhead trout *O. mykiss*, (formerly *Salmo gairdneri*) discussed on March 13 and 14, 1806. Kendall.

6. The cutthroat trout bears Clark's name, *Oncorhynchus clarki* (formerly *Salmo clarkii*); it was first described by Lewis on June 13, 1805. Kendall; Burroughs, 264.

7. Probably the mountain sucker, *Catostomus* (formerly *Pantosteum*) *platyrhynchus*, here compared with the northern sucker *C. catostomus*. Burroughs, 264–65; Cutright (LCPN), 426.

8. The shellfish may be identified as follows: the clams are probably from the family Veneridae, although Coues considers them from the family Mytilidae; the periwinkle is *Littorina* sp.; the mussel is *Mytilus* sp. if Lewis is referring to the salt water species, but if he means the freshwater variety of the Columbia River as Biddle suggests, then it would be of the family Unionidae, as given by Coues; the cockle is from the family Cardiidae (see December 9, 1805); and the final species "with a circular flat shell" is from the family Anomiidae, bivalves. Some of these species are described more fully on March 15, 1806, in Clark's entry. Coues (HLC), 3:896 and n. 100, 896–87, 896 n. 101, 897 nn. 102, 103.

9. The suggestion here that local Indians hunted whales offshore is significant, as maritime hunting of this nature is generally thought to have been restricted to native peoples living farther north on the Pacific Coast. Ray (LCEN), 115. Elsewhere, Lewis and Clark provide further support for this practice in their observation that representations of hunters in canoes harpooning whales often occurred on hats worn by these people (see entries of January 29 and 30, 1806).

10. See above, January 10, 1806.

11. This last sentence and a portion of the previous one have a dark "x" across them.

[Lewis] *Thursday March 13th 1806.*

This morning Drewyer Jos Feilds and Frazier returned; they had killed two Elk and two deer. visited by two Cathlahmahs who left us in the evening. we sent Drewyer down to the Clatsop village to purchase a couple of their canoes if possible. Sergt. Pryor and a party made another surch for the lost peroge but was unsuccessfull; while engaged in surching for the perogue Collins one of his party killed two Elk near the Netul below us. we sent Sergt. Ordway and a party for the flesh of one of the Elk beyond the bay with which they returned in the evening. the other Elk and two deer were at some distance. R. Fields and Thompson who set out yesterday morning on a hunting excurtion towards point Adams have not yet returned. The horns of some of the Elk have not yet fallen off, and those of others have shotten out to the length of six inches.¹ the latter are in the best order, from which it would seem that the poor Elk retain their horns longest.

Observed Equal Altitudes of the ☉ with Sextant.

A. M.	8	6	16	P. M.	2	45	10	} Altitude given by Sext.
"		8	6	"		47	3	at time of Obsert.
"		10	—	"		48	54	48° 26′ 45″

Chronometer too slow on Mean Time—

The Porpus² is common on this coast and as far up the river as the water is brackish. the Indians sometimes gig them and always eat the flesh of this fish when they can procure it; to me the flavor is disagreeable. the Skaite³ is also common to the salt water, we have seen several of them that had perished and were thrown out on the beach by the tide. The flounder⁴ is also an inhabitant of the salt water, we have seen them also on the beach where they had been left by the tide. the Indians eat the latter and esteem it very fine. these several speceis are the same with those of the Atlantic coast. the common Salmon⁵ and red Charr are the inhabitants of both the sea and rivers. the former is usually largest and weighs from 5 to 15 lbs. it is this speceis that extends itself into all the rivers and little creeks on this side of the Continent, and to which the natives are so much indebted for their subsistence. the body of this fish is from 2½ to 3 feet long and proportionably broad. it is covered with imbricated scales of a moderate size and is variagated with irregular black spots on it's sides and gills. the eye is large and the iris of a silvery colour the pupil black. the rostrum or nose extends beyond the under jaw, and both the upper and lower jaws are armed with a single series of long teeth which are subulate and infleted near the extremities of the jaws where they are also more closely arranged. they have some sharp teeth of smaller size and same shape placed on the tongue which is thick and fleshey. the fins of the back are two; the first is plaised nearer the head than the ventral fins and has [blank] rays, the second is placed far back near the tail is small and has no rays. the flesh of this fish is when in order of a deep flesh coloured red and every shade from that to an orrange yellow, and when very meager almost white. the roes of this fish are much esteemed by the natives who dry them in the sun and preserve them for a great length of time. they are about the size of a small pea nearly transparent and of a redish yellow colour. they resemble very much at a little distance the common currants of our gardens but are more yellow. this fish is sometimes red along the sides and belley near the gills particularly the male. The red Charr[6] are reather broader in proportion to their length than the common salmon, the skales are also imbricated but reather large. the nostrum exceeds the lower jaw more and the teeth are neither as large nor so numerous as those of the salmon. some of them are almost entirely red on the belley and sides; others are much more white than the salmon and none of them are variagated with the dark spots which make the body of the other. their flesh roes and every other particular with rispect to their form is that of the Salmon. this fish we did not see untill we decended below the grat falls of the Columbia; but whether they are exclusively confined to this portion of the river or not at all seasons, I am unable to determine.—

[Clark] *Thursday March 13th 1806.*

This morning Drewyer Jos. Fields and Frazer returned; they had killed two Elk and two deer. Visited by two *Cath-lah-mars* who left us in the evening. we Sent Drewyer down to the Clatsop Village to purchase a couple of their canoes if possible. Sergt. Pryor and a party made another Serch for the lost Canoe but was unsucksessfull; while engaged in Serching for the Canoe, Collins one of his party killed two Elk near the Netul below us. we Sent Sergt. Ordway and a party for the flesh of one of the Elk beyond the Bay with which they returned in the evening; the other Elk and 2 Deer were at Some distance— R. Field and Thompson who Set out on a hunting excursion yesterday morning towards point Adams have not yet returned. took equal altitudes to day this being the only fair day for Sometime past.

The Porpus is common on this coast and as far up the river as the water is brackish. the Indians Sometimes gig them and always eat the flesh of this fish when they Can precure it; to me the flavour is disagreeable. the *Skaite* is also common to the Salt water, I have Seen Several of them that had perished and were thrown out on the beach by the tide. The flounder is also an enhabitent of the Salt water. we have Seen them also on the beach where they had been left by the tide. the nativs eate the latter and esteem it very fine. these Several Species are the Same of those of the atlantic Coasts. The Common Salmon and red charr are the inhabitents of both the Sea and river. the former is usially largest and weighs from 5 to 15 lbs. it is this Species that extends itself into all the rivers and little creek on this Side of the Continent, and to which the nativs are So much indebted for their Subsistence. the body of this fish is from 2½ to 3 feet long and perpotionably broad. it is covered with imbricated scales of a moderate Size and is varigated with errigular black Spots on its Side and gills. the eye is large and the iris of a Silvery colour the pupil black. the rostrum or nose extend beyond the under jaws, and both the upper and the lower jaw are armed with a Single Series of long teeth which are Subulate and infleted near the extremities of the jaws where they are more closely arranged. they have Some Sharp teeth of Smaller Size and Same Shape on the tongue which is thick and fleshey. the fins of the back are two; the first is placed nearer the head than the Venteral fins and has [*blank*] rays, the Second is placed far back near the tail is small and has no rays. The flesh of this fish when in order of a deep flesh coloured red and every Shade from that to an orrange yellow, and when very meager almost white. the Roe of this fish are much esteemed by the nativs, who dry them in the Sun and preserve them for a great length of time. they are about the Size of a Small pea nearly transparrent and of a redish yellow colour. they resemble very much at a little distance the Common Current of our gardens but are more yellow. this fish is Sometimes red along the Sides and belly near the gills; particularly the male of this Species.

The Red Charr are reather broader in proportion to their length than the Common Salmon, the Skales are also embricated but reather large. the nostrum exceeds the lower jaw more and the teeth are neither So noumerous or large as those of the Salmon. Some of them are almost entirely red on the belly and Sides; others are much more white than the Salmon, and none of them are varigated with the dark Spots which mark the body of the other. their flesh roe and every other particular with respect to their is that of the Salmon. this fish we did not See untill we had decended below the Great falls of the Columbia; but whether they are exclusively confined to this portion of the river or not at all Seasons, I am unable to determine.

The *Salmon Trout*[7] are Seldom more than two feet in length, they are narrow in purportion to their length, at least much more So than the Salmon & red charr. their jaws are nearly of the Same length, and are furnished with a Single Series of Subulate Streight teeth, not so long or so large as those of the Salmon, the mouth is wide, and the tongue is also furnished with Some teeth. the fins are placed much like those of the Salmon. at the Great Falls are met with this fish of a Silvery white colour on the belly and Sides, and a blueish light brown on the back and head. in this neighbourhood we have met with another Species[8] which does not differ from the other in any particular except in point of Colour. this last is of a dark colour on the back, and its Sides and belley are yellow with transverse Stripes of dark brown. Sometimes a little red is intermixed with these Colours on the belly and Sides towards the head. the flesh & roe is like those described of the Salmon. the white Species which we found below the falls were in excellent order when the Salmon were entirely out of Season and not fit for use. The Species which we found here early in november on our arival in this quarter had declined considerably, reather more so than the Red charr with which we found them asociated in the little riverlets and creeks. I think it may be Safely asserted that the Red Charr and both Species of the Salmon trout remain in Season longer in the fall of the year than the common Salmon;[9] but I have my doubt whether of the Species of the Salmon trout ever pass the Great falls of the Columbia. The Indians tell us that the Salmon begin to run early in the next month; it will be unfortunate for us if they do not, for they must form our principal dependance for food in assending the Columbia above the Falls and it's S. E. branch Lewis's river to the Mountains.

The Speckled or Mountain *Trout* are found in the waters of the Columbia within the Rocky mountains. they are the Same of those found in the upper part of the Missouri, but are not So abundant in the Columbian Waters as in that river. The *bottle nose* is also found on the waters of the Columbia within the mountains.

1. Perhaps it was Biddle who drew a red vertical line through this sentence.
2. Perhaps the harbor, or common, porpoise, *Phocoena phocoena*. Hall, 2 : 897. Another red vertical line runs through several sentences.
3. Probably the big skate.
4. The starry flounder.
5. Presumably Lewis called it thus because it was the one he encountered most often; it is the king (or Chinook) salmon, *Oncorhynchus tshawytscha*, still of great economic importance to the Pacific Northwest. Burroughs, 261–62; Cutright (LCPN), 269–70.
6. The sockeye salmon.
7. Steelhead trout, a new species. Burroughs, 263; Cutright (LCPN), 426.
8. Apparently also steelhead trout. Thwaites (LC), 4 : 167 n. 1; Burroughs, 263.
9. On the salmon runs, see Cutright (LCPN), 269–70.

[Lewis] *Friday March 14th 1806.*

This morning we sent a party after the two Elk which Collins killed last evening, they returned with them about noon. Collins, Jos. Feilds and Shannon went in quest of the flock of Elk of which Collins had killed those two. this evening we heared upwards of twenty shot, and expect that they have fallen in with and killed a number of them. Reubin Fields and Thompson returned this evening unsuccessfull having killed one brant only. late in the evening Drewyer arrived with a party of the Clatsops who brought an indifferent canoe some hats and roots for sale. the hats and roots we purchased, but could not obtain the canoe without giving more than our stock of merchandize would lisence us. I offered him my laced uniform coat but he would not exchange.[1] The Salmon Trout are seldom more than two feet in length they are narrow in proportion to their length, at least much more so than the Salmon or red charr. the jaws are nearly of the same length, and are furnished with a single series of small subulate streight teeth, not so long or as large as those of the Salmon. the mouth is wide, and the tongue is also furnished with some teeth. the fins are placed much like those of the salmon. at the great falls we met with this fish of a silvery white colour on the belley and sides, and a bluish light brown on the back and head. in this neighbourhood we have met with another speceis which dose not differ from the other in any particular except in point of colour. this last is of a dark colour on the back, and it's sides and belley are yellow with transverse stripes of dark brown. sometimes a little red is intermixed with these colours on the belley and sides towards the head. the eye, flesh, and roes are like those discribed of the Salmon. the white speceis which we found below the falls was in excellent order when the salmon were entirely out of season and not fit for uce. the speceis which we found here on our arrival early in November had declined considerably, reather more so inded than the red Charr with which we found them ascociated in the little rivulets and creeks. I think it may be safely asserted that the red Charr and both speceis of the salmon trout remain in season longer in the fall of the year than the common Salmon; but I have my doubts whether either of them ever pass the great falls of the Columbia. The Indians tell us that the Salmon begin to run early in the next month; it will be unfortunate for us if they do not, for they must form our principal dependence for food in ascending the Columbia, above the falls and it's S. E. branch to the mountains. The mountain or speckled trout are found in the waters of the Columbia within the mountains. they are the same of those found in the upper part of the Missouri, but are not so abundant in the Columbia as on that river. we never saw this fish below the mountains but from the transparency and coldness of the Kooskooske I should not doubt it's existing in that stream as low as it's junction with the S E. branch of the Columbia.— The *bottle nose* is the same with that before mentioned on the Missouri and is found exclusively within the mountains.—

[Clark] *Friday March 14th 1806*

This morning we dispatched a party after two Elk which Collins killed last evening, they returned with them about noon. Jos: Field, Collins, Go: Shannon & Labiesh went in quest of the Gang of Elk out of which Collins had killed the 2 yesterday. this evening we herd upwards of twenty Shot and expect they have fallen in with and killed Several of them. Reuben Field and Thompson returned this evening unsuksessfull haveing killed only one Brant. late in the evening Geo: Drewyer arrived with a party of the Clatsops who brought an indifferent Canoe, three hats and Some roots for Sale we could not purchase the Canoe without giveing more than our Stock of merchandize would lisence us. Capt Lewis offered his laced uniform Coat for a verry indifent Canoe, agreeable to their usial way of tradeing his price was double. we are informed by the Clatsops that they have latterly Seen an Indian from the *Quin-na-chart* Nation[2] who reside Six days march to the N. W and that four vessels were there and the owners Mr. Haley, Moore, Callamon & Swipeton were tradeing with that noumerous nation, whale bone Oile and Skins of various discription.

1. The next few lines have a red vertical line through them, perhaps Biddle's work.
2. The Makah people lived in the area of Cape Flattery, Clallam County, Washington, at the mouth of the Strait of Juan de Fuca, where their reservation is now located. Lewis and Clark's name comes from their self designation in Makah, $q^w idičča^\prime a\cdot t\chi$, "people of the cape" (referring to Cape Flattery). They belonged to the Nootka branch of the Wakashan language stock, and were the only Wakashans in the present United States. Their culture was like that of the Nootka, including the hunting of whales. Hodge, 1: 791–92; Spier, 28; Swanton, 427–28. For Haley, Moore, Callamon, and Swipeton, see above, November 6, 1805, January 1, February 13, 1806.

[Lewis]   *Saturday March 15th 1806.*

This morning at 11 OCk. the hunters[1] arrived, having killed four Elk only. Labuish it seems was the only hunter who fell in with the Elk and having by some accedent lost the fore sight of his gun shot a great number of times but killed only the number mentioned. as the elk were scattered we sent two parties for them, they returned in the evening with four skins and the flesh of three Elk, that of one of them having become putrid from the liver and pluck[2] having been carelessly left in the animal all night. we were visited this afternoon by Delashshelwilt[3] a Chinnook Chief his wife and six women of his nation which the old baud his wife had brought for market. this was the same party that had communicated the venerial to so many of our party in November last, and of which they have finally recovered. I therefore gave the men a particular charge with rispect to them which they promised me to observe. late this evening we were also visited by Catel[4] a Clatsop man and his family. he brought a canoe and a Sea Otter Skin for sale neither of which we purchased this evening. The Clatsops who had brought a canoe for sale last evening left us early this morning.— Bratton still sick.

January 21–March 17, 1806

Observed Equal Altitudes of the ☉ with Sextant.

	h	m	s		h	m	s	
A. M.	7	58	29	P. M.	2	49	1	⎫ Altitude given at
	8	0	15	"	"	50	50	⎬ the time of obsert.
	"	2	8	"	"	52	41	⎭ 48°—′ —″

                                                                    h   m   s

Chronometer too slow on mean Time   [*blank*]

There is a third speceis of brant[5] in the neighbourhood of this place which is about the size and much the form of the pided brant. they weigh about 8½ lbs. the wings are not as long nor so pointed as those of the common pided brant. the following is a likeness of it's head and beak.[6] a little distance around the base of the beak is white and is suddonly succeeded by a narrow line of dark brown. the ballance of the

47. Head of a Brant
(greater white-fronted goose, *Anser albifrons*),
March 15, 1806, Codex J, p. 131

neck, head, back, wings, and tail all except the tips of the feathers are of the bluish brown of the common wild goose. the breast and belly are white with an irregular mixture of black feathers which give that part a pided appearance. from the legs back underneath the tail, and arond the junction of the same with the body above, the feathers are white. the tail is composed of 18 feathers; the longest of which are in the center and measure 6 Inches with the barrel of the quill; those sides of the tail are something shorter and bend with their extremeties inwards towards the center of the tail. the extremities of these feathers are white. the beak is of a light flesh colour. the legs and feet which do not differ in structure from those of the goose or brant of the other speceis, are of an orrange yellow colour. the eye is small; the iris is a dark yellowish brown, and pupil black. the note of this brant is much that of the common pided brant from which in fact they are not to be distinguished at a distance, but they certainly are a distinct speis of brant. the flesh of this fowl is as good as that of the common pided brant. they not remain here during the winter in such numbers as the white brant do, tho' they have now returned in considerable quantities. first saw them below tide-water.

[Clark] *Saturday March 15th 1806*

This morning at 11 oClock the hunters arived, haveing Killed four Elk only. Labiesh it Seams was the only Hunter who fell in with the Elk and haveing by some accident lost the foresight of his gun Shot a great number of times and only killed four. as the Elk were scattered we Sent two parties for them, they return in the evening with four Skins, and the flesh of three Elk, that of one of them haveing become putred from the liver and pluck haveing been carelessly left in the Animal all night. We were visited this Afternoon in a Canoe 4 feet 2 I. wide by *De-lash-hel-wilt* a Chinnook Chief his wife and Six women of his Nation, which the Old Boud his wife had brought for Market. this was the Same party which had communicated the venereal to Several of our party in November last, and of which they have finally recovered. I therefore gave the men a particular Charge with respect to them which they promised me to observe. late this evening we were also visited by *Ca-tel* a Clatsop man and his family. he brought a Canoe and a Sea Otter Skin for Sale neither of which we could purchase of him. the Clatsops which had brought a Canoe for Sale last evening left us this morning. Bratten is still very weak and unwell.—

There is a third Species of Brant in the neighbourhood of this place which is about the Size and much the form of the bided brant. they weigh about 8½ lbs. the wings are not as long nor So pointed as the Common pided brant. the following is a likeness of its head and beak.[7] a little distance arround the base of the beak is white and is Suddenly Succeeded by a narrow line of dark brown. the ballance of the neck, head, back, wings and tail all except the tips of the feathers are of the blueish brown of the Common wild goose, the breast and belly are white with an irregular mixture of black feathers which give that part a pided appearance. from the legs back underneath the tail, and around the junction of the Same with the body above, the feathers are white. the tail is composed of 18 feathers; the longest of which are in the center and measure

48. Head of a Brant
(greater white-fronted goose, *Anser albifrons*),
March 15, 1806, Voorhis No. 2

6 inches with the barrel of the quill; those on the Side of the tail are Something Shorter and bend with their extremities inwards towards the center of the tail. the extremities of these feathers are white. the beak is of a light flesh colour. the legs and feet which do not differ in Structure from those of the Goose or brant of the other Species, are of an orrange yellow Colour. the eye is Small; the iris is of a dark yellowish brown, and puple black. the note of this brant is much that of the common pided brant from which in fact they are not to be distinguished at a distance, but they Certainly are a distinct Species of brant. the flesh of this fowl is as good as that of the Common pided brant. they do not remain here dureing the winter in Such numbers as the white brant do, tho' they have now returned in Considerable quantities. we first met with this brant on tide water.

The *Clams* of this coast are very Small. the Shells consist of two valves which open with a hinge, the Shell is Smooth thin and of an oval form or like that of the Common Muscle and of a Skye blue colour; it is of every Size under a Inch & ¾ in length, and hangs in clusters to the moss of the rocks, the nativs Sometimes eate them.— The Periwinkle both of the river and Ocian are Similar to those found in the Same Situation on the Atlantic.— there is also an Animal which inhabits a Shell perfectly circular about 3 inches in diameetor, thin and entire on the marjin, convex and Smooth on the upper Side, plain on the under part and covered with a number of minute Capillary fibers by means of which it attaches itself to the Sides of the rocks. the Shell is thin and Consists of one valve. a Small circular opperture is formed in the Center of the under Shell the Animal is Soft and boneless &c.—.

1. Collins, Joseph Field, Shannon, and Labiche, according to Clark's previous entry.
2. Internal organs such as the heart, lungs, and liver.
3. The name is Chinookan *[i]tlašxilwilt*, meaning unknown.
4. The Clatsop chief's name is from Chinookan *qatl*, meaning also unknown.
5. The first description of the greater white-fronted goose, *Anser albifrons* [AOU, 171]. Burroughs, 197–98. A red vertical line goes through the first few lines of this passage, perhaps placed by Biddle.
6. A sketch of the greater white-fronted goose's head in Lewis's Codex J, p. 131 (fig. 47).
7. Another sketch of the greater white-fronted goose's head from Clark's Voorhis No. 2 (fig. 48).

January 21–March 17, 1806

[Lewis]   Sunday March 16th 1806.

Not any occurrence worthy of relation took place today. Drewyer and party did not return from the Cathlahmahs this evening as we expected. we suppose he was detained by the hard winds of today. the Indians remained with us all day, but would not dispose of their canoes at a price which it was in our power to give consistently with the state of our Stock of Merchandize. two handkercheifs would now contain all the small articles of merchandize which we possess; the ballance of the stock consists of 6 blue robes one scarlet do. one uniform artillerist's coat and hat, five robes made of our large flag, and a few old cloaths trimed with ribbon. on this stock we have wholy to depend for the purchase of horses and such portion of our subsistence from the Indians as it will be in our powers to obtain. a scant dependence indeed, for a tour of the distance of that before us.[1] the Clam of this coast are very small. the shell consists of two valves which open with a hinge. the shell is smooth thin of an oval form or like that of the common mussle, and sky blue colour. it is about 1½ inches in length, and hangs in clusters to the moss of the rocks. the natives sometimes eat them. the perewinkle both of the river and Ocean are similar to those found in the same situations on the Atlantic coast. the common mussle of the river are also the same with those in the rivers of the atlantic coast. the cockle is small and also much the same of the Atlantic. there is also an animal which inhabits a shell perfectly circular about 3 Inches in diameter, thin and entire on the margin, convex and smooth on the upper side, plain on the under part and covered with a number minute capillary fibers by means of which it attatches itself to the sides of the rocks. the shell is thin and consists of one valve. a small circular apperture is formed in the center of the under shell. the animal is soft & boneless.—

The *white Salmon Trout*[2] which we had previously seen only at the great falls of the Columbia has now made it's appearance in the creeks near this place. one of them was brought us today by an Indian who had just taken it with his gig. this is a likness of it;[3] it was 2 feet 8 Inches long, and weighed 10 lbs. the eye is moderately large, the puple black and iris of a silvery white with a small addmixture of yellow, and is a little terbid near it's border with a yellowish brown. the position of the fins may be seen from the drawing, they are small in proportion to the fish. the fins the rocks. the shell is thin and consists of one valve. a small circular apperture is formed in the center of the under shell. the animal is soft & boneless.—

The white salmon Trout which we had previously seen only at the great falls of the Columbia, has now made it's appearance in the creeks near this place. one of them was brought us today by an Indian who had just taken it with his gig. this is a likeness of it; it was 2 feet 8 Inches long, and weighed 10 lbs. the eye is moderately large, the pupil black with a small admixture of yellow, and iris of a silvery white, a little terbid near it's border with a yellowish brown. the position of the fins may be seen from the drawing, they are small in proportion to the fish. the fins are boney but not pointed except the tail and back fins which are a little so. the prime back fin and ventral ones, contain each ten rays; those of the gills thirteen, that of the tail twelve, and the small fin placed near the tail above has no bony rays, but is a tough flexable substance covered with a smooth skin. it is thicker in proportion to it's width than the salmon. the tongue is thick and firm beset on each border with small subulate teeth in a single series. the teeth of the mouth are as before described. neither this fish nor the salmon are caught with the hook, nor do I know on what they feed.————

49. White Salmon Trout
(coho salmon, *Oncorhynchus kisutch*),
March 16, 1806, Codex J, p. 133

are boney but not pointed except the tail and back fins which are a little so, the prime back fin and ventral ones, contain each ten rays; those of the gills thirteen, that of the tail twelve, and the small fin placed near the tail above has no bony rays, but is a tough flexable substance covered with smooth skin. it is thicker in proportion to it's width than the salmon. the tongu is thick and firm beset on each border with small subulate teeth in a single series. the teeth of the mouth are as before discribed. neither this fish nor the salmon are caught with the hook, nor do I know on what they feed.—

[Clark]   *Sunday March 16th 1806*

Not any occurrence worthy of relation took place today. Drewyer and party did not return from the *Cath lah mah's* this evening as we expected. we Suppose he was detained by the hard winds today. the Indians remain with us all day, but would not dispose of their Canoe at a price which it was in our power to give consistently with the State of our Stock of Merchandize. One handkerchief would contain all the Small articles of merchandize which we possess, the ballance of the Stock Consists of 6 Small blue robes or Blankets one of Scarlet. one uniform Artillerist's Coat and hat, 5 robes made of our larg flag, and a fiew our old Clothes trimed with ribon. on this Stock we have wholy to depend for the purchase of horses and Such portion of our Subsistence from the Indians as it will be in our power to obtain. a scant dependence indeed for the tour of the distance of that before us.

The pellucid jelly like Substance, called the *Sea nettle*[4] I found in great abundance along the Strand where it has been thrown up by the waves and tide, and adheres to the Sand.

There are two Species of the Fuci,[5] or (Seawead) Seawreck which we also found thrown up by the waves. the 1st Specie at one extremity consists of a large sesicle or hollow vessale which would contain from one to 2 gallons, of a conic form, the base of which forms the extreem End and is convex and Globelar bearing on its center Some Short broad and irregular fibers. the Substance is about the consistancy of the rind of a citron Mellon and ¾ of an inch thick, yellow celindrick, and regularly tapering the tube extends to 20 or 30 feet and is then termonated with a number of branches which are flat ½ inch in width, rough particularly on the

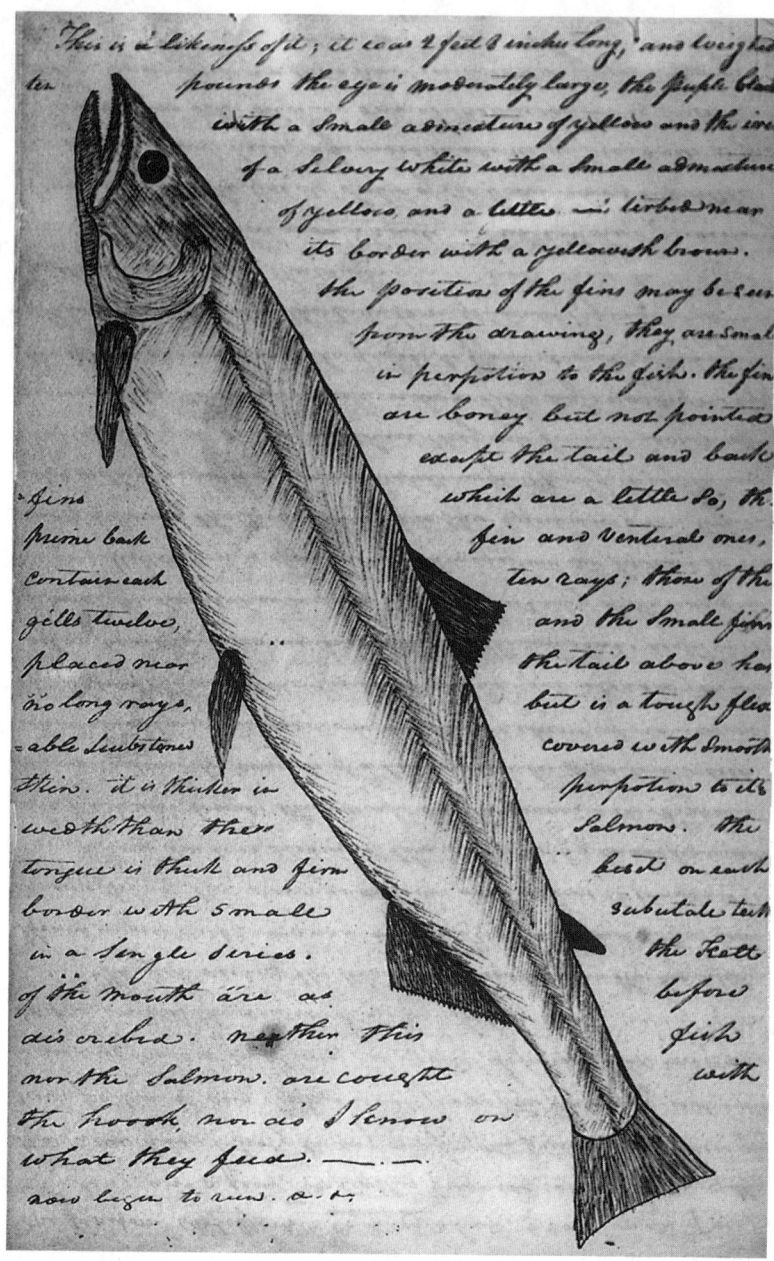

50. White Salmon Trout
(coho salmon, *Oncorhynchus kisutch*),
March 16, 1806, Voorhis No. 2

edges, where they are furnished with a number of little oval vesicles or bags of the Size of a Pigions egg. this plant Seams to be calculated to float at each extremity, while the little end of the tube from whence the branches proceed, lies deepest in the water.

The *white Salmon Trout* which we had previously seen only at the Great Falls of the Columbia, or a little below the Great Falls, has now made its appearance in the creeks near this place. one of them was brought us to day by an indian who had just taken it with his gig. This is a likeness of it;[6] it was 2 feet 8 inches long, and weighed ten pounds. the eye is moderately large, the puple black with a Small admixture of yellow and the iris of a Silvery white with a Small admixture of yellow and a little tirbed near its border with a yellowish brown. the position of the fins may be seen from the drawing, they are small in perpotion to the fish. the fins are boney but not pointed except the tail and back fins which are a little So, the prime back fin and venteral ones, contain each ten rays; those of the gills twelve, and the Small finn placed near the tail above has no long rays, but is a tough flexable Substance covered with Smooth Skin. it is thicker in perpotion to it's width than the Salmons. the tongue is thick and firm beset on each border with small subulate teeth in a Single Series. the Teeth of the mouth are as before discribed. neither this fish nor the Salmon are cought with the hook, nor do I know on what they feed.—.—. now begin to run &c. &c.

1. A red vertical line runs from beginning of the next sentence to near the end of the paragraph, perhaps done by Biddle.
2. The coho salmon. Burroughs, 261.
3. A sketch of the coho salmon from Lewis's Codex J, p. 133 (fig. 49).
4. Identified by Coues (HLC), 3:897, as a jellyfish, perhaps *Cyanea* sp. There is also the possibility of *Aurelia* sp. or *Velella* sp.
5. See Lewis's entry of March 17, 1805, next, where both species are described.
6. A sketch of the coho salmon from Clark's Voorhis No. 2 (fig. 50).

[Lewis] *Monday March 17th 1806.*

Catel and his family left us this morning. Old Delashelwilt and his women still remain they have formed a ca[m]p near the fort and seem to be determined to lay close sege to us but I beleive notwithstanding every effort of their wining graces, the men have preserved their constancy to the vow of celibacy which they made on this occasion to Capt C. and myself. we have had our perogues prepared for our departer, and shal set out as soon as the weather will permit. the weather is so precarious that we fear by waiting untill the first of April that we might be detained several days longer before we could get from this to the Cathlahmahs as it must be calm or we cannot accomplish that part of our rout. Drewyer returned late this evening from the Cathlahmahs with our canoe which Sergt. Pryor had left some days since, and also a canoe which he had purchased from those people. for this canoe he gave my uniform laced coat and nearly half a carrot of tobacco. it seems that nothing excep this coat would induce them to dispose of a canoe which in their mode of traffic is an article of the greatest val[u]e except a wife, with whom it is equal, and is generally given in exchange to the father for his daughter. I think the U' States are indebted to me another Uniform coat, for that of which I have disposed on this occasion was but little woarn.— we yet want another canoe, and as the Clatsops will not sell us one at a price which we can afford to give we will take one from them in lue of the six Elk which they stole from us in the winter.—[1]

The pellucid jellylike substance, called the sea-nettle is found in great abundance along the strad where it has been thrown up by the waves and tide.—

There are two speceis of the Fuci or seawreck [seaweed] which we also find thrown up by the waves. the 1st speceis[2] at one extremity consists of a large vesicle or hollow vessell which would contain from one to two gallons, of a conic form, the base of which forms the extreem end and is convex and globelar bearing on it's center some short broad and irregular fibers. the substance is about the consistence of the rind of a citron mellon and ¾ of an inch thick. the rihind is smooth. from the small extremity of the cone a long, hollow, celindrick, and regularly tapering tube extends to 20 or thirty feet and is then terminated with a number of branches which are flat ½ an inch in width rough particular on the edges where they are furnished with a number of little ovate vesicles or bags of the size of a pigeon's egg. this plant seems to be calculated to float at each extremity while the little end of the tube from whence the branches proceed, lies deepest in the water.—

The other speceis[3] I have never seen but Capt. Clark who saw it on the coast towards the Killamucks informed me that it resembled a large pumpkin, it is solid and it's specific gravity reather greater than the water, tho it is sometimes thrown out by the waves. it is of a yellowis brown colour. the rhind smooth and consistence hard[er] than that of a pumpkin tho' easily cut with a knife. there are some dark brown fibers reather harder than any other part which pass longitudinally through the pulp or fleshey substance wich forms the interior of this marine production.—

The following is a list of the names of the commanders of vessels who visit the entrance of the Columbia river in the spring and autumn fror the purpose of trading with the natives or hunting Elk. these names are spelt as the Indians pronounce them.[4]

Mr. Haley, their favorite trader visits them in a vessel with three masts, and continues some time
Youens, visits in a 3 masted vessel— Trader
Tallamon   do. 3   do. no trader
Callallamet   do. 3   do. Trader. has a wooden leg.
Swipton   do. 3   do. Trader.
Moore   do. 4   do. do.
Mackey   do. 3   do. do.
Washington   do. 3   do. do.
Messhipp   do. 3   do. do.
Davidson   do. 2   no trader   hunts Elk
Jackson   do. 3 masted vessel   Trader
Bolch   do. 3   do. do.
Skelley   do. 3   do. do. tho' he has been gone some years. he has one eye.

[Clark] *Monday March 17th 1806*

Catel and his family left us this morning. Old *Delashelwilt* and his women still remain, they have formed a Camp near the fort and Seam determined to lay Close Sege to us, but I believe notwithstanding every effort of their wining graces, the men have preserved their constancy to the vow of celibacy which they made on this Occasion to Capt L. and my self. we have had our Canoes prepared for our departure, and Shall Set out as Soon as the weather will permit. the weather is So precarious that we fear by waiting untill the first of April that we might be detained Several days longer before we could get from this to the Cath-lah-mahs, as it must be Calm or we cannot accomplish that part of the rout in our Canoes. Drewyer returned late this evening from the Cath-lah-mahs with our Indian Canoe which Sergt. Pryor had left Some days since, and also a Canoe, which he had purchased from those people. for this canoe he gave Captn. Lewis's uniform laced coat and nearly half a Carrot of tobacco. it Seams that nothing except this Coat would induce them to dispose of a Canoe which in their mode of traffic is an article of the greatest value except a wife, with whome it is nearly equal, and is generally given in exchange to the father for his Daughter. I think that the United States are in justice indebted to Captn Lewis another uniform Coat for that of which he has disposed of on this ocasion, it was but little worn.

We yet want another Canoe as the Clatsops will not Sell us one, a proposition has been made by one of our interpt[5] and Sever[al] of the party to take one in lieu of 6 Elk which they Stole from us this winter &c. [during?]

   1. The captains do not mention the matter further, but Sergeant Ordway notes in his entry for the next day (March 18, 1806) that four men went "over to the prarie near the coast" and took a canoe "as we are in want of it." They concealed it near the fort, as the Clatsop chief Coboway was visiting at the time. See the reflections on this incident in Ronda (LCAI), 211–12. The next paragraph and several lines of the third and fourth have red vertical lines through them, perhaps Biddle's work.
   2. This is actually two species. The one with the hollow vessel is *Nereocystis leutkeana*. Lewis erred in assuming he had one species by not realizing that a second plant had attached itself to the first with its holdfast; it is *Egregia menziesii*. Different species of kelp often grow together and can superficially appear as one. Since *Nereocystis* floats at one end only, the little ovate bags on the edges are the small gas bladders of the attached *Egregia*. Lewis was the first to describe these species. Abbott & Hollenberg, 244, 253–55.
   3. The description here is too vague to yield sure identification; it is not even certain that an alga is being described.
   4. For information on some of these traders see above, January 1, 1806.
   5. Probably either Drouillard or Charbonneau.

Chapter Twenty-Nine

The Start for Home

March 18–22, 1806

[Lewis] *Tuesday March 18th 1806.*
Drewyer was taken last night with a violent pain in his side. Capt. Clark blead him. several of the men are complaining of being unwell. it is truly unfortunate that they should be sick at the moment of our departure. we directed Sergt. Pryor to prepare the two Canoes which Drewyer brought last evening for his mess. they wanted some knees to strengthen them and several cracks corked and payed. he completed them except the latter operation which the frequent showers in the course of the day prevented as the canoes could not be made sufficiently dry even with the assistance of fire. Comowooll and two Cathlahmahs visited us today; we suffered them to remain all night. this morning we gave Delashelwilt a certificate of his good deportment &c. and also a list of our names, after which we dispatched him to his village with his female band. These lists of our names we have given to several of the natives and also paisted up a copy in our room. the object of these lists we stated in the preamble of the same as follows (viz)[1] "The object of this list is, that through the medium of some civilized person who may see the same, it may be made known to the informed world, that the party consisting of the persons whose names are hereunto annexed, and who were sent out by the government of the U' States in May 1804 to explore the interior of the Continent of North America, did penetrate the same by way of the Missouri and Columbia Rivers, to the discharge of the latter into the Pacific Ocean, where they arrived on the 14th November 1805, and from whence they departed the [*blank*] day of March 1806 on their return to

The Start for Home

the United States by the same rout they had come out."— on the back of some of these lists we added a sketch of the connection of the upper branches of the Missouri with those of the Columbia, particularly of it's main S. E. branch, on which we also delienated the track we had come and that we meant to pursue on our return where the same happened to vary. There seemed so many chances against our government ever obtaining a regular report, though the medium of the savages and the traders of this coast that we declined making any. our party are also too small to think of leaving any of them to return to the U' States by sea, particularly as we shall be necessarily divided into three or four parties on our return in order to accomplish the objects we have in view;[2] and at any rate we shall reach the United States in all human probability much earlier than a man could who must in the event of his being left here depend for his passage to the United States on the traders of the coast who may not return immediately to the U' States or if they should, might probably spend the next summer in trading with the natives before they would set out on their return. this evening Drewyer went in quest of his traps, and took an Otter. Joseph Fields killed an Elk.— The Indians repeated to us the names of eighteen distinct tribes residing on the S. E. coast who spoke the Killamucks language,[3] and beyound those six others who spoke a different language which they did not comprehend.

[Clark] *Tuesday March 17th 1806*[4]

Drewyer was taken last night with a violent pain in his Side. I bled him. Several of the men are complaining of being unwell. it is truly unfortunate that they Should be Sick at the moment of our departure. Derected Sergt. Pryor to prepare the two Indian Canoes which we had purchased for his mess. they wanted Some knees to Strengthen them, and Several cracks corked and payed. he compleated them except paying. the frequent Showers of rain prevented the Canoes drying Sufficient to pay them even with the assistance of fire.—

Commorwool and two Cathlahmahs visited us to day; we Suffered them to remain all night. this morning we gave Delashelwilt a certificate of his good deportment &c. and also a list of our names, after which we dispatched him to his village with his female band. Those list's of our Names we have given to Several of the nativs, and also pasted up a Copy in our room. the Object of these lists we Stated in the preamble of the Same as follows Viz: "The Object of this list is, that through the medium of Some civilized person who may See the Same, it may be made known to the informed world, that the party consisting of the persons whoes names are hereunto annexed, and who were Sent out by the Government of the United States in May 1804, to explore the interior of the Continent of North America, did penetrate the Same by way of the Missouri and Columbia rivers, to the discharge of the latter into the Pacific Ocian, where they arrived on the 14th of November 1805, and from whence they departed the [blank] day of March 1806 on their return to the United States by the Same rout they had come out."

On the back of lists we added a Sketch of the continent of the upper branches of the Missouri with those of the Columbia, particularly of its upper N. E. branch or Lewis's River, on which we also delienated the track we had Came and that we ment to pursue on our return, when the Same happened to vary. There Seemes So many chances against our governments ever obtaining a regular report, through the medium of the Savages, and the traders of this Coast that we decline making any. Our party are too small to think of leaveing any of them to return to the Unt. States by Sea, particularly as we Shall be necessarily devided into two or three parties on our return in order to accomplish the Object we have in View; and at any rate we Shall reach the U, States in all humain probabillity much earlier than a man Could who must in the event of his being left here depend for his passage to the U, State on the traders of the Coast, who may not return imediately to the U, States. or if they should, might probably Spend the next Summer in tradeing with the nativs before they would Set out on their return. This evening Drewyer went in quest of his traps, and took an otter. Joseph Field killd and Elk.— The Indians repeated to us Eighteen distinct Nati[ons?] resideing on the S S. E Coast who Speak the *Kil a mox* language or understand it. and beyend those Six other Nations which Speak a different language which they did not comprehend.

The 2d Species of Seawreck[5] which I saw on the coast to the S. S. E. near the *Kil â mox* nation. it resembles a large pumpkin, it is Solid and it's Specific Gravity reather greater than the water, tho' it is Sometimes thrown out by the waves. it is of a pale yellowish brown colour. the rhind Smooth and consistency harder than that of the pumpkin, tho' easily cut with a knife. there are Some fibers of a lighter colour and much harder than any other part which pass Longitudinally through the pulp or fleshey Substance which forms the interior of this marine production.—.—.

1. While the party was preparing to leave, the Russian ship *Juno,* out of New Archangel (Sitka) in Alaska, commanded by Nicolai Rezanov, was attempting to cross the Columbia bar. It was finally driven off by the storm of March 21. Rezanov was seeking a more hospitable place than Alaska for a Russian settlement. His failure at this time not only prevented a possible confrontation with Lewis and Clark but kept the Russians from gaining a foothold on the Columbia. On June 12, 1806, Captain Samuel Hill's *Lydia,* of Boston (see above, November 6 and 24, 1805), entered the mouth of the river. The Indians told him about their American visitors, showed him medals given them, and gave him at least one copy of the declaration and muster roll. The news did not reach the United States by this route until after the party's safe return to St. Louis. The ultimate fate of the documents is unknown. Jewitt, 174; Ruby & Brown (CITC), 108–10; Chevigny, 105–24; Jackson (LLC), 2:300.

2. The first indication of the captains' intention to divide the party on the return journey, which they did on leaving Travelers' Rest in Montana on July 3, 1806.

3. These "Nations" may well be villages belonging to some larger group, as on Clark's maps of the Columbia. The coast of Oregon and northern California was the home of peoples speaking a medley of languages of several major language families. The Tillamooks (Kilamox) were of the Salishan family. South of them were Alseas, Yaquinas, Coos, Siuslaws, and Umpquas, speaking languages sometimes grouped into the Penutian phylum. In southwest Oregon and northwest California were various groups speaking Athapascan languages. The Yuroks and Wiyots of northwest California spoke Algonquian languages, while the Karok language is difficult to relate to any others. Thompson (NW); Drucker, 104, 107–8. A red vertical line runs through this sentence, perhaps done by Biddle.

4. Actually March 18.

5. See note at March 17, 1806.

[Lewis] *Wednesday March 19th 1806.*

It continued to rain and hail today in such manner that nothing further could be done to the canoes. a pratry were sent out early after the Elk which was killed yesterday with which they returned in the course of a few hours. we gave Comowooll alias Connia, a cirtificate of his good conduct and the friendly intercourse which he has maintained with us during our residence at this place; we also gave him a list of our names.— do not.[1] The Killamucks, Clatsops, Chinnooks, Cathlahmahs and Wâc'-

ki-a-cums [*NB: Qu: Wackms.*] resemble each other as well in their persons and dress as in their habits and manners.— their complexion is not remarkable, being the usual copper brown of most of the tribes of North America. they are low in statue reather diminutive, and illy shapen; possessing thick broad flat feet, thick ankles, crooked legs wide mouths thick lips, nose moderately large, fleshey, wide at the extremity with large nostrils, black eyes and black coarse hair. their eyes are sometimes of a dark yellowish brown the puple black. I have observed some high acqualine noses among them but they are extreemly rare. the nose is generally low between the eyes.— the most remarkable trait in their physiognomy is the peculiar flatness and width of forehead which they artificially obtain by compressing the head between two boards while in a state of infancy and from which it never afterwards perfectly recovers.[2] this is a custom among all the nations we have met with West of the Rocky mountains. I have observed the heads of many infants, after this singular bandage had been dismissed, or about the age of 10 or eleven months, that were not more than two inches thick about the upper edge of the forehead and reather thiner still higher. from the top of the head to the extremity of the nose is one streight line. this is done in order to give a greater width to the forehead, which they much admire. this process seems to be continued longer with their female than their mail children, and neither appear to suffer any pain from the operation. it is from this peculiar form of the head that the nations East of the Rocky mountains, call all the nations on this side, except the Aliahtans or snake Indians, by the generic name of Flat heads. I think myself that the prevalence of this custom is a strong proof that those nations having originally proceeded from the same stock. The nations of this neighbourhood or those recapitulated above, wear their hair loosly flowing on the back and sholders; both men and women divide it on the center of the crown in front and throw it back behind the ear on each side. they are fond of combs and use them when they can obtain them; and even without the aid of the comb keep their hair in better order than many nations who are in other rispects much more civilized than themselves.— the large or apparently swolen legs particularly observable in the women are obtained in a great measure by tying a cord tight around the ankle. their method of squating or resting themselves on their hams which they seem from habit to prefer to siting,[3] no doubt contributes much to this deformity of the legs by preventing free circulation of the blood. the dress of the man consists of a smal robe, which reaches about as low as the middle of the thye and is attatched with a string across the breast and is at pleasure turned from side to side as they may have occasion to disencumber the right or left arm from the robe entirely, or when they have occasion for both hands, the fixture of the robe is in front with it's corners loosly hanging over their arms. they sometimes wear a hat which has already been discribed. this robe is made most commonly of the skins of a small animal which I have supposed was the brown mungo, tho' they have also a number, of the skins of the tiger cat, some of those of the Elk which are used principally on their war excursions, others of the skins of the deer panther and bear and a blanket wove with the fingers of the wool of the native sheep. a mat is sometimes temperarily thrown over the sholders to protect them from rain. they have no other article of cloathing whatever neither winter nor summer.   and every part except the sholders and back is exposed to view. they are very fond of the dress of the whites, which they wear in a similar manner when they can obtain them, except the shoe which I have never seen woarn by any of them.   they call us pâh-shish´-e-ooks, or *cloth men*.[4] The dress of the women consists of a robe, tissue, and sometimes when the weather is uncommonly cold, a vest.   their robe is much smaller than that of the men, never reaching lower than the waist nor extending in front sufficiently far to cover the body. it is like that of the men confined across the breast with a string and hangs loosely over the sholders and back. the most esteemed and valuable of these robes are made of strips of the skins of the Sea Otter net together with the bark of the white cedar or silk-grass.   these strips are first twisted and laid parallel with each other a little distance assunder, and then net or wove together in such manner that the fur appears equally on both sides, and unites between the strands. it make a warm and soft covering. other robes are formed in a similar manner of the skin of the Rackoon, beaver &c. at other times the skin is dressed in the hair and woarn without any further preperation. in this way one beaver skin, or two of those of the Raccoon or tiger catt forms the pattern of the robe. the vest is always formed in the manner first discribed of their robes and covers the body from the armpits to the waist, and is confined behind, and destitute of straps over the sholder to keep it up. when this vest is woarn the breast of the woman is concealed, but without it which is almost always the case, they are exposed, and from the habit of remaining loose and unsuspended grow to great length particularly in aged women in many of whom I have seen the bubby reach as low as the waist. The garment which occupys the waist, and from thence as low as nearly to the knee before and the ham, behind, cannot properly be denominated a petticoat, in the common acceptation of that term; it is a tissue of white cedar bark, bruised or broken into small shreds, which are interwoven in the middle by means of several cords of the same materials, which serve as well for a girdle as to hold in place the shreds of bark which form the tissue, and which shreds confined in the middle hang with their ends pendulous from the waist, the whole being of sufficient thickness when the female stands erect to conceal those parts usually covered from formiliar view, but when she stoops or places herself in many other attitudes, this battery of Venus is not altogether impervious to the inquisitive and penetrating eye of the amorite.[5] This tissue is sometimes formed of little twisted cords of the silk grass knoted at their ends and interwoven as discribed of the bark. this kind is more esteemed and last much longer than those of bark. they also form them of flags and rushes which are woarn in a similar manner. the women as well as the men sometimes cover themselves from the rain by a mat woarn over the sholders. they also cover their heads from the rain sometimes with a common water cup or basket made of the cedar bark and beargrass. these people seldom mark their skins by puncturing and introducing a colouring matter. such of them as do mark themselves in this manner prefer their legs and arms on which they imprint parallel lines of dots either longitudinally or circularly. the women more frequently than the men mark themselves in this manner.

    The favorite ornament of both sexes are the common coarse blue and white beads which the men wear tightly wound arond their wrists and ankles many times untill they obtain the width of three or more inches. they also wear them in large rolls loosly arond the neck, or pendulous from the cartelage of the nose or rims of the ears which are purforated for the purpose. the women wear them in a similar manner except in the nose which they never purforate. they are also fond of a species of wampum which is furnished them by a trader whom they call Swipton. it seems to be the native form of the shell without any preperation.[6] this shell is of a conic form somewhat curved, about the size of a raven's quill at the base, and tapering to a point which is sufficiently large to permit to hollow through which a small thred passes; it is from one to 1 ½ Inches in length, white, smooth, hard and thin. these are woarn in the same manner in which the beads are; and furnish the men with their favorite ornament for the nose. one of these shells is passed horizontally through the cartilage of the nose and serves frequently as a kind of ring to prevent the string which suspends other ornaments at the same part from chafing and freting the flesh. the men sometimes wear collars of bears claws, and the women and children the tusks of the Elk variously arranged on their necks arms &c. both males and females wear braslets on their wrists of copper brass or Iron in various forms. I think the most disgusting sight I have ever beheld is these dirty naked wenches. The men of these nations partake of much more of the domestic drudgery than I had at first supposed. they collect and prepare all the fuel, make the fires, assist in cleansing and preparing the fish, and always cook for the strangers who visit them. they also build their houses, construct their canoes, and make all their wooden utensils. the peculiar provence of the woman seems to be to collect roots and manufacture various articles which are prepared of rushes, flags, cedar bark, bear grass or waytape. the management of the canoe for various purposes seems to be a duty common to both sexes, as also many other ⟨domestic⟩ occupations which with most Indian nations devolves exclusively on the woman. their feasts which they are very fond are always prepared and served by the men.—

Comowool and the two Cathlahmahs left us this evening. it continued to rain so constantly today that Sergt. Pryor could not pitch his canoes.—

[Clark] *Wednesday March 19th 1806   Inds. Descd.*

It continued to rain and hail in Such a manner that nothing Could be done to the Canoes. a party were Sent out early after the Elk which was killed last evening, with which they returned in the Course of a fiew hours, we gave Commorwool alias Cania, a Certificate of his good conduct and the friendly intercourse which he has maintained with us dureing our residence at this place: we also gave him a list of our names &c.— The *Kilamox, Clatsops, Chinnooks, Cath lah mahs Wau ki a cum* and *Chiltz* I—resemble each other as well in their persons and Dress as in their habits and manners.— their complexion is not remarkable, being the usial Copper brown of the tribes of North America. they are low in Statue reather diminutive, and illy Shaped, possessing thick broad flat feet, thick ankles, crooked legs, wide mouths, thick lips, noses Stuk out and reather wide at the base, with black eyes and black coarse hair.

I have observed Some high acqualine noses among them but they are extreemly reare. the most remarkable trate in their physiognamy is the peculiar flatness and width of the forehead which they Artificially obtain by compressing the head between two boards while in a State of infancy, and from which it never afterwards perfectly recovers. This is a custom among all the nations, we have met with West of the Rocky Mountains. I have observed the head of maney infants, after this Singular Bandage had been dismissed, or about the age of 11 or 12 months, that were not more than two inches thick about the upper part of the forehead and reather thiner Still higher. from the top of the head to the extremity of the nose is one Streight line. this is done in order to give a greater width to the forehead, which they much admire. This process seams to be continued longer with their female than their male children, and neither appears to Suffer any pain from the opperation. it is from this peculiar form of the head that the nations East of the Rocky Mountains, call all the nations on this Side, except Aliahtans, So-so-ne, or Snake Indians by the General name of Flat Heads. I think my Self that the provalence of this custom is a Strong proof of those nations haveing originally proceeded from the Same Stock. The nations of this neighbourhood or those recpitulated above, ware their hair loosly flowing on their back and Sholders; both men and women divide it on the Center of the Crown in front and throw it back behind the ear on each Side. they are fond of Combs and use them when they Can obtain them; and even without the aid of Combs keep their in better order, than maney nations who are in other respects much more Civilized than themselves.—

The large or apparently Sweled legs particularly observable in the women, are obtained in a great measure by tying a cord tight around the leg above the ancle bone. their method of Squating or resting themselves on their hams which they Seam from habit to prefer to Setting, no doubt contributes much to this deformity of the legs by preventing free circulation of the blood. This is also the Custom of the nations above.

The dress of the men like those above on the Columbia river Consists of a Small robe, which reaches about as low as the middle of the thye and is attatched with a String across the breast and is at pleasure turned from Side to Side as they may have an occasion to disincumber the right or left arm from the robe entirely, or when they have occasion for both hands, the fixture of the robe is in front with it's corner loosly hanging over their Arms. they Sometimes wear a hat which have already been discribed (See 29th Jany.) Their Robes are made most commonly of the Skins of a Small animal which I have Supposed was the brown mungo, tho' they have also a number of the Skins of the tiger Cat, Some of those of the Elk which are used principally on their war excursions, others of the Skins of Deer, panthor, Bear, and the Speckle Loon, and blankets wove with the fingers of the wool of the native Sheep. and Some of those on the Sea Coast have robes of Beaver and the Sea Otter. a mat is Sometimes temperaly thrown over the Sholders to protect them from rain. they have no other article of Cloathing whatever neither winter nor Summer, and every part except the Sholders and back is exposed to view. they are very fond of the dress of the whites, which they ware in a Similar manner when they Can obtain them, except the Shoe or mockerson which I have never Seen worn by any of them. They Call us *pâh-shish-e-ooks* or *Cloath men*. The dress of the women consists of a roab, tissue, and Sometimes when the weather is uncommonly Cold, a vest. their robe is much Smaller than that of the men, never reaching lower than the waist nor extending in front Sufficiently far to cover the body. it is like that of the men confined across the breast with a String and hangs loosely over the Sholders and back. the most esteemed & valuable of those robes are made of Strips of the Skin of the Sea Otter net together with the bark of the white Cedar or Silk grass. these fish are first twisted and laid parallel with each other a little distance asunder, and then net or wove together in Such a manner that the fur appears equally on both Sides, and united between the Strands. it makes a worm and Soft covering. other robes are formed in a Similar manner of the Skins of the rackoon, beaver &c. at other times the Skins is dressed in the hair and worn without any further preperation. in this way one beaver Skin or two of the rackoon or one of the tiger Cat forms a vest and Covers the body from the Armpits to the waist, and is confined behind, and destitute of Straps over the Sholder to keep it up. when this vest is worn the breast of the woman in consealed, but without it which is almost always the case, they are exposed, and from the habit of remaining loose and unsuspended grow to great length, particularly in aged women, on many of whome I have Seen the bubby reach as low as the waist. The petticoat or tissue which occupies the waiste has been already described (See 7th Novr. 1805) formd. of the Bark of white cedar, Silk grass, flags & rushes. The women as well as the men Sometimes cover themselves from the rain by a mat worn over the Sholders. They also Cover their heads from the rain Sometimes with a common water cup or basket made of Cedar bark and bear grass.

Those people Sometimes mark themselves by punctureing and introducing a Colouring matter. Such of them as do mark themselves in this manner prefur the legs and arms on which they imprint parallel lines of dots either longitudinally or circularly. the woman more frequently than the men mark themselves in this manner. The favorite orniments of both Sexes are the Common coarse blue and white beads as before discribed of the Chinnooks. Those beads the men wear tightly wound around their wrists and Ankles maney times untill they obtain the width of three or four inches. they also wear them in large rolls loosly around the neck, or pendulous from the cartelage of the nose or rims of the ears which are purfarated in different places round the extremities for the purpose. the woman wear them in a Similar manner except in the nose which they never purfarate. they are also fond of a Species of wompum, which is furnished by a trader whome they call Swipton. it seams to be the nativ form of the Shell without any preperation. this Shell is of a conic form Somewhat curved about the Size of a ravens quill at the base, and tapering to a point which is Sufficiently large to permit a hollow through which a Small thread passes; it is from 1 to 1½ inches in length, white, Smooth, hard and thin these are worn in the Same manner in which the beeds are; and furnish the men with their favorite orniment for the nose. one of these Shells is passed horizontally through cartilage of the nose and Serves frequently as a kind of ring which prevents the string which Suspends other orniments at the Same part from Chafing

The Start for Home

and freting the flesh. The men Sometimes wear Collars of Bears Claws, and the women and children the tusks of the Elk variously arranged on their necks arms &c. both male and female wear bracelets on their wrists of Copper, Brass or Iron in various forms. The women Sometimes wash their faces & hands but Seldom. I think the most disgusting Sight I have ever beheld is those dirty naked wenches.

The men of those nations partake of much more of the domestic drudgery than I had at first Supposed. they Collect and prepare all the fuel, make the fires, cook for the Strangers who visit them, and assist in Cleaning and prepareing the fish. they also build their houses, construct their Canoes, and make all their wooden utensils. the peculiar province of the woman Seams to be to collect roots and manufacture various articles which are prepared of rushes, flags, Cedar bark, bear grass or way tape, also dress and manufacture the Hats & robes for Common use. the management of the Canoe for various purposes Seams to be a duty common to both Sexes, as are many other occupations which with most Indian nations devolve exclusively on the womin. their feasts of which they are very fond are always prepared and Served by the men.—.—.

it Continued to rain So constantly dureing the day that Sergt. Pryor Could not Pay his Canoes. The Clatsop Chief Commowool and the two Cath-lah-mahs left us this evening and returned to their village.

1. These two words are apparently in the same red ink as the "x" which crosses out the next passage about local Indians. The writing does not appear to be Biddle's; it may be Lewis's or Clark's hand, more likely the latter. Perhaps it is a note to Biddle to ignore this material for his *History*.

2. A good description of the head deformation practiced by the coastal tribes. It was a mark of superior status; slaves were not permitted to deform their heads. See fig. 23. Hodge, 1:96–97. See also Biddle Notes [ca. April 1810], Jackson (LLC), 2:500, 545.

3. Another red vertical line, from "apparently swolen" to about here.

4. This is a Clatsop term *[it]pašišxayukš*, "blanket people."

5. Clark copied this passage in his Codex H entry for November 7, 1805. For the significance of this copying, see notes there.

6. The shell of a mollusk of the genus *Dentalium*. Cutright (LCPN), 229.

[Lewis] *Thursday March 20th 1806.*[1]

It continued to rain and blow so violently today that nothing could be done towards forwarding our departure. we intended to have Dispatched Drewyer and the two Fieldses to hunt near the bay on this side of the Cathlahmahs untill we jounded them from hence, but the rain rendered our departure so uncertain that we declined this measure for the present. nothing remarkable happened during the day. we have yet several days provision on hand, which we hope will be sufficient to subsist us during the time we are compelled by the weather to remain at this place.—

Altho' we have not fared sumptuously this winter and spring at Fort Clatsop, we have lived quite as comfortably as we had any reason to expect we should; and have accomplished every object which induced our remaining at this place except that of meeting with the traders who visit the entrance of this river. our salt will be very sufficient to last us to the Missouri where we have a stock in store.— it would have been very fortunate for us had some of those traders arrived previous to our departure from hence, as we should then have had it our power to obtain an addition to our stock of merchandize which would have made our homeward bound journey much more comfortable. many of our men are still complaining of being unwell; Willard and Bratton remain weak, principally I beleive for the want of proper food. I expect when we get under way we shall be much more healthy. it has always had that effect on us heretofore. The guns of Drewyer and Sergt. Pryor were both out of order. the first was repared with a new lock, the old one having become unfit for uce; the second had the cock screw broken which was replaced by a duplicate which had been prepared for the lock at Harpers ferry where she was manufactured. but for the precaution taken in bringing on those extra locks, and parts of locks, in addition to the ingenuity of John Shields, most of our guns would at this moment been untirely unfit for use; but fortunately for us I have it in my power here to record that they are all in good order.

[Clark] *Thursday March 20th 1806*

It continued to rain and blow so violently to day that nothing could be done towards fowarding our departure. we intended to have dispatched Drewyer & the 2 Field'es to hunt above Point William untill we joined them from hense but the rain renders our departure So uncertain that we decline this measure for the present. nothing remarkable happened dureing the day. we have yet Several days provisions on hand, which we hope will be Sufficient to Serve us dureing the time we are compell'd by the weather to remain at this place.—.

Altho' we have not fared Sumptuously this winter & Spring at Fort Clatsop, we have lived quit as comfortably as we had any reason to expect we Should; and have accomplished every object which induced our remaining at this place except that of meeting with the traders who visit the enterance of this river. our Salt will be very sufficient to last us to the Missouri where we have a Stock in Store.— it would have been very fortunate for us had Some of those traders arrived previous to our departure from hence; as we Should then have had it in our power to obtain an addition to our Stock of merchandize, which would have made our homeward bound journey much more comfortable.

Maney of our men are Still Complaining of being unwell; Bratten and Willard remain weak principally I believe for the want of proper food. I expect when we get under way that we Shall be much more healthy. it has always had that effect on us heretofore.

The Guns of Sergt. Pryor & Drewyer were both out of order. the first had a Cock screw broken which was replaced by a duplicate which had been prepared for the Locks at Harpers Ferry; the Second repared with a new Lock, the old one becoming unfit for use. but for the precaution taken in bringing on those extra locks, and parts of locks, in addition to the ingenuity of John Shields, most of our guns would at this moment been entirely unfit for use; but fortunate for us I have it in my power here to record that they are in good order, and Complete in every respect—

1. This ends the daily entries in Lewis's Codex J; the rest of the codex consists of weather diaries for the months January-March 1806, reading backwards (pp. 145–52). On the flyleaf at the end of the notebook are the following figures:

$$\begin{array}{r} 35 \\ 8 \\ \hline 2[8?]0 \end{array}$$

See also Appendix C, vol. 2.

[Lewis]   *Friday March 21st 1806.*[1]

As we could not set out we thought it best to send out some hunters and accordingly dispatched Sheilds and Collins on this side the Netul for that purpose with orders to return in the evening or sooner if they were successfull. The hunters returned late in the evening unsuccessfull. we have not now more than one day's provision on hand. we directed Drewyer and the Feildses to set out tomorrow morning early, and indevour to provide us some provision on the bay beyond point William. we were visited to day by some Clatsop indians who left us in the evening. our sick men Willard and bratton do not seem to recover; the former was taken with a violent pain in his leg and thye last night. Bratton is now so much reduced that I am somewhat uneasy with rispect to his recovery; the pain of which he complains most seems to be seated in the small of his back and remains obstinate. I beleive that it is the rheumatism with which they are both afflicted.—

[Clark]   *Friday March 21st 1806*

as we could not Set out we thought it best to Send out Some hunters and accordingly dispatched Shields and Collins on this Side of the Netul for that purpose with orders to return in the evening or Sooner if they were Successfull. they returned late in the evening unsuccessfull. we have not now more than two days provisions on hand. we derected Drewyer and the two Fieldses to Set out tomorrow morning early, and indevour to provide us Some provision on the Bay beyond point William. we were visited to day by Some *Clatsops* who left us in the evening. our sick men willard and Bratten do not Seem to recover; the former was taken with a violent pain in his leg and thye last night. Bratten is now so much reduced that I am Somewhat uneasy with respect to his recovery; the pain of which he complains most Seems to be Settled in the Small of his back and remains obstenate. I believe that it is the Rheumatism with which they are both affected.—.

1. Here begin the daily entries in Lewis's Codex K that go to May 23, 1806. Preceding the entry on the flyleaf are the following words written in pencil upside down to the rest of the journal writing: Cohalo, Yeh-whal-te, Nerhe-e-ear. The writer is not known.

The Start for Home

[Lewis] *Saturday March 22cd 1806.*

Drewyer and the Feildses departed this morning agreably to the order of the last evening. we sent out seven hunters this morning in different directions on this side the Netul. about 10 A. M. we were visited by 4 Clatsops and a killamucks; they brought some dried Anchoveis and a dog for sale which we purchased. the air is perefectly temperate, but it continues to rain in such a manner that there be is no possibility of geting our canoes completed.— at 12 OCk. we were visited by Comowooll and 3 of the Clatsops. to this Cheif we left our houses and funiture. he has been much more kind an hospitable to us than any other indian in this neighbourhood.[1] the Indians departed in the evening. the hunters all returned except Colter, unsuccessfull. we determined to set out tomorrow at all events, and to stop the canoes temperarily with Mud and halt the first fair day and pay them. the leafing of the hucklebury[2] riminds us of spring.

[Clark] *Saturday March 22nd 1806*

Drewyer and the two Fieldses departed this morning agreably to the order of last evening. we Sent out Six hunters this morning in different directions on both Sides of the Netul. about 10 A. M. we were visited by *Que-ne-o* alias Commorwool 8 Clatsops and a *Kil-a-mox;* they brought Some dried Anchovies, a common Otter Skin and a Dog for Sale all of which we purchased. the Dog we purchased for our Sick men, the fish for to add to our Small Stock of provision's, and the Skin to cover my papers. those Indians left us in the evening. the air is perfectly temperate, but it continues to rain in Such a manner that there is no possibillity of getting our canoes completed in order to Set out on our homeward journey. The Clatsops inform us that Several of their nation has the Sore throat, one of which has latterly died with this disorder. the Hunters Sent out to day all returned except Colter unsessfull.

1. See Thwaites (LC), 4 : 196 n. 1, on Lewis and Clark's relations with local chiefs.
2. Perhaps mountain huckleberry, noted on February 7, 1806.

Chapter Thirty

Fort Clatsop Miscellany

Introduction

The following items represent another collection of miscellaneous documents comparable to the miscellany gathered at Fort Mandan (see Chapter 10). Here at Fort Clatsop, however, there was not the urgency to collect a mass of data to be shipped to Jefferson as an interim report of their work, as was the case from Fort Mandan. Instead, the captains themselves would be the messengers of these compiled documents, mainly tabular lists of geographic features and native peoples on their route from the eastern foothills of the Rocky Mountains to the Pacific Coast. Since they would carry these lists back with them, it was not necessary to have an additional narrative of events such as was sent from Fort Mandan. The journals they brought back would serve that purpose. However, tables would be valuable as additional, brief copies and security against loss. They would also provide quick reference to distances, latitudes, names, and numbers. Finally, the captains probably realized that Fort Clatsop provided the last opportunity to assemble such lists at leisure before reaching St. Louis. Time for developing tables, lists, and compilations would be difficult to find after the return.

Part 1: Estimated Distances from Fort Mandan to the Pacific Coast

Clark prepared this extensive list of estimated distances for the route from Fort Mandan to the Pacific Coast as an apparent supplement to his route maps. This document is found in Codex I, pp. 2–12, apparently wholly in Clark's hand. Two other versions of this table exist. One is in the little field book with Clark's draft of his trip to the coast, January 6–10, 1806, and the other is in Voorhis No. 4. The one in the draft notebook is labeled, "Distances of the Mouthes of Rivers Creeks and the Most remarkable places from Fort Mandan & Lattiduds in 1805." It does not have the remarks that are found in the final column of the Codex I and Voorhis versions. The title for the Voorhis table is quite similar to the codex piece, with only some spelling differences and minor word changes. The tables in the draft and Voorhis notebooks have been compared to the one printed below. From the start the mileage figures from point-to-point and the accumulated mileage are in disagreement. The draft version appears at first to have been just that for Codex I, but later it digresses while the codex and Voorhis items more regularly agree with one another, eventually the draft version exceeds the other tables by four miles in the accumulated mileage column and remains so to the end. The codex and Voorhis notebooks vary by up to nine miles in early entries. There are few dissimilarities for the latitudes between the three versions, while the column of remarks in the codex and Voorhis documents differ only slightly in wording. Another partial version of a similar table exists in microform and photostatic copies at the University of Virginia, Charlottesville, and the National Archives, Washington, D.C. (see Appendix C, vol. 2). That table lists geographic points from the mouth of the Missouri River to the Great Falls of the Missouri, together with mileage figures and occasional latitude readings. Here again there are discrepancies with other tables but mainly in terms of minor mileage differences. All of this material was eventually gathered with similar tables from Codex C and other documents (see Chapter 10) including information from the return journey and made into one comprehensive table for the entire trip and placed in Codex N and Voorhis No. 4. That table will appear in volume 8 of this edition. Clark had, of course, kept all these distances and other data carefully in his journals, and at Fort Clatsop he apparently brought them together in several versions. Unlike the record of streams and distances prepared at Fort Mandan (see Chapter 10), this compendium covers territory almost entirely unexplored previously by whites, which made it all the more significant. It also includes the names of the Indian tribes the party encountered and some explanations of names they bestowed on streams. The Indians are covered more fully in the next part of this chapter.

[Clark] [undated, winter 1805–6][1]

Estimated Distances in Miles Ascending the Missouri, Crossing the Rockey Mountains & decending the Kooskooskee, Louises River and the Columbia River of the remarkable places and Latitud partially anexed.

Names of remarkable places	from one place to another	Distanc to the mouth of Missourie	Latitude & remarks &c.
From Fort Mandan	—	1600	47° 21 47" N.
To Knife River on the Lard. side 100 yds. wide	6	1606	Mi-ne-ta-reis live
To an Island near the Std.	11	1617	small
To a Menatarras Wintering Village S	13½	1640½	abandoned
To Miry River on the Std.	2¼	1642¾	bold
To an Island in the little bason	28	1670¾	small
To the mo. of Little Missouri Lard. 134	29	1699¾	47° 31' 26.2" N.
To Wild Onion Creek Std. 16	12½	1712¾	a little water
To Goose eggs Lake run Std.	9¼	1722	Small
To Shabonoes Creek Lard. 20	16	1738	47° 47' 16⁸/₁₀" N.
To the Goat pen Creek Std. 20	15	1753	⟨47 42 16⁸/₁₀⟩ North near Mouse river
To Hall's Strand Lake & Creek Std.	40	1793	extream N. point
To White earth River Std. 60	46	1839	Still & deep
Rojhone or Yellow Stone River Ld. 858	48	1885	48° 00' 00" N.
To Marthys River Std. 50	57	1944	High coloured
To Porcupine River Std. 112	53	1997	Som timber on it
To 2000 mile Creek Lard. 30	3	2000	no water at prst.
To Indian Fort Creek Ld. dry	10	2010	a fort of logs
To Little dry Creek Ld. 25	27	2037	no water in it
To Lackwater Creek Std. Ld. 25	1½	2038½	do do do
To Big Dry Creek Ld. 100	7½	2046	do do do
To Little Dry River Ld. 200	5	2051	do do do

To the Gulph in bend to the Stard.	30	2081	47° 36' 11"
To Milk River on the Std. 150	13	2094	Color of tea
To Big Dry Run dry Ld. 400	25	2119	no water runing
to Warners run or Creek Std.	9	2128	47° 25' 33 1/10"
to Pine Creek Std. 20	33	2161	Saw 1st pine
to Gibsons Creek Std. 35	16	2177	a little running water
to Brown Bear defeated Creek Ld. 40	12	2189	do do do
to Brattins River Std. 100	24	2213	47° 13' 51" N.
to Burnt lodge Creek Ld. 50	6	2219	no water running
to Wisers Creek Std. 40	14	2233	a little running W.
to Blowing fly Creek Lard. 25	32	2265	do do do
to Muscle Shell River Ld. 110	5	2270	47° 0 24 6/10" N.
to Grouse Creek Std.	30	2300	no running water
to Tea pot Creek Std. 15	8	2308	do do do
to North Mountain C: Std. 30	28	2336	running water
to South Mountain Creek Ld. 30	18	2354	do do
to Ibex Island	15	2369	Killed a big horn
to Goodrich's Island	9	2378	
to Windsers Creek Std. 30	7	2385	Some water runs
to Sofshell turtle Creek Std 25	6	2391	do do do
to Elk rapid	9	2400	Doe Elk & faun Swam over
to Thompsons Creek Std. 28	27½	2427½	{ vally above Mts. bold stream
to Bull Creek Ld. 25	8½	2436	{ a Buffalow crossed a canoe & tho' C

to Big horn River Ld. 100	3	2439	Killed 3 big horns
to Vally Creek Std. 20	1	2440	thro a Vally N.
to Ash rapid	3	2443	Some ash trees
to the Slaughter River Lad. 40	11	2454	a great no. of buffalow drove down a Clift and dashed to picies on Std. I speared a wolf
to Stone wall Creek Std. 30	26	2480	Curious appearance of walls below
to Marias River Std. 186	41	2521	47° 25′ 17³/₁₀ N.
to Snow River Ld. 50	19	2540	Mtn Covd. with Snow head of this river
to Shields River Ld. 35²	28	2568	bold Stream
to the foot of the great rapids at a the great portage Lard. sd.	7	2575	47° 8′ 4⁹/₁₀″ N
to Portage River Lard. Side 55	1	2576	rapid & Sholey
to the first great fall of 87 feet pitch	6	2582	Continual Spray
to the Second fall of 19 feet pitch	3½		☞ 1718 poles
to the Grand Cascade of 47 feet 8 In pitch	½		102 poles
to the upper fall of 26.5 pitch total fall above portg. about 362 feet	2¾	2590½	881 poles
to Medicine River Std. 137	3¾	2594¼	1196 poles
to the head of the Portage on the Ld. at the white Bear Islands, the land portage 18 miles thro: a plain	3	2586¼	972 poles 47° 3′ 33″ N.
to Smith's River Lard. 80	30¾	2628	bold current & Vally
to the Rockey Mountains at Pine Island rapid	40¼	2668¼	46° 42′ 14⁷/₁₀″
to Dearbourne's River Std. 80	8¾	2676	bold current & in Mtn.

to Gun brook Ld. 10	2	2678	*found a fusee*
to Ordways' Creek Std. 25	10	2688	bold current Vly
to the Great gate of the rock Mounts. river confined in a narrow channel between Clifts of 1200 feet high	24	2712	W. Clark across Sd. mtn.
to Pott's Vally Creek Std. bold	6	2718	[*illegible, erased*] Wide vally N.
to Pryors Vally River Std. 28 yds	20	2738	Latd 46° 10' 32 9/10" N bold Current and wide extence Vally saw a smoke N W
to White Earth Creek Std.[3] bold	30	2768	bold 15
to White House Creek Lad bold	11	2779	Some timber on it 15
to Yorks 8 Islands	23	2802	W C on land York tired
to Gasses Vally Creek Std. 25	14	2816	bold & 3 forks &
to the Little Gate of the Mountain	5	2821	we saw a horse
to Howards Creek Lard. bold	6	2827	mistook the Spring of the Creaf for the [*illegible*]
to the *three* forks of Missouri at Jefferson, Madderson & Gallitins rivers. Gallintins on Ld. and 70 yds wide Maddison 90 yds wide & Jeffersons 90 yds wide and is the Std. fork	21	2848	W. C. return to the party verrry sick 45° 22' 34" N
Up Jeffersons River to Philosophy River on Ld. Side 30	15	2863	*bold rapid*
to the Narrows of the 3d Mountn.	17	2880	M. L. go a head
to Frazures Creek & rapid Ld. bold	8	2888	*bad rapid*
to R. Field's Vally Creek Sd. 28	4	2892	R. F. killed 4 deer

to Wisdom River Std. Side 40	55	2947	*45° 2′ 21 6/10″ N*
to Philanthrophy River Ld. 30	12	2959	river crooked
to Beaverhead Clifts Stad. Side	34	2993	do. do.
to McNeals Creak Ld. bold	37	3030	bold Stream 17
to the 4th Gap of the Mountain	28	3058	Saw Several rattle snakes
to Willards Creek Std. bold	6	3064	Willard discovered this the day before we got to it
to a rapid at the narrows of 5th Mtn.	21	3085	a bad rapid for half a mile
to the East fork of *Jeffersons* river at which place left the Canoes and Commened a portage	11	3096	*44° 35′ 28 1/10″*
to the 3 forks in Snake Indian vally	15	3111	W C. Camp with Inds.
to the head Spring of *Jeffersons* river in a Dividing ridge of the rock M	13	3124	meet an Ind. on a Mule
to the snake Indian or *So-so-nee* Nation on the East fork of Louieses River one of the Easterly forks of the great Columbia river from S. E. & 35 yds.	10	3134	*44° 23′ 22 7/10″*
to the main fork of Louises River Ld 90	18	3152	from the South
to Salmon Creek Std. Side bold	9	3161	Shields killed a fish
to tower run Std. Small	14	3175	*leave Lowis's river*
up tower run to the forks of the road	4	3179	road leave the river
Across the hills. To fish Creek six miles north of its mouth. 25	20	3199	hilly road

to the forks of the road & Creek	7½	3206½	cross the C. often
to the Top of a Snow Mountain at the head of the Creek	21½	3228	pilot lost to the right
to Clark's River[4] at a village of 33 tents of Flathead	12	3240	*river from right*

Down Clarks' River

to flour Camp Creek Ld. bold	7	3247	over a mountn.
to Horse Vally Creek[5] in Horse Vally	26	3273	bold Stream Sd.
to Scattered Creek do. Sd.	22	3295	46° 41' 38.9"
to Travellers rest Creek Ld. 30	21	3316	46° 48' 28⁸/₁₀"

Commencement of high hills up Travellers rest creek[6]

to the forks of the road and Creek Sd.	11	3327	road to our right
to the Hot Springs on the right	14	3341	nearly boiling
to the Glades on the Dividing Mtn.	10	3351	
to the forks of Glade Creek	6	3357	crossed to S E. side
to Koos-koos-ke river mo: Glade C:	9	3366	*Killed a coalt*
to the foot of the Great Mountains	6	3372	open pine Countrey
	56		

Across the Great Rocky Mountains[7]

to the top of a mountain Covered with Snow the 15th of Septr. the forks of the road from our right	8		Snow high rugid

to a branch running to the right on M	13		do do do Eat a Coalt
to a branch running to the left on M.	10		do do do Eat a coalt
to Hungry Creek on the left on M	32		do do do Killed a Horse
to the forks of Collinses Creek large	26		do do
to the foot of the Mountain west	8	3469	open pine Country
	97		
to the *Cho pun-nish* (Flathead) Villages	6		Seatd. in a prarie
to Koos-kooske River at the mouth of village Creek from the right	17		about 120 yds wide
to Rock dam Creek Stard. 20 yds	3		damed by rocks
to *Cho-pun-nish* River from the N. E (at Canoe Camp) 120	5	3500	*46° 34' 56²⁄₁₀" N.*
to Canister run Ld. (passd. 16 rapids)	19		passed 16 rapids
to Colters Creek Std. (psd. 14 rapids) 20	18		passed 14 rapids
to Lowises river at the mouth of the Kooskooske river	23	3560	*46° 29' 21⁷⁄₁₀" N.*
to the Swet house Village on Ld.	7	3567	Passed 1 rapid
to the Pilots Village on the Stard	11	3578	passed 4 rapids
to a village of Mat Lodges Std.	13	3591	" 3 "
to *Ki-moo-ê-nim* Creek Ld. 20	35	3626	" 8 "

to Drewyers River on the Std Side below the narrows of 2½ 30	5	3631	"	1	"
to the Cave rapid, a Canoe Sunk at this rapid	28	3659	"	5	"
to the bason rapid (bad)	34	3693	"	8	"
to the Discharge[8] rapid (bad)	14	3707	"	4	"
to the *Columbia* at the mouth of Lewis's River (on its Lard Side)	7	3714	"	1	" 46° 15' 13.9"
to a Village of 9 Mat Lodges of the *So-kulk* nation on the 4th Island	9	3723	above a bad rapd.
to 2 Lodges at the foot of a bad rapid	3	3726	a rapid
to *Wal-ler wal ler* river S. S. 40 yds[9] river enters range of high land	4	3730	hills about 200 feet
to *Yel-lep-pets* Village of 16 mat Lodges of the ⟨Sokulk⟩ nation Sd.	4	3734	passed 1 rapid
to the lower of 17 Lodges on three Islands opposit the hat rock Ld.	15	3749	"	1	"
to the Muscle Shell rapids (bad)	6	3755	Low Cty. comns. Ld.
to the upper Lodges of the fritened band of *Pish quit pahs*[10] nation on the Std.Side Comencement of the low countrey on either side	3	3758	low Country on both Sides of R
to Pelican rapid at the lower of 48 Lodges of the fritened band scattered on the Std. shore	19	3777	low Countrey on both Sides of R

to the Commencement of the high lands on the Std. Side at the lowest of 21 Lodges of *Wah-how pums*[11] nation on 4 Islands (horse scerfised to the Dead)	18	3795	passed 2 rapids
to the Commencement of the high land on the Lard Side at a rapid	16	3811	" 1 "
to a rapid at 8 Lodges of the Sd. side of the *Wah how pums*[12] nations—	9	3820	" 1 "
to the Short rapid	6	3826	" 1 "
to 9 Mat Lodges at the rockey rapd.	7	3833	" 1 "
to River *la page* on the Lard Side at a bad rapid 40 yds.	9	3842	" 2 "
to the lower of 16 mat Lodges of the E-nee-sher Nation on Std.	4	3846	Campd. 1 "
to 11 Lodges of the E-nee-sher Nation at fish Stacked rapid	6	3852	" 2 "
to the Towahnahiooks[13] River from the Lard Side *180* yd	8	3860	we all viewed it above its mouth
to the Falls of the Columbia of 37 feet 8 ins near which is 40 Mat Lodges of the *E-Nee-sher* Nation	4	3864	45° 42′ 57³⁄₁₀″
to the Short Narrows of 45 yds. wide	2		" 1 "
to the *E che lute* Town of 21 large wood houses at the long narrows of from 50 to 100 yds wide	4	3870	45 *1* "

to a *Chil luck it te quaw* town of 8 houses on the Stard. side.	14	3884	bought Dogs
to the friendly village of 7 wood houses of the *Chilluck it le quaw* N.	6	3890	resd. of Chiefs
to the mouth of *Cataract* River on the Std. Side of 60 yds wide at 11 houses of the *Chilluckittequaw*	4	3894	10 Nations live up this river. no fish
to *River Labeach* on the Ld. 40 yds. at a village of 26 houses scattered on each side of the river of the *Smack shop* Nation [14]	13	3907	the first houses we have seen on the south side
to Canoe Creek on the Std. 28	1	3908	Saw Several Canoes
to 3 houses of *Smack shop* Ntn. Std.	9	3917	Encamped
to Cruzatt's River Std. 60 yds.	12	3929	Stumps out from shore some diste.
to the Great Rapids near a Village of 8 large wod houses on the Stard Side above of the *Sha ha lah* Nation	6	3935	45° 44′ 3⁸⁄₁₀″
to a village below the great rapids of 4 houses abandaned opsd. a 2d bad rapid	1	3936	not inhabited.
to 4 houses of the *Sha ha lah* Nation at the lower rapids of the Columbia river at *tide water*	6	3942	do. do

Tide water

to a village of 9 Houses of the *Sha ha lah* Nation on the Stard Side near the beaten rock 800 feet hi	5	3947	a man with a brass barrel gun

Fort Clatsop Miscellany

to the *Pho ca* rock in midl. Rivr. 100 foot high	11	3958	Saw Seal's
to the Commencement of the Columbian vally wide & butifull	6	3964	rich & estincive
to the Quick Sand River on the Lard Side of 120 yds	3	3967	shallow & Spread over a wide base
to the Enterance of Seal River 80 yds opsd. upper pt. of white brant Isld.[15]	3	3970	emince No. of brant
to *Ne-cha-co-kee* village opposit the Dimond island on the S. Side—	4	3974	hunted a Pond at N.
to White goose Isld. opsd. Lowr. pt.	6	3980	I tho: white gees
to a Village of 25 houses of the *Shah-ha-la* Nation on the Lard Side	6	3986	grass houses &c.
to the head of image Canoe Isld.	4	3990	met 2 Canoes on which was images
to the enterance of *Moltno mah*[16] river from the S. E. 500 yards wide	10	4000	Inds. Stold Tomhk.
to the Mult-no-mah Nation and Village of [*paper torn*] at narrow part of the Columbia	6	4006	Campd. opst. a No. of noisey fowls
to the *Quath-láh-poh* the Grand Village on the North side	8	4014	Inds. vist. us in 7 Canos
to *Cah-wah-na-ki-ooks* river of 200 yds wide from the N. East	1	4015	
to the lower point of *Wap pa to* Island near the Lard. Side	1	4016	a Chanl. ¼ me. wide
to the Mouth of *Cath-la-haws* V[17] Creek Std	9	4025	I thought was a Id.

to the lower point of *E-lar-lar* or Deer Island near the Lard.[18]	6	4031	Indian names I saw 16 snakes
to the *Enterance* of *Cow-e-lis-kee* River on the Stard Side 150 yards wide about the mouth and up this river the *Skil-lute* Nation reside rong Inds. acct. [account?]	13	4044	Campd. I killd. phest.
to Fannys Isld. & bottom on Ld.	16	4060	bottom on the Ld.
to the Sea Otter Island	12	4072	foggy
to the upper village of the *War-ki â cum* Nation on Std.	6	4078	Petticoat women at this village landed for no.
to the lower village of the *Warki-â-cum* nation of 7 houses under a high hill on the Stard Side	9	4087	bought a Dog
to the Shallow Bay (or nitch) on Std. Side	16	4103	5 miles deep
to Point Distress on the Stard. Side	16	4119	lay 6 days
to Station Camp near an old Chinnook village of 36 houses in a Std. bottom	2	4121	lay 10 days
to Cape Disapointmint at the Enterance of the Columbia river into the Great Pacific Ocian in Latd. *46° 19′ 11 1/10″* N. and Longitude *124° 57′ 0″* W.	11	4132	*46° 19′ 11 1″*

On the Sea Coast to the N N W

From Cape Disapointment to the Comencement of a Sandy Coast & low land	5		W. C. Saw the Coast much further
Point Lewis N. of the Chinnook Villages is about	15		

Fort Clatsop Miscellany

to the *Chiltz* Nation about [19]	6		Indian account
to the *Que-ne-elt* Nation about Cape Shalwater & about [20]	15		"
to the *Chil-tar-ett* Nation near Grays Bay comencing about	<u>19</u>	"	
	60		

Note. 50 mile of the above from the information of Indians.
From the *War-ki a cum* upper Village on the South Side of the Grand Columbia to Point Adams [X: *Roand*] &c.   South Side

		miles	
To the upper War-ki-a-cum Village is [21]		4078	behind Islds.
to Point *Samuel g—* [22] Lard Side	6	4084	high land
to the *Cath-lâh-mâh* Town of 9 houses South of the Seal Islands	8	4092	on high land
to Point *William* opsd. the Shallow B.	10	4102	Curious pt. [23]
to Point *Meriwether* above *Meriwethers* Bay	9	4111	3 rivers mouth
to Fort *Clâtsop* on the west side of and 3 miles up the *Netul* river from Meriwether bay	7	4118	
to the *Clât sop* Village on Ld.—	10	4128	large wood houses
to Point Adams at the enterance of the Columbia into the Ocian	6	4134	low land

On the Sea coaste to the S. S. E from point Adams [24]

to *Ne er cawan a ca* Creek & village	8		3 houses

459

Fort Clatsop Miscellany

51. Tongue Point,
Oregon, Winter 1805–6, Codex I, p. 11

to the enterance of *Clât-sop* river at 3 houses remains of an old vilg.	9	3 old towns
to the Salt works at the foot of a mountain near 4 houses	2	Canoe Vaults
to the most projicted part of the Mountain of Clarks point of view of 1000 feet above the leavel of the water	7	one rock out
to an old *Kil â mox* Village	3	no. of rocks out
to the mouth of *E-cu-la* or whale Creek 35 yds wide, and 4 huts of *Kil a mox* boiling whale blubber	6	do— do

to 6 huts of Kil á mox boiling blubber	2		do— do
to the Great *Kil á mox* Town at the enterance of Ni-ê-lee Creek	20		Inds. net a Sand bar do
to *Kil-her-hurst's* Town of *Kil á mox* at the Enterance *Kil a mox* Bay	5		a rock in entrs—
to *Kil-her-ner's* town of *Kil a mox* on the Bay at the mouth of a Creek	2		on the bay
to *Chish ucks* town of *Kil â mox* at the Enterance of Kilamox river which is about 100 yds	2		heads near Columbia
to Tow-er-quot tons Creek & Town	2		
	68		
to *Chuck tins* Town and Creek at the bottom of the Bay (which I call Kilámox Bay)[25]	2 mile		
Miles	70		

note ☞ 30 miles of this coast is from the information of Indians, collected from differint persons. They further inform me that the *Kil á mox* have two Small villages on the Kil á mox river, it is very rapid without any purpindicular falls, that nation pass across from the head of this little river to the Columbian Vally, which is at no Great Distance from its head at *Wap pa to* Island and pass down the *Chock-âh lil' com* or Columbia river with the *Wappato* they purchase.

notes from the Mouth of Columbia.

To the Wappato Island, Center is	S. 20° E	108 miles
To quick Sand river is—	S. 32° E	121 "
to the grand rapids is—	S. 47° E	128 "
to the Great falls is—	S. 65° E	172 "
to the Mouth of Lewis's river	East	240 "

From the Mouth of Lewis'es river[26]

to the Mouth of Kooskooske is	N. 52° E 96 miles
to the Mouth of *Cho-pun-nish* R at the Canoe Camp is—	} East 144 Miles
to the long Shute or narrows above	N. 28° E. 55 Mile

LEWIS AND CLARK'S POINTS FROM FORT MANDAN TO THE PACIFIC COAST

Lewis and Clark's Name	*Present Name and Location*
Fort Mandan	McLean County, North Dakota, probably under Missouri River
Knife River	Knife River, Mercer County, North Dakota
Menatarras [*Hidatsa*] Wintering Village	McLean County, probably under Garrison Reservoir (see entry for April 9, 1805)
Miry River	Snake Creek, McLean County
Little Missouri	Little Missouri River, Dunn County, North Dakota
Wild Onion Creek	Deepwater Creek, McLean County
Goose Eggs Lake Run	Shell Creek, Mountrail County, North Dakota
Shabonoes [*Charbonneau's*] Creek	Bear Den Creek, Dunn-McKenzie county line, North Dakota
Goat Pen Creek	Little Knife River, Mountrail County
Hall's Strand Lake and Creek	Tobacco Creek, Williams County, North Dakota
White Earth River	Little Muddy River, Williams County
Rojhone or Yellow Stone River	Yellowstone River, McKenzie County
Marthys River	Big Muddy Creek, Roosevelt County, Montana
Porcupine River	Poplar River, Roosevelt County
2000 Mile Creek	Red Water Creek (River), McCone County, Montana
Indian Fort Creek	Nickwall Creek, McCone County
Little Dry Creek	Spring Creek, McCone County
Lackwater Creek	Wolf Creek, Roosevelt County
Big Dry Creek	Sand Creek, McCone County

Little Dry River	Prairie Elk Creek, McCone County
Milk River	Milk River, Valley County, Montana
Big Dry Run	Big Dry Creek, McCone-Garfield county line, Montana
Warners [*Werner's*] Run	Duck Creek, Valley County
Pine Creek	Seventh Point Coulee, Valley County
Gibsons Creek	Sutherland Creek, Valley County
Brown Bear Defeated Creek	Snow Creek, Garfield County
Brattins [*Bratton's*] River	Timber Creek, Phillips County, Montana
Burnt Lodge Creek	Seven Blackfoot Creek, Garfield County
Wisers [*Weiser's*] Creek	Fourchette Creek, Phillips County
Blowing Fly Creek	Squaw Creek, Garfield County
Muscle Shell River	Musselshell River, Garfield-Petroleum county line, Montana
Grouse Creek	Beauchamp Creek, Phillips County
Tea Pot Creek	CK, or Kannuck, Creek, Phillips County
North Mountain Creek	Rock Creek, Phillips County
South Mountain Creek	South Mountain, or Armells, Creek, Fergus County, Montana
Ibex Island	Grand Island, Phillips-Fergus county line
Goodrich's Island	Dry Island, Fergus County
Windsers [*Windsor's*] Creek	Cow Creek, Blaine County, Montana
Softshell Turtle Creek	Bullwhacker Creek, Blaine County
Elk Rapid	Bird Rapids, Blaine-Fergus county line
Thompsons Creek	Birch Creek, Chouteau-Blaine county line, Montana
Bull Creek	Dog Creek, Fergus County
Bighorn River	Judith River, Fergus County
Vally Creek	Chip Creek, Chouteau County, Montana
Ash Rapid	Deadman Rapids, Fergus-Chouteau county line
Slaughter River	Arrow Creek, Fergus-Chouteau county line
Stonewall Creek	Eagle Creek, Chouteau County

Marias River	Marias River, Chouteau County
Snow River	Shonkin Creek, Chouteau County
Shields River	Highwood Creek, Chouteau County
Great Rapids	Rapids near Cascade-Chouteau county line, Montana
Portage River	Belt Creek, Cascade-Chouteau county line
First Great Fall	Great Falls of the Missouri River, Cascade County
Second Fall	Crooked Falls, Cascade County
Grand Cascade	Rainbow Falls, Cascade County
Upper Fall	Black Eagle Falls, Cascade County
Medicine River	Sun River, Cascade County
White Bear Islands	Above Great Falls, Cascade County
Smith's River	Smith River, Cascade County
Pine Island Rapid	Half-Breed Rapids, Cascade County
Dearbourne's River	Dearborn River, Cascade-Lewis and Clark county line, Montana
Gun Brook	Probably Stickney Creek, Lewis and Clark County (see entry for July 18, 1805)
Ordways' Creek	Little Prickly Pear Creek, Lewis and Clark County
Great Gate of Rock Mountains	Gates of the Rocky Mountains, Lewis and Clark County
Potts's Vally Creek	Towhead Gulch or Spokane Creek, Lewis and Clark County (see entry for July 20, 1805)
Pryors Vally Creek	Spokane Creek, Lewis and Clark County
White Earth Creek	Beaver Creek, Broadwater County, Montana
White House [*Whitehouse's*] Creek	Duck Creek, Broadwater County
Yorks 8 Islands	Broadwater County, south of Townsend (see *Atlas* map 63)
Gasses Vally Creek	Crow Creek, Broadwater County

Little Gate of the Mountain	Broadwater County, between Toston and Lombard (see *Atlas* map 64)
Howards Creek	Sixteenmile Creek, Broadwater-Gallatin county line, Montana
Three Forks of Missouri	Three Forks of the Missouri River, Broadwater-Gallatin county line
Jeffersons River	Jefferson River, Broadwater-Gallatin county line
Madderson River	Madison River, Gallatin County
Gallintins River	Gallatin River, Gallatin County
Philosophy River	Willow Creek, Gallatin County
Frazures [*Frazer's*] Creek	South Boulder Creek, Madison County, Montana
R. Field's Vally Creek	Boulder River, Jefferson County, Montana
Wisdom River	Big Hole River, Madison County
Philanthrophy River	Ruby River, Madison County
Beaver head Clifts	Beaverhead Rock, Madison County
McNeals Creek	Blacktail Deer Creek, Beaverhead County, Montana
4th Gap of the Mountain	Rattlesnake Cliffs, Beaverhead County
Willards Creek	Grasshopper Creek, Beaverhead County
Rapid at the Narrows of the 5th Mountain	Vicinity of Clark Canyon, Beaverhead County
East Fork of Jeffersons River	Red Rock River, Beaverhead County, at junction with Horse Prairie Creek to form Beaverhead River
3 forks in Snake Indian vally	Junction of Coyote, Bloody Dick, and Horse Prairie creeks, near Red Butte, Beaverhead County (marked "W. C. Camp" on *Atlas* map 67)
Head of Jeffersons River	Head of Trail Creek, Beaverhead County, near Idaho border
East Fork of Louieses River	Lemhi River, Lemhi County, Idaho
Main Fork of Louises River	Salmon River, Lemhi County

Salmon Creek	Probably Carmen Creek, Lemhi County (see entry for August 21, 1805)
Tower Run	Tower Creek, Lemhi County
Forks of the Road	North branch of Tower Creek, Lemhi County (see *Atlas* map 67)
Fish Creek	North Fork Salmon River, Lemhi County
Forks of the Road and Creek	West Fork is North Fork Salmon River; East Fork is one of several creeks running into North Fork (see entry for September 2, 1805; *Atlas* maps 67, 68)
Top of a Snow Mountain	Lemhi County, Idaho, or Ravalli County, Montana, vicinity of Saddle Mountain (see entry for September 3, 1805)
Clark's River	East Fork Bitterroot River, Ravalli County
Flour Camp Creek	Warm Springs Creek or Laird Creek, Ravalli County, near camp of September 6, 1805 (see *Atlas* map 68)
Horse Vally Creek	Skalkaho Creek, Ravalli County
Scattered Creek	Mill, North Spring, and Burnt Fork creeks, and branches, Ravalli County (see entry for September 8, 1805; courses of September 9, 1805; *Atlas* map 68)
Travellers Rest Creek	Lolo Creek, Missoula County, Montana
Forks of the Road and Creek	Grave Creek, Missoula County
Hot Springs	Lolo Hot Springs, Missoula County (see entry for September 13, 1805; *Atlas* map 69)
Glades on the Dividing Mountain	Vicinity of Packer Meadows, Idaho County, Idaho
Forks of Glade Creek	Brushy Creek and Pack Creek, joining Crooked Fork Creek, Idaho County
Koos-koos-ke River at the mouth of Glade Creek	Lochsa River, Idaho County
Branch running to the right	Perhaps Moon Creek, Idaho County (see entry for September 16, 1805)

Branch running to the left	Unnamed stream east of Indian Grave Peak, Idaho County (see entry for September 17, 1805)
Hungry Creek	Hungery Creek, Idaho County
Forks of Collinses Creek	Lolo and Eldorado creeks, Clearwater-Idaho county line, Idaho
Foot of the Mountain	Weippe Prairie, Clearwater County
Chopun-nish Villages	South of Weippe, Clearwater County
Kooskooske River at the mouth of Village Creek	Clearwater River at mouth of Jim Ford Creek, Clearwater County
Rock Dam Creek	Orofino Creek, Clearwater County
Cho-pun-nish River	North Fork Clearwater River, Clearwater County
Canister Run	Canyon Creek, Nez Perce County, Idaho
Colters Creek	Potlatch River, Nez Perce County
Louises River	Snake River, at mouth of Clearwater River, Nez Perce County, Idaho-Asotin County, Washington border
Swet House Village	Mouth of Alpowa Creek, Asotin County
Pilots Village	Vicinity of present Wawawai, Whitman County, Washington (see entry for October 11, 1805; *Atlas* map 73)
Village of Mat Lodges	Below mouth of Almota Creek, Whitman County
Ki-moo-ê-nim Creek	Tucannon River, Columbia County, Washington
Drewyers [*Drouillard's*] River	Palouse River, Franklin-Whitman county line, Washington
Cave Rapid	Pine Tree Rapids (now under Lake Sacajawea), Franklin-Walla Walla county line, Washington (see entry for October 14, 1805)
Bason Rapid	Fishhook Rapids, Franklin-Walla Walla county line
Discharge Rapid	Five-Mile Rapids, Franklin-Walla Walla county line

Columbia at the mouth of Lewis's River	Columbia River, at the mouth of the Snake River, Franklin, Walla Walla, and Benton counties, Washington
Village . . . of the So-kulk nation	Walla Walla-Benton county line, Washington
2 lodges at the foot of a bad rapid	Vicinity of Hover, Benton County
Wal-ler Waller River	Walla Walla River, Walla Walla County
Yel-lep-pets Village	Benton County, opposite mouth of Walla Walla River, probably now under Lake Wallula (see *Atlas* map 75)
Hat Rock	Hat Rock, Hat Rock State Park, Umatilla County, Oregon
Muscle Shell Rapids	Vicinity of present McNary Dam, Benton County, Washington-Umatilla County, Oregon border
Upper lodges . . . of Pishquit-pahs Nation	Vicinity of Plymouth, Benton County
Pelican Rapid	Vicinity of Crow Butte State Park, Benton County
Wah-howpums nation	Klickitat County, Washington; "Wah-how pums" may be error for "Pish-quit-pahs" (see entry for October 20, 1805; *Atlas* map 76)
Commencement of the high land . . . at a rapid	Perhaps near Willow Creek, Gilliam County, Oregon (see entry for October 20, 1805; *Atlas* map 76)
Rapid at 8 Lodges of . . . Wahhowpums nation	Near mouth of Olive Creek, Klickitat County, Washington (see entry for October 21, 1805)
Short Rapid	Klickitat County, Washington-Gilliam County, Oregon border, now under Lake Umatilla
Rocky Rapid	Klickitat County, below Rock Creek (see *Atlas* map 77)
River la page [*Lepage*]	John Day River, Gilliam-Sherman county line, Oregon

E-nee-sher Nation	Klickitat County, above Miller Island; rapid is now under Lake Celilo (see *Atlas* map 77)
Towahnahiooks River	Deschutes River, Wasco-Sherman county line, Oregon
Falls of the Columbia	Celilo Falls, Klickitat County, Washington-Wasco County, Oregon border
Short Narrows	The Dalles of the Columbia, Klickitat County, Washington-Wasco County, Oregon border
Echelute Town . . . at the Long Narrows	The Dalles of the Columbia, Klickitat County, Washington-Wasco County, Oregon border; village in Klickitat County, Washington
Chilluckittequaw Town	Klickitat County, opposite the vicinity of Crates Point (see *Atlas* map 78)
Friendly Village	Klickitat County, above Klickitat River
Cataract River	Klickitat River, Klickitat County
River Labeach [*Labiche*]	Hood River, Hood River County, Oregon
Canoe Creek	White Salmon River, Skamania-Klickitat county line, Washington
Smackshop Nation	Skamania County, above Little White Salmon River
Cruzatt's [*Cruzatte's*] River	Wind River, Skamania County
Great Rapids	Cascades of the Columbia River, Skamania County, Washington-Hood River and Multnomah counties, Oregon border
Village below the Great Rapids	Above North Bonneville, Skamania County
4 houses of the Shahalah Nation	Skamania County, just below Bonneville Dam
Village of 9 houses of Shahalah Nation	Skamania County, below Beacon Rock State Park, and perhaps below Woodward Creek
Phoca Rock	Phoca Rock, Multnomah County
Quick Sand River	Sandy River, Multnomah County
Seal River	Washougal River, Skamania County

Ne-cha-co-kee Village	Eastern edge of Portland, Multnomah County
White Goose Island	Government Island, Multnomah County
25 houses of the Shah-ha-la Nation	Portland, Multnomah County
Image Canoe Island	Hayden Island, Multnomah County
Moltnomah River	Willamette River, Multnomah County
Mult-no-mah Nation	Sauvie Island, Multnomah County
Quath-láh-pohthe Grand Village	Clark County, Washington, just above Lewis River
Cah-wah-na-ki-ooks River	Lewis River, Clark-Cowlitz county line, Washington
Wappato Island	Sauvie Island, Multnomah County
Cathlahaws Village and Creek	Kalama River, Cowlitz County
Elallar or Deer Island	Deer Island, Columbia County, Oregon
Cow-e-lis-kee River	Cowlitz River, Cowlitz County
Fannys Island and Bottom	Crims Island and Bradbury Slough, Columbia County
Sea Otter Island	Perhaps Puget Island, Wahkiakum County, Washington (see entry for November 7, 1805)
Upper Village of the Warkiâcum Nation	Vicinity of Cathlamet, Wahkiakum County (see *Atlas* map 81)
Lower Village of the Warki-â-cum nation	Vicinity of Skamokawa, Wahkiakum County (see *Atlas* map 81)
Shallow Bay	Grays Bay, Wahkiakum County
Point Distress	Eastern side of Point Ellice, Pacific County, Washington
Station Camp	Southeast of Chinook Point, Pacific County
Cape Disappointment	Cape Disappointment, Pacific County
Commencement of a Sandy Coast	Vicinity of Seaview, Pacific County
Point Lewis	Vicinity of Leadbetter Point and Cape Shoalwater, Pacific County

Point Samuel	Cathlamet Point, Clatsop County (see entry for November 26, 1805)
Cath-lâh-mâh Town	Clatsop County, behind Karlson Island
Point William	Tongue Point, Clatsop County
Point Meriwether above Meriwethers Bay	Astoria and Youngs Bay, Clatsop County
Fort Clatsop . . . up Netul River	Fort Clatsop National Memorial, on Lewis and Clark River, Clatsop County
Clâtsop village	Near Point Adams, Clatsop County
Point Adams	Point Adams, Clatsop County
Neercawanaca Creek	Neacoxic Creek, Clatsop County
Clât-sop River	Necanicum River, Clatsop County
Salt Works	Seaside, Clatsop County
Clarks Point of View	Tillamook Head, Clatsop County
Kil-â-mox Village	North of Cannon Beach, Clatsop County
E-cu-la or Whale Creek	Ecola Creek, Clatsop County
6 huts of Kilámox	Cannon Beach, Clatsop County
Great Kilámox Town at entrance of Ni-ê-lee Creek	Perhaps at the mouth of Nehalem River, Tillamook County, Oregon
Kil-her-hurst's Town . . . at the entrance of Kilamox Bay	Tillamook Bay, Tillamook County
Kil-her-ner's Town . . . at the mouth of a Creek	Tillamook Bay, Tillamook County, perhaps at mouth of Kilchis or Wilson River
Chishucks Town . . . at the entrance of Kilamox River	Tillamook Bay, Tillamook County, mouth of Tillamook River
Tow-er-quottons Creek and Town	On Tillamook Bay, Tillamook County
Chucktins Town and Creek	On Tillamook Bay, Tillamook County

1. Vertically across pp. 2–3 of Codex I, in red ink in Clark's hand are the words, "See Book No. 14 for this part of the river more detale." A red vertical line runs through the two distance columns on pp. 2–3. Book number 14 is Codex N in Biddle's numbering system (see Appendix B and Appendix C, vol. 2).

2. At the top of this page in Codex I (p. 4) in red ink and apparently in Clark's hand, are the following words: "S Book No. 14. Nearest rout and acssess."

3. Clark reverses this item with the next in his draft field book.

4. Called "flathead River" in the field book. In Codex I and Voorhis No. 4, "Clark's" appears to have been added to a blank space.

5. "*Labrich* [Labiche] Creek" in the field book. In Codex I, "Horse Vally" appears to have been substituted for an erased word.

6. Next to this heading are these words by Clark in red ink: "See Book No. 14 or last Book."

7. Next to this heading are these words by Clark in red ink: "See in the last Book No. 14." The subtotals "56" above, and "97" below, are also written in red. Voorhis No. 4 adds cumulative mileages for each entry.

8. Called "portage rapid" in the field book. In Codex I the word appears to be a later entry.

9. This line in Codex I appears to have been substituted for some erasures. It does not appear in Voorhis No. 4.

10. This word in Codex I appears to have been added to a blank space.

11. Again perhaps an addition to a blank space in Codex I.

12. Another apparent addition in Codex I.

13. "Clarks River" in the field book. In Codex I and Voorhis No. 4 the word appears to have been substituted for some erasures. See note at October 22, 1805. The number "180" appears to be an addition to a blank space in Codex I.

14. The words appear to have replaced erasures in Codex I.

15. Much of this entry appears to replace erasures in Codex I.

16. Here and in the next entry of Codex I the name appears to replace erasures.

17. In Voorhis No. 4 this entry has it: "To the enterance of *Chah wah na hiook* river on the Stard Side." The mileage "4025" appears to be crossed out.

18. Following this entry Voorhis No. 4 adds: "To the *Narrows* of the Mountain and lower part of the Columbian Vally."

19. In Voorhis No. 4 Clark adds the "*Cla-mor-to-micks*" and "*Potoash*" tribes.

20. After this entry in Voorhis No. 4 Clark adds: "*Qui eet to, Chil lâte hackle, Qui ne chart,* and *Pailsh*" tribes.

21. This entry is missing from Voorhis No. 4.

22. Many of the place-names in this section appear to have been added to blank spaces or substituted for erasures in Codex I.

23. Here on the right margin of p. 11 of Codex I appears a small sketch of Point William, today's Tongue Point, Oregon (fig. 51).

24. Cumulative mileages are given for the following entries in Voorhis No. 4.

25. Following this entry in Voorhis No. 4 there appears some enumeration of Indian tribes as are given in part 2 of this chapter. There are some small differences in numbers.

26. After this section Clark adds the following in the field book. He is apparently estimating courses and distances for the return trip over the Rocky Mountains. See also some similar notes in part 3 of this chapter.

To the foot of the Mountain is	S. 85 E	28 miles
To Travelers rest over monts.	N 80° E.	107 miles

From Travelers rest to the dividing ridge at Snake Indian portage or Lewis's portage from Jeffersons R	S 24 E	175 miles
From Travelers rest creek to pine Island rapid comesmt [commencement?] of Mtns.	S 85 E	99 miles

Part 2: Estimate of the Western Indians

Lewis and Clark prepared these documents at Fort Clatsop and later, as rough equivalents of the "Estimate of the Eastern Indians" which was drawn up at Fort Mandan. However, the material here provides much less information than the earlier document, being largely confined to names, locations, and estimated numbers. The "Western Indians" are those located west of the Continental Divide, especially on the Columbia drainage and the Northwest Coast. Much of the information would have come from Indian informants, since it chiefly concerns tribes wholly unknown to whites, except for those on the coast and those met by the party on their route of travel. Some of these tribes the captains had never actually seen, and among those they had seen were many obscure bands, subdivisions of larger groups now long extinct or absorbed into others. Identification in a number of cases is problematical.

The first item is in both Lewis's and Clark's hands and is found in Codex I. Lewis's part covers the Indian tribes the party encountered from the Rocky Mountains to the coast, Clark then follows with a list of the coastal Indians to the north and south of the mouth of the Columbia River. The next item, also from Codex I and in Clark's hand, names tribes from the coastal region east toward the Rocky Mountains and appears to supplement the other list and account for additional tribes. The numbers to the side of the Indian tribal names appear to represent an attempt to bring some order to the multiple lists. This may have been done in preparation for the final estimate, called a supplement by Clark at the end of the second document; the supplement is here printed as the third item. Perhaps as a precaution to losing Codex I and as a preliminary to the supplement, a final list was made and arranged under the numbering system. This list was placed in Voorhis No. 4, clearly a compilation of the lists in Codex I, but set up under the numbering system with adjustments in tribal populations. The combined version of Voorhis No. 4 may be the one referred to on June 13, 1806, or that reference may be to the supplement. Lewis's and Clark's lists from Codex I are printed here with footnotes explaining the differences in Voorhis No. 4.

Two additional items are related to lists of Indians of this later period. Both are in Clark's hand and are loose sheets in the Voorhis Collection of the Missouri Historical Society (see Appendix C, vol. 2). One is titled "Indian Names" and appears to be a preliminary list of Indian tribal names but with no additional comments. Another, single sheet is titled, "A List of the Nations and tribs of Indians residing West of the Rocky Mountains &c." Clark there lists the following tribes, giving some marginal comments very similar to those in the lists below: Clat Sops, Chnnooks, Wau-ki-e-coms, Cath-lah-mahs, Skellutes, Cal-la-mah's, and Quath-lah-pottles.

[Lewis and Clark][1]

Estimate of the Western Indians

Name of Indian Nations and their Places of general residence	No of Lodges	Probable No. of Souls
1 *Oote-lash-schute* residing in spring & summer on the W. side of R. Mountains and winter and fall on the Missouri on it's waters	33	400
2 *Cho-pun-nish* of the Kooskooske River	220	3600
3 *Cho-pun-nish* of Lewis's River above the entrance of the Kooskooske	80	1200
4 *Cho-pun-nish* of Lewis's River below the entrance of the Kooskooske	30 h. 10 t.	2300
5 *Sokulk* residing on the Columbia near the entrance of Lewis's R.[2]	120	2400
54 *Cuts-sâh-nim* in the same neighbourhd and up the Tapteete river	60	1200
6 *Chim'-nah-pum'* residing at the forks of a large river which falls into the Columbia about 15 m. above Lewis's R.	42	1860
7 *Wal-low wal-low* from the entrance of Lewis's River down the Columbia to Musselshell rappid	46	1000
8 *Pish-quit-pahs* on the Columbia from Musselshell rappid to the commencement of the high country	71	1600[3]
9 *Wah-how-pum* on the Columbia from the commencement of the highlands to the neighbourhood of the great falls	33	700
10 *E-ne-shuh* residing at the great falls of the Columbia	41	1200

11	*E-che-lute* residing at the upper part of the great narrows of the Columbia	21 h.	600[4]
12 *	*Chil-luck-kit-te-quaw* residing next below the narrows and extending down on the N. side of the Columbia nearly to the River Labeach	56 h	1000[5]
14	*Shah-ha-la* residing at the grand rappid and extending down to Wappetoe Island	62 h.	1300[6]
20	*Skil-lutes* commencing at the wappetoe Island and extending down to the marsey Islands Cow-e-lis-kee river N	50 h	1500[7]
21	*Wack-ki-a-cums* on the North Side of the Columbia opposite to the marshey Islands.	11 h	100[8]
22	*Cath-lâh-mâhs* on the South side of the Columbia opposite the lower part of the mashey Islands.	9 h	200[9]
23	*Chin-nooks* on the North side of the Columbia to it's entrance and on Chinnook River	28 h.	400
24	*Clât-sops* on the South side of the Columbia and a few miles along the S. E. Coast on both sides of Point Adams.	14 h.	200
25	*Kil-la-mucks* from the Clâtsops of the coast along the S. E. Coast many miles	50 h.	1000
39	*Kil-laxt-ho-kles* from the Chinnooks along the N N W. Coast	8 h.	100
39	*Chiltz* from the Chiltz North Westwardly along the same coast	38 h.	700
39	*Cla-moi-to-mich's* from the Queneelt N. Westwardly along the same coast	12	200[10]
	Total		24,760

Febr. 8th 1805

Note— there are several other nations residing on the Columbia below the grand rappids and on some streams which discharge themselves into the same whose names we have learnt but have not any proper data from which to calculate ther probable number; therefor omitted

40	*Potoash's* reside North westerley of the S of the Cla moi to mich on the Sea Coast	10 h.	200

40	*Qun-ni-ites* from the potoashs North westwardly along the Same Coast	60	1000
40	*Qui eet so* from the qunaniite North westerly along the Sea coast	18 h.	250
41	*Chil-lâte* from the quieetso N Westerly along the Same Coast	8 h.	150
41	*Co-lâst-ho-cle* from the Chillate N. Westerly along the same coast	10 h.	200
41	*Quin-ne-chart* verry noumerous resideng from the Calasthocle's N Westerly along the Same Coast and on the Slashes and Creeks off the Coast	—	2000
40	*Pailsh* reside between the potoash and quineles [Qun-ni-ites?] on the Sea Cost	10	200
26	*Luck-ton* Tribe reside to S. E. E. of the Kil-â-mox on the Sea Coast and Speak the Kil-a-mox Language	Indians informs us that this nation is not noumerous	200
27	*Ka-hun-kle* Nation on the Same Coast to the S. S. E. & Speake or understand the Same Language	Noumerous	400
28	*Lick-â-wis* Nation do do do	large town	800
29	*Youck-cone* do do do do	large houses do	700
30	*Neck-ê-to* do do do do	large Town	700
31	*Ul-se-âh* do do do do	Small Town	150
32	*You-itts* Tribe do do do	do do	150
33	*Shi-â-stuck-kle* Nation do do do	large do	900
34	*Kil-la-wats* do do do do	do	500

The following Nations resid on the Same Coast to the S. W. of the abov and Speake differant Languages.

35	1st *Cook-koo-oose* Nation I saw Several prisones from this nation with the Clatsops and Kilamox, they are much fairer than the common Indians of this quarter, and do not flatten their heads		1500
36	2 *Shal-la-lah* Nation are Said to be noumerous		1200

37	*Luck-kar-So* Nation	do do do	1200
38	*Han-na-kal-lal* Nation	do do	600
			13,000

Extent Indian information

1. This first estimate is from Codex I, pp. 147–49, reading backwards. See also the note at January 29, 1806, for how this material fits into Codex I. Lewis wrote the first part (pp. 148–49) through the *"Note,"* then Clark completed the list (p. 147) from the Potoash to the Han-na-kal-lal. The numbers to the side may represent a later addition in order to arrange the tribes for the final list, here printed as the last document in this part. There is a red vertical line running through these three pages.
2. Voorhis No. 4 adds "and up the [Taptarle?] River."
3. Voorhis No. 4 has "91" lodges, and "2600" people.
4. Voorhis No. 4 has "20" and "1000."
5. Voorhis No. 4 has "1400." The asterisk at this entry probably relates to the one at the end of Clark's entry for the "Smack-shop Nation," which is listed as number 13.
6. Voorhis No. 4 has "1800."
7. Voorhis No. 4 has "2500." To this side of this entry is a symbol that resembles a circle with a cross through it; its purpose is unknown. "Cow-e-lis-kee river" appears to be a substitution for erasures.
8. Voorhis No. 4 has "200."
9. Voorhis No. 4 has "300."
10. Voorhis No. 4 has "260."

[Clark][1]

Estimate of Western Indians

	Name of Indian nations and their Places of General residence	No. of Lodges or Houses	Probable No. of Souls
	⟨*Cal-la-mak's* Tribe reside on a Creek which falls into the Columbia on the North Side at the lower part of the Columbia vally⟩	10	200
18	*Quath-lah-poh-tle* Nation reside on the N. Side of the Columbia above the enterance of Cah-wah-na-hi-oots river and opposit the lower point of the Wappatoe Island	14	300[2]
	Clan-nar-min-a-mon on the S W Side of the Wappato Island	12	280

477

	Cath-lah-cum-up's on the South Side of the Columbia opposit Wappato Isd.	6	150[3]
	Clan-in-na-tas on Wappato Island above the Cathlahcumups on S. Side	5	100[4]
19	*Cath-lah-nah-quiah* on Wappato Island above the Chaninnatas on the S. Side	6	150[5]
19	*Clack-Star* Nation on a Small river which falls in on the South Side of Wappeto Island	20	350[6]
19	*Cath-lah com-mah-tup* on the main Shore South of the Wappato Island	3	70[7]
17	*Ne-mal-quin-ner* Tribe reside on the Multnomah river on the N E Side above the wappato Island	4	100[8]
17	*Mult-no-mah* Nation imediately below the enterance of the Multnomah river into the Columbia on Wappato Island and on S. Side of Columbia	6	200[9]
17	*Clan-nah-queh* Tribe of Multnomahs on the S. Side of Columbia or on Wappato island a fiew miles below the Multnomah	4	130
16	*Shotos* Nation on the N. Side of the Columbia back of a pond and nearly opposit to the Clan nah quihs ½ me. from R.	8	160[10]
14	*Ne-er-cho-ki-oo* tribe on the S. Side of the Columbia above the Multnomah river this is a tribe of the Sha-a-lah Nation	2	40[11]
15th	*Ne-cha-co-kee* Nation on the S. Side of the Columbia opposit to the Dimond Isld.	large 1	100
		101	⟨2330⟩
41	*Clark-a-mus* Nation noums. reside on a river of the Same name which heads in Mt. Jefferson and falls into the Multnomah on its N E Side about 40 miles up it	Houses	800[12]
42	*Cush-hooks* on the N. E. Side of the Multnomah imediately below the falls 60 ms. up.	do	250[13]
43	*Char-cow-ah* N. on the S. W. Side of the Multnomah imediately above the falls of that river	do	200

478

44	Cal-lah-po-e-wahs Nation very noumerous and inhabid the Country on both Sides of the Multnomah above the Charcowah's		2000
52	Skâd-dâts Nation reside on the Catteract river about 25 miles North of the Falls of the Columbia live by hunting		200
52	Squân-nar-oos tribe on the Catteract river		120
52	Shal-lât'tos do on the Catteract river		100
53	Shan-wap-poms N. on do and Tap-teut Riv		400
		Soles	6400
	⟨To-war-nâh-hi-ooks or Snake Indians reside on a river high up of the Same name which discharges itself into the Columbia imediately above the falls⟩		1000
			7200
48	Wil-le-let-po Nation reside North of the S W. mountains on the heads of We-au-cum river which discharges itself into Lewis's river on the S W Side above Kooskooske river		250
49	Wil-le-wah's on a river of the Same name which discharges itself into Lewis's river above Kooskooske on the S. W. and on the Lower Side of that river		500
50	Sho-Sho-ne's on the South fork of Lewis's river as high up as the falls of that river, and on the Nemo, Watshlem, Shallett, Shust pellanimmo, She-com-shink, Timmooenumlarwas & the Cop coppahark rivers branches of the Said South Branch of Lewis's river		3000
51	Sho-Sho ne's of the East branch of Lewis's river near the head of Jeffersons river in the mountains	60	800
46	Sho-bar-boo-be-er a band of Shoshonies or Snake Indians reside on the S W Side of the Multnomah river high up the Said river		1000[14]

45	*Sho-Sho-nes* or Snake Indians resideing in winter and fall on the Multnomah river Southwardly of the S W. mounts. and in Spring and Summer on the heads of Wallar wallar, youmatolam, R. LaPage and the To-war-ne-hi ooks rivers and at the falls of the latter for the purpose of fishing for the Salmon on those river &c. not known	3000 8550
47	*Sho-Sho-nes* on the Multnomah and its waters the residence of whome is not particulary known	6000
57	*Whe-el-po* Nation on both Side of Clarks river of the great falls and down to the enterance of Lastaro river	2500
58	*Hi-high-e-nim-mo* from the forks to the enterance of the Lastaro river on both Sides	800[15]
59	*Lar-ti-e-lo's* at the falls of the Las-taro R. below the great Lake Waytom on both Sides of the Said river	600
60	*Sket-so-mish's* on a river of the Same name which falls into Las-taro River below the falls of that river around Waytom Lake and on 2 Islands in Lake	2000
61	*Mick-suck-seal-toms* Tribe on Clarks River above the falls of that river	300
61	*Ho-hil-po's* Tribe on Clarks river above the Micksuckscaltoms abve falls	300
61	*Tus kip âh* Nation or *Tush-she-pâh* a Northerly branch of Clarks river and on Clarks river occasionally. Sometimes pass over to the Missouri to kill Buffalow	430
61[16]	*Oat-lash-schute* tribe as mentioned on the other side of the next leaf a part of the Tush he pah Nation includes the Tush-she-pah Ho-hil-po's & Misk-Suck-Seal-tom Tribes all of them rove on Clark's river and occasionally cross over to the Missouri for the purpose of makeing robes and dried meat &c.	—
55	*La-hân-na* Nation reside on both sides of Columbia above Clarks river and as far up the Columbia as is known by the Chopunnish & other nations which we have Seen on the Columbian waters	2000

56	*Coos-pel-lars* Nation reside on a large fork of the Columbia which discharges itself into that river on it's East Side above the enterance of Clarks river, and heads with the waters of Hudsons bay	600 [17]
13*	*Smack-shop* Nation reside on the Columbia either Side below the Chil luck kit quaw nation and extending down to near the grand rapids	800
		16,330

The estimate of the Nations and tribes West of the Rocky Mountains may be Seen More Correctly Stated in a Supplement accompanying these Books   WC   80,000 Soles [18]

69,040

1. This item in Clark's hand is from Codex I, pp. 150–51, 153–55, reading backwards; it is interrupted by a map of the Cape Disappointment area (fig. 1). The numbering system is continued from the previous document (see note there) and the list itself appears to name additional tribes not accounted for on the previous list. Again red vertical lines run through these pages.
2. Voorhis No. 4 gives it as "900."
3. Voorhis No. 4 gives it as "450."
4. Voorhis No. 4 gives it as "200."
5. Voorhis No. 4 gives it as "400."
6. Voorhis No. 4 gives it as "28" and "1200."
7. Voorhis No. 4 gives it as "170."
8. Voorhis No. 4 gives it as "200."
9. Voorhis No. 4 gives it as "800."
10. Voorhis No. 4 gives it as "460."
11. Voorhis No. 4 gives it as "140."
12. Voorhis No. 4 gives it as "1800."
13. Voorhis No. 4 gives it as "650."
14. Voorhis No. 4 gives it as "1600."
15. Voorhis No. 4 gives it as "1300."
16. To the side of this entry Clark has written, "See next sheet." The reference is to p. 149 of Codex I, the "next sheet" reading backward from here on p. 151. See the first entry in the previous document here.
17. Voorhis No. 4 gives it as "1600."
18. This paragraph is written in red ink. The supplement is the next document as printed here. The "80,000" represents the total given in the next document.

[Clark][1]

Estimate of Western Indians

	Names of Indian Nations and their places of General Residence	No of Houses or Lodges	Probable No. of Souls
1	*Sho-sho-ne* Nation reside in Spring and Summer on the East fork of Lewis's river a branch of the Columbia, and winter and fall on the Missouri	60	800
2	*Oate-lash-schute* Tribe of the *Tush-she-pah* Nation reside in Spring and Summer in the Rocky Mountains on Clarks river, and winter and fall on the Missouri and its waters	33	400
3	*Chopunnish* Nation residing on the Kooskooske river below the forks and on Colters Creek &c. and who Sometimes pass over to the Missouri	large Lodges	2,000
4	*Pel-lote-pal-lah* [X: *Pel-loat-pal-lah*] Band of Chopunnish reside on the Kooskooske above the forks and on the Small Streams which fall into that river west of the rocky mountains, & chopunnish river and Sometimes pass over to the Missouri	do	1,600
5	*Ki-moo-e-nim* Band of Chopunnish N. reside on Lewis'es river above the enterance of the Kooskooske as high up that river as the forks	do	800
6	*Y-e-let po* Band of Choponish[2] reside under the S W. Mountains on a Small river which falls into Lewis's river above the entrance of the Kooskooke which they call *we-are-cum*	do	250
7	*Wil-le-wah* Band Choponish[3] on a river of the same name which discharges itself into Lewis's river on the S W Side below the forks of that river	do	500
8.	*So-yen-now* Band (of Choponiesh[)] on the N Side of the E fork of Lewis's river from it's junction to the rocky mountains and on La-mal-tar Creek	do	400
9	*Chopunnish* of Lewis's river below the entrance of Kooskooske on either Side of that river to it's junction with the Columbia	h Ld 30 10	2,300
10.	*Sokulk* Nation reside on the Columbia above the entrance of Lewis's river as high up as the enterance of Clarks river	120	2,400

11.	*Chim-nah-pum* on the N W side of the Columbia both above and below the enterance of Lewis's river and on the Tapteel R which falls into the Columbia 15 M. above Lewis's R.	42	1,860
[12?]	*Wal-low-wallow* Nation on both Sides of the Columbia from the enterance of Lewis's river as low as the Muscle shell rapid and in winter pass over to the waters of the Tapteel river	46	1,600
13	*Pish-quit-pah's Nation* reside from the Muscle rapid & on the the N. side of the Columbia to the Commencement of the high Country this N. winter on the waters of the Tapteel river	71	2600
14	*Wah-how-pum* Nation reside on the N. bank of th Columbia in different Bands from the pishquitpahs as low as River Lapage the differt. bands of the nation winter on the waters of Tapteel & Columbia Rvs.	33	700
15.	*E-ne-chur* Nation reside at the Great falls of Columbia on either Side are Stationary	41	1,200
16	*E-shel-lute* Nation reside at the upper part of the Great Narrows of Columbia on the N. Side (is the great mart for all the Country)	h 21	1,000
17	*Chil-luck-kit-te-quaw* N. residing next below the narrows and extending down on the N. Side of the Columbia to River Labeech	h 32	1,400
18	*Smock-Shop* Nation Band of Chil luck kit-te quaw[4] reside on the Columbia on each Side from the Enterance of River Labiech to the neighbourhood of the Great Rapids of that river	24	800
			22,610[5]
[19?]	*Sha-ha-la* Nation reside at the Grand rapids of the Columbia and extend down in different Villages as low as the Multnomah river Consisting of the following tribes viz: *y-e-huh* above the rapids, ⟨Wah-clel-lah⟩ Clah-clel-lah below the rapid, the ⟨Chah-hal lah⟩ Wah-clel-lah below all the rapids and the *Ne-er-cho-ki-oo* 1 House 100 sole on the S. side a few miles above the Multnomah R.	62	2800

20	*Wap-pa-to* Indians [6] *Ne-cha-co-kee* Tribe reside on the S. Side of the Columbia a fiew miles below quick Sand river & opposit the dimond Island—(remains)—	1	100
	Shoto Tribe resides on the N. Side of the Columbia back of a pond and nearly opposit the enterance of the multnomah river	8	460
	Mult-no-mah Tribe reside on Wap-pa-tow Island in the Mouth of the Multnomah, the remains of a large nation	6	800
	Clan-nah-quehs Tribe of Moltnomah's on Wappato Island below the Multnomars	4	130
	Ne-mal-quin-ner's a Tribe of Multnom's reside on the N E Side of the Multnomah River 2 ms. above its mouth	4	200
	Cath-lah-com-mah-tup's a Tribe of Multnoms South Side of the Wappato Island on a slew of the Miltnr	3	170
	Cath-lah-nah-qui-ah's Tribe of Multnomies reside on the S W. side of Wappato Island	6	400
	Clack Star N. resides on a Small river which discharges itself on the S W. Side of Wappato Island	28	1,200
	Clan-in-na-ta's resides on the S W. Side of Wappato Island	5	200
	Cath-lah-cum-ups on the main Shore South West of Wappato Island	6	450
	Clan-nar-min-na-mun's on the S. W. side of the Wappato Island	12	280
	Quath-lah-poh-tle's N. reside on the S W. of the Columbia above the Enterance of *Cah-wah-na-hi-ooks* river opposit the Low pt. of Wappato Isd.	14	900
	Cal-la-maks reside on a creek which falls into the Columbia on the N. Side at the lower part of the Columbia Valley N. Side	10	200
21	*Skil-lute* Nation resides on the Columbia on each Sides in different Villages from the lower part of the Columbian Vally as low as the Sturgeon Island and on either Side of the *Coweliskee* River	50	2500

	Hull-loo-et-tell on the Cow e lis kee ⟨above⟩[7]		
22	*Wack-ki-a-cums* reside on the N. Side of the Columbia opposite the Marshey Islands	11	200
23	*Cath-lâh-mâhs* reside on the S. Side of the Columbia opposit to the Seal Islands	9	300
24	*Chin-nook's* reside on the N. side of the Columbia to its enterance & on Chinnook river	28	400
25	*Clât Sops* N. reside on the S. Side of the Columbia and a few miles along the S. E. coast on both Sides of point Adams	14	200
26	*Kil-la-mucks* N. from the Clât sops of the coast along the S. E. coast for many ms.	50	1,000
27	Indian information those Nations Speak the Kil-a-mucks Lg:[8]		
	Luck-tons reside on the sea coast to the S. S E. of the Kil-la-mucks ⟨and speak their Lagg.⟩	houses	200
	Ka-hun-kle's do do do S. S E of the Luck-tons	—	400
	Lick-a-wis do do do to the S. S E large town	—	800
	Yorick-cone's do do do do do houses	—	700
	Neck-ê-to's do do do do large town	—	700
	Ul-se-âh's do do do do Small town	—	150
	You-ilts do do do do do	—	150
	She-a-stuck-kle's do do do do large town	—	900
	Kil-la-wats do do do do do	—	500 39,140[9]
28.	Indian information[10] reside to the South of the Killamox & Speak a Dift Language		
	Cook-koo-oose Nation reside on the Sea Coast to the South of the *Kil-la-wats*	hous	1500

	Shal-la-lah Nation on the Same Course to the South	—	1,200
	Luck-kar-So Nation on the Same Course to the South &c	—	1200
	Han-na-kal-lal Nation on the Same Course to the South &c	—	600
29.	Information of different Indians[11] on the N W Coast		
	Kil-laxt-ho-kle's T. on the Sea coast from the Chinooks to the N N W.	[8?]	100
	Chiltz N. from the Killaxthokles along the N N. W Coast	38	700
	Cla-moc-to-mich's from the chiltz along the N N W. Coast	12	260
	Potoash's reside on the Same Coast N Westwarly of the Clamochokle	10	200
	Pailsh T. reside from the potash on the N W. coast &c	10	200
	Qui-ni-ilt's from the pailsh along the N W Coast &c	60	1,000
	Qui-eet-so's from the quiniilts along the N W. Coast &c	18	250
	Chil-late's from the quieettso along the N W. coast &c	8	150
	Ca-last-ho-cle from the Chillâte N W. allong the Same Coast	10	200
	Quin-ne-chart N. reside on the Sea Coast & Creeks N. & N W. of the Calasthocles	—	2,000
30	*Clark-a-mus* Nation reside on a large river of the Same mame which heads in Mt. Jefferson and discharges itself into the Multnomah 40 m. up that river on its N. E. Side. this N. has Several villages on either Side	Houses	1,800
31	*Cush-hooks* N reside on the N E. bank of the Multnomah imediately below the falls of that river about 60 m. above its enterance into the Colm.	do	650

32	*Char-cow-ah* N. reside on the S W. bank of the Multnomah imediately above the falls and take the Salmon in that river	do	200
33	*Cal-lah-po-e-wah* Nation inhabit the Country on both Sides of the Multnomah above the Charcowahs for great extent	—	2,000
34	*Sho-Sho-ne* (or Snake indians) residing in winter and fall on the Multnomah river Southerly of the S. W. mountains, and in Spring and Summer on the heads of the *To-war-ne hi ooks, La Page, You-ma-tol-am*, and *Wal-lar-wal-lar* rivers, and more abundantly at the falls of the Towarnehiooks, for the purpose of fishing	—	3,000
35	*Sho-Sho-ne's* on the Multnomah and its waters, the residence of them is not well known to us, or Inds. of the Columbia Say abt.	—	6,000
36	*Sho-bar-boo-be-er* Band of Shoshones reside on the S W Side of the Multnomah river, high up the Said river	—	1,600
37	*Sho-Sho-ne's* resideing on the S. fork of Lewis's river and on the Nemo, Walshlemo, Shal-lett, Shushpel-lanimmo, She com skink, Timmoonumlarwas, and the Cop cop pahark rivers branches of the South fork of Lewises river	—	3,000
[38?]	We saw parts of those Tribes at the long narrows[12] *Skâd-dâts* N. reside on Cattaract river 25 m. N. of the big narrow. live by Hunting[13] hunt deer &c.	—	200
	Squân-nar-oos do do below the Skaddats	—	120
	Shal-lât-tos do do above do	—	100
	Shan-wap-pom's reside on the heads of Catteract river & Tapteel river		400
			67710[14]
39	*Cuts-sâh-nim* Nation reside on both Sides of the Columbia Above the Sokulks & on the Northerly branches of the tapteel river and also on the *Wah-na-a-chee*[15] river	60	1,200
	La-hân-na Nation reside on both Sides of the Columbia above the enterance of Clarks river	120	2,000

Coos-pel-lar's Nation reside on a river which falls into the Columbia to the N. of Clarks river	30	1600
Whe-el-po Nation reside on both Sides of Clarks river from the enterance of the Lastaw to the Great falls of Clarks R	130	2,500
Hi-high-e-nim-mo Nation from the enterance of the Lastaw into Clarks river on both Sides of the Lestaw as high as the forks	45	1300
Lar-ti-e-lo's Nation at the Falls of the Lastaw river below the great Waytom Lake, on both Sides of the river	30	600
Skeet-so-mish Nation resides on a Small river of the Same name which discharges itself into the Lastaw below the falls around the Waytom Lake and on two islands within the Said Lake	120	2,000
Mick-suck-seal-tom Tribe of the *Tushshepah* reside on Clark river above the great falls of that river, in the rocky Mounts.	25	300
Ho-hil-pos a tribe of do. on Clarks river above the *Micksuck-seal-toms* in the Rocky mountains	25	300
Tush-She-pah's Nation reside on a N. fork of Clarks river and rove on Clarks river in Spring and Summer and the fall and winter on the Missouri. The *Oat-lash-shut* is a band of this nation	35	430
		80,000

West of the Rocky Mountains is 80,000 [16] Sol

1. This table is from a separate document at the American Philosophical Society and called a "Supplement" by Clark in the previous document. It is in Clark's hand and written on four sheets of letter paper together with a map of Bonhomme Island; the map will appear in volume 8 of this edition. (See also Appendix C, vol. 2.) This table probably postdates the Fort Clatsop period and may have been made as late as June 1806, or even later. Lewis on June 13, 1806, wrote, "we made a digest of the Indian Nations West of the Rocky Mountains which we have seen and of whom we have been repeated[ly] been informed by those with whom we were conversant." That digest may be this supplement or it may be the list in Voorhis No. 4, which is a compilation of the lists in Codex I. If the map of Bonhomme Island in present Bon Homme County, South Dakota, and Knox County, Nebraska, relates to the timing of the supplement then it could have been written as late as September 1, 1806, when they passed the island. The former date is more plausible. It

is placed here because of its close association with the Fort Clatsop lists of western Indian tribes. There are small check marks next to many of the numbers that list the tribes. Following the list of tribes, on the final sheet are these figures (the longer set struck out and difficult to read):

     12230   ⟨22010
     29520   ??140
     41750   ?1770
            29520⟩

 2. The words "of Choponish" are an interlineation in red.
 3. "Choponish" is an interlineation written in red.
 4. "Band of Chil luck kit-te quaw" is an interlineation in red.
 5. This subtotal is given in red.
 6. This subheading is in the left margin of the document, outside a brace enclosing all the tribes under the number 20.
 7. Above this line in red is the number "32,890," perhaps a subtotal to this point. One word follows the deleted word "above" but is not legible.
 8. Another marginal subheading, including all the tribes under number 27.
 9. This subtotal is given in red.
 10. Another marginal subheading, including all the tribes under number 28. The remainder of the sentence is in red.
 11. Another marginal subheading, including all the tribes under number 29. The remainder of the sentence is in red.
 12. Another marginal subheading, including all the tribes under number 38.
 13. The words "live by Hunting" are in red.
 14. This subtotal is written in red.
 15. This word appears to be an addition to a blank space and written by Lewis.
 16. The number "80,000" is given in red.

IDENTIFICATION OF WESTERN INDIANS[1]

Lewis and Clark's Name	Modern Name
1. Sho-sho-ne	Shoshones
2. Oate-lash-schute or Tush-she-pah	Flatheads or Salish
3. Chopunnish	Nez Perces
4. Pel-lote-pal-lah	Nez Perces
5. Ki-moo-e-nim	Nez Perces
6. Y-e-let po [Wil-le-let-po]	Cayuses
7. Wil-le-wah	Nez Perces?
8. So-yen-now	Palouses?
9. Chopunnish	Nez Perces and Palouses
10. Sokulk	Wanapams

11. Chim-nah-pum	Yakimas
12. Wal-low-wal-low	Walulas or Walla Wallas
13. Pish-quit-pah's	Yakimas
14. Wah-how-pum	Teninos
15. E-ne-chur	Teninos
16. E-skel-lute	Wishram-Wascos
17. Chil-luck-kit-te-quaw	Wishram-Wascos
18. Smock-Shop	Wishram-Wascos
19. Sha-ha-la	Watlala Chinookans
Y-e-huh	Watlala Chinookans
Clah-clel-lah	Watlala Chinookans
Wah-clel-lah	Watlala Chinookans
Ne-er-cho-ki-oo	Watlala Chinookans
20. Wap pa to Indians	Chinookans of Sauvie Island
Ne-cha-co-kee	Chinookans
Shoto	Chinookans
Mult-no-mah	Chinookans
Clan-nah-queh's	Chinookans
Ne-mal-quin-ner's	Chinookans
Cath-lah-com-mah-tups	Chinookans
Cath-lah-nah-qui-ah's	Chinookans
Clack Star	Clatskanies
Clan-in-na-ta's	Chinookans
Cath-lah-cum-ups	Chinookans
Clan-nar-min-na-mun's	Katlaminimin Chinookans
Quath-lah-poh-tle's	Cathlapotle Chinookans
Cal-la-maks	Chinookans; perhaps Tillamooks
21. Skil-lute	Watlala Chinookans
Hull-loo-et-tell	Watlala Chinookans
22. Wack-ki-a-cums	Wahkiakums
23. Cath-lâh-mâhs	Cathlamets
24. Chin-nook's	Chinooks
25. Clât-sop's	Clatsops
26. Kil-la-mucks	Tillamooks
27. Kil-a-mucks language	Salishan language
Luck-tons	Salishans; perhaps Nestuccas
Ka-hun-kle's	Salishans
Lick-a-wis	Yaquinas
Yorick-cone's	Yaquinas
Neck-ê-to's	Alseas

Ul-se-âh's	Alseas
You-ilts	Yahaches (Alseas)
She-a-stuck-kle's	Siuslaws
Kil-la-wats	Lower Umpquas
28. South of Killamox	
Cook-koo-oose	Coos
Shal-la-lah	Nasomahs (Coquilles?)
Luck-kar-So	Tututnis
Han-na-kal-lal	Tututnis?
29. On the N. W. Coast	
Kil-laxt-ho-kle's	Athapascan Kwalhiokwas?
Chiltz	Chehalis
Cla-moc-to-mick's	Chinookans
Potoash's	Salishans
Pailsh	Copalis Salishans
Qui-ni-ilt's	Quinaults
Qui-eet-so's	Queets
Chil-lâte's	Quileutes
Ca-last-ho-cle	Hohs?
Quin-ne-chart	Makahs
30. Clark-a-mus	Clackamas Chinookans
31. Cush-hooks	Clowwewalla Chinookans
32. Char-cow-ah	Clowwewalla Chinookans
33. Cal-lah-po-e-wah	Calapooyas
34. Sho-sho-ne . . . on the Multnomah river	Northern Paiutes?
35. Sho-sho-ne's on the Multnomah	Northern Paiutes?
36. Sho-bar-boo-be-er	Mono-Paviotso division of Shoshones
37. Sho-sho-ne's . . . on the S. fork of Lewis's river	Shoshones
38. At the long narrows	
Skâddâts	Pisquows or Kittitas
Squân-nar-oos	Pisquows or Kittitas
Shal-lât-tos	Pisquows or Kittitas
Shan-wap-pom's	Pisquows or Kittitas
39. Cuts-sâh-nim	Yakimas
La-han-na	Pend d'Oreilles?
Coos-pel-lar's	Kalispels
Whe-el-po	Colvilles
Hi-high-e-nim-mo	Sanpoils or Spokanes

Lar-ti-e-to's	Spokanes
Skeet-so-mish	Skitswishes or Coeur d'Alenes
Mick-suck-seal-tom	Flatheads or Salish?
Ho-hil-pos	Flatheads or Salish
Tush-she-pah's	Flatheads or Salish

1. Modern and exact identification of many of these Indian groups is impossible because these people had often disappeared or had been absorbed into other tribes by the time systematic investigation of the native peoples of the area was undertaken. Many of them may have been only distant bands or small village units of larger cultural groupings and the explorers, moving quickly through the area, were not able to make the subtle distinctions and associations that would provide positive identification today. Moreover, many of these people were never seen by Lewis and Clark and their existence was based solely on Indian information, which may have been garbled. In fact, some groups may never have existed as separate or actual units. In some instances Lewis and Clark were the first and the last to note a band, village, or tribe. Later writers took the captains at their word and simply used the explorers' terminology to identify the Indians, putting us back to where we began. We have tried to correct this circle of confusion by identifying Lewis and Clark's more obscure western Indians by linguistic, geographic, and cultural relations where possible, "Chinookan" being a frequent designation. Some of the groups, particularly the more dominant ones, were discussed in the captains' daily entries and are identified in notes at those points, along with their certain identification here. Readers may wish to turn to those entries to obtain more complete information. For identifications we have relied on such entry notes and on sources and consultants listed in the present volume.

Part 3: Miscellany

The following are a collection of miscellaneous items that do not fit into other sections of this chapter. These notes were apparently made at Fort Clatsop or are related to the expedition since the party left Fort Mandan in April 1805. Some show elements of the captains' attempts to determine the most expeditious route across the Rocky Mountains on the return trip.

[Clark][1]

Moriah River[2]	47° 29' 10⁴/₁₀" N.
Lower part of the falls is in Latd.	47° 8' 4⁵/₁₀" N.
upper part of the rapids Latd. is	47° 3' 30" N.
Forks of Jefferson	43 30 43
Travelers rest	46 48 28

Up the Missouri to the forks of Jefferson River at the Portage	3096 miles
To the head of the river	24
To Columbia River³	14 = 38
To the Forks of do	18
To the mouth of Tower Creek	14
To Fish Creek	23
To ⟨Flat head⟩ [*NB: Clarks*] river 33 tents	41
To Travelers rest Creek	76
over the Snow mountains	160
To the Forks of *Kos kos ke* River	30⁴
To the mouth of *Kos kos kee* River	60
To the mouth of Ki-moo-e-nim	140
To the great falls of Columbia	168
To Snake Indian River South Sd. 6 miles above the falls	—
To *Timm* or the long narrows	6
To the *Cat-ter-ack* River N. Side	23
To the Grand Shute (or Rapid)	42
To the little rapid at Strawberry Island & last rapid	6
To Quick Sand river S. Side	26
To the Shallow Bey N. Side	136
To Cape Swells N. Side	6
	4149⁵

1. These notes in Clark's hand, giving various latitude readings and mileages from the Missouri to "Cape Swells" on Grays Bay in Wahkiakum County, Washington, appear on the front flyleaf and inside front cover of Codex G (the second item reading backwards). The figures here are frequently different from those in the daily journals. The identification of the places can be found at the end of part 1 of this chapter.

2. Marias River.

3. Not the Columbia itself but an affluent of that river and the men's first contact with its waters. Clark probably means the present Lemhi River or one of its branches.

4. To the side of this entry is the figure, "3496" and under it two figures crossed out, "362" and "401." Perhaps subtotals but arithmetically incorrect.

5. A correct total of these figures would be 4,109.

[Clark]¹

From Clarks point of view
To Cape Disapointment   N 20° W

493

to Point adams	North—
To Fort Clatsop—	N E
to Cape Lookout is	S 12° E
to a point at about 17 miles is	S. 5 E [*some letters illegible*]

Wood river is Latd.   *38° 55' 19" N.*
Longtd. *89° 57' 45"* W
Fort Mandan Latd.   *47° 12' 47"* N.
Longtd. *99 24 45* W.
Mouth of Columbia Latd.   *46° 19' 11.1"* N.
Longtd. *124 57   0*   W.
Head of Missouris

Distance from Wisdom river to the forks of Jefferson S. E. by E to the Creek—

Philanty Rivr 5 miles S W—

The 3 forks is 92 months [miles?] South of the Pine Island rapid at [*blank*] M Course is [*blank*]

Wisdom river is 23½ miles South of the 3 forks   Course S. W

The forks of Jefferson River is 32 miles South of Wisdom river.   Course S W [*blank*] miles

from the mouth of Columbia to the Wapp[ato Island?][2]

1. This material immediately follows Clark's draft of his trip to the coast, January 6–10, 1806, in the little field book at the American Philosophical Society. The items are written in different directions on the page, but apparently in these three parts.

2. This sentence is written sideways on the page. Similar wording is found toward the end of the material in part 1 of this chapter.

[Clark][1]

To pass across from Travelers Rest Creek to the Missouri at the Mouth Dearbourns River is 400 Miles nearer than the route we Came   the Distance across is about 100 Miles Direct and about it is 648 miles by water and 548 by land[2]

From the *Flathead* tents across direct to the mouth of Wisdom River is 100 Miles, and *Saves* 180 Miles to the Missouri—   and this rout Saves about 140 to the Canoes at the Forks of Jeffersons River to pass this rout—

up the Flathead river to the place we Met the first flat heads, thence on their trail to the Missouri River will be 140 miles nearer than around by the Snake Indian Villages on Lewis's River—

From Travelers rest Creek to the 3 forks of the Missouri on a Direct line is S 55° E 169 miles

From Same place to the Mouth of Wisdom R. is S. 38° ⟨W⟩ E 160 m

To Pryor Vally Creek from Same place is S 67° E. 135 Miles

1. This material is again from the draft field book; it follows the table of distances that duplicates the Codex I table in part 1 of this chapter. Clark appears to be trying to determine the most efficient route beyond Travelers' Rest on the return trip.

2. To the side of this paragraph is the following observation. It may have been for January 8, 1806; see Lewis's entry of that day.

Equal altituds the [*blank*] of January 1806 at Fort Clatsop

	h	m	s		h	m	s
A M	8	11	26.5	P M	—	—	—
"		13	43.5		—	—	—
"		16	8.5		—	—	—

[Clark][1]

Ca-la-mox Chief is *O co no*

Call a black rute	She-ne-tock-we
a black berry	Shel-will
a Liquorice root	Cul-wha-mo
whale	E-cu-lah
red berrys grow just over ground	Sol-me
Buzzard	E-pe-ea[2]

3316	3240	46—48
2668	2947	34
648	293	14
		62
100	100	128
548	193	84
		⌊967
		16

From Flat head at the Mouth Travelers rest to Deerborn River at Missouri *Save* 548 100 by land Miles—of *648*

From Flat head Village to Wisdom river *Save* 193 Miles, 170 by land

3316	3244
3096	3090
220	144
200	36
400	180

1. This material is found on the back cover of the draft field book and relates to linguistic information of ethnobotany and ethnozoology, and mileage calculations for the return trip. Some of the figures are uncertain, due to the faded ink.

2. The term is Chinookan *ipa'uwi*, "cormorant." Boas (Ch), 607.

[Lewis][1]

Latitudes of certain points or places from Fort Mandan to Fort Clatsop.

Names of Places			Latitude N. in ° ′ & ″
No.	1.[2]	entrance of the Little Missouri—	47° 31′ 26.2″
No.	7.	on the Eastern bank of the Yellow stone river 2 M. S E of it's Junction with the Missouri—	47° 59′ 40.6″
No.	2.	On Stard ¼ m. above the extremity of 3ed Couse Apl. 14th	47 47 16.8
	17.[3]	On Lard. Shore middle of the 8th course of May 11th—	47 25 33.6
	19.	at Panther Camp wher our perogue upset. took altd. of ☉ May 16th	47 13 51.2
	24.	On Lard. shore 1 m. short of the extremity of the 2d couse of May 27th	47 19 55.9
		Mouth of Maria's river by the Error of Instrument 2° 11′ 40″ is in	47 56 25.3
No.	30	on Std. 5 M. below the R. M.—	46 46 50.2
No.	42	At the Rattlesnake bluff—on Lard. side	44 —[48.1?]

1. This is an undated, loose sheet in the Voorhis Collection of the Missouri Historical Society, giving selected latitudes from Fort Mandan to Fort Clatsop (see Appendix C, volume 2). These may be checked against those given in the journals and those in the table of distances in part 1 of this chapter. The readings are not always in agreement among the various sources.

2. In the margin are the following words which apply to the first three readings: "calculate with Lat. Error of 2° 11′ 40″."

3. In the margin are the following words which apply to readings for numbers 17, 19, and 24: "with error of 2° 40′—."

Volume 6

Sources Cited

Abbot & Hollenberg — Abbot, Isabella A., and George J. Hollenberg. *Marine Algae of California.* Stanford: Stanford University Press, 1976.

Abramowitz — Abramowitz, Alan W. "Cultural Resources Assessment of the Carty Unit, Ridgefield National Wildlife Refuge, Clark County, Washington." University of Washington, Office of Public Archaeology, Institute for Environmental Studies, Report to the U.S. Fish and Wildlife Service. Seattle, 1980.

Allen (MG) — Allen, John Eliot. *The Magnificent Gateway: A Layman's Guide to the Geology of the Columbia River Gorge.* Portland, Oreg.: Timber Press, 1979.

Allen (PG) — Allen, John L. *Passage Through the Garden: Lewis and Clark and the Image of the American Northwest.* Urbana: University of Illinois Press, 1975.

Anderson (SSGV) — Anderson, Bern. *Surveyor of the Sea: The Life and Voyages of Captain George Vancouver.* Seattle: University of Washington Press, 1960.

AOU — American Ornithologists' Union. *Check-list of North American Birds.* 6th ed. Baltimore, Md.: American Ornithologists' Union, 1983. [AOU] in brackets with numbers refers to a species item-number in the book.

Appleman (LC) — Appleman, Roy E. *Lewis and Clark: Historic Places Associated with Their Transcontinental Exploration (1804–06).* Washington, D.C.: United States Department of the Interior, National Park Service, 1975.

Atlas	Moulton, Gary E., ed. *Atlas of the Lewis and Clark Expedition*. Lincoln: University of Nebraska Press, 1983.
Bailey	Bailey, L. H. *Manual of Cultivated Plants*. Rev. ed. New York: Macmillan, 1949.
Barkley	Barkley, T. M., ed. *Atlas of the Flora of the Great Plains*. Ames: Iowa State University Press, 1977.
Barry (BOC)	Barry, J. Neilson. "Broughton on the Columbia in 1792." *Oregon Historical Quarterly* 27 (December 1926): 397–411.
Benson (HLCE)	Benson, Keith R. "Herpetology on the Lewis and Clark Expedition: 1804–1806." *Herpetological Review* 3 (September 1978): 87–91.
Berreman	Berreman, Joel V. "Tribal Distribution in Oregon." *Memoirs of the American Anthropological Association* 47 (1937): 1–67.
Boas (Ch)	Boas, Franz. "Chinook." In *Handbook of American Indian Languages*. Bureau of American Ethnology, Bulletin 40, pt. 1, 559–677. Washington, D.C.: Government Printing Office, 1911.
Boas (KT)	———. *Kathlamet Texts*. Bureau of American Ethnology, Bulletin 26. Washington, D.C.: Government Printing Office, 1901.
Boyd	Boyd, Robert T. "The Introduction of Infectious Diseases among the Indians of the Pacific Northwest, 1774–1874." Ph.D. diss., University of Washington, 1985.
Boyd & Hajda	Boyd, Robert T., and Yvonne P. Hajda. "Seasonal Population Movement Along the Lower Columbia River: The Social and Ecological Context." *American Ethnologist* 14 (May 1987): 309–26.
Burroughs	Burroughs, Raymond Darwin. *The Natural History of the Lewis and Clark Expedition*. East Lansing: Michigan State University Press, 1961.
Butler (PLCV)	Butler, B. Robert. "Perspectives on the Prehistory of the Lower Columbia Valley." *Tebiwa* 8 (Spring 1965): 1–16.
Caywood	Caywood, Louis R. "The Exploratory Excavation

of Fort Clatsop." *Oregon Historical Quarterly* 49 (September 1948): 205–10.

Chevigny — Chevigny, Hector. *Russian America: The Great Alaskan Venture, 1741–1867.* New York: Viking Press, 1965.

Chuinard (MMFC) — Chuinard, Eldon G. "A Medical Mystery at Fort Clatsop." *We Proceeded On* 3 (May 1977): 8–9.

Chuinard (OOMD) — ———. *Only One Man Died: The Medical Aspects of the Lewis and Clark Expedition.* Glendale, Calif.: Arthur H. Clark, 1979.

Chuinard (TJCD) — ———. "Thomas Jefferson and the Corps of Discovery: Could He Have Done More?" *American West* 7 (November 1975): 4–13.

Cook — Cook, Warren L. *Flood Tide of Empire: Spain and the Pacific Northwest, 1543–1819.* New Haven: Yale University Press, 1973.

Coues (HLC) — Coues, Elliott, ed. *History of the Expedition under the Command of Lewis and Clark.* . . . 1893. Reprint. 3 vols. New York: Dover Publications, 1965.

Coues (NLEH) — ———, ed. *New Light on the Early History of the Greater Northwest.* 3 vols. New York: Harper, 1897.

Cox — Cox, Ross. *The Columbia River.* Edited by Edgar I. Stewart and Jane A. Stewart. Norman: University of Oklahoma Press, 1957.

Criswell — Criswell, Elijah Harry. *Lewis and Clark: Linguistic Pioneers.* University of Missouri Studies, vol. 15, no. 2. Columbia: University of Missouri Press, 1940.

Culin — Culin, Stewart. *Games of North American Indians.* Bureau of American Ethnology, Annual Report. Washington, D.C.: Government Printing Office, 1907.

Curtis — Curtis, Edward S. *The North American Indian.* Edited by Frederick W. Hodge. 20 vols. Cambridge: The University Press (vols. 1–5); Norwood, Mass.: Plimpton Press (vols. 6–20), 1907–30.

Cutright (LCIPM) — Cutright, Paul Russell. "Lewis and Clark and Indian Peace Medals." *Bulletin of the Missouri Historical Society* 24 (January 1968): 160–67.

Cutright (LCPN)	———. *Lewis and Clark: Pioneering Naturalists.* Urbana: University of Illinois Press, 1969.
DeVoto	DeVoto, Bernard. *The Course of Empire.* Boston: Houghton Mifflin, 1952.
Dorsey (ST)	Dorsey, J. Owen. "The Gentile System of the Siletz Tribes." *Journal of American Folklore* 3 (July–September 1890): 227–37.
Drucker	Drucker, Philip. *Cultures of the North Pacific Coast.* San Francisco: Chandler Publishing Company, 1965.
Dunlay	Dunlay, Thomas W. "'Battery of Venus': A Clue to the Journal-Keeping Methods of Lewis and Clark." *We Proceeded On* 9 (August 1983): 6–8.
Fernald	Fernald, Merritt Lyndon. *Gray's Manual of Botany.* 8th ed. New York: D. Van Nostrand, 1950.
Frachtenberg	Frachtenberg, Leo J. *Alsea Texts and Myths.* Bureau of American Ethnology, Bulletin 67. Washington, D.C.: Government Printing Office, 1920.
Franchère (AA)	Franchère, Gabriel. *Adventure at Astoria, 1810–1814.* Translated and edited by Hoyt C. Franchère. Norman: University of Oklahoma Press, 1967.
Franchère (JV)	———. *Journal of a Voyage on the North West Coast of North America during the Years 1811, 1812, 1813 and 1814.* Translated by Wessie Tipping Lamb and edited by W. Kaye Lamb. Toronto: Champlain Society, 1969.
Franklin & Dyrness	Franklin, Jerry F., and C. T. Dyrness. *Natural Vegetation of Oregon and Washington.* United States Department of Agriculture, Forest Service General Technical Report PNW-8. Washington, D.C.: Government Printing Office, 1973.
Gassner	Gassner, Julius S., trans. *Voyages and Adventures of La Pérouse.* Trans. from 14th ed., 1875. Honolulu: University of Hawaii Press, 1969.
Gehr	Gehr, Keith D. "The Bay View Cannery-Skamokawa Village Site." *Northwest Anthropological Research Notes* 9 (Spring 1975): 121–38.
Gibbs (AVC)	Gibbs, George. *Alphabetical Vocabulary of the*

	Chinook Language. 1863. Reprint. New York: AMS Press, 1970.
Gibbs (TWO)	———. "Tribes of Western Washington and Northwestern Oregon." *Contributions to North American Ethnology* 1 (1877): 157–241.
Gibson (BMNC)	Gibson, James R. "Bostonians and Muscovites on the Northwest Coast, 1788–1841." In Vaughan, 81–119.
Gough	Gough, Barry M. "The Northwest Coast in Late 18th Century British Expansion." In Vaughan, 47–80.
Gunther (EWW)	Gunther, Erna. *Ethnobotany of Western Washington: The Knowledge and Use of Indigenous Plants by Native Americans.* Rev. ed. Seattle: University of Washington Press, 1973.
Gunther (ILNC)	———. *Indian Life on the Northwest Coast of North America, As Seen by the Early Explorers and Fur Traders during the Last Decades of the Eighteenth Century.* Chicago: University of Chicago Press, 1972.
Hajda	Hajda, Yvonne, P. "Regional Social Organization in the Greater Lower Columbia: 1792–1830." Ph.D. diss., University of Washington, 1984.
Hall	Hall, E. Raymond. *The Mammals of North America.* 2d ed. 2 vols. New York: John Wiley and Sons, 1981.
Hitchcock et al.	Hitchcock, C. Leo, Arthur Cronquist, Marion Ownbey, and J. W. Thompson. *Vascular Plants of the Pacific Northwest.* 5 vols. Seattle: University of Washington Press, 1955–69.
Hodge	Hodge, Frederick Webb, ed. *Handbook of American Indians North of Mexico.* 1912. Reprint. 2 vols. St. Clair Shores, Mich.: Scholarly Press, 1968.
Holmgren	Holmgren, Virginia C. "A Glossary of Bird Names Cited by Lewis and Clark." *We Proceeded On* 10 (May 1984): 28–34.
Horr	Horr, David A. *Oregon Indians.* 2 vols. New York: Garland Publishing Company, 1974.
Howay (1930)	Howay, F. W. "A List of Trading Vessels in the Maritime Fur Trade, 1795–1804." *Proceedings*

	and *Transactions of the Royal Society of Canada*, 3d ser., vol. 24, sec. 2 (1930): 111–34.
Howay (1931)	——. "A List of Trading Vessels in Maritime Fur Trade, 1795–1804." *Proceedings and Transactions of the Royal Society of Canada*, 3d ser., vol. 25, sec. 2 (1931): 117–49.
Howay (1932)	——. "A List of Trading Vessels in Maritime Fur Trade, 1805–1814." *Proceedings and Transactions of The Royal Society of Canada*, 3d ser., vol. 26, sec. 2 (1932): 43–86.
Hymes	Hymes, Dell. *"In Vain I Tried To Tell You": Essays in Native American Ethnopoetics*. Philadelphia: University of Pennsylvania Press, 1981.
Irving (Astor)	Irving, Washington. *Astoria*. 1836. Reprint. Portland, Oreg.: Binfords and Mort, 1967.
Jackson (LLC)	Jackson, Donald, ed. *Letters of the Lewis and Clark Expedition with Related Documents, 1783–1854*. 2d ed. 2 vols. Urbana: University of Illinois Press, 1978.
Jefferson	Jefferson, Thomas. *Notes on the State of Virginia*. Edited by William Peden. Chapel Hill: University of North Carolina Press, 1955.
Jewitt	Jewitt, John R. *The Adventures and Sufferings of John R. Jewitt, Captive of Maquinna*. Edited by Hilary Stewart. Seattle: University of Washington Press, 1987.
Jones et al.	Jones, J. Knox, Jr., David H. Armstrong, Robert S. Hoffmann, and Clyde Jones. *Mammals of the Northern Great Plains*. Lincoln: University of Nebraska Press, 1983.
Kendall	Kendall, Robert L. "Editorial: Taxonomic Changes in North American Trout Names." *Transactions of the American Fisheries Society* 117 (July 1988): 321.
Kidd	Kidd, Robert S. "The Martin Site, Southwestern Washington." *Tebiwa* 10 (Autumn 1967): 13–38.
Large (EA)	Large, Arlen J. "The Empty Anchorage: Why No Ship Came for Lewis and Clark." *We Proceeded On* 15 (February 1989): 4–11.

Lavender	Lavender, David. *The Way to the Western Sea: Lewis and Clark Across the Continent.* New York: Harper and Row, 1988.
Lee et al.	Lee, David S., Carter R. Gilbert, Charles H. Hocutt, Robert E. Jenkins, Don E. McAllister, and Jay R. Stauffer, Jr. *Atlas of North American Freshwater Fishes.* Raleigh: North Carolina State Museum of Natural History, 1980.
Little (CIH)	Little, Elbert L., Jr. *Atlas of United States Trees.* Vol. 1, *Conifers and Important Hardwoods.* Washington, D.C.: United States Department of Agriculture, Forest Service, 1971.
Little (MWH)	———. *Atlas of United States Trees.* Vol. 3, *Minor Western Hardwoods.* Washington, D.C.: United States Department of Agriculture, Forest Service, 1976.
Martin	Martin, Irene. "Ethnohistorical Notes on the Wahkiakum Indians." In Minor (FSS), 40–52.
Meany	Meany, Edmond S. *Vancouver's Discovery of Puget Sound.* New York: Macmillan, 1907.
Menzies	Menzies, Archibald. *Menzies's Journal of Vancouver's Voyage, April to October, 1792.* Edited by C. F. Newcome. Victoria, B.C.: W. H. Collin, 1923.
Minor (ASCR)	Minor, Rick. "Aboriginal Settlement and Subsistence at the Mouth of the Columbia River." Ph.D. diss., University of Oregon, 1983.
Minor (EAS)	———. "An Evaluation of Archaeological Sites on State Park Lands Along the Oregon Coast." Report to the Oregon State Historic Preservation Office, Heritage Research Associates Report No. 44. Eugene, 1986.
Minor (SS)	———. "Archaeological Testing at the Skamokawa Site (45-WK-5), Wahkiakum County, Washington." University of Washington, Office of Public Archaeology, Institute for Environmental Studies, Report to the Soil Conservation Service, Reconnaissance Report 19. Seattle, 1978.
Minor (CAC)	———. "The Carty Artifact Collection from Cathlapotle Village." Report to the U.S. Fish and Wildlife Service, Heritage Research Associates Report No. 78. Eugene, 1989.

Minor (FSS)	———. "Further Archaeological Testing at the Skamokawa Site (45-WK-5), Wahkiakum County, Washington." University of Washington, Office of Public Archaeology, Institute for Environmental Studies, Report to the Soil Conservation Service, Reconnaissance Report 36. Seattle, 1980.
Minor (PH)	———. "Prehistory." In "Prehistory and History of Columbia River Gorge National Scenic Area, Oregon and Washington," by Stephen Dow Beckham, Rick Minor, Kathryn Anne Toepel, and Jo Reese, 31–80. Report to the U.S. Forest Service, Columbia River Gorge National Scenic Area, Heritage Research Associates Report No. 75. Eugene, 1988.
Minor & Toepel	Minor, Rick, and Kathryn Anne Toepel. "Archaeological Investigations at 45CL4, Ridgefield National Wildlife Refuge, Clark County, Washington." Report to the U.S. Fish and Wildlife Service, Heritage Research Associates Report No. 37. Eugene, 1985.
Minor, Toepel, & Beckham	Minor, Rick, Kathryn Anne Toepel, and Stephen Dow Beckham. "An Overview of Investigations at 45SA11: Archaeology in the Columbia River Gorge." Report to Portland District U.S. Army Corps of Engineers, Heritage Research Associates Report No. 39. Eugene, 1985.
Moulton (SJ)	Moulton, Gary E. "The Specialized Journals of Lewis and Clark." *Proceedings of the American Philosophical Society* 127 (June 16, 1983): 194–201.
Murray & Marrant	Murray, Thomas A., and Joel Marrant. "Preliminary Sampling of the Three Rox Site, 35-LNC-33, on the Oregon Coast." In "Contributions to the Archaeology of Oregon, 1981–1982," edited by Don E. Dumond, 47–55. Association of Oregon Archaeologists, Occasional Papers No. 2. Portland, 1983.
Newman	Newman, Thomas M. "Tillamook Prehistory and its Relation to the Northwest Coast Culture Area." Ph.D. diss., University of Oregon, 1959.

Olson (TNC)	Olson, Ronald L. "Adze, Canoe, and House Types of the Northwest Coast." University of Washington *Publications in Anthropology* 2 (November 1927): 1–38.
Pettigrew	Pettigrew, Richard M. "A Prehistoric Culture Sequence in the Portland Basin of the Lower Columbia Valley." University of Oregon Anthropological Papers No. 22. Eugene, 1981.
Phebus & Drucker	Phebus, George, Jr., and Robert M. Drucker. *Archaeological Investigations at Seaside, Oregon.* Seaside: Seaside Museum and Historical Society, 1977.
Prucha (IPM)	Prucha, Francis Paul. *Indian Peace Medals in American History.* Lincoln: University of Nebraska Press, 1971.
Ray (CI)	Ray, Verne F. "The Chinook Indians in the Early 1800s." In Vaughan, 121–50.
Ray (LCEN)	———. "Lower Chinook Ethnographic Notes." University of Washington *Publications in Anthropology* 7 (May 1938): 29–165.
Ray & Lurie	Ray, Verne F., and Nancy Oestreich Lurie. "The Contributions of Lewis and Clark to Ethnography." *Journal of the Washington Academy of Sciences* 44 (November 1954): 358–70.
Ronda (LCAI)	Ronda, James P. *Lewis and Clark among the Indians.* Lincoln: University of Nebraska Press, 1984.
Ross	Ross, Alexander. *Adventures of the First Settlers on the Oregon or Columbia River.* Edited by Milo Milton Quaife. Chicago: R. R. Donnelly and Sons, 1923.
Ruby & Brown (CITC)	Ruby, Robert H., and John A. Brown. *The Chinook Indians: Traders of the Lower Columbia River.* Norman: University of Oklahoma Press, 1976.
Ruby & Brown (IPN)	———. *Indians of the Pacific Northwest: A History.* Norman: University of Oklahoma Press, 1981.
Russell (GEF)	Russell, Carl P. *Guns on the Early Frontiers: A History of Firearms from Colonial Times through the Years of the Western Fur Trade.* Berkeley: University of California Press, 1962.
Saleeby & Pettigrew	Saleeby, Becky M., and Richard M. Pettigrew. "Seasonality of Occupation of Ethnohistorically-

Documented Villages on the Lower Columbia River." In *Prehistoric Places on the Southern Northwest Coast,* edited by Robert E. Greengo, 169–93. Thomas Burke Memorial State Museum Research Report No. 4. Seattle, 1983.

Shaw   Shaw, Robert D. "Report of Excavations: the Martin Site (45PC7), 1974." Washington Archaeological Society, Occasional Paper No. 5. Seattle, 1977.

Silverstein   Silverstein, Michael. "Chinookans of the Lower Columbia." In *Handbook of North American Indians.* Vol. 7, *Northwest Coast,* edited by Wayne Suttles. Washington, D.C.: Smithsonian Institution, forthcoming.

Spier   Spier, Leslie. "Tribal Distribution in Washington." General Series in Anthropology No. 3. Menasha, Wis.: George Banta, 1936.

Spier & Sapir   Spier, Leslie, and Edward Sapir. "Wishram Ethnology." University of Washington *Publications in Anthropology* 3 (May 1930): 151–300.

Strong (CC)   Strong, Thomas Nelson. *Cathlamet on the Columbia.* Portland, Oreg.: Binfords and Mort, 1906.

Suphan   Suphan, Robert J. "An Ethnological Report on the Identity and Localization of Certain Native Peoples of Northwestern Oregon." In Horr, 1 : 167–256.

Swan (ICF)   Swan, James G. "The Indians of Cape Flattery, at the Entrance to the Strait of Fuca, Washington Territory." Smithsonian Contributions to Knowledge No. 220. Philadelphia: Collins, 1869.

Swan (NC)   ———. *The Northwest Coast.* 1857. Reprint. Fairfield, Wash.: Ye Galleon Press, 1966.

Swanton   Swanton, John R. *The Indian Tribes of North America.* Bureau of American Ethnology, Bulletin 145. Washington, D.C.: Government Printing Office, 1952.

Taylor (CsI)   Taylor, Herbert C., Jr. "Anthropological Investigation of the Chehalis Indians Relative to Tribal Identity and Aboriginal Possession of

	Lands." In *Coast Salish and Western Washington Indians*, 5 vols., edited by David A. Horr, 3:117–57. New York: Garland Publishing Company, 1974.
Taylor (CkI)	———. "Anthropological Investigation of the Chinook Indians Relative to Tribal Identity and Aboriginal Possession of Lands." In Horr, 1:103–165.
Taylor (TI)	———. "Anthropological Investigation of the Tillamook Indians Relative to Tribal Identity and Aboriginal Possession of Lands." In Horr, 1:25–102.
Thompson (NW)	Thompson, Laurence C. "The Northwest." In *Current Trends in Linguistics*. Vol. 10, *Linguistics in North America*, edited by Thomas A. Sebeok, pt. 2, 979–1045. The Hague: Mouton, 1973.
Thwaites (LC)	Thwaites, Reuben Gold, ed. *Original Journals of the Lewis and Clark Expedition, 1804–1806*. 8 vols. New York: Dodd, Mead, 1904–5.
Vaughan	Vaughan, Thomas, ed. *The Western Shore: Oregon Country Essays Honoring the American Revolution*. Portland, Oreg.: American Revolution Bicentennial Commission of Oregon, 1975.
Warren (RSWA)	Warren, Claude N. "A Re-evaluation of Southwestern Washington Archaeology." *Tebiwa* 2 (Winter 1958–59): 9–26.
Waterman	Waterman, T. T. "The Whaling Equipment of the Makah Indians." *University of Washington Publications in Anthropology* 1 (June 1920): 1–67.
Waterman & Coffin	Waterman, T. T., and Geraldine Coffin. *Types of Canoes on Puget Sound*. Indian Notes and Monographs No. 5. New York: Museum of the American Indian, Heye Foundation, 1920.
Wheeler	Wheeler, Olin D. *The Trail of Lewis and Clark, 1804–1806*. 2 vols. New York: G. P. Putnam's Sons, 1904.
Woodward (ECT)	Woodward, John. "An Early Ceramic Tradition on the Pacific Coast." *Masterkey* 51 (April–June 1977): 66–72.

Woodward (PSOC) ———. "Prehistoric Shipwrecks on the Oregon Coast? Archaeological Evidence." In "Contributions to the Archaeology of Oregon, 1983–1986," edited by Kenneth M. Ames, 219–64. Association of Oregon Archaeologists, Occasional Papers No. 3. Portland, 1986.

Index

Abies amabilis, 284 n
Abies grandis, 28 n. See also Fir, grand
Accipiter cooperii, 378 n. See also Hawk, Cooper's
Acer circinatum, 296 n. See also Maple, vine
Acer macrophyllum, 19 n. See also Maple, bigleaf
Acipenser medirostris, 70 n. See also Sturgeon, green
Acipenser transmontanus, 346 n. See also Sturgeon, white
Acorn, 345
Actitis macularia, 383 n. See also Sandpiper, spotted
Aechmophorus occidentalis, 98 n, 391 n. See also Grebe, western
Agropyron spicatum, 368 n. See also Wheatgrass, bluebunch
Air gun, 233, 235
Alcoholic beverages. See Liquor
Alder, black. See Alder, red
Alder Creek, 276 n
Alder, Oregon, 29 n. See Alder, red
Alder, red: observed, 9, 26–27, 65, 96, 98, 103; marked on, 81; habitat of, 284 n; described, 290, 293, 293 n, 297; mentioned, 29 n, 98 n, 104 n
Aldrich Point, 41 n
Algae, 426–27, 428 n
Algonquian language, 432 n
Allogona townsendiana, 405 n
Allspice, 174, 197
Almota Creek, 467
Alnus rubra, 29 n. See also Alder, red
Alsea (Neck-ê-to, Ul-se-ah) Indians, 201, 202 n, 237 n, 432 n, 476, 485, 490–91
Alsean language, 202 n, 237 n
Anas discors, 384 n. See also Teal, blue-winged
Anas platyrhynchos, 98 n. See also Mallards
Anas sp., 384 n. See also Teals
Anchovies, 344. See also Eulachon
Anomiidae, 409 n
Anser albifrons, 420 n. See also Goose, great white-fronted
Antelope. See Pronghorn
Anthus spragueii, 383 n. See also Pipit, Sprague's
Antilocapra americana, 317 n. See also Pronghorn
Aplodontia rufa, 78 n. See also Beaver, mountain
Apocynum sp., 217 n. See also Dogbane
Appaloosas, 313, 315, 317 n
Aquila chrysaetos, 94 n. See also Eagle, golden
Arborvitae. See Redcedar, western
Arbutus menziesii, 105 n. See also Madrone, Pacific
Arcostaphylos uva-ursi, 237 n. See also Bearberry
Ardea herodias, 98 n. See also Heron, great blue
Arikara (Ricare) Indians, 169, 172 n, 191, 405–6
Ariolimax columbianus, 146 n. See also Slug, Pacific woods
Ar-lo-quat, 148 n
Armells Creek. See South Mountain Creek
Arms and ammunition: powder, 15, 74, 76, 138, 187, 205–6, 208–9, 273 n; stolen, 48–49; balls and shot, 74, 76, 187, 205–6, 208–9; examined, 265, 272; repaired, 441–42; mentioned, 151, 153, 158, 456. See also specific weapons and Guns
Arrow Creek (Slaughter River), 449, 463
Arrowhead. See Wapato
Arrows. See Bows and arrows
Arrowwood, 44, 45 n
Artiodactyla, 405 n
Arwarharmay (and similar spellings) Indians. See Hidatsa Indians
Ash, 9, 17
Ash, Oregon, 20 n, 96, 98, 98 n, 294–95, 296 n
Ash, volcanic, 14 n
Assiniboine Indians, 169, 191
Astagus sp., 398 n. See also Crayfish
Astor, John Jacob, 94 n
Astoria (Point Meriwether), 92, 94 n, 459, 471
Astoria Formation, 67 n, 179 n, 185 n
Astorians, 37 n, 61 n, 91 n, 94 n, 148 n, 333 n
Astronomical observations, 71 n, 82–83, 179, 255, 257, 259, 277, 347, 410, 417, 495
Athapascan Kwalhiokwa (Kil-laxt-ho-kle) Indians, 475, 486, 491
Athapascan language, 432 n
Atlantic Ocean, 397
Audubon, John James, 148 n
Aurelia sp., 425 n. See also Jellyfish
Awls, 214, 216

509

Index

Axes, 16, 17, 90, 113, 158, 243–44, 265, 271, 327
Aythya valisineria, 37n. *See also* Canvasback

Bachelor Island, 21, 23, 24n, 56
Backgammon, 118–19
Badger, 19, 21n, 313, 315, 317n, 352–53, 355n, 357–58
Baggage: portaged, 7; wet, 39–40, 48–49, 91–92, 108, 127, 169; unloaded, 40–43; dried, 83, 85; mentioned, 328–29
Bags, 135, 172n, 216, 305, 307
Baker (Haleys) Bay: search for, 46–47; maps of, 47n; arrive at, 49–50, 66; Indians of, 53–54, 81, 154; distance on, 113; described, 201–2; trees of, 282, 284; animals of, 387; mentioned, 51n, 61, 202n, 284n
Baker, James, 47–48n
Balaenoptera musculus, 185n
Balch. *See* Bowles, William
Balls. *See* Arms and ammunition
Balsam, 281, 283. *See also* Fir, grand
Bands, arm, 173n
Bark, Peruvian, 318, 321n
Barton, Benjamin Smith, 98
Basalts, 9n, 10n, 179n
Baskets: stolen, 47; purchased, 74; types of, 77n; materials for, 78n, 296n, 307n, 435, 439; as gift, 137; described, 215–17; mentioned, 336–37
Bats, 405–6, 409, 409n
Beacon Rock, 7–9, 9n, 54
Beads: as clothing, 15, 142, 435, 439; as trade items, 72–74, 81, 83, 85, 88, 113, 118, 120–21, 123, 134, 144, 165, 168, 172n, 181, 187, 190, 199, 204–5, 214, 216, 221–22, 314, 316, 360; Indian name for, 81, 82n; gambling with, 119

Bearberry: observed, 116; as food, 118, 373, 375; as trade item, 133; scarcity of, 134; described, 235–36, 245–46, 251, 253; mentioned, 237n
Bear, black, 290–91, 293n, 312, 315, 317n, 318, 324
Bear Den (Charbonneau's) Creek, 447, 462
Beargrass, 7–8, 9n, 77n, 78n, 215, 217, 221, 246, 335, 337, 435–36, 439–40
Bear, grizzly, 312, 315, 317n, 318, 324
Bears: signs of, 116, 122; and Indians, 206; skins of, 208, 434, 438; claws of, 440
Beauchamp (Grouse) Creek, 448, 463
Beaver, American: skins of, 25, 27, 31, 33, 74, 76, 161–62, 187, 205, 434, 438; hunted, 135, 215–16, 290–91, 293; as food, 166–67, 307, 309; bait for, 174–75, 197–98; castoreum, 178n; Indians and, 208; as trade item, 358, 360; mentioned, 77n, 313, 315, 317n, 337–38
Beaver (White Earth) Creek, 450, 464
Beaverhead Rock, 451, 465
Beaver, mountain (sewelel): discovered, 3; skins of, 76, 206, 208, 434, 438; described, 351, 353–54, 355n; mentioned, 78n, 210n, 313, 317n
Bedding, 48–49, 85, 91–92, 108, 122–23
Beech. *See* Alder, red
Beech, eastern, 98n
Bells, 113
Belt Creek (Portage River), 449, 464
Berberis aquifolium, 28n. *See also* Grape, Oregon
Berberis nervosa, 28n. *See also* Grape, dull Oregon
Berries, 32, 119, 139, 161–63, 214, 216–17, 307, 366, 368

Betsy, 160n
Betula occidentalis, 29n. *See also* Birch, water
Bible, 272–73n
Biddle, Nicholas: emendations, 14n, 25n, 30n, 34n, 37n, 42n, 68n, 145n, 202n, 239n, 257n, 317n, 409n; writes expedition history, 19n, 59n, 440n; marks, 29n, 71n, 94n, 99n, 148n, 158n, 162n, 164n, 179n, 185n, 198n, 214n, 221n, 225n, 227n, 230n, 232n, 235n, 237n, 242n, 244n, 248n, 249n, 278n, 280n, 284n, 286n, 290n, 293n, 296n, 307n, 316n, 317n, 321n, 324n, 327n, 330n, 333n, 335n, 342n, 346n, 351n, 355n, 358n, 362n, 368n, 387n, 391n, 394n, 397n, 401n, 405n, 408n, 414n, 416n, 420n, 425n, 428n, 432n; collaboration with Clark, 41n, 51n, 120n, 172n, 206n; editorial methods, 471n
Big Dry Creek (Big Dry Run), 448, 463
Big Hole (Wisdom) River, 451, 465, 494–95
Big Muddy Creek (Marthy's River), 447, 462
Bile, 318–19
Birch (Thompson's) Creek, 448, 463
Birch, water, 26–27, 29n
Bird (Elk) Rapids, 448, 463
Birds. *See specific species*
Biscuits, 187, 205
Bitterroot (Flathead, Clark's) River, 308–10, 311n, 325n, 472n, 494–95
Bitterroot (Snow) Mountains, 493
Bivalves, 407, 409n, 420
Blackberry, Pacific, 16, 18, 20n, 26–27, 103, 104n, 297–98, 298n, 302–3
Blackbird, Brewer's, 375, 377, 378n
Blackbird, rusty, 378n
Black Eagle Falls, 449, 464
Black Hills, 337–38

510

Index

Blacktail Deer (McNeal's) Creek, 451, 465
Blankets: Indian, 17, 74–75, 195, 336, 434, 438; drying out, 40; trading, 49, 88, 187, 205, 423; wet, 69; scarcity of, 92; infested, 138, 142; mentioned, 77n, 181, 189, 192n
Blechnum spicant, 307n. *See also* Fern, deer
Bloody Dick Creek, 465
Blubber: and Indians, 143, 166, 176, 178, 183, 189, 193, 199, 460–61; as food, 162–63, 167–68, 188, 407–8; purchased, 180; scarcity of, 245–46. *See also* Whales
Bluebird, mountain, 131n
Boards, 133
Boats. *See* Canoes
Bobcat, 327, 328n, 333
Bobcat, Oregon: discovered, 3; skins of, 76, 77n, 124n, 208, 352, 354, 434–35, 438–39; as trade item, 187, 192n, 205–6; habitat of, 313, 315; described, 327, 328n, 333–34; mentioned, 114, 317n
Bobwhite, northern, 375, 377n
Bogs, 117
Boils. *See* Medical problems
Bolch. *See* Bowles, William
Bonasa umbellus, 24n
Bonasa umbellus sabini, 24n. *See also* Grouse, Oregon ruffed
Bonhomme Island, 488n
Botany. *See specific species*
Boulder River (Reubin Field's Creek), 450, 465
Bowles, William, 155, 160n, 427
Bowls, 118–19, 215–16
Bowmon, J., 74–75
Bows and arrows, 16–17, 19, 27, 206–7, 209–10, 210n, 211n, 248, 274, 336
Bradbury Slough (Fanny's Bottom), 470
Bradford Island, 7, 9n
Brains, 230, 232n
Branding iron, 82n
Branta bernicla, 9n. *See also* Brants

Branta canadensis, 10n. *See also* Goose, Canada
Branta canadensis leucopareia, 10n. *See also* Goose, lesser Canada
Brants: hunted, 8, 16, 19, 60–62, 71, 73, 81, 83, 85, 119–21, 414–15; described, 9n; abundance of, 11–13, 21–23, 75, 88, 92–93, 96, 457; observed, 53–54, 59–60n, 161–62, 171, 261; as food, 65–67; mentioned, 383, 385, 391–94, 394n, 417–20
Brant, white. *See* Goose, snow
Brarow. *See* Badger
Brass, 15, 139, 142, 187, 195, 205, 221–22
Bratton, William: sent out, 42–43; volunteers, 60; duties of, 65, 138, 140, 172n, 177; votes, 83; hunting, 166; illness of, 293, 295, 297, 307, 311n, 318, 321, 324, 329–30, 332–33, 336–37, 384–85, 388, 390–91, 393–96, 416, 419, 441–43; information of, 312, 314
Bread, 96–97, 113, 118, 121, 166, 238–39
Brier, green. *See* Blackberry, Pacific
British, 36n, 62n, 94n, 148n, 160n
Broughton, William Robert, 14n, 29n, 47–48n, 115n
Brushy Creek, 466
Bubo virginianus, 378n. *See also* Owl, great horned
Bubo virginianus occidentalis, 378n
Bubo virginianus saturatus, 378n
Bucephala albeola, 98n. *See also* Bufflehead
Buffalo, 162, 449, 480
Bufflehead, 96, 98n, 383, 384n, 385, 397–98, 398n, 401n
Bullwhacker (Softshell Turtle) Creek, 448, 463
Bulrushes, 26, 29n, 305, 307, 307n
Bunchberry, 44–45, 45–46n

Bunks, 138
Burke Island, 23, 25n
Burnt Fork Creek, 466
Buteo jamaicensis, 94n. *See also* Hawk, red-tailed
Buteo swainsoni, 378n
Buttons. *See* Clothes
Buzzard. *See* Condor, California

Cactus, prickly pear, 370
Cah-wah-na-ki-ooks River. *See* Lewis River
Calapooya Indians, 479, 487, 491
Callallamet, 156, 161n, 427
Callamon, 156, 160–61n, 416, 427
Camas, 139, 139n, 193, 226–27, 227n
Camassia quamash, 139n. *See also* Camas
Camps. *See individual states* (e.g., Oregon, camps in)
Canadians, 236
Candle fish, 346n. *See also* Eulachon
Candles, 200–201
Canio. *See* Coboway
Canis latrans, 317n. *See also* Coyote
Canis lupus, 210n. *See also* Wolf, gray
Canis lupus fuscus, 317n
Canis lupus nubilus, 317n
Canisters, 265, 272
Cannon Beach Member, 179n, 185n
Canoe Camp, 462
Canoe Creek. *See* White Salmon River
Canoes: Indian, 1, 3, 12–18, 22–23, 26, 30–33, 34n, 40, 53, 55, 65–66, 81, 88–89, 103, 106, 122, 124–25, 135–36, 146–47, 201–2, 207, 210, 232–34, 249, 272, 336, 342, 346, 414–16, 418, 421, 423, 456; stolen, 4, 428n; navigational problems, 7–9, 35–41, 43–49, 92–93, 114, 272, 312, 314, 325–26; carvings, 16, 18, 22–23, 55, 263, 267, 272n; obtained, 72;

511

Canoes (*continued*)
damaged, 79, 90–91, 374, 376; burial, 97, 98n, 176, 180, 182, 186, 188, 194, 286, 460; portaged, 117–18; lost, 198–99, 203–4, 401, 403, 406–7, 409, 411; construction of, 243–44, 262–63, 265, 267, 270, 272; sketches of, 272n, 273n; found, 278, 280; purchased, 426, 428; repaired, 427, 429–30; problems with, 432, 436, 440, 444, 448; cached, 451, 494; mentioned, 68, 96–97, 101, 105–6, 108, 125–26, 133, 158, 167, 169, 171, 181, 194, 196, 215, 246, 260, 275, 284–85, 290, 297, 351, 367, 381–82, 402
Canvasback, 35–36, 37n, 96, 161–62, 383, 385, 395, 397
Canyon Creek (Canister Run) (Idaho), 453, 467
Canyon Creek (Oreg.), 176, 178n
Cape Disappointment: named, 36n; located, 50, 109, 113–15, 188, 470, 493; distance to, 88, 458; maps of, 248n, 481n; mentioned, 47n, 49, 51n, 53, 59, 60–62, 66–67, 67n, 69–70, 71n, 182, 193, 201–2
Cape Flattery, 161n, 416n
Cape Horn, 9n, 29n
Cape (Lookout) Meares, 494
Cape Shoalwater, 459, 470
Cape Swells. *See* Grays Point
Cardiidae, 120n, 409n
Cardinal-flower, blue, 240, 241, 242n
Carex sp., 217n, 307n. *See also* Sedges
Carmen Creek, 451, 466
Cascades Indians, 10n
Cascade Range, 3, 29n, 284n, 325n, 370, 374n
Cascades of the Columbia River (Great Rapids, Great Shute): portage of, 7–8, 9n; Indians of, 10n, 203,

270–71, 475, 483; animals of, 161–62, 318, 335–36, 351, 354, 371, 402; plants of, 285–86, 299–300; arrive at, 456; distance to, 461, 493; mentioned, 1, 29n, 73, 338, 469
Castor canadensis, 77n. *See also* Beaver, American
Castoreum, 174–75, 178n, 197
Catel, 416, 418, 420n, 425, 427
Cataract (and similar spellings) River. *See* Klickitat River
Cathlamet Bay, 36, 37n, 397n
Cathlamet (Cath-lâh-mâh) Indians: 41n; language, 34n, 236, 281; culture, 34n, 432; clothes, 40–41; seamanship, 40, 41n; encountered, 41; located, 41n, 201–2, 475, 485; villages, 58, 87–88, 89, 89n, 154, 459, 471; customs, 97; chiefs, 155, 159n, 185n; visits, 192, 195–96, 409, 411, 429–30, 436, 440; trade, 199, 224; artifacts, 206, 208; canoes, 263, 270; relations with expedition, 401–2, 426, 428; listed, 490; mentioned, 421, 423, 441, 474
Cathlamet Point (Point Samuel), 89, 90n, 459, 471
Cathlapotle (Quath-lah-pohtle) Indians, 23, 24n, 457, 470, 474, 477, 484, 490
Catostomus catostomus, 409n
Catostomus platyrhynchus, 409n. *See also* Sucker, mountain
Cat-tail, common, 26, 27, 29n, 74, 77n, 135, 146–47, 192, 196, 216–17, 305, 307, 307n, 366, 368n, 370, 435, 439–40
Cat, tiger. *See* Bobcat, Oregon
Cayuse (Y-e-letpo, Wil-le-letpo) Indians, 479, 482, 489
Cedar, white. *See* Redcedar, western

Celilo (Great) Falls: animals of, 142, 144, 328, 338, 340–41, 345, 347, 351, 354–55, 360, 390, 411, 414–15, 421; Indians of, 201–4, 270, 313, 329, 334, 474, 483; conditions of, 315, 318, 324, 331, 335–36, 370–71, 402; distance to, 455, 461, 493; mentioned, 84, 86n, 91–92, 136–37, 211–12, 320, 323, 413, 469, 479
Centrocercus urophasianus, 373n. *See also* Grouse, sage
Cervus elaphus, 20n. *See also* Elk
Ceryle alcyon, 384n. *See also* Kingfisher, belter
Chah-clel-lah Indians. *See* Watlala Indians
Chahulklilhum Village, 34n
Chairs, 138
Charbonneau, Jean Baptiste, 1–2, 172n
Charbonneau, Toussaint: duties of, 2, 62, 65; volunteers, 60; votes, 84; interpreter, 157, 428n; scouting party, 168, 171, 172n; discovers varied thrush, 254–55; mentioned, 137
Char, red. *See* Salmon, sockeye
Chehalis (Chiltz) Indians: 77n; language, 51n; name, 73; visits, 75; located, 77n; chiefs, 154, 159n; numbers, 201–2, 475, 486; appearance, 437; mentioned, 459, 491
Chen caerulescens, 10n
Chicken, 370–71, 373n
Chil-lar-la-wil. *See* Shelathwel
Chil-luck-kit-te-quaw (and similar spellings) Indians. *See* Wishram-Wasco Indians
Chiltz Indians. *See* Chehalis Indians
Chim-nah-pum (and similar spellings) Indians. *See* Yakima Indians
Chimneys, 138
Chinking, 134, 134n
Chin-ni-ni, 154, 159n

Chinookan Indians: language, 34n, 61n, 76n, 82n, 91n, 98n, 120n, 159n, 164n, 184n, 185n, 185–86n, 198n, 317n, 342n, 434, 496n; games, 273–74; disease among, 286–87n; located, 457; villages, 470; numbers, 475, 478, 484, 486; mentioned, 472n, 490–92
Chinook Indians: 51n; canoes, 1, 272n; relations with expedition, 18, 50, 72, 164–65, 189, 239, 241; language, 34n, 76n, 82–83, 192, 196, 236, 351, 353; located, 51n, 70, 201–2; trade, 53, 221–22, 224; villages, 59, 68n, 182, 458; customs, 60–61, 97, 142, 168, 179, 186, 190, 368n; disease among, 65; dress, 75–76, 439; chiefs, 83, 85, 154, 159n, 330, 332, 416, 418; culture, 89, 180, 194; war, 155; lodges, 184, 218–21; encountered, 188; artifacts, 206, 208, 211, 213, 218; visits, 325, 327; appearance, 432–34, 437–38; numbers, 475, 485; mentioned, 474
Chinook jargon, 121, 122n, 178, 179n, 186n
Chinook Point, 51n, 73n, 115n, 470
Chinook River, 62, 65, 67n. *See also* Wallacut River
Chip, 221–22, 223n
Chip (Valley) Creek, 449, 463
Chipmunk, eastern, 347n
Chipmunk, Townsend's, 313, 315, 317n, 346, 347n, 348
Chippewa Indians, 240–41
Chisels, 265, 271
Chishuck, 461, 471
Chopunnish Indians. *See* Nez Perce Indians
Chopunnish River. *See* North Fork Clearwater River
Chronometer, 255, 257–58, 410, 417
Chucktins Creek, 461, 471
Ci-in-twar, 154

Cinnamon, 135, 174, 197
Circus cyaneus, 378n. *See also* Harrier, northern
Cirsium edule, 77n. *See also* Thistle, edible
Cisco, 346n. *See also* Whitefish
Civet, 355n
CK (Tea Pot) Creek, 448, 463
Clackamas (Clark-a-mus) Indians, 478, 486, 491
Clams, 407, 409n, 420–21
Clark Fork (East Fork Clark's) River, 308, 310, 311n, 325n, 480–82, 488, 493
Clark, Frances, 29n
Clark, William: journal-keeping methods, 2–3, 9n, 25n, 33n, 34n, 46n, 60n, 71n, 77n, 115n, 146n, 148n, 151n, 158n, 159–60n, 172n, 198n, 230n, 248n, 253n, 257–58n, 261n, 262n, 290n, 311n, 374n, 440n, 445, 446, 472n, 473–74, 477n, 481n, 488–89n, 492, 493n, 494n, 496n
Clark's Point of View. *See* Tillamook Head
Clark's River. *See* Bitterroot River; Clark Fork River; Deschutes River; Pend Oreille River
Clatskanie (Clax-ter) Indians, 155, 159n, 478, 484, 490
Clatsop Indians: 76–77n; relations with expedition, 4, 177, 276, 335, 349, 381–82, 384, 409, 411, 414, 416, 418–19, 426, 428; located, 73, 75, 112, 201–2, 459, 471; culture, 76n; trade, 81, 106, 189, 199, 221, 224; visits, 81, 122–24, 135–36, 138–39, 147, 152–53, 162–63, 216, 232, 299–300, 325, 327, 333, 335, 337, 358, 395–96, 443–44; disease among, 81, 286; movements, 87, 140, 143; information of, 95, 302, 305; villages, 117–18, 120n, 122, 136, 167, 171–72, 182, 275; utensils, 118–19; games, 118–19; customs, 119, 136, 142, 163–65, 168, 179–80, 186, 190, 192, 194, 221–23, 285; lodges, 119, 184, 218–21; appearance, 142, 432–35, 437–38; chiefs, 154, 159n, 342, 346, 420n; encountered, 188; language, 195–96, 243–44, 351, 353, 440n; located, 201–2, 459, 471; artifacts, 206, 208–14; clothes, 249, 251; numbers, 475, 485; mentioned, 2, 184n, 235–36, 474, 490
Clatsop River. *See* Necanicum River
Clax-ter (and similar spellings) Indians. *See* Clatskanie Indians
Clay, 179n, 194, 230n
Clayoquot Sound, 191n
Clearwater (Kooskooskee) River: plants of, 284–86; maps of, 308–10; animals of, 331–32, 376–77, 387–88, 415; distances on, 446, 453, 462, 493; Indians of, 474, 479, 482; mentioned, 311n, 467
Climate. *See* Weather conditions; Weather observations
Cloth, 113, 144n, 187, 205
Clothes: moccasins, 3, 130, 137, 186, 249, 339–40, 407, 438; jackets, 17; overalls, 17, 20n, 407; Indian, 17, 74–76, 78n, 88, 97, 249, 262n, 434–36, 438–39; hats, 17, 78n, 142, 144, 187, 221–22, 223n, 246, 249, 253n, 335, 337, 342, 346, 381–82, 409n, 414–15, 434–35, 438, 440; shirts, 17, 137, 187, 407; capote, 18, 20n, 123, 407; wet, 42, 47; scarcity, 44, 93; general, 85, 181, 187; mending, 103–4; socks, 103, 137; shoes, 104; as presents, 137; drawers, 137; woolens, 137, 138n; vests, 137,

513

Index

Clothes (continued)
346; making, 186, 219,
339–40, 407; trousers,
187; buttons, 187, 205;
coats, 187, 208, 346, 416;
trading, 205, 346, 381,
416; leggings, 249. See also
Blankets; Robes
Cloves, 174, 197
Clowwewalla (Cush-hooks,
Char-cow-ah) Indians,
478, 486–87, 491
Coal Creek, 26, 28 n
Coast Ranges, 25 n
Coats. See Clothes
Coboway: presents for, 123,
141; biographical sketch,
123 n; visits, 138–39,
162–63, 214, 216, 232,
234, 342, 346, 384–85,
429, 430; listed, 154; departs, 164–65, 235–36,
387, 390, 436, 440; trading, 336–37; certificate
for, 432; mentioned, 112,
115 n, 144 n, 185 n, 428 n
Cockles, 119, 120 n, 407,
409 n, 421
Codex journals: Codex J discussed, 34 n, 290 n, 346 n;
begins, 158 n; ends, 442;
Codex H ends, 71 n; Codex I begins, 71 n; discussed, 172 n, 445–46,
471 n, 473, 477 n, 481 n,
495 n; list in, 160 n, 488 n;
ends, 248 n; Codex Ia begins, 94 n; ends, 104 n;
Codex P discussed, 232 n;
Codex R discussed, 346 n;
Codex C discussed, 446;
Codex N discussed, 446,
471 n; Codex G discussed,
493 n. See also Elkskinbound Journal; First
Draft; Voorhis journals
Coeur d'Alene Indians, 492
Coffee, 113
Coin, 81
Colaptes auratus, 381 n. See also
Flicker, northern
Col-chote, 154
Colic. See Medical problems
Colinus virginianus, 377 n. See
also Bobwhite, northern
Collins, John: hunting, 8–10,
12, 40, 138, 140, 172 n,
179, 186, 192, 221, 321,
324, 330, 333, 335, 356,
387 n, 394, 409, 411; votes,
83; separated, 125–26;
returns, 162, 164, 198,
293, 295, 325–26, 331,
366–67, 391, 393, 396,
420 n; duties of, 223 n; information of, 235–39;
sent out, 240, 290–91,
358, 360, 414–15, 443
Colorado River, 311 n
Colter, John: sent out, 45,
296–97; information of,
46, 235–36; gun stolen,
47; volunteers, 60; duties
of, 62, 65, 92, 172 n,
229 n; hunting, 71,
215–16, 223 n, 444; votes,
83; separated, 125; returns, 167, 293, 295
Colter's Creek. See Potlatch
River
Columbian Plain. See Great
Columbian Plain
Columbia Rediviva, 36 n, 160 n
Columbia River Basalt Group,
9–10 n, 28 n
Columbia River: characteristics of, 1, 36 n, 46, 51 n,
179 n, 182; conditions of,
2, 12, 14 n, 19 n, 34 n, 98,
282, 284, 284 n, 294, 310–
11, 323; arrive at, 24; described, 35 n; Indians of,
41 n, 61 n, 75, 76 n, 98 n,
154–56, 195–96, 214,
240–41, 246, 262, 267,
281, 313, 315, 438, 474–
75, 478, 480–87; traders
of, 85, 160 n, 314, 316,
427; explored, 86 n, 87;
bearings on, 115 n; animals of, 131, 142, 144;
Indian name of, 184; Indians trade on, 203–4,
368 n; plants of, 229, 233;
maps of, 248 n, 308–9,
430–31, 432 n; distances
on, 446, 456–59, 461; distances to, 454; latitude,
494; mentioned, 57, 71 n,
77 n, 94 n, 276 n, 295, 318,
320, 335, 337, 340–41,
349, 351, 353, 355, 365,
371, 381–82, 387–89,
393, 395, 397, 413, 415,
451, 468, 493, 493 n. See
also Cascades of the Columbia River; The Dalles
of the Columbia River;
Celilo (Great) Falls
Colville (Whe-el-po) Indians,
480, 488, 491
Combs, 437
Comcomly, 60, 61 n, 73 n,
154, 159 n, 333 n
Comowool. See Coboway
Compass, 84
Condor, California: hunted,
63, 66, 100; discovered,
67 n; specimen, 69; observed, 162–63; described, 319–23; sketch
of, 324 n; Indian name
for, 495; mentioned, 96,
379, 381, 381 n
Conia. See Coboway
Continental Divide, 473
Con-year. See Coboway
Cook, James, 36 n
Cooks, 158
Coos (Cook-koo-oose) Indians, 237 n, 432 n, 476,
485, 491
Coosan language, 237 n
Coot, American, 96–97, 98 n,
398–400, 401 n
Copalis (Pailsh) Indians,
472 n, 476, 486, 491
Copper, 15, 187, 205, 207,
210, 440
Coquille Indians, 491
Coregonus sp., 346 n. See also
Whitefish
Cormorant, double-crested,
13, 14 n, 96, 161–62, 261,
383, 385, 387, 388–89
Corn, 235 n
Cornel, dwarf, 45 n. See also
Bunchberry
Cornus canadensis, 45 n. See
also Bunchberry
Cornus sericea, 29 n. See also
Dogwood, red osier
Cornus stolonifera, 29 n
Corvus, blue-crested. See Jay,
Steller's
Corvus brachyrhynchos, 94 n
Corvus caurinus, 164 n. See also
Crow, northwestern
Corvus corax, 94 n. See also
Raven, common
Corvus corax principalis, 378 n

514

Index

Corvus corax sinuatus, 378n
Corylus cornuta, 347n. *See also* Hazelnut
Cottontail, eastern, 313, 315, 317n, 362n
Cottontail, Nuttall's, 313, 315, 317n, 360, 362n
Cottonwoods, 366, 368
Cottonwood, black, 7, 9, 11, 15, 17, 20n
Cottonwood Island, 28n
Coues, Elliott, 29n, 346n, 362n
Cougar. *See* Mountain lion
Cous, 187, 192n, 205
Cow (Windsor's) Creek, 448, 463
Coweliskee River. *See* Cowlitz River
Cowlitz (Coweliskee) River: arrive at, 26, 28; located, 28n, 470; Indians of, 202, 475, 484–85; animals of, 346n; distance to, 458; mentioned, 29n, 477n
Cowlitz Formation, 30n
Cowlitz language, 28n
Cows, 302, 305, 307n
Coyote, 312–13, 315, 317n, 331, 333n, 335
Coyote Creek, 465
Crabapple, Oregon, 3, 15–17, 19n, 98, 103, 105n, 235, 237n, 243–44, 244n
Crabapple, western, 19n
Cranberrybush, American, 45n
Cranberry, wild, 45–46n, 74, 77n, 103, 116–18, 235, 237n, 243–44, 330–31
Cranes, 53–54, 73
Cranes, sandhill, 11, 13, 14n, 21, 96, 161–62, 261, 379–80
Crayfish, 396–97, 398n
Cree language, 235n
Crims (Fanny's) Island, 27, 29n, 458, 470
Cronin Point, 185n
Crooked Falls, 449, 464
Crooked Fork (Glade) Creek, 452, 466
Crow, American, 94, 94n, 96
Crow (Gass's) Creek, 450, 464
Crow, northwestern, 162–63, 164n, 261, 375, 377, 378n
Cruzatte, Pierre: votes, 84; illness of, 141, 143; duties of, 172n; sent out, 355n; and Indians, 358, 360; returns, 370
Culho-mo. *See* Lupine seashore
Cullaby Creek, 316n
Cul-te-ell, 155, 159n
Cul-wha-mo. *See* Lupine, seashore
Cups, 435
Curlew, long-billed, 382–83, 384n
Cus-ka-lah (and similar spellings), 120–21, 120n, 136, 171, 358, 360, 365, 367
Cuts-sâh-nim (and similar spellings) Indians. *See* Yakima Indians
Cutwhamo. *See* Lupine, seashore
Cyanea sp., 425n. *See also* Jellyfish
Cyanocitta cristata, 133n. *See also* Jay, blue
Cyanocitta stelleri, 94n. *See also* Jay, Steller's
Cygnus buccinator, 14n. *See also* Swan, trumpeter
Cygnus columbianus, 14n. *See also* Swan, tundra
Cynomys ludovicianus, 347n. *See also* Dog, prairie

Dalles. *See* The Dalles of the Columbia River
Davidson, 156, 160n, 427
Day, John, 91n
Deadfalls, 206, 208, 210n, 344, 347
Deadman (Ash) Rapids, 449, 463
Dearborn River, 308–9, 449, 464, 494–95
Deep River, 37n
Deepwater (Wild Onion) Creek, 447, 462
Deer: hunted, 12, 16, 19, 53–54, 60–61, 68–69, 73, 81, 91–93, 105, 108, 140, 163–64, 188, 191, 206, 208, 232–34, 236, 242–43, 409, 411, 450; signs of, 17, 101; and Indians, 19; observed, 23, 70; skins of, 74, 76, 434, 438; as food, 84–85, 114, 166–67, 215–16, 325–26; scarcity of, 95, 186; use of, 231, 351, 354; habits of, 403; mentioned, 71n, 328, 405n
Deer, Columbian black-tailed, 3, 68, 70, 70n, 317n, 328, 330n, 405n
Deer, Columbian white-tailed, 312, 315, 317n, 328, 330n
Deer (E-lal-lar) Island, 23, 25n, 458, 470
Deer, mule, 312, 315, 317n, 328, 331–32, 403–4, 405n
Deer, white-tailed, 405n
Delashelwilt, 77n, 416, 418, 425, 427, 429–30
Delaware River, 395, 397
Dendragapus canadensis, 377n. *See also* Grouse, spruce
Dendragapus obscurus, 377n
Dentalium sp., 436, 439, 440n
Deschutes (Clark's, Towarnahiooks) River: Indians of, 13, 14n, 204, 314, 316, 317n, 480, 487; conditions of, 324; name of, 325n; animals of, 368; distance to, 455, 493; mentioned, 469, 472n
Detachment orders, 156–58, 161n. *See also* Orderly Book
Devil's club, 44, 45n
Diamond Island. *See* Government Island
Diarrhea. *See* Medical problems
Dibblee Island, 28n
Diggers, 231–32, 234
Distichlis spicata, 307n. *See also* Saltgrass, seashore
Dogbane (silk grass), 211, 214, 216–17, 217n, 434–35, 438–39
Dog (Bull) Creek, 448, 463
Dog, prairie, 346, 347n, 348, 352, 354
Dog, turnspit, 329, 330n, 352, 357
Dogs: observed, 27; purchased, 30–31, 33, 192, 196, 346, 358, 360, 395–96, 444, 456, 458; as food, 162–63, 166; and Indians, 274–75, 299–300,

515

Index

Dogs (*continued*)
312, 315, 318–19, 336–37, 401, 403; mentioned, 218–19. *See also* Mastiff; Spaniels
Dogwood, red osier (red wood), 26–27, 29n
Dolphin, Risso's, 67n
Dominique, 373, 374n
Dove, mourning, 379–80, 381n
Drawers. *See* Clothes
Drewyer. *See* Drouillard
Drouillard, George: sent out, 46–47, 101, 179, 242–43, 312, 314, 351, 353, 391, 401, 401n, 403, 443–44; votes, 84; duties of, 92, 117n, 140; hunting, 103, 118, 135, 161–62, 172n, 174, 186, 196, 198–200, 215–16, 229n, 275, 277, 281–82, 293, 307, 309, 387n, 393, 431; returns, 124, 192, 232–34, 275–76, 323–24, 342, 346, 368, 370, 387, 390, 395–96, 409, 411, 414–15, 428; information of, 137–38, 145, 290–91, 333, 335–37; separated, 421, 423; interpreter, 428n; illness of, 429–30; gun repaired, 441–42
Dry (Goodrich's) Island, 448, 463
Dryocopus pileatus, 381n. *See also* Woodpecker, pileated
Duck, black and white. *See* Bufflehead
Duck, fishing. *See* Merganser
Duck (Werner's) Creek (Valley County, Mont.), 448, 463
Duck (Whitehouse's) Creek (Broadwater County, Mont.), 450, 464
Duckinmallard. *See* Mallard
Ducks: hunted, 10–13, 16, 19, 53–54, 60–61, 81, 93, 120–21, 188; abundance of, 21–23, 35, 88, 96; as food, 72; observed, 161–62, 261, 385; mentioned, 171, 383, 385
Dysentery. *See* Medical problems

Eagle, bald, 94, 94n, 96, 162–63, 363, 405–6
Eagle, golden, 94n, 321, 323, 404–6, 405n
Eagle (Stone Wall) Creek, 449, 463
East Fork Bitterroot River, 452, 466
E-chee-lute (and similar spellings) Indians. *See* Wishram-Wasco Indians
Ecola Creek, 180, 183–84, 185n, 284, 460, 471
Ectopistes migratorius, 373n. *See also* Pigeon, passenger
Egregia menziesii, 423, 426, 428n, 431–32
Elderberry, blue, 104n, 285–86, 286n
Elderberry, common, 286n
Elderberry, red, 103, 104n
Eldorado Creek, 467
Elk: as food, 2, 84–85, 105, 107, 137–39, 142, 145–46, 152–53, 162, 177, 186, 200–201, 211–12, 223–24, 245–46, 255, 284–85, 325–27, 368, 370; stolen, 4, 281–82, 299–300, 336, 426, 428; observed, 17, 103, 448; and Indians, 19, 60–61, 74, 76, 87, 89, 219–21, 243–44, 274, 318; named, 20n; signs of, 38, 42, 44–45, 134; hunted, 53, 105–9, 116–18, 121–22, 124–27, 151n, 156, 161, 166–67, 171–72, 188, 191–92, 194–96, 208, 210, 215–16, 226–27, 232–34, 239–42, 244, 253, 275, 279–80, 293, 295, 312, 321, 323–24, 335, 351, 353, 356, 358, 360, 365, 367, 387, 390–91, 393–94, 396, 409, 411, 414–16, 418, 430–32, 436; skins of, 66, 74, 76, 144, 187, 204, 230–31, 328–29, 434, 438; informed of, 92–93, 95–97; spoiled, 114, 287–88; as trade item, 180, 205; abundance of, 184; sent for, 198–99; use of,

202–3, 206–7, 354, 440; scarcity of, 243, 342, 344, 381–82; search for, 262, 267; food of, 276–77; habitat of, 315, 331, 333, 403; described, 404, 408; mentioned, 317n, 405n
Elkskin-bound Journal, 67n, 68n, 127n, 148n, 158–59n. *See also* Codex journals; First Draft; Voorhis journals
Elymus cinereus, 368n. *See also* Wildrye, basin
Empidonax hammondii, 381n. *See also* Flycatcher, Hammond's
E-ne-shur (and similar spellings) Indians. *See* Tenino Indians
Engraulidae, 346n
Enhydra lutris, 86n, 166n. *See also* Otter, sea
Equisetum talmateia, 225n. *See also* Horsetail, giant
E-skel-lute (and similar spellings) Indians. *See* Wishram-Wasco Indians
Ethnology. *See specific Indian tribes*
Eulachon (anchovy): discovered, 3; described, 342–44, 349–51; fished for, 346, 353; and Indians, 358, 360; migration of, 364; as food, 368, 37c, 378–79, 384–85, 402–3; purchased, 444; mentioned, 346n
Euphagus carolinus, 378n
Euphagus cyanocephalus, 378n. *See also* Blackbird, Brewer's
Eutamias townsendii, 317n. *See also* Chipmunk, Townsend's
Ewen, 155–56, 160n, 427

Falco sparverius, 378n. *See also* Kestrel, American
Fallawan. *See* Callamon
Felis concolor, 136n. *See also* Mountain lion
Fern, Christmas, 303, 305, 307n
Fern, deer, 304, 306, 307n

516

Index

Ferns, 44–45, 45 n, 276–77
Fern, western bracken, 193, 224, 224 n, 228–29, 230 n
Ferret, 355 n
Fever. *See* Medical problems
Field, Joseph: hunting, 8–9, 68, 71, 177, 188, 190–91, 368 n, 391, 393, 420 n, 430–31; sent out, 40–41, 106 n, 140, 262, 267, 351, 353, 401, 401 n, 403, 441, 443–44; duties of, 47, 62, 65, 166, 172 n, 297, 414–15; volunteers, 60; votes, 83; information of, 105, 253, 255, 321, 324; illness of, 122; gives gift, 136, 138; returns, 358, 360, 395–96, 409, 411
Field, Reubin: hunting, 8, 140, 284–85, 296–97, 450; illness of, 35; information of, 38, 278, 280, 356, 390, 400, 401 n; scouting party, 46–47; volunteers, 60; duties of, 62, 65–66, 92, 172 n; discovers condor, 69, 100, 320; sent out, 72, 138, 281–82, 351, 358, 360, 441, 443–44; votes, 83; returns, 162, 164, 366–67, 391, 393, 414–15; separated, 227, 229, 239–40, 275–76, 409, 411; mentioned, 287–88, 401, 403
Files, 134–36, 153, 173 n, 176–77, 181, 187, 265, 271
Fir, balsam. *See* Fir, grand
Fir, Douglas, 3, 19 n, 45 n, 124 n, 282–83, 284 n, 290–91, 293 n
Fir, grand (balsam): observed, 65; use of, 124; described, 281–83; mentioned, 3, 26, 28 n, 45 n, 124 n, 279–80, 284 n
Fir, Pacific silver, 284 n
Firs, 183, 194, 262, 267, 373, 375
First Draft, 172 n, 178 n, 446 n. *See also* Codex journals; Elkskin-bound Journal; Voorhis journals

Fish: as food, 2, 30–33, 39–40, 44–45, 65, 67, 87, 92–93, 97, 103–5, 118–19; and Indians, 7–8, 60–61, 74, 76, 121, 154, 168, 180, 184, 190, 215–17, 219, 221, 248, 307, 440; purchased, 35, 89, 349, 381–82, 401–2, 444; fished for, 46, 451; spoiled, 48–49; as trade item, 85, 124, 126–27, 134–38, 146–47, 181, 204, 395–96; observed, 116; informed of, 302, 305. *See also specific species*
Fish Creek. *See* North Fork Salmon River
Fisher, 313, 315, 317 n, 329, 330 n, 333–35
Fisher Island, 28 n
Fishhook (Bason) Rapids, 454, 467
Fishhooks: as trade item, 25, 27, 30–31, 35, 40, 72, 89, 106, 120–21, 123, 134–36, 139, 146–47, 161–62, 168, 175, 181, 187, 196, 205, 221–22, 358, 360; Indian, 211, 213–14; use of, 423; mentioned, 172 n, 177
Five-Mile (Discharge, Portage) Rapids, 454, 467, 472 n
Flag, cooper's. *See* Cat-tail, common
Flags, 72, 173 n
Flathead (Oote-lash-shute, Tush-she-pah) Indians, 310, 474, 480, 482, 488–89, 492, 494–95
Flathead River. *See* Bitterroot River
Fleas: habitat of, 26–27, 48, 50; abundance of, 35–36; problems with, 120, 122–23, 138, 161–62, 188; and Indians, 142, 144, 191; mentioned, 29 n
Flicker, northern, 379–80, 381 n
Flies, 259, 365
Flies, crane, 94, 139, 139 n, 145, 147
Flies, sand, 259
Flint, 146–47

Flitches, 183, 185 n, 193
Flounder, starry, 63, 67, 67 n, 407, 410, 412, 414 n
Flour, 96–97
Flycatcher, Hammond's, 379, 381, 381 n
Fog. *See* Weather conditions
Fort Clatsop: building of, 2, 122–24, 126–27, 134–36, 138, 140, 143, 146–47, 152; party at, 77 n, 158 n, 179, 273–74, 284–85, 288, 374, 376; site of, 90 n, 112, 115 n, 243–44, 471; given up, 123 n; documents prepared at, 133 n, 445–46, 473, 488 n, 492; guarding, 156–58; infested, 161–62; party from, 172 n, 200; distance from, 189, 193; Indians visit, 195, 299, 330–32, 425; astronomical observations at, 257, 347, 349, 495 n; conditions at, 312, 314, 353, 441–42; animals of, 363; distance to, 459; mentioned, 104 n, 131 n, 233–34, 278, 280, 293, 295, 297, 362 n, 382–83, 496, 496 n
Fort George, 94 n
Fort Mandan: party at, 2; latitude of, 71 n, 494; longitude of, 71 n, 494; party leaves, 86 n, 492; located, 462; documents prepared, 473; party leaves, 492; mentioned, 307, 445–47, 496, 496 n
Fort River. *See* Lewis and Clark River
Fourchette (Weiser's) Creek, 448, 463
Fowls, water, 30, 32
Fox, 76, 205, 208, 210, 315
Fox, Cross, 329, 330 n
Fox, red, 187, 192 n, 313, 315, 317 n, 329–30, 330 n, 334
Fox, swift, 313, 315, 317 n, 329, 330 n, 334
Fragaria vesca, 9 n. *See also* Strawberry, woodland
Fraxinus latifolia, 20 n. *See also* Ash, Oregon

517

Index

Frazer, Robert: sent out, 46–47, 318, 403; votes, 83; duties of, 172n; discipline, 195, 198n; returns, 321, 324, 391, 393, 409, 411; information of, 390, 400–401; mentioned, 401n
Friendly Village, 456, 469
Frow, 113, 115n
Fulica americana, 98n. *See also* Coot, American
Fulmar, northern, 3, 386, 387n, 388, 391n
Fulmarus glacialis, 387n. *See also* Fulmar, northern
Fusil, 60–61, 74

Gallatin River, 450, 465
Gallinago gallinago, 383n. *See also* Snipe, common
Game. *See specific species*
Gass, Patrick: votes, 83; sent out, 162–64, 257n, 262, 267, 278–79, 281–82, 296–97, 325–26, 358, 360, 365, 367, 401, 403; duties of, 172n, 177, 194–95; separated, 179, 284–85, 318, 321; returns, 200, 275–76, 287–88, 323, 328–29; hunting, 324; mentioned, 59n, 86n, 130n, 384n
Gates of the Rocky Mountains, 450, 464
Gaultheria shallon, 120n. *See also* Salal
Gavia arctica, 391n
Gavia arctica pacifica, 391n. *See also* Loon, Pacific
Gavia immer, 391n
Gavia stellata, 391n
Geese: hunted, 8, 10, 35–36, 53–54, 91, 93; abundance of, 9, 11, 13, 21–23, 35, 88, 96; scarcity of, 73; observed, 161–62, 171, 261
Gibson, George: scouting party, 42–43; votes, 84; hunting, 106, 106n, 177, 190; illness of, 122, 135, 239, 241, 242n, 293, 295–97, 307, 311n, 312, 314, 316n, 318–19, 321, 324, 330, 332–33, 335–37; duties of, 138, 140, 166, 172n, 253, 255; returns, 194–95
Gigs, 44–47, 206, 208, 210–11, 213, 421
Glands, perineal, 178n
Glass, 113
Glass, looking, 113
Gluts, 243, 244n
Glycyrrhiza glabra, 61n, 230n. *See also* Liquorice, common
Glycyrrhiza lepidota, 230n. *See also* Liquorice, wild
Goat, mountain, 195, 313, 315n, 317n, 336–38, 339n, 434, 438
Goats, 305, 307n
Gonorrhea. *See* Medical problems
Goodrich, Silas: votes, 84; gives gift, 137; illness of, 239, 241, 242n, 356–57, 391, 393; mentioned, 242n
Goose, Canada, 8, 9–10n, 383, 384n, 385, 391–92, 394, 394n
Goose, greater white-fronted, 3, 417–19, 420n
Goose, lesser Canada, 8, 10n
Goose, snow: abundance of, 9, 21–23, 96; observed, 16, 18–19, 73, 161–62; island named for, 20n; hunted, 22–23, 53–54; habits of, 75; described, 391–93; mentioned, 10n, 60n, 261, 383, 385, 394n, 418, 420, 457
Gorget, 254, 257n
Government (Diamond, White Goose) Island, 13, 14n, 15–16, 20n, 55, 457, 470
Grampus, 62, 67n
Grampus griseus, 67n. *See also* Grampus
Grand (Ibex) Island, 448, 463
Grape, dull Oregon, 3, 26, 28n, 299, 301, 302n
Grape, Oregon, 3, 26, 28n, 297–300, 298n, 302n
Grasses, 77n, 116, 122, 276, 304, 307, 313, 316
Grasshopper (Willard's) Creek, 451, 465
Grass, silk. *See* Dogbane
Grave Creek, 452, 466
Gravel, 230n
Gray, Robert, 36n, 37n, 51n, 160n
Grays Harbor, 77n
Grays Point (Cape Swells), 35, 37n, 493
Grays River, 37n
Grays (Shallow) Bay, 35–36, 37n, 51n, 86–87, 87n, 112, 458–59, 470, 493
Greasewood, 370–71, 373n
Great Basin, 312n
Great Columbian Plain: conditions of, 211, 213, 311; Indians of, 313, 315; animals of, 318, 324, 331–32, 335–36, 346, 348, 352, 355–56, 359–60, 366–70, 382
Great Falls of the Columbia River. *See* Celilo (Great) Falls
Great Falls of the Missouri River, 3, 309–10, 446, 449, 464, 492
Great Lakes, 344, 346n, 351, 392, 394
Great Rapids. *See* Cascades of the Columbia River
Great Shute. *See* Cascades of the Columbia River
Grebe, horned, 399, 401, 401n
Grebe, pied-billed, 399–400, 401n
Grebe, red-necked, 399, 401, 401n
Grebe, western, 96, 98n, 390, 391n
Green Lake, 21n
Green River, 312n
Greensward, 304, 307, 307n
Griping. *See* Medical problems: bowels
Grouse, blue, 375–76, 377n
Grouse, Columbian sharp-tailed, 366–67, 368n
Grouse, Oregon ruffed, 22, 24, 24n, 278–80, 280n, 375–76, 377n
Grouse, ruffed, 374, 377n
Grouse, sage, 3, 368–71, 373, 373n
Grouse, spruce, 371, 374–76, 377n
Grus canadensis, 14n. *See also* Crane, sandhill

518

Index

Gulf of California, 316
Gull, Bonaparte's, 385, 387n, 388
Gull, glaucous-winged, 385, 387n, 388
Gulls, 9, 11, 13, 39, 42, 88, 96, 181, 383, 385
Gull, western, 383, 384n, 385, 387n, 388
Guns: Indian, 13, 15, 60–61, 76, 206, 208; stolen, 48–50; repaired, 147, 441–42; as trade item, 205, 360, 405; damaged, 416, 418; found, 450; mentioned, 113. *See also specific weapons and* Arms and ammunition
Guterich (and similar spellings). *See* Goodrich
Gymnogyps californianus, 67n. *See also* Condor, California
Gymnorhinus cyanocephalus, 131n

Hackmatack, 26, 28n
Hail. *See* Weather conditions
Haley. *See* Hill, Samuel
Haley's Bay. *See* Baker Bay
Half-Breed (Pine Island) Rapids, 449, 464, 473, 494
Haliaeetus leucocephalus, 94n. *See also* Eagle, bald
Hall, Hugh, 83, 384–85, 447, 462
Hamilton Creek, 7, 9n
Hamilton (Strawberry) Island, 7, 8–9, 9n, 54, 493
Handkerchiefs, 81, 136–37, 421
Hare. *See* Jackrabbit
Harpers Ferry, 441–42
Harpooners, 246, 249
Harrier, northern, 375, 377, 378n
Hat Rock, 454, 468
Hats. *See* Clothes
Hawaiian Islands, 192n, 307n
Hawk, Cooper's, 375, 378n
Hawk, fishing. *See* Osprey
Hawk, red-tailed, 94, 94n, 96, 375, 377, 378n
Hawks, 96–97, 101
Hawk, sparrow. *See* Kestrel, American
Hawk, Swainson's, 375, 377, 378n

Hayden (Image Canoe) Island, 16–17, 20n, 23, 55, 457, 470
Haystack Rock, 185n
Hazelnut, 345, 347n
Heceta, Bruno de, 36n
Hemlock, western, 3, 19n, 45n, 279–80, 280n, 284n
Hemp, Indian, 217n. *See also* Dogbane
Heron, great blue, 96, 98n, 383, 385, 388
Herpestes sp., 355n. *See also* Mongoose
Herring, 302, 305, 336–37
Hidatsa (Arwarharmay, Minetare) Indians, 169, 172n, 191, 405–6, 447, 462
Highwood Creek (Shields's River), 449, 464
Hill, Samuel, 27, 29n, 48n, 86n, 155–56, 160n, 416, 427, 432n
Hoh (Ca-last-ho-cle) Indians, 476, 486, 491
Holly, mountain, 297, 298n, 299, 302, 302n
Hominy, 235n
Honeysuckle, orange, 284–85, 286n
Hood (Labiche's) River, 456, 469, 472n, 475, 483, 487
Hooks, 134
Horse Prairie Creek, 465
Horses: left with Indians, 3; as food, 166, 452–53; food of, 211; Indians, 312–16, 317n, 336, 405–6; purchased, 421, 423; observed, 450; sacrificed, 455. *See also* Appaloosas
Horsetail, giant, 224, 225n, 230–31, 232n. *See also* Rushes
Hosiery, 83, 137, 230–31, 237, 242–43, 465
Howard, Thomas P., 83, 230–31, 237, 242–43
Huckleberries, 276–77, 373
Huckleberry, evergreen, 237–38, 239n, 297, 298n
Huckleberry, mountain, 285–86, 286n, 444, 444n
Hudson Bay, 481
Hungery Creek, 453, 467
Hull-loo-et-tell Indians. *See* Watlala Indians

Ilex montana, 302n. *See also* Holly, mountain
Illness. *See* Medical problems
Image Canoe Island. *See* Hayden Island
Indian Grave Peak, 467
Indians: relations with, 4, 31, 46–49, 50–51, 60, 72, 79, 81, 84–85, 90–91, 157, 234, 421, 428n, 444, 444n; clothing, 15–17, 30, 74–75, 144, 221, 235, 246, 336, 338, 405; housing, 15, 17, 218, 221; encountered, 22, 106, 126; visits, 43, 133–34, 145, 161, 347; villages, 53, 87; camps, 58; hunting, 73; utensils, 97, 215–17, 231–32, 234; food, 136, 228, 233, 239, 246, 251, 297, 370, 378, 388, 421; trade, 144, 165, 201, 204–5, 221, 314, 316; appearance, 144, 190, 433–34, 436–37, 439–40; information of, 160n, 204–5, 211, 213, 290–91, 305, 308, 406, 413; chiefs, 223; disease among, 240–41; tools, 243–44; artifacts, 296n; whaling, 407, 409n, 416n; fishing, 410–11; presents for, 421, 423, 426, 428, 441–42; mentioned, 86n. *See also specific Indian tribes and* Clothes: Indian
Indians, beliefs and customs of: 168–69, 190–91, 222–23, 233, 436, 440; head deformation, 3, 15, 159n, 253n, 368n, 433, 437, 440n, 476; sexual, 73, 75, 136, 137n, 416, 418, 427; tattooing, 74–75, 435, 439; burial, 89, 98–99n, 176, 182, 185n, 186, 455, 460; games, 118–19, 120n; treatment of elderly, 168–69, 172n, 190–91; pipe, 179, 405–6; medical, 240; slavery, 360, 365–67, 368n, 440n
Influenza. *See* Medical problems
Ink, 173n

519

Index

Insects, 94, 96, 145, 147
Interpreters, 158. *See also* Charbonneau; Drouillard
Iron, 207, 210, 440
Ixoreus naevius, 257 n. *See also* Thrush, varied

Jackets. *See* Clothes
Jackrabbit, white-tailed, 313, 315, 317 n, 359–62, 362 n
Jackson, 155–56, 427
James River, 395, 397
Jay, blue, 132, 133 n
Jay, gray, 130, 131 n, 162–63, 164 n, 379–80, 381 n
Jay, pinyon, 131, 131 n
Jay, Steller's, 94, 94 n, 131–32, 131 n, 133 n, 162–63, 261, 379–80, 381 n
Jefferson River: maps of, 307–11; distance to, 450; distance from, 473 n; Indians of, 479; latitude of, 492; distances on, 494; mentioned, 465
Jefferson, Thomas, 86 n, 445
Jellyfish, 423, 425 n, 426
Jerking, 186, 200, 203–4, 290, 293, 295, 302, 305, 365, 367
Jim Ford (Village) Creek, 453, 467
John Day (Ke-ke-mar-que) River (Clatsop County, Oreg.), 91, 91 n, 105
John Day (Lepage's) River (Sherman-Gilliam counties, Oreg.), 91 n, 455, 468, 480, 483
Johnson Slough, 125, 126 n
Jonah, 184
Journals. *See* Codex journals; First Draft; Elkskin-bound Journal; Orderly Book; Voorhis journals; Weather Diary
Judith River, 449, 463
Juno, 432 n

Kalama (Cath-la-haw's) River, 23, 25 n, 57, 457, 470
Kalispel (Coos-pel-lar) Indians, 481, 488, 491
Kalmia latifolia, 28 n
Kannuck Creek. *See* CK Creek
Kansa (Kanza) Indians, 405

Karlson Island, 397 n, 471
Karok Indians, 432 n
Kathlamet language, 34 n, 41 n
Katlaminimin (Clan-nar-minna-mun) Indians, 477, 484, 490
Kegs, 321, 324, 333, 335
Ke-ke-mar-que River. *See* John Day River
Kestrel, American, 375, 377, 378 n
Kettles, 113, 139–40, 187, 205, 275–76
Kilchis River, 185 n, 471
Kil-her-hurst, 461, 471
Kil-her-ner, 461, 471
Kilhow-â-nah-kle River. *See* Youngs River
Killamox (and similiar spellings) Indians. *See* Tillamook Indians
Ki-moo-ê-nim Creek. *See* Tucannon River
Kingbird, 130, 131 n
Kingfisher, belted, 383, 384 n, 385, 388
Kinnikinnick. *See* Bearberry
Kittita Indians, 491
Klaskanine River, 384 n
Klickitat (Cataract) River, 112, 294–95, 296 n, 456, 469, 479, 487, 493
Knife River, 447, 462
Knives: stolen, 31, 33, 46; as trade item, 74, 165, 187, 205, 214, 216, 221–22; lost, 195, 198 n; Indian, 246–51; mentioned, 172 n, 249 n, 253 n
Kooskooskee River. *See* Clearwater River
Kuske-lar. *See* Cus-ka-lah

Labiche, François: hunting, 8–10, 12, 38, 71–72, 226, 275–76, 279–80, 318, 328–29, 387 n, 415–16, 418, 420 n; duties of, 62, 65–66, 92, 172 n; votes, 83; sent out, 138, 140, 221, 391, 393; separated, 227, 229, 239–40; returns, 287–88, 324; discovers condor, 319, 322; information of, 321, 323, 342, 344, 387, 390

Lady (White Brant) Island, 11, 14 n
Lady Washington, 155–56, 160 n, 427
Laird Creek. *See* Warm Springs Creek
Lake Pend Oreille, 480, 488
Lake River, 24 n
Lake Winnipeg, 245, 248 n, 251
Lakjalama Indians, 25 n
Languages, Indian. *See specific Indian languages*
La Pérouse, Jean-François de Galaup, Comte de, 36 n, 50, 51 n
Larch, western, 28 n
Larix occidentalis, 28 n
Larus glaucescens, 387 n. *See also* Gull, glaucous-winged
Larus occidentalis, 384 n. *See also* Gull, western
Larus philadelphia, 387 n. *See also* Gull, Bonaparte's
Larus sp., 387 n. *See also* Gulls
Lastaro River. *See* Pend Oreille River
Lastaw River. *See* Pend Oreille River
Laudanum, 312, 316 n
Laurel. *See* Rhododendron, California
Laurel, mountain, 28 n
Lava, 179 n
Lead, 113, 205–6, 265, 272
Leadbetter Point, 470
Leggings. *See* Clothes
Lelia Bird, 29 n
Lemhi (East Fork Lewis's) River, 451, 465, 479, 482, 493, 493 n, 495
Lemon, 156
Lepage, Jean Baptiste: votes, 84; duties of, 172 n; sent out, 217 n, 242–43; hunting, 229 n; returns, 234, 275–76; illness of, 337, 357, 374, 376; information of, 338
Lepage's River. *See* John Day River
Lepus townsendii, 317 n. *See also* Jackrabbit, white-tailed
Lewis and Clark (Fort, Netul) River: site of Fort Clatsop, 2, 90 n, 242–43; arrive at, 95, 109, 114; animals of,

520

Index

108, 277; visits to, 221–22; hunting on, 241–42, 262, 267, 275–76, 287–88, 290, 296–97, 312, 314, 325–26, 328–29, 351, 353, 356, 360, 382, 388, 390–91, 393, 398–99, 409, 411, 443; Indian name of, 243; ice on, 253, 255; frozen, 363; listed, 459, 471; mentioned, 89, 98n, 115n, 171, 223n, 230n, 278–79, 390, 400–401, 403, 406–7
Lewis (Cah-wah-na-ki-ooks) River, 24n, 457, 470, 472n, 484. *See also* Salmon River; Snake River
Lewis, Meriwether: journal-keeping methods, 2–3, 24n, 34n, 77n, 94n, 98n, 101n, 104n, 131n, 151n, 158n, 257–58n, 261n, 262n, 406, 442n, 443n, 445, 473, 477n
Lewis, Samuel, 90n
Lice. *See* Fleas
Licorice. *See* Liquorice
Linnaean system, 346n
Liquor, 179, 196
Liquorice, common, 61, 61n, 229, 230n, 233. *See also* Lupine, seashore
Liquorice, wild, 229, 230n, 233
Little Gate of the Mountain, 450, 465
Little Knife River (Goat Pen Creek), 447, 462
Little Missouri River, 337–38, 447, 462, 496
Little Muddy (White Earth) River, 447, 462
Little Prickly Pear (Ordway's) Creek, 450, 464
Little White Salmon River, 469
Littorina sp., 409n. *See also* Periwinkles
Lizards, 94, 96
Lizard, western fence, 402, 405n, 408
Lobelia siphilitica, 242n. *See also* Cardinal-flower, blue
Lochsa River, 452, 466
Lolo (Collins's) Creek (Idaho), 453, 467

Lolo Hot Springs, 452, 466
Lolo Trail, 286n
Lolo (Travelers' Rest) Creek (Mont.): distance to, 308–10, 452, 493; distance from, 473n, 494–95; latitude of, 492; mentioned, 311n, 466
Lomatium cous, 192n. *See also* Cous
Lone Ridge, 383, 384n
Long Narrows. *See* The Dalles of the Columbia River
Lonicera ciliosa, 286n. *See also* Honeysuckle, orange
Loon, arctic, 391n
Loon, common, 391n
Loon, Pacific, 389–90, 391n, 438
Loon, red-throated, 390, 391n
Loons, 11, 74, 261, 383, 385, 391n
Loon, speckled. *See* Loon, Pacific
Louis veneri. *See* Medical problems: syphilis
Lower Chehalis language, 28n
Lower Chinook Indians, 218n
Lower Chinook language, 34n, 76n, 78n, 185n
Lower (Kil-la-wats) Umpqua Indians, 476, 485, 491
Lupine, seashore (cul-wha-mo), 60–61, 61n, 74, 76, 118, 133, 135, 139, 153–54, 224, 229, 230n, 233, 495
Lupinus littoralis, 61n. *See also* Lupine, seashore
Lutra canadensis, 162n. *See also* Otter
Lydia, 29n, 86n, 432n
Lye, 230–31
Lynx, Canada, 124, 124n, 327, 328n, 334
Lynx canadensis, 124n
Lynx rufus, 328n. *See also* Bobcat
Lynx rufus fasciatus, 77n. *See also* Bobcat, Oregon

Mace, 175, 178n, 197
McGee, 155–56, 160n, 427

McGuire Island, 14n, 15–16, 20n. *See also* Government Island
Mackenzie, Alexander, 107n
McKenzie Head, 63, 67n
Mackey. *See* McGee
McNeal, Hugh: illness of, 35, 242n, 254–55, 330, 332, 333n, 336–37, 356–57, 391, 393; votes, 84; separated, 125–26; duties of, 172n; and Indians, 181, 189, 194
Madison River, 308, 310, 450, 465
Madisons Cave, 356, 358n
Madrone, Pacific, 103, 105n
Magnesia, 178
Magpie, black-billed, 379–80, 381n
Makah (Quin-ne-chart) Indians, 161n, 416, 416n, 472n, 476, 486, 491
Ma-laugh, 73, 77n
Mallard, 96, 98n, 161–62, 383, 385, 395–96, 398, 400
Mallet, 113
Malus diversifolia, 19n. *See also* Crabapple, Oregon
Mammals. *See specific species*
Mandan Indians, 191, 405–6
Maple, bigleaf, 15, 17, 19n, 103, 104n, 294–95, 296n
Maples, 7, 26, 96, 98n
Maple, vine, 294–95, 296n
Maple, white, 294–95
Maps, 3, 47n, 181, 307, 309, 311n
March Island, 397n
Margaret, 160n
Marias River, 449, 464, 492, 493n, 496
Mar-lock-ke, 77n, 154
Martes pennanti, 317n. *See also* Fisher
Martin Island, 23, 25n
Mary, 160n
Mastiff, 339–40
Mats: use of, 33, 118–20, 216–17, 219–20, 378, 380, 435, 438–39; purchased, 74, 135–36, 146; as trade item, 90, 133, 153, 192, 196; making of, 305, 307, 307n

521

Index

Meadowlark, eastern, 379–80, 381 n
Meadowlark, western, 379–80, 381 n
Meares, John, 36 n, 191 n
Medals, Indian peace, 72–73, 75, 123, 142, 144, 172 n, 192, 196, 198 n, 330, 332, 432 n
Medical problems: venereal disease, 3, 65, 74, 76, 77 n, 416, 418; sea sickness, 35–36; cuts, 44; colds, 53–54, 122, 140–41, 143, 312, 336–37; syphilis, 74, 239, 241, 242 n, 254–55, 330, 332, 333 n, 356–57, 391, 393; smallpox, 81, 285–86, 286–87 n; diarrhea, 97, 98 n, 105; bowels, 97, 98 n, 105, 125; unidentified illness, 105–6, 121, 293, 295, 333, 335–36, 339–40, 342, 344, 356, 368, 370, 374, 384–85, 429–30, 441–42, 450; dislocated shoulder, 122; dysentery, 122; strains, 122, 126; boils, 122, 135; colic, 125; bruises, 135; muscle strain, 140; gonorrhea, 240–41; accidents, 293, 295; fever, 312, 314, 318–19, 321, 324, 336–37; back, 318–19, 330, 332, 388, 390, 393, 395–96, 443; coughs, 330, 332; influenza, 336–37; feet, 384–85; rheumatism, 395; legs, 443; sore throat, 444
Medicine: roots and herbs, 239; mercury, 239, 241, 242 n, 333 n, 391, 393; potassium nitrate, 312, 315, 316 n, 318–19; laudanum, 312, 315, 316 n, 388, 390; Rush's pills, 318–19, 321 n; barks, 318, 321, 321 n, 324, 333, 335; Scott's pills, 329, 330 n, 333, 335, 374, 376; alcohol, 388, 390, 390 n; camphor, 388, 390; castile soap, 388, 390, 390 n; liniment, 388, 390, 395–96; bleeding, 429–30

Melospiza melodia, 383 n. *See also* Sparrow, song
Members of the party, 235–36, 351, 353
Mephitis mephitis, 317 n. *See also* Skunk, striped
Merganser, common, 383, 384 n
Merganser, red-breasted, 383, 384 n, 385, 396–97
Mergus merganser, 384 n
Mergus serrator, 384 n. *See also* Merganser, red-breasted
Meriwether's Bay. *See* Youngs Bay
Meship, 155–56, 427
Meteorology. *See* Weather observations
Mexico, 160 n
Miami River, 355
Mice, 313, 315, 317 n
Microtus pennsylvanicus, 355 n. *See also* Mouse, meadow
Middle Chinook language, 34 n
Milk River, 448, 463
Mill Creek, 466
Minetare (and similar spellings) Indians. *See* Hidatsa Indians
Mink, 313, 315, 317 n, 341, 355 n
Mississippi River, 392, 394, 399–400
Missouri River: distance from, 59; animals of, 131, 161, 329, 331–32, 352, 355, 359–60, 366–67, 371, 379, 382, 402, 404, 406–7; Indians of, 190–91, 474, 480, 482; cache on, 275–76, 321, 441–42; maps of, 308–10, 430–31; White Cliffs, 329, 330 n, 334; mentioned, 311 n, 462
Mitchell, David D., 148 n
Moccasins. *See* Clothes
Mole, eastern, 355 n
Moles, 313, 315, 317 n
Mole, western, 355–56, 355 n
Monadenia fidelis, 405 n
Mongoose, 352, 354, 355 n, 434, 438
Mono-Paviotso (Sho-bar-boo-

be-er) Indians, 314, 316, 317 n, 479, 487, 491
Moon Creek, 466
Moore, Hugh, 155–56, 160 n, 302, 305, 307 n, 416, 427
Moose, 405 n
Mosquitoes, 139
Mount Adams, 21 n
Mountain lion, 114, 135, 136 n, 313, 315, 317 n, 355–56, 356 n, 434, 438
Mount Coffin, 27, 29 n
Mount Hood, 11–13, 14 n
Mount Jefferson, 478, 486
Mount Rainier, 87, 87 n, 112
Mount St. Helens, 16, 18, 20 n, 21 n, 56, 87, 112
Mouse, meadow, 355–56, 355 n
Mouse River. *See* Souris River
Mudstones, 179 n, 185 n
Mules, 314, 316, 317 n, 451
Muskets, 17, 121, 122 n, 146, 187, 205, 208
Muskrat, 402, 408
Mussels, 120 n, 407, 409 n, 421
Musselshell Rapids, 18, 454, 468, 474, 483
Musselshell River, 448, 463
Mustela, 355 n
Mustela frenata, 138 n. *See also* Weasel, long-tailed
Mustela vison, 317 n. *See also* Mink
Mycteria americana, 14 n. *See also* Stork, wood
Myristica fragrans, 178 n. *See also* Nutmeg
Mytilidae, 409 n
Mytilus sp., 409 n. *See also* Mussels

Nahpooitle Village, 24 n
Narrows of the Columbia River. *See* The Dalles of the Columbia River
Nasomah (Shal-la-lah) Indians, 476, 486, 491
Neacoxic (Neercawanaca) Creek, 171–72, 173 n, 175, 177, 194, 459, 471
Necanicum (Clatsop) River: Indians of, 120 n, 154, 184 n; conditions of, 175,

177, 193–95; distance to, 46 n; mentioned, 159 n, 178 n, 198 n, 471
Needles, 173 n, 333, 335
Ne-er-cho-ki-oo Indians. *See* Watlala Indians
Nehalem Bay, 185 n
Nehalem River (Ni-ê-lee Creek), 461, 471
Neotoma cinerea, 355 n. *See also* Woodrat, bushy-tailed
Neotoma floridana, 355 n. *See also* Woodrat, eastern
Nereocystis leutkeana, 423, 426, 428 n, 431–32
Nestucca Indians, 490
Nets, 211, 213–14, 216, 346, 349
Nettles, 217 n
Nettle, stinging, 26–27, 29 n
Netul River. *See* Lewis and Clark River
New Archangel, Alaska, 432 n
New Mexico, 311, 314, 316, 317 n
Newt, rough-skinned, 402, 405 n, 408
Nez Perce (Chopunnish, Ki-moo-ê-nim, Pel-lote-pal-lah, Wil-le-wah) Indians: relations with expedition, 3; language, 148 n; horses of, 313, 315; beliefs and customs of, 317 n; villages, 453; numbers, 474, 479–80, 482; mentioned, 284, 286, 328, 331–32, 489
Nickwall (Indian Fork) Creek, 447, 462
Ninebark, 103, 104 n, 285–86, 286 n
Nootka Indians, 272 n, 416 n
Nootka Sound, 187, 191 n, 205, 302, 305, 307 n
Nor-car-te, 154, 159 n
North Fork Clearwater (Chopunnish) River, 387–88, 453, 462, 467, 482
North Fork Salmon River (Fish Creek), 451, 466, 493
North Spring Creek, 466
North West Company, 94 n, 236, 329, 333 n
Northern Paiute (Shoshone) Indians, 479–80, 487, 491

Numenius americanus, 384 n. *See also* Curlew, long-billed
Nutmeg, 174, 178 n, 197

Oak, Oregon white, 15, 17, 19 n
Oak Point, 41 n
Oak, white, 3, 17, 345
O'Cain, 160 n
O'Cain, Joseph, 160 n
O-co-no, 154, 495
Octant, 317
Odderway (and similar spellings). *See* Ordway
Odocoileus hemionus columbianus, 70 n. *See also* Deer, Columbian black-tailed
Odocoileus virginianus, 405 n
Odocoileus virginianus leucura, 317 n
Ohio River, 392, 394, 397, 399–400
Oil, fish, 215, 217
Oil, train. *See* Oil, whale
Oil, whale: purchased, 2, 221–22; and Indians, 141–43, 178, 180, 183, 189, 193, 199, 233, 416; as food, 188, 407–8; mentioned, 175, 178 n, 197. *See also* Whales
Old Toby, 452
Olive Creek, 468
Oncorhynchus clarki, 414 n. *See also* Trout, cutthroat
Oncorhynchus kisutch, 409 n. *See also* Salmon, coho
Oncorhynchus mykiss, 409 n. *See also* Trout, steelhead
Oncorhynchus nerka, 41 n. *See also* Salmon, sockeye
Oncorhynchus tshawytscha, 414 n. *See also* Salmon, king
Oplopanax horridum, 45 n. *See also* Devil's club
Orderly Book, 152–53, 158 n, 161 n, 198 n. *See also* Detachment orders
Ordway, John: volunteers, 60; scouting party, 62, 65; votes, 83; separated, 125; illness of, 135, 336–37, 339; sent out, 199 n, 281, 287–88, 325–26, 329,

409, 411; returns, 229 n, 284–85, 333, 335; mentioned, 59 n, 244 n, 257 n, 327 n, 408 n, 428 n
Oreamnos americanus, 317 n. *See also* Goat, mountain
Oregon, camps in: Multnomah County, 10 n, 14 n; Columbia County, 24 n, 30 n; Clatsop County, 90 n, 91 n, 94 n, 115 n. *See also* Fort Clatsop
Orofino (Rock Dam) Creek, 453, 467
Osage Indians, 405–6
Osprey, 383, 384 n, 385, 388
Otter, river: hunted, 161–62, 174, 196, 430–31; as trade item, 187, 205, 444; and Indians, 208; mentioned, 162 n, 337–38, 313, 315, 317 n
Otter, sea: abundance of, 11; skins of, 72, 74, 76, 194–95, 214, 216, 354, 434, 438; as trade item, 73, 81, 83, 85, 121, 123–25, 165, 180, 187, 205, 221–22, 325, 327, 346, 395–96, 416, 418; and Indians, 208, 210; described, 339–42; named, 342 n; mentioned, 86 n, 166 n, 313, 315, 317 n. *See also* Seal, harbor
Overalls. *See* Clothes
Owl, dusky horned, 378 n
Owl, great horned, 376–77, 378 n
Owl, Montana horned, 378 n

Pacific Fur Company, 94 n
Pacific Ocean: observed, 31, 33, 48; conditions of, 50, 61, 103–4; arrive at, 51 n, 58–59; islands of, 205; map of, 309; trade of, 314, 316; animals of, 318, 324, 327, 335, 366–67; distance to, 458–59; mentioned, 71 n, 107 n, 311, 384 n
Pack Creek, 466
Packer Meadows, 466
Paddles, 97, 180, 182, 186, 263, 270, 272 n, 273 n

523

Index

Paint, 172 n
Paiute Indians, 13, 14 n
Palouse (Drouillard's) River, 454, 467
Palouse (So-yen-now) Indians, 482, 489
Pandion haliaetus, 384 n. *See also* Osprey
Panther camp, 495
Pantosteum platyrhynchus, 409 n
Paper, 173 n
Passerella iliaca, 164 n
Peale, Charles Willson, 66, 68 n, 144, 145 n
Peale's Museum, 144–45
Pelican Rapids, 454, 468
Pen, 173 n
Pend d'Oreille (La-hân-na) Indians, 480, 487, 491
Pend Oreille (Clark's, Lastaro or Lastaw) River, 325 n, 480, 482, 487–88
Pennyweight, 192 n
Penutian language family, 432 n
Perisoreus canadensis, 131 n. *See also* Jay, gray
Periwinkles, 407, 409 n, 420–21
Personnel. *See* Members of the Party
Phalacrocorax auritus, 14 n. *See also* Cormorant, double-crested
Philanthropy River. *See* Ruby River
Phoca Rock, 9, 10 n, 457, 470
Phoca vitulina richardii, 10 n. *See also* Seal, harbor
Phocoena phocoena, 414 n. *See also* Porpoise, harbor
Phoenix, 160 n
Physocarpa capitatus, 104 n. *See also* Ninebark
Physocarpa opulifolius, 104 n
Pica pica, 381 n. *See also* Magpie, black-billed
Picea engelmannii, 19 n
Picea sitchensis, 19 n. *See also* Spruce, Sitka
Pigeon, passenger, 369, 371, 373 n
Pillar Rock, 33, 34 n, 87 n
Pilot. *See* Old Toby
Pine Island Rapids. *See* Half-Breed Rapids

Pine, ponderosa, 3, 19 n
Pines: abundance of, 7, 22–26, 43–44, 89, 114, 183, 194; observed, 8–9, 11, 15, 27, 42, 96, 98, 116–17, 183; habitat of, 70; use of, 107, 124, 172, 230–31, 249, 251; seeds of, 373, 375; mentioned, 19 n, 237
Pine, shore, 44, 45 n
Pine, spruce. *See* Spruce, Sitka
Pine Tree (Cave) Rapids, 454, 467
Pine, western white, 3, 207, 279–80, 282–84, 284 n
Pinus contorta, 45 n. *See also* Pine, shore
Pinus monticola, 284 n. *See also* Pine, western white
Pipe, 83, 147, 179, 196, 223–24, 405–6
Pipit, Sprague's, 382–83, 383 n
Pirogues. *See* Canoes
Pish-quit-pah (and similar spellings) Indians. *See* Yakima Indians
Pisquow (Shal-lât-to, Shan-wap-pom, Skâddât, Squân-nar-oo) Indians, 479, 487, 491
Pistols, 16–17
Pitch, 124 n
Pits, 206, 208, 210
Plants. *See specific species*
Plates, 187, 216–17
Platichthys stellatus, 67 n. *See also* Flounder, starry
Platte River, 11–12
Platters, 119
Plovers, 9, 13, 62, 66, 383
Pluck, 416, 418, 420 n
Podiceps auritus, 401 n. *See also* Grebe, horned
Podiceps grisegena, 401 n. *See also* Grebe, red-necked
Podilymbus podiceps, 401 n. *See also* Grebe, pied-billed
Point Adams: observed, 49–50, 188; named, 51; located, 62, 65, 88, 109, 114–16; conditions of, 67; Indians of, 76 n, 133 n, 140, 177, 475, 485; sketch

of, 104 n; distance to, 189, 192–93, 459; visits to, 221–22; listed, 471, 494; mentioned, 53–54, 59, 95, 98 n, 115 n, 138, 228–29, 233–36, 275, 276 n, 312, 321, 324, 351, 353, 356, 382, 391, 393, 409, 411
Point Ellice (Point Distress), 40 n, 48–50, 51 n, 53, 458, 470
Point Lewis, 458, 470
Point Meriwether. *See* Astoria
Point Vancouver, 14 n
Point William. *See* Tongue Point
Polecat. *See* Skunk
Polygonatum biflorum, 242 n
Polystichum munitum, 307 n. *See also* Fern, Christmas
Pomona Basalt flow, 34 n
Poplar (Porcupine) River, 447, 462
Populus trichocarpa, 20 n. *See also* Cottonwood, black
Porcupine, 353, 358
Pork, 113
Porpoise, harbor, 407, 410–11, 414 n
Post Office Lake, 21 n
Potassium nitrate. *See* Medicine
Potlatch River (Colter's Creek), 453, 467, 482
Potoash Indians. *See* Salishan Indians
Potomac River, 395, 397
Pots, 187
Potts, John, 83, 162, 164, 172 n
Powder. *See* Arms and ammunition
Pox. *See* Medical problems: syphilis
Prairie-chicken, greater, 366, 368 n
Prairie Elk Creek (Little Dry River), 447, 463
Prince William Henry, 160 n
Procyon lotor, 211 n. *See also* Raccoon
Pronghorn, 313, 315, 317 n, 336, 338, 339 n
Provisions, 113, 223, 259
Pryor, Nathaniel: volunteers,

524

Index

60; scouting party, 62, 65; votes, 83; sent out, 106n, 133, 181, 189, 275–77, 296–97, 336, 381–82, 409, 411; information of, 106–7; returns, 114, 281–82, 287–88, 312, 314, 401–2; illness of, 122; duties of, 172n, 428–30; separated, 307, 309, 395–96; mentioned, 426, 436, 440–42
Pryor's Valley Creek. See Spokane Creek
Pseudotsuga menziesii, 19n. See also Fir, Douglas
Pteridium aquilinium, 224n. See also Fern, western bracken
Puddingberry, 45n. See also Bunchberry
Puget (Sturgeon, Sea Otter) Island, 27, 29n, 30, 33n, 41n, 458, 470
Pulicidae family, 29n
Puncheons, 133–34, 136
Pyrus fusca, 19n

Quannio. See Coboway
Quartz, 179n
Quath-lah-poh-tle (and similar spellings) Indians. See Cathlapotle Indians
Queet (Qui-eet-so) Indians, 472n, 476, 486, 491
Quercus garryana, 19n. See also Oak, Oregon white
Quicksand River. See Sandy River
Quileute (Chil-lâte) Indians, 472n, 476, 486, 491
Quill wood. See Holly, mountain
Quinault (Qui-ni-ilt) Indians, 221n, 459, 476, 486, 491
Quioo, 155, 159n
Quiver. See Bows and arrows

Rabbits. See Cottontail
Rabelais, François, 164n
Raccoon: skins of, 162, 434, 438; and Indians, 208, 210; habitat of, 313, 315, 317n, 344, 347; mentioned, 211n
Raft, 72, 116–18

Rain. See Weather conditions
Rainbow Falls, 449, 464
Rainier, Peter, 87n
Raja binoculata, 178n. See also Skate, big
Ramsay, Jack, 147, 148n
Rats, 313, 315, 317n
Rattlesnake Cliffs, 451, 465, 496
Rattlesnakes, 402, 408, 451
Raven, common, 94, 94n, 96, 181, 261, 375, 377, 378n
Razor, 141–42
Redcedar, western (arborvitae, white cedar): observed, 25–27, 176, 183, 194, 284; abundance of, 26; and Indians, 30, 32, 74, 77n, 186, 206, 209, 211, 214–16, 221, 246, 262, 267, 325, 327, 434–36, 438–39; mentioned, 28n, 45n, 284n, 293n
Red Rock (East Fork Jefferson) River, 451, 465
Red Water (2000 Mile) Creek, 447, 462
Reed Island, 14n
Rezanov, Nicolai, 432n
Rheumatism. See Medical problems
Rhododendron, California (laurel), 26–27, 28–29n, 97, 98n, 117
Rhododendron macrophyllum, 28n
Rhus copallina, 242n. See also Sumac, dwarf
Ribbons, 139, 142, 144, 172n
Ricare (and similar spellings) Indians. See Arikara Indians
Rifles: stolen, 50; use of, 119, 120–21, 181; and Indians, 206, 208; and party, 224, 233, 235
Rio Grande, 311n, 316
Robes: rotten, 33, 42–43, 47, 91; Indian, 40, 72, 75–76, 90, 142, 144, 248, 262n, 327, 345, 348, 351, 354, 434, 438, 480; as trade item, 49, 123–25, 206, 208, 358, 360; burial, 97, 186; infested, 122–23; mentioned, 421, 423

Robin, American, 254, 256, 257n, 363–64, 379–80
Rock Creek, 468
Rock (North Mountain) Creek, 448, 463
Rocky Mountains: conditions of, 2–3; crossing, 84, 211, 213, 311; plants of, 104n, 240, 245, 251; animals of, 131, 254–55, 318, 324, 328, 331–32, 338, 371, 376–77, 379–80, 396–97, 404–5, 413; maps of, 308–9; Indians of, 310, 313, 474, 482, 488; distances in, 472n, 492; mentioned, 315, 336, 346, 355–56, 358, 360, 366–67, 402, 406, 481
Rocky Rapids, 455, 468
Roots: as food, 2, 106, 118, 138, 188; purchased, 16, 18, 61, 76, 85, 89–90, 120–21, 142, 161–63, 414–15; and Indians, 60, 74, 154, 168, 190, 205, 216–17, 224, 307; as trade item, 123–24, 134, 136, 145, 152, 164–65, 214, 360; as gift, 137, 139; described, 228, 233; mentioned, 358
Roses, 96, 98
Rosin, 277–83
Rover, 160n
Rubus spectabilis, 104n. See also Salmonberry
Rubus ursinus, 20n. See also Blackberry, Pacific
Ruby (Philanthropy) River, 451, 465, 494
Ruminantia, 405n
Rush, Benjamin, 321n
Rushes: observed, 26; and Indians, 77n, 119, 135, 146–47, 188, 192–93, 196, 216–17, 439–40; and elk, 276; mentioned, 29n. See also Horsetail, giant
Russians, 2, 432n

Sacagawea: and Indians, 1–2; votes, 84, 86n; gives gifts, 97, 137; cooking, 106–7; volunteers, 168, 171; mentioned, 172n

525

Index

Saccacommis. *See* Bearberry
Saddle Mountain (Idaho), 452, 466
Saddle Mountain (Oreg.), 127, 127n, 383, 384n
Sagamity, 233, 235n
Sagittaria latifolia, 19n. *See also* Wapato
Sagittaria sagittifolia, 20n
Saint Helena, 20n
Saint Louis, Mo., 148n, 445
Salal: discovered, 3; and Indians, 119, 139, 235–36; named, 120n; Indian name for, 120n, 495; and elk, 276–77; described, 287–90; mentioned, 237n, 239n, 278n, 290n
Salishan Indians, 472n, 475–76, 485–86, 489, 490–91
Salishan language, 184n, 186n, 237n, 432n, 477n, 490
Salish Indians. *See* Flathead Indians
Salix lasiandra, 29n
Salix scouleriana, 29n
Salix sitchensis, 29n
Salmo clarkii, 414n
Salmo gairdneri, 409n
Salmon: purchased, 36, 76; fished for, 42–43; as gift, 74; and Indians, 118, 180, 184, 192, 196, 211, 214, 480, 487; as trade item, 187, 203–5; scarcity of, 308, 310; migration of, 336, 338, 414n; observed, 407
Salmon, coho, 407, 409n, 421, 425
Salmon Creek, 21n
Salmon, king, 410, 412, 414n
Salmon (Lewis's, Main Fork Lewis's, Southeast Fork of Columbia) River, 308–10, 311n, 314, 316, 451, 465, 482
Salmon, sockeye, 40–41, 41n, 407, 411–13, 414n, 415
Salmonberry, 102, 104n, 298, 299n
Salt: need for, 84–85, 441–42; making, 140, 140n, 166–67, 171, 195,
275–76; use of, 211–12, 245–46; scarcity of, 227, 229; sent for, 230, 237; quantity of, 235–36, 321, 324, 333, 335; brought in, 242–43; mentioned, 113, 116, 138
Saltgrass, seashore, 305, 307n
Saltmaking camp: established, 2, 140, 166–67; maps of, 127n; site of, 140n, 192n; arrive at, 175, 177, 188; men at, 194–95, 200, 223n, 235–36, 307, 309, 312, 314; visits, 230–31, 237–40, 275–76, 297, 325–26, 328–29; conditions at, 242–43, 253, 255, 321, 324; evacuated, 333, 335; mentioned, 162, 293, 295, 460, 471
Sambucus canadensis, 286n
Sambucus cerulea, 104n. *See also* Elderberry, blue
Sambucus glauca, 104n
Sambucus racemosa, 104n
Sand, 230n
Sand (Big Dry) Creek, 447, 462
Sand Island, 50, 51n
Sandpiper, spotted, 382–83, 383n
Sandstones, 67n, 179n, 185n
Sandwich Islands, 307n
Sandy (Quicksand) River: arrive at, 11–12, 14n, 55, 101n; conditions of, 24; distance to, 112, 457, 493; plants of, 229, 233, 298, 298n; animals of, 324, 325n; located at, 461, 469; Indians of, 484; mentioned, 13, 18, 59, 83–84, 86n
Sanpoil (Hi-high-e-nim-mo) Indians, 480, 488, 491
Sapsucker, red-breasted, 379–80, 381n
Sarcobatus vermiculatus, 373n. *See also* Greasewood
Sassafras, 174, 197
Sauvie (Wapato) Island: Indians of, 21n, 475, 477–78, 484, 490; maps of, 24n, 186n; distance to,
457; mentioned, 20n, 25n, 461, 470, 494
Scalopus sp., 355
Scapanus sp., 355n. *See also* Mole, western
Sceloporus occidentalis, 405n. *See also* Lizard, western fence
Scirpus sp., 29n, 307n. *See also* Bulrushes; Rushes
Sciurus griseus, 317n. *See also* Squirrel, western gray
Sciurus niger, 347n. *See also* Squirrel, fox
Scott, Hugh, 330n
Scumar-qua-up, 155, 159n
Seal, harbor: abundance of, 13, 55; described, 340–42; mentioned, 10n, 14n, 313, 315, 317n, 342n, 457
Seal River. *See* Washougal River
Seaweed, 431
Sedges, 77n, 216–17, 217n, 304, 307
Serviceberry, 45–46n
Sevenbark. *See* Ninebark
Seven Blackfoot (Burnt Lodge) Creek, 448, 463
Seventh Point Coulee (Pine Creek), 448, 463
Sewelel. *See* Beaver, mountain
Sextant, 82, 255, 257, 277, 317, 410, 417
Sha-ha-la Indians. *See* Watlala Indians
Shâh-hâr-wâr-cap, 192, 196
Shakespeare, William, 164n
Shaler, William, 29n
Shallow Bay. *See* Grays Bay
Shal-lun. *See* Salal
Shannon, George: hunting, 16, 177, 190, 227, 229, 244n, 275–76, 279–80, 328–29; sent out, 45, 118, 138, 140, 162, 164, 221, 317–18, 351, 353, 414–15; returns, 47–48, 124, 194–95, 226, 239–40, 287–88, 324, 358, 360, 420n; information of, 50, 342, 344; volunteers, 60; scouting party, 62, 65, 92; votes, 83; duties of, 172n, 368n; separated, 179; discovers condor, 319, 321–22; discovers eagle, 323

526

Index

Sha-no-ma, 154, 159n
Shappelell. *See* Cous
Sharbono (and similar spellings). *See* Charbonneau
Shaw-natâhque (and similar spellings). *See* Thistle, edible
Sheep, bighorn, 448
Shelathwell, 72, 73n, 154, 159n, 333n
Shelewele (and similar spellings). *See* Salal
Shell Creek (Goose Eggs Lake Run), 447, 462
She-ne-tock-we. *See* Thistle, edible
Shields, John: votes, 83; blacksmith, 158, 441–43; duties of, 172n, 368n, 395–96; sent out, 351, 353, 401; returns, 358, 360, 391, 393; information of, 390; hunting, 400, 401n, 403; fishing, 451
Shil-lar-la-wit. *See* Shelathwell
Shirts. *See* Clothes
Shoalwater Bay, 69
Shocatilicum, 184, 185n
Shoes. *See* Clothes
Shonkin Creek (Snow River), 449, 464
Short Narrows. *See* The Dalles of the Columbia River
Short Rapids, 455, 468
Shoshonean language, 317n
Shoshone (Snake) Indians: information of, 3, 310, 316; language, 13, 14n; tobacco, 123; games, 273–74; located, 311, 313–15, 451, 495; numbers, 479, 482, 487; mentioned, 433, 437, 483, 489, 491
Shot. *See* Arms and ammunition
Sialia currucoides, 131n
Siletz River, 202n
Silica, 178, 179n
Silt, 230n
Siltstone, 67n
Sioux Indians, 169, 191
Sitka. *See* New Archangel
Sitka spruce vegetation zone, 45n, 104n, 284n, 307n
Siuslaw (She-a-stuck-kle) Indians, 237n, 432n, 476, 485, 491
Siuslawan language, 237n
Sixteenmile (Howard's) Creek, 450, 465
Skalkaho (Horse Valley) Creek, 452, 466
Skate, big, 175, 177, 178n, 407, 410, 412, 414n
Skelley (or Shellie), 155–56, 427
Skewers, 215–16
Skil-lute (and similar spellings) Indians. *See* Watlala Indians
Skipanon River, 95, 98n, 116–18, 117n, 275–76, 276n, 312, 316n, 325–26, 327n
Skitswish (Skeet-so-mish) Indians, 480, 488, 492
Skunk, eastern spotted, 355n
Skunk, striped, 313, 315, 317n, 355, 356n, 360
Slavery, 365, 367n
Slug, Pacific woods, 145, 146n, 147
Smilacina racemosa, 242n. *See also* Solomon's seal, false
Smilacina sessilifolia, 242n
Smilacina stellata, 242n. *See also* Solomon's seal, false
Smith River, 449, 464
Smith, Silas B., 123n, 185n
Smock-Shop (and similar spellings) Indians. *See* Wishram-Wasco Indians
Snails, 96, 402, 408
Snake Creek (Miry River), 447, 462
Snake, garter, 100, 408
Snake Indians. *See* Shoshone Indians
Snake (Lewis's, Southeast Fork of Columbia) River: Indians of, 204, 474, 479, 482, 487, 491; maps of, 309, 430–31; described, 311; animals of, 368, 370, 413, 415; distances on, 446, 453; distance to, 461; mentioned, 311n, 467–68
Snake, Pacific red-sided garter, 22, 24, 100, 101n, 402, 405n, 408
Snakes, 94, 96, 137–38, 145, 147, 259, 458. *See also specific species*
Snares, 206, 208, 345, 347
Snipe, common, 382–83, 383n
Snow. *See* Weather conditions
Snow (Brown Bear Defeated) Creek, 448, 463
Snow Mountains. *See* Bitterroot Mountains
Soap, 230–31, 388, 390n
Socks. *See* Clothes
Sokulk Indians. *See* Wanapam Indians
Sol-me, 45, 45n, 235–36, 237n, 240–42, 242n, 495. *See also* Bunchberry; Solomon's seal, false
Solomon's seal, 242n
Solomon's seal, false, 240–42, 242n
Soto, 148n
Souris (Mouse) River, 447
South Boulder (Frazer's) Creek, 450, 465
Southeast Fork of Columbia River. *See* Salmon River; Snake River
South Mountain Creek, 448, 463
Spaniels, 120, 122n
Spanish, 86n, 148n, 160n, 314, 316
Sparrow, fox, 162, 164n
Sparrow, golden-crowned, 162–63, 164n
Sparrow, song, 382–83, 383n
Spears, 17, 206, 208, 210
Spenser, Edmund, 164n
Spermophilus tridecemlineatus, 347n. *See also* Squirrel, thirteen-lined ground
Sphyrapicus ruber, 381n. *See also* Sapsucker, red-breasted
Spiders, 94, 96
Spilogale putorius, 355n
Spokane (Hi-high-e-nim-mo, Lar-ti-e-to) Indians, 480, 488, 491–92
Spokane (Pryor's Valley) Creek, 450, 464, 495
Spoons, 134, 215–17
Spring (Little Dry) Creek, 447, 462
Spruce, Engelmann, 19n

Index

Spruce, Sitka (spruce pine): abundance of, 26, 43–44; observed, 42–44, 176, 398, 400; use of, 77n; described, 276–78, 291–93, 325–26; mentioned, 3, 7, 9, 15, 19n, 45n, 124n, 278n, 293n, 327n, 401n
Spuck. *See* Otter, sea
Squaw (Blowing Fly) Creek, 448, 463
Squawmash. *See* Camas
Squirrel, Douglas's, 313, 315, 317n, 345, 347n, 348
Squirrel, fox, 345, 347n
Squirrel, red, 345, 347n, 348
Squirrel, Richardson's red, 101–2, 104n, 313, 315, 317n, 345, 347n, 348
Squirrel, thirteen-lined ground, 346, 347n, 348
Squirrel, western gray, 313, 315, 317n, 344, 347, 347n
Station Camp, 458, 470. *See also* Chinook Point
Sterna forsteri, 387n
Stickney Creek (Gun Brook), 464
Stil-la-sha, 73, 76–77n
Stock-home. *See* Tàh-cum
Stork, wood, 13, 14n
Storms. *See* Weather conditions
Strait of Juan de Fuca, 416n
Strawberry Island. *See* Hamilton Island
Strawberry, woodland, 9n, 54
Sturgeon: as gift, 72, 74; and Indians, 121, 184, 206, 209; as food, 344, 368, 370, 378–79, 402–3; as trade item, 346; fished for, 351, 353; purchased, 358, 360; migration of, 364
Sturgeon, green, 68, 70, 70n
Sturgeon, white, 342, 346n
Sturnella magna, 381n. *See also* Meadowlark, eastern
Sturnella neglecta, 381n. *See also* Meadowlark, western
Sucker, mountain, 407, 409n, 414–15
Sucker, northern, 409n
Sugar, 113
Sumac, dwarf, 240–41, 242n
Sun (Medicine) River, 449, 464

Sunken Village, 20–21n
Susquehanna River, 395, 397
Sutherland (Gibson's) Creek, 448, 463
Swans: observed, 9, 11; hunted, 11–12, 22–23, 91–92; abundance of, 11, 13, 35, 88, 92; mentioned, 21, 73, 171, 261, 391
Swan, trumpeter, 11, 13, 14n, 161–62, 383, 385, 395–96, 397n
Swan, tundra, 11, 13, 14n, 161–62, 383, 385, 395–96, 397n
Swan, whistling. *See* Swan, tundra
Swepeton (and similar spellings), 155–56, 416, 427, 436, 439
Sword, 15
Sylvilagus floridanus, 317n. *See also* Cottontail, eastern
Sylvilagus nuttallii, 317n. *See also* Cottontail, Nuttall's
Syphilis. *See* Medical problems

Table, 138
Tàh-cum, 154, 159n, 330, 332, 333n
Tallamon. *See* Callamon
Tallow, 107, 201–2
Tamarack, 28n
Tamiasciurus douglasii, 317n. *See also* Squirrel, Douglas's
Tamiasciurus hudsonicus, 347n. *See also* Squirrel, red
Tamiasciurus hudsonicus richardsoni, 104n. *See also* Squirrel, Richardson's red
Tamias striatus, 347n
Tanner's ooze, 102, 104n, 175, 197
Tanning, 230–31, 232n
Tansey Creek, 276
Tapteete (and similar spellings) River. *See* Yakima River
Taricha granulosa, 405n. *See also* Newt, rough-skinned
Taxidea taxus, 21n. *See also* Badger
Teal, blue winged, 383, 384n, 385, 398–99, 400–401
Teals, 383, 384n, 398–400
Tenasillahe Island, 32, 34n, 58

Tenino (E-ne-shur, Wah-howpum) Indians, 201, 455, 468–69, 474, 483, 490
Tern, Forster's, 387n
Thaleichthys pacificus, 346n. *See also* Eulachon
Thamnophis sirtalis concinnus, 101n. *See also* Snake, Pacific red-sided garter
The Dalles of the Columbia River (Long Narrows, Short Narrows), 355, 360, 455, 462, 469, 483, 493
The Needles, 185n
Thermometers, 259. *See also* Weather observations
Thimbles, 113
Thistle, edible (shaw-natâhque): purchased, 74, 123; use of, 76, 183, 224, 233; gift, 139; trade, 146–47, 183; described, 226–27; mentioned, 77n, 123n, 227n
Thompson, John B.: votes, 83; sent out, 296–97, 409, 411; duties of, 365, 367; returns, 414–15
Thread, 173n, 192, 214, 216
Three Forks of the Missouri River, 450, 465, 494–95
Thrush, varied: described, 254–56; observed, 261, 363; habitat of, 379–80; mentioned, 257n, 262n, 365n, 381n
Thuja plicata, 28n. *See also* Redcedar, western
Tides: height of, 8–10, 15–16, 34n, 60–61, 107–9; effect of, 27, 30, 32–33, 35–46, 48, 50, 73, 75, 114, 175, 181, 196, 199, 203, 275–76, 278, 280
Tillamook (Kilamox) Bay, 184n, 185n, 461, 471
Tillamook Head (Clark's Point of View): observed, 67, 68n; Indians of, 76n, 120, 122n; crossing, 176; conditions of, 178, 178n, 182–83, 188, 193–94; distance to, 460; mentioned, 184n, 471, 493
Tillamook (Killamox) Indians: 184n; food of, 2,

528

193, 230–31; customs, 99n, 168, 180, 182, 188, 365, 367; located, 112, 144n, 164n, 201–2, 284; chiefs, 154, 159n, 495; trade, 162–63, 183, 199, 224; lodges, 166–67, 180, 184; villages, 182–84, 185n, 460–61, 471; language, 186n, 237n, 430–32, 432n; relations with expedition, 189–90; culture, 194–95; bands, 202n, 236, 490; artifacts, 208; canoes, 265, 271; war, 365, 367; appearance, 433–40; visits, 444; numbers, 475–76, 485; mentioned, 115n, 143, 176, 192n, 262n, 286, 427
Tillamook (Killamox) River, 461, 471
Timber (Bratton's) Creek, 448, 463
Tipi, 127
Tipulidae, 139n
Tlashgenemaki Village, 34n
Tobacco: Indian, 123; as trade item, 134, 187, 192, 205, 426, 428; as present, 137; purchased, 146–47; and Indians, 179, 196; mentioned, 113
Tobacco (Hall's Strand) Creek, 447, 462
Tomahawk Island, 20n
Tomahawks, 15, 17–18, 117, 293, 295, 457
To-mar-lar, 148n
Tongue Point (Point William): located, 37n, 471; Indians of, 41n, 76n; named, 90–91, 91n; arrive at, 101; conditions of, 104, 151n; distance to, 459; sketch of, 472n; mentioned, 441, 443
Tonquin, 94n
Tools, 203. *See also individual items*
Towarnahiooks. *See Deschutes River*
Tower Creek, 451, 466, 493
Tow-er-quottons Creek, 461, 471
Towhead Gulch (Pott's Valley Creek), 450, 464

Tow-wâll, 73, 77n, 112
Traders: and Indians, 2, 19, 48n, 148n, 179, 202–4, 206; messages left for, 4, 430–31; explorations of, 36n, 37n; information about, 47, 50, 62, 66, 84–85, 186–87, 190, 201; named, 155–56, 159–61n, 302, 307n, 416, 416n, 427; posts, 191n, 307n; information of, 329; mentioned, 314, 428n, 441. *See also names of individual traders*
Trail Creek, 451, 465
Traps, 161–62, 296n, 430
Trask River, 185n
Travelers' Rest, 432n, 472–73
Travelers' Rest Creek. *See Lolo Creek (Mont.)*
Trenchers, 118–19
Triticum sp., 368n
Troglodytes troglodytes, 94n. *See also Wren, winter*
Trousers. *See Clothes*
Trout, 211, 214
Trout, cutthroat, 407, 409n, 413, 415
Troutdale Formation, 94n
Trout, salmon. *See Trout, steelhead*
Trout, steelhead, 3, 27, 30, 42–43, 45, 407, 409n, 413–15, 414n
Tsuga heterophylla, 45n. *See also Hemlock, western*
Tucannon River (Ki-moo-ê-nim Creek), 453, 467, 493
Turdus migratorius, 257n. *See also Robin, American*
Tututni (Han-na-kal-lal, Luck-kar-So) Indians, 477, 477n, 486, 491
Tympanuchus cupido, 368n. *See also Prairie-chicken, greater*
Tympanuchus phasianellus, 368n
Tympanuchus phasianellus columbianus, 368n. *See also Grouse, Columbian sharp-tailed*
Typha latifolia, 29n. *See also Cat-tail, common*
Tyrannus tyrannus, 131n. *See also Kingbird*

Umatilla (Youmatolam) River, 480, 487
Umpqua Indians, 237n, 432n
Unionidae, 409n
Upper Chinook language, 20n, 21n, 25n, 34n, 41n, 76n
Ursus americanus, 293n. *See also Bear, black*
Ursus horribilus, 317n. *See also Bear, grizzly*
Urtica dioica, 29n. *See also Nettle, stinging*

Vaccinium membranaceum, 286n. *See also Huckleberry, mountain*
Vaccinium ovatum, 239n. *See also Huckleberry, evergreen*
Vaccinium oxycoccos, 77n. *See also Cranberry, wild*
Vancouver, George, 1, 14n, 20n, 29n, 46–47, 47n, 50, 51n, 87n, 115n, 160n
Vancouver Island, 191n, 272n, 307n
Vancouver Lake, 21n
Vanilla, common, 175, 178n, 197
Vanilla fragrans, 178n. *See also Vanilla, common*
Varnish, 206, 210n
Velella sp., 425n. *See also Jellyfish*
Venereal disease. *See Medical problems*
Veneridae, 409n
Vests. *See Clothes*
Viburnum trilobum, 45n
Volcanics, Goble, 28n
Voorhis journals: Voorhis No. 2 begins, 248n, 253n; discussed, 290n; Voorhis No. 4 discussed, 446, 473, 488n. *See also Codex journals; Elkskin-bound Journal; First Draft*
Vulpes velox, 317n. *See also Fox, swift*
Vulpes vulpes, 192n, 330n. *See also Fox, red*
Vulture. *See Condor, California*

Wah-clel-lah Indians. *See Watlala Indians*

Index

Wah-how-pum Indians. *See* Tenino Indians
Wahkiakum (War-ci-â-cum) Indians: 34n; language, 31–32, 41n; clothes, 32, 75, 251; lodges, 32, 221n; appearance, 32, 433, 437; villages, 33, 37n, 58, 458–59, 470; name, 33n; beliefs, 34n; culture, 34n; relations with expedition, 47; encountered, 50; visits, 142, 144–47; chiefs, 155, 159n; canoes, 263, 270; numbers, 475, 485; mentioned, 89, 281, 401–3, 474, 490
Wah-na-a-chee River. *See* Wenatchee River
Wakashan language, 416n
Walker Island, 27, 28n
Wallace Island, 29n, 30n. *See also* Puget Island
Wallacut (Chinook) River, 62, 66, 67n, 68–70, 71n, 113, 475, 485
Walla Walla (and similar spellings) Indians. *See* Walula Indians
Walla Walla (Waller Waller) River, 454, 468, 480, 487
Walula Indians, 148n, 474, 483, 490
Wampum, 135–36, 172n, 215–16, 436, 439
Wanapam (Sokulk) Indians, 313, 315, 454, 468, 474, 482, 487, 489
Wannershia, 235n
Wapato: as food, 15, 17, 44, 152–53, 368, 370, 378–79, 402–3; habitat of, 24, 229, 233; purchased, 25, 27, 30–33, 79, 89, 106, 146–47; as trade item, 49–50, 123, 142, 144, 185n, 195–96, 199, 336–37, 461; and Indians, 53, 76, 87, 154, 193; as present, 60, 72, 74, 192; scarcity of, 165–66; mentioned, 19n, 20n
Wapiti. *See* Elk
War-ci-â-cum (and similar spellings) Indians. *See* Wahkiakum Indians
War-ho-lote, 154, 159n

Warm Springs (Flour Camp) Creek, 452, 466
Warner. *See* Werner
Washington, camps in: Clark County, 21n; Wahkiakum County, 34n, 87n; Wahkiakum-Pacific counties, 37n; Pacific County, 40n, 51n, 59n, 67–68n, 71n, 73n
Washougal (Seal) River, 11–12, 14n, 457, 469
Watap, 262, 267, 272n, 325, 327, 436, 440
Watch, 81, 165
Watlala (Sha-ha-la, Skil-lute) Indians: 10n; villages, 8, 17, 20n, 55–56, 456–57, 469–70; culture, 19; visits, 146–47; relations with expedition, 146–47; located, 201, 458; trade, 203–4, 224; clothes, 249, 251; numbers, 475, 478, 483–84; mentioned, 485, 490
Waves. *See* Weather conditions
Waytom Lake. *See* Lake Pend Oreille
Weapons. *See specific weapons* and Arms and ammunition
Weasel, long-tailed, 137, 138n
Weasels, 355n
Weather conditions: wind, 1, 38–43, 46, 48–49, 53, 59, 73, 75, 79, 92, 100, 104, 107–9, 126–27, 130, 138, 150, 201–2, 312, 314, 344, 347, 349, 364, 387, 390, 398, 401–2, 441; rain, 2, 22, 24, 35–36, 38, 40–44, 48, 69, 79, 90, 107–8, 126–27, 429–30, 432, 436, 440–41; fog, 10–12, 30–31, 33, 58, 100; waves, 35–38, 40–43, 46, 48–49, 53, 59–60, 90, 103–4, 109; storms, 37, 39, 92, 100–101, 101n, 108, 118, 126–27, 135, 138, 163, 259, 344, 347, 349; hail, 43–44, 100, 126–27, 130, 133–35, 150, 163, 432, 436; general, 84, 86;

snow, 130, 150, 239, 241–42, 244, 260, 262, 267, 363
Weather observations: November 1805, 99–101; December 1805, 148–51; January 1806, 258–62; February 1806, 362–65
Weippe Prairie, 467
Weiser, Peter: illness of, 35; volunteers, 60; scouting party, 62, 65; votes, 83; duties of, 139–40, 172n; separated, 152, 161–64; information of, 166–67; returns, 284–85, 293, 295, 370; sent out, 290–91, 297, 355n
Wenatchee (Wah-na-a-chee) River, 487
Werner, William: votes, 84; illness of, 122; duties of, 172n, 177; sent out, 230–31; separated 237; returns, 242–43
Whale, blue, 185n
Whales: remains of, 66, 320, 322; bones of, 68, 70, 407–8; informed of, 141, 143; and Indians, 162–63, 166, 178, 180, 189, 199, 409n, 416, 416n, 460; seeking, 167–68, 171, 172n, 176–77, 182–84, 192, 262; purchased, 180, 235–36; as food, 188, 235–36; scarcity of, 245–46; figures of, 249; Indian name for, 495; mentioned, 2, 68n, 144n, 198n, 407. *See also* Blubber; Oil, whale
Wheat, 368n
Wheatgrass, bluebunch, 366–68, 368n
Wheeler, Olin D., 123n
White Bear Islands, 354, 449, 464
Whitefish, 344, 346n, 349
Whitehouse, Joseph: votes, 84; separated, 125–26; gives gift, 137; sent out, 312, 314; returns, 323–24; mentioned, 59n
White Salmon River (Canoe Creek), 456, 469
Wildrye, basin, 366, 368, 368n

Index

Willamette (Multnomah) River: learn of, 311, 311n; Indians of, 314, 317n, 478–80, 483–84, 486–87, 491; listed, 457, 470; mentioned, 1, 13, 14n
Willapa Bay, 51n, 70n, 77n
Willard, Alexander: scouting party, 42–43, 45, 47; and Indians, 48, 50; votes, 83; sent out, 138, 140, 221; separated, 152, 161–64; returns, 166–67; hunting, 229n, 235–36, 255; duties of, 253; injured, 293, 295; illness of, 332–33, 335–37, 347, 356–57, 393, 441–43
Willow Creek (Oreg.), 468
Willow Creek (Philosophy River) (Mont.), 450, 465
Willow, Pacific, 29n
Willows, 26–27, 77n, 366, 368
Willow, Scouler, 29n
Willow, Sitka, 29n
Wilson, Alexander, 37n
Wilson (Kilamox) River, 184, 185n, 461, 471
Wind. *See* Weather conditions
Wind (Cruzatte's) River, 112, 115n, 456, 469
Windsor, Richard, 83, 86n, 172n, 321, 324–26
Winship, Charles, 160n
Winship, Jonathan, 160n
Wire, 144, 173n, 187, 196
Wisdom River. *See* Big Hole River
Wiser. *See* Weiser
Wishram-Wasco (Chil-luck-kit-te-quaw, E-skel-lute, Smock-Shop) Indians: language, 19; trade, 201; canoes, 263; horses of, 313, 315; villages, 455–56, 469; numbers, 475, 481, 483; mentioned, 10n, 477n, 490
Wiyot Indians, 432n
Wolf, gray, 208, 210, 210n, 312–13, 315, 317n, 331, 333n, 335, 449
Wolf (Lackwater) Creek, 447, 462
Wolomped River, 112, 115n
Wolves, 166, 200–201, 312–13, 315, 317n
Woodpecker, pileated, 379–80, 381n
Woodrat, bushy-tailed, 354, 355n, 356
Woodrat, eastern, 354, 355n, 356
Wood River, 494
Woodward Creek, 469
Worms, 94, 96
Wren, winter: observed, 94, 162–63, 261, 363, 365, 379, 381; mentioned, 94n, 164n, 262n, 365n, 381n

Xerophyllum tenax, 9n. *See also* Beargrass

Yahache (You-ilt) Indians, 476, 485, 491
Yakima Basalt Subgroup, 10n
Yakima (Chim-nah-pum, Cuts-sâh-nim, Pish-quit-pah) Indians, 313, 315, 454, 468, 474, 483, 487, 490–91
Yakima (Tapteete) River, 474, 483, 487
Yaquina (Lick-a-wi, Yorick-cone) Indians, 201, 202n, 237n, 432n, 476, 485, 490

Y-e-huh Indians. *See* Watlala Indians
Yelleppit, 148n, 454, 468
Yellowstone (Rochejhone) River, 3, 86n, 311n, 447, 462, 496
York: votes, 2, 84, 86n; hunting, 53–54; volunteers, 60; scouting party, 62, 65; sent out, 105; separated, 109, 114; illness of, 125, 135, 140–41, 143; islands named for, 450, 464
Yorks 8 Islands, 450, 464
Youens, Youin. *See* Ewen
Youmatolam River. *See* Umatilla River
Young, Sir George, 115n
Youngs (Kilhow-â-nah-kle) River: arrive at, 95; explore, 164; hunting on, 317–18, 381–83, 391, 393, 398, 400; falls on, 383, 384n; mentioned 98n, 112, 114, 115n, 164n, 321n
Youngs (Meriwether's) Bay: arrive at, 92–93, 95; animals of, 108, 147; visits to, 109, 133, 171, 199, 318; explore, 114–15; hunting on, 409, 411; listed, 459, 471; mentioned, 94n, 115n, 133n, 164, 275–76, 276n, 384n, 398–99
Youngs River Falls, 383, 384n
Yurok Indians, 432n

Zenaida macroura, 381n. *See also* Dove, mourning
Zonotrichia atricapilla, 164n. *See also* Sparrow, golden-crowned
Zoology. *See specific species*